CO ANF 907

Handbook to The Hymnal

WILLIAM CHALMERS COVERT, D.D., Litt.D., *Editor*

CALVIN WEISS LAUFER, D.D., *Associate Editor*

*"A hymn book is a transcript from real life. . . .
The heart of the Christian Church is revealed in its
hymns; and if we will take the trouble to relate them
to the circumstances that gave them birth, we shall
find that they light up with new meaning and have
fresh power to help us in our daily lives."
—"The Evolution of the English Hymn," page 30.*

Presbyterian Board of Christian Education

PHILADELPHIA

1935

Copyright, 1935, by the Presbyterian Board of Christian Education

LA
5465
P92
1933 /c

155696

Printed by The Lakeside Press, R. R. Donnelley & Sons Co., Chicago

Dedication

THIS HANDBOOK IS DEDICATED TO THAT GROWING
COMPANY IN PULPIT, CHOIR LOFT, AND PEW, WHO
SEEK TO QUICKEN A DEEPER INTEREST IN PRESENT-
DAY CHURCH WORSHIP THROUGH A MORE INTEL-
LIGENT USE OF HYMNS. THOSE WHO HAVE HERE
WROUGHT CONFIDENTLY EXPECT THAT WHAT THEY
HAVE BEEN PRIVILEGED TO DO WILL BE OF HELP
IN DEVELOPING IN ALL WORSHIPING GROUPS A
MORE UNDERSTANDING AND FERVENT APPRECIA-
TION OF THE HYMNS OF THE CHURCH, TO THE
HONOR AND GLORY OF OUR LORD JESUS CHRIST.

Contents

Contents

Principal Sources Consulted

The contributors to this Handbook wish to acknowledge their indebtedness to the following authorities, and recommend their use for further study:

Baker's "Biographical Dictionary of Musicians."

Benson, Louis F., "Studies of Familiar Hymns" (First Series).

Benson, Louis F., "Studies of Familiar Hymns" (Second Series).

Benson, Louis F., "The English Hymn."

Brownlie, John, "The Hymns and Hynm Writers of the Church Hymnary."

Brown, Theron, and Butterworth, Hezekiah, "The Story of the Hymns and Tunes."

Cowan, William, and Love, James, "The Music of the Church Hymnary."

Dearmer, Percy, "Songs of Praise Discussed."

Duffield, Samuel Willoughby, "English Hymns: Their Authors and History."

Grove's "Dictionary of Music and Musicians."

Jones, James Edmund, "The Book of Common Praise" (Annotated Edition).

Julian, John, "A Dictionary of Hymnology."

Lightwood, James T., "Hymn-Tunes and Their Story."

Metcalf, Frank J., "American Writers and Compilers of Sacred Music."

Metcalf, Frank J., "Stories of Hymn Tunes."

Moffatt, James, "Handbook to the Church Hymnary."

Ninde, Edward S., "The Story of the American Hymn."

Pratt, Waldo Selden, "The History of Music."

Smith, H. Augustine, "Lyric Religion."

Introduction

PURPOSE OF THE "HANDBOOK TO THE HYMNAL": There is between the lines and behind the stanzas of every hymn in "The Hymnal" a background of inspiring facts, personal and otherwise, not available to the average worshiper. Such facts and incidents illumine the personality of the writers and add significance to the message of the hymns. To place these facts before the hymn lovers of the Church, and to quicken their interest in hymns in general and especially in the hymns of the new Hymnal, is the purpose of this Handbook. The spiritual experience of public and private worship will be vitalized and deepened through a better understanding, on the part of pastors, choir members, and congregations, of the 513 hymns and 95 responses, ancient hymns, and canticles now included in "The Hymnal" (1933).

PLAN OF THE HANDBOOK: In meeting the growing demands of leaders in both church and academic groups for handbook materials covering the current hymns, old as well as new, nothing is here attempted beyond a brief treatment of four phases of the hymn. There is a short biographical statement about the *author*, with a few facts calculated to reveal personality, religious and hymn-writing experience, and major life motives. The *hymn* is dealt with in a manner to indicate its thought content and something of the history of its appearance and service, the treatment varying as the interest of the commentators differs. The *composer* is held to be of equal importance with the author in unfolding the spiritual significance of the worship ideals of the hymn. Biographical matter is here presented and the place of the musician in contemporary life established where possible. The *tune* is the subject of brief, instructive comments, with a view to its more effective rendering in public worship.

The facts given by various contributors to the Handbook are not in many instances the result of original research. The field has been worked so thoroughly by hymnological scholars and the historical data of most of the hymns, meager at best, have been so widely published in various types of commentaries that to assume any originality would be an affectation.

The bibliography preceding this sketch indicates the chief sources from which material has been drawn. It should also be said that much material has been gathered from the files of the late Dr. Louis F. Benson.

PRACTICAL USES: There is a widespread and urgent desire for new vitality and spiritual power in the public worship of the Church. It is hoped that hymn-singing may come again into the place it had in the Apostolic Church and in the Church of the Reformation. The spiritual value of the hymn has generally been neglected in our

Handbook to The Hymnal

orders of worship. The hymn is too often treated casually by pastors and choir leaders, and unintentionally suppressed beneath the orderly routine of the services. The informative materials in connection with authors, composers, hymns, and tunes in "The Hymnal" may be used to intensify the spiritual meaning of the hymns and enhance the personal interest and singing coöperation of the people. Information concerning practices already in vogue show that the "HANDBOOK TO THE HYMNAL" may be used in some of the following ways:

1. In connection with the daily personal uses of "The Hymnal" as a book of private devotion.

2. In the conduct of hymn services of various kinds by pastors and choir leaders who wish to arouse more general participation than now exists on the part of the people.

3. In preliminary comments by the pastor when he is announcing the hymns of the ordinary worship services, or in insertions of explanatory material in the weekly calendar.

4. By choirmasters at rehearsals when choirs need to be put *en rapport* with the spirit of the hymns to be used in the services.

5. For courses in hymnology now carried on in young people's summer conferences throughout the United States.

6. In the theological seminaries and colleges where the study of hymnology is being systematically carried on.

THE CONTRIBUTING PERSONNEL: That the "HANDBOOK *to* THE HYMNAL" in its treatment of hymns might make available the best from representative minds and hearts among the pastors, the following clergymen were asked to deal with certain sections of hymns as to their authors and thought content:

Hugh T. Kerr, D.D., LL.D.	J. Harry Cotton, D.D.
Charles R. Erdman, D.D., LL.D.	James M. Howard, D.D.
Cleland B. McAfee, D.D., Ph.D., LL.D.	John B. Ferguson, D.D.
	Arthur B. McCormick, D.D.
William R. Taylor, D.D.	J. Shackelford Dauerty, D.D.
William Hiram Foulkes, D.D., LL.D.	Stanley A. Hunter, D.D.
Harry C. Rogers, D.D.	Edwin F. Hallenbeck, D.D.
Arthur A. Hays, D.D.	John J. Moment, D.D.
George N. Luccock, D.D.	Jesse Halsey, D.D.
Edwin A. McAlpin, Jr., D.D.	William C. Laube, D.D.

That further material might represent the results of specialized training, research, and long choir experience, the following church musicians

Introduction

were asked to deal with certain sections of hymns in regard to their composers and tunes:

Professor Charles N. Boyd
Professor Harry S. Mason
Dr. John Finley Williamson
Mr. N. Lindsay Norden
J. V. Moldenhawer, D.D.
Mr. Reginald L. McAll
Professor John Warren Erb
Mr. Edward Shippen Barnes
Mr. David Hugh Jones
Mr. R. Buchanan Morton

Mr. W. Lawrence Curry
Mr. Henry Barraclough
Miss Emily S. Perkins
Mr. Hugh Porter
Mr. Frederick E. Drechsler
Mr. Donald B. Kettring
Mr. Paul Ambrose
Paul W. McClintock, D.D.
Mr. George Edward Fisher
Robert M. Donaldson, D.D.

These gifted clergymen and church musicians, out of lives burdened with heavy responsibilities, have here rendered a volunteer service of greatest value to the Church. With deep personal interest in the cause of intelligent and spiritually uplifting worship they have given of their consecrated talents, without any remuneration whatever, to the achievement of this joint enterprise now prepared and dedicated to the worship of Almighty God through the nobler uses of Christian hymns.

WILLIAM CHALMERS COVERT, *Editor.*

Original Sources

THE PSALTERS IN EARLY PRESBYTERIAN WORSHIP: The Reformed Churches, immediately following the break with the Roman Catholic Church, were sorely hindered in their worship, since the Mass Book was the only directory for worship available.

John Knox and others made such use of the amended Mass Book itself as would meet the needs of Protestant worship until the Psalters began to appear. As early as 1539 the Church in France used a small collection of seventeen metrical psalms, five of which Calvin prepared while exiled in Strasbourg. This book, edited by Marot, the converted Parisian ballad singer, was carried to Geneva and there adopted about 1541. The following year Marot issued in Paris a collection of his own versified psalms, about thirty in number. In consequence he was compelled to flee from an indignant Sorbonne to Geneva about 1542. Calvin recognized both the talents and the spirit of Marot and put upon him the responsibility for developing the psalmody and worship aids of the Genevan Church. After Marot's death, in 1544, versification of the psalms for worship lagged until in 1548 Theodore Beza arrived in Geneva. This scholarly coworker of Calvin, who became Calvin's successor and also his very competent biographer, produced a collection of metrical psalms containing 101 of his own versions and forty-nine by Marot. For the music to which the psalms were set during this period in Geneva, Calvin was indebted to Louis Bourgeois. No one did more to quicken the singing of the congregations and give Protestantism its needed psalm- and hymn-singing accessories than Bourgeois, who practically completed the Psalter by 1557, although a completely versified Psalter with 125 tunes was not available until 1562. This is known as the "French-Genevan Psalter" and covers the years 1539–1562.

In 1556 a collection of metrical psalms was printed at Geneva with the following title-page: "The Forme of Prayers and Ministration of the Sacraments, Etc. Used in the Englishe Congregation at Geneva; and Approved by the Famous and Godly Learned Man, John Calvyn." This was brought out by the group of Protestants who, fleeing Queen Mary's persecution, settled in Frankfurt, but later, finding Geneva more to their liking, arrived there and organized a group under John Knox. Their Psalter had tunes, the collection being made up from those used in England from Sternhold and Hopkins' version with some additions from William Whittingham, the "French Psalter," and William Kethe. These editions—and there are several—are known as the "Anglo-Genevan Psalters."

The "English Psalter," a single surviving copy of which is now in the library of Christ Church College, Oxford, appeared in 1560. It is a reproduction of the "Anglo-Genevan Psalter" with but three additions. A later edition, in 1561, marked the first real divergence between the worship ideals of the English Protestants and those of the Scottish Churches. The edition of 1562, published by John Day, was even more important than those which preceded it. The entire 150 psalms were versified and improved. The book included other metrical versions, together with the Creed, the Ten Commandments, The Lord's Prayer, the "Veni Creator," the "Venite," the "Te Deum," and other ancient hymns and modern originals. The title-page read: "The whole Booke of Psalmes, collected into Englysh metre by T. Starnhold, I. Hopkins, and others: conferred with the Ebrue, with apt Notes to synge them withal, Faithfully perused and alowed according to th' ordre appointed in the Quenes maiesties Injunctions. Very mete to be used of all sortes of people privately for their solace and comfort: laying apart all ungodly Songes and Ballades, which tende only to the norishing of vyce, and corrupting of youth. . . . Imprinted at London by John Day, dwelling over Aldersgate, *Cum gratia et privilegio Regie Maiestatis, per septennium. An* 1562." Here was a great achievement that held its place for more than a hundred years. Some of the tunes, which appeared in four parts, continue to this day. They are generally marked as 'Old Psalm ———." In 1592, Thomas Este, a music printer, issued a Psalter in which for the first time the tunes were harmonized in four parts, and printed "the cantus and tenor . . . on the left-hand page and the altus and bassus on the right." Later printers produced Psalters with an increasing number and variety of tunes.

As John Knox was in close contact with Geneva, the early worship forms used in Scotland were those in use at Geneva. They became known as the "Order of Geneva." The "Anglo-Genevan Psalter" as a whole was adopted in Scotland in 1561. In 1562 the General Assembly lent the sum of £200 to a printer for bringing out the Psalter as a part of the "Book of Common Order," containing eighty-seven psalms, of which forty-two were from the "English Psalter," 1562, and twenty-one from Scottish versifiers like John Craig, Robert Pont, and others. "Common" tunes, or tunes adapted to several psalms, now appeared, and in 1635 came the "Scottish Psalter," with both "proper" and "common" tunes, all of which were harmonized by Edward Millar.

In 1643 the House of Commons, upon the advice of the Westminster General Assembly and in the interest of general uniformity between England and Scotland in both government and worship, authorized the use of the version of Francis Rous, who was the provost of Eton. This book, further revised by the General Assembly of the Church of Scotland, finally appeared in 1650 and continues to be used to the present day, although, unfortunately for the cause of good church music in Scotland, no tunes were supplied in Rous's version. Memorized tunes and hymns lined out by a precentor have always been a notable feature in the order of Scottish churches.

Original Sources

CHURCH HYMNS IN GREAT BRITAIN AND AMERICA: Christian hymns now in use in the two great English-speaking nations have so much in common that a brief review of their development may well be summarized under one caption. The Lollards, followers of Wycliffe, gathering in and about Oxford in 1384, were doubtless the original hymn singers of England, excepting the choristers of the Roman Catholic Church. The earliest printed English hymns are those found in "Marshall's Primer," c. 1534, and the "Sarum Primer," 1538. These were crude translations from the Latin. The first book containing hymns was Miles Coverdale's "Goostly Psalmes and Spiritualle Songes," 1539. Among the forty-one hymns in this book were seventeen chorals from Luther and fifteen versified psalms. In 1545 Henry VIII, assisted by Cranmer, issued the "King's Primer," hoping to halt the growing popularity of German hymns by establishing the English hymn in the churches. When the effort to establish hymn-singing was abandoned John Calvin, by this time the leader of English Protestantism rather than Luther, was credited with its failure. But Thomas Sternhold, John Hopkins, William Kethe, and others soon came forward and with their coming a broader spirit took hold of worship, resulting in a generous use of hymns in addition to the metrical psalms. The "Gude and Godlie Ballates" did for the Reformation in Scotland what Coverdale's "Goostly Psalmes and Spiritualle Songes" did for popular worship in England. This book has disappeared. The oldest known copy was printed in 1578 at Edinburgh. It contains 116 hymns in Scottish dialect. It is interesting to note that to the twenty-two psalms in the book are added thirty-four hymns, eight graces, and forty-two ballads, together with some satirical verses at the expense of Rome that to-day would be considered coarse and unworthy.

It is a matter of great regret that the Genevan prejudices were so effective in the restraint of the use of other than metrical psalms that from the 130 known English writers of religious verse in the latter part of the sixteenth century there are no hymns. A few poems of John Donne, George Herbert, and Phineas Fletcher, notable religious poets of the day, appear in the hymn books following the death of Elizabeth.

George Wither, who wrote profusely, producing more than a hundred books, eight on hymnology, is regarded as the first to produce an English hymnal. His "Hymnes and Songs of the Church," appearing in 1623, met with the approval of almost everyone, including the king, but encountered the selfish opposition of the Stationers' Company and its deserved success was blocked. Wither, undaunted, came forward in 1641 with "Hallelujah, Britain's Second Remembrancer," containing more than two hundred hymns.

The Psalter of Sternhold and Hopkins now gave way in England to a demand for other versions. Parliament did its part to effect unity between England and Scotland in the matter. A committee was appointed to pre-

Handbook to The Hymnal

pare a uniform Psalter based on the version of Francis Rous. There followed a noble edition, ever to be known as "the Scots' version" because it was adopted by the General Assembly of the Church of Scotland in 1650. Bishop Ken's manual of prayers, written for the boys at Winchester School, contained, in the edition of 1695, three hymns, one each for morning, evening, and midnight. Tate and Brady, in 1696, produced the "New Version," which by reason of its improved literary quality held its place in the worship life of the Church for a hundred and fifty years.

In 1695 Isaac Watts, a young Nonconformist living at Southampton, objected to the literary character of the rimed psalms used and was asked to write something better. He responded and a new day in English hymnology dawned. There followed rapidly "Hymns and Spiritual Songs," 1707, with 210 hymns; "Divine and Moral Songs for Children," 1715; and "The Psalms of David Imitated," 1719. Before Watts died, in 1748, six hundred of his hymns were in common use. He may well be called the founder of English hymnology, and, from that day to this, through his own hymns and those of his followers, the most potent influence in the worship of the Calvinistic Reformed Churches.

Charles Wesley (1707–1788), the greatest of English hymn writers, who produced more than 6500 hymns, began his career as the lyric leader of the greatest revival England had ever known. The Moravian School of English hymnists, led by Bishop Gambold (1711–1771), produced, in 1754, "Hymns of the Children of God in All Ages." William Cowper (1731–1800), collaborating with John Newton (1725–1807), produced the famous "Olney Hymns," first published in 1779. These hymns, 348 in number, are of varied excellence. The romantic character and widely contrasted experiences of these two marked authors gave prominence to the book.

George Whitefield's "Hymns for Social Worship," 1753, passed through thirty-six editions, being widely used in the many revivals that stirred the period. Many hymns written by Anglican clergymen of the evangelical type now appeared. They were strongly Calvinistic but reflected the spirit of the Wesley and Whitefield era. John Wesley's "A Collection of Hymns for the Use of the People Called Methodists" was issued in 1780.

So brief a story of English hymns omits salient and illuminating features of a period such as English hymnology was never to know again. Only the major points of creative interest and development are referred to here. An enormous output speaks of the depth and power of sacred song in expressing the religious feelings of English Christians. Between 1800 and 1900, 500 hymnals were compiled for the churches of Great Britain, including 250 for the Anglican churches and 250 for the Nonconformist churches. The long and rich development has culminated in such monumental collections as "Hymns Ancient and Modern," 1861,

Original Sources

"The English Hymnal," "The New Congregational Hymn Book," "Songs of Praise," and "The Church Hymnary."

Against this fine background of English hymnody the hymn in America should have had a much more rapid development. Perhaps the over-mastering influence of the hymnal ideals of England and Scotland explains the fact that up to the time of the American Revolution very few hymns of American origin are known to have existed.

When on December 11, 1620, the Pilgrim Fathers anchored off Cape Cod and went ashore, leaving the women on board, they "worshiped God with prayers and the singing of psalms." In all probability they sang from Ainsworth's "The Booke of Psalms: Englished Both in Prose and Metre with Annotations Opening the Words and Sentences by Conference with Other Scriptures," 1612. No tunes were given until the second edition of Ainsworth in 1618 and then but five were included.

In 1636 a committee was appointed to prepare a more satisfactory psalm book for the colonial Christians. Among the members was John Eliot, later to be the great apostle to the Indians. After four years the committee produced what was called "The Bay Psalm Book," first published in 1640 and passing through nine editions. Crude as it was from a literary point of view, the first edition, with hymns, was printed seventy times; also, thirty editions were printed in Scotland and eighteen in England. For a hundred years this book held chief place in the public singing of the colonial churches. Stephen Day, who introduced the printing press to America, was the printer. Music was in a low state, only three or four tunes being available. It was not unusual for more than one tune to be sung at the same time. Amid the jargon it is not to be wondered at that Thomas Walter, in 1721, rebelled at the "horrid and discordant noises" in worship.

The leadership in early American hymnology of the brilliant Presbyterian pioneer preacher, Rev. Samuel Davies, is recognized as notable in Julian's "A Dictionary of Hymnology." Dr. Davies succeeded Jonathan Edwards as president of the College of New Jersey, located at Princeton, in 1753. Sixteen of his hymns appear in "Hymns Adapted to Divine Worship," issued by Dr. T. Gibbons in 1769. Dr. Davies' hymn on "God's pardoning love," the first line of which is "Great God of wonders, all Thy ways," appeared in more than a hundred hymn books in England alone.

An American appendix of twenty-seven hymns was added to Tate and Brady's version and issued in 1789 by the Episcopal Church, while the Dutch Reformed Church published a small collection of psalms and hymns in 1789. The Methodist Church in America issued a "Pocket Hymn Book" in 1790. In all these hymnals less than fourteen per cent of the hymns were contributed by American writers.

With the "Great Awakening" a tide of interest and productivity in hymns by American church musicians rose. In 1828–1829 "Psalms and

Hymns" appeared. Later amended editions followed in 1830–1834 and 1843. There seems to have been no Hymnal authorized by the Presbyterian General Assembly until 1831. The New School body issued "The Church Psalmist" with a supplement in 1847. A notable collection of hymns appeared in 1874 as "The Presbyterian Hymnal," superior in every way to "The Hymnal of the Presbyterian Church," 1866. The Presbyterians were largely responsible for the success of the hymnals, edited by prominent Presbyterian musicians, that appeared in rapid succession; among them were the following: "Spiritual Songs," 1831, by Thomas Hastings; "Songs for the Sanctuary," 1865, and "Spiritual Songs," 1878, by Charles S. Robinson. In 1872, Dr. E. F. Hatfield, a great hymnologist, issued "The Church Hymn Book," a work specially mentioned by Julian's "A Dictionary of Hymnology." Dr. Louis F. Benson, who devoted his life to the development of hymnology in the Presbyterian Church, began his work with the epoch-making edition of the Hymnal of 1895. This was revised in 1911, and finally gave way, in 1933, to the new Hymnal, of which Dr. Clarence Dickinson was editor in chief.

The following chronological table summarizes fairly well the story of the antecedents of "The Hymnal" (1933).

1539—"The Genevan Psalter," organized by Calvin, Marot, and others.

1719—Publication of Dr. Watts's "The Psalms of David Imitated," to which hymns were added.

1802—"The Psalms of David Imitated in the Language of the New Testament, and Applied to the Christian State and Worship," by Dr. Watts. Approved and allowed by the General Assembly.

1813—"An Imitation of the Psalms of David, Carefully Suited to Christian Worship, Being an Improvement of the Presbyterian Church in the United States, to Be Used in Churches and Private Families." Approved by the General Assembly.

1831—"Psalms and Hymns Adapted to Public Worship, and Approved by the General Assembly of the Presbyterian Church in the United States of America."

1842—"Psalms and Hymns, Adapted to Social, Private, and Public Worship."

1843—Report of a Hymnal committee appointed in 1838, submitting a revision of "Psalms and Hymns," published as the official Hymnal.

1847—A New School Hymnal, "The Church Psalmist."

1852—An Old School Hymnal, "The Presbyterian Psalmodist," edited by Hastings.

1857—"The Church Psalmist," to which 155 hymns were added.

1866—"The Hymnal of the Presbyterian Church," representing the final break with metrical psalmody.

Original Sources

1874—"The Presbyterian Hymnal," recognized as official, following the Reunion, 1870.

1895—"The Hymnal," Dr. Benson's epoch-making work, setting a new standard for church hymns.

1911—"The Hymnal," Revised, with many changes designed to render the book more adaptable to congregational uses. This is the Church's great Hymnal and has found its place in more than three thousand churches.

1933—"The Hymnal" (1933), edited by Dr. Clarence Dickinson and Dr. Calvin W. Laufer.

GERMAN HYMN SOURCES: It was John Huss and the Bohemian Brethren, later called Moravians, who gave Martin Luther, the singing Reformer, the idea of using hymns in worship and in propagating the new gospel. In 1504 a book of chorals was published in the Bohemian language by the United Brethren. It is to Martin Luther, however, that full credit is to be given for the restoration of the apostolic practice of hymn-singing in the churches. Following Gregory's day, congregational singing gradually had been suppressed in order that the beauty and order of worship might be preserved from ignorant and unworthy singers. Luther, touched to tears by hearing a street beggar singing a hymn by Speratus, determined to give his best efforts to the adaptation for church worship not only of the "psalms and hymns and spiritual songs" but also of the popular airs and folk-song melodies. Even the "Passion Chorale" was the adaptation of a secular tune long used with an amatory poem. This did not prevent its use with "O Sacred Head, Now Wounded" or hinder Bach from introducing it into his "St. Matthew Passion" score.

No more striking illustration of the contagious spread of choral-singing under Luther is to be had than what followed after he set the Forty-sixth Psalm to the thrilling tune known as "Ein' Feste Burg." This rugged tune spread throughout Germany and central Europe and became the battle hymn of the new movement. Melanchthon heard a child singing it, as he and his friends entered Weimar as exiles, and spoke of its cheering power. Gustavus Adolphus and his soldiers in the great struggle at Leipzig sang it, and as late as 1870, in the struggle between France and Germany, this hymn rang out from the war camps and homes of Germany as in Luther's day. Mendelssohn, in his "Reformation" symphony, and Meyerbeer, in his opera "Les Huguenots," introduced this historic choral; while Wagner gave it a noble interpretation in his "Kaisermarsch," written to welcome home the victorious soldiers of 1870.

Some of the oldest German chorals are from plain-song melodies of the old Latin Church. "Soldau" (Hymns 102, 182), found in the first collection of tunes issued in 1524, is an example. "Nun Danket" (Hymn 459), known as the "Te Deum" of Germany and sung everywhere; Nicolai's "Sleepers, Wake," which Handel used in the "Hallelujah Chorus" with great effect; and many other chorals in common use in German churches have come out of the melodies of the past.

Immediately following Luther, choral-writing became the passion of choirmasters and every region had its "Gesangbuch." The classic collection of these chorals will probably always be Bach's "Vierstimmige Choralgesange." The choral reached England through Coverdale, who had visited the Continent before issuing, in 1537, his "Goostly Psalmes and Spiritualle Songes." He hoped to assist the youth of England to change their "foul and corrupt ballads into sweet songs and spiritual songs in God's honor." Henry VIII, however, suppressed Coverdale's singing plans. Later, in "Lyra Davidica," 1708, these chorals appear once more, and in "Psalmodia Germanica," 1722, edited by Jacobi, a varied collection of fifty chorals appeared, designed, according to the editor, to meet the needs of all worship occasions, "so that a lover of psalmody may entertain his singing faculty either rising or going to bed, at work or at ease, at home or abroad; and thus, on all occasions, trim his lamp with the oil of devotion."

John Wesley gave added impulse to the use of the German chorals, including them in his tune books. The Moravian singers, scattering to all parts, carried with them the choral as a native possession.

Catherine Winkworth, in "Christian Singers of Germany," provides much interesting information as to the rise and progress of the chorals, which are said to number more than four thousand. In response to special requests, particularly from the younger church singers, many choral tunes are found in "The Hymnal." In every instance they lend musical strength and spiritual vigor to the singing in our corporate worship.

WELSH HYMNODY: The musical history of the Welsh people goes back to druidical times. From earliest days bards and harpists led the people in song, so that the Welsh have become an inspiring race of singers. At the close of Armistice Day, in November, 1920, when the first united "Hymn Tune and Singing Festival" of Welsh Nonconformist Churches of London convened in Westminster Chapel, Lloyd George stated that "Wales is the land of song." He added that, according to Geraldus Cambrensis, the Welsh were skilled in part singing as early as the tenth century. Lloyd George, taught to sing in childhood, was able to sing before he could talk. The first prize he won was for singing. "Training young and old to sing," he declared, "was a kind of conscription in the little town in which I lived." That is characteristically true of Welsh tradition and practice.

The recovery of Welsh hymns and tunes is due to folk-song societies, to the National Council of Music in Wales, and to many hymn writers and

Original Sources

organists. Welsh hymns and tunes, some of them centuries old, have been made available to the world through the efforts of such hymnologists as Dr. Mary Davies, Dr. Lloyd Williams, Mr. D. W. Evans, Mr. G. O. Williams, Professor Gwym Jones, Professor T. H. Parry Williams, Dr. Basil Howard, Dr. R. Vaughan Williams, H. Walford Davis, and Dr. David Evans, professor of music at University College, South Wales. Preceding them, however, were others who in their time rendered service to perpetuate and enrich Welsh hymnody and praise. A number of these should be mentioned.

Vicar Rees Prichard (1579–1644) came on the field when sacred song and praise needed counsel and leadership. He provided both, for he was an accepted popular preacher in Wales and a poet of ability. His book called "Canwyll Y Cymry," or "The Welshman's Candle," a volume of verse, was, for want of a better, made to do service as a hymn book. With its use a new era began.

A greater work was achieved by Archdeacon Prys (c.1541–1624), who set the psalms into meter in order that, as he wrote, "the Welsh people might be enabled to praise God from their hearts." It proved to be an unusual work, and exerted a great influence not only in Wales but also among the Welsh colonists in America. This volume, "Salmau Cau," bound with the Welsh Book of Common Prayer, was used at St. Davids, Radnor, Pennsylvania, and St. Deiniol-Bangor Church, Churchtown, in the same state. Three hundred years after its appearance in 1621 Welsh people are still singing from this book.

Further stimulus to Welsh hymnody was given by Rev. Griffith Jones (1683–1761), vicar for forty-five years in one parish, who compiled a hymnal from the writings of different authors; by Rev. Evan Evans (d. 1850), the chief Welsh hymnologist of his time; and by Rev. Robert Davies, who issued a hymnal based on "the feasts and fasts of the Church of England."

Through the efforts of Nonconformist leaders and others of the Established Church, the works of Watts and the Wesleys were translated into Welsh, and were extensively used.

In the meantime, and through several centuries, Welsh music was collected and made available to classrooms, choral groups, churches, pastors, precentors, and organists. The collection of manuscripts made in the seventeenth century by Robert Vaughan is now the priceless nucleus of the National Library of Wales at Aberystwyth. From such collections as these, contemporaneous editors and musicians have drawn valuable materials for modern hymnals. Among the greatest of these, according to competent judges, is the Welsh "Hymn and Tune Book" (1917), which was published by Haydn Jones, M.D. Forty years before, his father, Rev. J. D. Jones, won distinction by rendering a similar service for the Welsh Congregational Church.

Handbook to The Hymnal

Through such outstanding hymn writers and musicians, the praise of the Church has been greatly enriched. What Professor Edward Reuss admirably states of Hebrew poetry may also be observed concerning the Welsh: "All that moved the souls of the multitude was expressed in song; it was indispensable to the sports of peace, it was a necessity for the rest from battle, it cheered the feast, and the marriage; it lamented in the hopeless dirge for the dead, it united the masses, it blessèd the individual, and was everywhere the lever of culture." Welsh verse and song are plaintive and tender, vigorous and daring, emotional and spiritual, simple and transparent, grave and jubilant. Of Williams of Pantycelyn, Rev. W. G. Thomas, late vicar of St. Asaph, writes that he "surpasses all in the expression of the yearnings of the heavenly homesickness; in devout tenderness, often rising into rapture, wherewith his faith clasps the crucified Saviour, when wrapt in contemplation of the glory of Jesus as the Head of the Church militant and triumphant; and also in the depth and maturity of his theological thoughts."

The several Welsh hymns included in "The Hymnal" not only meet the requisites of worship in our many Welsh congregations but add to the collection an element of unique beauty and fervor that marks all the singing of this gifted race.

Index of First Lines

Handbook to The Hymnal

Index of First Lines

Handbook to The Hymnal

Index of First Lines

xxix

Handbook to The Hymnal

Index of First Lines

xxxi

Handbook to The Hymnal

Unto the hills around do I
lift up 96
Upward where the stars
are burning 428

Watchman, tell us of the
night 109
We are living, we are
dwelling 374
We bear the strain of earthly care 179
We come unto our fathers' God . 342
We give Thee but Thine own . 394
We know not a voice of that river 432
We plow the fields, and scatter . 464
We praise Thee, O God, our Re-
deemer, Creator 461
We thank Thee, Lord, Thy paths
of service lead 367
We worship Thee, almighty Lord 17
We would see Jesus; for the shad-
ows lengthen 263
"Welcome, happy morning!" . 169
What a Friend we have in Jesus . 257
What grace, O Lord, and beauty
shone 143
What, ye ask me, is my prize . . 331
Whate'er my God ordains is right 291

When all Thy mercies, O my God 81
When, His salvation bringing . 149
When I survey the wondrous
cross 152
When morning gilds the skies . 3
When mothers of Salem 446
When shadows gather on our
way 323
When the great sun sinks to his
rest 72
When the Lord of love was here 141
When wilt Thou save the people 375
Where cross the crowded ways of
life 410
Where is the Friend for whom
I'm ever yearning 329
While shepherds watched their
flocks by night 120
Who is on the Lord's side . . . 272
With happy voices singing . . . 441
With songs and honors sounding
loud 75

Ye christian heralds, go
proclaim 381
Ye servants of God, your
Master proclaim 198

Index of Responses

Index of Ancient Hymns and Canticles

Alphabetical Index of Tunes

xxxvii

Handbook to The Hymnal

xxxviii

Alphabetical Index of Tunes

Handbook to The Hymnal

Alphabetical Index of Tunes

Metrical Index of Tunes

Handbook to The Hymnal

Metrical Index of Tunes

Index of Authors

ABÉLARD, Pierre (1079–1142), 430.
  Adams, Mrs. Sarah Flower (1805–1848), 261.
Addison, Joseph (1672–1719), 69, 81.
Alexander, Mrs. Cecil Frances Humphreys (1823–1895), 157, 211, 223, 454.
Alexander, Rev. James Waddell (1804–1859), 151.
Alford, Rev. Henry (1810–1871), 369, 427, 460.
Ambrose of Milan (340–397), 32, 59; Plain Song 84.
Andrew, St., of Crete (660–732), 275.
Anon.:
  American, 324; Response 16.
  English, 52, 129, 131, 288, 458; Response 44.
  German, 194; Chant 90.
  Greek, 187; Chants 82, 83.
  Latin, 116, 130, 142, 163, 164, 309, 336, 354, 472.
Argyll, John Campbell, Duke of (1845–1914), 96.
Armstrong, Rev. John (1813–1856), 480.
Ash and Evans' "Collection" (1769), 209.
Auber, Harriet (1773–1862), 205.

BABCOCK, Rev. Maltbie Davenport (1858–1901), 70, 72, 488.
  Bacon, Rev. Leonard (1802–1881), 462.
Baker, Rev. Sir Henry Williams (1821–1877), 99, 421, 463, 498; Plain Song 85.
Baring-Gould, Rev. Sabine (1834–1924), 35, 345, 365.
Bateman, Christian Henry (1813–1889), 191.
Bates, Katharine Lee (1859–1929), 411.
Bax, Clifford, 424.
Baynes, Rev. Robert Hall (1831–1895), 361.

Beach, Rev. Seth Curtis, 101.
Ben Judah, Daniel (14th century), 8.
Benson, Rev. Louis FitzGerald (1855–1930), 29, 32, 138, 253, 359, 400, 433, 490; Plain Song 84.
Bernard of Clairvaux (1091–1153), 151.
Bernard of Cluny (12th century), 435.
Bevan, Mrs. Emma Frances (1827–1909), 227.
Bickersteth, Bishop Edward Henry (1825–1906), 62, 301, 372.
Blackie, John Stuart (1809–1895), 76.
Blew, Rev. William John (1808–1894), 226.
Bode, Rev. John Ernest (1816–1874), 268.
Bonar, Rev. Horatius (1808–1889), 60, 188, 196, 236, 352, 376, 428, 500.
Borthwick, Jane Laurie (1813–1897), 30, 280, 281, 366.
Bowie, Rev. Walter Russell, 409.
Bowring, Sir John (1792–1872), 80, 89, 109, 154.
Brady, Rev. Nicholas (1659–1726), 19, 83, 317.
Bridges, Rev. Matthew (1800–1894), 153, 190, 232.
Bridges, Robert (1844–1930), 158; Response 82.
Bright, Rev. William (1824–1901), 355.
Brooke, Rev. Stopford Augustus (1832–1916), 74, 141, 303, 444.
Brooks, Bishop Phillips (1835–1893), 121, 123.
Browne, Rev. Simon (1680–1732), 209.
Brownlie, Rev. John (1859–1925), 187.
Bryant, William Cullen (1794–1878), 476.
Buckoll, Rev. Henry James (1803–1871), 487.
Bull, Rev. John (1777–1871), 318.
Bunyan, John (1628–1688), 276.
Burleigh, William Henry (1812–1871), 262.

xlvii

Burns, Rev. James Drummond (1823–1864), 100.

Butler, Henry Montague (1833–1918), 258.

Byrne, Mary, 325.

Byrom, John (1691–1763), 508.

CAMPBELL, Jane Montgomery (1817–1878), 464.
Campbell, John, Duke of Argyll (1845–1914), 96.

Canitz, Friedrich Rudolph Ludwig, Freiherr von (1654–1699), 487.

Carlyle, Thomas (1795–1881), 451.

Caswall, Rev. Edward (1814–1878), 3, 226, 309, 313.

Cennick, Rev. John (1718–1755), 347, 511.

Chadwick, Rev. John White (1840–1904), 406.

Chandler, Rev. John (1806–1876), 472, 510.

Chatfield, Rev. Allen William (1808–1896), 239.

Chenez, Charitie Lees de, 298.

Chesterton, Gilbert Keith, 419.

Chorley, Henry Fothergill (1808–1872), 420.

Claudius, Matthias (1740–1815), 464.

Clephane, Elizabeth Cecilia (1830–1869), 162.

Clute, Oscar (1840–1901), 84.

Coffin, Rev. Charles (1676–1749), 510.

Cook, Joseph Simpson, 453.

Copenhaver, Laura S., 379.

Cory, Mrs. Julia Bulkley Cady, 461.

Coster, George Thomas (1835–1912), 273.

Cotterill, Rev. Thomas (1779–1823), 237.

Cousin, Mrs. Anne Ross (1824–1906), 434.

Cowper, William (1731–1800), 103, 224, 241, 259, 296; Response 12.

Coxe, Bishop Arthur Cleveland (1818–1896), 334, 374.

Crewdson, Mrs. Jane Fox (1809–1863), 295, 512.

Croly, Rev. George (1780–1860), 204.

Cross, Rev. Allen Eastman, 494.

DAVIS, Rev. Ozora Stearns (1866–1931), 179.
Davis, Rev. Robert, 397.

"Day's Psalter" (1563), 503.

Dearmer, Canon Percy, 24; Ancient Hymn 86.

Denny, Sir Edward (1796–1889), 143.

Dickinson, Rev. Charles Albert (1849–1906), 244.

"Disciples' Hymn Book," Response 8.

Dix, William Chatterton (1837–1898), 135, 222.

Doane, Bishop George Washington (1799–1859), 34, 254, 384.

Doane, Bishop William Croswell (1832–1913), 58.

Doddridge, Rev. Philip (1702–1751), 98, 278, 279, 470.

Draper, Rev. Bourne Hall (1775–1843), 381.

Duffield, Rev. George, Jr. (1818–1888), 265.

Duncan, Mrs. Mary Lundie (1814–1840), 449.

Dwight, Rev. Timothy (1752–1817), 337.

EDMESTON, James (1791–1867), 47, 304.
Ellerton, Rev. John (1826–1893), 20, 45, 55, 169, 386, 420, 440, 509.

Elliott, Charlotte (1789–1871), 230, 306.

Elliott, Ebenezer (1781–1849), 375.

Elliott, Emily Elizabeth Steele (1836–1897), 231.

Evans, William E., 483.

F B. P." (16th century), 436.
Faber, Rev. Frederick William (1814–1863), 93, 159, 267, 431.

Farrington, Rev. Harry Webb (1880–1931), 181.

Fawcett, Rev. John (1740–1817), 54, 343.

Index of Authors

Findlater, Mrs. Sarah Borthwick (1823–1907), 115.

Fletcher, Frank, 177.

Fortunatus, Bishop Venantius H. C. (530–609), 169.

Foster, Frederick William (1760–1835), 51.

Foulkes, Rev. William Hiram, 245.

"Foundling Hospital Collection" (1796), 10.

Freeman, Rev. Robert, 418.

GATES, Mrs. Mary Cornelia Bishop (d. 1905), 383.
Gerhardt, Rev. Paul (1607–1676), 125, 151, 294, 299, 314, 505.

Gilder, Richard Watson (1844–1909), 499.

Gill, Thomas Hornblower (1819–1906), 342, 469.

Gilmore, Rev. Joseph Henry (1834–1918), 106.

Gladden, Rev. Washington (1836–1918), 364, 486.

Goadby, Rev. Frederic William (1845-1880), 473.

Grant, Sir Robert (1779–1838), 2.

Greek Service (6th or 7th century), 44.

Greenwell, Dora (1821–1882), 134, 326.

Gregory the Great (540–604), 24; Ancient Hymn 86.

Grigg, Rev. Joseph (c. 1720–1768), 225.

Gurney, Mrs. Dorothy Frances Blomfield, 484.

Gurney, Rev. John Hampden (1802–1862), 145.

HAM, Rev. Marion Franklin, 370.
Hammond, Rev. William (1719–1783), Response 11.

Hankey, Katherine (1834–1911), 443.

Harbaugh, Rev. Henry (1817–1867), 246.

Hastings, Thomas (1784–1872), 293, 391.

Hatch, Rev. Edwin (1835–1889), 213.

Havergal, Frances Ridley (1836–1879), 186, 200, 229, 242, 272, 287, 311, 399, 456, 467, 468.

Hawks, Mrs. Annie Sherwood (1835–1918), 332.

Heber, Bishop Reginald (1783–1826), 41, 53, 57, 136, 271, 349, 353, 385.

Hedge, Rev. Frederick Henry (1805–1890), 266.

Heermann, Rev. Johann (1585–1647), 158.

Herbert, Rev. George (1593–1632), 9.

Hernaman, Mrs. Claudia Frances Ibotson (1838–1898), 144.

Hickson, William Edward (1803–1870), 413.

Higginson, Rev. Thomas Wentworth (1823–1911), 90.

Hill, Rev. Rowland, "Psalms and Hymns" (1783), 288.

Hodder, Edwin (1837–1904), 219.

Holland, Rev. Henry Scott (1847–1918), 417.

Holmes, Oliver Wendell (1809–1894), 87.

Hopper, Rev. Edward (1818–1888), 286.

Hopps, Rev. John Page (1834–1912), 445.

Hosmer, Rev. Frederick Lucian (1840–1928), 176, 323, 363, 425.

How, Bishop William Walsham (1823–1897), 137, 160, 161, 170, 215, 228, 394, 429; Responses 31, 32.

Hull, Eleanor, 325.

Hunter, Rev. John (1848–1917), 507.

Hutchings, William Medlen (1827–1876), 446.

INGELOW, Jean (1820–1897), 330.
Ingemann, Bernhardt Severin (1789–1862), 345.

JOHN of Damascus (8th century), 166, 168.
Johns, Rev. John (1801–1847), 404.

Johnson, Rev. Samuel (1822–1882), 95, 256, 338.

Handbook to The Hymnal

"K" in Rev. John Rippon's "Selection" (1787), 283.

Keble, Rev. John (1792–1866), 31, 37, 61; Chant 83.

Kelly, Rev. Thomas (1769–1854), 195, 201.

Ken, Bishop Thomas (1637–1711), 42; Doxologies 94, 95.

Kennedy, Rev. Benjamin Hall (1804–1889), 312.

Kerr, Rev. Hugh Thompson, 88.

Kethe, Rev. William (16th century), 1.

King, Rev. John (1789–1858), 149.

Knapp, Rev. Shepherd, 368.

LATHBURY, Mary Artemisia (1841–1913), 39, 216.

Laufenberg, Heinrich von (d. c. 1458), 351.

Laufer, Rev. Calvin Weiss, 13, 367.

Laurenti, Laurentius (1660–1722), 115.

Lee, Harry, 497.

Leeson, Jane Eliza (1807–1882), 452.

Leyda, Ida F., 493.

"Liturgy of St. James," 112; Response 12.

Logan, Rev. John (1748–1788), 98.

Longfellow, Rev. Samuel (1819–1892), 79, 208, 335; Responses 29, 30, 45.

Lowell, James Russell (1819–1891), 373.

Lowry, Rev. Robert (1826–1899), 332.

Lowry, Somerset Corry, 393.

Luke, Mrs. Jemima Thompson (1813–1906), 442.

Luther, Rev. Martin (1483–1546), 118, 119, 126, 266.

Lynch, Rev. Thomas Toke (1818–1871), 82, 128, 214.

Lyte, Rev. Henry Francis (1793–1847), 12, 14, 33, 274, 465.

MACALISTER, Edith F. B., 350.

MacFayden, H. R., 496.

Macnicol, Rev. Nicol, 234.

Mahlmann, Siegfried August (1771–1826), 413.

Mant, Bishop Richard (1776–1848), 15.

Marckant, Rev. John (16th century), 503.

Marriott, Rev. John (1780–1825), 392.

Mason, Rev. John (1645–1694), Response 9.

Masterman, Rev. John Howard Bertram, 405.

Mathams, Rev. Walter John (1853–1932), 277.

Matheson, Rev. George (1842–1906), 247, 307.

Maude, Mrs. Mary Fawler Hooper (1819–1913), 248.

Medley, Rev. Samuel (1738–1799), 203.

Mercer, Rev. William (1811–1873), 41.

Merrill, Rev. William Pierson, 250, 401, 416.

Miller, Emily Huntington (1833–1913), 447.

Miller, Rev. John (d. 1810), 51.

Milman, Rev. Henry Hart (1791–1868), 150.

Milton, John (1608–1674), 64, 185, 463.

Mohr, Rev. Joseph (1792–1848), 132.

Moment, Rev. John James, 4, 290.

Monsell, Rev. John Samuel Bewley (1811–1875), 7, 56, 189, 251, 270, 422, 485.

Montgomery, James (1771–1854), 11, 92, 111, 124, 207, 255, 292, 356, 358.

Moore, Thomas (1779–1852), 293.

Morison, Rev. John (1750–1798), 360.

Morrell, Rev. T. B., and How, Bishop William Walsham, "Psalms and Hymns" (1867), 457.

Morris, Mrs. Eliza Fanny (1821–1874), 252.

Moultrie, Rev. Gerard (1829–1885), 112; Response 14.

Muhlenberg, Rev. William Augustus (1796–1877), 348.

Munger, Mrs. Harriet Osgood, 395.

Murray, Rev. Robert (1832–1910), 390.

Myers, Frederick William Henry (1843–1901), 110.

1

Index of Authors

NEALE, Rev. John Mason (1818–1866), 44, 59, 108, 130, 142, 146, 166, 167, 168, 221, 275, 336, 430, 435; Plain Song 85.

Neander, Joachim (1650–1680), 6, 27.

Nelson, Horatio, Earl (1823–1913), 25.

Neumark, Georg (1621–1681), 105.

Neumeister, Rev. Erdmann (1671–1756), 227.

Newman, Cardinal John Henry (1801–1890), 289; Response 40.

Newton, Rev. John (1725–1807), 310, 339, 495; Responses 10, 17, 41.

Nicolai, Rev. Philipp (1556–1608), 321.

North, Rev. Frank Mason, 410.

O B. C.," 25.

Oakeley, Rev. Frederick (1802–1880), 116.

Osler, Edward (1798–1863), 10, 482.

Oxenham, John, 322, 341.

PADERBORN GESANGBUCH" (1726), 513.

Palgrave, Francis Turner (1824–1897), 46.

Palmer, Rev. Ray (1808–1887), 285, 319, 354.

Parker, Rev. Edwin Pond (1836–1925), 407.

Parker, Rev. Theodore (1810–1860), 174.

Pennefather, Rev. William (1816–1873), Response 13.

Perkins, Emily S., 67.

Perronet, Rev. Edward (1726–1792), 192.

Phelps, Rev. Sylvanus Dryden (1816–1895), 396.

Pierpoint, Folliott Sandford (1835–1917), 71.

Pigott, Jean Sophia, 327.

Plumptre, Rev. Edward Hayes (1821–1891), 180, 297.

Pollock, Rev. Thomas Benson (1836–1896), 238.

Pope, Alexander (1688–1744), 346.

Pott, Rev. Francis (1832–1909), 164, 455.

Potter, Rev. Thomas Joseph (1827–1873), 457.

Prentiss, Mrs. Elizabeth Payson (1818–1878), 315.

Procter, Adelaide Anne (1825–1864), 36, 73, 305.

Prudentius, Aurelius Clemens (348–413), Plain Song 85.

"Psalms and Hymns," Rev. Rowland Hill (1783), 288.

"Psalms and Hymns," Morrell and How (1867), 457.

"Psalms and Hymns," S. P. C. K. (1869), 457.

"Psalter Hymnal, The" (1927), 102.

REED, Rev. Andrew (1787–1862), 212.

Richard of Chichester (c. 1197–1253), Response 39.

Rinkart, Rev. Martin (1586–1649), 459.

Rippon, Rev. John (1751–1836), 192, 283.

Roberts, Rev. Daniel C. (1841–1907), 414.

Roberts, Rev. Robert Rowland, 183.

Robinson, Rev. Robert (1735–1790), 235.

Rodigast, Samuel (1649–1708), 291.

Romanis, Rev. William (1824–1899), 502.

Rosenroth, Christian Knorr von (1636–1689), 30.

Rossetti, Christina Georgina (1830–1894), 133, 432, 439, 448, 504.

Rous, Francis (1579–1659), 97.

Russell, Rev. Arthur Tozer (1806–1874), 156, 172.

SANGSTER, Mrs. Margaret E. (1838–1912), 387.

Schaff, Rev. Philip (1819–1893), 357; Response 36.

Schlegel, Katharina von (b. 1697), 281.

Schmolck, Rev. Benjamin (1672–1737), 21, 280.

Index of Authors

Index of Composers

Handbook to The Hymnal

Clark, Jeremiah (1670–1707), 185, 195, 490; Response 35.

"Collection" (Greatorex), Boston (1851), 94.

"Collection of Hymns and Sacred Poems, A," Dublin (1749), 49, 340.

"Collection" (Petrie's), 145.

"Collection, The" (Valerius') (1625), 461.

Conkey, Ithamar (1815–1867), 154.

Converse, Charles Crozat (1832–1918), 257.

Cooper, A. S., Chant 74.

Cooper, Joseph Thomas (1819–1870), 501.

Cottman, Arthur (1842–1879), 143, 259, 338, 358; Response 10.

Courteville, Raphael (d. 1772), 254, 335.

Croft, William (1678–1727), 2, 77, 334, 476.

Crüger, Johann (1598–1662), 158, 212, 329, 459.

Cummings, William Hayman (1831–1918), 117.

Cutler, Henry Stephen (1824–1902), 271.

DABOVITCH, Rev. Sebastian, Chant 66.
Damon, William, "Psalter" (1579), 239.

Darwall, Rev. John (1731–1789), 50, 193.

Davies, E. T., 250.

Davies, Sir Henry Walford, 282, 300.

"Day's Psalter" (1563), 86, 144, 356.

Dickinson, Rev. C. J. (1822–1883), 359.

Dix, Leopold L., 508.

Doane, William Howard (1832–1916), 315.

Dougall, Neil (1776–1862), 28, 176.

Douglas, Canon Charles Winfred, 276; Chant 85.

Downes, Lewis Thomas (1827–1907), Response 41.

Drese, Adam (1620–1701), 502.

Drewett, Edwin (1850–1924), 383.

Duckworth, Francis, 32, 72.

Dyer, Samuel (1785–1835), 474.

Dykes, Rev. John Bacchus (1823–1876), 53, 57, 99, 150, 159, 205, 206, 218, 224, 233, 236, 255, 275, 289, 309, 322, 323, 356, 392, 398, 426, 427, 440, 485, 492.

EBELING, Johann Georg (1620–1676), 125.
Edwards, E., Response 6.

Edwards, Rev. F. Llewellyn, 323.

Elliott, James William (1833–1915), 268, 473.

Elvey, Sir George Job (1816–1893), 109, 175, 190, 230, 460; Chant 68.

Emerson, L. O. (1820-1915), 41.

"Essay on the Church Plain Chant" (1782), 304.

"Este's Psalter" (1592), 91, 229, 503; Response 24.

Evans, David, 177.

Evans, David Emlyn (1843–1913), 511.

Evans, D., "Hymnau a Thonau" (1865), 222, 371, 419.

Ewing, Lt. Col. Alexander (1830–1895), 435.

FARRANT, Richard (c. 1530–1580), Response 9; Chant 48.
Felton, Rev. William (c. 1715–1769), Chant 61.

Filitz, Rev. Friedrich (1804–1876), 252; Response 13.

Fink, Rev. Gottfried Wilhelm (1783–1846), 478.

Fischer, William Gustavus (1835–1912), 443.

Flemming, Friedrich Ferdinand (1778–1813), 306.

"Foundery Collection, The" (Rev. John Wesley's) (1742), 264, 288; Response 17.

"Freylinghausen's Gesangbuch," Halle (1704), 27, 30.

GARDINER, William (1770–1853), 410.
Gastorius, Severus (fl. 1675), 291.

Index of Composers

Gauntlett, Henry John (1805–1876), 454.

"Geistliche Kirchengesäng," Cologne (1623), 13, 388.

"Geistliche Lieder," Leipzig (1539), 118, 351, 506.

"Geistliche Lieder," Wittenberg (1535), 342.

"Genevan Psalter" (1549), Chant 82.

"Genevan Psalter" (1551), 185, 386, 481; Doxologies 94, 95.

"Genevan Psalter" (1552), 424.

"Gesangbuch der Herzogl. Wirtembergischen Katholischen Hofkapelle" (1784), 65, 147.

Giardini, Felice de (1716–1796), 52, 378, 483.

Gibbons, Orlando (1583–1625), 68, 240, 488.

Gläser, Carl Gotthilf (1784–1829), 179.

Goodson, Richard, Chant 47.

Goss, Sir John (1800–1880), 14, 272, 273.

Gottschalk, Louis Moreau (1829–1869), 208.

Goudimel, Claude (c. 1510–1572), 227.

Gould, John Edgar (1822–1875), 225, 286.

Gounod, Charles François (1818–1893), 26, 38.

Gower, John Henry (1855–1922), 157.

Greatorex, Henry Wellington (1811–1858), "Collection" (1851), 94.

Greatorex, W., 148, 258.

Greene, Maurice (1696–1755), 16.

Grenoble Church Melody, Response 29.

Grüber, Franz (1787–1863), 132.

Gwyllt, Ieuan (Rev. John Roberts), (1822–1877), 183.

HANDEL, George Frederick (1685–1759), 120, 122, 278, 313, 421.

Harding, John P., 136.

Harrington, Karl Pomeroy, 497.

Hassler, Hans Leo (1564–1612), 151.

Hastings, Thomas (1784–1872), 197, 237.

Hatton, John C. (d. 1793), 377, 462.

Havergal, Frances Ridley (1836–1879), 56, 169, 456.

Havergal, Rev. William Henry (1793–1870), 97; Chant 49.

Haweis, Rev. Thomas (1734–1820), 199, 363.

Haydn, Franz Joseph (1732–1809), 69, 339.

Haydn, Johann Michael (1737–1806), 198, 400.

Hayes, William (1706–1777), 482.

Hayne, Rev. Leighton George (1836–1883), 425.

"Heilige Seelenlust" (1657), 43.

Hemy, Henri Frederick (1818–1888), 267.

Hewlett, William Henry, Response 25.

Hews, George (1806–1873), 209.

Hiles, Henry (1826–1904), 36.

Hill, G. Everett, 201.

"Hirschberg Gesangbuch" (1741), 79, 397.

Hodges, Rev. John Sebastian Bach (1830–1915), 353.

Holbrook, Joseph Perry (1822–1888), 62, 280.

Holden, Oliver (1765–1844), 192.

Hopkins, Edward John (1818–1901), 55, 71.

Horsley, William (1774–1858), 157.

Howard, Samuel (1710–1782), 188, 294, 383.

Hoyte, W. Stevenson, 467.

Hughes, Rev. John, 104.

Hullah, John (1812–1884), 284, 296.

Hurst, William, 498.

Husband, Rev. Edward (1843–1908), 228.

"Hymnau a Thonau" (D. Evans') (1865), 222, 371, 419.

"Hymns and Sacred Poems, A Collection of," Dublin (1749), 49, 340.

ISAAK, Heinrich (c. 1455–1517), 505.

Isalaw (John Richards) (1843–1908), 15.

Handbook to The Hymnal

JACKSON, Robert (1842–1914), 84, 213, 246.

Jacob, B., "National Psalmody" (1819), 400.

James, Philip, 496; Amen 92.

Jeffery, J. Albert (1851–1928), 58.

Jenkins, David (1849–1915), 247.

Jones, John (Talysarn) (1797–1857), 247.

Jones, Rev. William (1726–1800), 187, 232.

Joseph, Georg (17th century), 43.

Jowett, Rev. Joseph (1784–1856), 511.

Jude, William Herbert (1851–1892), 223.

KATHOLISCHES GESANGBUCH," Vienna (c. 1774), 37.

Keeler, Walter Bradley, 433.

Kirkpatrick, William J. (1838–1921), 126.

Knapp, William (1698–1768), 470.

Knecht, Justin Heinrich (1752–1817), 228.

Kocher, Conrad (1786–1872), 71, 135.

LA FEILLÉE, François de (c. 1750), "Méthode du Plain Chant' (1808), 24, 196, 290, 430.

Lane, Spencer (1843–1903), 255.

Langran, James (1835–1909), 174; Response 8.

"Laudi Spirituali," Response 45.

Laufer, Rev. Calvin Weiss, 245, 324, 350, 367; Response 5.

Le Jeune, George Fitz-Curwood (1842–1904), 308, 435.

Lloyd, Charles Harford, 432.

Lloyd, R. F., 493.

Lockwood, Mrs. Charlotte Mathewson, 4.

Lomas, George (1834–1884), 277.

Lowry, Rev. Robert (1826–1899), 332, 396.

Luther, Rev. Martin (1483–1546), 266, 342.

Lutkin, Peter Christian (1858–1931), Chant 72.

Lwoff, Alexis Theodore (1799–1870), 346, 420.

"Lyra Davidica" (1708), 163.

MACALISTER, Robert Alexander Stewart, 9, 330.

MacMillan, Ernest, 453.

"Magdalen Chapel Hymns" (c. 1760), 445.

Maker, Frederick Charles (1844–1927), 29, 73, 162, 220, 302.

Malan, Rev. Henri Abraham César (1787–1864), 312, 316.

Mann, Arthur Henry (1850–1929), 200, 268, 380, 468.

Marsh, Simeon Butler (1798–1875), 233.

Martin, George W. (1828–1881), 247.

Mason, Henry Lowell, 181.

Mason, Lowell (1792–1872), 18, 152, 179, 203, 217, 241, 256, 261, 263, 279, 285, 343, 385, 391, 413.

Mason and Webb's "Cantica Laudis," Boston (1850), 362, 394.

Matthews, Henry E. (b. 1820), 450.

Matthews, Rev. Timothy Richard (1826–1910), 123, 161, 231.

"M. B. F." (1886), 361.

McCartney, Robert Hyslop (1844–1895), 311.

McCutchan, Robert G., 423.

"Melodienbuch von Rautenburg" (J. Cammin's), 331.

Melody of 1529, 17.

Mendelssohn-Bartholdy, Jakob Ludwig Felix (1809–1847), 11, 107, 117; Response 19.

Merbecke, John (1523–c. 1585), Chants 62, 65, 73, 75, 78.

Merrill, Rev. William Pierson, 269, 415, 418.

Messiter, Arthur Henry (1831–1916), 297.

"Méthode du Plain Chant" (La Feillée's) (1808), 24, 196, 290, 430.

Miller, Edward (1731–1807), 152, 360.

Moffatt, Rev. James, 439.

Monk, William Henry (1823–1889), 33, 164, 171, 201, 355, 406.

Index of Composers

Morley, Thomas (1845–1891), 202.
Morris, R. O., 133.
Mountain, James, 327.
Mozart, Wolfgang Amadeus (1756–1791), 203, 242.
"Musikalisches Handbuch," Hamburg (1690), 150.

Nägeli, Hans Georg (1768–1836), 279.
Nares, James (1715–1783), 264.
"National Psalmody" (B. Jacob's) (1819), 400.
Neander, Rev. Joachim (1650–1680), "Bundes-Lieder" (1680), 51.
Nettleton, Rev. Asahel (1783–1844), 235.
"Neu Leipziger Gesangbuch" (1682), 326, 491.
Neumark, Georg (1621–1681), 105.
"Neuvermehrtes Meiningisches Gesangbuch" (1693), 215.
Nicolai, Rev. Philipp (1556–1608), 321.
Noble, T. Tertius, 366; Chant 55.

Oakeley, Sir Herbert Stanley (1830–1903), 46, 101.
Oliver, Henry Kemble (1800–1885), 90; Response 2.
Oxford Chant, Chant 52.

Palestrina, Giovanni Pierluigi da (1526–1594), 164; Chant 77.
Palmer, G. H., 331.
Palmer, Horatio Richmond (1834–1907), 40.
"Parish Choir, The" (1850), 25.
Parker, Rev. Edwin Pond (1836–1925), 407.
Parker, Horatio William (1863–1919), 19, 193, 270, 370, 404.
Parr, Rev. Henry (b. 1815), 243.
Parry, Joseph (1841–1903), 233.
Peace, Albert Lister (1844–1912), 303, 305, 307.
Pearsall, R. L. de (1795–1856), 62.

"Pensum Sacrum," Görlitz (1648), 475; Response 27.
Perkins, Emily S., 67.
Petrie's "Collection," 145, 510.
"Plain Chant, Méthode du" (La Feillée's) (1808), 24, 196, 290, 430.
Pleyel, Ignaz Joseph (1757–1831), 22, 347.
Poole, Clement William (1828–1924), 82, 140, 219.
Praetorius, Michael (1571–1621), 119.
"Praxis Pietatis Melica" (1668), 6.
"Praxis Pietatis Melica" (Crüger's) (1653), 197, 212.
Price, John (Beulah), 512.
Prichard, Rowland Hugh (1811–1887), 113, 416.
"Psalmodia Evangelica" (Williams') (1789), 114, 405, 423.
"Psalmodia Sacra," Gotha (1715), 113.
"Psalter" (Damon's) (1579), 239.
"Psaumes Octante Trois," Geneva (1551), 292.
Purcell, Henry (1658–1695), 232.
Purcell, Thomas (d. 1682), Chant 57.
Purday, Charles Henry (1799–1885), 88, 96.

Quaile, Robert Newton, 446.

Redhead, Richard (1820–1901), 214, 237.
Redner, Lewis Henry (1831–1908), 121.
Reinagle, Alexander Robert (1799–1877), 81, 310, 341.
"Reinhardt MS.," Üttingen (1754), 7.
Richards, John (Isalaw) (1843–1908), 15
Rimbault, Edward Francis (1816–1876), 434.
Roberts, Rev. John (Ieuan Gwyllt) (1822–1877), 183.
Rouen Church Melody, 72, 141; Response 42.

Handbook to The Hymnal

SACRED MELODIES" (Gardiner's) (1815), 410.
"St. Alban's Tune Book" (1875), 160.
"St. Gall Gesangbuch" (1863), 62.
Sandys, W., "Christmas Carols" (1833), 129.
Schicht, Johann Gottfried (1753–1823), 172.
"Schlesische Volkslieder," Leipzig (1842), 194.
Scholefield, Rev. Clement Coterrill (1839–1904), 45.
"School Worship," England (1926), 141, 489.
Schulz, Johann Abraham Peter (1747–1800), 464.
Schumann, Robert Alexander (1810–1856), 78, 399.
Scott-Gatty, Alfred (1847–1918), 110, 368, 403; Response 7.
"Scottish Psalter" (1615), 98, 103, 479.
"Scottish Psalter" (1635), 185, 234, 295.
"Serbian Liturgy," Chant 66.
Shaw, Geoffrey Turton, 265.
Sherwin, William Fisk (1826–1888), 39, 216.
Shrubsole, William (1760–1806), 192.
Sibelius, Jean, 281, 499.
Smart, Sir George T. (1776–1867), 83.
Smart, Henry (1813–1879), 61, 68, 115, 124, 166, 274, 336, 369, 372, 390, 431.
Smith, Rev. Henry Percy (1825–1898), 364.
Smith, Robert Archibald (1780–1829), 299, 328; Responses 23, 32.
Somervell, Arthur, Responses 31, 39.
Spiess, Johann Martin (1715–c. 1766), 20, 253.
Spohr, Louis (1784–1859), 317.
Stainer, Sir John (1840–1901), 130, 131, 155, 495, 500; Chant 83; Amen 91.
Stanley, Samuel (1767–1822), Response 12.
Stebbins, George Coles, 47.

Steggall, Charles (1826–1905), 409.
Stewart, Sir Robert Prescott (1825–1894), 395.
Stocks, George Gilbert, 509.
Storer, Henry John, 408, 437.
"Stralsund Gesangbuch" (1665), 6.
Strattner, Georg Christoph (1650–1705), 452.
Strong, Thomas Banks, Response 40.
"Students' Hymnal, A," University of Wales (1923), 100, 213, 444.
Sullivan, Sir Arthur Seymour (1842–1900), 128, 168, 247, 365, 455, 457.
"Supplement to the New Version" (1708), 77, 334, 476.
Sweetser, Joseph Emerson (1825–1873), 299; Response 15.

TALLIS, Thomas (1520–1585), 42; Chants 80, 81.
Taylor, Virgil Corydon (1817–1891), 87.
Teschner, Rev. Melchior (c. 1615), 146.
Thalben-Ball, George, 76.
"Thesaurus Musicus" (1740), 412.
Tonus Peregrinus, Chant 60.
Tonus Regius, Response 28.
Torrance, Rev. George William (1836–1907), Response 43.
Tours, Berthold (1838–1897), 111, 137, 149, 441.
Traditional:
Austrian, 501.
Bohemian, Response 34.
Danish, Amen 89.
Dutch, 93, 393, 461.
English, 70, 80, 95, 131, 138, 248, 276, 298, 314, 442, 447, 448, 451, 453, 471, 486, 503; Responses 11, 16, 37.
Finnish, 284.
French, 25, 112, 141, 167, 489; Responses 14, 29, 42.
German, 18, 130, 134, 449, 465, 474, 513; Response 1; Amen 90.
Greek, 442; Amen 87.
Hebrew, 4, 8; Response 18.
Irish, 145, 325, 508, 510.

Index of Composers

Adoration

*

HYMN: All People That on Earth Do Dwell
TUNE: Old Hundredth

Author: *Rev. William Kethe*   Composer: *Louis Bourgeois*

AUTHOR: The first hymn of this collection, calling to universal praise, comes from the pen of an exiled reformer who fled before the persecution of Mary in 1555–1558 and found refuge in Geneva. William Kethe was without question a native of Scotland, but the time and place of his birth are lost in obscurity. During his exile he became a messenger of comfort to English refugees scattered through western Europe. His gifts in psalmody were evidently recognized, for it is intimated that he was active in the work of completing the metrical version of The Psalms later to be known as the "Anglo-Genevan Psalter" (see the article, "The Psalters in Early Presbyterian Worship," under "Original Sources," page xv). In the version of 1561 of this Psalter Kethe has twenty-five of his versified psalms. All these were set into the "Scottish Psalter," which was issued in 1564–1565. Kethe was known to be chaplain to the forces under the Earl of Warwick for a period and to have been in charge of the parish of Childe Okeford in Dorsetshire. His death in all probability occurred in the closing years of the century.

HYMN: This well-known version of Psalm 100 is the only hymn of Kethe's in common use. It is taken from the "Psalter," published in 1561 by that enterprising printer John Day, who suffered much for his loyalty to the reformed faith and who has put both English literature and typography under lasting debt. This version, composed by Kethe, who was a faithful friend of John Knox, has resisted many proposed alterations, and in its quaintness and rugged diction calls us to praise with practically the same idioms as well as the same tune known to the original group of Presbyterians at Geneva. This hymn expresses the dominant motive of the entire Hymnal and sets for it the pitch of triumphant and grateful praise with which every hymn chant and canticle harmonizes.

COMPOSER: Louis Bourgeois was born in Paris at the beginning of the sixteenth century. An adherent of John Calvin, he was invited to Geneva, in 1541, to teach and organize the music of the Church. He was appointed cantor in one of the churches at Geneva, and later, 1545, master of the choristers. Apart from notices in the registers of the Council of Geneva, little is known of him. He was admitted to the rights of citizenship "in consideration of his being a respectable man and willing to teach children."

In his work he was highly successful, and congregational singing in Geneva was an inspiring experience. A visitor to Geneva in 1557 writes of the large attendance upon Protestant worship, where "each one draws from his pocket a small book which contains the psalms with notes and out of full hearts, in native speech, the congregation sings before and after the sermon." This was largely due to Bourgeois. However, he was a man of some independence and was thrown into prison for having without permission altered several tunes of the psalms. Through Calvin's intervention he was released on the following day. His chief claim to notice is his work in the preparation and publication of the various Genevan Psalters. Bourgeois left Geneva in 1557, and probably died in Paris. Dr. Robert Bridges writes, "Historians who wish to give a true philosophical account of Calvin's influence at Geneva ought probably to refer a great part of it to the enthusiasm attendant on the singing of Bourgeois' melodies."

TUNE: "Old Hundredth" was either composed or adapted by Bourgeois to Beza's version of Psalm 134. It appeared in the "Genevan Psalter" of 1551. There are those who consider it of secular origin and maintain that it is an arrangement. In its present form it is ascribed to Bourgeois, who edited the Genevan Psalters from 1542 to 1557. The name "Old Hundredth" is peculiar to England, where it was associated with Kethe's version of Psalm 100, and so published in John Day's "Psalter" in 1560–1561. There are several variations of the tune, the changes relating to the value of the notes. As it appears here, the original rhythm is preserved, though it closes with an English version of the last phrase.

---

2   HYMN: O Worship the King All Glorious Above
         TUNE: Hanover

Author: *Robert Grant*   Composer: *William Croft*

AUTHOR: Scholar, statesman, philanthropist, jurist, Sir Robert Grant will be remembered as the author of this noble hymn. He was born in Bengal, India, in 1779; educated at Magdalen College, Oxford; admitted to the bar at the age of twenty-eight; and became a member of the British Parliament at twenty-nine. He inherited the philanthropic qualities of his father, and through his efforts a bill was enacted in 1833 emancipating the Jews. In 1831 he became a privy councilor and in 1834 governor of Bombay. He died in India in 1838, at the age of fifty-nine. A medical college bearing his name was erected as a memorial.

Adoration

Twelve hymns which he had written were published by his brother in 1839. One of these, "Saviour, When in Dust to Thee," is in the form of a litany.

HYMN: Like so many of our best hymns, "O Worship the King All Glorious Above" is based on one of the Hebrew psalms. It is a free and lyrical paraphrase of Psalm 104 and first appeared in Bickersteth's "Christian Psalmody" in 1833. It was included in the collection published in 1839. As printed in 1833, the second line read "O gratefully sing his unchangeable love" and line 4, stanza 3, read "girdle" instead of "mantle." The hymn originally consisted of six stanzas. The sixth stanza, not in this Hymnal, usually beginning "O measureless Might! Ineffable Love!" originally read "O Lord of all might, how boundless thy love!" The nobility of the hymn is better appreciated after a thoughtful reading of Psalm 104 on which it is based: "Bless the Lord, O my soul. O Lord my God, thou art very great; thou art clothed with honour and majesty" (King James Version).

COMPOSER: As a boy, William Croft was a chorister in the Chapel Royal and received instruction from Dr. Blow. He afterwards became organist of St. Anne's, Soho, and later of the Chapel Royal. In 1708 he succeeded Dr. Blow as organist of Westminster Abbey. He received the degree of Doctor of Music in 1713. He was one of the greatest English composers of church music, publishing thirty anthems and, with Purcell, a burial service unsurpassed "for solemn grandeur." Handel is said to have been influenced by him in the style of his oratorios. He died at Bath in 1727.

To-day Croft is chiefly known for the superb tunes he contributed to hymnody. "They are the earliest examples of the English psalm tune as distinguished from the Genevan."

TUNE: The tune, "Hanover," first appeared in 1708, in the sixth edition of "A Supplement to the New Version of Psalms," by Tate and Brady. In this collection it did not bear a name, nor was the composer's name mentioned, but it was called "A New Tune to the 149th Psalm of the New Version, and the 104th Psalm of the Old." It was first called "Hanover" in Gawthorn's "Harmonia Perfecta" in 1730. This was in honor of the House of Hanover, then reigning in England. The tune appeared later under various names, among them "Bromswick," "Old 104th," and "Tally's."

The tune is now definitely attributed to William Croft, although others have at various times been credited with its composition. It is thought that Croft may have had some concern in the publication of the Tate and Brady supplement, which might explain his leaving the tune unsigned. At one time the claim was made that Handel was its composer, but this seems unlikely as the tune had been published two years prior to Handel's coming to England. The tune was also attributed to Tallis, hence the name "Tally's." But in the index of "The People's Music Book," 1844, appears the following note: "This tune has been ascertained to be the composition of Dr. Croft, by satisfactory evidence."

---

3   HYMN: When Morning Gilds the Skies
TUNE: Laudes Domini

Translator: *Rev. Edward Caswall*   Composer: *Joseph Barnby*

SOURCE: For comments on the source, see the article, "German Hymn Sources," under "Original Sources," page xxi.

TRANSLATOR: Rev. Edward Caswall was born at Yately, England, July 15, 1814. He was an unusual student and took special honors at Brasenose College, Oxford. He joined the Tractarian Movement, which carried many English churchmen into the Roman Church. Upon the death of his wife, he entered the oratory at Edgbaston, Birmingham. This unusual parish was presided over by Cardinal John Henry Newman, who in 1845, after three years of mental distress, found a meager welcome, and for forty years an obscure seclusion, in the Roman Church. Caswall devoted the twenty-eight years of his semimonastic life to the interests of the sick poor and the little children of poverty in Birmingham and to the composition of original hymns and the translation of Latin hymns. Caswall's translations, together with those of Dr. John Mason Neale, make up the great majority of Latin hymns now in use. He has a permanent place in hymnology by reason of the lyric quality of his own hymns and his faithful transcriptions of the ancient hymns. Caswall and Newman were buried side by side in a rural churchyard near Birmingham.

HYMN: The hymn comes from unknown German sources and first appears in the "Katholisches Gesangbuch," 1828. Here, with fourteen stanzas, it bore the title "A Christian Greeting." A radiant morning hymn of adoration, it breathes the joy and rest of a complete faith in Christ. It was the favorite hymn of Canon Liddon (1829–1890), the great pulpit orator of his time, and was sung at his funeral.

COMPOSER: Sir Joseph Barnby was born in York in 1838 and died in London in 1896. He was well known in England, equally as organist, composer, editor, and choral conductor. Trained as a chorister at York Minster, he held important positions as organist,

Adoration

finally serving as precentor at Eton College from 1875 to 1892. He is known for his numerous services and anthems, but especially for his hymn tunes, 246 of which, after his death, were published in one volume. He edited five hymn books. As conductor of the Royal Choral Society in London, he continued its tradition for splendid performances of the great oratorios. Dvorák's "Stabat Mater" and Wagner's "Parsifal" were first performed in England under his baton, the latter being given in concert form in November, 1884.

Barnby belongs to the group of English church musicians of the later nineteenth century whose work, though often secular, was reverent in spirit. "Laudes Domini" is a good example of his tuneful and vigorous style.

TUNE: "Laudes Domini" was written to the hymn "When Morning Gilds the Skies" and was first published in the appendix to "Hymns Ancient and Modern" in 1868. The composer, Sir Joseph Barnby, slightly altered the last two measures for his edition of "Original Tunes," published the following year.

The hymn is well adapted for the opening of the service and, set to "Laudes Domini," makes a good processional. Due to its fluent harmony and strong rhythm, this tune is often played too fast. While it is joyful in character, care must be taken to interpret it with proper dignity.

---

4   HYMN: Men and Children Everywhere
     TUNE: Rock of Ages

Author: *Rev. John J. Moment*   Arranger: *Charlotte Mathewson Lockwood*

AUTHOR: John James Moment was a member of the Presbyterian Hymnal Committee. He was born in Orono, Ontario, in 1875. He won an A.B. from Princeton University in 1896, and a B.D. from Hartford Theological Seminary in 1906, and was awarded the honorary degree of Doctor of Divinity by Washington and Jefferson College. He began his professional career as a teacher at Lawrenceville School, 1898–1904, but from 1906 to 1908 was assistant minister of the First Presbyterian Church, East Orange, New Jersey, and from 1908 to 1911 associate minister of the Bergen Reformed Church, Jersey City, New Jersey. He was pastor of the High Street Presbyterian Church, Newark, New Jersey, from 1911 to 1918 and has been pastor of the Crescent Avenue Presbyterian Church, Plainfield, New Jersey, since 1918. Hymn 290, "God of Compassion, in Mercy Befriend Us," is also from his pen.

Handbook to The Hymnal

HYMN: The hymn was written to be rendered as an anthem. The music was written by Charlotte M. Lockwood, organist of the Crescent Avenue Presbyterian Church, Plainfield, New Jersey. The music and the words follow in spirit the ancient Hebrew hymn "Moot Zoor," or "Fortress Rock," here named "Rock of Ages." It is a true hymn and lingers after each stanza on the high theme of adoration: "Holy, holy, To our God all glory be!" It strikes the true note of psalmody.

SOURCE: The source of this hymn is an ancient Hebrew melody.

ARRANGER: Charlotte Mathewson Lockwood, F.A.G.O., S.M.M., was born at Granby, Connecticut, in 1903. Her childhood was spent in Reidsville, North Carolina, where at the age of eleven she was organist of the First Methodist Church. In 1923 she became a pupil of Dr. Clarence Dickinson in New York, and since then has been closely associated with him. She also studied with Widor in Paris and Ramin at Leipzig. She is at present organist of the Crescent Avenue Presbyterian Church, Plainfield, New Jersey, and of the West End Synagogue, New York, and is a member of the faculty of the School of Sacred Music at Union Theological Seminary, New York, from which she graduated as Master of Sacred Music.

TUNE: The tune, "Rock of Ages," derived its name from the first line of a hymn used in the Jewish ritual for the festival of lights. It is set to this hymn in "The Union Hymnal." The date of its first use in this connection is not known. The harmonization here used was made by Charlotte M. Lockwood.

The tune has a majestic sweep, the climactic fifth line of the music being well matched by the text. Notice the skill with which the sonorous descending progression in the sixth line is lightened by the eighth notes in the air. Care should be taken not to stress the second syllable of the word "holy" in the refrain.

---

5   HYMN: Joyful, Joyful, We Adore Thee
      TUNE: Hymn to Joy

Author: *Rev. Henry van Dyke*   Composer: *Ludwig van Beethoven*

AUTHOR: The author, Dr. Henry van Dyke, one of the most distinguished literary men of his generation, was born November 10, 1852, on one of America's historic streets in Germantown, Pennsylvania. His birthplace was near the site of the Battle of Germantown,

6

Adoration

where the son of John Witherspoon was killed and now lies buried. He graduated from the Polytechnic Institute of Brooklyn and entered Princeton College, where he received the degree of Bachelor of Arts in the Class of 1873 and his A.M. in 1876. He graduated from Princeton Theological Seminary in 1877, was ordained in 1879, and began his career as pastor of the United Congregational Church in Newport, Rhode Island, coming to the Brick Presbyterian Church, New York City, in 1883. It was in this noted pulpit that Dr. van Dyke's rare sermonic abilities were revealed. His sermons were characterized by great freshness and vitality of style, by beauty of diction, and by breadth of view, as well as by a fearlessness in the declaration of his convictions.

He became professor of English literature in Princeton University in 1900. Here his estate, "Avalon," with its rare library, became a favorite rendezvous of writers from both sides of the ocean. He was elected Moderator of the General Assembly in 1902. He was a warm personal friend and intimate comrade of President Woodrow Wilson. Recognizing his distinguished abilities, the latter appointed Dr. van Dyke United States Minister to the Netherlands and Luxemburg in 1913. Previously he had been the American lecturer at the University of Paris, in 1909, and he was elected a Fellow of the Royal Society of Literature in 1910. He was honored by Oxford University with the degree of D.C.L. in 1917, and made commander in the Legion of Honor in 1918. Meanwhile he had received the degrees of Doctor of Divinity and Doctor of Laws from several universities in the United States.

His world-wide distinction rests upon his authorship. He wrote more than twenty-five notable books. Among them were: "The Reality of Religion," 1884; "The Story of the Psalms," 1887; "The Poetry of Tennyson," 1889; "Sermons to Young Men," 1893; "Little Rivers," 1895; "The Story of the Other Wise Man," 1896; and "The Gospel for an Age of Doubt," 1896, in addition to other volumes and a great variety of casual writing in current church periodicals.

No work gave Dr. van Dyke more satisfaction than his leadership of the Committee on Revision of "The Book of Common Worship," adopted in 1905. It was on his own motion that it was ordered revised in 1928, and finally adopted by the General Assembly in 1931. This he regarded as the final task of life allotted to him. With this done, and his advisory work on the new Hymnal concluded, his life closed in great peace at "Avalon" on April 10, 1933.

HYMN: This hymn was written in 1907. It is found in "The Music of the Gospel," issued in 1932. According to Rev. Tertius van Dyke, the hymn was written by his father during a preaching visit at Williams College. Coming down to the breakfast room, he placed a manuscript on the table before President Garfield, saying: "Here

7

Handbook to The Hymnal

is a hymn for you. Your mountains were my inspiration. It must be sung to the music of Beethoven's 'Hymn to Joy.' " No literary man of his generation loved nature with deeper spiritual understanding than did Dr. van Dyke, and this hymn reveals something of the glorious message it had for his soul.

COMPOSER: Ludwig van Beethoven was born at Bonn in 1770, and his early training and career as a musician began in that city. In 1792 he removed to Vienna, where the rest of his work was done and where he died in 1827. He revealed his notable genius first as a violinist then as a pianist, being very specially noted for his improvisations. In 1795 he began to publish compositions which reflected the influence of Haydn, with whom he studied, and of Mozart, who had already prophesied great things for him. From 1800 onward major works in various forms were composed in rapid succession. During this time he began to be afflicted with deafness. As early as 1815 he was unable to hear without artificial aid and soon became totally deaf. From that time his work, which now was his sole means of self-expression, changed in character. In this later period five of the greatest piano sonatas, the chief string quartets, the "Missa Solemnis," and the immortal "Ninth Symphony" came from his pen.

During his tempestuous life this master produced an amazing output, his last formal opus number being 138, in addition to 120 other distinct compositions. He was "the first composer to utilize the capacity of the modern piano and the first to bring out the latent powers of the modern orchestra."

The "Ninth Symphony" was begun in 1817. Its final movement was at first intended to be orchestral, and the early sketches show no trace of choral treatment, though Beethoven made notes of a companion symphony employing voices in two movements. In 1822 he conceived the idea of employing Schiller's "Ode to Joy" in the final movement, which was completed in September, 1823. The first performance was in Vienna on May 7, 1824, though the score was actually composed for use by the London Philharmonic Society. The whole symphony excited the greatest enthusiasm. "The subject of the vocal portion of the symphony was what gave him the greatest trouble," writes one biographer. Adequate rendition of the vocal portion has given some trouble to choral units ever since.

TUNE: "Hymn to Joy" was arranged from Beethoven's "Ninth Symphony" as a hymn tune by Edward Hodges (1796–1867), who came from Bristol, England, in 1838, to Canada and from there, in 1839, to serve for more than twenty years as an organist in New York, first at St. John's Episcopal Chapel and then at Trinity Church.

The hymn tune should never be sung so fast as the tempo indicated for the choral movement in the symphony. Its use by the congregation

8

Adoration

demands a firm, steady rhythm, allowing sufficient time for a good breath at each pair of lines. Only one distinct accent should be allowed in each bar, the secondary accent on the third beat being eliminated.

---

6   HYMN: Praise Ye the Lord, the Almighty, the King
                of Creation
        TUNE: Lobe den Herren

Author: *Joachim Neander*   Source: *"Stralsund Gesangbuch"*

AUTHOR: Joachim Neander had a careless youth. He was converted under the ministry of Undereyk, and later became his associate in St. Martin's Church at Bremen, where he was born and educated, lived and died (1650–1680). For a period he was under the influence of the Pietists. In 1674 he was appointed head master of the Reformed Grammar School at Düsseldorf, whence his religious zeal sent him forth on evangelistic and preaching missions. So eager was he in forwarding the Pietist faith that he was dismissed from his position. He lived in a cave on the banks of the Rhine near Mettman, which is still known as Neander's Cave. He returned to Bremen in 1679 to associate himself with St. Martin's. His ministry here was brief and stormy. He died in 1680 at the age of thirty. He was a scholar, interested in literature and music, and he has been called "the first poet of the Reformed Church in Germany." He wrote sixty hymns and many tunes.

TRANSLATOR: Catherine Winkworth, the foremost translator of German hymns, was born in London in 1829 and died suddenly of heart disease in 1878. Her life was devoted to unselfish service for the higher education of women through the Clifton Association and other societies. Her spirituality and devotional feelings, coupled with rare poetic gifts and a perfect knowledge of the German language and people, account for the beauty and simplicity of her translations. A tablet on the wall of Bristol Cathedral indicates that Catherine Winkworth "opened a new source of light, consolation, and strength in many thousand homes." Her "Lyra Germanica" is a devotional classic.

HYMN: The hymn was written during Neander's troubled days at Düsseldorf and first published in 1680. Neander himself selected the tune to which it has always been set, "Lobe den Herren." There are four stanzas in the original hymn, the third being omitted in "The Hymnal." The hymn is a noble and felicitous paraphrase of Psalms 103 and 150, and therefore a hymn of adoring praise.

9

SOURCE: The earliest known publication of the tune, "Lobe den Herren," was in the "Stralsund Gesangbuch" in 1665. In 1668 it appeared in Johann Crüger's "Praxis Pietatis Melica," and later in various collections of German chorals. It was first set to this hymn by Neander in 1680.

Many variants of the melody and harmonization have appeared, due to the widespread use of the choral. It is as well known in Scandinavia as in Germany. The origin of the tune is uncertain; it was probably based upon a traditional folk song.

TUNE: "Lobe den Herren" is a tune of great vigor and strength. It is expressive of joy and thanksgiving and most fitting in services of praise and adoration. Care should be taken to avoid too rapid a tempo.

---

7   HYMN: O Worship the Lord in the Beauty of Holiness
         TUNE: Was Lebet, Was Schwebet

Author: *Rev. John S. B. Monsell*   Source: *"Reinhardt MS."*

AUTHOR: Rev. John S. B. Monsell, LL.D., is described by Dr. Moffatt as "a persuasive preacher, and a singularly devout and sunny-hearted man." He was a son of the rectory. His father was an archdeacon in St. Columb's, Ireland. He was educated in Dublin University and ordained in 1834. Though a conscientious and devoted preacher and pastor, nothing hindered his constant writing of much fine prose and very worthy poetry. More than three hundred hymns were found in his eleven volumes of poetry. Over seventy of these hymns are in common use to-day. He died from injuries received from a stone falling from the roof of his parish church, where he was inspecting repairs. Dr. Julian considers Monsell's hymns lacking in "massiveness, concentration of thought, and strong emotion," but "as a whole bright, joyous, and musical." Although "a few only are of enduring excellence," Monsell's hymns live in the hymnology of the universal Church. Seven of his best-loved hymns are found in "The Hymnal."

HYMN: The meter of this hymn gives it a pleasing and singable rhythm and adds to its worship uses an atmosphere of joy and activity. Monsell urged that hymns for corporate singing should be fervent and spontaneous, not rigid and reserved. His home life is described as "full of the beauty of holiness" and "of genial brightness and gayety playing like sunshine over all the troubles of life." The theme of the hymn is that God hears, cares, and guides and, therefore, mental equilibrium and spiritual serenity are the part of every true worshiper.

Adoration

SOURCE: "Was Lebet, Was Schwebet" comes from the Reinhardt Manuscript of Üttingen of 1754. We are unable to trace the melody to an earlier time, although it must be much older.

TUNE: The melodic curve and smooth, flowing meter suggest that "Was Lebet, Was Schwebet" may have a folk-tune origin.

The meter of the tune deserves mention. Almost all tunes in triple time give two beats to each of the accented syllables of a trochaic text, as in Hymn 287, "Bullinger." This tune, however, is in true triple time, with one note to each beat of the three beats in the bar. The hymn is consistently dactylic in meter, so that each syllable fits one note of the music. The rhythm should be marked by making the second and third beats of each bar slightly weaker than the first beat.

---

8   HYMN: The God of Abraham Praise
                  TUNE: Yigdal (Leoni)

Author: *Daniel Ben Judah*   Source: *Hebrew Melody*

AUTHOR: The translation of this hymn used in "The Union Hymnal," edited by the Central Conference of American Rabbis, and beginning, "Praise to the Living God," is attributed to Newton Mann, who based his paraphrase upon the Hebrew version attributed to Daniel Ben Judah, about whom little is known but who probably belonged to the fourteenth century. The translation by Thomas Olivers is in twelve stanzas, divided into three parts of four stanzas each, dated 1770, and inscribed: "A Hymn to the God of Abraham. In Three Parts. Adapted to a Celebrated Air, Sung by the Priest, Signior Leoni, Etc., at the Jews' Synagogue, in London: By Thomas Olivers."

HYMN: The version in "The Hymnal" is substantially the same as that used in the Jewish Hymnal. The original version is based upon the Hebrew Yigdal, or Doxology, which is sung by Jews at morning worship and at the close of the evening service.

As found in the Hebrew Prayer Book, it reads:

" 1. Magnified and praised be the living God: he is, and there is no limit in time unto his being.

" 2. He is One, and there is no unity like unto his unity; inconceivable is he, and unending is his unity.

" 3. He hath neither bodily form nor substance: we can compare nought unto him in his holiness.

" 4. He was before anything that hath been created—even the first: but his existence had no beginning.

" 5. Behold, he is the Lord of the universe: to every creature he teacheth his greatness and his sovereignty.

" 6. The rich gift of his prophecy he gave unto the men of his choice, in whom he gloried.

" 7. There hath never yet arisen in Israel a prophet like unto Moses, one who hath beheld his similitude.

" 8. The Law of truth God gave unto his people by the hand of his prophet, who was faithful in his house.

" 9. God will not alter nor change his Law to everlasting for any other.

"10. He watcheth and knoweth our secret thoughts: he beholdeth the end of a thing before it existeth.

"11. He bestoweth loving-kindness upon a man according to his work; he giveth to the wicked evil according to this wickedness.

"12. He will send our anointed at the end of days, to redeem them that wait for the end—his salvation.

"13. In the abundance of his loving-kindness God will quicken the dead. Blessed for evermore be his glorious name."

SOURCE: The origin of the Hebrew melody is not clear. Idelsohn gives nine tunes which seem in part to bear some resemblance to the tune as it is now used.

TUNE: The tune, "Yigdal," or, as it is often called, "Leoni," was introduced into Christian worship about the year 1770. Thomas Olivers, a Wesleyan minister, happened to attend a service at the Duke's Place Synagogue in London, where he heard a melody "which so completely enraptured him that he resolved to have it sung in Christian congregations." He secured the tune from Meyer Lyon (Leoni) and to it wrote the stanzas of "The God of Abraham Praise." The hymn set to this tune became widely known and ran through thirty reprints.

"Yigdal" is a tune of great breadth and power. Although it is in a minor key, it strikes a note of praise. The strength and dignity of the music are very fitting for the noble words in honor of the Eternal One. Because of the clear duple rhythm and the vigorous movement of the tune it is useful as a processional or recessional hymn. It should, however, by no means be confined to the beginning or the end of the service.

Adoration

9   HYMN: Let All the World in Every Corner Sing
        TUNE: St. Darerca

Author: *Rev. George Herbert*   Composer: *Robert Alexander Stewart Macalister*

AUTHOR: For intimate data concerning the life and work of "Holy George Herbert," as Rev. George Herbert was known among his neighbors, we turn to his biography written by quaint Izaak Walton, author of "The Compleat Angler," 1653. Walton is said to have spent much of his time with "families of the eminent clergy of whom he was most beloved." Herbert was esteemed by the poets Sir Henry Wotton and John Donne, and by Lord Bacon as well. He was born in a family castle in Montgomery and, according to Walton, seemed "marked out for piety and to become the care of heaven." His pastoral and preaching work was marked by a life of sacrificial devotion. His chief literary work, "The Temple," is a collection of quaint devotional poems, including his hymns. Humor, naïve figures of speech, and great sincerity characterize the poems of this pioneer Elizabethan hymn writer. Shortly before his death he took up his viol and sang Donne's lines:

> "The Sundays of man's life
> Threaded together on time's string
> Make bracelets to adorn the wife
> Of the eternal glorious King."

HYMN: Herbert's hymns have long since secured a firm place in the worship life of the Church. No finer example of childlike simplicity and spiritual fervor in worship can be found than in this hymn.

COMPOSER: Robert Alexander Stewart Macalister, A.R.C.O., F.S.A., Litt.D., LL.D., was born in Dublin in 1870, and was educated in Germany and at Cambridge, England. He is now professor of Celtic archæology in University College, Dublin. He has been active in promoting archæological discovery in Palestine, and has many publications in that field. Dr. Macalister is organist and choirmaster of the Adelaide Road Presbyterian Church in Dublin, where he resides. He served on the Revision Committee and the Subcommittee on Music in the preparation of "The Church Hymnary," Revised, 1927.

TUNE: "St. Darerca" was written by Dr. Macalister for this hymn for "The Church Hymnary" as revised in 1927.
     The tune requires close study before being introduced for congregational use. It amply repays the effort, however, especially if it is sung first as a choir hymn.

A distinct pause should follow the stately refrain of the second line, "My God and King!" The character of the two succeeding couplets demands a smooth, unhurried firmness which will prevent the contrapuntal runs from sounding jerky. The seventh line may well be sung slowly and in unison. Notice the effective reiteration of the progression of the last four notes of the first line, in the second, the seventh, and finally the majestic eighth line.

IO   HYMN: Praise the Lord: Ye Heavens, Adore Him
               FIRST TUNE: Alleluia (Wesley)

Source: *"Foundling Hospital Collection"*   Composer: *Samuel*
Author (Stanza 3): *Edward Osler*   *Sebastian Wesley*

AUTHORS: The author of the first two stanzas of this hymn is unknown. The hymn was found in a four-leafed folder attached to copies of "Psalms, Hymns, and Anthems of the Foundling Hospital," 1796. The folder bears the title "For Foundling Apprentices, Attending Divine Service to Return Thanks." It is the only one of five hymns printed in the folder that is familiar. The hymn as originally printed contained four stanzas.

In 1836 Edward Osler added stanza 3 as used in "The Hymnal." Edward Osler was born at Falmouth, England, in 1798. He prepared for the medical profession and gave several years to its practice, then turned to religious and literary work. He served the Society for Promoting Christian Knowledge and later became editor of the Royal Cornwall Gazette, a position which he held until his death in 1863. His hymnological work was distinguished, and chiefly in connection with the "Mitre Hymn Book" and "Psalms and Hymns Adapted to the Services of the Church of England." There were in the above collection fifteen psalm versions and fifty hymns by Osler. This doxology, with which this noble hymn closes, is worthy of a place at the side of Bishop Ken's doxology and Watts's "Give to the Father Praise."

HYMN: The title of the original hymn is "Hymn from Psalm 148, Haydn." It is a free and open rendering of some of the appealing lines of this great psalm, in which heaven and earth join in a magnificent anthem of praise and adoration. Writing of the death of his brother, Bernard of Clairvaux says: "Who could ever have loved me as he did? He was a brother by blood, but far more in the faith. God grant, Gerard, that I may not have lost thee, but that thou hast only gone before me; for, of a surety, thou hast joined those whom, in thy last night below, thou didst invite to praise God, when suddenly, to the surprise of all,

Adoration

thou, with a serene countenance and cheerful voice, didst commence chanting that psalm, 'Praise ye the Lord from the heavens: praise him in the heights. Praise ye him, all his angels: praise ye him, all his hosts.' At that moment, O my brother, the day dawned on thee, though it was night to us; the night to thee was all brightness."

COMPOSER (First Tune): Samuel Sebastian Wesley, Mus.D., was born in London in 1810 and died in Gloucester in 1876. He came from a line of church musicians. His father, Samuel Wesley, was a noted composer of music for the Church, and his grandfather was Charles Wesley, the evangelist and prolific hymn writer. Wesley became an organist at the age of sixteen. He served in five parish churches and in the following cathedrals: Hereford, Exeter, Winchester, and finally at Gloucester. The choral establishments in the cathedrals with which he was connected were generally unsatisfactory, but he continually labored to introduce higher standards in the cathedral service. His organ-playing was renowned and he was famed for his ability in improvisation. His organ compositions and anthems were widely used. He was also greatly interested in hymn music, and in 1872 he published a collection of hymn tunes, "The European Psalmist," which contained 130 tunes from his pen.

TUNE (First): "Alleluia" was written by Samuel Sebastian Wesley for the hymn "Alleluia! Sing to Jesus," which appeared in 1868 in the appendix to "Hymns Ancient and Modern." This tune is suitable for a processional.

SECOND TUNE: Faben

Composer: *John H. Willcox*

COMPOSER (Second Tune): The composer of "Faben" was John Henry Willcox, who was born in Savannah, 1827, and died in Boston in 1875. He graduated at Trinity College, Hartford, in 1849, and later became an organist in Boston. He was noted as a talented player, and was also an expert in organ construction. He wrote much music for the Roman Catholic church service.

TUNE (Second): "Faben" is one of a large group of tunes that enjoyed great popularity toward the end of the last century. The patterns of rhythm and melody are simple and consistently developed so that they are easy to sing.

Care must be taken not to take this tune too fast; otherwise the short notes become choppy and the effect of the tune as a whole is spoiled. The obvious climax in the last pair of lines, prepared for in lines 5 and 6, should be given out broadly, preferably with a slight retard. Good vocal leadership will prevent slurring some of the intervals of the melody, especially the descending fourth at the end of the first line, repeated twice later.

Handbook to The Hymnal

I I
    HYMN: Songs of Praise the Angels Sang
    TUNE: Mendelssohn

Author: *James Montgomery*   Composer: *Felix Mendelssohn*

AUTHOR: James Montgomery is classed by the literati as a minor English poet. Nevertheless the Church ranks him with Wesley, Watts, and Doddridge. He has left behind him a dozen volumes of verse. There are three volumes of hymns, numbering four hundred, from which more than one hundred have been drawn that to-day are widely sung. Nine of Montgomery's hymns are in "The Hymnal."

He was born in November, 1771, in Irvine in Ayrshire, near the birthplace of Robert Burns, and he shared something of Burns's native gift of rhythm and intimate understanding of the common experiences of life. His father was a Moravian minister, belonging to a devout but humble peasant family. In 1778 James Montgomery entered the Moravian School at Fulneck, near Leeds, England, to be educated for the ministry. He spent more time writing poetry, however, than in his studies. He left school in 1787 and spent four years in very precarious and doubtful modes of living. He became an editor in Sheffield and for his outspoken political opinions was twice imprisoned. He drifted away from the Church but turned to it again at forty-three years of age when he joined the old Moravian church of his boyhood with the following pathetic confession of unhappy years:

> "Now to you my spirit turns—
> Turns a fugitive unblest;
> Brethren, where your altar burns,
> Oh, receive me into rest."

He died in his sleep, April 30, 1854.

HYMN: No hymns show a wider knowledge of the Scriptures than do those of Montgomery. In this hymn he brings together as ground of praise the act of God in the creation of the world and the angels' song at the birth of Christ. He also ties into his theme the reference in Job 38:7: "The morning stars sang together, and all the sons of God shouted for joy." During his last illness his physician read aloud for his comfort many of his hymns. Montgomery said that each hymn had been born of a distinct Christian experience.

COMPOSER: Felix Mendelssohn-Bartholdy, Ph.D., was born at Hamburg in 1809 and died in Leipzig in 1847. His father was a banker and his grandfather was the famous Jewish philosopher, Moses Mendelssohn. He himself, however, was brought up as a Lutheran. His extraordinary musical talent developed early. At the age of twelve he

Adoration

began to compose with great rapidity in all the major forms, and was only seventeen when he wrote the overture to "A Midsummer Night's Dream." Thus began his brilliant career as a composer, pianist, and organist.

He revived the study and the performance of the works of Bach, securing a public performance of the "St. Matthew Passion" at Berlin in 1829. This was its first rendition since the death of Bach in 1750. The same year he made his first visit to England, beginning a series of triumphant tours of that country. Some of his music was inspired by these visits, including the "Scotch Symphony." His oratorio "Elijah" was first performed in England in 1846. "St. Paul," 1836, and the "Hymn of Praise," 1840, were enthusiastically received there. His organ-playing produced a lasting impression upon English organists. He was received with signal honor by Queen Victoria and Prince Albert.

Mendelssohn went to Leipzig in 1835 as conductor of the concerts and as teacher at the Gewandhaus. He was the friend of every important musician of his day, especially Rossini, Cherubini, Liszt, Chopin, and the singer, Jenny Lind. His compositions include, in addition to songs and orchestral works, concertos for the violin and piano, chamber music, sonatas, and preludes and fugues for the organ.

Mendelssohn was beloved by all who knew him. He was unselfish and pure in his private life, unspoiled by wealth and applause. As a humble and earnest Christian he consecrated his genius to the highest ends.

TUNE: This music first appeared in Mendelssohn's "Festgesang for Male Chorus and Orchestra," which was written for a festival held at Leipzig in 1840 to commemorate the invention of printing. It was adapted by Dr. William H. Cumming, organist at Waltham Abbey, England, as a setting for Charles Wesley's "Hark! the Herald Angels Sing," and was first published in this form in 1856. Prior to that time this great hymn had no definite association with any tune.

---

12   HYMN: Praise the Lord, His Glories Show
TUNE: Llanfair

Author: *Rev. Henry Francis Lyte*   Composer: *Robert Williams*

AUTHOR: Although he had intended to enter the medical profession, Henry Francis Lyte, A.M. (1793–1847), was led into the gospel ministry and was ordained in 1815. He graduated from Trinity College, Dublin, where three times he won the prize for the best English poem. Early in his ministry he experienced a change of heart. He had been called to minister to a dying clergyman friend whose faith was clouded, and together they found peace in Christ. Of the change that came to him he wrote: "I was greatly affected by the whole matter, and brought to look at life and its issue with a different eye than before; and I began to study my Bible and preach in another manner than I had previously done." He cared for the children of his friend and, although he was always poor, carried the burden cheerfully. He was "jostled from one curacy to another" until he settled at Lower Brixham, a fishing village. The parish was new and consisted of fisher folk. He was delicate and sensitive; his health was undermined and he sought rest and restoration on the Continent. He died at Nice, where in his last illness he was attended by Henry Edward Manning, afterwards a Roman Catholic cardinal. Five of Lyte's hymns are in "The Hymnal."

His last words, as he pointed upward, were "Peace; joy!" He published "Tales on the Lord's Prayer in Verse," 1826; "Poems, Chiefly Religious," 1833; "The Spirit of the Psalms," 1834.

HYMN: This hymn is taken from the author's "The Spirit of the Psalms," published in 1834, in which most of Lyte's hymns are found. His versions of the psalms have been criticized as being sad and tinged with gloom, but here the criticism is beside the point. This hymn, based on Psalm 150, originally consisted of two eight-line stanzas.

As a hymn writer, Lyte obtained a full answer to his own prayer which he expressed in the following verse:

"Might verse of mine inspire
    One virtuous aim, one high resolve impart—
Light in one drooping soul a hallowed fire,
    Or bind one broken heart,

"Death would be sweeter then,
    More calm my slumber 'neath the silent sod,
Might I thus live to bless my fellow men,
    Or glorify my God."

COMPOSER: Robert Williams was born in Anglesey, an island to the northwest of Wales, about 1781, and died at Mynydd Ithel in 1821. He was born blind, and was trained to earn his living as a basket maker. He was an able musician, as may be seen from this tune. He was also a good singer, with a quick ear and ready memory.

TUNE: "Llanfair" is dated July 14, 1817, in the composer's manuscript book and appears there under the caption "Bethel." It appeared in J. Parry's collection of 1837, "Peroriaeth Hyfryd," harmonized by John Roberts, of Henllan. In its simplicity, smoothness, and the ease with which it attains its climax, "Llanfair" is ideal for congregational singing. It provides an interesting effect to give the alleluias to an antiphonal choir.

Adoration

13

HYMN: Thee, Holy Father, We Adore
TUNE: Lasst Uns Erfreuen

Author: *Rev. Calvin W. Laufer*   Source: *"Geistliche Kirchengesäng"*

AUTHOR: As a church musician, devotional poet, and writer of hymns for special occasions as well as for general use, Dr. Calvin W. Laufer has rendered a distinct service to the Church at large. He was born in Brodheadsville, Pennsylvania, in 1874; graduated from Franklin and Marshall College in 1897, and from Union Theological Seminary in 1900. Ordained to the Presbyterian ministry, he entered upon the pastorate of the Steinway Reformed Church, Long Island City, and later of the First Presbyterian Church, Union City, New Jersey. He began work with the Board of Christian Education of the Presbyterian Church in 1913, and later became its editor of musical publications. Under his direction were prepared "The Church School Hymnal for Youth," "Junior Church School Hymnal," and "Primary Music and Worship." With Dr. Clarence Dickinson as editor, Dr. Laufer was the associate editor of the new Presbyterian Hymnal (1933). He was long associated with Dr. Louis F. Benson in his several hymnals. The hymns and tunes of Dr. Laufer are in wide use throughout the churches in America.

HYMN: This triumphant and joyous hymn of faith was born out of a great domestic sorrow that left the author's heart and home bereft of an inspiring companionship. The experience of God's grace, in its ministry of comfort and a sense of victory in this soul crisis, not only illumined the darkness that fell but revealed the majesty and greatness of God in unforgettable glory. As an anthem text by Lawrence Curry, the hymn is published in both England and the United States.

SOURCE: "Lasst Uns Erfreuen" was published in 1623 in the "Geistliche Kirchengesäng." The composer of the tune is not known. There is a similarity between the first line of the melody and the first line of the tune to "Verzage Nicht, Du Häuflein Klein," written by Matthäus Greiter, who lived during the first half of the sixteenth century.

TUNE: "Lasst Uns Erfreuen" has interested many modern composers. There are several settings of it as an Easter anthem for male and mixed choruses. It has also been arranged for the organ. The tune can be sung by the whole congregation as indicated, or antiphonally with the choir. In some churches it may be introduced by being used first as a hymn anthem by the choir, and in this case the following treatment is suggested. The first stanza may be sung in unison by the men,

19

the alleluias being taken by all parts in harmony, except the last line, which will be sung in unison. In the second stanza the unison portions may be taken by the sopranos and altos, the harmonized alleluias being given to the men. The stanza ends with all voices in unison. The third stanza may be sung as marked by the full choir, the second alleluias in lines 3 and 6 being taken as an echo. The alleluia preceding the final one may be harmonized, leaving the latter to be sung *forte*, in unison, and with a broad retard.

---

14   HYMN: Praise, My Soul, the King of Heaven
             TUNE: Benedic Anima Mea

Author: *Rev. Henry Francis Lyte*   Composer: *John Goss*

AUTHOR: For comments on the author, Henry Francis Lyte, see Hymn 12.

HYMN: This hymn is taken from Lyte's "The Spirit of the Psalms," 1834. It is a free and felicitous paraphrase of Psalm 103. The original hymn contained five stanzas of seven lines each. The fourth stanza, omitted in "The Hymnal," is as follows:

> "Frail as summer's flower we flourish;
> Blows the wind and it is gone;
> But, while mortals rise and perish,
> God endures unchanging on:
> Praise Him! praise Him!
> Praise Him! praise Him!
> Praise the high eternal One!"

J. McLeod Campbell, touching the same note, said: "The feeling which caused the psalmist to call on the 'angels, that excel in strength' to praise the Lord, one enters into, in realizing a great cause for thanksgiving and praise, with which the heart feels its deepest response altogether inadequate and unworthy."

COMPOSER: Sir John Goss, Mus.D., was born in Fareham, Hants, in 1800 and died in London in 1880. He was the son of Joseph Goss, organist at Fareham. Having sung in the Chapel Royal as a boy, he continued his studies under Thomas Attwood, whom he finally succeeded as organist of St. Paul's Cathedral in 1838. He wrote many anthems, services, chants, and hymn tunes as well as glees, songs, and orchestral pieces. His anthems, "The Wilderness" and especially "O

Adoration

Saviour of the World," are sung in English-speaking churches everywhere. His "Introduction to Harmony and Thorough Bass," 1833, reached thirteen editions. It was designed for use in the Royal Academy of Music. Later he edited a collection of "Chants, Ancient and Modern," 1841, and in 1856, with Dr. William Mercer, he issued "The Church Psalter and Hymn Book."

Goss's sacred compositions are noted for their melodious and well-designed treatment, as well as for the quality of reverence that pervades them. "It is said that he never began the writing of an anthem without asking a blessing upon his work. He meant every anthem of his to be what an anthem should be—a sermon in music."

TUNE: The tune, which was first called "Praise, My Soul," was written by Sir John Goss for this hymn. It first appeared in two forms in "The Supplemental Hymn and Tune Book," edited by Rev. R. Brown-Borthwick, third edition, 1869. The first was a set of harmonizations for each stanza of the complete hymn, in the key of D. They are quite varied and most effective. Goss also took the harmonies for the second stanza in four-part vocal score, and set them in the key of E. This is the form in which the tune now appears in "The Hymnal."

"Benedic Anima Mea" is an ideal tune for processional use, owing to its stately rhythm and the long note at the end of each line. When sung in unison, especially by men, it may well be played in the key of D, in which it may be found in many hymn books.

15

HYMN: Round the Lord in Glory Seated
TUNE: Sanctus

Author: *Bishop Richard Mant*   Composer: *John Richards (Isalaw)*

AUTHOR: On February 12, 1776, in Southampton, the birthplace of Isaac Watts a century earlier, Richard Mant was born. He was the son of the master of a grammar school and a student of much promise, receiving the degree of A.B. from Trinity College, Oxford, in 1797 and his A.M. two years later. He was the chancellor's prize essayist, Fellow of Oriel, and the recipient of other student honors. He was ordained and became an assistant to his father, and later chaplain to the archbishop of Canterbury and in 1820 a bishop. His intellectual leadership was recognized in his appointment to the Bampton Lectureship in 1811. He was a voluminous writer of prose as well as of poetry, little of which is current to-day. His metrical version of the psalms, which he published in 1824, and his translations of the Latin hymns, together with "The

21

History of the Church in Ireland," 1840, and his many hymns, have given Richard Mant a permanent, if not conspicuous, place in English church history. He died November 2, 1848.

HYMN: The hymn in all probability found its originating theme in the worship experience described in Isa. 6:1–3. The dramatic episode of Jehovah's appearance to the depressed prophet in a Temple scene of grandeur and mystical meaning is in the background. We here have the purest possible vocabulary of adoration.

COMPOSER: John Richards (Isalaw) was born in Bangor, North Wales, in 1843 and died there in 1908. Nothing is known of his musical education, but he had "an unusual melodic gift" and "composed a large number of hymn tunes, glees, and anthems," which have been very popular in Wales.

TUNE: "Sanctus" was composed by John Richards, and was first published in "Hymns and Tunes of the Presbyterian Church of Wales" in 1900.
This tune can be used as a processional. The last stanza may well be sung a trifle more slowly, the last line being taken in unison.

---

16 HYMN: O Thou My Soul, Bless God the Lord
FIRST TUNE: St. Nicholas

Source: *"Scottish Psalter"* Composer: *Maurice Greene*

SOURCE: For comments on the source, "Scottish Psalter," 1650, see the article, "The Psalters in Early Presbyterian Worship," under "Original Sources," page xv.

HYMN: This is a majestic metrical version of Psalm 103. The hymn as given in the version now in use in the "Scottish Psalter and Church Hymnary" has twenty-two stanzas. The first five stanzas are used in the version in "The Hymnal." It is familiar in all churches that carry forward the principles of the Reformation.

COMPOSER (First Tune): Maurice Greene—born in London in 1695 or 1696; died in 1755—was an important figure in English church music in his day. In 1727 he succeeded Dr. Croft as organist and composer at the Chapel Royal, and three years later was appointed professor of music at Cambridge University. Greene was intimately acquainted with Handel, but the friendship was broken off when Handel discovered that his rival Buononcini was among Greene's friends.
Greene wrote much church service music. Near the close of his life he made a notable collection of the best English cathedral music.

Adoration

TUNE (First): This virile psalm tune, "St. Nicholas," has met the test of centuries and holds a place of first rank, not merely in Scotland but in other parts of the world. It is a majestic setting for Psalm 103 and brings out certain elements of the psalm which the second tune, "Martyrdom," cannot possibly express. The minor mode has much to do with it.

SECOND TUNE: Martyrdom

Composer: *Hugh Wilson*

COMPOSER (Second Tune): Hugh Wilson (1766–1824), of Fenwick, Ayrshire, was the son of a Scottish shoemaker. He was greatly interested in mathematics and held responsible positions in the mills at Pollokshaws as calculator and draftsman. He often led the psalmody in the Secession Church. For a while he lived and worked at Duntocher, where he acted as a manager in the Secession Church. Many psalm tunes came from his pen.

TUNE (Second): "Martyrdom," at first called "Fenwick," was published in 1825 by R. A. Smith in "Sacred Music Sung in St. George's Church, Edinburgh." In this publication Smith claimed the harmonization as his own, and described the tune as an old Scottish melody. It has been shown, however, that the tune had been printed previously in sheet form at the end of the eighteenth century by Hugh Wilson, though it appeared then in common time. It is not known whether the composer produced the present arrangement in triple time or whether Mr. Smith made the alteration for his collection.

This tune is a splendid example of Scottish psalmody. It lends itself well to unison singing, preferably with men's voices alone.

---

17   HYMN: We Worship Thee, Almighty Lord
      TUNE: Wallin

Author: *Johann Olaf Wallin*   Source: *Melody of 1529*

AUTHOR: Johann Olaf Wallin represents one of the most brilliant men in the history of the Swedish pulpit and hymnology. He was born at Stora, Tuna, Sweden, in 1779. As a student in the University of Uppsala, he won several competitions and was the prize student of poetry. He achieved national repute as a preacher of rare ability, being named "pastor primarius" at Stockholm in 1815. Later, he was dean of Vesterås and archbishop of Uppsala. In 1818 he began the revision of the hymn book for Sweden. It was a notable contribution to Swedish

23

Handbook to The Hymnal

worship, approved by the king and adopted by the Church, and remains to this day the popular Swedish hymn book. It contains nearly 150 of Wallin's own hymns and translations. He died in 1839.

TRANSLATOR: The translator of the hymn is Charles Wharton Storck.

HYMN: The hymn breathes the atmosphere of The Psalms. References are evident to Ps. 72:11; Ps. 122:1–5; and Psalm 24. The universality of the Kingdom of God and the sure foundations of the Church inspire the chorus of the adoring seraphim and the victory song of earthly worshipers.

SOURCE: The source is a sixteenth century melody.

TUNE: The tune, "Wallin," is printed in "The Swedish Psalmbook" of the Church of Sweden, published in 1819, where the date of its first known use as a hymn tune is given as 1529.

If the tune here printed dates from 1529, it must have been one of the earliest chorals to be used in Sweden and undoubtedly had an earlier German origin.

The tune itself, set in a minor key, reflects the majesty of the words. The last note of each line is a major triad, which is uncommon in minor chorals except in Sweden.

Times of Worship
The Lord's Day
*

18

HYMN: O Day of Rest and Gladness
TUNE: Mendebras

Author: *Bishop Christopher Wordsworth*   Source: *Old German Melody*

AUTHOR: Christopher Wordsworth, D.D. (1807–1885), a nephew of the poet Wordsworth, was a brilliant Cambridge scholar, athlete, and poet. He became Fellow and classical lecturer at Trinity College, Cambridge, and head master at Harrow at thirty years of age, when he began his notable service in the interest of moral reform. For nineteen years he was minister in a country parish and in 1868 was made bishop of Lincoln. He was a constant writer, publishing an entire commentary on the Bible. In 1862 he published "The Holy Year," containing hymns for the Christian year. He held that "the first duty of a hymn is to teach sound doctrine, and thus save souls." Most of the hymns are forgotten, but a few having irresistible charm survive (see Hymns 173, 398, 426). Of Bishop Wordsworth Canon John Ellerton wrote, "He was a most holy, humble, loving, self-denying man."

HYMN: This hymn is taken from "The Holy Year," 1862. As originally written it contained six stanzas of eight lines each. Sometimes stanzas 5 (omitted in "The Hymnal") and 6 (stanza 3 in "The Hymnal") are used as a separate hymn, beginning "To-day on weary nations." Dr. Louis F. Benson says: "There is a small group of familiar hymns that do not take the form of praise or prayer or exhortation, but the form of teaching. They are called didactic hymns, and consist of a series of statements setting forth some doctrine. . . . Bishop Wordsworth's 'Gracious Spirit, Holy Ghost,' expounding the doctrine of love, and his 'O Day of Rest and Gladness,' setting forth the history and benefits of the Christian Sunday, are examples."

SOURCE: The source is an old German melody.

ARRANGER: Lowell Mason was born at Medfield, Massachusetts, in 1792, and died at Orange, New Jersey, in 1872. At the age of sixteen he had charge of the church choir at Medfield. In 1812 he settled at Savannah, Georgia, working as a bank clerk but continuing his activity in church music as a choirmaster of a Presbyterian church. There he also began to write hymn tunes. In 1827 he returned to his native state and pursued his musical work in Boston. He became president of the Handel and Haydn Society, which had previously made it possible for him to publish his first collection of tunes. It was the success of this venture that encouraged him to begin his unique work of teaching music and arousing greater interest in music through lectures, conventions, and musical publications. He founded the Boston Academy of Music in 1832. In 1835 he received the degree of Doctor of Music from New York University. Two tune books which he produced had wide popularity in both America and England. Their permanent value is indicated by the fact that thirty-three of his tunes appeared in the Presbyterian Hymnal (1895) of which fifteen are retained in the edition of 1933.

TUNE: This setting of "Mendebras," arranged by Lowell Mason, was first published in 1839 in "The Modern Psalmist," set to the hymn "I Love Thy Kingdom, Lord," which is in short meter. Its earliest printing in its present form—as a 7.6.7.6.D.—was in "The Psaltery," 1845, compiled by Mason and Webb, associated with the words "The Gloomy Night of Sadness." The tune seems to have appeared first with the present hymn in "Songs for the Sanctuary," edited by Dr. Charles S. Robinson, in 1865.

19

HYMN: O 'Twas a Joyful Sound to Hear
TUNE: Mount Sion

Source: *Tate and Brady*   Composer: *Horatio Parker*

SOURCE: Nahum Tate shared with Nicholas Brady in the courageous task of preparing the "New Version," 1696. This was a metrical version of The Psalms that displaced the version of Sternhold and Hopkins, which had been in use for 150 years. The "New Version" was dedicated to King William III who had made Tate poet laureate and had provided a London living for Brady. Authorized by the king in council and approved by the bishop of London as revised in 1698, this collection of pioneer paraphrases was used for more than one hundred years. For further comments on the source, Tate and Brady, see the article, "Church Hymns in Great Britain and America," under "Original Sources," page xvii.

HYMN: This hymn is the metrical translation of Psalm 122 as given in the "New Version," by Tate and Brady. This noble call to public praise breaks with the slavish literalism of older translations and undertakes to respond to those lyric requisites demanded by true poetry. The original sentiment of this pilgrim psalm is here perfectly preserved. Beginning the journey in joy, the procession ends in the rapturous attainment of the holy place with great spiritual satisfaction. As some one has said, "The psalmist here no longer feels the sadness but the sanctity of the past."

COMPOSER: Horatio W. Parker, Mus.D. (Cantab.), A.M. (Yale), was born at Auburndale, Massachusetts, in 1863, and died at Cedarhurst, New York, in 1919. He early revealed the talent for musical composition which made him outstanding among the native composers of his generation. After advanced musical study in Boston he went, in 1882, to Munich for three years and was a favorite pupil of Rheinberger. When Dr. Parker returned to this country in 1885 after his student days in Munich, he became organist and professor of music at the Cathedral School, Garden City, Long Island. The next year he became organist and choirmaster at St. Andrew's in New York City, and two years later he went to the Church of the Holy Trinity in Boston. For a number of years he was interested in the composition of music for the church service, even when he was known as a composer of larger works. Later on he was a teacher at the National Conservatory of Music in New York, of which Dvořák was director. This contact undoubtedly stimulated him in his creative musical work.

In 1893 Parker became organist at Trinity Church, Boston. At this time he had finished "Hora Novissima," the first work to bring him world-wide recognition. It was performed in May, 1893, by the Church Music Society of New York. Within a few years his choral compositions began to appear at the cathedral festivals in England.

The following year Parker was appointed professor of music at Yale University, and under his guidance the musical department flourished remarkably. One result was the gift of Woolsey Hall to the University, with its superb organ, which made possible the performance of all kinds of choral and instrumental music under ideal conditions. In 1901 he accepted a call to be organist at St. Nicholas Collegiate Church, New York. His opera "Mona" was performed in the Metropolitan Opera House in 1912.

TUNE: "Mount Sion," written for this hymn by Horatio W. Parker in 1888, is one of the most stirring processional tunes of the Anglican type produced in America. The melodic line is strong, it contains six four-note scale progressions, and the descending curves of the second pair of lines make an admirable preparation for the climax in the second half of the tune. The success of the tune lies entirely in its interpretation. It must have motion, but the tempo should be well controlled. The time signature is in reality $\frac{2}{1}$, giving two beats in each bar. The tune may be used as a processional, with either two steps or one step to each bar.

27

Handbook to The Hymnal

The former is preferable when children are marching, or in a large church, at a marching tempo of about 60. With an adult choir or in a small church one step is taken for each bar, and the marching tempo is about 44, or less.

20	HYMN: This Is the Day of Light
	TUNE: Swabia

Author: *Rev. John Ellerton*   Composer: *Johann M. Spiess*

AUTHOR: John Ellerton's name belongs to eight hymns in "The Hymnal" (Hymns 20, 45, 55, 169, 386, 420, 440, 509). He was born in 1826 and died in 1893. He was educated at Trinity College, Cambridge, and was a close friend of Bishop Wordsworth. During student days he came under the influence of Frederick Denison Maurice. Ellerton was a man of broad human sympathies and evangelical zeal. He was ordained in 1850 and was minister in various parishes until he became domestic chaplain to Lord Crewe. In this position he became deeply interested in welfare movements, conducting classes in Scriptural history, English, and music. His work as a hymnologist is of great importance. He compiled "Church Hymns" and "The Children's Hymn Book" and was joint compiler of the classic book of the English Church, "Hymns Ancient and Modern." He advised in the preparation of the "Hymnal Companion to the Book of Common Prayer," and various other volumes of hymns. Of him it is said, "His hand may be traced and his voice heard in every hymn book of importance during the last thirty years before his death." He is the author of eighty-six hymns published in his own volume, "Hymns, Original and Translated." He copyrighted none of his hymns, holding that he wrote in the interest of the gospel. During his last illness he repeated hymns unceasingly, even when semiconscious. He received the honorary title of "Canon" during his last illness but he was never installed.

HYMN: This hymn is taken from "Hymns for Special Occasions and Festivals," 1867, a collection of one hundred hymns for Chester Cathedral, compiled by Dean Howson. The hymn consisted originally of six stanzas. It is a didactic hymn, teaching the value of Sunday as a day of light, of rest, of peace, and of prayer, but it succeeds in introducing, more definitely than do most didactic hymns, the note of true worship.

COMPOSER: Johann Martin Spiess was born in Bavaria in 1715. He became organist in St. Peter's Church at Heidelberg and was also professor of music in the gymnasium there. In 1745 he published a book of chorals, among which was the tune afterwards known as

Times of Worship

"Swabia." There it is set to the hymn "Auf Wachet! Wachet Auf!" Very little is known definitely about his life. He settled in Berne and was organist there in 1766. He died in June, 1772.

TUNE: The present arrangement of "Swabia" was made by Rev. W. H. Havergal, and is found in his "Old Church Psalmody," 1847. The tune is well constructed, containing four equal lines of music, three of which end with a long note. Thus it is well adapted for processional use.

21
HYMN: Light of Light, Enlighten Me
FIRST TUNE: Liebster Jesu

Author: *Rev. Benjamin Schmolck*   Composer: *Johann R. Ahle*

AUTHOR: Benjamin Schmolck, an outstanding preacher, poet, and hymn writer, was born in Silesia in 1672. Graduating from the University of Leipzig, he was ordained, in 1701, to the Lutheran ministry. His first sermon in his father's pulpit made such an impression that a hearer urged him to continue the study of theology, providing him an allowance for three years. He supported himself through later schooling by writing poetry. Following the Thirty Years' War, the Peace of Westphalia (1648) imposed severe restrictions upon Lutheran churches and changed the whole order of things. Only one church building was allowed to the district of Schweidnitz, and that was to be made of timber and clay, without bells, and outside the town walls. Under these painful hindrances three clergymen looked after thirty-six villages but were not allowed to administer Communion to the sick without a permit from a local Roman priest. In the church town of Schweidnitz, Schmolck lived until his death. During his last few years he continued his productive labors with a paralyzed right hand and a cataract blinding him. As a popular preacher and a voluminous writer of devotional books, he became widely known throughout Germany. He was the best-loved hymn writer of his day, being called a "second Gerhardt." He wrote nine hundred hymns, besides cantatas and wedding and funeral pieces. More than one hundred are still in use in Germany, two appearing in this Hymnal.

TRANSLATOR: For comments on the translator, Catherine Winkworth, see Hymn 6.

HYMN: This hymn is from "Lyra Germanica," a classic in devotional literature which was published by Miss Winkworth in 1855, with a second series in 1858. It is touched with the joy and brightness of the Sunday morning hour of worship, for which it is

29

appointed. It is a happy affirmation of the light, peace, and joy that the day of rest brings to the worshiper.

COMPOSER (First Tune): Johann Rudolf Ahle, who wrote the melody of this choral, was born in Mühlhausen in 1625 and died in 1673. He was a student in the gymnasium at Göttingen, and at the University of Erfurt, later becoming cantor at St. Andrea's Church, Erfurt. He was distinguished as a church musician and composer.

ARRANGER (First Tune): Johann Sebastian Bach, the youngest son of Johann A. Bach and a member of a large family of church musicians, was born in Eisenach in 1685. He died at Leipzig in 1750. From early boyhood he was given the best possible musical instruction by his father, and afterwards by his eldest brother. At the age of eighteen he was an able composer and organist and also an accomplished violinist. He became in turn organist at Arnstadt, Mühlhausen, where he succeeded the son of J. R. Ahle, and at Weimar, where for nine years he was court organist and violinist. Here he began to write his large organ works as well as church cantatas. In 1717 he began his appointment as court director at Köthen, where he was chiefly occupied with chamber music.

He occasionally visited other cities, including Leipzig, where he finally settled in 1723 as cantor of the *Thomasschule*, in addition to having oversight of the music in the two leading churches and in the University. The school supplied singers for several choirs in the city. The *Thomaskirche* is forever associated with his name for here he played the Sunday services and produced the vocal compositions written by him specially for them.

Only a few more than two hundred of Bach's cantatas, which were short verse anthems written for the choirs of the two churches, have survived, though he wrote nearly three hundred. He composed five Passions, six motets, several masses, including the immortal "Mass in B Minor," as well as over forty fugues and six sonatas for the organ, and a wealth of clavier and other chamber music.

Very few of his works were published during his lifetime, or for many years afterwards. However, the influence of Bach on the composers of his day was tremendous and Mozart, Beethoven, Chopin, Schumann, and Wagner were earnest students of his music. He created choral music for Protestant liturgical worship that equaled the sublimest compositions of the school of Palestrina. The whole congregation was expected to sing the chorals that were included in his cantatas and major choral works.

Not only was Bach the greatest organist of his day but his mastery of the architecture of music remains unique in the history of the art. He produced thematic material in endless variety, and reached the highest development of polyphonic style in its treatment. An intellectual, he yet was possessed by the mysticism and emotions of his religion, and "his

Times of Worship

greatest works have a singular universality that has given them permanent influence upon the whole of later musical progress."

TUNE (First): As composed by Ahle, the tune, "Liebster Jesu," appeared in 1664 with the words "Ja, Er Ists, das Heil der Welt." It was first set to the text "Liebster Jesu" in 1687, having been modified considerably from the original.

It is interesting to note that the melody was brought to America early in the nineteenth century. It appeared in 1834 in "Musica Sacra," of which Thomas Hastings was editor, in an altered version under the name "Nuremburg," and probably was in use here before that date. The same version was used in the Presbyterian Hymnals of 1895 and 1911.

Bach set the tune in the form here printed and added the present harmonization. It was arranged by him also as a choral prelude for the organ, two treatments of it appearing in his "Little Organ Book."

SECOND TUNE: Hinchman

Composer: *Uzziah C. Burnap*

COMPOSER (Second Tune): Uzziah C. Burnap, the composer of "Hinchman," was for many years a well-known dry-goods merchant in Brooklyn and New York. Born in 1834, he studied music in Paris and graduated at the University of Paris, taking his degree in music. He was a prolific composer, and wrote a great many hymn tunes. For thirty-seven years he served as organist in the Reformed Church on the Heights in Brooklyn, New York. According to competent authority he was one of the early improvisers in the United States and ranked with Buck and Wood in that field. He died in Brooklyn in 1900.

TUNE (Second): "Hinchman" was written in 1869. The tune is constructed conventionally. The fourth line repeats the form of the third line, and the last couplet is identical with the first. The tune finds a place here because, for many worshipers, it is closely associated with the words of the hymn.

---

22   HYMN: Sweet Is the Work, My God, My King
      TUNE: Grace Church

Author: *Rev. Isaac Watts*   Composer: *Ignaz J. Pleyel*

AUTHOR: Isaac Watts (1674–1748) is the largest contributor to "The Hymnal." There are twenty-two hymns and responses which bear his name appearing in this book. (See the index of authors.) Isaac Watts was the son of a Nonconformist boarding-house keeper. Isaac was offered an education if he would study for ordination in the

31

Church of England, but he refused. He succeeded in preparing for the ministry, and in 1702 he became pastor of the Independent Church in Mark Lane, London. His health failed and during the last thirty-six years of his life he was a semi-invalid. He wrote a work on logic which was a textbook at Oxford and in 1728 received the degree of Doctor of Divinity from Edinburgh. He wrote about six hundred hymns and paraphrases. His work is a median between the strict translation of the psalms into meter and the modern English hymn. Isaac Watts said, "We preach the gospel and pray in Christ's name, and then check the aroused devotions of Christians by giving out a song of the old dispensation." He entitled his first edition "The Psalms of David Imitated in the Language of the New Testament, and Apply'd to the Christian State and Worship." In the edition entitled "Hymns and Spiritual Songs," published in 1707, the title-page bears the inscription: "With an Essay Towards the Improvement of Christian Psalmody, by the Use of Evangelical Hymns in Worship, as Well as the Psalms of David." Most of his hymns were written when he was in his twenties. The hymn "Behold the Glories of the Lamb" was his first hymn and was written purposely to raise the standard of praise. He was buried in the Puritan cemetery, Bunhill Fields, and a memorial monument was erected to him in Westminster Abbey. He ranks among the greatest of English hymn writers.

HYMN: This hymn is a free paraphrase of Psalm 92. It originally contained seven stanzas and was entitled "A Psalm for the Lord's Day." Psalm 92 was called *"Il Salmo Delectasti"* by Dante because the first words of stanza 4 in the Latin begin with the words *"Quia delectasti me"* ("Thou hast made me glad").

COMPOSER: Ignaz Joseph Pleyel was born near Vienna in 1757 and died in Paris in 1831. He was the twenty-fourth son of a poor village schoolmaster. As a pupil of Haydn in composition, beginning in 1772, he formed a lasting friendship with the great Austrian composer. He became chapelmaster at Strasbourg. In 1795 he went to Paris. Here he started to publish music, producing the first complete edition of Haydn's string quartets, and in 1807 he established the piano factory which still bears his name. He was a prolific composer of instrumental music. Some of his quartets attracted the attention of Mozart.

TUNE: The tune, "Grace Church," is an arrangement from a string quartet by I. J. Pleyel, dated 1815. Its wide and continued popularity is readily explained. It is well constructed, it is easy to sing, and its meter suits admirably the smooth iambic rhythm of the text. It has often been set to the hymn "Lord of All Being, Throned Afar."

Times of Worship

23 HYMN: This Is the Day the Lord Hath Made
TUNE: Arlington

Author: *Rev. Isaac Watts*   Composer: *Thomas A. Arne*

AUTHOR: For comments on the author, Isaac Watts, see Hymn 22.

HYMN: This hymn is a liberal versification of a portion of Psalm 118. Watts treated the psalms with great freedom in order to meet what he considered metrical necessities and the evangelical purposes of worship. Verses 24–26 of the psalm constitute the theme, providing a joyful character to the hymn as appointed for worship on the Sabbath. The original title to the hymn, showing Watts's double purpose in versifying the psalms, was "Hosanna; the Lord's Day; or, Christ's Resurrection, and Our Salvation." Watts strove through all his career, as in this hymn, to modify the rigidity of much of the psalmody and to bring into the worship of the Church through his psalms the softer notes of Christianity. His critics said of him that he undertook to "make David speak like an English Christian of the eighteenth century." In this Christianizing of the psalms, Watts followed in the footsteps of others, notably Phineas Fletcher, who versified six psalms in 1633 in a poetic work entitled "The Purple Island," an allegorical description of man.

COMPOSER: Thomas Augustine Arne, Mus.D., was born in London in 1710, and died there in 1778. Though educated for the legal profession, he early showed his love of music, his first compositions being in the form of light opera. His distinctive style was first shown in the music for Dalton's adaptation of Milton's "Comus," 1738, which fully established his reputation as a composer. Two years later he wrote the most popular of all his airs, "Rule, Britannia," which occurred in his masque of "Alfred." Many lovely English ballads came from his pen. He also wrote several oratorios, including "Judith."

Arne married Cecilia Young, daughter of an organist at Barking. She was a noted singer and was frequently engaged by Handel in performances of his music. Arne was at one time composer for Drury Lane Theater. He received his degree of Doctor of Music from Oxford in 1759. He excelled as a writer of popular melodies, and he was the foremost English composer of his day.

TUNE: "Arlington" was adapted by Rev. Ralph Harrison, a Presbyterian minister, from a minuet in the opera "Artaxerxes," by Thomas A. Arne, which was produced in 1762. The tune was published in "Sacred Harmony," compiled by Harrison in 1784.

33

Handbook to The Hymnal

Morning

*

24 HYMN: Father, We Praise Thee, Now the Night Is Over
TUNE: Christe Sanctorum

Author: *Gregory the Great*   Source: *La Feillée's*
"Méthode du Plain Chant"

AUTHOR: Gregory the Great (540–604) takes us across the ages to the afterglow of early Christianity. He is known as Pope Gregory I. He was born of a noble Roman family and at an early age was a prætor in the city of Rome. He gave up position and fortune and dedicated his life to monastic service. The story of the beginning of his interest in England is familiar. Seeing some fair-haired youths in the slave market, he asked about them and was told they were Angles. "Not Angles," he said, "but angels. From what country came they?" The reply was, "From Deira." "Then," he said, "they must be plucked '*de ira*,' from the wrath of God. Who is their king?" "Aella," was the answer. "Then shall alleluia be sung in that kingdom." When Gregory became bishop of Rome, four years later, he sent Augustine on his celebrated mission to England. Gregory is noted for his missionary zeal, for he sent missionaries through Europe and Asia and the known world. He was gentle toward heretic, infidel, slave, and Jew. His work in connection with church liturgies has made the "Gregorian chant" immortal. He founded a school of singers in Rome and made the plain chant the basis of his instruction. "The contributions of St. Gregory to our stores of Latin hymns are not numerous, nor are the few generally attributed to him quite certainly proved to be his. But few as they are, and by whomsoever written, they are most of them still used in the services of the Church. In character they are well wedded to the grave and solemn music which St. Gregory himself is supposed to have written for them."

TRANSLATOR: Percy Dearmer, D.D., an accomplished present-day hymnologist and interpreter of hymns, was born in London in 1867. He was educated in the ancient Westminster School and at Christ Church College in Oxford. His faithful parish work at various points did not hinder his special devotion to the scholarly study of liturgics and to much diversified religious writing of a high order. He was officially active in the program of the London Christian Social Union and the League of Arts. His lengthy war service was followed by his becoming, in 1919, professor of ecclesiastical art in King's College, London, a position to which he brought the results of wide study and deep spiritual

34

appreciation. In 1931 he became canon of Westminster. One may judge of the scope of his interests by the books from different fields that have come rapidly from his pen. Among them are "The Parson's Handbook," "The English Carol Book," "The Art of Public Worship," and "The Church at Prayer and the World Outside." Canon Dearmer was secretary of the committee that prepared "The English Hymnal" and in reality was its editor. His own late collection, "Songs of Praise," is written for use in both churches and public schools. Corporate worship in the Church of this generation is already deeply in Dr. Dearmer's debt.

HYMN: The hymn was first contributed by Dr. Dearmer to "The English Hymnal" in 1906. It translates the Latin "*Nocte surgentes vigilemus omnes*." It fittingly begins the section of hymns for morning worship in "The Hymnal."

SOURCE: The tune is taken from a book published by François de la Feillée entitled "Méthode du Plain Chant." An edition of this work in the British Museum is called a "new edition" and was published in 1782. Another edition was published in 1808.

TUNE: "Christe Sanctorum" is well adapted for congregational singing. It should be sung in unison as is indicated in "The Hymnal." This is particularly easy to do as the range of the melody is such that no one will find notes either too high or too low. The slant of the melody is upward for the first half of the tune. The key also changes at the first half to B flat. The slant of the melody for the last half is downward, beginning on high E flat and ending on low E flat. The effect of this hymn when sung somewhat slowly is very fine.

25

HYMN: As the Sun Doth Daily Rise
TUNE: Innocents

Author: *Horatio Nelson*   Source: *The Parish Choir*

AUTHOR: Horatio Nelson was the third earl and a nephew of the great admiral whose immortality rests as much on his famous slogan, "England expects every man to do his duty," as upon his naval conquests. The third earl was born August 7, 1832. He graduated from Eton, and Trinity College, Cambridge. He was associated with the saintly John Keble, who with all his spiritual worth was rated among the "inferior clergy." Nelson edited "The Salisbury Hymn Book," called in its later revision of 1868 "The Sarum Hymnal." Besides his hymns, his devotional leadership was proclaimed in such helps to spirituality as "A

Form for Family Prayer" and "A Calendar of Lessons for Every Day," 1857. He was a man of great fervor and evangelical force in his preaching and parish work.

HYMN: This old Latin morning hymn is attributed, without foundation in fact, to the good Saxon king, Alfred (849–901). Alfred rose like a star of hope in a darkened era, and with him began the rise of Anglo-Saxon culture. The translation by "O.B.C." was included in Earl Nelson's collection of "Hymns for Saint's Day, and Other Hymns," published in 1864. With childlike simplicity of faith the author associates the never-failing sunrise with the unchanging goodness of God. From daily bread provided he sees proof of spiritual nourishment and growth in grace.

SOURCE: The tune is arranged from a thirteenth century French melody in The Parish Choir, 1850.

TUNE: The Parish Choir, the periodical from which this tune, "Innocents," is taken, was a publication which owed its inception to the Oxford Movement in England. It was issued by the "Society for Promoting Church Music," a society which was interested principally in the setting of plain-song melodies to old Latin hymns.

This tune is simple. The melodic figure in the first line is repeated in the third line, while the second line of the hymn has the same melodic figure but sung at a lower pitch. In the second line of the hymn the key changes to B. The last line is similar to the second but ends in the key of E, instead of B, as it is necessary for the tune to end in the key in which it begins.

If it is desired to sing either the whole or part of the hymn in unison, it would be better to put it in the key of E flat.

---

26 HYMN: Christ, Whose Glory Fills the Skies
TUNE: Lux Prima

Author: *Rev. Charles Wesley*   Composer: *Charles F. Gounod*

AUTHOR: Rev. Charles Wesley (1707–1788) is too well known to need extended notice. His name is immortal. He was the sweet singer of Methodism and the support and inspiration of his evangelist brother, John Wesley. Dr. James Moffatt calls him the greatest hymn writer of any age. In "The Hymnal" fifteen hymns are from his hand. (See index of authors.)

Times of Worship

Charles Wesley was educated at Christ Church, Oxford, where he graduated in 1729. He belonged to the group called "Oxford Methodists." He accompanied his brother John to America, going, however, as secretary to Governor Oglethorpe. On his return he came under Moravian influences and in 1738 he "found rest to his soul." He refused to leave the Church of England and he disapproved of the ordinations of his brother John. His latter years were spent in hymn-writing. His hymns number at least sixty-five hundred, many of which are now forgotten. These hymns, as much as the forty thousand sermons preached and the two hundred and fifty thousand miles traveled by his brother John as an itinerant preacher, had to do with the great spiritual movement of Methodism and also with a revived English and American Protestantism.

HYMN: This hymn is taken from Wesley's "Hymns and Sacred Poems," published in 1740. In speaking of this hymn an American authority on hymnology says: "It was printed for a long time in Toplady's volume as if it had been his; but some good Wesleyan brother found out that Toplady was born in 1740, and that was the date of publication on the title-page of Wesley's book. And then no less a man than Dr. Morley Punshon quoted it in one of his sermons, which was printed, ascribing it to Sir Robert Grant. The fact is, there was one stanza, put first in the old hymn book, and beginning, 'O disclose thy lovely face,' which was of no special value, but rather got in the way of the rest of the hymn and blocked the frequent choice of it. Nobody knows who wrote those lines or how they, in the first instance, found their way into Charles Wesley's poetry. He never wrote them, and when they were discarded at last every true singer discovered what a fine lyric had come all at once into popularity and use."

COMPOSER: Charles François Gounod was born in 1818. He was of a deeply religious nature and expected to take holy orders. He took two years of theology and in 1846 became an out pupil at the Séminaire in Paris. However, he decided that he could serve his religion best by his music, and it is significant that his first compositions were all of a sacred character. Gounod will always be remembered as the composer of the opera "Faust." The horrors of the Franco-Prussian War made a deep impression on him and he was compelled to reside for several years in England. He returned to the composition of sacred music and wrote "Gallia," a lamentation for France. Later, in 1882, he produced his great religious work, "The Redemption." "It is intended to illustrate three great parts," to quote the composer's own words in his prefatory commentary, "on which the existence of the Christian Church depends: The Passion and death of the Saviour, his glorious life on earth from his resurrection to his ascension, and, finally, the spread of Christianity in the world through the mission of the apostles." These three parts of the trilogy are preceded by a prologue on the Creation and Fall of our first parents and the promise of a Redeemer. It is said that while composing this work Gounod used to spend hours in Notre Dame Cathedral in prayer and meditation. He died in 1893.

T UNE: The interest in this tune, "Lux Prima," is kept up most skillfully by the building of the melody toward a climax which occurs at the word "Day-Star," at the beginning of the last line.

---

27 HYMN: Heaven and Earth, and Sea and Air
TUNE: Gott Sei Dank Durch Alle Welt

Author: *Joachim Neander*   Source: *"Freylinghausen's Gesangbuch"*

A UTHOR: For comments on the author, Joachim Neander, see Hymn 6.

H YMN: This is one of the most beautiful hymns of thanksgiving for the glory and wonder of nature. It is a recognition of the providence of God as witnessed in the "rains and fruitful seasons." It once had a footnote which read, "Is also a traveler's hymn by land and water." Marked by robust piety and genuine Christian experience, this hymn first found its place in Freylinghausen's book of Pietist hymns.

S OURCE: Johann Anastasius Freylinghausen's "Geistreiches Gesangbuch" was published at Halle, Germany, in 1704. In it appeared nearly all his hymns and others of the Pietistic school. The volume contained many hymns which survive to this day. Soon after its publication it became the standard collection of the Halle School, by virtue of which it influenced many editors and writers in subsequent hymn books. The volume appeared in another edition, which was greatly enriched. Many of the tunes are widely used either in original or revised form. Freylinghausen ranks as one of the best writers of the Pietistic school. His hymns are well written and are distinguished for their wholesome piety and depth, their Scriptural background and variety of style. He was born at Gandersheim, December 2, 1670. He studied at Jena and, attracted by the preaching of A. H. Francke, became his associate and married his daughter. At Francke's death in 1727, he succeeded him as pastor and director of the institution founded by him. He died on February 12, 1739, and was buried by the side of Francke.

Times of Worship

TUNE: The tune, "Gott Sei Dank Durch Alle Welt," appears on page 5 of the "Geistreiches Gesangbuch," issued in 1704. It has appeared since in various hymn books and has been known under the names of "Berline" and "Carinthia."

---

28   HYMN: Lord, in the Morning Thou Shalt Hear
      TUNE: Kilmarnock

Author: *Rev. Isaac Watts*   Composer: *Neil Dougall*

AUTHOR: For comments on the author, Isaac Watts, see Hymn 22.

HYMN: This hymn is a free paraphrase of Psalm 5 after the method of Watts. It does not appear in "The Church Hymnary" of the Scottish Church, a rather strange omission. Isaac Watts wrote the name of Christ into the psalm.

Bishop Bury, in his account of his mission to Costa Rica, tells this happy incident: "As I stood one morning, according to custom, at the door of one of my timber churches in Costa Rica, to say 'good-by' to the people after an early Communion service, before leaving them for that year, a tall, strong Negro came out, leading his little boy of seven. When he and I had expressed our mutual good will in the usual 'God bless you' and 'God speed,' he glanced down at his little son, who at once, looking timidly up at me as he did so, recited a text, 'In the morning will I direct my prayer unto thee, and will look up.' It was a text I had taken weeks before at their children's service, and the father wished his bishop to see that one small person out of the congregation remembered what had been said."

COMPOSER: Neil Dougall was born in Greenock, Scotland, in 1776. At fifteen he became an apprentice seaman on board the ship Britannia. In 1793 war broke out with France, and Dougall joined the Clarence, a boat fitted out to make reprisals on the high seas. In 1794 an unfortunate accident befell him. An accidental discharge of a gun during a salute deprived him of both his sight and his right arm. He was urged to join a singing class in Greenock and such was his progress that a year later he opened a singing class of his own. His compositions include about a hundred psalm and hymn tunes, an anthem from Psalm 136, and about a dozen songs and other pieces. He died in Greenock in 1862.

39

Handbook to The Hymnal

TUNE: "Kilmarnock" first appeared in the second edition of "Parochial Psalmody: A New Collection of the Most Approved Psalm Tunes," by J. P. Clark, published in 1831. The following account of its composition is taken from "Poems and Songs by Neil Dougall, with a Memoir of the Author":

"One day R. A. Smith and the late John Taylor, who was then precentor in the Middle Parish Church, Greenock, paid him (Dougall) a visit. . . . After some conversation Smith said: 'Anything new doing, Mr. Dougall? No scraps to divert us?' Mr. Dougall went to a drawer and brought the first few scraps of paper he could lay his hands on. Smith took up one and hastily humming it over, said, 'A very pretty melody; and what do you call it?' 'It's not christened yet,' was the answer; 'but do you observe anything peculiar about it?' 'I do,' said Smith; 'it is on the Caledonian scale, the same as "Morven."' 'Yes; the same as your tune.' 'No, no; not my tune,' said Smith. 'Will you oblige me with a copy of your nameless tune?' 'With pleasure,' said the composer, 'and we'll christen't "Kilmarnock"'; and this ended the conference."

---

29 HYMN: The Sun Is on the Land and Sea
      TUNE: Wentworth

Author: *Rev. Louis F. Benson*   Composer: *Frederick C. Maker*

AUTHOR: The name of Louis F. Benson is ever to be associated in the minds of the present generation of hymn lovers with a career of lifelong devotion to the study of hymnology and the task of enriching the corporate worship of the Church. He was born in Philadelphia in 1855 and was educated for the law, graduating from the University of Pennsylvania. After seven years before the bar, he entered Princeton Theological Seminary and was ordained to the Presbyterian ministry in 1886.

After a pastorate of six years he resigned to begin his long and fruitful services as editor of a notable series of hymn books issued under the authority of the General Assembly of the Presbyterian Church. He served as an influential member of the committee that prepared "The Book of Common Worship of the Presbyterian Church in the U.S.A." in 1905, and of its committee on revision. His scholarship and wide information gave him and his books preëminent authority in the realm of hymnology. Among his books are "The Best Church Hymns," "Studies of Familiar Hymns," "The Hymnody of the Christian Church," and "The English Hymn." His high standards for church music are registered in "Christian Song," 1926. He possessed one of the world's most valuable private hymnological libraries. Upon his death it was given to the library of Princeton Theological Seminary. Dr. Benson died in 1930.

40

Times of Worship

HYMN: Written at the apex of Dr. Benson's vigor and enthusiasm as a student of hymnology, this hymn reflects his keen response to the inspiring surroundings of the physical world. On the tide-washed shores of Mount Desert, Maine, in a summer home blessed by long and loving family residence, this hymn was born. Dr. Benson's simple faith illumined every sunrise and mountain ridge and underwrote every day with the promised peace of God.

COMPOSER: Frederick Charles Maker was born in Bristol, England, in 1844. He was a chorister in Bristol Cathedral and later organist of Milk Street Methodist Free Church, Clifton Downs Congregational Church, and Redland Park Congregational Church. He composed a cantata entitled, "Moses in the Bulrushes," and contributed tunes to "The Bristol Tune Book." He died in Bristol in 1927.

TUNE: The tune, "Wentworth," is divided into three parts consisting of two lines each. The first two lines are in the key of C, as are the last two lines. Lines 3 and 4 pass from the key of C to A minor and D major and G major. This illustrates an important principle in music, namely, that of contrast. The reason the composer placed the middle section in other keys was to make an effective contrast with the key of C, in which the tune begins and ends.

---

30   HYMN: Jesus, Sun of Righteousness
             TUNE: Morgenglanz der Ewigkeit

Author: *Christian Knorr von Rosenroth*   Source: *"Freylinghausen's Gesangbuch"*

AUTHOR: Baron Christian Knorr von Rosenroth (1636–1689) was born in Silesia and died in Bavaria. He was a pastor in Silesia and traveled in France, Holland, and England. He was a distinguished scholar and devoted himself to Oriental studies, chemistry, and the occult sciences. He found rest in Christ for his intellectual questions and later was made prime minister of the palsgrave, Christian August, of Sulzbach. He wrote seventy hymns full of ardent spiritual devotion.

TRANSLATOR: The hymn was translated from the German by Jane Laurie Borthwick (1813–1897). Between 1854 and 1862 she and her sister published four series of "Hymns from the Land of Luther." Sixty-nine were translated by herself and fifty-three by her sister. She achieved marked success in translating hymns from the German, a task which she undertook at the suggestion of her father.

Handbook to The Hymnal

HYMN: Baron Von Rosenroth's hymn first appeared in 1684, under the title "Morning Prayer." It is based on a still older German hymn. It has been spoken of as "one of the freshest, most original and spirited of morning hymns as if born from the dew of the sunrise." Stanzas 2 and 5 of the original hymn are usually omitted.

SOURCE: For comments on the source, "Freylinghausen's Gesangbuch," see Hymn 27.

TUNE: The tune, "Morgenglanz der Ewigkeit," appears in the first edition (1704) of Freylinghausen's "Geistreiches Gesangbuch." The first and the last stanzas may be sung in unison and the middle two stanzas in harmony.

31
HYMN: New Every Morning Is the Love
TUNE: Melcombe

Author: *Rev. John Keble* Composer: *Samuel Webbe*

AUTHOR: John Keble is ever to be remembered as the author of "The Christian Year," a book of devotions which is the product of a saintly mind and a profound spiritual experience. During his lifetime Keble saw his book pass through ninety editions. It has influenced the devotional life of educated people as has no other devotional poetry. Keble was born in Fairford, England, in 1792. He entered Oxford at fourteen, passing directly from his father's study, where he had been trained, into the university. He was a student of great ability, taking the Oriel Fellowship. Tutoring for several years in Oxford, this modest poet-preacher entered a tiny parish where for a dozen years he served as a curate for his father during his declining years. In 1827 friends urged him to publish the poems of "The Christian Year." This he did anonymously. The profits from "The Christian Year" enabled Keble to rebuild his church at Hursley in 1833. He was, in that same year, honored by being made professor of poetry at Oxford. It was, according to Cardinal Newman, a sermon preached by Keble on national apostasy that started the historic Oxford Movement. Keble was grieved at the defection to the Roman Church of Newman, Pusey, and others. Although he is remembered for "The Christian Year," he was the author of other books, besides a hundred hymns and twelve volumes of sermons. He died March 29, 1866. Three of Keble's hymns and one chant are included in "The Hymnal."

42

Times of Worship

HYMN: Taken from a long poem entitled, "Hues of the Rich Unfolding Morn," written in 1822, this hymn was published in "The Christian Year," in 1827. Keble knew Wordsworth, Southey, and Coleridge, and one catches hints of a Christian world view shared with these great poets. This is regarded as Keble's most widely used hymn. With a deep appreciation of the beauties of the natural world is closely linked the satisfying experience of worship.

COMPOSER: Samuel Webbe was born in 1740. In early life he was apprenticed to a cabinetmaker. His fame rests on his secular compositions called "glees," of which he produced a great number. He gained eleven prizes for glees alone. He wrote a number of simple services for small choirs and much religious music, and also published a collection of shorter sacred pieces. He was an excellent scholar, a poet of fair ability, and a good linguist. He died in London in 1816.

TUNE: "Melcombe" appears in a number of Scottish psalm-tune and hymn books. In the 1896 edition of "The Scottish Hymnal" the tune is called "O Salutaris." The tune appears in "A Collection of Motetts, Etc.," published by Webbe in 1792, but it had appeared in an "Essay on the Church Plain Chant" in 1782. This is a very beautiful tune in regard to both melody and harmony.

32
HYMN: O Splendor of God's Glory Bright
TUNE: Rimington

Author: *Ambrose of Milan*   Composer: *Francis Duckworth*

AUTHOR: Ambrose of Milan, commonly called St. Ambrose, is one of the greatest names in church history. Ambrose (340–397) studied law and became governor of the district in which Milan was situated. In the controversy with the Arians he displayed learning and courage, and while not yet even a communicant he was baptized and consecrated bishop of Milan in 374. He was exceedingly popular although firm. He refused to recognize political preference and princes bowed to his authority. He was an eloquent preacher and was the means of bringing the great Augustine into the service of Christ. Like Gregory, Ambrose contributed much to the liturgy and music of the Church. He introduced antiphonal singing in the Western Church. He has been called "The Father of Church Song." "A beautiful tradition makes the 'Te Deum Laudamus' to have been composed under inspiration, and recited alternately, by Saints Ambrose and Augustine immediately after the baptism of the latter in 387. But the story rests upon a passage which there is every reason to consider spurious." Two hymns by Ambrose are included in "The Hymnal."

TRANSLATOR: For comments on the translator, Louis F. Benson, see Hymn 29.

HYMN: The hymn in its present form is the translation of Dr. Louis F. Benson. It bears the characteristics of the style of Ambrose, being theological, thoughtful, and penetrating. "Great he was indeed, as a scholar, an organizer, a statesman; still greater as a theologian, the earnest and brilliant defender of the Catholic faith against the Arians of the West, just as Athanasius (whose name, one cannot but remark, is the same as his in meaning) was its champion against those of the East."

COMPOSER: Francis Duckworth was born in Rimington, a Yorkshire village in Ribblesdale, England. When he was five years old the family removed to Stopper Lane, near by, where his father took over the village store situated next door to the Wesleyan chapel. At the age of twelve the modest sum of ten shillings was invested in music lessons for the boy, and these constitute the only formal instruction he received. With this meager training, Mr. Duckworth began to play the organ at the services in the village chapel. Leaving his native village for Colne, Lancashire, at the age of twenty, he entered into business with two of his brothers. After working for them for about six years, he commenced business on his own account. Shortly after establishing his residence at Colne, he became deputy organist, then organist at Albert Road Wesleyan Chapel, where he continued playing until January, 1929, when he resigned. With his resignation he had completed fifty years of service as an organist. Though music was only his avocation, Mr. Duckworth made good use of his talents, as the wide popularity of some of his compositions shows.

TUNE: "Rimington" was first published in 1904. However, the origin of it, so the composer reveals, goes back to Duckworth's boyhood days, to the overhearing of a conversation between his uncle and several others in which the merits of hymn writers were discussed. The uncle showed marked partiality for Isaac Watts, from whose hymns he quoted "Jesus Shall Reign Where'er the Sun." This conversation inspired the boy with the hope that he might write a tune for his uncle's favorite hymn. Many years elapsed before the tune was written. It was named "Rimington" after his native village and is now recognized in England as the best musical setting for Dr. Watts's hymn. Over two million copies are in circulation. The tune, which appears in more than eight foreign hymnals, is a favored number for community singing and broadcasting. Incidentally, "Rimington" was sung on Mount Calvary on the Sunday following the capitulation of Jerusalem during the World War.

The first two lines of this tune are modeled on the form of the Genevan psalm tune. One of the characteristics of the Genevan psalm tune was the "gathering" notes, or notes of double length, at the beginning of the lines. The last two lines are freer in their rhythmic expression. The tune can easily be sung in unison if desired.

Evening

*

33 HYMN: Abide with Me: Fast Falls the Eventide
TUNE: Eventide (Monk)

Author: *Rev. Henry Francis Lyte*   Composer: *William H. Monk*

AUTHOR: For comments on the author, Henry Francis Lyte, see Hymn 12.

HYMN: This hymn was not written for an evening hymn. It is rather a hymn for one who is entering the shadows of life's evening. After visiting an old friend, W. A. Le Hunte, who in his dying moments continued to repeat the words, "Abide with me," Lyte returned home and wrote the hymn, sending it to the family of the sick friend, in whose private papers the original copy is found to-day.

COMPOSER: William Henry Monk was born in London, March 16, 1823. He was a well-known organist, choir trainer, and musical editor. He edited "Hymns Ancient and Modern," 1861, and also assisted in the last revision of "The Congregational Psalmist Hymnal." He edited the tunes for "The Scottish Hymnal" published in 1870.

Monk was a man of deep religious conviction. He regarded the organ as a means of touching the hearts of men and not as a vehicle for any display of skill. He was a great advocate of congregational singing. For nearly forty years he was organist of St. Matthias, Stoke Newington, England, a church known as a hymn-loving church. He died in 1889.

Handbook to The Hymnal

TUNE: It is interesting to know that Henry F. Lyte, author of the hymn, "Abide with Me: Fast Falls the Eventide," also wrote a tune for it. This tune, however, contained several very awkward intervals which made it difficult for inexperienced singers. So it is by the tune of another man that Lyte's great hymn has been carried to popularity. William Henry Monk composed this tune, "Eventide," in ten minutes. When "Hymns Ancient and Modern" was about ready to go to press, it was found that there was no suitable tune for "Abide with Me: Fast Falls the Eventide." Monk sat down and wrote this beautiful tune. Such was his power of concentration that a pupil sat within two yards of him playing an elaborate piano piece without disturbing him in the least. "Eventide" needs no description: it is too well-known and too beloved. It has brought consolation to many hearts in the darkest hours.

---

34   HYMN: Softly Now the Light of Day
              TUNE: Seymour

Author: *Bishop George W. Doane*   Composer: *Carl M. von Weber*

AUTHOR: Bishop George Washington Doane, D.D., LL.D. (1799–1859), was born in Trenton, New Jersey. He was educated at Union College, Schenectady, New York, and ordained in the Episcopal Church in 1821. He was made professor of literature at Trinity College, Hartford, Connecticut, and in 1828 became rector of Trinity Church, Boston. He was made bishop of New Jersey in 1832. In 1834 he edited the first American edition of Keble's "The Christian Year" and had published "Songs by the Way" in 1824. Under his influence were established St. Mary's School for Girls, founded in 1837, and Burlington College, founded in 1846, both at Burlington, New Jersey.

HYMN: In "Songs by the Way," 1824, this hymn was entitled "Evening," and over against the title was written: "Let my prayer be set forth before thee as incense; and the lifting up of my hands as the evening sacrifice." Bishop Doane's life was full of many severe trials and a suggestion of tender sadness is reflected in this beautiful hymn.

COMPOSER: Carl Maria von Weber was born in 1786. His father had been a soldier, but had left the career of arms and led a vagrant and desultory life as a musician. At the same time he gave his son an excellent musical education, placing him with the best teachers. At the age of seventeen Carl became a pupil of the great Abbé Vogler, one of the greatest teachers of his day. Afterwards Weber became connected with the Royal Court at Württemberg, his position being that of secretary

46

to the king's brother. Here Weber was obliged to witness the caprice and vices of the court of King Frederic, whom he heartily despised and under whom he suffered unmerciful ignominy. But in spite of these discouraging conditions, his creative spirit was active and at this time he composed some of his most beautiful songs. He will always be remembered for his operas, "Der Freischütz," "Preciosa," "Euryanthe," and "Oberon." The latter work was written by Weber for Covent Garden, London, and produced by him there while he was ill and depressed. He survived only two months after its production and died in London in 1826.

TUNE: The tune, "Seymour," is intimately associated with the words to which it is set. Weber was a great lover of nature and when he was composing this melody the calm and peace of the evening were in his soul. The hymn should be sung softly and slowly.

35

HYMN: Now the Day Is Over
TUNE: Merrial

Author: *Rev. Sabine Baring-Gould*   Composer: *Joseph Barnby*

AUTHOR: Rev. Sabine Baring-Gould is said to have had more book titles to his credit in the literary catalogue of the British Museum than any writer of his generation. He was born at Exeter, January 28, 1834, and, after graduating at Clare College, Cambridge, in 1857, took orders and settled for a time in the small parish of Horbury. He was well endowed financially and became a great traveler and a noted antiquarian. His capacity for writing induced an active and influential life. His "The Lives of the Saints" (15 volumes), "The Origin and Development of Religious Belief" (2 volumes), together with travel books, histories, novels, and finally a book of hymns, gave his fruitful pen a total of nearly fifty publications. His three immortal hymns are "Onward, Christian Soldiers," Hymn 365; "Through the Night of Doubt and Sorrow," Hymn 345; and "Now the Day Is Over."

HYMN: The hymn theme is said to have been taken from Prov. 3:24, "When thou liest down, thou shalt not be afraid." It was first published in The Church Times in 1867 and appeared in "Hymns Ancient and Modern," in 1868. It is the most widely used evening hymn. It combines the element of trustful worship with the childlike dependence and earnest desire for God's care and keeping.

COMPOSER: For comments on the composer, Joseph Barnby, see Hymn 3.

Handbook to The Hymnal

TUNE: Baring-Gould, the author of the hymn, composed a tune for it called "Eudoxia." The tune in "The Hymnal," "Merrial," has, however, become intimately associated with the words to which it is set. It is known all over this country. It should be sung softly and slowly, with the thought that the words constitute an evening prayer.

---

36 HYMN: The Shadows of the Evening Hours
TUNE: St. Leonard (Hiles)

Author: *Adelaide A. Procter*   Composer: *Henry Hiles*

AUTHOR: Adelaide Anne Procter (1825–1864) used the pen name "Mary Berwick." She sent her first poems to Charles Dickens, then editor of Household Words, who continued publishing her verses for two years before he discovered who she was. Her parents were personal friends of Dickens. She published two series of poems with the title, "Legends and Lyrics, a Book of Verse," in 1858 and 1862 respectively. In 1851 she became a Roman Catholic. Some of her songs have become familiar, especially "The Lost Chord." She was musical and skilled in languages. Of her, Dickens said: "Now it was the visitation of the sick that had possession of her; now it was the sheltering of the homeless; now it was the elementary teaching of the densely ignorant; now it was the raising up of those who had wandered and got trodden underfoot; now it was the wider employment of her own sex in the general business of life; now it was all these things at once. Perfectly unselfish, swift to sympathize, and eager to relieve, she wrought at such designs with a flushed earnestness that disregarded season, weather, time of day or night, food, rest." She died in her mother's arms, saying, "It has come at last." Two others of her hymns are in "The Hymnal," Hymns 73 and 305.

HYMN: This hymn is taken from "Legends and Lyrics," 1858. It contains four stanzas. The third stanza, omitted in "The Hymnal," is:

> "Slowly the rays of daylight fade;
>   So fade within our heart
> The hopes in earthly love and joy
>   That one by one depart.
> Slowly the bright stars, one by one,
>   Within the heavens shine;
> Give us, O Lord, fresh hopes in heaven,
>   And trust in things Divine."

48

Times of Worship

In the introduction to her "Collected Poems," Charles Dickens says: "She never by any means held the opinion that she was among the greatest of human beings; she never suspected the existence of a conspiracy on the part of mankind against her; she never recognized in her best friends her worst enemies; she never cultivated the luxury of being misunderstood and unappreciated; she would far rather have died without seeing a line of her composition in print, than that I should have maundered about her, here, as 'the poet,' or 'the poetess.' "

COMPOSER: Henry Hiles, Mus.D., was born in Shrewsbury, England, in 1826. He was a well-known organist and composer, "The Crusaders" being the best known of his many sacred cantatas. He was a resident of Manchester, a lecturer on music at Owen's College and Victoria University, and professor of composition at the Manchester College of Music. From 1885 to 1888 he was editor and proprietor of the Quarterly Musical Review. He also wrote books on harmony and the theory of music. He died at Worthing in 1904.

TUNE: "St. Leonard (Hiles)" is an effective tune in spite of its weak melodic outline. In small gatherings where the singing is likely to be in unison, it would be well to transpose the whole tune into the key of F in order to avoid the high F in the seventh line. The hymn should be sung somewhat slowly and meditatively.

37

HYMN: Sun of My Soul, Thou Saviour Dear
TUNE: Hursley

Author: *Rev. John Keble*   Source: *"Katholisches Gesangbuch"*

AUTHOR: For comments on the author, John Keble, see Hymn 31.

HYMN: This is one of the one hundred or more hymns by Keble. It is taken from his "The Christian Year," which sold 305,500 copies in forty-six years. Wordsworth is said to have proposed to Keble that they go over the hymn together, that its lyric faults might not hinder its larger spiritual influence. This was never done. The obvious sincerity of the poem, with its love of nature and delight in God's care, wins for it at once a place in the hearts of all worshipers. The original poem represents a lone traveler, after the sun has set, pressing on his darkening way and trusting confidently in God's protection and guidance. He thinks, too, of the sick, the poor, and of helpless childhood.

Handbook to The Hymnal

SOURCE: The tune, "Hursley," otherwise known as "Pascal," has been attributed to Peter Ritter. This is due in a large measure to the fact that Dr. Rimbault, in his Notes and Queries for April 11, 1868, states that, in a manuscript collection of German chorals in his possession, the tune "Pascal" is ascribed to Ritter and dated 1792. Dr. Rimbault considered the ascription authentic. However, the tune is known to have appeared in a Vienna choral book, published not earlier than 1774 and not later than 1780. Hursley was the name of the parish in which Keble, the author of the words, spent the closing years of his ministry and where his body is buried, in the churchyard. In addition to the names "Hursley" and "Pascal," the tune is known as "Stillorgan," "Framingham," and "Te Deum."

TUNE: The tune, "Hursley," has been arranged from the old choral in the Vienna "Katholisches Gesangbuch." It is intimately associated with the words. This tune should not be sung slowly but at a moderately quick tempo. It is a fine tune rising to a climax on the note D at the beginning of the last line. Much of its charm lies in the three repeated notes at the beginning of the first, second, and last lines and in the fact that the rhythmic pattern in the first line is carried out with only slight modifications in all the other lines.

---

38   HYMN: The Radiant Morn Hath Passed Away
      TUNE: The Radiant Morn

Author: *Rev. Godfrey Thring*   Composer: *Charles F. Gounod*

AUTHOR: Godfrey Thring (1823–1903) was the son of the rector of Alford, in Somerset, England. He was educated at Balliol College, Oxford, and ordained a clergyman of the Church of England. He succeeded his father as rector of Alford-with-Hornblotton. Afterwards, he became dean of Wells Cathedral. In 1866 he published "Hymns Congregational and Others," and "Hymns and Verses"; in 1874, "Hymns and Sacred Lyrics." Thring was strongly against all "party" hymn books and sought to incorporate in his hymn books all the best hymns of the Church Universal. "A Church of England Hymn Book," which he compiled in 1880, set a high standard. A revised edition appeared in 1882 and laid the foundation of the present literary standards prevailing in the best hymnals of the Church. Godfrey Thring's closing days were lived in retirement. He was a courageous, true, loyal Christian. His published verses in "Hymns and Poems for the Holy Days and Festivals of the Church" gave Keble the idea for his "The Christian Year."

Times of Worship

HYMN: Taken from Thring's own "Hymns Congregational and Others," 1866, this hymn was adopted as the opening hymn of the 1868 Appendix of "Hymns Ancient and Modern." It was first printed under the heading "The Lord Shall Be Thine Everlasting Light," Isa. 60:20. The second stanza has been changed. The author himself said that the hymn "was composed as an afternoon hymn, as in most of the parishes in that part of Somersetshire in which I lived, the second service was nearly always held in the afternoon and not in the evening." The tune, "St. Gabriel," by Sir F. Ouseley, was written for the hymn but is not used in "The Hymnal." This hymn is used in one of the most popular anthems of the Church.

COMPOSER: For comments on the composer, Charles F. Gounod, see Hymn 26.

TUNE: Few hymn tunes have a better constructed melody than has "The Radiant Morn." While the melody in lines 1 and 2 has the general direction of ascent, the melody in line 3 has the general direction of descent. This makes for good balance, and the hymn tune is beautifully rounded off by the concluding short line.

---

39   HYMN: Day Is Dying in the West
              TUNE: Evening Praise

Author: *Mary A. Lathbury*   Composer: *William F. Sherwin*

AUTHOR: Mary A. Lathbury was the daughter of a Methodist minister and was born in Manchester, New York, August 10, 1841. She became a teacher of art and later entered upon a life of editorial writing, especially for children and young people. Her recognized ability brought her in touch with Bishop John H. Vincent in the work of the Methodist Sunday School Union. She was likewise from the beginning associated with the Chautauqua Movement. Because of the worth and popularity of her poems and literary readings, she was known as the "laureate of Chautauqua." She founded the "Look-Up Legion" after the pattern of Edward Everett Hale's "Harry Wadsworth Club," which had for its motto: "Look up, and not down; look forward, and not back; look out, and not in; and lend a hand." Miss Lathbury died in 1913.

HYMN: While writing for the Bible study groups in the Sunday Schools of the country and for the Chautauqua vesper services, made famous by the devotional leadership of Bishop Vincent, Miss Lathbury produced "Day Is Dying in the West" and "Break Thou

Handbook to The Hymnal

the Bread of Life." Perhaps no evening hymn has so large a place in the worship life of the American churches as has "Day Is Dying in the West."

COMPOSER: William Fisk Sherwin was born in 1826 in Buckland, Massachusetts. He began the study of music under Lowell Mason at the age of fifteen and became a teacher of vocal music at the New England Conservatory and elsewhere. He died in 1888. Sherwin is remembered by his connection with Chautauqua, where he was the director of music. It was here that he wrote his best tunes for Miss Lathbury's poems.

TUNE: The tune, "Evening Praise," sometimes called "Chautauqua," has been very popular for the last forty years. The refrain should be begun very softly, rising in a gradual crescendo.

---

40   HYMN: The Sun Declines; O'er Land and Sea
      TUNE: Vincent

Author: *Robert Walmsley*   Composer: *Horatio Richmond Palmer*

AUTHOR: Robert Walmsley (1831–1905) was a Congregationalist layman. He was a jeweler and an ardent Sunday School worker. Most of his hymns were written for festivals of the Manchester Sunday School Union. In "Sacred Songs for Children of All Ages," published in 1900, forty-four of his hymns were printed.

HYMN: This hymn appeared in "Sacred Songs for Children of All Ages," 1900. In its original form it has three stanzas. The third stanza is as follows:

> "And when with morning light we rise,
>   Kept by Thy care,
> We'll lift to Thee, with grateful hearts,
>   Our morning prayer.
> Be Thou through life our Strength and Stay,
>   Our Guard and Guide
> To that dear home where there will be
>   No eventide."

As one reads the stanzas the words "Abide with us; for it is toward evening," Luke 24:29, are suggested.

52

Times of Worship

COMPOSER: Horatio Richmond Palmer was born April 26, 1834, at Sherburne, New York. He was director of Rushford Academy of Music, New York, and studied in Berlin and Florence. Settling in Chicago in 1861, he established a magazine called "Concordia." In 1874 he went to New York and from 1887 to 1891 held the office of dean of the Chautauqua School of Music. From 1867 to 1886 he published a number of musical works of which his "A Theory of Music," 1876, is perhaps the best known. He received the degree of Doctor of Music from Chicago University in 1879 and from Alfred University in 1880. He died in 1907.

TUNE: The first and second lines of this tune, "Vincent," should be sung very softly and the next line just a little stronger and the fourth line softly. The fifth and seventh lines should be sung crescendo. The sixth line is in B flat, but, with the last chord, comes back to the home key, E flat. The last two lines should be gradually softer to the end of the hymn.

41

HYMN: God, That Madest Earth and Heaven
TUNE: Ar Hyd Y Nos

Authors: (Stanza 1) *Bishop Reginald Heber*   Source: *Welsh*
(Stanza 2) *Rev. William Mercer*   *Traditional Melody*
(Stanza 3) *Rev. Richard Whately*

AUTHORS: This hymn of deep personal faith is by Bishop Reginald Heber, D.D., with two stanzas added by other well-known men. Born in Malpas, England, April 21, 1783, Heber graduated from Brasenose College, Oxford, where as a student he was marked for distinction. Even in childhood his poetic gifts were noted. His university prize poem on Palestine won him not only the Newdigate Prize but also the approbation of Sir Walter Scott, who read the manuscript at his breakfast table. Among Heber's friends were such distinguished literary men of his day as Dean Milman, Robert Southey, and William Gifford. For sixteen years Heber occupied an ancestral manor and served with great devotion the parish at Hodnet in Shropshire. His brilliant contributions to The Quarterly Review attracted attention. His Bampton lectures on the Holy Spirit, 1815, together with his sermons as preacher at Lincoln's Inn, 1822, and his hymns and poems, woke England to the fact that Heber was an intellectual as well as a spiritual leader. Made bishop of Calcutta in 1822, he concluded his literary work, giving his life instead in the most unwearied devotion to missionary travel and service. His was the privilege of baptizing the first native Christian. Debilitated

53

by fever and exhausting labors, he died suddenly at the close of a day in which he had baptized forty-two persons in the city of Trichinoply on April 3, 1826. He did much to popularize congregational hymn-singing. Before going to India he wrote "From Greenland's Icy Mountains." "Thou Art Gone to the Grave" was written upon the death of his little child. The lyric spirit of Scott and Byron lived in Heber's hymns. When a man can leave behind him such hymns as "The Son of God Goes Forth to War," "Brightest and Best of the Sons of the Morning," "Holy, Holy, Holy! Lord God Almighty," his immortality is assured. Heber has eight hymns in "The Hymnal."

William Mercer, D.D. (1811–1873), the writer of stanza 2, issued "The Church Psalter and Hymn Book" in 1857, with the help of Sir John Goss as musical editor. By 1864, 100,000 copies were being sold annually. The book had no rival in the field.

Archbishop Whately, D.D., who added stanza 3 to this hymn, was born in 1787. Newman says in his "Apologia" that it was Whately who taught him to think. He was Bampton lecturer in 1822 and author of several books, including "Difficulties of the Writings of the Apostle Paul." He died in 1863.

HYMN: This composite hymn originally consisted of the first stanza only. It was published after Heber's death, when other stanzas were added as indicated. As an evening hymn it breathes the atmosphere of quiet trust in God and expectancy of his care.

SOURCE: The tune is a traditional Welsh melody. Folk music owes its original conception to no known individual but is the free expression of the people, handed down traditionally. Folk music was the secular music of its day. Sacred music was the composition of monks and clerics and was composed according to certain specified rules. It is fitting perhaps that as the voice of the people in the Church has become more clearly defined in modern times than formerly, the use of folk music should find a place there.

HARMONIZER: Luther Orlando Emerson was born in 1820 and died in 1915. He published "The Romberg Collection" of tunes in 1853 and was active in Salem, Boston, and Greenfield, Massachusetts.

TUNE: "Ar Hyd Y Nos," the adaptation of the old Welsh folk-song melody, "All Through the Night," or "Poor Mary Ann," to Bishop Heber's hymn, "God That Madest Earth and Heaven," is in accordance with the growing practice of hymn-tune composers either to adapt a folk-song melody for hymn tunes or to compose a tune founded on such a melody.

54

Times of Worship

42 HYMN: All Praise to Thee, My God, This Night
        TUNE: Tallis' Canon

Author: *Bishop Thomas Ken*   Composer: *Thomas Tallis*

AUTHOR: Thomas Ken (1637–1711) was educated at Winchester and New College, Oxford, and early showed musical genius. He served as curate of the Isle of Wight, where the hymns that we know best were written. He returned to Winchester at twenty-nine years of age as Fellow of the college and there prepared his "Manual of Prayers" for use in the college. He was appointed, in 1679, chaplain to Princess Mary at The Hague, but because of his outspokenness he was forced to return to England. He was made chaplain at the court of Charles II, but after refusing to obey the order of the king to give the use of his house to Nell Gwyn, he was made bishop of Bath and Wells by the amused and good-natured monarch. Later Ken refused to obey the order to read the Declaration of Indulgence and was one of seven bishops committed to the Tower. James II pronounced Bishop Ken the most eloquent preacher among the Protestants of his time.

HYMN: In "A Manual of Prayers for the Use of the Scholars of Winchester College," 1674, reference is made to the Morning, Midnight, and Evening Hymns. Thomas Ken himself sang these hymns to the viol. His counsel was: "Be sure to sing the Morning and Evening Hymn in your chamber devoutly, remembering that the psalmist, upon happy experience, assures you that it is a good thing to tell of the loving-kindness of the Lord early in the morning and of his truth in the night season." These hymns have found a place in the hymnals of the Church for a hundred and fifty years. The "Morning Hymn," beginning, "Awake my soul, and with the sun," consists of fourteen stanzas and closes with "Praise God, from whom all blessings flow." The "Midnight Hymn," beginning with, "My God, now I from sleep awake," consists of thirteen stanzas and closes with the Doxology. The "Evening Hymn," beginning, "All praise to Thee, my God, this night," consists of twelve stanzas and concludes again with the Doxology. In the edition of 1695 it began with the line, "Glory to Thee, my God, this night," but the 1709 edition has "All praise to Thee, my God, this night." The first four stanzas in "The Hymnal" and the closing Doxology are taken from the 1709 edition, with a slight change in the third stanza.

COMPOSER: Thomas Tallis, or Tallys, was born sometime between 1510 and 1520. He has deservedly been styled, "The Father of English Cathedral Music." His work ranks almost with that of Palestrina. He was a chorister at St. Paul's Cathedral, London, organist of Waltham Abbey, and organist to Queen Elizabeth. He became one of the gentlemen of the Chapel Royal, taking his turn as organist there. He held this post during the latter part of the reign of Henry VIII and the reigns of Edward VI, Mary, and Elizabeth, until his death in 1585.

TUNE: About 1561 Tallis wrote nine tunes and several anthems for Archbishop Parker's Psalter. The tune in "The Hymnal," "Tallis' Canon," is abridged by Ravenscroft from the eighth tune in the series. It was set by Ravenscroft to "A Psalme Before Morning Prayer," but since late in the seventeenth century it has been associated with Bishop Ken's "Evening Hymn." In this tune the tenor sings the melody five notes after the soprano. This is what is known as a "canon."

---

43   HYMN: At Even, When the Sun Was Set
            TUNE: Angelus

Author: *Rev. Henry Twells*   Composer: *Georg Joseph*

AUTHOR: Henry Twells was born in Birmingham in 1823. He was a schoolmate at King Edward's School of two young men who were to become England's most distinguished Greek scholars and Churchmen, Bishop Westcott and Bishop Lightfoot, not to speak of Archbishop Benson, primate of all England. Twells was ordained in 1849 and served as rector in Stratford-on-Avon and other parishes. He served as master of St. Andrew's House School and as head master of Godolphin School, and later he was canon of Peterborough Cathedral. He died at Bournemouth in 1900, where by his own means he had built a church which he served until his death. He is to be remembered chiefly by this beautiful evening hymn and his contributions to "Hymns Ancient and Modern."

HYMN: This hymn, which is included in practically all standard hymnals on both sides of the sea, is based on the impressive evening episode described in Mark 1:32: "At even, when the sun did set, they brought unto him all that were sick." The confession of human weakness in the third and fourth stanzas of the hymn is followed by the prayer for help and healing.

COMPOSER: Very little is known regarding the composer, Georg Joseph. He lived in the second half of the seventeenth century and was a musician in the service of the bishop of Breslau. He set to music a number of sacred songs by "Angelus Silesius," or Johann Scheffler, who lived from 1624 to 1677 and was famous as a mystic and poet. Georg Joseph was the musical editor of Scheffler's "Heilige Seelenlust."

TUNE: The key of the tune, "Angelus," changes in the first line to B flat. After a few notes in E flat it returns to B flat again. Shortly afterwards the key changes to C minor before the final return to E flat. This frequent change of key imparts a sense of restlessness to the hymn and probably for this reason it has been less popular than many others which have a clearer tonality. At the same time there is much of beauty in the tune and it makes an effective hymn for the beginning of the evening service.

44

HYMN: The Day Is Past and Over
TUNE: St. Anatolius (Brown)

Source: *A Greek Service*   Composer: *Arthur H. Brown*

SOURCE: This hymn has been ascribed to Anatolius, a Greek hymn writer about whom nothing is known. He is not to be identified with Anatolius the Patriarch, A.D. 449.

TRANSLATOR: John Mason Neale, D.D., fourteen of whose translations appear in this Hymnal, was born in London, England, January 24, 1818. His father was an Evangelical clergyman of distinction, who provided his son with every advantage for a notable career. At eighteen John entered Cambridge University, where he was a student of rank and gained a scholarship at Trinity College. While at the university he joined the High Church movement. According to Dr. Louis F. Benson, "he passed his whole ministry under the shadow of reproach and disfavor." His only preferment was the wardenship of Sackville College at East Grinstead, where he remained from 1846 to 1866. He was deeply interested in the hymns of the Latin and Greek Churches, which he translated with brilliant success. Among his leading publications are "Mediæval Hymns and Sequences," 1851, and "Hymns of the Eastern Church," 1862. His "memory," writes Dr. Benson, "is kept green by such hymns as 'Jerusalem the Golden' and 'Art Thou Weary, Art Thou Languid.' " He passed away on the feast of transfiguration, August 6, 1866.

HYMN: The Greek original of this hymn is used in the Evening Service of the Greek Church and belongs to the sixth or seventh century. Dr. John M. Neale says: "This little hymn, which, I believe, is now used in the public service of the Church, is a great favorite in the Greek Isles. Its peculiar style and evident antiquity may well lead to the belief that it is the work of . . . [St. Anatolius]. It is to the scattered hamlets of Chios and Mitylene what Bishop Ken's 'Evening Hymn' is to the villages of our own land; and its melody is singularly plaintive and soothing." The Greek text appears in the Great After-Supper Service of the Greek Church. A literal translation given by Dr. Julian is as follows:

"God is with us, let the nations know and be discomfited: for God is with us.

"The day is passing on, I thank thee, O Lord: that the evening with the night may be sinless, I beseech—Grant to me, Saviour, and save me.

"Glory to the Father, and to the Son, and to the Holy Ghost.

"The day is passing away, I glorify thee, O Master: that the evening with the night may be offenceless, I beseech—Grant to me, Saviour, and save me.

"Both now, and ever, and to ages of ages. Amene.

"The day has passed away, I hymn thee, O Holy: that the evening with the night may be plotless, I beseech—Grant to me, Saviour, and save me."

The translation was first published in 1853. The stanzas in "The Hymnal" are from the revised edition of Neale's "Hymns of the Eastern Church," 1862.

COMPOSER: Arthur Henry Brown was born at Brentwood, Essex, England, in 1830. He was organist of the Church of St. Thomas the Martyr, Brentwood, from 1842 until 1853, when he became organist of the Church of St. Edward the Confessor, Romford, Essex, returning to Brentwood, however, five years later. Brown wrote many hymn tunes and edited several publications, among them "The Altar Hymnal." In 1916 he won a silver medal, given by the Guild of Church Musicians, for his hymn tune "High Laver."

TUNE: "St. Anatolius (Brown)" was composed for the words to which it is set. It was composed on February 8, 1862, and published, with a few other hymns, the following November. The climax of the hymn is at the beginning of the fifth line, and the melody has, from there to the end of the hymn, a downward slant from high E flat to low E flat.

---

45 HYMN: The Day Thou Gavest, Lord, Is Ended
TUNE: St. Clement

Author: *Rev. John Ellerton*   Composer: *Rev. Clement C. Scholefield*

AUTHOR: For comments on the author, John Ellerton, see Hymn 20.

Times of Worship

HYMN: This hymn was written in 1870 for use as a "liturgy for missionary meetings" and appeared the following year in "Church Hymns." The striking feature of this hymn is its recital of the majestic procession of the sunrise and sunset around the earth and the continuous praise, morning and evening, that greets this token of God's ceaseless love.

COMPOSER: Rev. Clement Cotterill Scholefield, A.M., was born at Edgbaston, Birmingham, England, June 22, 1839. He was educated at Pocklington Grammar School, Yorkshire, and graduated from St. John's College, Cambridge. He was ordained pastor of Hove Church, near Brighton, in 1867. Two years later he became pastor of St. Peter's, South Kensington, London. For ten years he was chaplain of Eton College, Windsor. Scholefield was a self-taught musician and composer of hymn tunes. He died in 1904.

TUNE: "St. Clement" appeared in a collection of "Church Hymns with Tunes," published by Sir Arthur Sullivan in 1874. The first and third lines are identical. The second line ends in the key of E flat but the last line remains in the key of A flat.

---

46   HYMN: O Light of Life, O Saviour Dear
      TUNE: Abends

Author: *Francis T. Palgrave*   Composer: *Herbert S. Oakeley*

AUTHOR: Francis Turner Palgrave (1824–1897) was the son of Sir Francis Palgrave, the historian. He was educated at Oxford and for five years served as vice principal of Kneller Hall. Later he served as examiner and assistant secretary in the education department of the Privy Council. In 1885 he became professor of poetry at the University of Oxford. His writings include: "Idylls and Songs," 1854; "Essays on Art," 1866; "Hymns," 1867; "Lyrical Poems," 1871. He is best known as editor of "The Golden Treasury of English Lyrics," 1864, and "The Treasury of Sacred Song," 1889.

HYMN: This is an evening hymn, written in 1865. Palgrave was the author of many hymns, few of which are now in use. His purpose in writing has been interpreted in this statement: "Professor Palgrave's hymns are marked by much originality of thought and beauty of diction, as well as great tenderness. His object was 'to try and write hymns which should have more distinct matter for thought and feeling than many in our collections offer, and so, perhaps, be of little use and comfort to readers' and he has admirably succeeded in his object."

COMPOSER: Sir Herbert Stanley Oakeley, D.C.L., was born at Ealing, Middlesex, England, on July 22, 1830. He was educated at Rugby, and at Oxford, where he was a pupil of Dr. Stephen Elvey. Afterwards he went abroad and studied in Germany under Moscheles, Schneider, and others. From 1865 until 1891 he occupied the chair of music at Edinburgh University. The archbishop of Canterbury conferred on him the degree of Doctor of Music in 1871, as did nine universities, and Aberdeen University conferred the degree of Doctor of Laws in 1881. He was knighted by Queen Victoria in 1876. He died in 1903.

TUNE: The tune, "Abends," was originally composed for "Sun of My Soul, Thou Saviour Dear." It was probably composed in 1871, but its first appearance seems to have been in 1874, in the Irish "Church Hymnal," edited by Sir R. P. Stewart. The tune in many respects reveals the hand of an educated composer but is probably too ornate ever to become really popular.

---

47   HYMN: Saviour, Breathe an Evening Blessing
TUNE: Evening Prayer

Author: *James Edmeston*   Composer: *George C. Stebbins*

AUTHOR: James Edmeston was a London architect and surveyor, born in 1791. A devout and lifelong Churchman, in his later years he was warden of St. Barnabas' Church at Homerton. The special object of his interest throughout his active life was little children, particularly those in the London Orphan Asylum. In this Christlike work he found inspiration for many of his children's hymns. To meet the demand of the Evangelical movement, a prize was offered for the fifty best hymns for use in cottage meetings. His "Cottage Minstrel" was awarded the prize and was in wide use for years. Edmeston is said to have written a hymn every Sunday for his own family devotions. More than two thousand hymns are credited to his pen, which are found in such collections as "Sacred Lyrics," "Infant Breathings," and other hymnals. His two best-known hymns are this evening hymn and "Lead Us, Heavenly Father, Lead Us," Hymn 304, written for the children in the London orphanage. He died in 1867, leaving twelve volumes, mostly hymns and poems.

Times of Worship

HYMN: This hymn first appeared in Edmeston's "Sacred Lyrics," 1820. It was suggested to him by a simple incident recounted by Salte in his "Travels in Abyssinia," where in the night the native Christians' "short evening hymn, 'Jesus, Forgive Us,' stole through his camp."

COMPOSER: George Coles Stebbins was born in East Carlton, Orleans County, New York, on February 26, 1846. His early life was spent on a farm in his native county. He studied at Rochester and began his musical career as director of the First Baptist Church of Chicago. Afterwards he became director of music at Tremont Temple, Boston. He became associated with Dwight L. Moody in 1876 and organized the choir for Mr. Moody's first great campaign in Chicago. He was coeditor with Ira D. Sankey and James McGranahan in publishing various editions of "Gospel Hymns." He compiled and edited "The Northfield Hymnal," published in 1904.

TUNE: This tune, "Evening Prayer," should be sung slowly and softly. The last two lines of the hymn, however, should be sung with a note of triumph.

Opening

*

48 HYMN: Father, Again in Jesus' Name We Meet
    TUNE: Longwood

Author: *Lucy E. G. Whitmore*   Composer: *Joseph Barnby*

AUTHOR: The author of this hymn is Lucy Elizabeth Georgina Whitmore (1792–1840). Lady Whitmore was the daughter of Orlando Bridgeman, second Baron and first Earl of Bradford. She married William W. Whitmore in 1810. In 1824 she published "Family Prayers for Every Day in the Week." This small volume contained fourteen of her hymns. The eighth hymn was "Father, Again in Jesus' Name We Meet."

HYMN: The hymn appeared in one of the "Staffordshire Hymn Books," the first of which was published in 1805. The hymn is based on Luke 15:20: "And he arose, and came to his father. But while he was yet afar off, his father saw him, and was moved with compassion, and ran, and fell on his neck, and kissed him." Dora Greenwell

61

says: "Let such be consoled in remembering that the Father who draws us to Christ beholds us, yea, sets forth to meet us, while we are yet a great way off. A great way off, and yet upon the way—herein lies all the difference between resistance and returning."

COMPOSER: For comments on the composer, Joseph Barnby, see Hymn 3.

TUNE: "Longwood" made its first appearance in "The Hymnary" of 1872, Barnby's greatest achievement in editing. He composed this tune especially for the hymn "Saviour, Again to Thy Dear Name We Raise."

---

49   HYMN: O Come, Let Us Sing to the Lord
           TUNE: Irish

Source: *"Scottish Psalter"*   Source: *"A Collection of*
                                                Hymns and Sacred Poems"

SOURCE: For comments on the source, "Scottish Psalter," 1650, see the article, "The Psalters in Early Presbyterian Worship," under "Original Sources," page xv.

HYMN: This is the metrical version of Psalm 95. It was the war song of the Knights Templars, the rival order to the Knights of St. John. Spurgeon said of this psalm: "It has a ring like that of the church bells and like the bells it sounds both merrily and solemnly, at first ringing out a lively peal, and then dropping into a funeral knell as if tolling at the funeral of the generation which perished in the wilderness." This is the "Venite" that has called to worship the Christians of all ages.

SOURCE: The source is "A Collection of Hymns and Sacred Poems," Dublin, 1749.

TUNE: The name "Irish" may probably be ascribed to the fact that the tune first appeared in Dublin, Ireland. It is found at the end of the collection without name, under "Tunes Adapted to the Foregoing Hymns." In Ashworth's "Collection of Tunes," c. 1760, we find it published under the caption "Irish Tune." Other than this, the tune gives no evidence of an Irish origin. It may have some association with John Wesley, as he is thought to have edited the Dublin collection while in Ireland in 1749. However, this is a matter of conjecture. The tune appears in "The Church Hymnary" and other hymnals associated with Hosmer's hymn "'Thy Kingdom Come,' on Bended Knee." It makes, in the present Hymnal, a well-adapted setting to the metric version of Psalm 95.

---

50   HYMN: Lord of the Worlds Above
                           TUNE: Darwall's 148th

Author: *Rev. Isaac Watts*   Composer: *Rev. John Darwall*

AUTHOR: For comments on the author, Isaac Watts, see Hymn 22.

HYMN: This hymn was first published in Isaac Watts's "The Psalms of David Imitated," 1719. It consisted of seven stanzas of eight lines each. This is one of the best of Watts's paraphrases of the psalms and has been passed down to us with several alterations. It was much used in the collection of hymns in the services of Wesley and White-field and appeared also in Toplady's "Psalms and Hymns," 1776. From there it passed into the hymnals of the Church of England. The hymn is written in the peculiar metrical style introduced by John Pullain in his version of Psalm 148. The hymn is based on Psalm 84.

COMPOSER: John Darwall, was born at Haughton, Staffordshire, in 1731. He was educated at Manchester Grammar School and Brasenose College, Oxford, graduating from the latter in 1756. He became curate and later vicar of Walsall. An enthusiastic poet and amateur musician, he composed a tune for each of the 150 metrical psalms. Some of these are to be found in Dr. Mann's "Church of England Hymnal" and also in the late eighteenth century tune books. He also published two volumes of pianoforte sonatas: "A Christmas Hymn and Tune" and "A Charity Hymn and Tune"; and "A Hymn to Which Is Prefixed a Biographical Notice." He died at Walsall in 1789.

TUNE: "Darwall's 148th" was published in Aaron Williams' "New Universal Psalmodist," 1770, as the musical setting for Psalm 148. It is one of the 150 tunes composed for the complete Psalter by Darwall, and has been widely used as a setting for hymns such as "Rejoice, the Lord Is King" and "Ye Holy Angels Bright." The melody has a mounting note of triumph and praise in it which undoubtedly obtains from Darwall's original conception of Psalm 148.

Handbook to The Hymnal

51
HYMN: God Himself Is with Us
TUNE: Arnsberg

Author: *Gerhard Tersteegen*   Composer: *Rev. Joachim Neander*

AUTHOR: Gerhard Tersteegen was a profound mystic who, after his conversion at sixteen, spent much of his time in seclusion for prayer and fasting. He withdrew to a hovel near his native town and lived the life of a devout ascetic, making the barest living by weaving ribbons, eating but once a day, and serving the poor. He passed into a long period of melancholy, but, coming out with hope and courage, wrote a covenant of dedication to God in his own blood. His reputation as a spiritual counselor grew. Multitudes came from all the surrounding countries to interview this godly man at his loom. His house was known as "The Pilgrims' Cottage." It was a center of comfort and spiritual guidance. To Tersteegen's passion for preaching is to be added his hymn-writing gifts. He wrote 111 hymns, all reflecting the deep inner experience of the mystical school. They were published in what he called "The Spiritual Flower Garden." One of his most widely known hymns is "God Calling Yet! Shall I Not Hear." He was born in Mörs, Germany, in 1697 and died April 3, 1769.

TRANSLATORS: Frederick William Foster (1760–1835), a translator of many old German hymns, was a provincial superintendent of the Moravian Church and the editor of the Moravian hymn book, 1826.
   Rev. John Miller preached in England and Ireland from 1768 to 1810 and contributed largely to the Moravian hymnal, 1789.

HYMN: The hymn reflects the worship feelings of one who realizes, without any elaborate means of grace, the immediate contact of the soul with God and the possession of an inner light through direct fellowship with him.

COMPOSER: For comments on the composer, Joachim Neander, see Hymn 6.

TUNE: "Arnsberg" appears in "Bundes-Lieder," a collection of Neander's hymns, and is believed on good authority to have been composed by him. It is set to the hymn, "Wunderbarer König, Herrscher Von Uns Allen." In later German collections it is associated with the hymn, "Gott Ist Gegenwärtig," of which the present hymn is a translation.

64

52

HYMN: Come, Thou Almighty King
TUNE: Trinity (Italian Hymn)

Author: *Anonymous*   Composer: *Felice de Giardini*

A UTHOR: This hymn is anonymous. It was written about 1757 and has been mistakenly attributed to Charles Wesley.

H YMN: The hymn was first found with the title "An Hymn to the Trinity" in a tract containing also Charles Wesley's hymn, "Jesus, Let Thy Pitying Eye." The tract is bound up with Whitefield's collection of 1757 and is in the British Museum. The earliest form in which the hymn appears is in five stanzas of seven lines each. The hymn is used throughout the English-speaking world and has been translated into many foreign languages.

C OMPOSER: Felice de Giardini was born in Turin, Piedmont, Italy, in 1716. He was trained as a chorister in Milan Cathedral. In 1750 he made his London début as a violinist. His success was such that he became the leader at the Italian opera in London. After a long residence in England he went to Naples in the service of Sir William Hamilton, British ambassador to the Sardinian court. On his return to England after five years' absence, Giardini found himself with only the shell of his former popularity. In hope of better fortune he went to Moscow, but failed to retrieve his former fame. Poverty and distress hastened his death in that city in 1796. Despite his love for a few and his enmity for many, history has marked him for a great artist.

T UNE: Although bearing two captions in the present Hymnal, "Trinity" and "Italian Hymn," the tune has still a third, "Moscow," which is an even more widely used name, especially in Great Britain and its colonies. The tune was composed by De Giardini for this specific hymn. It made its appearance in what is known as "The Lock Collection," 1769. Here it is found as "Hymn to the Trinity." As it appears in the present Hymnal, the tune is, with one melodic exception, the original version.

53
　　　HYMN: Hosanna to the Living Lord
　　　TUNE: Hosanna

Author: *Bishop Reginald Heber*　　　Composer: *Rev. John B. Dykes*

AUTHOR: For comments on the author, Reginald Heber, see Hymn 41.

HYMN: Bishop Heber, in protest against what he felt to be irreverent familiarity with the name of God and divine things on the part of many hymn writers, wrote a letter to The Christian Observer in October, 1811, and with it appended four hymns, of which this was one, designed for Advent Sunday. It is a jubilant hymn, now used in all parts of the English-speaking world. This is the revised form as it appeared in 1827 after Bishop Heber's death.

COMPOSER: John Bacchus Dykes, A.M., Mus.D., was born in Hull, England, in 1823. He was the son of a banker and the grandson of a prominent evangelical clergyman in Hull. He early showed a talent for music, playing the organ in his father's church at the age of ten. Educated at Wakefield and at St. Catharine's College, Cambridge, he helped, as an undergraduate along with William Thomson, who was afterwards Lord Kelvin, to found the university musical society. He took orders in 1847, and went from the curacy of Malton to become a minor canon at Durham and soon the precentor in the cathedral there. His doctorate was conferred in 1861 by Durham University. A year later he became vicar of St. Oswald's, in the same city, and remained in that position for fourteen years. His health finally broke under the burdens of his parish. During his active ministry he published various sermons and liturgical writings, wrote several popular services and anthems, and composed some three hundred hymn tunes. For these latter he is best known. His contribution to that monumental work in hymnody, "Hymns Ancient and Modern," marked the entrance of a newer type of hymn based on the secular part song of the period. As Dr. Benson has so aptly stated in his volume "The English Hymn," Dykes, together with Monk, Elvey, Gauntlett, and others, "crystallized the musical tendencies of the time into a definite form of Anglican hymn tune, with restrained melodies and close harmonies wonderfully adapted to liturgical worship and yet appealing to the taste of the people."

TUNE: "Hosanna" is not one of the best known of Dykes's tunes. Since the beginning of the twentieth century, approximately, the tune has been widely associated with this hymn, especially in the United States. Moving in jubilant rhythm and with a rising climax in the recurring refrain, it provides a very effective setting for the hymn.

Times of Worship

Closing

*

54
HYMN: Lord, Dismiss Us with Thy Blessing
TUNE: Sicilian Mariners

Author: *Ascribed to Rev. John Fawcett*   Source: *Sicilian Melody*

AUTHORS: This hymn has been ascribed to John Fawcett, D.D. (1740–1817), who is known best as the author of "Blest Be the Tie That Binds." At the age of sixteen he came under the influence of Whitefield and later joined the Baptist Church in Bradford. Fawcett became a Baptist minister in 1765 and in due time settled near Halifax. He was invited to become pastor of Carter's Lane Chapel in London but declined, owing to the loving entreaty of his people. This occasion gave rise to the writing of "Blest Be the Tie That Binds." He declined, also, the presidency of the Baptist Academy at Bristol. He published a number of theological books and a devotional commentary on the Scriptures. He received from America the degree of Doctor of Divinity. For each sermon he preached he is said to have written a hymn. One hundred and sixty-six such hymns were published in "Hymns Adapted to the Circumstances of Public Worship and Private Devotion."

For comments on Godfrey Thring, who recast stanza 3, see Hymn 38.

HYMN: This hymn is ascribed to Fawcett in the York collections of 1786 and 1791. The editors of these collections were Nonconformists and residents of the neighborhood in which Fawcett labored. The hymn has been much altered with the passing of the years. Stanza 1, line 6, originally read: "In this dry and barren place." Stanza 3, afterwards revised by Godfrey Thring, originally read as follows:

> "So whene'er the signal's given
> Us from earth to call away,
> Borne on angels' wings to heaven,
> Glad the summons to obey,
>   May we ever
> Reign with Christ in endless day."

SOURCE: The source of the tune is a Sicilian melody.

TUNE: "Sicilian Mariners," sometimes called "Sicily," is a tune of doubtful origin. It is unknown in Sicily to-day. "The Lutheran Book of Worship with Hymns and Tunes," 1899, ascribes the tune to Marcos Antonio Portogallo. The tune was very much in vogue in

Handbook to The Hymnal

the Nonconformist churches. In Rev. W. Tattersall's edition of Merrick's "Psalms," published in 1794, we find it set to the old Latin hymn, "O Sanctissima, O Purissima." This is in all probability its original association, although since then it has been set to several different hymns. The fourth volume of Corri's "Select Collection of the Most Admired Songs, Duetts, Etc.," c.1794–1795, contains the tune under the title "The Prayer of the Sicilian Mariner." It also appears in Hyde's collection, 1798, and in Dr. Miller's "Dr. Watts's Psalms and Hymns," 1800.

---

55   HYMN: Saviour, Again to Thy Dear Name We Raise
       TUNE: Ellers

Author: *Rev. John Ellerton*   Composer: *Edward J. Hopkins*

AUTHOR: For comments on the author, John Ellerton, see Hymn 20.

HYMN: Of the more than fifty hymns written by John Ellerton, this is by far the most popular, because, according to Dr. Julian, it is "the most beautiful and tender." In this, as well as in others of his hymns, Ellerton combines a fluent diction with the gentle mood of a soul in perfect dependence on God as the shadows of the night gather. His hymns appeal to experienced and cultured worshipers, while satisfying the less rigorous demands for literary merit on the part of the uneducated. This hymn was written for a choral festival at Nantwich, Cheshire, in 1866, and later appeared in "Hymns Ancient and Modern," 1868.

COMPOSER: Edward John Hopkins, Mus.D., was born in Westminster, England, in 1818. He was trained in the Chapel Royal and played the organ in Westminster Abbey at an early age. When he was sixteen years of age he was appointed organist of Mitcham Parish Church. Thereafter he played in several other churches and finally received the appointment to Temple Church, where he served from 1843 to 1898. He was eminently successful there, raising the music to a very high standard. He wrote much church music—services, anthems, hymn tunes, and organ compositions. His edition of "The Temple Choral Service Book" was a notable piece of work. Besides all this, he edited hymnals for the Wesleyan and Congregational communions, the Free Church of Scotland, and the Presbyterian Churches of England and Canada. He died in 1901 in London. Dr. Hopkins was considered "the greatest representative of the old school of English church musicians." His music is quiet and unobtrusive and "hallowed with a devotional fervor which lifts it into a region not far removed from the perfection of sanctified art."

Times of Worship

TUNE: "Ellers" was composed for this hymn. It appeared in "The Supplemental Hymn and Tune Book," compiled by Rev. R. Brown-Borthwick (third edition, with new appendix, 1869). Originally arranged for unison voices with organ accompaniment, the tune later was published in parts in the "Appendix to the Bradford Tune Book," in which Hopkins himself harmonized the tune. It has other arrangements in "Church Hymns," 1874, and Dr. Allon's "The Congregational Psalmist," 1875, respectively. The hymn is restrained and reflective and should be sung with dignity and feeling.

56
HYMN: On Our Way Rejoicing
TUNE: Hermas

Author: *Rev. John S. B. Monsell*   Composer: *Frances R. Havergal*

AUTHOR: For comments on the author, John Samuel Bewley Monsell, see Hymn 7.

HYMN: The hymn appeared first in Monsell's "Hymns of Love and Praise," 1863, and was designated for use on the first Sunday after Trinity. It was rewritten for Monsell's own "The Parish Hymnal," 1863, the principal change being the addition of a refrain containing the first four lines of the first stanza in order to adapt the hymn for processional use.

COMPOSER: Frances Ridley Havergal was born at Astley, England, in 1836. She was the youngest child of Rev. William H. Havergal, pioneer of reform in metrical psalmody. At the age of seven she began to write verses which soon gained circulation in such religious periodicals as Good Words and others. Her maturer works reveal a sympathetic and attractive spirit, tempered by faith and consecration. Her life was one of constant comradeship with her "Master," her favorite name for Christ. Unfortunately her health was frail, which became a great hindrance both in her early studies and in her later religious and philanthropic work. Her collected "Poetical Works" were published in 1884, as well as a volume of "Memorials" containing a partial autobiography. She also wrote a number of tunes. She died at Caswell Bay in 1879, leaving behind her a glorious hymnody, rich in lines of beautiful thought and hallowed by years of close communion with her Lord.

TUNE: "Hermas" appeared in "Havergal's Psalmody" of 1871. It is one of Frances Havergal's best-known tunes and has been widely used as a setting to her own ascension hymn, "Golden Harps Are Sounding." In its present setting it strikes a fitting note of praise and joy.

69

The Holy Trinity

*

57
HYMN: Holy, Holy, Holy! Lord God Almighty
TUNE: Nicæa

Author: *Bishop Reginald Heber*   Composer: *Rev. John B. Dykes*

AUTHOR: For comments on the author, Reginald Heber, see Hymn 41.

HYMN: This hymn was written at Hodnet, where all Bishop Heber's literary work was done. It ranks as his finest hymn. Based on the apocalyptic vision recorded in Rev. 4:8-11, the hymn retains all the majestic rhythm of the Bible, breathing the purest spirit of adoration. It was the favorite hymn of Alfred, Lord Tennyson, and was sung at his funeral at Westminster Abbey, April 12, 1892.

COMPOSER: For comments on the composer, John B. Dykes, see Hymn 53.

TUNE: "Nicæa" was composed for this hymn in "Hymns Ancient and Modern," 1861, and was thus named because the text deals with the doctrine of the Trinity as expounded in the Nicene Creed. Its universal use makes comment unnecessary. Suffice it to say that the union of Heber's hymn and Dykes's tune makes the hymn one of the best known and most widely used in English hymnody.

58
HYMN: Ancient of Days, Who Sittest Throned in Glory
TUNE: Ancient of Days

Author: *Bishop William C. Doane*   Composer: *J. Albert Jeffery*

AUTHOR: William Croswell Doane was an American bishop of the Protestant Episcopal Church. He was born in Boston in 1832 and died in 1913. In 1850 he graduated from Burlington College, New Jersey, which had been founded by his father, Bishop George Washington Doane, in 1846. (See Hymn 34.) William Doane was ordained by his father in 1856 and became his assistant at St. Mary's Church, Burlington. He was rector of St. John's, in Hartford, Connecticut, from 1863 to 1867, and of St. Peter's, in Albany, New York. In 1869 he was consecrated first bishop of the Diocese of Albany. He received the degree of Doctor of

The Holy Trinity

Divinity from Oxford and of Doctor of Laws from Cambridge. He founded St. Agnes School for Girls at Albany. In 1902 he became chancellor of the regents of the University of the State of New York. He published a biography of his father, several religious books, and a volume of poems, "Rhymes from Time to Time."

HYMN: This hymn is a teaching hymn and belongs in the group dedicated in this Hymnal to "The Holy Trinity." It begins with an ascription of praise to God, the "ancient of days," Dan. 7:9. It ascribes praise in each following verse to Father, Son, and Holy Spirit, and closes with an ascription to the Triune God. This noble and stately hymn has been confined almost exclusively to American hymnals.

COMPOSER: John Albert Jeffery was born in Plymouth, England, on October 26, 1851. He inherited his musical talent from his father, who was organist at St. Andrew's Cathedral, in Plymouth, where his son succeeded him when but a boy of fourteen years. He afterwards studied at the Conservatory of Music in Leipzig, under Reinecke and other great masters. Here he received the honorary degree of Doctor of Music, following his graduation. He also studied with Liszt at Weimar. He was among the earliest musicians to become prominent in the Wagnerian movement. Coming to America in the eighties, he became the head of the music department of St. Agnes Episcopal School in Albany, New York, where he was also organist of All Saints' Cathedral under Bishop William C. Doane. After leaving Albany he became identified with the New England Conservatory of Music in Boston and continued there until his death in June, 1929.

TUNE: "Ancient of Days" is a stately and celebrated tune. It was written in 1886 for the bicentennial of the city of Albany, New York, for which Bishop William C. Doane wrote the words of the hymn. The hymn was first sung in the Cathedral Church under the direction of the composer and proved very successful. The tune calls for breadth of tone, full organ, and marked rhythm. For festal occasions where a processional hymn is desired, the tune is most effective. It is equally useful as a national hymn of thanksgiving.

59
    HYMN: O Trinity of Blessèd Light
    TUNE: Adesto Sancta Trinitas

Author: *Ambrose of Milan*   Source: *Chartres Church Melody*

AUTHOR: For comments on the author, Ambrose of Milan, see Hymn 32.

71

Handbook to The Hymnal

TRANSLATOR: For comments on the translator, John M. Neale, see Hymn 44.

HYMN: This is an old Latin hymn, to which first reference was made by Hincmar of Rheims, in A.D. 857. In this and other ancient Latin hymns we have, as Dr. Percy Dearmer indicates in "Songs of Praise Discussed," many fine qualities, such as simplicity, terseness, directness, singableness, but not poetry. Already the decay of Greco-Roman culture had driven poetry into rhetoric. This hymn is ascribed to Ambrose with reasonable certainty, though this cannot be said of ninety-two others attributed to him. It is the best-known hymn of Ambrose, with whom we ever associate the "Te Deum," as well as the greater incident—the conversion of Augustine.

SOURCE: The source of the tune is a Chartres church melody.

TUNE: "Adesto Sancta Trinitas" is a Chartres church melody and probably belongs to the latter half of the sixteenth, or early half of the seventeenth, century. Found among the people, it has been harmonized and arranged by a number of composers. The form in which it appears here is an arrangement by the editors of this Hymnal. Like most traditional tunes it is simple in structure and popular in style.

---

60   HYMN: Glory Be to God the Father
           TUNE: St. Peter's Westminster

Author: *Rev. Horatius Bonar*   Composer: *James Turle*

AUTHOR: Horatius Bonar, D.D. (1808–1889), has been called "the prince of Scottish hymn writers." He was educated at Edinburgh University under Thomas Chalmers and was ordained at Kelso, in 1838. Immediately he became a religious influence throughout the country because of his missionary and evangelistic zeal. His numerous tracts and devotional books had wide circulation. At the disruption of the Church of Scotland in 1843 he entered the Free Church and became joint editor of the church paper, The Border Watch. Following a visit to Palestine he became interested in the Jews. He believed firmly in the immediacy of the Second Advent and this expectation inspired much of his writing. In 1866 he became pastor of the Chalmers Memorial Free Church, Edinburgh, and was elected Moderator of the General Assembly of the Church of Scotland in 1883. He was a man of deep piety and careful scholarship.

72

The Holy Trinity

He is remembered as theologian, poet, preacher, and saint. His love for children inspired his first hymns. He wrote many hymns and over one hundred are still in use. "The best of them rank with the classics; one or two of them have been acclaimed by exacting judges to be the best hymns ever written."

HYMN: This hymn was written for the hymnal of the English Presbyterian Church, "Psalms and Hymns for Divine Worship," 1867. It appeared in the author's "Hymns of Faith and Hope," 1866. The tune originally chosen for it, and now used in the hymnals of Great Britain, was written by Henry Smart, and named "Regent Square" after Regent Square Church, the cathedral of the English Presbyterian Church, London. The first stanza is often used as a doxology and is sometimes made the fourth stanza of the hymn. Its original title was "Praise." It calls to mind the ascription of praise in the Apocalypse: "Unto him that loved us, and washed us from our sins in his own blood, And hath made us kings and priests unto God and his Father; to him be glory and dominion for ever and ever. Amen," Rev. 1: 5, 6 (King James Version).

COMPOSER: James Turle, who was born in 1802, began his musical career when at the age of eight years he became a chorister at Wells Cathedral. In 1819 he entered on his first charge as organist of Christ Church, Blackfriars. At the same time he became assistant to Thomas Greatorex and on his death succeeded him as organist of Westminster Abbey. He was organist at a number of musical festivals, notably the festival at Norwich when Spohr directed his oratorio, "Calvary," and at the Handel Festival at Westminster Abbey. A canon of Westminster said of him, "Mr. Turle makes the organ talk to him." He composed a number of hymn tunes, chants, and anthems, and edited "The People's Music Book" in 1844. In conjunction with Professor E. Taylor, in 1846, he edited "The Art of Singing at Sight." At the request of The Society for Promoting Christian Knowledge, he compiled "Psalms and Hymns," which appeared in 1862. He died in London, June 28, 1882.

TUNE: "St. Peter's Westminster" is a tune of considerable range. The melody covers an octave and three tones above. This wide compass makes the tune quite colorful and versatile in emotional utterance. Profound and exultant feeling are combined in marked manner. It should be sung joyously and in correct rhythm.

God the Father

His Eternity and Power

*

61   HYMN: God, the Lord, a King Remaineth
TUNE: Regent Square

Author: *Rev. John Keble*   Composer: *Henry Smart*

AUTHOR: For comments on the author, John Keble, see Hymn 31.

HYMN: In 1839 Keble set out to make English metrical versions of the psalms, although he thought the task impossible because of the difference between Hebrew parallelism and English rhythm. This hymn is one of the finest in the collection which he then published. It is a version of Psalm 93, with the insertion of the Hebrew word "Alleluia" (Praise Ye the Lord), which does not occur in this psalm. There are two attitudes that may be taken toward the might of God— "The Lord reigneth; let the people tremble," Ps. 99:1 (King James Version), and "The Lord reigneth; let the earth rejoice," Ps. 97:1 (King James Version). This hymn rejoices in the power of God in nature but closes with rejoicing in the word of God as it is spoken in many ways. Note its mingling of declaration about God and address to him.

COMPOSER: Henry Smart (1813–1879) was born into a musical family, being the nephew of Sir George Smart, organist of St. George's, Windsor, and the son of a violinist. After being a lawyer for four years, he decided to become a musician. He had little formal training, and for the most part was his own teacher. However, he became not only a fine organist but a composer for the organ equaled by few. He was especially successful in planning and supervising the construction of organs. He acted as organist at the Parish Church, Blackburn; at St. Giles's, Cripplegate; at St. Philip's, Regent Street; at St. Luke's, Old Street; and also at St. Pancras. In 1865 he became blind, but this did not interfere with his work. He favored congregational singing, and the slow, dignified style of the old psalm tunes rather than the quicker measures which his contemporaries were beginning to use. He wrote some very fine music; some parts of his complete "Service in F" have been considered worthy of Beethoven. His hymn tunes and anthems are also of a high order.

God the Father

TUNE: "Regent Square" was written by Henry Smart for the English Presbyterian hymnal, "Psalms and Hymns for Divine Worship," 1867. In that volume it was set to Dr. Horatius Bonar's hymn, "Glory Be to God the Father." The tune is named after the Regent Square Church of London. It is a jubilant tune, vigorous in progression, and inspiring in its sweep.

---

62   HYMN: O God, the Rock of Ages
                        FIRST TUNE: Pearsall

Author: *Bishop Edward H. Bickersteth*   Composer: *R. L. de Pearsall*

AUTHOR: This is the first of three hymns in "The Hymnal" by Bishop Bickersteth. Edward Henry Bickersteth, D.D., was the son of Rev. Edward Bickersteth, once a missionary to West Africa and later the first resident secretary of the Church Missionary Society, a hymn writer of some distinction. Edward was born in January, 1825, and died in 1906. Most of his hymns, including this one, were written when he was rector of Christ Church, Hampstead, England. Later, in 1885, he became bishop of Exeter. One writer says of him: "His thoughts are usually with the individual, and not with the mass: with the single soul and his God, and not with the vast multitude bowed in adoration before the Almighty." We are always in danger of losing our sense of personal relation to God in our sense of his greatness.

HYMN: Bishop Bickersteth's familiarity with the Bible text appears in the imagery of this hymn. While the title "Rock of Ages" is nowhere applied to God in Scripture, nor to Christ as in Toplady's familiar "Rock of Ages, Cleft for Me," yet the idea is sustained by many passages and is actually used in the margin of Isa. 26:4 in the American Standard Version. The metaphor of the "rock" is used for God thirty-five times in the Scriptures. The transiency of human life and the unsleeping mercy and goodness of God are familiar teachings. Ps. 102:11; 40:7a; 121:4.

COMPOSER (First Tune): Robert Lucas de Pearsall (1795–1856) was a descendant of an ancient English family. After completing his studies he practiced law for four years. In 1825 he went to Mainz, and thereafter for several years he divided his time between England and the Continent, occupying himself with the study and composition of music. In 1842 he bought a castle on the Lake of Constance where he spent the rest of his life. He wrote a great variety of music, including a cantata, a ballet opera, an overture to Macbeth, a number of madrigals, some settings for psalms, a requiem mass, and other compositions for both the Roman Catholic and the Anglican Church.

TUNE (First): "Pearsall," according to the preface of "St. Gall Gesangbuch," 1863, was composed by Robert Lucas de Pearsall. In that volume it is associated with "Singt Heilig, Heilig, Heilig, Ist Unser Herr und Gott." It is a very serviceable tune and in several English hymnals is set to "Jerusalem the Golden." Its characteristics are dignity, stateliness, and strength. Consequently it is an effective musical setting for "O God, the Rock of Ages."

SECOND TUNE: Miriam

Composer: *Joseph P. Holbrook*

COMPOSER (Second Tune): Joseph Perry Holbrook (1822–1888) was born near Boston, Massachusetts. He is remembered as the compiler and musical editor of several books of music, including "Songs for the Sanctuary" and a Methodist hymnal, which he edited with Dr. Eben Tourjée. It is said of the former of these books, which was under the editorship of Dr. Charles S. Robinson, that much of its popularity was due to Joseph Holbrook, who was a tune writer in the "parlor music" style. As a composer he was greatly influenced by the popular melodies of Lowell Mason, Thomas Hastings, William B. Bradbury, and others.

TUNE (Second): "Miriam" appeared in "Songs for the Sanctuary" in 1865. This proved to be a volume of extraordinary success, for, according to Dr. Louis F. Benson, it was adopted by nearly two thousand congregations and was kept in print until the end of the century. "Miriam" is a melodic tune, subjective in mood, and characterized by evangelistic fervor. Its use in revival meetings, where it was associated with "I Lay My Sins on Jesus," always proved successful. Thus related it was included in the Presbyterian Hymnal of 1911. As a hymn contemplative in character, it should be sung with dignity and assurance.

63

HYMN: Before Jehovah's Awful Throne
TUNE: Park Street

Authors: *Rev. Isaac Watts and Rev. John Wesley*

Composer: *Frederick M. A. Venua*

AUTHORS: For comments on the author, Isaac Watts, see Hymn 22. John Wesley, who altered stanza 1, is the outstanding preacher and evangelist of the eighteenth century. His early mission to Georgia, in 1735, may have thoroughly disappointed him as he testifies,

God the Father

but it gave to America its first hymn book, which he published under the direction of the Society for the Propagation of the Gospel. It was the singing of Moravian missionaries on shipboard during that dreary voyage that revealed to Wesley the power in hymns and hymn-singing for propagating the gospel. Spiritually revived, he became, following his return, the greatest evangelist of his day and the greatest force in spiritualizing the cold, formal life of the English Church of the period. He traveled 250,000 miles, chiefly on horseback, preached 40,000 sermons, and reached uncountable thousands of hearers with his stirring messages. As a writer he was amazingly productive: He was a translator of many of the classics, besides being the author of several grammars and dictionaries; he was editor of the works of John Bunyan, Richard Baxter, and other religious worthies; he translated many German hymns and improved the style and phraseology of many of the hymns of his brother, Charles, as well as those of Isaac Watts. He died in London in 1791, leaving to the world as his richest legacy the Methodist Church and a world-wide evangelistic movement.

HYMN: This is a version of Psalm 100. The first stanza of the hymn includes verses 1 and 2 and part of verse 3 of the psalm; the other stanzas include one verse each. The hymn has caught singularly well the mingled reverence and exultation of the psalm. The throne is awful, "awesome," yet we bow before it in joy. The note of redemption is not so clear in the psalm as in Watts's version of verse 2, but it is implied in the fact that we are "the sheep of his pasture." The shepherd will care for his sheep. Stanza 3 opens the world-wide prospect of divine control at times when chaos seems impending. Such times recur frequently both in life as a whole and in personal experience. After all these changes have come, when everything is unsettled, it is good to feel that something is firm as a rock and will stand after the rolling of the years has ended.

COMPOSER: Frederick M. A. Venua, born in 1788, was a French organist and a native of Paris. He was a member of the Royal Society of Musicians and was held in high esteem. After many years of activity he retired, about 1858, to Exeter, England, where he died in 1872.

TUNE: "Park Street" is a favorite hymn tune in America. It was introduced to this country by the Handel and Haydn Society of Boston in a hymnal published in 1820. Since that time the tune has been included in most hymnals. Beginning with "The Presbyterian Psalmodist" of 1852, "Park Street" has been in constant use in the Presbyterian Church. Invariably it is associated with "Before Jehovah's Awful Throne."

64

HYMN: Let Us with a Gladsome Mind
TUNE: Monkland

Author: *John Milton*   Arranger: *John B. Wilkes*

AUTHOR: This is the first of three hymns, Hymns 64, 185, and 463, by John Milton, the main facts of whose life are available in any encyclopedia. He was born December 9, 1608, and died November 8, 1674. His father, John Milton, had become a Protestant and had been disinherited by an earnest Roman Catholic father, so that the son knew the difficulties of sincere belief. He matriculated at Christ Church, Cambridge, at sixteen. Among his fellow students he had the nickname of "the Lady," partly because of his graceful appearance and manner and partly because of "the haughty fastidiousness of his tastes and morals." His writing began very early. In deep patriotism he devoted his powers to the British nation, joining Oliver Cromwell as his Latin secretary. After the Restoration, Milton barely escaped the scaffold. He became totally blind in his forty-fourth year from excessive use of his weak eyes. His greatest writings came from this later period: "Paradise Lost," "Paradise Regained," "Samson Agonistes" were all dictated to others.

HYMN: Written when Milton was fifteen and still a pupil in preparatory school, this hymn consisted at first of twenty-six stanzas, following closely the movement of Psalm 136, on which it is based. That psalm tells the story of Israel, using in every verse the refrain, "For his mercy endureth for ever." Some of Milton's original stanzas are very boyish, but a selection has been made which the maturest worshiper can use with gratitude. The stanzas selected here are from Ps. 136: 1, 2, 7-9, 25, the closing stanzas returning to verse 1.

ARRANGER: John Bernard Wilkes, born in 1785, though an organist of ability, is chiefly remembered by his tune "Monkland" which is used three times in this Hymnal. Wilkes was organist in the parish of Sir Henry W. Baker at Monkland, near Leominster, England. Subsequently he served in like capacity at St. David's, Merthyr Tydvil, and at Llandaff Cathedral. In 1865 he retired to London, where he died in 1869.

TUNE: The source of "Monkland" has not been ascertained. It appeared in "Hymn Tunes of the United Brethren," edited by John Less, at Manchester, in 1824. No composer's name was there given. When "Hymns Ancient and Modern," 1861, was in the course of preparation, Mr. Wilkes made an arrangement of the melody and named it "Monkland" after the place where he was then organist. The arrangement has proved very satisfactory.

God the Father

65

HYMN: I Sing the Mighty Power of God
TUNE: Ellacombe

Author: *Rev. Isaac Watts*   Source: *"Gesangbuch der Herzogl. Wirtembergischen Katholischen Hofkapelle"*

AUTHOR: For comments on the author, Isaac Watts, see Hymn 22.

HYMN: God is here praised for his power, wisdom, goodness, and omnipresence as revealed, from the earth to the sky, in mountains, seas, the sun, the moon, creatures, plants, flowers, clouds, tempests, and in man himself. Our Lord found evidence of God's power, wisdom, and goodness in nature, which, of course, is subject to second causes and operates through processes increasingly well-known. This does not shut out the presence and operation of God. Paul expresses the same idea in I Cor. 14:10, where he speaks of the many kinds of voices in nature, every one meaning something. If our wise men should some day discover the origin of life, this would not affect our assurance that everything "borrows life" from God, for it is he who made and maintains the forces through which life comes. Watts counted this a hymn for children and gave it the heading: "Praise for Creation and Providence."

SOURCE: The source of the tune is "Gesangbuch der Herzogl. Wirtembergischen Katholischen Hofkapelle," 1784.

TUNE: "Ellacombe" appears in the "Gesangbuch der Herzogl. Wirtembergischen Katholischen Hofkapelle," 1784. Hartig there dates it 1700, but Bäumker believes that "Ellacombe" is no older than the beginning of the nineteenth century.

66

HYMN: Immortal, Invisible, God Only Wise
TUNE: Joanna

Author: *Rev. Walter Chalmers Smith*   Source: *Welsh Hymn Melody*

AUTHOR: The Scottish Church has given the world some of its worthiest hymns. Walter Chalmers Smith, D.D., LL.D. (1824–1908), writer of this hymn, was an eminent scholar, a leader in the Free Church (Presbyterian) of Scotland and Moderator of its Assembly

79

at the time of its jubilee in 1893. The story of the forming of this Free Church, now united again with the Church from which it separated, must be read in larger works than this, but it reveals plainly the devotion to God which this hymn clearly expresses. Dr. Smith expresses here the mind and heart of his colleagues. He once spoke of his poetry as "the retreat of his nature from the burden of his labors." Everyone needs such a retreat; most men must find it in the poetry of others, for nothing is better calculated to uplift downcast or overburdened hearts than worthy poetry that turns the mind toward the great things of faith.

HYMN: In the sixteen long lines of this hymn more than a score of divine attributes are named, each a call to worship and praise. They combine the sense of divine majesty and inaccessibility with the sense of God's nearness to us so that all our dependence is on God. Dr. Charles H. Parkhurst once said that while it is true that "the veil of the temple [is] rent in the midst," yet it is not becoming to rush in and eat from the mercy seat! This hymn is a serious challenge to our arrogance of approach to God as if the rights were on our side; yet it puts no barrier in the way of our coming into the divine presence. The text for the hymn, as given by Dr. Smith, is I Tim. 1:17. The closing line of the hymn suggests Ps. 36:9 and Ps. 104:2.

SOURCE: For comments on the source, a Welsh hymn melody, see the article, "Welsh Hymnody," under "Original Sources," page xxii.

TUNE: "Joanna," a Welsh air, is believed to be the tune of a ballad sung in the early nineteenth century. This arrangement is from "The Church Hymnary," Revised, 1927, where it is used to the same words. It is a fluent, joyful tune, easily sung and readily recalled.

---

67 HYMN: Thou Art, O God, the God of Might
TUNE: Burg

Author: *Emily S. Perkins*   Composer: *Emily S. Perkins*

AUTHOR: Emily S. Perkins is a resident of Riverdale-on-Hudson, New York, and is an active member of The Hymn Society of New York. She has written several hymns to match the message which her tunes have suggested. A collection of fifty-four of her hymn tunes, four of which have also words by Miss Perkins, was privately printed in 1921 with the title, "Stonehurst Hymn Tunes." This hymn is Hymn 6 in that collection.

God the Father

HYMN: Different from most instances the tune "Burg" here came first and the words followed. The author was seeking that verbal interpretation which she felt most illuminative of her tonal message of adoration. Here is grateful recognition of the attributes and gifts of God—might, power, truth, justice, righteousness, love, mercy, care, grace, and pardon. The permanence of these attributes and their availability for transient and sinful lives may well be considered in services of worship. The assurances of the hymn can be traced both to Christian experiences and to a Christian faith based on the nature and character of God.

COMPOSER: For comments on the composer, see "Author."

TUNE: "Burg," as its name suggests, is majestic in strength. It is a forward-moving tune which, beginning with a tonic of the scale, rises to a third above the octave. The concluding phrases are direct and forceful, and remind one of the slow, steady measures of a choral. It appeared first in "Stonehurst Hymn Tunes," in 1921, a private collection of Miss Perkins' hymns and tunes.

---

68   HYMN: O Sing a New Song to the Lord
      TUNE: Song 67 (Gibbons)

Source: *"Scottish Psalter"*   Composer: *Orlando Gibbons*

SOURCE: For comments on the source, "Scottish Psalter," 1650, see the article, "The Psalters in Early Presbyterian Worship" under "Original Sources," page xv.

HYMN: This version of Psalm 96 dates from the middle of the seventeenth century and was first used in Scotland. The psalm has thirteen verses and the original version in the "Scottish Psalter" covered them all. The stanzas selected here end with the ninth verse, but they carry much of the message of the later verses, especially where they reassert the right of God to the whole earth and all its peoples. The psalm, like this hymn version, is a declaration about God addressed to fellow worshipers. The thought of "a new song" occurs frequently with reference to divine praise. The expression comes to its climax in Rev. 5:9, where "they sing a new song" before the throne of God. Every day gives occasion for a new song of praise, even though it is expressed in old and familiar words. This idea is found in the most unexpected places in the Bible: in Lam. 3:23, 24, for instance, where the compassions of God are described as "new every morning." In Zeph. 3:5 a similar truth appears: "Every morning doth he bring his justice to light." It requires a new song to give human gratitude its opportunity.

COMPOSER: Orlando Gibbons' father was one of the town "waits," or musical watchmen, of Cambridge. Orlando was born in 1583. At thirteen he joined the choir of King's College. At twenty-one he became organist of the Chapel Royal. In 1623 he was made organist of Westminster Abbey. He was an organist of renown and a composer of distinction. Royalty honored him and the best positions were at his disposal. He officiated at the organ at the funeral of James I. He died in 1625 at Canterbury and is buried in the cathedral there. His tunes are once again receiving the favor which is their due.

ARRANGER: For comments on the arranger, Henry Smart, see Hymn 61.

TUNE: "Song 67 (Gibbons)" was composed originally for a hymn in celebration of St. Matthias' Day. Henry Smart changed the tempo of the tune to the more "stately, dignified, measured beat and slow movement of the old psalm tunes."

God in Nature

*

69 HYMN: The Spacious Firmament on High
TUNE: Creation

Author: *Joseph Addison*   Composer: *Franz Joseph Haydn*

AUTHOR: This hymn and Hymn 81 are the two in this Hymnal by Joseph Addison, the English essayist, poet, and man of letters. His father was an Anglican clergyman, who later became dean of Lichfield. Joseph Addison was born in his father's rectory on May 1, 1672. He died on June 17, 1719, after a prominent public life largely spent in government service and literary work. He was one of the founders, with Steele, of The Spectator. The choice English there used has been a standard for writers ever since. Addison counted it impossible, even in that age of doubt, to look fairly at the facts of nature without reaching an assurance of God. As his death neared, he called the earl of Warwick and said, "See in what peace a Christian can die!"

God the Father

HYMN: The basis of the hymn is Ps. 19: 1-6. These verses magnify the discovery of God in nature; the remainder of the psalm consists of a vigorous statement of the law of God as apprehended by rational beings. The hymn was published in No. 465 of The Spectator, August 23, 1712, at the end of "an essay on the proper means of strengthening and confirming faith in the mind of man." Addison spoke of the psalm as "a bold and sublime manner of thinking." Every advance in natural science adds weight to the argument. If the heavens seemed "spacious" in Addison's day, to say nothing of the psalmist's day, what ought they to seem to us? How much more we know of the nightly scene than did they! In the mere astronomical laws and forces we have a revelation of a divine hand. The silence of the heavens is to the outer ear; to the inner ear they sing as they shine.

COMPOSER: Franz Joseph Haydn (1732–1809) was the son of a wheelwright of Rohrau, Lower Austria. After singing for ten years in the Cathedral Church of Vienna, St. Stephen's, he was cast out, penniless, at the age of eighteen because his voice changed. However, after living in poverty for several years, he won the recognition of Glück, the composer, who saw in him a rare musical genius. Haydn became chapelmaster to Prince Anton Paul Esterhazy and for thirty years while he held this position he had a special band at his disposal. In 1791 he visited England and received a degree of Doctor of Music from Oxford. He composed various forms of music which were popular both in England and on the Continent. At sixty-five he composed his masterpiece, "The Creation," a beautiful and inspiring work. Haydn invented the symphony and the string quartet, in fact he was called the "father of modern instrumental music." Besides four oratorios he wrote twenty-two operas, forty-four sonatas, eighty-three instrumental quartets, and one hundred and twenty symphonies, as well as other works. To Haydn religion was a completely cheerful thing. He was full of the joy of life and his music reflects this spirit of happy gratitude. He considered his talents always as a gift from God and over every one of his scores he wrote the words, "*In nomine Domini*," and at the end the ascription, "*Laus Deo*."

TUNE: "Creation" was taken from the oratorio, "The Creation." As a hymn tune it appeared quite early in American hymnals. "The Choral," edited by B. F. Baker and I. B. Woodbury, published in 1845, uses it. Thomas Hastings included it in "The Presbyterian Psalmodist," 1852, and since then, with the exception of the Hymnal of 1867, Presbyterian editors have appropriated it. The tune is vast in concept, majestic in form, and heartening in spirit.

70   HYMN: This Is My Father's World
     TUNE: Terra Patris

Author: *Rev. Maltbie D. Babcock*   Arranger: *Edward Shippen Barnes*
Composer: *Franklin L. Sheppard*

AUTHOR: Maltbie Davenport Babcock, D.D., was an American Presbyterian minister of peculiar gifts and powers. He was born August 3, 1858, at Syracuse, New York, and died in Italy, March 18, 1901. He was educated at Syracuse University and Auburn Theological Seminary. In both places he took high rank as a student and in addition showed his gifts as a musician and athlete. He was leader of the glee club, director of the orchestra, active on the baseball team, a member of the dramatic club, a participant in all kinds of outdoor life, and at the same time an earnest and effective worker in religious activities. He had an agile mind and a magnetic personality. His pastorates in Lockport, New York, Baltimore, Maryland, and the Brick Church, New York City, were notable and in them he left an enduring influence.

HYMN: This hymn is a fraction of a much longer poem in Dr. Babcock's "Thoughts for Everyday Living." It is a call to take the point of view of Christ regarding the world and all experiences in it. The Ruler of this world is not a remote, detached sovereign, nor a potentate who governs arbitrarily. God is our "Father"; thus our Lord taught us always to address him. The hymn finds evidence of his hand in rocks, trees, skies, seas, birds, morning light, the lily, and rustling grass. But out of all this the third stanza brings assurance of the ultimate triumph of God, who is "the Ruler yet." In Dr. Babcock's mind the fatherhood of God gave no occasion for human arrogance or presumption but only for peace and humble gratitude.

COMPOSER: Franklin Lawrence Sheppard, who modestly published this beautiful tune in 1915 as an arrangement of an English traditional melody, is, it has since been found, the composer. He was born in Philadelphia, Pennsylvania, on August 7, 1852. He prepared for college at the Classical School of William Fewsmith and then entered the University of Pennsylvania in 1868, from which he graduated at the head of his class in 1872. When the Delta chapter of Phi Beta Kappa was subsequently established there, he became a charter member. He entered the employment of his father's firm, Isaac A. Sheppard & Co., stove and heater manufacturers, and in 1875 went to Baltimore, Maryland, as manager of its foundry in that city. From earliest childhood he attended Zion Protestant Episcopal Church, in which he was confirmed in 1864. On April 6, 1874, he was elected a vestryman. Mr. Sheppard was

God the Father

an active Churchman. Later, becoming a Presbyterian, he was elected to the eldership in the Second Presbyterian Church of Baltimore, which he also served with distinction in the Sunday School and as director of music. He was a man of many interests. He served several times as a commissioner to the General Assembly, and was a member of the Board of Publication and Sabbath-School Work, later becoming its president. The Witherspoon Building in Philadelphia owes its existence to his leadership and labor. An accomplished musician, he was for a time the organist of the church in which he was confirmed. He was deeply interested in the music of the Sunday School, and edited "Alleluia," published by the Board of Publication in 1915, which has had a sale of over 400,000. He was an efficient member of the committee that edited and published the Hymnal of 1911. He died in Germantown, Philadelphia, on February 15, 1930.

ARRANGER: Edward Shippen Barnes, an American organist and composer, was born at Seabright, New Jersey, on September 14, 1887. His early training was received at Lawrenceville Academy, Lawrenceville, New Jersey. At Yale, where he graduated, he studied under Horatio W. Parker. He spent several years in Paris, where he continued his musical studies at the Schola Cantorum. Returning to America, he became organist in the Church of the Incarnation, New York City, and later in the Rutgers Presbyterian Church of the same city. He is now organist of St. Stephen's Episcopal Church, Philadelphia. Mr. Barnes is a versatile composer and has many works to his credit, including anthems, cantatas, hymn tunes, and organ suites.

TUNE: "Terra Patris," an arrangement of "Terra Beata," in 1915 appeared in "Alleluia" as a traditional English melody arranged by S. F. L. The "S.F.L." stands for Franklin L. Sheppard, who in this way for some years concealed his identity. The tune is not an English melody but the work of Mr. Sheppard, who could not believe that it was his but thought it must be reminiscent of something that his mother taught him as a boy. However, it came to him as an inspiration, and his son, Walter L. Sheppard, a Presbyterian elder and lawyer, states that his father felt about this melody very much as Lewis Redner felt about the music which he wrote for "O Little Town of Bethlehem"—that it was inspired. Mr. Sheppard and Dr. Maltbie D. Babcock were intimate friends. This friendship contributed greatly to the writing of this tune, which in the original appears in almost every school and church hymnal in America.

71
HYMN: For the Beauty of the Earth
FIRST TUNE: St. Athanasius

Author: *Folliott S. Pierpoint*   Composer: *Edward J. Hopkins*

AUTHOR: Born at Bath, England, October 7, 1835, Folliott Sandford Pierpoint was educated at Cambridge. He contributed widely to church hymnody but this hymn is the one by which he is best known. He died in 1917.

HYMN: This was originally written for use at the Communion service, injecting the note of joy into this solemn service. It has been more often used at Thanksgiving, however, and for children's services. The hymn is entirely given to praise with no petition. It moves from "the beauty of the earth" to the Church, lifting "holy hands above." In all the range between, there is cause for new thanksgiving. There is an old story of God's sending out two angels into the earth— the angel of petition and the angel of thanksgiving, each with a basket to bring back what he found. The two came back presently, the angel of petition loaded down and with an overflowing basket, the angel of thanksgiving with an almost empty basket, grieving that men were so much more ready to ask than to return thanks for gifts received. In this hymn are twenty-four causes of praise, apart from those personal blessings which are so easily omitted in our reckoning.

COMPOSER (First Tune): For comments on the composer, Edward J. Hopkins, see Hymn 55.

TUNE (First): "St. Athanasius" was introduced to the Church of America through the Episcopal Hymnal of 1872, in which it was wedded to Bishop Wordsworth's hymn, "Holy, Holy, Holy, Lord." Twenty-three years later, Dr. Benson included it in the Hymnal of 1895, a decision that has been respected in subsequent revisions.

SECOND TUNE: Dix
Composer: *Conrad Kocher*

COMPOSER (Second Tune): Conrad Kocher, Ph.D., was born in the year 1786, in Ditzingen, Württemberg. After studying music in St. Petersburg he returned to Germany, where he published several promising compositions. During a stay in Italy he became interested in church choral music and decided to found a school of sacred song for such study in Germany. He was offered the position of organist of Stiftskirche, Stuttgart, and this he held from 1827 until 1865. The school

God the Father

which Kocher founded became so popular that others like it were established throughout Württemberg. In 1852 he received a degree from Tübingen University. Besides chorals he composed oratorios, operas, and sonatas. He died in 1872.

TUNE (Second): "Dix" first appeared in 1838 in a collection of chorals edited and published by Kocher in Stuttgart. Here it was set to the hymn "Treuer Heiland, Wir Sind Hier." It was not until about seventy years ago that the tune came to be known as "Dix." This name has since been associated with it because of its long use with the words "As with Gladness Men of Old." "Dix" is strong and vital, joyous, and full of pageantry. The tempo is as the tread of a stately procession.

---

72   HYMN: When the Great Sun Sinks to His Rest
      FIRST TUNE: St. Venantius

Author: *Rev. Maltbie D. Babcock*   Source: *Rouen Church Melody*

AUTHOR: For comments on the author, Maltbie D. Babcock, see Hymn 70.

HYMN: Dr. Babcock rejoiced to find God everywhere. This hymn is a prayer for the spirit of worship under varied circumstances— in the evening at sunset, in the later night when the stars appear, and in the depth of the forest. It is well to pray that God will teach us as this hymn suggests. There is reason for bowing before God in all places. We are more apt to miss the worship of God in the darkness than in the daylight. Dr. Babcock's hymn calls us to see God in the dark periods of the day and of life. There are those who put us to shame by their humble recognition of God in the dark experiences. They have found the stars when the night has come.

SOURCE (First Tune): "St. Venantius" is a Rouen church melody.

TUNE (First): During the sixteenth and seventeenth centuries in France the music used in cathedrals and churches underwent a serious change. Many tunes in measured form were introduced into the services where before there had been only plain-song melodies. These tunes were sometimes not wholly new but were based on the old plain-song melodies or on folk songs.

SECOND TUNE: Rimington
Composer: *Francis Duckworth*

COMPOSER (Second Tune): For comments on the composer, Francis Duckworth, see Hymn 32.

TUNE (Second): For comments on the tune, "Rimington," see Hymn 32.

---

73 HYMN: My God, I Thank Thee, Who Hast Made
TUNE: Wentworth

Author: *Adelaide A. Procter*   Composer: *Frederick C. Maker*

AUTHOR: For comments on the author, Adelaide A. Procter, see Hymn 36.

HYMN: This hymn appeared in 1858 in Miss Procter's "Legends and Lyrics." Like others in this section, it is a hymn of pure gratitude with no petition. It expresses gratitude for blessings already received and for those yet to come, which are assured by those already here. It finds cause for gratitude in the limitations of life, which make us discontented with merely temporal and temporary things. Eternal souls ought not to find full satisfaction in even the richest experiences of the present life. In the first stanza the mind is directed away from those things that make nature seem "red in tooth and claw" to the many "glorious things," "noble and right." There are such things for any eye that will look. The change in direction of thought occurs at the beginning of stanza 3. Stanzas 1 and 2 speak of blessings already received; stanzas 3 and 4 speak of these blessings as only a foretaste of greater ones to come. God's blessings are not meant to stupefy our souls but to make us yearn for larger things from his hand.

COMPOSER: For comments on the composer, Frederick C. Maker, see Hymn 29.

TUNE: For comments on the tune, "Wentworth," see Hymn 29.

God the Father

74

HYMN: Let the Whole Creation Cry
TUNE: Monkland

Author: *Rev. Stopford A. Brooke*   Arranger: *John B. Wilkes*

AUTHOR: Rev. Stopford Augustus Brooke, LL.D., an Anglican clergyman, was born in 1832 and died in 1916. He was a popular preacher with a strong poetic bent. Becoming restive under the doctrinal requirements of the Anglican Church, he resigned his orders therein but did not join any other group or church. He remained an independent clergyman until the end of his life, preaching and lecturing widely.

HYMN: Like our familiar Doxology, this hymn is a call to praise rather than an expression of praise. It is not addressed to God but to those who should praise him. It ranges the field from "the whole creation" to "children." Characteristic Christian optimism appears at the end of the first stanza. Most people say instinctively, "God is *great* and therefore King." Christ has taught us to say that "God is *good* and therefore King." It is his goodness that makes us worship, for Christian worship includes, always, an element of love. His goodness leaves us saying, "Holy, holy, holy!" When we think of the goodness of God, we think of none to compare with his. We gladly give glory to him alone.

ARRANGER: For comments on the arranger, John B. Wilkes, see Hymn 64.

TUNE: For comments on the tune, "Monkland," see Hymn 64.

75

HYMN: With Songs and Honors Sounding Loud
TUNE: Bedford

Author: *Rev. Isaac Watts*   Composer: *William Wheale*

AUTHOR: For comments on the author, Isaac Watts, see Hymn 22.

HYMN: This metrical version of Psalm 147 was originally in eight stanzas. The stanzas selected for this hymn are especially those which disclose reasons to praise God in nature and its seasons. The long series of facts in nature, undeniable in themselves, is

89

Handbook to The Hymnal

seen as a revelation of God's love only by those whose hearts are tuned to praise. The first two lines and the last two form a kind of parenthesis of appeal for the spirit of praise while in between are the warranting facts. These facts lie in nature. No draft is made on personal experiences, which have their place in the psalm itself. The facts of nature remain, whatever one's personal experiences may be. Stanza 3 deserves special observation because of its description of the "steady counsels" of God in the midst of the varying and swiftly moving seasons. The years flash by, but the steadying reality is the abiding counsel of God to which life may be committed without fear. Even the fleeting clouds and wind move in obedience to the mighty word of God. Strange that men should at times lose assurance of God in an increased knowledge of his world and its laws!

COMPOSER: William Wheale was born in 1690. He graduated from Cambridge in 1719 with the degree of Bachelor of Music. Four years before, after an organ had been installed in St. Paul's Church, Bedford, Wheale had been appointed organist. According to the burial register of St. Paul's Church, he died in September, 1727. He is remembered chiefly for having written this very popular and useful tune.

TUNE: The first book found to contain the tune, "Bedford," is probably "The Divine Musick Scholars Guide," collected and printed by Francis Timbrell about 1723. The tune appears twice in this book, first with Psalm 27 and again with Psalm 84, headed by the words, "Bedford Tune. By Wm. Wheale." Various other English books, chiefly psalmodies, also contain this tune. It is written, as in Timbrell's book, in triple time in the key of F. It was changed later to common time, probably by William Gardiner in his "Sacred Melodies," 1812. It has here been restored to its original tempo.

---

76   HYMN: Angels Holy, High and Lowly
       TUNE: Llanherne

Author: *John Stuart Blackie*   Composer: *George Thalben-Ball*

AUTHOR: The author, John Stuart Blackie, LL.D., was a layman, "a Scottish scholar and man of letters." He was born July 28, 1809, and died March 2, 1895. The year of his birth is notable. It was the birth year of Tennyson, Gladstone, Abraham Lincoln, Oliver Wendell Holmes, and Darwin. Professor Blackie was a classical scholar, professor of Latin in Marischal College, Aberdeen, and later professor of Greek in the University of Edinburgh. His father was a banker and the son was educated for the law, but teaching and its opportunities.

God the Father

of scholarly pursuits won him. Of himself he said in late life, "I am rather a young old boy and I am one of the happiest creatures under the sun at this moment and my amusement is to sing songs." He advises his hearers to do the same, adding, "Your soul will become a singing bird, and then the Devil won't get near it."

HYMN: This hymn comes from the "Benedicite," Chant 55 of the Ancient Hymns and Canticles in this Hymnal. The words come from the apocryphal section of The Book of Daniel, and are alleged to be the prayer of the three "children" in the fiery furnace. They came into early use in the Church. Professor Blackie's hymn sweeps a wide circle in its call to praise and worship. In stanza 1 the call is to angels, nature, and man; in stanzas 2 and 3, to nature with its varied powers; in stanza 4, to man with glad soul and voice, combining the idea of gladness and freedom. Careless thinking does not combine the ideas. Praise here is for the lordship of God. His fatherhood shines through but it is not here used as ground for praise.

COMPOSER: George Thomas Thalben-Ball was born at Sidney, N.S.W., in 1896. After private tutoring he entered the Royal College of Music and graduated with distinction. As organist he has held the following positions: Whitefield's Tabernacle; Holy Trinity Church, Castelnau; and Paddington Parish Church. He is the present organist of the Temple Church, London. He is on the faculty of the Royal College of Music, an examiner to the associated board of the Royal Academy of Music and the Royal College of Music, a Fellow of the Royal College of Organists, and associate of the Royal College of Music. As editor of "School Worship," which was published in 1926 by the Congregational Union of England and Wales, he has rendered distinguished service to young people. The book owes much of its popularity to his expert workmanship and skillful arrangements as well as to his own compositions.

TUNE: Among the many original compositions in "School Worship," "Llanherne" is one of the most interesting. The tune is in the style of a carol, well arranged for choir or congregation, and, as one of the new tunes in "The Hymnal," should become a favorite.

His Love and Fatherhood

*

77 HYMN: Our God, Our Help in Ages Past
TUNE: St. Anne

Author: *Rev. Isaac Watts*   Composer: *William Croft*

AUTHOR: For comments on the author, Isaac Watts, see Hymn 22.

HYMN: When Jowett, of Balliol, asked a tea party of Oxford dons to put down a short list of the "best hymns," the lists came back with this hymn alone on each. It is clearly a setting of Psalm 90. Both the psalm and the original version of this hymn are much longer than could be used here. The heading Watts gave to the hymn was, "Man Frail, and God Eternal." The singer is supposed to be standing where the past and the future meet—in the instant of the present. He looks back to a Help in ages past; he looks forward to a Hope for years to come; he has had a Shelter from stormy blasts; he needs a Guard while time shall last; and all the while he has an eternal Home in God. It is a joyous assurance. The family of Robert Browning asked to have the hymn sung at his funeral service. It expresses a robust faith which yet realizes the difficulties and dangers of human life. John Wesley changed the first word from "our" to "O" and it often appears in this form. Watts wrote the more intimate "our." The word suggests The Lord's Prayer, in which we claim the Father for ourselves and for all who will call him so.

COMPOSER: For comments on the composer, William Croft, see Hymn 2.

TUNE: The "Supplement," 1708, to Tate and Brady's "The New Version of Psalms" made hymnological history. The Supplement contained several tunes by Dr. Croft, and all of them survive to this day. Of these "St. Anne" is foremost. "St. Anne" is a majestic tune and has been wedded to many different texts. It was originally set to Psalm 42. Johann Sebastian Bach valued the tune highly and appropriated it in his "Fugue in E Flat," popularly known as "St. Anne's Fugue." The tune is now recognized the world over as the most satisfactory setting for Dr. Watts's version of Psalm 90, "Our God, Our Help in Ages Past."

God the Father

78
HYMN: My God, How Endless Is Thy Love
TUNE: Canonbury

Author: *Rev. Isaac Watts*   Composer: *Robert Schumann*

AUTHOR: For comments on the author, Isaac Watts, see Hymn 22.

HYMN: Watts's heading for this hymn was "A Song for Morning or Evening." The hymn follows the order of Gen., ch. 1: "The evening and the morning," where ordinarily the terms are reversed. The Scriptural order is the order of faith—no matter how dark the evening, the morning will come. The idea of recurrent blessings is familiar in Scripture. Stanza 1 might be taken from Lam. 3:22, 23, a most unlikely place to discover so beautiful a word of assurance: "His compassions fail not. They are new every morning." Stanza 2 might come from Isa. 45:7: "I form the light, and create darkness," each a great gift of God to man. Stanza 3 expresses that dialogue which ought always to go on between God and the soul—God's blessings being perpetually answered by the soul's praises. The response of the soul, once it realizes the goodness of God, is the full surrender of all powers to his command.

COMPOSER: Robert Alexander Schumann (1810–1856) during his forty-six years covered a wide range of musical activity. Director of music at both Leipzig and Dresden, he also composed for voice, chorus *a capella*, strings, orchestra, piano, and organ. The worldwide popularity of his compositions is no doubt due to their fine lyric quality. Romanticism marks his writings.

TUNE: "Canonbury" is taken from "Nachtstücke, Opus 23, No. 4," 1839, one of the many delightful airs written by Robert Schumann. It appears in Jones's "Book of Common Worship."

93

79

HYMN: I Look to Thee in Every Need
TUNE: O Jesu

Author: *Rev. Samuel Longfellow*   Source: *"Hirschberg Gesangbuch"*

AUTHOR: Samuel Longfellow, a brother of Henry W. Longfellow, the poet, was born June 18, 1819, in Portland, Maine, and died October 3, 1892. An ardent theist and devoted pastor, he spent his life in active service of others. Since he was always in delicate health, death was to him a familiar thought. In his first sermon after the death of his eminent brother, he said: "I bring you a message from the chamber of death and from the gateway of the tomb. And that message is life, life immortal, life uninterrupted, unarrested, not cut off." He retired from the active ministry, partly because of ill health and partly to write the definitive life of his brother which is widely known and used.

HYMN: Here is a word for nervous, overwrought, discouraged, disheartened people. Even though the word "God" is not mentioned no one but God could supply the content of which this is the framework. In The Book of Esther the name of God does not occur, yet that Biblical story carries clear evidence of the ruling and overruling hand of God. In stanza 4 there is a clear connection between the law of God and the love of God. They are not in opposition, for the law of God is simply the love of God made available for daily guidance.

SOURCE: The source is a melody in the "Hirschberg Gesangbuch," 1741. For comments on German hymnody see the article, "German Hymn Sources," under "Original Sources," page xxi.

TUNE: In 1747, J. B. Reimann published his "Sammlung Alter und Neuer Melodien Evangel. Lieder, Etc.," in which the tune, "O Jesu," appears set to the hymn, "O Jesu, Warum Legst Du Mir," the first words of the hymn giving the name to the tune. There has been some slight change from the original, notably the first and last notes of each line, which are varied.

80

HYMN: God Is Love ; His Mercy Brightens
TUNE: Sussex

Author: *John Bowring*   Source: *English Traditional Melody*

AUTHOR: This is the first of four hymns by Sir John Bowring, LL.D., F.R.S., in this Hymnal, (Hymns 80, 89, 109, and 154). Bowring was a layman, a government official, and British consul

God the Father

at Canton, and later governor at Hong Kong. He was born October 17, 1792, and died November 23, 1872. Though a professing Unitarian, his heart turned trustfully to the cross of Christ. Dr. Charles S. Robinson says of him, "His heart rested for his salvation upon an atonement wrought out by the infinite Son of God." His scholarship ran in several lines—philology, poetry, politics. He was proficient in five languages before he was sixteen years of age. On his gravestone are engraved the words of his best-known hymn, "In the Cross of Christ I Glory."

HYMN: The construction of this hymn deserves notice because of the closing line of each stanza. The same form is used in John Milton's boyhood hymn, Hymn 64, but Milton found it in Psalm 136, which he was using. It is used in Hymns 3, 9, 71, 72; in such Christmas hymns as Hymns 116 and 124; and not infrequently elsewhere. The method gives a unity which is helpful, suggesting the common goal of paths which start at many points. It is often said that the profoundest words anywhere about God are the three words of I John 4:8, "God is love." It is said of Christ that he has been made Wisdom to us, I Cor. 1:30, but the Bible nowhere says directly that God is Wisdom. Anyone knows the rich truth of the saying, however, and the hymn joins the two ideas helpfully and properly. Unwise love and unloving wisdom would be equally dangerous. Our hope lies in both these attributes of God in the midst of life's changes and chances. Some versions of the hymn say, "From the gloom His brightness streameth"; Bowring wrote, "From the mist," as here given.

SOURCE: The source of this tune is an English traditional melody.

TUNE: "Sussex" is an arrangement of an English traditional melody. It was made by Dr. R. Vaughan Williams for "The English Hymnal," which was published in 1906. Since its appearance in that volume it has been included in "The Hymnary," 1930, Canada; "The Church Hymnary," 1930, England; "Songs of Praise," 1925, England. The tune is of simple structure, joyous and vigorous in movement, and calls for marked rhythm. For group singing it is a very successful tune and in "Songs of Praise" it is used with the patriotic hymn of Thomas Campbell (1777–1844), beginning, "Men of England, who inherit."

95

81   HYMN: When All Thy Mercies, O My God
             TUNE: St. Peter

Author: *Joseph Addison*   Composer: *Alexander R. Reinagle*

AUTHOR: For comments on the author, Joseph Addison, see Hymn 69.

HYMN: At the close of an article on "Gratitude" in The Spectator for August 9, 1712, this poem is given. In the article itself a paragraph occurs which sheds light on Addison's thought: "If gratitude is due from man to man, how much more from man to his Maker? The Supreme Being not only confers upon us those bounties which proceed more directly from his hand, but even those blessings which are conveyed to us by others." This is sustained by the saying in Scripture that "every good gift and every perfect gift is from above," James 1 : 17. As all our earthly heat can be traced at last to the sun, though much of it comes from secondary channels, so all blessings come from God, however they are brought to us. Addison mentions a thankful heart as being itself a gift of God. God would doubtless confer this gift more frequently if it were more willingly received. Dr. Henry van Dyke did not like the little song, "Count your blessings, name them one by one." He refused to be mathematical in his attempt to praise God, giving so much thankfulness for so many blessings.

COMPOSER: Alexander R. Reinagle, who was born in 1799 and died in 1877, at Kidlington, Oxford, came from a noted musical family. His uncle was a well-known violinist and his father was a violoncellist. John Wesley speaks of attending a concert where the latter performed. The composer himself was organist at St. Peter's-in-the-East, Oxford, from 1822 to 1853. The hymn derives its name from the church which he so long served.

TUNE: Few Western tunes are pleasant to Oriental ears, but "St. Peter" is one of the exceptions. The writer of this article has seldom been so thrilled by mass singing as when he was leading a congregation of nearly one thousand Hainanese as they sang it in unison with stately rhythm. This is one of our majestic hymns, to be sung in moderate time and with strong rhythmic accent.

God the Father

82 HYMN: The Lord Is Rich and Merciful
     TUNE: Petersham

Author: *Rev. Thomas Toke Lynch* Composer: *Clement William Poole*

AUTHOR: This is the first of three hymns by Rev. Thomas Toke Lynch in this Hymnal (Hymns 82, 128, and 214). Lynch was an independent minister of England, who was born July 5, 1818, and died May 9, 1871. He was never strong in body. His personal appearance and manner of preaching were much against him, but the "individuality, freshness, and spirituality of his pulpit work" overcame this difficulty, and he had a thoughtful hearing, though his congregations were always small. His spirit may be caught in a remark he made when controversy rose around him: "The air will be clearer for this storm. We must conquer our foes by suffering them to crucify us, rather than by threatening them with crucifixion." When some one told him that he was about to die, he said, "Now I am going to begin to live." Lynch wrote a book of hymns for his congregation, called "The Rivulet," in which this hymn occurs. He explained the title by saying, "Christian poetry is indeed a river of the water of life, and to this river my rivulet brings its contribution."

HYMN: The title given by the author to this hymn, which appeared in "The Rivulet," 1868, is "Have Faith in God." The suggestion of the first line of each stanza is carried out in the remainder of the stanza. Since God is what the first line suggests, believers may expect the experience named. The call is to come to him, trust in him, learn of him—three definite duties of Christian discipleship. The closing figure of the evening hours and their call to rest is worth careful thought. After all, working and living are not all; there is also resting.

COMPOSER: Clement William Poole (1828–1924) was the son of a bencher of Gray's Inn, London. His deeply religious nature, with his intense love of music, led him, after a greatly varied life, to devote himself to sacred music. He was at one time clerk in the Audit Office. Later he engaged in business, in which he was not oversuccessful. He became honorary organist of the Parish Church at Kingston-on-Thames; Christ Church, Ealing; and Holy Trinity, Ramsgate. His compositions comprise a "Magnificat," several songs, and over thirty hymns. He died at Ealing at the age of ninety-six.

TUNE: "Petersham" was originally set to the words of "The Roseate Hues of Early Dawn." It was included in "The Congregational Psalmist," Second Appendix, published in 1875.

97

83   HYMN: Through All the Changing Scenes of Life
         TUNE: Wiltshire

Source: *Tate and Brady's "New Version"*   Composer: *George T. Smart*

SOURCE: For comments on the source, Tate and Brady's "New Version," see Hymn 19.

HYMN: This hymn is from a version of Psalm 34 that originally had eighteen stanzas, covering the entire psalm. Stanza 4 is added as a Trinitarian doxology to bring the Old Testament psalm into full accord with the Christian service. It is probable that the familiar "Gloria Patri" was originally prepared for this purpose, to be used in the liturgical service at the end of each psalm. Psalm 34 is a call to share religious experience. The writer of the psalm is not content to praise by himself alone; he tells others of it and calls them to join him in giving praise to God. If they cannot do it on their own account, they must join in corporate worship on the psalmist's account. Whoever tests the love of God finds the same unfailing goodness. His truth is a sure foundation, and no one who confides in it will be put to shame. The closing part of the psalm, omitted here, carries the plea farther, making it into a challenge to a corrected and obedient life. Trials and difficulties may come, but the deliverance of God will come also.

COMPOSER: Sir George T. Smart (1776–1867) was born in London. As in the case of many Englishmen, his interest in music was developed by his training as a chorister. He served in the Chapel Royal under Ayrton. Later he became organist of St. James's Chapel, Hampstead Road, London. His musical life covered a number of notable achievements: From 1813 to 1844 he was conductor of the Philharmonic Society, of which he was one of the original members; in 1822 he became one of the organists at the Chapel Royal where in his earlier days he had been a member of the choir; in 1838 he was appointed composer to the Chapel Royal. To him was given the honor of arranging and conducting the music at the coronations of William IV and of Victoria. After a series of concerts in Dublin, in 1811, he received the honor of knighthood. He was a great friend of Weber and it was at his home that the latter died. His publications include a collection of glees and canons, published in 1863, "Collection of Sacred Music" (two volumes), and several anthems. He died in London.

TUNE: The tune, "Wiltshire," first appears in Smart's "Divine Amusement," c.1795, set to Psalm 48. The melody appeared again later, somewhat changed by the composer.

God the Father

84

HYMN: O Love of God Most Full
TUNE: Trentham

Author: *Rev. Oscar Clute*   Composer: *Robert Jackson*

AUTHOR: Rev. Oscar Clute was born in Bethlehem, New York, March 11, 1837. After his ordination in 1868, he held the following pastorates: Vineland, New Jersey; Keokuk, Iowa; Iowa City, Iowa; and Pomona, California. Subsequently he was president of the Agricultural College of Michigan and later of a similar institution in Florida. He was a man of great missionary zeal and of deep religious convictions. He felt a deep interest in the entrance of women into the ministry. Well-equipped with scientific knowledge, he was among the foremost of the western ministers in the work of maintaining men's loyalties to spiritual things, which for a time seemed to be threatened by the scientific theories of the latter part of the nineteenth century. He died at the Soldiers' Home in Sawtelle, California, in January, 1902.

HYMN: This hymn is a rhapsody of gratitude for the love of God. Stanza 1 prays for it in the heart and soul; stanza 4 is an experience of the answer. In Christian experience the "wildest sea" subsides, but through the storm the heart is kept steady and unafraid. Sometimes the darkness is dissipated by rays of light; sometimes the darkness settles down more thickly, but the Christian soul moves on without fear in the confidence of faith. Our Lord said that he would give his disciples a peace which the world cannot give. It would be the peace of an untroubled heart in the midst of any experience that might come. The world would remove all causes for anxiety; Christ gives courage in the midst of those causes.

COMPOSER: Robert Jackson was a native of Oldham, Lancashire, England. He was born in 1840 and died in 1914. He was educated at the Royal Academy of Music, Hanover Square, London, where he gained the silver medal. For some years he held the position of organist at St. Mark's Church, North Audley Street, London. On the death of his father he was appointed organist and choirmaster at St. Peter's Church, Oldham, in his father's place. His father had held the position for over 47 years, and father and son together had a record of continuous service at the same church of about 92 years. Robert Jackson composed a considerable quantity of music—anthems, hymn tunes, songs, and part songs. For many years he was a member of Sir Charles Halle's orchestra and he was the conductor of the Oldham Musical Society. Robert Jackson devoted his whole life to music and was successful in the training of numerous pupils.

99

Handbook to The Hymnal

TUNE: "Trentham" is a tune of simple pattern but great beauty. As a voice for the expression of devotion, it is most effective. In the rendering of the tune, careful attention should be given to the tenor, which is very melodious. "Trentham" first appeared in 1894 and was published in Robert Jackson's "Sacred Leaflets."

85

HYMN: O Gracious Father of Mankind
TUNE: Old 22nd

Author: *Rev. Henry H. Tweedy*   Source: *"Anglo-Genevan Psalter"*

AUTHOR: Professor Tweedy is a member of the faculty of Yale Divinity School. He was born August 5, 1868, and educated at Yale University and Union Theological Seminary. He has been a pastor in Utica, New York, and Bridgeport, Connecticut. His Yale appointment dates from 1909. Dissatisfied with many current hymns and finding many most difficult for a Christian believer to sing, he set himself to prepare something that would express more nearly the experience and desire of believers. This hymn was part of the result. When the Homiletic Review, in 1925, offered a prize for new hymns, Dr. Tweedy submitted his hymn, which had not been written for the contest but before it was announced. It was awarded first prize. Several other hymns have followed this one and have gained wide usage.

HYMN: The hymn, though dealing with prayer, expresses so well the Christian thought of God that it is well classified in "The Hymnal." Many earnest believers are troubled about praying to an all-wise and all-knowing God. If God knows everything already, why pray? And certainly prayer is not for the information of God, nor to reveal to him anything that he does not know. There is an aspect of it expressed here which is the unburdening of our hearts before him for our sakes, as an inspiration to "labor for those gifts we ask on bended knee." Every prayer is a pledge of effort to secure what we pray for. Our prayers are a response to the desire of God to do for us more than we have been willing to allow him to do. They are not inducements to an unwilling Deity.

SOURCE: For comments on the source, "Anglo-Genevan Psalter," 1556, see the article, "The Psalters in Early Presbyterian Worship," under "Original Sources," page xv.

TUNE: "Old 22nd" was used in the "Anglo-Genevan Psalter" for a setting of Psalm 16, but in all other Psalters it is set to Psalm 22.

100

God the Father

86   HYMN: My Soul with Expectation Doth
           TUNE: St. Flavian

Source: *"Scottish Psalter"*   Source: *"Day's Psalter"*

SOURCE: For comments on the source, "Scottish Psalter," 1650, see the article, "The Psalters in Early Presbyterian Worship," under "Original Sources," page xv.

HYMN: The hymn is a part of Psalm 62, the original version being longer and covering the whole of the psalm. In the American Standard Version the psalm opens with the verse, "My soul waiteth in silence for God only." This hymn follows the more familiar King James Version. The entire psalm, as also the hymn, implies that the soul has not yet received what it longs for and expects. There is no fretting, however, and no condemnation of God for the delay. The psalm uses the figure of the rock, portraying the stability of God when all else seems unsettled. We are saved *out of* some things; we are saved *from* some things. In either case God is our salvation. Stanza 3 suggests the sense of shame of the believer when he realizes that his life and experiences are no better or finer than those of unbelievers; in such a time a man glories not in himself or in his prospects but in God alone. The hymn closes with a plea to all men to pour out their hearts to God and find his abundant strength for life.

SOURCE: For comments on the source, "Day's Psalter," 1563, see the article, "The Psalters in Early Presbyterian Worship," under "Original Sources," page xv.

TUNE: "St. Flavian" is the first part of the tune that was originally included in "Day's Psalter," 1563, set to Psalm 132. With some rhythmic changes it was retained in more recent editions. "St. Flavian" in its present form is from Richard Redhead's "Ancient Hymn Melodies and Other Church Tunes," 1853, taken from Thomas Ravenscroft's "Whole Booke of Psalmes," 1621.

---

87   HYMN: Lord of All Being, Throned Afar
           TUNE: Louvan

Author: *Oliver Wendell Holmes*   Composer: *Virgil C. Taylor*

AUTHOR: Oliver Wendell Holmes, M.D., LL.D., D.C.L., was born August 29, 1809. He died October 7, 1894. His father was minister of the First Congregational Church of Cambridge,

Handbook to The Hymnal

Massachusetts. Oliver Wendell Holmes was "essayist, poet, and teacher of anatomy," according to one biographer. He was a medical teacher at Harvard University, rather than a practitioner. Certain types of theological orthodoxy offended him in early life; in later life he fell back more and more on old evangelical truths. He said that he "believed more than some and less than others," and he liked "those who believed more better than those who believed less." In a letter to Elizabeth Stuart Phelps he said, "There is a little plant called 'reverence' in the corner of my soul's garden, which I love to have watered about once a week." So he regularly frequented the sanctuary of worship.

HYMN: The poem that closes the last chapter of "The Professor at the Breakfast-Table," in the Atlantic Monthly for December, 1859, called "A Sun-Day Hymn," is this hymn. M. A. DeWolfe Howe says, "This hymn speaks for the place which, for all his rebellion against the Calvinism of his youth, he gave to religion in his life and thought." Beginning with the physical figure of the sun, the hymn moves by natural stages to God, the Lord of all being, spiritual and temporal. The clouds of sin around us are not his, save that in his light we know them for what they are. All forgiveness and new light come from him and under his shining the clouds of sin disperse.

COMPOSER: Virgil Corydon Taylor, who devoted all his life to the advancement of music, was born in Barkhamstead, Connecticut, April 2, 1817. His ancestry can be traced directly to Elder William Brewster, who drew up the Mayflower Covenant in 1620. To encourage his musical talent, his father placed a church organ in the home for his use. At this organ many of his compositions were written and played. Greatly influenced by the musical activities of Thomas Hastings and Lowell Mason, he directed singing schools and institutes. He was proficient as teacher and organist and contributed greatly to musical intelligence and appreciation. In his work he had the coöperation of his wife, who was an accomplished soprano. He served in Hartford, Connecticut, from which he removed to Poughkeepsie, where he conducted the Union Musical Association and presided at the organ of the Central Baptist Church. In 1861 he became organist of the Strong Place Baptist Church of Brooklyn, and from there he went to become organist of St. Paul's Church at Des Moines, Iowa. He died on January 30, 1891. A number of hymnals are to his credit, among which may be mentioned "The Sacred Minstrel" and "The Golden Lyre."

TUNE: "Louvan" first appeared in 1846 in "The Sacred Minstrel." From the first it was well received and consequently was included in other books which Taylor published. The tune has been used

God the Father

in the hymnals of the Presbyterian Church since the appearance of "The Presbyterian Psalmodist" in 1852. The tune was first used with a text by Thomas Moore, "There's nothing bright above, below."

---

88 HYMN: God of Our Life, Through All the Circling Years
TUNE: Sandon

Author: *Rev. Hugh T. Kerr*   Composer: *Charles Henry Purday*

AUTHOR: This hymn is from the pen of the pastor of the Shadyside Presbyterian Church, Pittsburgh, Pennsylvania, Hugh Thomson Kerr, D.D., LL.D. Dr. Kerr was born in Canada on February 11, 1872, and was educated in the University of Toronto and Western Theological Seminary, Pittsburgh. He was ordained to the Presbyterian ministry in 1897 and has been pastor in Hutchinson, Kansas, and Chicago, Illinois, his Pittsburgh pastorate beginning in 1913. He has taken a leading place in the Presbyterian Church in the U.S.A. and in 1930 was Moderator of its General Assembly.

HYMN: In the fall of 1916 the Shadyside Presbyterian Church of Pittsburgh celebrated its fiftieth anniversary. This hymn was written for that occasion. Madame Louise Homer, well-known in grand opera, a daughter of an earlier pastor of the church, was present and led in the singing of what she described as "this noble hymn." Every day is in some true sense an anniversary, closing the preceding years and opening the new ones. The hymn is, therefore, appropriate for use at all times. We stand, it suggests, on the dividing line between the past and the future and both are under the sheltering hand of God. This is the warrant for our expectation of his leadership into hope's ultimate Promised Land.

COMPOSER: Charles Henry Purday, born at Folkestone, England, in 1799, was the son of a bookseller. His musical life was active and varied. A vocalist of note, he sang at the coronation of Queen Victoria. He was a publisher of music, a lecturer, a conductor of psalmody in the Scots Church, Crown Court, Covent Garden, and a strong advocate of the reform of the copyright laws relating to music. On this subject he published a book entitled, "Copyright, a Sketch of Its Rise and Progress," 1877. He died in London in 1885.

TUNE: "Sandon," set to the hymn, "Lead, Kindly Light, Amid th' Encircling Gloom," appeared in 1860 in "The Church and Home Metrical Psalter and Hymnal," edited by Charles Purday. The tune was written especially for those words.

89 HYMN: Father and Friend! Thy Light, Thy Love
TUNE: Quebec

Author: *John Bowring*   Composer: *Henry Baker*

AUTHOR: For comments on the author, John Bowring, see Hymn 80.

HYMN: A skeptic once wrote that if there were a God he would surely write the fact in letters miles high on the clouds in the sky. Sir John Bowring would say that God has done this. Men with closed eyes do not always see, but their blindness does not blot out the writing of God. This hymn reminds us that wherever strength, wisdom, and goodness are found, we are seeing traces of God. His omnipresence insures that no child of his can ever be deserted or alone. Sir John must often have needed this assurance. Psalm 19:3 reads, in the American Standard Version,

> "There is no speech nor language;
> Their voice is not heard."

No; but

> "Their line is gone out through all the earth,
> And their words to the end of the world."

Mrs. Browning wrote:

> "Earth's crammed with heaven,
> And every common bush afire with God:
> But only he who sees, takes off his shoes,
> The rest sit round it and pluck blackberries."

God is there, a Father and Friend, but men who need him most may miss him because they will not see.

COMPOSER: Henry Baker, Mus.B. (1835–1910)—sometimes confused with Sir Henry W. Baker, editor of "Hymns Ancient and Modern"—was the son of Rev. James Baker who was rector of Nuneham Courtney and afterwards chancellor of the diocese of Durham. Henry Baker was born at Nuneham, Oxfordshire, England, and received his education at Winchester. He studied civil engineering at Cooper's Hill, afterwards giving many years of service to railway work in India. His interest in church music led him later to devote a great part of his life to it. Dr. John B. Dykes was influential in inducing him to seek his musical degree at Exeter College, Oxford.

TUNE: "Quebec" appears in English, and in some American hymn books as "Hesperus," and in J. Grey's "A Hymnal for Use in the English Church," 1866, as "Whitburn."

God the Father

90

HYMN: To Thine Eternal Arms, O God
TUNE: Federal Street

Author: *Thomas Wentworth Higginson*   Composer: *Henry K. Oliver*

AUTHOR: Colonel Thomas Wentworth Higginson was a precocious youth, entering Harvard University at 13 and graduating from there, second in his class, at 17. He inclined early to the ministry, but as he observed theological students he described them as "mystics, skeptics, and dyspeptics," and for some time turned away from that calling. However, he did finally enter the Divinity School and became a minister. He was a strong antislavery advocate, a personal friend of John Brown, and colonel of the first Negro regiment formed for the Civil War. He remained in the formal ministry only a short time and then gave himself to writing and lecturing. No cloud came over his personal Christian faith and many of his references to Christ indicate a deeply reverent and trustful attitude toward him.

HYMN: The hymn expresses a feeling common among older people that childhood faith is no longer possible for them; they wonder if they have the right to look to God in the same trustful way as when they were children. But after all, as the hymn suggests, we never outgrow our childhood feeling for God. Our experiences have taught us that we cannot trust hope and pride and strength as we once did. Now we know that we must fall back into the "everlasting arms." When our steps tremble, we need a power which can come from none but God.

COMPOSER: Henry Kemble Oliver was related to Oliver Wendell Holmes and to Wendell Phillips, his mother being a great-aunt of the former. Born at Beverly, Massachusetts, in 1800, he was educated at Harvard and was also given a degree at Dartmouth. He taught at Salem until 1844, when he became superintendent of the Atlantic Cotton Mills. In 1859 he served as mayor of Lawrence and, later, as head of the Massachusetts Bureau of Statistics of Labor. He was a judge at the Centennial in 1876 and also served in the state militia as colonel and adjutant. The degree of Doctor of Music was conferred on him by Dartmouth in 1883. His early musical training was received in Park Street Church, Boston, where he was first a chorister and later, in 1819, became organist. "Federal Street" was his first attempt at composition and was followed later by "Beacon Street," "Chestnut Street," "Salisbury Plain," "Walnut Grove," and others.

TUNE: It is related of "Federal Street" that Henry Oliver, after reading Theodore Hook's novel, "Passion and Principle," was greatly disturbed by its seriousness. While the composer was pacing the floor, deep in thought, a stanza of Anne Steele's hymn, "So Fades the Lovely Blooming Flower," came to his mind and seemed to resolve itself into this tune, which he immediately wrote, naming it after the street on which he lived in Salem. At the great Peace Jubilee in Boston, in 1872, "Federal Street" was sung by a large chorus with a still larger assembly uniting and the composer conducting.

---

91 HYMN: God Is Our Refuge and Our Strength
TUNE: Winchester Old

Source: *"Scottish Psalter"*   Source: *"Este's Psalter"*

SOURCE: For comments on the source, "Scottish Psalter," 1650, see the article, "The Psalters in Early Presbyterian Worship," under "Original Sources," page xv.

HYMN: The psalm here paraphrased is the familiar Forty-sixth, often called "Luther's Psalm" because of Luther's use of it in his best-known hymn, Hymn 266. This psalm has been the bulwark of faith in many trying hours. The hymn covers only the earlier half of the psalm, verses 1–5; the "Scottish Psalter" covered the entire psalm. The phrasing is quaint and unfamiliar, but no one can miss its meaning. This quaintness illustrates again the contrast between English poetry, with its demand for rime and meter, and Hebrew poetry, with its parallelisms and disregard of limiting meter. The riming short lines carry themselves into the mind and heart.

SOURCE: For comments on the source, "Este's Psalter," 1592, see the article, "The Psalters in Early Presbyterian Worship," under "Original Sources," page xv.

TUNE: The tune, "Winchester Old," comes to us from "Este's Psalter," published in 1592. It is of interest to know that this Psalter is the first one in which tunes were named, three having a name assigned to them, namely, "Glassenburie," "Kentish," and "Cheshire." The experiment was successful, and the plan was followed by Ravenscroft in his Psalter of 1621, and has been in vogue ever since. "Winchester Old" seems to have lain hidden and undiscovered for many years, until it was incorporated in "Hymns Ancient and Modern," in 1861, where it was set to "While Shepherds Watched Their Flocks by Night." The tunes in "Este's Psalter" were arranged for four voices. Richard Allison, one of the men employed by Este, published in 1599 a "Folio for Private Use," with the music arranged as "Table Music." It was so printed that, seated around a table on which the folio was placed, each performer had his part directly in front of him.

God the Father

92

Author: *James Montgomery*   Composer: *Melchior Vulpius*

AUTHOR: As a Moravian minister James Montgomery was notable for his intimate knowledge of the Scriptures. He said of himself that he "lay in wait for his heart, to catch its highest emotions." When he was asked which of his poems would live, he replied, "None, sir; nothing, except perhaps a few of my hymns." It has proved a true prophecy. For further comments on the author, James Montgomery, see Hymn 11.

HYMN: Obviously this version of Psalm 27 loosely follows some earlier versions. Contrasting it with Hymn 91, one observes the difference in style—the quaintness there, the naturalness and modernity here. The psalm maintains the note of courage and assurance to the end. Dangers are recognized, enemy hosts encamped near by, but reliance on God provides courage even for the waiting which so often baffles a Christian believer. In the last stanza the might, love, mercy, and peace of God render for the believer the services most needed. There is no guarantee against being faint and desolate, but an escape is provided.

COMPOSER: Melchior Vulpius was born at Wasungen, Canton of Henneberg, Thuringia, about 1560. He became cantor at Weimar about 1600. Little is recorded concerning him, but we know that he composed a number of tunes, which were published in the two important collections that he edited and issued in 1604 and 1609. Some others were published, after his death, in the "Cantonial" of Gotha. He is known as a composer and musical theorist. He died in 1616, at Weimar.

TUNE: "Mein Leben" is marked by its German origin. The tune is admirably adapted to the words from Psalm 27. Sung in moderate time with marked rhythm and careful attention to the phrasing, it adds to the majesty of the psalm.

93
HYMN: There's a Wideness in God's Mercy
TUNE: In Babilone

Author: *Rev. Frederick W. Faber*   Source: *Dutch Traditional Melody*

AUTHOR: This is the first of four hymns in "The Hymnal" by Frederick W. Faber, D.D. (Hymns 93, 159, 267, and 431). He left 150 hymns that are still in more or less general use. An

Anglican clergyman, he entered the Roman Catholic Church in 1846, all his hymns being written after that date. He was born on June 28, 1814, and died September 26, 1863. He was a Balliol College man and one of the first to be influenced by the Tractarian Movement. He established and conducted for a time a brotherhood in London and wrote extensively in the hope of strengthening the movement toward Rome.

HYMN: This is part of a much longer hymn which begins, "Souls of men, why will ye scatter?" It is a plea for trust instead of fear of God, and for greater kindliness toward others instead of the severity that demands their agreement with ourselves. It was easier for Faber to write this than to experience it himself, though he must have longed many times to be done with controversy and every form of bigotry.

SOURCE: The source of "In Babilone" is a Dutch traditional melody.

HARMONIZER: "In Babilone," as used here, was harmonized by Professor Julius Röntgen (1855–1933), of Amsterdam, Holland. Since its appearance in "The English Hymnal," 1906, it has won the recognition of hymnal editors in Canada and in the United States.

TUNE: The heart and the voice of the common people is in the tune, "In Babilone." The melody is fluent and joyous and has the healthy robustness of the Dutch people. Its mood is far removed from many of the contemplative tunes of the Church, and is characterized by virile and buoyant progressions.

---

94   HYMN: Begin, My Tongue, Some Heavenly Theme
      TUNE: Manoah

Author: *Rev. Isaac Watts*   Arranger: *Henry W. Greatorex*

AUTHOR: For comments on the author, Isaac Watts, see Hymn 22

HYMN: Here is a purely personal hymn; even the "our" at the end of stanzas 1 and 2 seems rather meditative than social in its significance. There are hymns whose aspirations are realized when several believers are together, but there are others, such as this one, which speak their message to one person whether he be in solitude

God the Father

or in a mass of worshipers. Public worship maintains the sense of individuality along with the corporate relationship of a group to God. Note in stanza 2 the four marked evidences of God's relation to each believer: his faithfulness, his power, his grace, his redemption. The next stanza brings the reminder that all the power that maintains nature and its forces is back of the promises of grace. The same figure is used in Isa. 40:10, 11, where the arm of God both rules the world and carries the lamb with equal strength available for each.

ARRANGER: Henry Wellington Greatorex (1813–1858) was born at Burton-on-Trent. He was one of a family noted through several generations for their musical ability. His grandfather, Anthony Greatorex, was at one time organist at Burton, and to him is ascribed the tune "Tottenham." Henry's father, Thomas, was organist at Westminster Abbey during the reign of King George IV. Henry Greatorex probably received his musical training from his father. In 1839 he came to the United States as organist in the Center Congregational Church, Hartford, Connecticut, where he remained two years. Afterwards he was organist in New York City at St. Paul's, but changed to Calvary Protestant Episcopal Church. In 1853 he went to Charleston, South Carolina, as organist of an Episcopal church and died there of yellow fever. He was twice married and the children of both families were noted for their musical and artistic work.

TUNE: "Manoah" is an arrangement by Henry W. Greatorex. It seems to have been arranged from several sources. In the Presbyterian Hymnals of 1867, 1874, and 1895, the melody is attributed to Rossini, but that position cannot be maintained. In the "Annotated Edition of the Book of Common Praise," by James Edward Jones, Toronto, Canada, the opinion is expressed that it "seems to be partly arranged from E. H. Méhul's "Joseph," 1807, and partly from the chorus, "God of Light," in Franz Joseph Haydn's "Seasons," 1801. Greatorex gives no clue to its origin in his "Collection of Sacred Music," published in 1851, in which it appears for the first time.

95
HYMN: Life of Ages, Richly Poured
TUNE: Horsham

Author: *Rev. Samuel Johnson* Source: *English Traditional Melody*

AUTHOR: Rev. Samuel Johnson was an American clergyman who was never connected with any one denomination or group. He formed the Free Church at Lynn, Massachusetts, and was for some time its minister. Born on October 10, 1822, educated at Harvard

University and Cambridge Divinity School, he was a close friend of and collaborator with Samuel Longfellow, brother of the poet, in hymnals and books of poetry. He died February 19, 1882.

H YMN: Here is a poem of unusual construction. It consists of only one sentence. The subject of the sentence occurs at the very beginning and recurs at the opening of the fourth stanza with an added petition. When a congregation is asked to sing it, this fact should be noted. The hymn suggests that God works through many channels—the prophet's word, the people's liberty, the thinker's creed, the hero's blood, art and song, holy books, and pilgrim tracks. Then comes the prayer that in the present day as in the past this manifestation of the life and love of God may continue. The hymn is useful for national days.

S OURCE: The tune is an arrangement of an English traditional melody and seems to have been taken from a collection made by Miss L. E. Broadwood.

T UNE: "Horsham," since its appearance in "The English Hymnal," 1906, has achieved wide use. Because of its adaptability to various texts, it is used four times in "The Hymnal." It is a tune of short compass, but exquisite in harmonic thought and beauty. In England it has been included in hymnals for children and young people. "Horsham" is a tune which fits every period of life, being popular with young and old alike.

His Abiding Presence

*

96   HYMN: Unto the Hills Around Do I Lift Up
          TUNE: Sandon

Author: *John Campbell, Duke of Argyll*   Composer: *Charles Henry Purday*

A UTHOR: John Campbell, the ninth duke of Argyll, was born August 6, 1845, succeeded to the dukedom in 1900, and died on May 2, 1914. He was a great Highland chieftain, with many and varied activities. His wife was Princess Louise, fourth daughter of Queen Victoria, the marriage occurring at St. George's Chapel, Windsor, on March 21, 1871. He was at one time governor-general of Canada and commander in chief of Prince Edward Island. At the coronations of both

God the Father

Edward VII and George V he carried the royal scepter. He was keeper of the great seal of Scotland. Like so many of his line, he was at the same time an earnest Christian student and writer who found high pleasure in the study of the psalms and in making them available for Christian worship.

HYMN: Obviously this is a setting of Psalm 121, widely known as the "Traveler's Psalm." The hymn covers the entire psalm. It is loved throughout the English-speaking world, especially in Scotland and America. Several fine touches in the lines deserve attention: "longing eyes," "my certain aid," "no careless slumber," "thy keeper true," "thy changeless shade," "the silent night." The idea of the watchfulness of God over men is not unknown in other faiths, but it was left for the Jewish and Christian faiths to bring out the fact that this watchfulness had behind it the thought of loving protection, not detection of men's sins. Even Christians have sometimes read the beautiful word of Gen. 16:13, "Thou God seest me," as if it were a forbidding aspect of God's omniscience, whereas it is a glorious assurance of God's care.

COMPOSER: For comments on the composer, Charles Henry Purday, see Hymn 88.

TUNE: For comments on the tune, "Sandon," see Hymn 88.

---

97 HYMN: The Lord's My Shepherd, I'll Not Want
TUNE: Evan

Source: *"Scottish Psalter"*   Composer: *Rev. William H. Havergal*

SOURCE: For comments on the source, "Scottish Psalter," 1650, see the article, "The Psalters in Early Presbyterian Worship," under "Original Sources," page xv.

HYMN: Of the multitude of versions of the Twenty-third Psalm, this one and the one found in Hymn 99 are probably the most widely used and most loved. The two are easily compared, this version having the quaint touches of an older English style and Rev. Sir Henry Baker's, Hymn 99, the more familiar phrases of later usage. It is the foremost of all the psalms in the hearts of Christian believers. It is the first extended portion of Scripture learned by most children in their homes and Bible schools, and it is always safe to assume the ability of any English-speaking congregation to repeat it. In spite of its familiarity, however, it is sometimes wise to explain its figures of speech to young people, who do not understand about the rod and staff and how they "comfort" anyone, nor about the table spread in the presence of foes, nor especially about anointing the head with oil.

COMPOSER: Rev. William H. Havergal (1793–1870) graduated from Oxford in 1815. He was ordained in the Church of England, 1816, and became rector of a church at Astley, near Bewdley, in 1829. While there he suffered from a severe carriage accident, which caused him to relinquish his clerical duties for several years, and during this time he devoted himself to the study of church music. At a time when English church music was at a low ebb, the publication, in 1847, of his "Old Church Psalmody" drew attention to the classical school of church music and paved the way for numerous excellent collections of hymns, chants, and anthems which are now the rich heritage of the Anglican Church. Havergal also wrote many secular songs, which were later collected into a volume called "Fireside Music," 1847. After his death his works were collected and edited by his youngest daughter, Frances Ridley Havergal (1836–1879), whose religious poetry is well known.

TUNE: "Evan" was originally a setting by Mr. Havergal for Burns's poem, "O Thou Dread Power, Who Reign'st Above." Dr. Lowell Mason, who visited Havergal in England, described the musical service that he heard in Havergal's church as in advance of anything that he had heard in England. In 1850 Mason arranged the first, second, seventh, and eighth lines of this melody as a psalm tune in the form here printed, and called it "Eva." Mr. Havergal later made a revision of the hymn tune in which he used Mason's arrangement but cast it in a different meter, making the notes of equal length, except for a longer note at the ends of the second and fourth lines. Mason's arrangement has always been deservedly popular, because, while he has preserved the quaint richness of the original melody, he has provided an interesting rhythmic pattern.

---

98   HYMN: O God of Beth-el, by Whose Hand
        TUNE: Dundee

Authors: *Philip Doddridge and John Logan*   Source: *"Scottish Psalter"*

AUTHORS: The son of a merchant in London, Philip Doddridge was born January 26, 1702, the youngest of twenty children. He died October 26, 1751. His home was a godly one and in it, before he could read, he learned the stories of the Old and New Testaments, outlined to him by his mother as they were depicted on the blue Dutch tiles. He had opportunities to enter the Anglican ministry, but his real affiliations were always with the Nonconformists; so he studied for that ministry, entering it in 1723. He was a practical preacher, seeking "to cultivate in his hearers a spiritual and devotional frame of mind." His theological books are still used, especially his "The Rise and Progress of Religion in the Soul." Three others of his hymns are used in "The Hymnal" (Hymns 278, 279, and 470). It was on a visit to Lisbon in search of health, which hard work and tuberculosis had impaired, that Doddridge died.

John Logan (1748–1788), who made editorial alterations in this hymn, was an editor of other men's work, which he sometimes claimed as his own. He had been a minister in Scotland, but fell into intemperate habits and came to London to live, leaving the active ministry. His life reminds us that appreciation of religious expression does not necessarily indicate religious vitality.

HYMN: This hymn is a good instance of what is properly called a "paraphrase"—not a translation, not a version, yet not independent or original. No one could follow its chief phrases intelligently without a fairly clear knowledge of Gen. 28:20–22. Yet the hymn passes easily from one Scripture truth to another and unites them in a plain body of Scriptural thinking.

SOURCE: For comments on the source, "Scottish Psalter," 1615, see the article, "The Psalters in Early Presbyterian Worship," under "Original Sources," page xv.

TUNE: "Dundee" first appeared as one of the twelve "common" tunes in "The CL Psalms of David," published in Edinburgh, 1615, by A. Hart. In the English and Scottish hymnals this tune often appears under the name "French." It appears in Ravenscroft's "Whole Booke of Psalmes," 1621, where it is called "Dundy" and is indexed among the "Scottish Tunes." It is a reasonable conjecture that this tune, in spite of its long association with Scottish and English psalmody, had its origin in Protestant Europe, perhaps being an adaptation of a secular melody cast into the psalter-tune form. For many years it was written in equal notes, after the manner of the German choral, but present musical editors seem inclined to restore it to its earlier form, which to a large degree allows it to be sung with more spontaneity. It is notable for its smooth, flowing style, moving almost step by step in a melody which rises to its highest point in the third line and comes to a substantial and dignified cadence at the close.

99   HYMN: The King of Love My Shepherd Is
TUNE: Dominus Regit Me

Author: *Rev. Henry W. Baker*   Composer: *Rev. John B. Dykes*

AUTHOR: Rev. Sir Henry Williams Baker is best known as the editor and director of "Hymns Ancient and Modern," the accepted hymnal of the Anglican Church. Three other hymns from his pen are in this Hymnal (Hymns 421, 463, and 498), and many others are still in use. He was an Anglican clergyman, who was born May 27, 1821, and died February 12, 1877. He published a book of "Family Prayers for the Use of Those Who Work Hard," indicating his care for the people of his parish. He was often a severe critic of other people's hymns. In the hour of his death, he repeated stanza 3 of this hymn as his word of final comfort. Rev. John B. Dykes, the organist, was a close friend of Baker and composed for this hymn the tune here used.

HYMN: Baker has added to the psalm the suggestion of the cross, stanza 4. In using the hymn it would be well to call the attention of young people to the unfamiliar terms that are used in stanza 5, such as, "unction," "pure chalice." Both are historically familiar: the grace of God gives the believer his anointing and supplies him full refreshment from God's cup of blessing. Care should be taken in using this hymn to sing all the stanzas, though six are given.

COMPOSER: For comments on the composer, John B. Dykes, see Hymn 53.

TUNE: This tune, "Dominus Regit Me," was composed for this hymn by Dr. Dykes and was first published in "Hymns Ancient and Modern," Appendix, 1868. Both hymn and tune were sung at Dr. Dykes's funeral on January 28, 1876. As in all the tunes of this master composer, one finds the character of the words expressed in music that suits the thought of each stanza. The melody is scalewise and flows along evenly with just enough rhythmic variety to avoid monotony and still maintain the quiet thought of spiritual confidence, which this psalm, one of the most beloved of all the psalms, carries in all its versions and many paraphrases. It is interesting to note, also, that each of the four harmonic parts has motion and vitality and, except in the last line where the bass has one full measure on the dominant, there is no monotonous repetition.

God the Father

IOO
HYMN: Still with Thee, O My God
TUNE: Rhiw

Author: *Rev. James D. Burns*   Source: *"A Students' Hymnal"*

AUTHOR: James D. Burns was a young student of the great Dr. Chalmers of Scotland when the Disruption took place and went out with him to the Free Church in 1843. Burns was born on February 18, 1823. His ministry was often interrupted by ill health. In preaching his first sermon he completely broke down, but his spirit so won the people that he was immediately called to the church where he had failed. For a time he was in charge of the Free Church congregation at Funchal, Madeira Islands. Writers mention his beautiful voice, which, with all his powers, he had dedicated to Christ. At the General Assembly of the Free Church at Edinburgh, in 1863, he caught a severe cold and was sent to Mentone on the Riviera for recovery; but it was too late and he died there on November 27, 1864. His spirit constantly rose above his limitations and was in harmony with this hymn.

HYMN: The theme of the hymn is taken from Ps. 139: 18, "When I awake, I am still with thee." The same idea underlies Harriet Beecher Stowe's hymn, Hymn 107. The omnipresence of God is here gladly accepted as a ground for joy. Sometimes believers and unbelievers alike speak with dread of the fact that God is everywhere and cannot be escaped. This hymn bears out a familiar idea that the only way to flee from God is to flee to him. There is awe in the thought of omnipresence, but in this hymn the awe is caught up in adoration. To realize God's loving presence, by day, by night, in life, in death, is a believer's supreme privilege.

SOURCE: The source is "A Students' Hymnal," University of Wales, 1923. For comments in Welsh hymnody see the article, "Welsh Hymnody," under "Original Sources," page xxii.

TUNE: James T. Lightwood, in "Hymn Tunes and Their Story," in making a comparison of the psalter tunes and Welsh tunes, says, "The Welsh tunes . . . are . . . lively, and contain certain awkward 'skips' or intervals." This seems an acute observation, yet it must be granted that "awkward 'skips' " are the exception rather than the rule. When this tune, "Rhiw," is sung at a dignified pace and a steady, even beat, it assumes the characteristic quality which is so universal in the Welsh tunes—singableness. A quietly sung fourth stanza, followed by a full-voiced fifth at a slightly broader tempo, will afford contrast and intensify the confident aspiration with which the hymn closes.

101 HYMN: Mysterious Presence, Source of All
TUNE: Abends

Author: *Rev. Seth Curtis Beach*   Composer: *Herbert S. Oakeley*

AUTHOR: Dr. Seth Curtis Beach lived most of his life in New England, although he was born in Marion, New York, on August 8, 1837. After attendance at Antioch College, Ohio, he graduated from Union College, Schenectady, New York, and from Harvard Divinity School. He was ordained in 1867. This hymn, published in 1866, comes from his student days. After several pastorates he was for a short time superintendent of foreign missionary work. Later he retired to Watertown, Massachusetts, where he died.

HYMN: It requires a certain imagination to hear behind the wind and within the leaf and the flower the voice of God, but it is a valid use of this high power. There are men like William Blake who live and think "in the borderland between the world of reality and the world of dreams," so that they become mystics and seers. The two worlds do not differ in that one is reality and the other not, but in the nature of the reality which each world expresses.

Psalmists, seers, and prophets join with nature in voicing God's mysterious presence for those who could not otherwise penetrate the mystery of it. There is ever with us the problem of finding God in nature and human history without falling into the pit of pantheism and losing the personality of God. God is in the world without and the soul within, blessing them without being absorbed in them.

COMPOSER: For comments on the composer, Herbert S. Oakeley, see Hymn 46.

TUNE: For comments on the tune, "Abends," see Hymn 46.

---

102 HYMN: Lord, Thou Hast Searched Me, and Dost Know
TUNE: Soldau

Source: *"The Psalter Hymnal"*   Source: *"Wittenberg Gesangbuch"*

SOURCE: The source is "The Psalter Hymnal," 1927, the Hymnal of the United Presbyterian Church. For comments on American hymnody, see the article, "Church Hymns in Great Britain and America," under "Original Sources," page xvii.

God the Father

HYMN: This hymn, from "The Psalter Hymnal," is a modern version of Psalm 139, covering only the first twelve of the twenty-four verses of the psalm. It is a rich statement of the omnipresence and omniscience of God. Here the all-knowing attribute of God is taken as a ground for gratitude and praise. When some one tried to comfort a distressed man with the assurance that God knew all, he replied, "All the worse; if God knows me even as well as I know myself, that adds to the distress of the hour." But when it can be added that this omnipresence and omniscience is that of a loving Father, as our Lord assures us, then we find peace again. Stanza 3 of the hymn asks the question, "Whither can we flee from God?" Neither heaven nor Sheol nor the farthest boundary of the sea is a place of escape from God. This is a rhetorical question; the author of the hymn does not want to escape from God, but only to come near to him, and his comforting word is that one's path can never run so far afield that it may outrun God.

SOURCE: The source is the "Wittenberg Gesangbuch."

ARRANGER: Johann Walther has the distinction of having been an intimate friend of Martin Luther. He assisted the great reformer in making provision for the musical ministries of the Church and in that capacity became the editor of the first Lutheran choral book, "Geystliche Gesangk Buchleyn," which was published at Wittenberg in 1524. This volume contained thirty-two hymns; twenty-four by Luther, and five of Latin origin. Most of the music was arranged by Walther.

He was born at Gotha, near Cola, in Thuringia, in 1496. His musical talents developed early and in the course of time brought to him eminence. Among the positions he held are the following: *Kappellmeister* to the elector of Saxony, in 1526; singing master of the music school at Torgau, in 1534; organizer and leader of a choir for the Elector Moritz, in 1548, where he remained until 1554. From there he returned with a pension to Torgau, where he resided until his death, April 24, 1570. His musical compositions were of a high order and were intended for the use of the choir and not the congregation. Notable is his Passion music, which was based on the Gospels of Matthew and John. Walther was also a hymn writer of distinction.

TUNE: "Soldau" is of pre-Reformation origin. It was arranged by Walther and appeared in "Geystliche Gesangk Buchleyn," Wittenberg, 1524. The version used in "The Hymnal" appeared in Dibdin's "Standard Psalm Tune Book," in 1851. The tune is virile and straightforward and should be sung in exact time and with full and sustained tones.

103 HYMN: God Moves in a Mysterious Way
TUNE: Dundee

Author: *William Cowper*   Source: *"Scottish Psalter"*

AUTHOR: The place of William Cowper in literature is secure. He is spoken of as "the greatest English poet of his age." He was only incidentally a religious poet and hymn writer. This is the first of five of his hymns in this Hymnal.

He was born in Berkhampstead, England, November 26, 1731, and died on April 25, 1800, after a life in which sadness and joy were strangely mingled. He was a man of unstable, nervous temperament. From time to time he came under the influence of various friends, notably Rev. John Newton, rector at Olney, three of whose excellent hymns and three responses are in this book. Newton was a worker of prodigious energy who could not measure others except by himself, and when he invited Cowper to collaborate with him, Cowper broke. In intervals of mental normality and creative quiet Cowper translated an edition of "Homer" and produced "The Task," his greatest poem, and several minor but meritorious hymns and poems. Two women, Lady Austen, who encouraged him to write "The Task," and his cousin, Lady Hesketh, gave him great encouragement in his writing.

HYMN: It is frequently said that this hymn was written after an attempt at suicide that was mysteriously defeated. Many modern hymnologists do not agree. However, Dr. Marshall Broomhall, former editorial secretary of the China Inland Mission, writing from Berkhampstead, believes this to be the accurate story: Cowper's mania included a belief that God had decreed his suicide. He drove to the Thames for the purpose of taking his own life, but found the water low and a porter seated on some goods, as if intended to hinder Cowper's casting himself into the river. So much hindrance broke the spell of his mania and he ordered the cab to return to his lodgings. Immediately he wrote this hymn.

SOURCE: For comments on the source, the "Scottish Psalter," 1615, see "The Psalters in Early Presbyterian Worship," under "Original Sources," page xv.

TUNE: For comments on the tune, "Dundee," see Hymn 98.

God the Father

104

HYMN: Guide Me, O Thou Great Jehovah
FIRST TUNE: Dismissal

Author: *Rev. William Williams*   Composer: *William L. Viner*

AUTHOR: The chief hymn writer of Wales, William Williams, was born in 1717 and died January 11, 1791. The son of a farmer, he intended to enter the medical profession. On hearing a certain powerful sermon, however, he was so moved that he decided to enter the ministry. He appeared for admission to the priesthood in the Anglican Church but was declined because of his evangelical views. He knew that his call was from God, whatever men said, and he became a flaming evangelist. In the progress of his ministry, his itinerations averaged three thousand miles a year for fifty years. He knew the power of sacred song in reaching the hearts of men and wrote eight hundred Welsh hymns and more than a hundred in English. Several hands have retouched parts of this hymn, but its substance is his own.

TRANSLATORS: The translator of stanza 1 was Peter Williams, who was an eloquent preacher in the Methodist movement in Wales, where the Williams family is prominent to this day for its contribution to hymnological literature. He was converted under the preaching of George Whitefield, by whose inspiring leadership he was influenced to enter the ministry. His preaching was too fervent in the Established Church, so that he cast in his lot with the Methodists. Little is known of him as a writer of hymns, and apart from his association with "Guide Me, O Thou Great Jehovah" his name does not appear elsewhere in "The Hymnal." He was born at Laugharne, Carmarthenshire, in 1722, and died at Carmarthen in 1796.

For comments on the translator of stanzas 2 and 3, William Williams, see "Author."

HYMN: The entire hymn is based on the wilderness journey toward Canaan. The manna becomes the "bread of heaven," the smitten rock becomes "the crystal fountain," the fire and cloudy pillar are clearly understood, while crossing Jordan at the last as an illustration of death and the Land of Canaan as heaven have become common usage. The habit of the Israelites of recounting their history appears in certain psalms, such as Psalms 104 to 106, and Christian believers have adopted that history as their own. In this hymn a general experience of a whole people is taken over and made purely personal. Only one "pilgrim" appears in the hymn, for no plural pronouns are used. If the pronouns were changed the hymn would lose much, for it would lose the intimacy of its personal meaning. There are parts of the life pilgrimage which must be taken alone, and we ought to face that fact.

Handbook to The Hymnal

COMPOSER (First Tune): William L. Viner (1790–1867) was born in Bath, England, where for eighteen years he was organist of St. Michael's Church. Later, in 1825, he moved to Cornwall and from there migrated to America, in 1859, where he spent the remainder of his life and where he died at Westfield, Massachusetts. He wrote some music in other forms, but is best known by his psalm and hymn tunes, one of the most notable collections of which is "One Hundred Psalm and Hymn Tunes in Score," published in 1838. It is interesting to know that Viner came under the influence of England's greatest hymn writer, Charles Wesley.

TUNE (First): "Dismissal," apparently, was written before Viner left England, though it bears the quality of some of the American tunes of the same age, and has been a favorite in this country for many years. The tune has a singable melody, undisturbing harmony, and a sufficiently varied rhythmic pattern. When it is sung with firmness it well carries out the "pilgrim" idea and should maintain a steady course, due and accurate regard being had for the three white notes at the cadences.

SECOND TUNE: Cwm Rhondda

Source: *Welsh Hymn Melody*

SOURCE (Second Tune): For comments on the source, a Welsh hymn melody, see the article, "Welsh Hymnody," under "Original Sources," page xxii.

ARRANGER (Second Tune): John Hughes was born at Dowlais Wales, in 1873. He was the eldest son of Mr. and Mrs. Evan Hughes, who removed from Dowlais to Llantwit Fardre in 1874. He started work as a door boy at Glyn Colliery when he was twelve years of age. Later he served as clerk and subsequently as an official in the traffic department of the Great Western Colliery Company. In 1905 he married Hannah Maria David, daughter of Mr. and Mrs. Caradoc David. Music was a natural gift with him and he used it in the service of the Church. Mr. Hughes was a lifelong member of Salem Baptist Church, in Llantwit Fardre, in which he succeeded his father as deacon and precentor, positions which he held until his death, May 14, 1932. In addition to tunes, he wrote anthems and Sunday School marches. He died at "Tregath," Tonteg, Llantwit Fardre, in 1932.

TUNE (Second): "Cwm Rhondda," originally known as "Rhondda," was composed in 1907 for the anniversary services at Capel Rhondda, Pontypridd. The name of the tune is that of the principal, coal town in Glamorganshire. As a setting for "Guide Me, O Thou Great Jehovah," "Cwm Rhondda" is a favorite among Welsh people.

God the Father

105
    HYMN: If Thou But Suffer God to Guide Thee
    TUNE: Neumark

Author: *Georg Neumark*   Composer: *Georg Neumark*

AUTHOR: As his name suggests, Georg Neumark was a German. He was born March 16, 1621, and died July 18, 1681. As a young man he set out for Königsberg to attend the university. On the way he was robbed of all his possessions except his prayer book and a small amount of money. This made university attendance at that time impossible and brought on a period of extreme poverty. He had little food, poor clothing, indifferent shelter. Quite unexpectedly at the very darkest hour he received an appointment as a tutor in a judge's family. It cleared his way so fully that he said, "On that very day I composed to the honor of my beloved Lord" this hymn, adding that he "had certainly cause enough to thank the divine compassion for such unlooked-for grace" shown to him. In 1681 Neumark became blind. Critical observers consider that the hymns he wrote during his most trying experiences are superior to those which came out of more favored days.

TRANSLATOR: For comments on the translator, Catherine Winkworth, see Hymn 6.

HYMN: Neumark gives Ps. 55:22 as the text for this hymn. The second stanza opens with a reference to Ps. 46:10 and closes with reference to Matt. 6:32b. Notice how carefully the hymn avoids the extreme of trust that becomes fatalistic weakness. We must do our part faithfully and must "swerve not from His ways." The hymn has been a favorite in more than one preparatory school where the sheer common sense of it has commanded acceptance of its challenge.

COMPOSER: For comments on the composer, Georg Neumark, see "Author."

TUNE: "Neumark" is from "Fortgepflanzter Musikalisch-Poetischer Lustwald," Jena, 1657, in which it is set to one of Neumark's hymns. The tune is an imposing one and has various versions. It appears in Mendelssohn's oratorio, "St. Paul," a version of which is used in "The Church Hymnary." The one used in "The Hymnal" is from "The Common Service Book" of the United Lutheran Church and is an arrangement by Jeremiah F. Ohl, D.D. The hymn should be sung in exact time, confidently, and not too fast. The dominant mood of the music is hopeful and, therefore, should be rendered with confidence and strength.

106   HYMN: He Leadeth Me: O Blessèd Thought
TUNE: He Leadeth Me

Author: *Rev. Joseph H. Gilmore*   Composer: *William B. Bradbury*

AUTHOR: Joseph H. Gilmore (1834–1918), a Baptist minister, preached in the First Baptist Church, Philadelphia, on March 26, 1862, on the Twenty-third Psalm and wrote this hymn immediately afterwards. His wife sent it to a Baptist paper, whence it was copied into a hymnal. The United Gas Improvement Company of Philadelphia, which erected its building on the site of this church, has placed a tablet on its wall, containing the first line of the hymn.

HYMN: This is another hymn whose initial suggestion is clearly from the Twenty-third Psalm, though it takes material freely from other parts of Scripture. There is a way of looking at the Christian life as one in which the gracious, kindly arms of God bear us up, as a life of rest and peace and security. The other more common way is the one described here: life as following through all sorts of experiences—hardship, ease, joy, pain—but always with a sense of Some One on ahead who knows the way and will stretch out a helping, guiding hand at critical places.

COMPOSER: William Batchelder Bradbury was a pupil of Dr. Lowell Mason and of G. J. Webb. He was one of the three men, the others being George F. Root and Lowell Mason, who made a distinct contribution to early church music. Bradbury was born in Maine in 1816. In 1830 he moved to Boston, where he began the study of the organ, and where, by 1840, he had gained recognition as an organist, choirmaster, and composer. For a number of years Bradbury lived in New York City, until he went to Europe in 1847. From his return to America, in 1849, until 1854 he devoted his time to teaching and composing and to the organization and conducting of music festivals, which were then very popular. Bradbury edited over fifty collections of music, in all of which are many of his own compositions. He was editor of The New York Musical Review and collected a large and valuable musical library. He died in 1868.

TUNE: The tune, "He Leadeth Me," is too well known and too well liked to need comment. In singing it due attention should be paid to the "holds" at the ends of lines 2, 3, and 4 of the stanzas, and of lines 2 and 4 of the refrain. They are logically placed and, while they should be observed, should not interrupt the progression of the tune.

God the Father

HYMN: Still, Still with Thee, When Purple
Morning Breaketh

TUNE: Consolation

Author: *Harriet Beecher Stowe*   Composer: *Felix Mendelssohn*

AUTHOR: Of the 323 writers definitely named in The Hymnal, 53 are women, several of whom contribute more than one hymn. Though Mrs. Stowe wrote a considerable number of hymns once in common use, this is her only hymn in this collection. She was the seventh child of Dr. Lyman Beecher, notable in his period for his eloquence and his vigor in preaching a sound orthodoxy, from which he afterwards felt that his son, Henry Ward Beecher, somewhat departed. Harriet's birth occurred on June 14, 1811, in Litchfield, Connecticut, where her father was pastor. Later her father became president of the Lane (Presbyterian) Theological Seminary, at Cincinnati, Ohio, and it was there that Harriet spent her girlhood and developed her strong feeling regarding slavery. She married Calvin Ellis Stowe, a professor in the seminary, and went with him to a new appointment at Bowdoin College, Maine, in 1850, where she wrote "Uncle Tom's Cabin," in 1852. Her husband subsequently became a professor at Andover Theological Seminary, and retired in 1863 to Hartford, Connecticut, where Mrs. Stowe died on July 1, 1896.

HYMN: The idea underlying this hymn comes from Ps. 139:18: "When I awake, I am still with thee." This verse is also the theme of Hymn 100. This hymn is personal throughout. It is an early-morning hymn. Effort is made to reproduce the glad surprise of waking after a dark night to find that the Light of life has not failed.

COMPOSER: For comments on the composer, Felix Mendelssohn, see Hymn 11.

TUNE: Among the great mass of Mendelssohn's compositions none perhaps are more popular than the piano collection of forty-eight pieces known as "Songs Without Words." In style these compositions range through many forms and many degrees of difficulty, yet each has a distinctive lyric quality. "Consolation" appears as number 9 of this collection. It is in the key of E major, and in a rhythmic pattern which has been slightly modified to qualify it more satisfactorily as a hymn tune. Its success as a hymn tune depends, to a large extent, upon clearly defined rhythm and a steady pace which does not encourage dragging, the besetting fault in the rendition of this tune.

Jesus Christ the Lord

His Advent

*

108 HYMN: O Come, O Come, Emmanuel
TUNE: Veni Emmanuel

Translator: *Rev. John M. Neale*   Source: *Ancient Plain Song*

TRANSLATOR: For comments on the translator, John M. Neale see Hymn 44.

HYMN: As early as the ninth century the singing and ritualistic services of Gregory entirely dominated the Church. This Latin hymn was used as a short antiphon to be sung at vesper services. The story of the Babylonian Exile has left a deep impression upon the imagination of the Christian Church, and here, as elsewhere, it has become a symbol of the exile of believers from the presence of God. Sin and sorrow, failure and suffering, have seemed to put great distance between God and his people, and the cry is for a Redeemer who will ransom his captive people and restore them to the status of children. The name "Emmanuel" is found in only one passage in the New Testament, Matt. 1:23, which in turn is a quotation from Isa. 7:14. It appears also in Isa. 8:8. The word literally means, "God with us." This hymn implies that the Advent season is a time of great joy, for it is a time when God draws near to deliver men from bondage. The refrain, beginning "Rejoice! Rejoice!" is an echo of Zech. 9:9. The title "Dayspring" is used once in the New Testament in Luke 1:78. The "Key of David" appears in Rev. 3:7. Its use here refers to the Christ who opens doors that lead to God, and to life eternal. This hymn is a stately song of gladness because the Promised One is coming.

SOURCE: The source of the tune is a thirteenth-century plain song.

TUNE: "Veni Emmanuel" is one of the rich "heritage tunes" which has been too late in finding its way into Protestant hymn books. It has a distinctive ecclesiastical flavor and is melodic rather than harmonic, having a melody which flows blithely in the joyfully expectant mood of the words. The season of Advent in the church year is a time for the serious consideration of the coming of Christ in all its aspects.

Jesus Christ the Lord

"Veni Emmanuel" is written in the first Gregorian mode, and this version is based on an adaptation by Thomas Helmore, in 1854, of a version in a French missal. The harmony is largely in the normal minor mode, which gives it a quaint and distinctive flavor. It should be sung with spirit and can be sung throughout in unison. It is also effective with men's voices singing in unison, the refrain being sung by all voices in harmony. This hymn also lends itself to interesting effects in antiphonal singing.

---

109 HYMN: Watchman, Tell Us of the Night
        TUNE: St. George's, Windsor

Author: *John Bowring*   Composer: *George J. Elvey*

AUTHOR: For comments on the author, John Bowring, see Hymn 80.

HYMN: The author told Dr. A. P. Happer in China that the first time he heard this hymn used was in 1834 or 1835, when he attended a prayer meeting of American missionaries in Asiatic Turkey and heard it sung by them. The hymn repeats the question of Isa. 21:11, "Watchman, what of the night?" The figure is that of a traveler who cries out to the watchman standing guard through the darkness of the night. It is a question when darkness is oppressive, when impatient ones wait for the dawn and cry, "How long?" How long the desolation of darkness? The star that shines over Bethlehem belongs to the ages to come. Its light will grow until the dawn of the perfect day.

COMPOSER: Sir George J. Elvey, Mus.D., was born in Canterbury, England, in 1816, and died in 1893. He was baptized in the Presbyterian Chapel in Canterbury and was educated in the Canterbury Cathedral Choir School. In 1838 he graduated from Oxford. From 1835 to 1882 he was organist and choirmaster of St. George's Chapel, Windsor, for which the tune is named, and had charge of the music for many important events connected with the royal house. Elvey was knighted in 1871. He was buried outside the west front of St. George's Chapel. Most of his compositions are for the Church and include many anthems.

TUNE: It would be natural to conjecture that this tune, "St. George's, Windsor," was written for "Come, Ye Thankful People, Come," by Henry Alford, dean of Canterbury, both because Elvey had grown up in the Cathedral Choir School there and because of the long association of the tune with this hymn. This may be true, though there seems to be no direct evidence. It is a forceful tune, which progresses to a splendid climax in the last line and moves strongly throughout. It lends itself readily to antiphonal singing.

I IO HYMN: Hark, What a Sound, and Too Divine for Hearing
TUNE: Welwyn

Author: *Frederick William Henry Myers* Composer: *Alfred Scott-Gatty*

AUTHOR: Frederick William Henry Myers was born in Keswick, Cumberland County, England, on February 6, 1843. He was educated at Cheltenham School. At 17 he entered Trinity College, Cambridge, where five years later he became classical lecturer. He soon discontinued his teaching, but made his permanent residence in Cambridge in 1872, when he became a school inspector under the education department. His spiritual life reached its peak in a profound experience which resulted in his great poem, "St. Paul," from which this hymn is taken. Yet afterwards he said that this was merely a shallow, emotional conversion to Christianity. Referring to his religious experience of that period, he said: "That faith looks to me now like a mistaken short cut in the course of a toilsome way. Disillusion came from increased knowledge of history and science. . . . In those days when my own hope ran lowest, my zeal for other men ran lowest too. . . . My history has been that of a soul struggling into the conviction of its own existence." He accepted the fact of immortality and in 1882 helped to found the Society of Psychical Research, the work for which he is best known.

HYMN: The last three stanzas of this hymn are taken from the author's great poem, "St. Paul." Above the waiting, silent earth there breaks a sound almost too good to be true. The writer's own desolate longing is voiced in the third stanza. The Christ is the hope of every desolate heart, the answer to every question, the fulfillment of all our desires. He is the end of life, that which gives all life meaning and purpose, and that which we really seek in all our blind striving.

COMPOSER: Alfred Scott-Gatty, K.C.V.O. (1847–1918), was the son of the subdean of York Cathedral and, by royal license, he assumed as an additional surname his mother's name of Scott. His mother was the author of "Parables from Nature." His chief concern in life seemed to be an interest in heraldry, in which connection he held many important offices. He was the author of much vocal music for children and of hundreds of popular songs.

Jesus Christ the Lord

TUNE: The tune, "Welwyn," by the distinguished Sir Alfred Scott-Gatty, is most promising. It is taken from the "Arundel Hymns," published in England in 1902. For depth of feeling, breadth of sentiment, and musical grandeur, it is difficult to equal. The composer was subdean of York Cathedral, and this tune reflects his surroundings. The hymn may be sung in unison, but in that event should be supported by full organ. Published in "The Church Hymnary" in England in 1927, "Welwyn" has won recognition throughout the Church.

III   HYMN: Hail to the Lord's Anointed
            TUNE: Tours

Author: *James Montgomery*   Composer: *Berthold Tours*

AUTHOR: For comments on the author, James Montgomery, see Hymn 11.

HYMN: This hymn has always been used as a missionary hymn. It was first sung at a Moravian convocation on Christmas Day, 1821, possibly at Fulneck, Yorkshire, a Moravian settlement of which Montgomery was then a member. In the next month the manuscript was sent to Mr. George Bennett, who was making a mission tour of the South Sea. Later, in 1822, it appeared in Montgomery's book, "Songs of Zion." In Dr. Julian's "A Dictionary of Hymnology," this paraphrase of Psalm 72 has been called the finest of all Montgomery's renderings of the psalms. It has been widely used and translated into several languages. It deals with the purpose of the Messiah, which Jesus himself defined in terms of meeting human need. The author's own passion for the underprivileged appears in this hymn of promise for the coming Messiah is to reign in every area of human experience.

COMPOSER: Berthold Tours (1838–1897) was born in Rotterdam' The Netherlands. His early lessons in organ-playing were under the guidance of his father, who was organist of the St. Lawrence Church in his native city. He later studied in Brussels and Leipzig, and traveled for two years in Russia. In 1861 he took up residence in London where, in 1878, he became adviser and editor for Novello & Co., the well-known music publishers. His compositions are numerous, and his best work is to be found in his hymn tunes, anthems, and services.

TUNE: "Tours," used three times in "The Hymnal," bears the name of its composer, and is an example of the splendid type of tune which evolved in England and was imitated by men of other nations who came under the influence of English church music (Gounod, for example), as well as being recognized by American composers as a pattern worthy of consideration. Note the upward trend of the melody line in each of the phrases and the interesting, rhythmic variety.

I I2   HYMN: Let All Mortal Flesh Keep Silence
          TUNE: Picardy

Source: *"Liturgy of St. James"*   Source: *French Traditional Carol*

SOURCE: This hymn is taken from what is known as the "Prayer of the Cherubic Hymn," a portion of the "Liturgy of St. James."

TRANSLATORS: This old Latin liturgic poem was rendered into prose in 1868 by Dr. Neale, one of the most famous of Latin translators. On eleven occasions Dr. Neale gained the Seatonian prize for poetry. All his life he struggled with poverty, and with sacrifice devoted the proceeds of his writing to various institutions that he founded. One hundred and six of his hymns were composed for children and for the sick.

The hymn was translated into English poetry by Rev. Gerard Moultrie and appeared in four stanzas in his book, "Lyra Eucharistica," in 1864. Moultrie was born in 1829. His translation and metrical rendering of the magnificent Midnight Hymn of the Greek Church, "Behold, the Bridegroom Cometh," is considered a notable achievement.

HYMN: Rising out of the reverence and spiritual joy of an unknown period of the Church, this hymn lifts the heart with a most exalted vocabulary of adoration. Its four stanzas call the worshiper to a state of spiritual-mindedness, portray the amazing paradoxes of the incarnation, affirm the glory, honor, and victory of the Christ-child, and fill the whole Advent scene with the apocalyptic majesty of seraphs shouting their alleluias.

SOURCE: The tune was originally an old French carol.

TUNE: "Picardy" seems to have appeared first in its present form in "The English Hymnal" of 1906, and, no doubt largely from its folk-song quality, soon found its way into the hymnals of Britain, appearing in America in the Hymnal of the Protestant Episcopal Church, in the edition of 1916. It is recognized as being a carol, probably of the seventeenth century, and, in Tiersot's "Mélodies," printed in Paris in

Jesus Christ the Lord

1887, bears the title "Romancero." A comparison of "Picardy" with modern tunes offers many points of interest, the first being its minor mode. The words of the hymn express reverence and joyful mystery as due and pertaining to "Christ our God," and the solemn minor strains reflect this mood. An effective rendering would be to begin this hymn quietly, and gradually to build a climax through the third stanza to the close of the hymn by a gradual crescendo and increasingly defined rhythm, closing with the triumphal ascription, "Alleluia, Lord Most High!" It lends itself also to "passive participation"; that is, having the congregation follow the words silently while the choir sings a thoughtful interpretation.

----

113   HYMN: Come, Thou Long-Expected Jesus
            FIRST TUNE: Hyfrydol

Author: *Rev. Charles Wesley*   Composer: *Rowland Hugh Prichard*

AUTHOR: For comments on the author, Charles Wesley, see Hymn 26.

HYMN: This hymn first appeared in 1744, in "Hymns for the Nativity of Our Lord." Later it was published in one of several tracts which bore the name "Festival Hymns." It was not included in the "Wesleyan Hymn Book" until the revised edition of 1875. Since then it has been found in great numbers of hymn books in England and America, especially those of the Church of England. It is one of the most dignified, yet stirring, of the Advent hymns. Its simple words contain the essence of the gospel, the fulfillment of Israel's hope, the source of her strength, and the consolation for her soul. Jesus is the "Hope of all the earth," the answer to human longing, the "dear Desire of every nation." The Child who is born is to reign as King; yet his reign is not the reign of outward force, but the compulsion of an eternal Spirit.

COMPOSER (First Tune): Rowland Hugh Prichard (1811–1887) was born near Bala, in Holywell, Wales, where he spent most of his life. In 1880 he moved to Holywell Mill, where he became the assistant to a loom tender in a flannel factory. He was an earnest Christian, gifted with a good voice and with ability to lead others in singing. He wrote many tunes, which appeared from time to time in Welsh periodicals. In 1844 he published "The Singer's Friend," a collection made up for the most part of his own tunes. Later he published a book of songs and hymns for children.

TUNE (First): "Hyfrydol" was written before Prichard was twenty years old. In keeping with the spirit of the words, it sings joyously in unison as well as in harmony, and, as it becomes better known, will encourage congregational participation.

SECOND TUNE: Stuttgart

Source: *"Psalmodia Sacra"*

SOURCE (Second Tune): The source of this tune is "Psalmodia Sacra," 1715.

ARRANGER (Second Tune): Christian Friedrich Witt (1660–1716) was born in Altenburg and died in Gotha, Germany. He was court organist and composed a number of tunes which appeared in his book, "Psalmodia Sacra," published in Gotha in 1715. Though little information regarding Witt is available, it is found that he lived at a period of German hymnology when the Pietistic, the Moravian, and the German Reformed Churches were producing hymns equal to the best in the Lutheran Church of the same period. From the source indicated—"Psalmodia Sacra"—it might be inferred that "Stuttgart" was originally written as a psalm tune and later, because of its merit, was used for "man-made" hymns.

TUNE (Second): "Stuttgart" is one of the hymn tunes in the book "Psalmodia Sacra," where it is set to the hymn, "Sollt Es Gleich Bisweilen Scheinen." It is a straightforward, singable tune of simple rhythmic pattern, made familiar by its use with the same words in the two preceding editions of "The Hymnal." Unlike some of the older tunes, it provides ample movement in the parts other than the soprano. It is a stately tune for one of four lines, though perhaps it lacks the warmth of "Hyfrydol."

---

114 HYMN: Lift Up Your Heads, Ye Mighty Gates
TUNE: Truro

Author: *Rev. Georg Weissel*   Source: *"Psalmodia Evangelica"*

AUTHOR: Georg Weissel, born at Domnau, near Königsberg, in 1590, was the son of Johann Weissel, a judge and afterwards burgomaster of the town. He studied at the University of Königsberg between 1608 and 1611, and later for short periods at Wittenberg, Leipzig, Jena, Strasbourg, Basel, and Maribor. In 1614, he was appointed rector of the school at Friedland, near Domnau, but resigned after three years to resume his studies in theology at Königsberg. In 1623 he became

Jesus Christ the Lord

pastor of the newly erected Altrossgart Church in Königsberg, where he remained until his death on August 1, 1635. He was the author of about twenty hymns, all "good in style, moderate in length, and varied in meter."

TRANSLATOR: For comments on the translator, Catherine Winkworth, see Hymn 6.

HYMN: This is one of the finest of German Advent hymns. It was first published in the "Preussische Fest-Lieder." Since its translation by Catherine Winkworth in 1855, it has been widely used in English-speaking lands. The imagery of Psalm 24 is sublime. It is the picture of the gates of the city whose towers are lifted high in pride and whose portals are opened wide with joy. So at Christmas time the earthly receives the heavenly and finds its true meaning. All nature sings in praise of Him for whom nature was created. Humanity reaches its perfect flower in him who is the perfect Man. The sublime experience of motherhood is here raised to its greatest height. Here the little Child is adored and is the Instrument through which God comes into the life of men.

SOURCE: This tune is found in Thomas Williams' collection, "Psalmodia Evangelica." It has sometimes been ascribed, but without sufficient evidence, to Dr. Charles Burney (1726–1814), an English organist, composer, and author of the four-volume book, "General History of Music."

TUNE: "Truro" appeared in a two-volume edition of "Psalmodia Evangelica," published in 1789 and edited by Thomas Williams, where it is written for three voices. In this collection Dr. Burney's name is attached to the tunes he is known to have written, but "Truro" bears no composer's name. This lack of definite information, however, does not lessen the virility of this excellent tune, which, in its associations with many different hymns, has been chosen invariably for a hymn of praise, aspiration, and exaltation.

---

115   HYMN: Rejoice, Rejoice, Believers
       TUNE: Lancashire

Author: *Laurentius Laurenti*   Composer: *Henry Smart*

AUTHOR: Laurentius Laurenti was born at Husum, in Schleswig, Germany, June 8, 1660, the son of Herr Laurenti, a burgess. At the age of twenty-one he entered the University of Rostock. A

131

Handbook to The Hymnal

year and a half later he went to Kiel to study music. In 1684 he was appointed cantor and director of music at the cathedral church in Bremen. He died there on May 29, 1722. Laurenti was the product of the Pietistic school and was one of their best hymn writers. Dr. Julian's "A Dictionary of Hymnology" says of his hymns, "They are of noble simplicity; are Scriptural, fervent, and often of genuine poetical worth."

TRANSLATOR: Sarah B. Findlater, born on November 26, 1823, was the daughter of James Borthwick, manager of the North British Insurance Office in Edinburgh. She married Rev. Eric John Findlater, of Lochearnhead, Perthshire. In company with her sister Jane she translated many hymns from the German. These translations are a joint work and it is impossible to set the name of one or the other to most of the hymns. They have attained a general acceptance in hymnals, second only to the translations of Miss Winkworth. Since the middle of the last century scarcely a hymnal has appeared in England or America that has not contained some of these translations.

HYMN: Advent hymns are adaptable to any season of the year as hymns of hope and anticipation. This hymn is inspired by the parable of the Wise and Foolish Virgins. It seeks to meet the need for that spiritual readiness or sensitivity that precedes all genuine and worthy worship, and does so without suppressing in any way the note of joy and expectancy.

COMPOSER: For comments on the composer, Henry Smart, see Hymn 61.

TUNE: "Lancashire" was composed about 1836 for the hymn "From Greenland's Icy Mountains," to be used at a missionary meeting at Blackburn, England. In a former edition of "The Church Hymnary," the authorized hymnal of the Church of Scotland, the tune, used for the well-known Easter hymn, "The Day of Resurrection," is preceded by a series of three Alleluias, set to music by Sir John Stainer. This tune may be classified as one of thrilling gladness because of its steady swing, almost entire absence of dotted notes, similarity of melody line in many of its phrases, and strong sense of climax, ending in the whole last line of the music.

Jesus Christ the Lord

His Birth

*

116   HYMN: O Come, All Ye Faithful
          TUNE: Adeste Fideles

Source: *Anonymous*   Source: *J. F. Wade's "Cantus Diversi"*

SOURCE: This hymn has been attributed to Saint Bonaventura, who lived in the thirteenth century; but it is found in no edition of his works. It is more probably a hymn of the seventeenth or of the eighteenth century, composed in Latin by a French or a German author.

TRANSLATOR: Rev. Frederick Oakeley, the youngest son of Sir Charles Oakeley, at one time governor of Madras, was born at Shrewsbury, September 5, 1802. He was educated at Christ Church, Oxford, where he received the degree of A.B. in 1824. In 1827 he was elected a Fellow of Balliol. He took holy orders in 1832. In 1845 he resigned all his appointments in the Church of England and was received into the communion of the Roman Catholic Church. Later he became canon of the procathedral in the Roman Catholic Church district of Westminster. He died January 29, 1880.

HYMN: The origin of this great Christmas hymn is obscure. It is known that it was sung as early as 1797. Oakeley's translation is the most popular. It appeared in Murray's "Hymnal" in 1852. This is a great Christian hymn because it deals with the center of the Christian message—the incarnation. God has clothed himself with human flesh and has opened unto man the secret of the Father's heart. He has provided a way of reconciliation to God and quieted the fears of men by the promise of his own glorious triumph. Here this incarnation is not primarily the subject of theological argument but a theme to be sung in glorious triumph. It is one of the most popular Christmas hymns. Its imagery is dignified, yet jubilant, calling upon the choirs of angels to echo their praises through the high arches of heaven.

SOURCE: Few tunes have gained such universal popularity as has "Adeste Fideles," and few have given such slender reward to seekers after definite authorship. It was found in manuscript long before it appeared in print and is known to have had wide use among Roman Catholics early in the eighteenth century, especially in the private chapels of the great families. It was the custom of these families to encourage priests with musical ability to copy out and carry to other chapels suitable music for use in the various services. One John

Wade, in 1751, a pensioner in the household of Nicholas King in Lancashire, copied three melodies: "Adeste Fideles" (called here "In Nativitate Domini Hymnus"), "Stabat Mater," and "Tantum Ergo," along with several others, in a collection which he called "Cantus Diversi." The manuscript volume is preserved in the library of Stonyhurst College, Lancashire, and is dated 1751. The tune appeared in print in 1782 in a Catholic collection called "An Essay on the Church Plain Chant." Samuel Webbe, Senior, is believed to have been the editor of the part of this book in which the tune appears without the composer's name.

TUNE: An interesting line of investigation suggests itself from the title, "Portuguese Hymn," by which this tune is sometimes designated. It is, in some of the early books, credited to Portogallo. Marcos Antonio Portogallo (1762–1830) was a Portuguese operatic composer. In addition to his voluminous operatic compositions he also wrote much church music. Previous to his settling in Brazil with his brother, Simão, also a church composer, he had spent much time in Spain, Italy, and Portugal. It is possible that this melody may have been taken from some of his numerous works and modified to suit the requirements of church music, thus finding its way into the Portuguese Chapel in London. It is known that, about 1785, after he had heard it in the Portuguese Chapel, the duke of Leeds introduced the tune at the "antient concerts," of which he seems to have been the patron, thinking it "antient" because it was a striking melody, new to him, and because the composer was unknown. Vincent Novello, then organist of the Portuguese Chapel, assigned the tune to John Reading, with the date 1680, but it has never been found in the works of either of the two composers of this name. To Vincent Novello, however, does belong the credit for the splendid arrangement in which this tune has come down to the present time.

"Adeste Fideles" belongs, first of all, by long association to the Christmas hymn in Latin, the first two words of which are used for the name of the tune, and to this same hymn in English translation. By second choice, it belongs to "How Firm a Foundation," and it is much to be deplored that these two sacred associations of the tune should be weakened by its use with too many other hymns of widely different content.

---

117 HYMN: Hark! the Herald Angels Sing
TUNE: Mendelssohn

Author: *Rev. Charles Wesley*   Composer: *Felix Mendelssohn*

AUTHOR: For comments on the author, Charles Wesley, see Hymn 26.

Jesus Christ the Lord

HYMN: This was the only hymn by Charles Wesley to be included in the Church of England's "Book of Common Prayer." It was written and first published in 1739. This hymn can best be appreciated if one hears it sung as a carol in the darkness of the night under the open sky, when the hard lines of daylight are obscured and the sensible objects are lost to sight, when the mystery of the night stirs the imagination, and when we can take our place with the humble shepherds of Bethlehem to whom the wondrous news first was revealed. The beautiful imagery deals with the incarnation, the regeneration, and the glorious hope of things to come. When we gather all the wealth of the meaning of Jesus to men into the simplicity of the Christmas story, its sacred beauty can be celebrated only by the song of angels.

COMPOSER: For comments on the composer, Felix Mendelssohn, see Hymn 11.

ARRANGER: William H. Cummings was born at Sidbury, Devon, in 1831. He served as choir boy at St. Paul's Cathedral. At sixteen he sang among the altos at the first of four performances of "Elijah" at Exeter Hall, April 16, 1847, under the direction of Mendelssohn. He was noted for his impressive rendering of the tenor solos in Bach's "St. Matthew Passion." For fourteen years he was principal of the Guildhall School of Music, resigning in 1910. He died in June, 1916.

TUNE: For comments on the tune, "Mendelssohn," see Hymn 11.

----

118   HYMN: Ah, Dearest Jesus, Holy Child
TUNE: Vom Himmel Hoch

Author: *Rev. Martin Luther*   Source: *"Geistliche Lieder"*

AUTHOR: Martin Luther was born in Eisleben, in 1483, the son of a peasant family. He was educated at Erfurt University, and grew up a devout Catholic. In 1505 he entered the Augustinian Convent at Erfurt as a monk, and was ordained to the priesthood in 1507. In 1508 he went to Wittenberg and became a lecturer at the university there. The fame of his lectures soon spread throughout Germany. Luther's break with the Catholic Church was slow. In 1517 he posted his famous Ninety-five Theses on the door of the church at Wittenberg, protesting against the sale of indulgences as the means of raising money to build St. Peter's Cathedral in Rome. These theses did not attack the practice of selling indulgences, but only the abuses connected with their sale. Throughout the year 1518 the controversy over the theses raged on. In August of that year Luther was cited to appear at Rome, but he refused to go. His break with the Catholic Church occurred during the Diet of Worms in 1521. He was asked to recant his heresies, but asked for time to consider. The next day he replied that he should not be asked to recant forthwith but was willing to be shown his errors from the Scriptures. He was rebuked for his arrogance. It was then that he uttered his famous words, appealing from the authority of the Church to the authority of the Scriptures—an appeal that marked the beginning of the Protestant Reformation.

Luther spent most of his life in Wittenberg. His greatest work was the translation of the Bible into the German language. During a brief visit to his birthplace at Eisleben, he died in 1546 at the age of 63. Luther wrote thirty-seven hymns, twenty-one of them in the year 1524. His best-known hymn is "A Mighty Fortress Is Our God." Luther composed several fine tunes. His Christmas hymns for children are among the tenderest and best loved in Christendom.

TRANSLATOR: For comments on the translator, Catherine Winkworth, see Hymn 6.

HYMN: In the simple, tender language of childhood this hymn calls upon the Child of Bethlehem to enter into the heart and to bring there the highest joy and peace. It is a hymn of childlike trust, yet worthy to be sung by adults who, to enter the Kingdom of heaven, must become as little children.

SOURCE: The tune came from the book "Geistliche Lieder."

TUNE: "Vom Himmel Hoch," the tune of this hymn, is taken from "Geistliche Lieder," published in Leipzig in 1539. It was composed in that year for the carol "From Heaven Above to Earth I Come," and is supposed to have been written by Martin Luther, the author of the words. It has come to be recognized as one of the fine tunes of the German choral type and was used with greatly enriched harmony by Bach in his "Christmas Oratorio" with the words here used, "Ah, Dearest Jesus, Holy Child," this being a portion of the original carol of fifteen stanzas. In the comparison with some of the more modern Christmas tunes, melodies like this show a deeply reverent dignity.

Jesus Christ the Lord

119

HYMN: All Praise to Thee, Eternal Lord
TUNE: Puer Nobis Nascitur

Author: *Rev. Martin Luther*   Composer: *Michael Praetorius*

AUTHOR: For comments on the author, Martin Luther, see Hymn 118.

HYMN: Many of Luther's hymns are translations of old Latin hymns. This hymn is a versification of a Latin sequence, variously ascribed to a ninth-century writer and to Gregory the Great in the sixth century. Dr. Julian's "A Dictionary of Hymnology" gives an early German form of the hymn, dated about 1370, but attributes the present form of the hymn, except the first stanza, to Luther. The hymn voices the paradoxes of Christmas: the eternal Lord clothed in the garb of flesh and blood, the little Child in whom the weary find rest, the lowly birth which enables men to rise from earth to heaven, the darksome night that makes us children of the light.

COMPOSER: Michael Praetorius (1571–1621) was born in Thuringia, Germany. After completing his education, soon after 1604 he become prior of a monastery. He was a serious student of music and began to write a complete encyclopedia of the art and practice of music, of which he finished three volumes. Among his compositions was "Musae Sioniae," a collection of vocal numbers in nine parts, most of which was sacred music.

HARMONIZER: George Ratcliffe Woodward, a clergyman of the English Church, has served in conspicuous parishes, among them St. Mark's Marylebone Road, London. He brought to his study of hymnology linguistic abilities of a high order and has made many translations from both the Latin and the German, many of which are included in his own collection, "Songs of Syon," published in 1904.

TUNE: "Puer Nobis Nascitur" is one of those tunes written for carols of mixed language, in this case part German and part English. (Note the traditional English "Boar's Head Carol," which is a mixture of Latin and English.) While essentially choral in type, it should be sung with a carol-like lilt, giving the shorter notes their full allotted time in order to avoid undue stress on the first notes of the following measure.

137

I20   HYMN: While Shepherds Watched Their Flocks by Night
       TUNE: Christmas

Author: *Nahum Tate*   Composer: *George Frederick Handel*

AUTHOR: In writing this hymn Nahum Tate worked independently of Nicholas Brady, his famous collaborator in the "New Version," a metrical arrangement of The Psalms, appearing in 1696. The son of a clergyman, he was born in Dublin in 1652. He wrote poetry with great facility, but as it was lacking in weight and worth it met with the scorn of Swift, Pope, and others of the classicists of the period. He won Dryden's good will and wrote a continuation of Dryden's poem "Absalom and Achitophel." He was made poet laureate in 1690 and royal historiographer in 1702. He wrote versions of "King Lear," "Richard II," and other Shakespearean plays. Tate and Brady's "New Version" displaced Sternhold and Hopkins' book and held its place for many years in the worship of the Church. Involved in debts, due to careless and dissolute habits, this man, whose lovely Christmas hymn is sung wherever the English language is spoken, died in poverty, in 1715, holding a sinecure in the mint, a position to which he was appointed by George I in recognition of a birthday ode he had penned to the king.

HYMN: The hymn is a recital of the gospel narrative of the birth of Jesus and is in fairly well-measured rime. It has all the realistic scenic features and vivid interlocutory addresses of Luke's description of the shepherds, and closes with a doxology. The hymn appears in the "Supplement," which was bound with the "New Version" and contained sixteen hymns. All have been forgotten except this one which, linked to the happy Christmas season and appealing especially to the imagination of childhood, lives on.

COMPOSER: George Frederick Handel (1685–1759) was born at Halle, in Saxony. At the age of seven he overcame his father's prejudice against music as a profession and advanced so quickly in acquiring skill on the organ and several other instruments, as well as the technique of composition in well-nigh all forms, that he soon won wide recognition for his unusual musical ability. In Italy he came under the influence of the then-flourishing Italian opera and in 1710 he went to England, where, in 1726, he became a naturalized British subject. Handel was a man of honor and integrity, as well as one of uncompromising independence. His irascible temper was not always well under control. He lived a simple, hard-working life and was noted for charitableness and liberality. He was endowed with unusual bodily strength. Handel was a profound student of the Bible and himself chose the texts for which he

Jesus Christ the Lord

desired to write the music. He is known to have written a few hymn tunes (James T. Lightwood, in his book, "Hymn-Tunes and Their Story," lists three: "Gopsal," "Cannons," and "Fitzwilliam"), but the habit he had of borrowing themes from his own works for other uses, as well as of appropriating the melodies of other composers, seems to have operated through his followers, for several extant tunes are indicated as "arranged from Handel." This habit, it should be noted, is not confined to the field of hymnody alone. (Witness "Marche Religeuse," on a theme by Handel, an organ composition by Guilmant.)

TUNE: "Christmas," in common with all the tunes of Handelian source, is joyous, uplifting, and well suited to the words which it carries. This tune, under the same name and ascribed to Handel, is to be found in the "Handel and Haydn Society of Church Music," published in 1830 and edited by Dr. Lowell Mason.

---

121   HYMN: O Little Town of Bethlehem
TUNE: St. Louis

Author: *Bishop Phillips Brooks*   Composer: *Lewis H. Redner*

AUTHOR: Phillips Brooks, one of the foremost preachers that America has yet produced, was born in Boston, December 13, 1835. His ancestry on both sides went back to the Puritans. Brooks took his preparatory work at the Boston Latin School and graduated from Harvard in 1855. Disappointed by his subsequent failure as a Latin teacher, he went to Alexandria, Virginia, to study theology. In 1869, after a notable service as rector of Holy Trinity Church, in Philadelphia, he became rector of Trinity Church, in Boston, where he preached to great congregations Sunday after Sunday. He was consecrated bishop of Massachusetts in 1891, but lived to enjoy this new honor less than two years. He had a keen sense of humor and was gifted with swift and powerful speech, rich in metaphor. His sermons reflected a deep understanding and genuine sympathy with men of different views and of other communions.

HYMN: In Christmas week of 1865 Phillips Brooks rode on horseback from Jerusalem to Bethlehem. The view of this little town set on the eastern slope of a Judean hill, with terraced vineyards about it, is thought to have inspired this hymn. He wrote it three years later as a carol for the Christmas Sunday School service in his Philadelphia church. Neither he nor his organist, Lewis H. Redner, thought that the music would live beyond that single service. It has become to-day one of the best-known of Christmas hymns. As Christ was born in Bethlehem centuries ago in the silent watches of the night, so in silence he comes to-day and is born in the hearts of those who will receive him.

COMPOSER: Lewis H. Redner (1831–1908) was organist and choir-master of Holy Trinity Church in Philadelphia during the rector-ship of Phillips Brooks. He was also superintendent of the Sunday School and teacher of one of the classes.

TUNE: "St. Louis" was written for the hymn "O Little Town of Bethlehem" for the Christmas service of the year 1868, at the request of the rector. Redner is said to have written the melody during the Saturday night before Christmas and filled in the harmony the next morning. It was published in The Church Porch in 1874, and later in the Hymnal of the Episcopal Church in 1892.

---

122   HYMN: Joy to the World! The Lord Is Come
TUNE: Antioch

Author: *Rev. Isaac Watts*   Composer: *George Frederick Handel*

AUTHOR: For comments on the author, Isaac Watts, see Hymn 22.

HYMN: In this hymn the believer finds nature responsive to his religious moods. To him there is a rich metaphorical meaning to nature that harmonizes with the divine purpose of revelation. When the Prophet Isaiah calls Israel to judgment, he calls on the heavens and earth as witnesses, Isa. 1:2. Before the coming of the Lord "every valley shall be exalted, and every mountain and hill shall be made low," Isa. 40:4. Frequently the psalmists speak of the gladness of mountains and hills, Ps. 114:4; 98:8; God will make a covenant for his people with the beasts of the field, the birds, and the creeping things, Hos. 2:18. Nature suffers because of man's degradation, Rom. 8:22. So the writer of this hymn feels all nature thrilling with joy at the Christmas season. So, in a similar mood, Robert Browning, in his poem "Saul," pictures David returning from his singing before King Saul with a new vision of the coming Christ. All nature seemed to respond to him:

> And the little brooks witnessing murmured,
> persistent and low,
> With their obstinate, all but hushed voices—
> "E'en so, it is so!"

Jesus Christ the Lord

COMPOSER: For comments on the composer, George Frederick Handel, see Hymn 120.

TUNE: "Antioch" has a distinctly Handelian flavor, the first four notes being the same as the opening notes of the "Messiah" chorus, "Lift Up Your Heads"; while the fourth line bears close resemblance to the rhythm and melody of the fourth (et seq.) measures of the "Messiah" tenor recitative "Comfort Ye." James T. Lightwood, a dependable English authority, says that the tune seems to be of American origin and that its source is usually stated to be "from Handel." Its first appearance in America is said to be in a collection edited by Dr. Lowell Mason and published in 1836. In many books Mason is credited with the arrangement, but the fact is that he seems to have taken it from an English collection by Clark of Canterbury. In style, "Antioch" bears close resemblance to many early American tunes, but examination of the tunes written or arranged by Mason would not warrant ascribing the tune to his editorship, since it is too much after the pattern of the fugue tunes which he so much abhorred and so much wished to replace with tunes more dignified in form. For the Church "Joy to the World! The Lord Is Come" to the stirring strains of "Antioch" has always had an important place in the yearly remembrance and celebration of the Nativity of our blessed Lord.

123

HYMN: The Sky Can Still Remember
TUNE: Chenies

Author: *Bishop Phillips Brooks*　　　　　Composer: *Rev. Timothy Richard Matthews*

AUTHOR: For comments on the author, Phillips Brooks, see Hymn 121.

HYMN: That which stirs a man deeply finds its echo in nature about him. The lover is awake to new beauties in nature and finds all things reminding him of his loved one. So Emerson once wrote,

> "O friend, my bosom said,
> Through thee alone the sky is arched,
> Through thee the rose is red."

How much more do all things remind the Christian of the greatness of God at Christmas time! The faithful stars, the night wind, the beauty of a December sunset find new meaning because of the star that once announced Christ's birth.

COMPOSER: Rev. Timothy Richard Matthews (1826–1910) was educated at Cambridge. He was a lifelong friend of Sir George J. Elvey. Ordained to the ministry of the Church of England in 1853, he served until his retirement from the active ministry in 1907. His musical works include over a hundred hymn tunes, many morning and evening services, and a Christmas carol. He was editor of "The North Coates Supplemental Tune Book" and a serial book, "The Village Organist."

TUNE: "Chenies" was composed for "From Greenland's Icy Mountains" about 1855 and was published in "The Village Church Tune Book," compiled in 1859. It should be sung after the happy style of a carol, steadily and, because of the thoughtful words, not too rapidly.

---

124   HYMN: Angels, from the Realms of Glory
        TUNE: Regent Square

Author: *James Montgomery*   Composer: *Henry Smart*

AUTHOR: For comments on the author, James Montgomery, see Hymn 11.

HYMN: One of the most popular of James Montgomery's compositions, this hymn first appeared in his newspaper, The Sheffield Iris, published in Sheffield, December 24, 1816. The hymn celebrates the comprehensiveness of the appeal of the Christ. The angels from heaven know the divine secret and rejoice. The lowly shepherds, representing the humble toilers of earth, acclaim the light of the star. The wise of earth find in him their deepest wisdom and their most sublime thought. The saints of every age, torn between hope and fear, find in his coming the promise of fulfilled hope.

COMPOSER: For comments on the composer, Henry Smart, see Hymn 61.

TUNE: For comments on the tune, "Regent Square," see Hymn 61

Jesus Christ the Lord

HYMN: All My Heart This Night Rejoices
TUNE: Ebeling (Bonn)

Author: *Rev. Paul Gerhardt*   Composer: *Johann Georg Ebeling*

AUTHOR: Paul Gerhardt ranks next to Luther as the most gifted
and popular hymn writer that Germany has produced. His was
a tragic career. The son of a burgomaster, he was born at Gräfen-
hainichen, near Wittenberg, in 1607. He studied in Wittenberg University
until 1642. He settled in Berlin. After the Thirty Years' War was over, he
was ordained there in 1651, and married four years later. Then followed
the happiest years of his life, in which he enjoyed universal love and
esteem and became one of the outstanding ministers of Germany. In
1665, along with other Lutheran ministers, he was ordered to sign an
edict of Elector Frederick William. Gerhardt decided that he could not
sign the edict and was deposed from his post. His wife and four of his
children having died, he went with the one remaining child to Lübben,
where he preached and suffered amidst an uncongenial environment and
unappreciative people until he died in 1676.

TRANSLATOR: For comments on the translator, Catherine
Winkworth, see Hymn 6.

HYMN: One authority dates this hymn in 1653, just at the time
when the author was in the midst of most severe personal
suffering. Except for the call in stanza 2 to "come; from all
that grieves you," one would never gather from its dominant, triumphant
tone the travail through which the author was then passing. Peace is not
determined by outer conditions; it is the product of a deep faith which in
every age has made men triumphant over the sufferings that life imposes.

COMPOSER: Johann Georg Ebeling (1637–1676) was cantor of
St. Nicholas Cathedral, Berlin, in 1662, and director of music in
a college of the same name. Later, in 1668, he was chosen to be
professor of music at the College of St. Charles, Stettin, and was also a
publisher of note. Many of his chorals are still in favor.

TUNE: The tune here called "Ebeling" is known often as "Bonn."
In a collection called "Spiritual Devotional Poems," by Paul
Gerhardt, set to music by J. G. Ebeling, and published in 1666,
"Bonn" is set to Gerhardt's hymn "Warum Sollt Ich Mich Denn
Grämen." While this tune has not the swing of "Stella," written by
Horatio Parker in 1893, it is nearer to the folk-song quality and, in addi-
tion, is hallowed by long devotional use. It should be sung joyously but
reverently and in accord with the mystical significance of the words.

126   HYMN: Away in a Manger, No Crib for a Bed
            TUNE: Cradle Song

Author: *Rev. Martin Luther*   Composer: *William J. Kirkpatrick*

AUTHOR: For comments on Martin Luther, to whom this hymn has been popularly ascribed, see Hymn 118.

HYMN: Martin Luther did not often appear as a gentle character. He was generally brusque and uncouth; yet it has not been considered an incongruity to ascribe to him this tender and lovely carol that for centuries, in the several tongues of many lands, has been the lullaby sung over the beds of countless children. This Christmas hymn has been the message to unnumbered little children, by which they have learned to know and to love "the little Lord Jesus."

COMPOSER: William J. Kirkpatrick (1838–1921) was a native of Pennsylvania. He always remained a business man, yet from 1858 to the end of his busy life he devoted his musical and scholarly skill to editing and compiling camp-meeting songs and gospel hymns. He was associated with A. S. Jenks in collecting material for the book "Devotional Melodies," and with J. R. Sweeney in compiling forty-seven songbooks. After the death of Sweeney, he published forty more.

TUNE: "Cradle Song" was composed for this hymn, but the date and title of the book in which it first appeared is unknown. The carol is one of the purest "lullaby carols," which are gentle in rhythm and quiet in tone. It is especially suited for unison singing by children's voices.

---

127   HYMN: It Came Upon the Midnight Clear
            TUNE: Carol

Author: *Rev. Edmund H. Sears*   Composer: *Richard S. Willis*

AUTHOR: Edmund H. Sears, pastor, author, and hymn writer, was born at Sandisfield, Massachusetts, on April 6, 1810. He was educated at Union College, Schenectady, New York, and at Harvard University. In 1838 he became the pastor of the First Unitarian Church at Wayland, Massachusetts. Save for an interval of seven years, he was pastor there for twenty-seven years. For twelve years he was associated with Rev. Rufus Ellis in the editorial work of The Monthly Religious Magazine, in which most of his hymns and poems appeared. He died in 1876.

Jesus Christ the Lord

HYMN: This hymn first appeared in The Christian Register in 1850. It quickly attained a wide usage and has been popular ever since. It is a magnificent vision of the angel chorus proclaiming peace on earth. This calm and lovely scene in which heaven draws near to earth, is in striking contrast to the marching legions of Rome, the clashing armies, the clamor for blood and power which dominated the era. The weariness of the world, the mute appeal of the accusing hands of soldier dead, the silent sorrows of mothers of every generation, the restless fears of nations cry out for Him who alone is able to heal the hurt of the nations. The sound of strife dies away. Eternal triumph belongs to the Child of Bethlehem.

COMPOSER: Richard Storrs Willis was born in Boston, in 1819, the son of Deacon Nathaniel Willis, who founded The Youth's Companion. He graduated from Yale and studied in Germany. There he formed a friendship with Mendelssohn, who revised some of his compositions. He returned to New York in 1847, and died in Detroit at the age of eighty-one. He wrote much vocal music, including a number of student and patriotic songs, as well as church music. He published a volume called "Our Church Music."

TUNE: "Carol" is an arrangement of Willis' "Study No. 23," made in 1850 by Uzziah C. Burnap (see Hymn 21), a resident of Brooklyn, New York. It is essentially a modern carol tune and should be sung at a moderate speed, smoothly and without undue emphasis on the first and fourth beats of the measure, and always with due regard for the full value of the shorter notes.

---

128 HYMN: A Thousand Years Have Come and Gone
TUNE: Noel

Author: *Rev. Thomas Toke Lynch*   Arranger: *Arthur S. Sullivan*

AUTHOR: For comments on the author, Thomas Toke Lynch, see Hymn 82.

HYMN: This hymn celebrates the joy of angels. Heaven's joy is in man's redemption. Man's joy comes when that which destroys joy is conquered. The deep secrets of unhappiness in men are hatred and the fear born of hatred, selfishness, the torture of inward division, the separation of man from his fellows, and the separation of man from God. His enemies can be destroyed only by One who himself,

145

"for the joy that was set before him," identified himself with our sorrows and "was bruised for our iniquities."

ARRANGER: Sir Arthur Seymour Sullivan, Mus.D. (1842–1900), was one of the most attractive of the English composers of his generation. He was an organist, professor of composition, and conductor of choral concerts and music festivals. He manifested conspicuous cleverness in the field of comic opera and, with Sir W. S. Gilbert as librettist, is noted for many highly popular light operas, among them being "H.M.S. Pinafore." He wrote music for two Shakespearean plays, "The Tempest" and "Merchant of Venice"; several oratorios; and a "Festival Te Deum." Among his many songs is "The Lost Chord." Most of his hymn tunes were written in the years following 1867, and these appeared chiefly in "The Church Hymnary" and "Church Hymns with Tunes." In the 1928 edition of "The Church Hymnary" there are seventeen of his tunes.

TUNE: "Noel" appeared in "Church Hymns with Tunes," in 1874, of which Sir Arthur Sullivan was editor. From a friend he received a melody which, altered slightly, comprises the first four lines. He wrote the concluding four lines and harmonized the whole. In "Church Hymns with Tunes" it was used with the hymn "It Came Upon the Midnight Clear." It is a sturdy tune and is well suited to "A Thousand Years Have Come and Gone," in its historical record of joy.

---

129 HYMN: The First Nowell the Angels Did Say
TUNE: The First Nowell

Source: *Old English Carol*   Source: *Traditional Melody*

SOURCE: This hymn was an old English carol.

HYMN: This traditional English carol, as is the case with many carols, has little to commend it as a specimen of poetry. It could well be called riming prose. To read the words aloud without any suggestion of the music is to be confronted with a very plain and unimaginative, and rather poorly told, story of the first Christmas. Perhaps its popularity lies in the music with which these words are firmly connected. The exaltation of the star is appropriate. As stars are a guide to travelers by land and by sea, so the star of Bethlehem is a guide for pilgrims of every age and leads to the One who alone can give meaning to life.

Jesus Christ the Lord

SOURCE: This tune was a traditional English melody.

TUNE: The first collection of which we have any record where this carol, "The First Nowell," appeared is "Christmas Carols Ancient and Modern," published by William Sandys, in London in 1833. The melody, which seems to have come from the west of England, where it still flourishes, has remained practically the same, though it has been harmonized by many different composers, one of the most scholarly arrangements being by Sir John Stainer. It is a joyous tune and sings well. The third and fourth of the repeated "Nowells" of the refrain are always interesting for the men's voices. Good contrast is gained by singing the fifth stanza softly.

---

130   HYMN: Good Christian Men, Rejoice
              TUNE: In Dulci Jubilo

Source: *Medieval Latin Hymn*   Source: *Medieval German Melody*

TRANSLATOR: For comments on the translator, John M. Neale, see Hymn 44.

HYMN: This medieval Latin hymn is a song of happy Christmas fellowship, expressing an abandon of joy that children feel and that adults should share more vividly. Such a song has a highly appropriate place in our Christmas worship. In the singing of its joyous affirmations of Christ's birth a world-wide sense of fellowship unites all Christians. The implications of that birth in victory over the grave and in endless bliss, in stanzas 2 and 3, are themes of joy to which Christian men everywhere respond.

SOURCE: This tune was a fourteenth-century German melody.

HARMONIZER: Sir John Stainer, whose compositions and arrangements are well represented in this Hymnal, was born in London in 1840. He was the son of a schoolmaster, who saw to it that his son received careful training. Stainer began his career as a choir boy at St. Paul's Cathedral, London, at the age of seven, and continued there for nine years. At an early age he was an accomplished player

and composer. As a choir boy he became acquainted with Arthur Sullivan, born in 1842, who was a choir boy in the Chapel Royal. As boys
they became fast friends and remained such all through their careers. At
fourteen, Stainer became organist of St. Benet and St. Peter's, at Paul's
Wharf. Two years later Sir F. Gore Ouseley appointed him the first
organist of St. Michael's, Tenbury. At nineteen years of age he matriculated at Christ Church, Oxford; soon afterwards he was appointed organist
of Magdalen College, and later of the University. In 1872 he became
organist of St. Paul's, where he had begun as a choir boy, and succeeded
the celebrated Sir John Goss. In that position many honors came to him.
He was a prolific composer and one of the best loved of the Victorian
composers. Queen Victoria knighted him in 1888. He died at Verona
in 1901. Two years later a bronze tablet was installed in his honor in St.
Paul's. At the dedication of the tablet, parts of his cantatas were sung.
The service closed with his "Sevenfold Amen."

TUNE: This tune, "In Dulci Jubilo," appears in the "Gesangbuch," edited by Klug and printed in Wittenberg in 1535, where
it is set to words which are a mixture of Latin and German. The
melody is probably earlier than the date above indicated. Sometimes it
has been ascribed to Peter of Dresden, who died about 1440; however,
it is believed to be even older than that. This arrangement by Sir John
Stainer is best suited for congregational singing, because it omits the
florid "passing notes" which figure in some of its harmonizations. It
sings jubilantly, not too rapidly, and should be kept smooth and steady.

---

131   HYMN: God Rest You Merry, Gentlemen
           TUNE: God Rest You Merry, Gentlemen

Source: *Traditional English Carol*   Source: *Traditional Melody*

SOURCE: This hymn is from a traditional English carol.

HYMN: This old English carol is so full of Christian joy as to be
almost boisterous in its meter. The hymn, however, is restrained
by a beautiful humility before the mystery of Him who was
born of a Virgin. It is a hymn of good fellowship, celebrating the joyous
companionship of those who know the power of God that was born at
the manger. One needs to understand England and its traditions in order
to appreciate this hymn and its expression of the soul of English folk.

Jesus Christ the Lord

SOURCE: The tune, "God Rest You Merry, Gentlemen," is an English traditional melody.

HARMONIZER: For comments on the harmonizer, John Stainer, see Hymn 130.

TUNE: Definite knowledge as to the source of this melody, "God Rest You Merry, Gentlemen," is so difficult to obtain that it seems wise to be content with "traditional melody" as the source. It has been slow in finding its way into church hymnals. One reason for this may be that it is in the minor mode, which has seldom been used in tunes of rejoicing. However, it will amply repay increasing familiarity and is due to find a permanent place among favorite carols because of its quaintness and its simple sincerity.

---

132   HYMN: Silent Night! Holy Night
          TUNE: Stille Nacht

Author: *Rev. Joseph Mohr*   Composer: *Ascribed to Franz Grüber*

AUTHOR: Joseph Mohr was born in Salzburg in 1792, and later became a priest in the Roman Catholic church there. He spent his life in several parishes, all within the diocese of Salzburg. He died in 1848, while serving as vicar at Wagrein.

HYMN: This carol was prepared for a Christmas festival in 1818 and was set to music by Franz Grüber. Many variations in the text of this lovely hymn appear in the translations; but the tender, mystical beauty of the Nativity incidents here rehearsed in such simplicity of style remain unmarred. This translation is a composite of several sources.

COMPOSER: Franz Grüber was an Austrian, born in Hochburg in 1787. He was a schoolmaster of the town of Arnsdorf, near where his friend Joseph Mohr was priest. He was also a musician and served as parish organist. His life was always greatly circumscribed, and he died at Hallein, in 1863, only about twelve miles from where he was born.

TUNE: The words of the hymn were written and given to Grüber by his friend Joseph Mohr as a Christmas present in 1818. Grüber immediately wrote the tune, "Stille Nacht," and the hymn was sung at the Christmas exercises in the village. It is said that, owing to some accident, the organ failed and Mohr, who sang tenor, sang the melody and played his accompaniment on the guitar. The choir of village girls joined in the melody, repeating the last two lines of each stanza. Wandering Tyrolese singers soon made the hymn known over all Germany and Austria.

---

133 HYMN: Love Came Down at Christmas
TUNE: Hermitage

Author: *Christina Rossetti*   Composer: *R. O. Morris*

AUTHOR: Christina Rossetti, the daughter of an Italian exile, the last child of a notable family, was born in London, December 5, 1830. She received her education at home. A High Church Anglican in her faith, she rejected two suitors on religious grounds. The sorrow of these experiences is reflected in her early poems. She was a woman of unusual beauty and sat as a model for her brother, Dante Gabriel Rossetti, and also for Holman-Hunt, Madox Brown, and Millais. In 1871 she suffered a severe illness and for two years her friends despaired of her life. She was often straitened by poverty. Almost nunlike, she had little experience with the world. There was in her an austerity, coupled with a sweetness of tone and a strong religious faith, that made her religious poems of abiding worth. She died in 1894, after two years of illness during which she endured great suffering.

HYMN: Few hymns have been born out of more exquisite cultural surroundings than those of Christina Rossetti. The language of this special Christmas hymn makes up in childlike vividness of devotion for the slight lack of that perfect lyric quality that characterizes this saintly woman's religious poetry. This hymn appears in her volume, "Verses," published in 1893.

COMPOSER: Reginald Owen Morris was born at York, England, in 1886. He was educated at both Harrow and New College, Oxford, and at the Royal College of Music in London, where he is now on the teaching staff. From 1926 to 1931 he was director of theory and composition in the Curtis Institute of Music, in Philadelphia, Pennsylvania. He is the author of textbooks on harmony and counterpoint, and the composer of a "Fantasy for String Quartet," several symphonies, *concertos* for violin, popular songs, and hymn tunes.

TUNE: "Hermitage" was especially written for "Songs of Praise," published by the Oxford University Press in 1925. It is of singular beauty and is written in a scholarly manner. It is cast in the minor tonality and is reverent and grave, with a quiet and somewhat medieval flavor and a gentle major ending.

Jesus Christ the Lord

134 HYMN: And Art Thou Come with Us to Dwell
        TUNE: Ein Kind Geboren

Author: *Dora Greenwell*   Source: *Old German Carol*

AUTHOR: Dora (sometimes called Dorothy) Greenwell, the daughter of a well-to-do country gentleman, was born in Durham County, England, in 1821. Owing to reverses of fortune, her home was sold when she was twenty-seven. From then on her portion was poverty, poor health, and a deepening religious faith. At the age of forty-eight she published the first volume of her poems. Of her work Whittier said, "It bears unmistakable evidence of a realization on the part of the author of the truth that Christianity is not simply historical and traditional, but present and permanent, with its roots in the infinite past and its branches in the future."

HYMN: Few hymns portray more clearly the scope of the incarnation. The coming of Christ frees us from everything that cramps and narrows our lives, until there "is light, is space, is breadth and room." The world in which we live somehow takes on a fairer proportion and clearer perspective, until each thing has "its hour of life and bloom." One is reminded of the lines of Robert Browning:

> I say, the acknowledgment of God in Christ
> Accepted by the reason, solves for thee
> All questions in the earth and out of it,
> And has so far advanced thee to be wise.

SOURCE: This tune was originally an old German carol.

TUNE: The source of this choral, "Ein Kind Geboren," seems lost in obscurity, although melodies somewhat similar appear under different titles. It provides an effective vehicle for the words of this hymn, which is suggestive of the mystery of the incarnation, emphasizing the word "Emmanuel" and its interpretation. It sings at a steady pace and is effective for unison singing by men's voices.

His Epiphany

*

135   HYMN: As with Gladness Men of Old
TUNE: Dix

Author: *William C. Dix*   Composer: *Conrad Kocher*

AUTHOR: William Chatterton Dix, born at Bristol, England, June 14, 1837, was the son of Dr. John Dix, a surgeon. He studied at the grammar school of Bristol. Trained to be a merchant, he moved to Glasgow in 1863 to take an important position in a marine insurance office. He was a scholarly layman and several of his hymns are translations from the Greek. About forty of his hymns are in use.

HYMN: This hymn was written about 1860, during an illness. Since then it has been incorporated in nearly every hymn collection in English-speaking countries. Sir Roundell Palmer said of this hymn, in 1866, before the Church Congress at York, that he held high hopes for the future of British hymnody, "when among its most recent fruits is a work so admirable in every respect as the Epiphany hymn of Mr. Chatterton Dix."

COMPOSER: For comments on the composer, Conrad Kocher, see Hymn 71.

TUNE: It is well in the singing of this tune, "Dix," to contrast the "joyful steps" of stanza 2 with the humble offering of "gifts most rare" of stanza 3. The last stanza may be taken at a slightly slower pace. For further comments on the tune, "Dix," see Hymn 71.

---

136   HYMN: Brightest and Best of the Sons of the Morning
TUNE: Morning Star

Author: *Bishop Reginald Heber*   Composer: *John P. Harding*

AUTHOR: For comments on the author, Reginald Heber, see Hymn 41.

HYMN: This hymn was first published in the Christian Observer in November, 1811. The author said of this and of other similar hymns that he intended them for the principal holy days of

Jesus Christ the Lord

the year and designed them to be sung between the Nicene Creed and the sermon. He added, in answer to unexpected criticisms, that in these hymns "no fulsom or indecorous language has been knowingly adopted; no erotic addresses to Him whom no unclean lips can approach; no allegory ill understood and worse applied."

COMPOSER: John P. Harding was born in 1850 and died in 1911. He was organist and choirmaster at St. Andrew's Church, Thornhill Square, Islington, London. Many of his compositions were inspired by children's festivals in connection with Gifford Hall Mission, Gifford Street, Caledonian Road, Islington. Not much is known of his musical activities. However, he contributed two tunes to "The Congregational Hymnary," published in London in 1916. He also composed anthems, church services, part songs, and carols.

TUNE: "Morning Star" appeared in "The New Hymnal" of the Episcopal Church in 1916. It is a carol tune in long phrases of generously curved melody line. The absence of dotted notes makes it possible to sing it with flowing smoothness. The rhythm of each line of the music is the same, yet in this tune this does not produce monotony. It should not be sung too rapidly.

It was in the Old Hymnal.

---

137   HYMN: O One with God the Father
            TUNE: Rotterdam

Author: *Bishop William Walsham How*   Composer: *Berthold Tours*

AUTHOR: William Walsham How, D. D., to whom, as Moffatt says, "modern hymnody owes . . . some of its richest treasures," was the son of an Irish lawyer and was born in 1823. After a thorough education he was ordained in 1846. His services as rector, dean, and canon in the Established Church of England are all characterized by self-sacrifice and total indifference to personal preferments. It is recorded that he declined a bishopric without ever indicating the fact to his family, and also another appointment doubling his stipend. He was a man who sincerely loved the humblest people of his several parishes and was known as "the poor man's bishop." He had a deep interest in hymnology and great ability as a hymn writer. He was joint editor of "Psalms and Hymns," 1854, and "Church Hymns," 1871, a notable collection issued under the auspices of the Society for the Promotion of Christian Knowledge. His "Poems and Hymns," 1886, brought his creative period to a close. He died in 1897.

HYMN: This hymn was written for "Church Hymns" in celebration of the manifestation of Christ to the Gentiles, especially the visit of the Magi to Bethlehem, set by consent for twelve days after Christmas, or January 6. In the calendar of the Church, this occasion is known as Epiphany. With this background in mind, How's hymn takes on not only literary beauty but special missionary significance. It thrills with the spirit of joy and confidence in the achieved fact of the incarnation and also in the presence in our life, gradually being appreciated, of God through Christ. Among the more notable hymns by Bishop How are "For All the Saints Who from Their Labors Rest," "O Word of God Incarnate," "We Give Thee but Thine Own," all found in this book.

COMPOSER: For comments on the composer, Berthold Tours, see Hymn 111.

TUNE: "Rotterdam" was composed in 1875 and was named for the city of the composer's birth, Rotterdam, The Netherlands. It is a dignified and inspiring tune of the better English type, and has qualities that make it a good processional.

His Life and Ministry

*

138   HYMN: O Sing a Song of Bethlehem
        TUNE: Kingsfold

Author: *Rev. Louis F. Benson*   Source: *English Traditional Melody*

AUTHOR: For comments on the author, Louis F. Benson, see Hymn 29.

HYMN: This simple hymn describes four stages in the life of Jesus. Referring to four geographical sites, these stages are rich with meaning for Christ's followers. On Bethlehem there shone a Light that still dispels the darkness. From Nazareth there came the fragrance of flowers, a symbol of the beauty which Jesus brings to darkened lives to-day. Over Galilee came the peace of the Ruler of wind and waves, who still speaks peace to troubled souls. From Calvary there comes a redeeming Power, adequate to-day to meet the moral needs of men.

Jesus Christ the Lord

SOURCE: The tune of this hymn is an English traditional melody.

TUNE: "Kingsfold" is an arrangement by Miss L. E. Broadwood of an English traditional melody. It appeared in "The English Hymnal" of 1906 and was published with Dr. Benson's words in "The Hymnary," the hymnal of the United Church of Canada, in 1930. It is a joyous and quaint carol tune in a minor mode, yet with a quality flexible enough to be interpretive of each of the stanzas. The last stanza differs from the others in that it begins with "a song of Calvary" and ends with Easter and salvation eternal.

139

HYMN: O Love, How Deep, How Broad, How High
TUNE: Deo Gracias

Translator: *Rev. Benjamin Webb*   Source: *"The Agincourt Song"*

TRANSLATOR: Benjamin Webb, A.M., was born in London in 1820. He received his education in St. Paul's School and Trinity College, Cambridge. He was ordained to the ministry in 1843 and held appointments in several churches. He became vicar of St. Andrew's, Wells Street, London, in 1862, and died in London in 1885.

HYMN: The Latin original of this hymn is variously dated from the fourteenth to the seventeenth centuries. The present hymn is a selection of stanzas from the Latin poem entitled "Apparuit Benignitas." It is "somewhat heavy and somnolent," as John Brownlie says in his book, "The Hymns and Hymn Writers of the Church Hymnary," yet it individualizes the message of the incarnation. Religious truth remains abstract, and so only partly true, until its meaning "for us" becomes clear.

SOURCE: This tune comes from "The Agincourt Song," an English melody of the fifteenth century.

TUNE: "Deo Gracias" is "The Agincourt Song," a fifteenth-century English melody, so-called from the words to which it was originally sung, which recalled the success of the British army in Normandy and ended with the words of thanksgiving to God, in quaint Latin, *"Deo gracias."* The two Latin words were taken for the name of the tune when it was brought over into the realm of hymnology. With even this slight background of knowledge concerning its origin, the majestic quality of the music is made more obvious. Its native character is tempered by the association with words which portray the idea of the greatness of the love of God—"deep, . . . broad, . . . high"— and there results a noble, sacred song. It sings well in unison, always at a moderate pace, clear and steady in rhythm and full-voiced, except in the third stanza.

---

140   HYMN: O Master Workman of the Race
        TUNE: Petersham

Author: *Rev. J. T. Stocking*   Composer: *Clement William Poole*

AUTHOR: Rev. Jay Thomas Stocking was born at Lisbon, New York, in 1870. He was educated at Amherst College, Yale Divinity School, and the University of Berlin. He has held a number of prominent pastorates in the Congregational Church and is the author of several books. In 1934 Dr. Stocking was made Moderator of the Congregational Council.

HYMN: Christian thought about Jesus Christ our Lord has emphasized now his divinity and now his humanity. This hymn lays emphasis upon the human Jesus. The vision of his early youth, his faithful adherence to life's purpose, all centered in his desire to do his Father's work. This is the secret of the character of the human Jesus. It should be the prayer of every believer that he will impart his secret to us.

COMPOSER: For comments on the composer, Clement William Poole, see Hymn 82.

TUNE: For comments on the tune, "Petersham," see Hymn 82.

---

141   HYMN: When the Lord of Love Was Here
        TUNE: Windrush

Author: *Rev. Stopford Augustus Brooke*   Source: *Rouen Church Melody*

AUTHOR: For comments on the author, Stopford Augustus Brooke, see Hymn 74.

HYMN: This hymn has no unified message. Its final impression upon the worshiper will be, as the author intended, varied. It celebrates the earthly life of our Lord. The primary emphasis

Jesus Christ the Lord

of the hymn is on his ministry to the discouraged. Jesus came chiefly to those who had given up hope for themselves. He told them that God had not given up hope; that forgiveness, new life, and new character were theirs by faith. It was a new vision of God that brought joy and gladness. The hymn is from Dr. Brooke's "Christian Hymns," published in 1881.

SOURCE: This tune was originally a Rouen church melody.

TUNE: "Windrush" in this form is adapted from the book "School Worship," published in 1926, where it is apparently an adaptation of "Prompto Gentes Animo," which is this melody as it appears for Hymn 653 in "The English Hymnal" of 1908. "The Rouen Church Melodies," as they are commonly called, are a collection of melodies based on plain songs and folk songs. They were made and used for group singing. Some of them have a decided ecclesiastical quality and many of them are obviously of the folk-song type. They are similar to carols, and are often in the minor mode.

Transfiguration

*

142 HYMN: O Wondrous Type, O Vision Fair
  TUNE: Deo Gracias

Translator: *Rev. John M. Neale*   Source: *"The Agincourt Song"*

TRANSLATOR: For comments on the translator, John M. Neale, see Hymn 44.

HYMN: This is an anonymous hymn from a fifteenth-century manuscript. The Latin original was included in the "Sarum Breviary," among the poems designated for use on the festival of the transfiguration. It is a reverent and deeply devotional hymn of the transfigured glory of Christ, a splendor that shall one day transfigure the Church and reflect the brighter glory of the Sun of righteousness.

SOURCE: This tune comes from "The Agincourt Song," an English melody of the fifteenth century.

TUNE: For comments on the tune, "Deo Gracias," see Hymn 139.

143 HYMN: What Grace, O Lord, and Beauty Shone
TUNE: Dalehurst

Author: *Edward Denny*   Composer: *Arthur Cottman*

AUTHOR: Sir Edward Denny, Bart., was born in 1796, and, in 1831, succeeded his father as fourth baronet of Tralee Castle, County Kerry, Ireland. A member of the Plymouth Brethren, he wrote largely for that sect. Many of his hymns have to do with the Second Coming of our Lord.

HYMN: This hymn from Denny's "Selection of Hymns," published in 1839, is a graceful and tender specimen of religious devotion. It celebrates the patient, forgiving love of Jesus, rising above all the calumny and venom of those who hated him, and pouring itself forth in unfailing forgiveness. Since Christ has so loved, if we are to follow him, then we too must have a love far above the hate and suspicion of others. This love comes from union with Christ.

COMPOSER: Arthur Cottman, whose compositions seem to have wider recognition in America than in his home country, England, was born in 1842. His parents, George and Susan Cottman, had him trained for the bar. Not much is known of his career as a solicitor. What is evident, however, is his keen interest in sacred music. Two of his tunes are known throughout the world. They are "Dalehurst" and "Mirfield." The first of these is used four times in "The Hymnal," an evidence of its adaptability to various texts. Both of these tunes were first published in Cottman's "Ten Original Tunes, "published in 1874. Two years later "Dalehurst" was included in "The Bristol Tune Book." From that source American editors began to include it in new publications. Cottman died at Ealing, England, June 3, 1879, at the age of thirty-seven.

TUNE: "Dalehurst" is a tune of simple pattern. The melody, which is a flowing one, ranges between the tonic and the sixth of the scale, with the exception of one note. The tune is contemplative in mood and should be sung in an even, moderate tempo.

---

144 HYMN: Lord, Who Throughout These Forty Days
TUNE: St. Flavian

Author: *Claudia F. Hernaman*   Source: *"Day's Psalter"*

AUTHOR: Claudia Frances Ibotson, the daughter of W. H. Ibotson, at one time vicar of Edwinstowe, was born at Addlestone, England, October 19, 1838. Her churchly and literary

Jesus Christ the Lord

environment challenged her fine talents and at an early age she began to write for church papers and magazines. When she was nearly twenty years old, she married Rev. J. W. D. Hernaman, who was an inspector of schools. Stimulated by the educational outlook of her husband's work and encouraged by her ability to understand youth, Mrs. Hernaman wrote verses, stories, and carols for children. Among her books may be mentioned: "The Child's Book of Praise," 1873; "Christmas Carols for Children," first series in 1884 and second series in 1885; "The Crown of Life," 1886; and "The Altar Hymnal," 1884. The themes of her verses include the great ideas of the Christian life, the Christian year, and the wonder and glory of childhood. While her hymns are not so widely used in children's hymnals in America as they are in England, those in current use exhibit literary skill of no mean order. Mrs. Hernaman was successful as a short-story writer and also as a translator of Latin hymns. From her pen have come more than one hundred and fifty hymns, many of which are for children. She died on October 10, 1898.

HYMN: "Lord, Who Throughout These Forty Days" appeared in "The Child's Book of Praise," published in 1873. In that volume it is designated as a Lenten hymn. The stanzas seek to portray in simple language the temptation of the Lord in the wilderness and the more trying days of his Passion. Over against these experiences is included the prayer that Christ's followers may truly mourn their sins, have power to withstand Satan, be found worthy of Christ's abiding presence, and have part in "an Easter of unending joy."

SOURCE: For comments on the source, "Day's Psalter," 1563, see the article, "The Psalters in Early Presbyterian Worship," under "Original Sources," page xv.

TUNE: For comments on the tune, "St. Flavian," see Hymn 86.

---

145 HYMN: Lord, as to Thy Dear Cross We Flee
TUNE: St. Columba (Irish)

Author: *Rev. John Hampden Gurney*   Source: *Old Irish Melody*

AUTHOR: Rev. John Hampden Gurney, the eldest son of Sir John Gurney, baron of the Court of Exchequer, was born in London in 1802. He was educated at Trinity College, Cambridge, where he graduated in 1824. He took holy orders and became curate of Lutterworth in 1827, where he labored for seventeen years. This was the same place where John Wycliffe lived, worked, and died. During his residence in this humble field Gurney refused several complimentary offers,

159

believing that the best interests of his rural position required him to remain. He was a man of wealth and position. In 1844 he became rector of St. Mary's, Marylebone, London, and in 1857 a prebendary of St. Paul's Cathedral. John Gurney died in London in 1862.

HYMN: John Brownlie calls this the author's best hymn. It was first published in 1838 and has since been included in many collections in both England and America. This hymn is one of the best examples of worship expressing itself in definite devotion to Christ. It asks that Christ may live in the worshiper's heart, that thereby he may purpose to do his Father's will through unselfish and sacrificial love for his fellow men.

SOURCE: This tune was an old Irish melody.

TUNE: This tune, "St. Columba (Irish)," is one of two tunes by the same name, the other being a more modern one by H. S. Irons. As the additional title, "Irish," indicates, it is of Irish origin. It is taken from "The Church Hymnal," authorized by the Irish Episcopal Church in 1874, and is one of the traditional Irish melodies collected by Dr. George Petrie in 1855. These quaint old melodies, strong in folk-song quality, lend themselves readily to congregational singing. "St. Columba (Irish)" sings equally well in unison or in harmony, and moves at a dignified pace.

His Triumphal Entry

*

146   HYMN: All Glory, Laud, and Honor
TUNE: St. Theodulph

Author: *Theodulph of Orleans*   Composer: *Melchior Teschner*

AUTHOR: The time and place of the birth of Theodulph of Orleans, an obscure but evidently influential saint, is not accurately determined. The church historians place his period about 820 and his place somewhere in Italy, where he was known as the abbot of a Florentine monastery. Charlemagne, whose influence dominated the culture and religion of Europe for five hundred years, though he was unable to read until he was forty and never able to write, brought Theodulph to France and made him bishop of Orleans. Here his troubles increased and he is said to have died in prison, on suspicion of a conspiracy against the Emperor Louis, Charlemagne's son.

Jesus Christ the Lord

TRANSLATOR: For comments on the translator, John M. Neale, see Hymn 44.

HYMN: Emperor Louis the Pious, son of Charlemagne, having trouble with his relatives and suspecting that Theodulph was supporting them, imprisoned him in the cloister of Angers. An old tale, not well supported, relates that on Palm Sunday, 821, the king was celebrating the day with his people. As he was passing in a royal procession he saw the venerable face of Theodulph at a window of the cloister, and paused. The bishop was singing this hymn that he had composed while in prison. The king was so pleased with this evidence of religious devotion that he released the singer and restored him to his bishopric. The hymn is now used as a processional in both Roman Catholic and Protestant churches.

COMPOSER: Melchior Teschner, who was precentor at Fraustadt, in Silesia, about 1613, was born toward the close of the sixteenth century. He was brought up in the Lutheran Church and is known to have been pastor of Oberprietschen, near Fraustadt. He was a musician of considerable ability and was greatly interested in enriching public worship.

TUNE: "St. Theodulph" first appeared in a small tract published in Leipzig in 1615, in which it was set to Valorius Herberger's "Valet Will Ich Dir Geben." A second tune, also by Teschner, was set to the same words, but only the first tune is now used. Later "St. Theodulph" was received into the "Gothaer Cantional" of 1648, and from there it found its way to choral books and hymnals. The tune is associated with a hymn by Paul Gerhard, entitled "Wie Soll Ich Dich Empfangen." It is of interest to note that Bach used the tune in his "St. John's Passion."

147

HYMN: Hosanna, Loud Hosanna
TUNE: Ellacombe

Author: *Jennette Threlfall*   Source: *Gesangbuch der Herzogl. Wirtembergischen Katholischen Hofkapelle*

AUTHOR: Jennette Threlfall, a child of misfortune and suffering, was born in the village of Blackburn, Lancashire, in 1821. Her father was a village merchant, whose courtship of her mother was seriously opposed by the latter's family, but to no purpose. Death early claimed both parents of Miss Threlfall and she lived successively with various relatives. An accident lamed and deformed her for life, and subsequent illness made her a complete invalid. Nevertheless, her beautiful, overflowing personality touched rich and poor alike in the community. It was in this atmosphere of superb tranquillity through trust in God that she wrote her verses for "Woodsorrel; or, Leaves from a Retired Home," in 1856, and "Sunshine and Shadow," in 1873. After her death in 1880, she was eulogized by both Dean Stanley and Canon Farrar.

HYMN: This hymn is intended to arouse in the worshiper a sense of victorious praise. It gathers kindling force from the author's own unbroken hope and courage in the face of lifelong disappointments and ever-present physical sufferings serenely met. The hymn is found in "Sunshine and Shadow."

SOURCE: The tune of this hymn came originally from the "Gesangbuch der Herzogl. Wirtembergischen Katholischen Hofkapelle."

TUNE: For comments on the tune, "Ellacombe," see Hymn 65.

---

148   HYMN: Draw Nigh to Thy Jerusalem, O Lord
TUNE: Woodlands

Author: *Bishop Jeremy Taylor*   Composer: *W. Greatorex*

AUTHOR: Bishop Jeremy Taylor was born at Cambridge in 1613. He was of very humble parentage, his father being a barber. He entered Caius College, Cambridge, in 1626. Following a brilliant career at the university, he was appointed Fellow of All Souls College, Oxford, in 1632. He became rector of Uppingham, Rutlandshire, in 1638. Early in 1660, after spending some time in Ireland, he returned to London and signed a Loyalist declaration thirty-five days before the Restoration. His loyalty was rewarded in 1661 with his consecration as bishop of Down and Connor. Later the same year he was chosen to be the vice chancellor at the University of Dublin. He was the author of several well-known devotional books. He died at the age of fifty-four.

HYMN: In the allegorical language of this hymn the triumphant Lord is welcomed to the heart of his people. Before the Lord enters our hearts, "passions, lusts, and proud wills" must, like the leaves of the palms, be laid in the dust at his feet. There is eager expectation for One to come and rule. Even as the children cried out with praise throughout the Temple, so in the hearts that receive him there is deep and permanent joy.

Jesus Christ the Lord

COMPOSER: Walter Greatorex, born in 1877 at Mansfield, Nottinghamshire, England, perpetuates with increasing honor the musical tradition of his family. The son of H. E. Greatorex, a banker, his training for a professional career was of the highest order. He was educated at Derby School and St. John's College, Cambridge. From 1888 to 1893 he served as a chorister at King's College, Cambridge. After completing his studies, in 1900 he became assistant music master at Uppingham School, and taught there for ten years. Since 1911 he has filled the position of music director in Gresham's School, Holt.

TUNE: "Woodlands" was written for Gresham's School choir in 1916 and was subsequently published in "The Public School Hymn Book," of Norfolk, England, in 1919. It derives its name from one of the houses at Gresham's School. Since its publication hymnal editors in England and America have found delight in perpetuating it. The tune should be sung with marked rhythm and animation.

---

149 HYMN: When, His Salvation Bringing
TUNE: Tours

Author: *Rev. John King*   Composer: *Berthold Tours*

AUTHOR: This hymn, with the signature, "J. King," first appeared in "The Psalmist, A Selection of Songs and Hymns," published in London in 1830. Rev. John Gwythe, one of the compilers of this book, said that this writer was "Joshua King, late vicar of Hull." But no one by the name of King was ever vicar of Hull. From the records of Eyton Church, Wellington, Shropshire, where Mr. King was at one time curate, it is clear that his Christian name was John; that he graduated from Queen's College, Cambridge, in 1814; and that he became an incumbent of Christ's Church, Hull, in 1822. Mr. King published several sermons and other works, and edited a volume of hymns and poems.

HYMN: This hymn is filled, as a hymn in honor of Christ's triumphal procession should be, with the spirit of human joy. Its pitch is set by the children who "stood singing hosanna to His Name." To it old and young respond, even though the hymn is chiefly for children's worship uses.

COMPOSER: For comments on the composer, Berthold Tours, see Hymn 111.

TUNE: For comments on the tune, "Tours," see Hymn 111.

150 HYMN: Ride On! Ride On in Majesty
TUNE: St. Drostane

Author: *Rev. Henry H. Milman*   Composer: *Rev. John B. Dykes*

AUTHOR: Henry H. Milman, D.D., was born in 1791, the youngest son of Sir Francis Milman, court physician to George III. He was appointed professor of poetry at Oxford in 1821. His Bampton lectures of 1827 mark a transition to theological study; this trend was further marked by his "History of the Jews," published in 1829. It was said of the latter work that "it was the first decisive inroad of German theology into England." He became canon of Westminster, rector of St. Margaret's, and in 1849 dean of St. Paul's. From then until his death in 1868 he wrote many valuable works on history and biography. An excellent conversationalist, he numbered among his intimate friends Bishop Heber, Hallam, Macaulay, and Dean Stanley. He wrote only thirteen hymns, all of them of a high standard and all in common use.

HYMN: This has been called the most popular Palm Sunday hymn in the English language. It was first published in Heber's posthumous "Hymns," in 1827. No superficial triumph is here celebrated. There is a majestic movement in the oft-repeated "Ride on!" In its meter there is the tone of triumph. The last stanza is a burst of joyous confidence in the ultimate reign of a glorified Christ.

COMPOSER (First Tune): For comments on the composer, John B. Dykes, see Hymn 53.

TUNE (First): "St. Drostane" is one of John Bacchus Dykes's finest tunes, written specifically for these words thirty-five years after Milman wrote them. Augustine Smith writes of this tune, in his book "Lyric Religion," "Naturally, other tunes have been used with Milman's text, such as 'Winchester New' and 'Park Street,' but 'St. Drostane,' composed especially for these words, carries them, it seems, with peculiar appropriateness, through awe and grief to the high rapture of redemption."

SECOND TUNE: Winchester New
Source: *"Musikalisches Handbuch"*

SOURCE (Second Tune): This tune came from the old German songbook "Musikalisches Handbuch."

Jesus Christ the Lord

TUNE (Second): "Winchester New" was set to the hymn "Wer Nur den Lieben Gott Lässt Walten" in the "Musikalisches Handbuch," printed in Hamburg in 1690. The earlier history of this tune is not known, but it became very popular after its publication in 1690. In its original form it appeared in England in the "Foundery Tune-Book" of 1742, under the caption "Swift German Tune" and as a long-meter tune. In Moore's "The Psalm-Singer's Delightful Pocket Companion," published in Glasgow in 1762, it was used in long-meter form and was named "Winchester." In various other collections the tune appeared under the captions "Frankfort" and "Crasselius."

His Passion

*

151   HYMN: O Sacred Head, Now Wounded
TUNE: Passion Chorale

Author: Ascribed to *Bernard of*   Composer: *Hans Leo Hassler*
    Clairvaux

AUTHOR: "O Sacred Head, Now Wounded" is ascribed to Bernard of Clairvaux (1091–1153).

TRANSLATORS: For comments on the first translator, Paul Gerhardt, see Hymn 125.

The English-speaking world owes this hymn to the scholarship and the poetic genius of Dr. James Waddell Alexander, one of the most eminent of American Presbyterian clergymen. Born in Louisa County, Virginia, March 13, 1804, educated at New Jersey College (now Princeton) and at Princeton Seminary, he served as pastor of the Presbyterian Church at Charlotte Court House, Virginia, in 1827, and the First Presbyterian Church of Trenton, New Jersey, in 1829. He was professor of *belles-lettres* and rhetoric in the College of New Jersey from 1833 to 1844, pastor of the Duane Street Church, New York, from 1844 to 1849, and professor of ecclesiastical history, church government, and sacred rhetoric in Princeton Seminary from 1849 to 1851. When the Duane Street Church was reorganized as the Fifth Avenue Presbyterian Church, he again became its pastor and so continued until his death at Sweetsprings, Virginia, July 31, 1859. Brilliant, scholarly, beloved, and revered, he was one of the most influential ministers of his generation. Author of many volumes, pastor, teacher, poet, it is probable that upon his version of this hymn his abiding fame in no small measure will depend.

Handbook to The Hymnal

HYMN: The hymn is a translation of a translation, and each translator has taken large liberties with the text. However, in passing from language to language, instead of sustaining any loss, the hymn has gained in loveliness and power. The Latin original is quite commonly ascribed to Bernard of Clairvaux (1091–1153). It was of great length and consisted of seven parts, each part in the form of a prayer addressed to some member of the body of the suffering Saviour as he hung upon the cross. The seventh section, which this hymn embodies, begins with the words "*Salve caput cruentatum*," which form the Latin title by which the hymn has been designated. Whoever was the author of the Latin original of this medieval hymn, it is almost certain that its translation into German was made in 1656 by Rev. Paul Gerhardt, who, with the possible exception of Martin Luther, was the most efficient hymn writer in the German tongue. This translation, entitled "O Haupt Voll Blut und Wunden," gave to the hymn its distinct evangelical note, which has been sustained and strengthened in the English version.

COMPOSER: Hans Leo Hassler (1564–1612), the celebrated German organist, was born in Nuremberg. His father was the town musician and his first teacher. He was the first notable German composer to go to Italy for study, where, in Venice, he was a fellow pupil with G. Gabrieli under Andrea Gabrieli. Hassler held in succession the positions of organist to Count Octavianus Fugger at Augsburg, organist at the Frauenkirche, in Nuremberg, and from 1608 at the court of the elector of Saxony. He died in Frankfurt. He is considered one of the greatest and most significant composers of his epoch and, along with Gumpeltzhaimer, Erbach, Melchior, and Franck, Hassler is held to be one of the founders of German music. His style was strongly influenced by the Gabrielis. His works included numerous sacred and secular canzonets, motets, psalms, litanies, and instrumental works.

HARMONIZER: For comments on the harmonizer, Johann S. Bach, see Hymn 21.

TUNE: The practice of adapting sacred texts to secular tunes is as frequent in early German hymnody as in that of Geneva and England. The "Passion Chorale" was originally written for a secular song, "Mein Gmüt Ist Mir Verwirret," appearing in 1601. Twelve years later, in "Harmoniae Sacrae," published in Görlitz, it is set to the hymn "Herzlich Thut Mich Verlangen." In later books it is associated with the hymn "O Haupt Voll Blut und Wunden," of which the present hymn is a free translation. (For another German hymn tune originally used with a secular text, see Hymn 505.) Here is another example of a tune, in itself a melody of beauty and simplicity, which with the matchless harmonizations of Johann S. Bach has become one of the most profoundly reverent musical expressions in all hymnody. The melody was used by the great master five times in his "St. Matthew Passion," each time with exquisite harmonization. The tune should be performed with great dignity and smoothness.

---

152 HYMN: When I Survey the Wondrous Cross
FIRST TUNE: Rockingham Old

Author: *Rev. Isaac Watts* Composer: *Edward Miller*

AUTHOR: For comments on the author, Isaac Watts, see Hymn 22.

HYMN: "The finest hymn in the English language"—such is the common verdict, and it is confirmed by the opinion of most competent judges. This very phrase is attributed to the famous literary critic Matthew Arnold. He is said to have repeated the third stanza just before his sudden death. He had heard the hymn sung on the last Sunday of his life, when attending a Communion service at the Sefton Park Presbyterian Church, Liverpool. The hymn was composed to be sung at Communion; at least, it first appears in a group of hymns designated for such use. These were found in a volume by Isaac Watts, entitled "Hymns and Spiritual Songs," all the hymns in the collection coming from his pen. The volume was published in 1707, although this hymn, like most of the other numbers, was written several years earlier. It appeared at a time when there was the most intense opposition to using in public worship any compositions except versions of the psalms. In this volume Watts also printed an essay setting forth the duty of the Church to prepare hymns expressing the faith of Christians, as the Psalter had expressed the faith of devout Hebrews.

As was the custom of the author, he provided for this particular Communion hymn a title and a text: "Crucifixion to the World by the Cross of Christ. Gal. 6:14." The text as usually rendered is: "But God forbid that I should glory, save in the cross of our Lord Jesus Christ, by whom the world is crucified unto me, and I unto the world" (King James Version). The first part of this text is embodied in these words of the second stanza:

> "Forbid it, Lord, that I should boast,
> Save in the death of Christ my God."

The second part of the text was expressed in the last lines of what was originally the fourth stanza, which is now commonly omitted:

"His dying crimson, like a robe,
　Spread o'er His Body on the tree;
Then am I dead to all the globe,
　And all the globe is dead to me."

In the second edition of "Hymns and Spiritual Songs," published in 1709, this verse appears in brackets to indicate that it might "be left out in singing without disturbing the sense." The only other change from the original form is an alteration of the second line of the hymn, which originally read, "Where the young Prince of Glory dy'd."

In addition to the reference from Gal. 6:14, there is in the first stanza a distinct reference to Phil. 3:7: "Howbeit what things were gain to me, these have I counted loss for Christ." Then, too, the superb closing stanza and the spirit of the entire hymn reproduces the sentiment of another verse from Galatians: "I have been crucified with Christ . . . who loved me, and gave himself up for me," Gal. 2:20.

COMPOSER (First Tune): Edward Miller, Mus.D., was born at Norwich, England, in 1731. He studied music under Dr. Burney, and was elected organist of Doncaster Parish Church, on July 25, 1756. He received the degree of Doctor of Music at Cambridge in 1786. He was a composer of ability and wrote elegies, songs, sonatas, flute solos, and psalm tunes. In 1787, a year after leaving Cambridge University, he published a book, "Elements of Thorough-Bass and Composition," and a history of Doncaster in 1804. In his book "The Psalms of David," published in 1790 for use in English churches, his famous tune, "Rockingham," appeared seven times. The book was a great success, and its subscribers included King George III, who sent Dr. Miller a present of twenty-five pounds to show his approval. Dr. Miller died at Doncaster, September 12, 1807.

TUNE (First): "Rockingham Old" (or "Rockingham," or "Communion") is first found in Miller's "The Psalms of David," 1790, where it is headed "Rockingham, L.M., Part of the Melody Taken from a Hymn Tune." The name of the tune thus reconstructed was "Tunbridge," which is found in a tiny volume, published about 1780, called "Supplement to Psalmody in Miniature." In his copy of the book Dr. Miller wrote at the foot of this tune, "Would make good long-meter," and "Rockingham" is the result of his reflection. It takes its name from the marquis of Rockingham, a friend and patron of the composer.

SECOND TUNE: Hamburg

Source: *A Gregorian Chant*

SOURCE (Second Tune): The tune, "Hamburg," is an arrangement of an old Gregorian chant. Gregory the Great (540–604) was powerful in shaping the musical destiny of the Early Christian Church.

Jesus Christ the Lord

He arranged the Ambrosian and Greek scales into eight tones or scales, thus establishing a system of chanting which has prevailed through the centuries in the Roman Church. Gregory wrought into completed form the High Mass of the Roman Church, wrote hymns, and encouraged congregational singing. He founded the Schola Cantorum, where monks were taught the various forms of liturgical chant.

ARRANGER (Second Tune): For comments on the arranger, Lowell Mason, see Hymn 18.

TUNE (Second): Lowell Mason arranged "Hamburg" from the first Gregorian tone. The tune was originally called "Gregorian Chant," and was set to the hymn "Sing to the Lord with Joyful Voice." Dr. Breed, in his "History and Use of Hymns and Hymn Tunes," writes, "The dignity, solemnity, and breadth of the old Gregorian music is well reproduced in 'Hamburg,' most appropriately set to that greatest of all hymns, 'When I Survey the Wondrous Cross.' "

"Hamburg" is an excellent illustration of the greatness that simplicity achieves in hymn tunes. Only five tones of the scale are employed, and yet this simple melody breathes the hushed reverence and solemnity of the text.

---

153   HYMN: Behold the Lamb of God
       TUNE: Ecce Agnus

Author: *Matthew Bridges*   Composer: *George William Warren*

AUTHOR: Matthew Bridges, born at Maldon, Essex, July 14, 1800, was brought up as a member of the Church of England, but later in life he entered the Roman Catholic Church. He was a student of history and in 1828 wrote a book, entitled "The Roman Empire Under Constantine the Great," with a view to disproving the historical claims of the Roman Church. His works include volumes of poetry, sermons on "The Passion of Jesus," and treatises on ancient and modern history. He died in Canada in 1894.

HYMN: The hymn is a personal declaration of adoration and devotion. It originally consisted of seven stanzas of seven lines each. Each stanza began, not with the words "Behold the Lamb of God," but with "Behold the Lamb." The hymn has been much altered and abbreviated in common use. However, the three stanzas which appear in "The Hymnal" follow the original closely.

COMPOSER: George William Warren (1828–1902) was an American organist, born at Albany, New York. He was self-taught, and held positions as organist at St. Peter's Church and St. Paul's

Handbook to The Hymnal

Church in Albany. In 1860 he went to New York and became organist at Holy Trinity Church. Later he was organist and director of music at St. Thomas' Church, New York. He wrote considerable church music and in 1888 edited a hymnal, entitled "Warren's Hymns and Tunes, as Sung at St. Thomas's Church."

TUNE: "Ecce Agnus," after its first appearance in the Hymnal of the Episcopal Church of 1894, has been included in several outstanding hymnals. From the first it has been associated with Matthew Bridges' text. This setting is respected by most editors. It is less contemplative than most Passion tunes and combines the elements of strength and tenderness. The fifth and sixth musical phrases are more subjective in their mood than the first two braces of music. The closing measures should be sung with evident feeling. As the marks of expression indicate, the entire tune requires a majestic rendering.

154

HYMN: In the Cross of Christ I Glory
TUNE: Rathbun

Author: *John Bowring*   Composer: *Ithamar Conkey*

AUTHOR: For comments on the author, John Bowring, see Hymn 80.

HYMN: The real inspiration of the hymn undoubtedly came from the words of the Apostle Paul, "Far be it from me to glory, save in the cross of our Lord Jesus Christ, through which the world hath been crucified unto me, and I unto the world," Gal. 6: 14. It will be remembered that this same text was prefixed by Dr. Watts to his famous hymn, "When I Survey the Wondrous Cross." The latter composition concerns itself with the whole verse of Scripture to which it is attached. Sir John Bowring, however, uses only the first line, and then with a somewhat altered train of thought sets forth in immortal phrases not so much the experience of being crucified with Christ as the imperishable power of the cross, its symbolizing of all the central truths of revelation, and the joy and cheer and gladness which fill the heart of a believer who realizes and appropriates what is meant by the redeeming work of Christ.

COMPOSER: Ithamar Conkey (1815–1867) was a prominent bass soloist who took part in many oratorio performances in New York. He was born in Shutesbury, Massachusetts, and was successively organist and choir director at the Central Baptist Church, Norwich, Connecticut, and bass soloist at Calvary Episcopal Church, New York. He was connected at one time with the choir at Grace Church, New York, and

170

Jesus Christ the Lord

was bass soloist and conductor of the quartet choir at the Madison Avenue Baptist Church, New York.

TUNE: Conkey has written a number of tunes, but "Rathbun" is the tune by which he will be remembered. This tune was composed while he was in Norwich, and H. Augustine Smith, in his book "Lyric Religion," tells of its creation:

"Dr. Hiscox, pastor of the Central Baptist Church, Norwich, was preaching in 1849 a series of sermons on the 'Words on the Cross.' One very rainy Sunday Ithamar Conkey, organist and choirmaster of the church, keenly disappointed that so few choir singers reported, closed the organ after the prelude, locked it, slipped out of the choir gallery, and went home. He sat down to practice, with the sermon in mind and the words of the one particular hymn, 'In the Cross of Christ I Glory,' and then and there composed the music 'Rathbun,' naming it after the leading soprano of his choir, Mrs. Beriah S. Rathbun."

The tune was first published in Greatorex's "Collection of Church Music," 1851, where it is set to Muhlenberg's hymn, "Saviour, Who Thy Flock Art Feeding."

155

HYMN: Cross of Jesus, Cross of Sorrow
TUNE: Cross of Jesus

Author: *Rev. William J. S. Simpson*   Composer: *John Stainer*

AUTHOR: The libretto of "The Crucifixion," by Sir John Stainer, was prepared by William J. Sparrow Simpson, A.M., D.D., a clergyman in the Church of England, chaplain of St. Mary's Hospital, Great Ilford. Dr. Simpson was educated at Trinity College, Cambridge, and was ordained in the year 1882. He is widely known because of his theological writings. His works include "The Catholic Conception of the Church" and "The History of the Anglo-Catholic Movement."

HYMN: This hymn, marked by reverence and a deep comprehension of the meaning of the cross of Christ, is taken from the oratorio "The Crucifixion," where it appears as "number four" under the caption "The Mystery of the Divine Humiliation." The original consists of ten stanzas.

COMPOSER: For comments on the composer, John Stainer, see Hymn 130.

TUNE: "Cross of Jesus" appeared with the publication of Stainer's "The Crucifixion," in 1887, of which it is a part and in which it is introduced for congregational singing. The cantata contains

171

several other hymns "to be sung by the congregation." This is the one, however, which has been lifted from its original setting and included in numerous hymnals. The tune is characterized by depth of feeling and may fail of its purpose if sung at too quick a tempo.

---

156   HYMN: O Jesus, We Adore Thee
TUNE: Meirionydd

Author: *Rev. Arthur T. Russell*   Source: *Welsh Hymn Melody*

AUTHOR: Arthur T. Russell was born at Northampton, England, in 1806. He was the son of Rev. Thomas Clout, a Congregational minister who changed his name to Russell. He early indicated his scholarly traits, both at Manchester College, York, and at St. John's College, Cambridge, where as a freshman at nineteen years of age he gained the Hulsean Prize, the subject of his thesis being "In What Respects the Law Is a Schoolmaster to Bring Men to Christ." Appointed rector in various parishes, he became one of the most productive writers on church subjects in his day. The following titles out of many indicate the major field of religious literature to which he made contributions: "The Claims of the Church of England Upon the Affections of the People," "A Critique Upon Keble's Sermon on Tradition," "Memorials of the Works and Life of Dr. Thomas Fuller." His "Memorials of the Life and Works of Bishop Andrewes" is considered his best prose work. Russell's interest in hymnology was revealed in the third edition of the hymn book that his father compiled for the Congregationalists. Several of his own hymns and translations appeared in 1848 in "Hymns for Public Worship." Because of his studies of Augustine, he parted company with his High Church views, and became a Calvinist. He died in 1874, leaving behind numerous unpublished hymns, notes on the Greek New Testament, and four volumes in manuscript on the "History of the Bishops of England and Wales."

HYMN: This hymn appeared first in Russell's book "Psalms and Hymns," published in 1851. It was written to be used on Good Friday, but is admirably adapted also for Communion services and for all occasions where the death of Christ is especially in mind. It is suited also for such other times as it is desired, either in private or public worship, to express adoration and devotion to the Redeemer who by his death "hath brought salvation" to those who bow their hearts before him.

SOURCE: For comments on the source, a Welsh hymn melody, see the article, "Welsh Hymnody," under "Original Sources," page xxii.

Jesus Christ the Lord

TUNE: The original air of this tune, "Meirionydd," is found in a manuscript book at one time in possession of William Lloyd, where it is called "Berth." Lloyd (1786–1852) was a self-educated musician, born in Rhos Goch, Llaniestyn, Carnarvon, and is said to have been a farmer dealing in cattle. He had a fine voice and held many singing meetings and music classes throughout the districts of Lleyn.

---

157 HYMN: There Is a Green Hill Far Away
FIRST TUNE: Meditation

Author: *Cecil Frances Alexander*   Composer: *John H. Gower*

AUTHOR: This hymn was written by Miss Cecil Humphreys, who, a few years after it was written, became Mrs. Alexander. Her father, an Englishman, was a major in the Royal Marines and as a landowner and government agent came to reside in County Tyrone, Ireland. There Cecil Humphreys was born in the year 1823. She began writing creditable verses while still a child, and in her early years manifested real poetic genius and deep religious convictions. Almost at its inception she became interested in the High Church movement, which originated in Oxford and was led by Newman, Pusey, and Keble. This movement laid great stress upon apostolic succession, the priesthood of the clergy, and Catholic ceremonial.

In 1850 Miss Humphreys married Rev. William Alexander, who later was appointed bishop of Derry and Raphoe and finally archbishop of Armagh and primate of all Ireland. She died in the bishop's palace, Londonderry, October 12, 1895. Probably her best-known literary production is the poem "The Burial of Moses." Unlike most poets, she did not enjoy hearing the praise of her own verses. One notable exception is recorded. When told that the influence of the hymn "There Is a Green Hill Far Away" had been the beginning of a new life for a certain worldly man, she exclaimed, "Thank God! I do like to hear that."

HYMN: The hymn appeared first in her volume, "Hymns for Little Children," published in 1848. It accords perfectly with evangelical beliefs which Miss Humphreys never abandoned. As a hymn dealing with the atonement and intended for children, it is beautifully written in language that can be easily understood. Its simplicity constitutes much of its charm. It makes its appeal to believers of all ages and has become one of the most beloved and widely used hymns of the Church.

Handbook to The Hymnal

COMPOSER (First Tune): "John Henry Gower (1855–1922) was an English musician, an organist at fourteen years of age, a concert artist throughout England, and later organist and professor of music at Trent College, Nottingham. Coming to America, he was identified with mining interests in Denver, Colorado, but did not lose his interest in music, becoming organist and choirmaster of St. John's Cathedral, Denver, and later at Central Presbyterian and Unity Churches. During the World's Fair, 1893, he became organist of the Church of the Epiphany, Chicago."

TUNE (First): "Meditation" appeared in John H. Gower's "Original Tunes" in 1890. In that collection it is set to "There Is a Land of Pure Delight." However, it has become closely attached to Mrs. Alexander's hymn, which it expresses with feeling and felicity.

SECOND TUNE: Horsley

Composer: *William Horsley*

COMPOSER (Second Tune): William Horsley, an intimate friend of Mendelssohn, is the author of the second tune of Mrs. Alexander's hymn. It bears his name, and is now invariably linked to the hymn. He was born in London in 1774 and struggled for his musical education against poverty and the poor instruction and neglect of a pianist in whose care he was early placed. In spite of his difficulties, however, he rose to preëminence, becoming organist in Ely Chapel and Belgrave Chapel, and finally of the Charterhouse. The Charterhouse is the survival of an ancient Carthusian monastery of England, taken by Henry VIII and finally transformed into a richly endowed institution for use as school and hospice for bachelors, in which a generation of great men like Addison, Blackstone, Thackeray, and John Wesley were educated. Horsley was a public-spirited musician, being one of the founders of the Philharmonic Society of London. He died in 1858, leaving several collections of songs, psalm and hymn tunes, and several sonatas.

TUNE (Second): "Horsley," which was written for children but has been appropriated by adults, first appeared in Horsley's "Twenty-Four Psalm Tunes and Eight Chants," which was published in 1844. The tune has wide use in England, where it is one of the tunes associated with Mrs. Alexander's "There Is a Green Hill Far Away." The tune was late in being introduced to America. However, since the Presbyterian Hymnal of 1895, in which it was used three times, it has appeared in subsequent hymnals of the denomination. "Horsley" is a straightforward tune and, unlike most common-meter tunes, moves from one musical phrase to another without duplication. It should be sung with dignity and in exact tempo.

Jesus Christ the Lord

158 HYMN: Ah, Dearest Jesus, How Hast Thou Offended
TUNE: Herzliebster Jesu

Author: *Rev. Johann Heermann*   Composer: *Johann Crüger*

AUTHOR: The life of Johann Heermann illustrates the truth that "poets learn in suffering what they teach in song." His long years of ill health, his privations, persecutions, and self-sacrificing service, enabled him to write with deep sympathy and to enter far into the meaning of the cross. He was born at Raudten, in Silesia, October 11, 1585. He died at Lissa, in Posen, in 1647. In his childhood he was dedicated to the ministry by his mother. He became a pastor, but his work was greatly hampered by physical weakness. He was finally compelled to retire, and devoted himself to literary work. His great service to the German Church was that of a hymn writer. Heermann was regarded by many as second only to Gerhardt. He began to write Latin poems in 1605. In 1608 he was crowned as a poet at Brieg. His work marks a transition from the objective hymns of the Reformation period to the more experimental and subjective school of the later period. His compositions are characterized by tenderness and depth of feeling, by trust and confidence, by devotion to Christ and humble submission to God's will.

TRANSLATOR: Robert Bridges, one of the great literary scholars of England, who has given serious attention to hymnology, was born on the tiny island of Thanet, off the Kentish coast, in 1844. After passing through Eton and Oxford, he turned to the study of medicine in St. Bartholomew's Hospital, London. He later achieved distinction as a casualty surgeon at the Great Northern Hospital. Along with the successful practice of his profession, he early became known as a poet of unusual versatility and power. Retiring from the practice of medicine in 1882, he gave himself to literature and the study of music. He was recognized by King George V, and made poet laureate of England in 1913. His musical ability and delicate poetic sense are notably revealed in his "Eros and Psyche," which he dedicated to the memory of the great Henry Purcell, who succeeded Christopher Gibbons as organist in Westminster Abbey in 1681. Bridges' most significant bequest to posterity in the field of hymnology is the famous "Yattendon Hymnal." This is a sumptuous edition of one hundred hymns, with music taken largely from the "Genevan Psalter" and arranged for unaccompanied singing. Forty-four of these noble hymns are from the pen of Bridges himself as author, adapter, or translator, and are of the highest literary and devotional character. He was the translator of the old hymn of Heermann here used. Robert Bridges died in 1930.

HYMN: This beautiful hymn of consecration was written for Passiontide. It first appeared in Heermann's "Devoti Musica Cordis," in 1630, and was entitled "The Cause of the Bitter Sufferings of Jesus Christ and Consolation from His Love and Grace. From Augustine." It is based upon a Latin meditation which appears as number seven in the "Meditationes" of Augustine. However, this collection was not made by Augustine, but is a medieval compilation, mainly from Anselm of Canterbury, who was the author of that particular portion of the book which gave to Heermann the inspiration for this hymn.

COMPOSER: Johann Crüger (1598–1662) was one of the most distinguished musicians of his time. Born at Grossbriesen, near Guben, Prussia, he was educated at the Jesuit College of Olmütz and at the school of poetry at Regensburg. He traveled extensively throughout Austria, Hungary, and Bohemia, and settled in Berlin in 1615. There, except for a short residence in the University of Wittenberg in 1620, he employed himself as a private tutor until 1622, when he was appointed cantor of the Cathedral of St. Nicholas at Berlin, and also one of the masters of the Greyfriars' Gymnasium. He founded the celebrated choir at St. Nicholas and continued in his position with that church until his death. Crüger wrote *concertos*, motets, and magnificats, but is chiefly remembered for his chorals, about twenty of which are now in general use. He is also to be remembered for the collections which he edited. Through his various collections flowed the main stream of seventeenth-century Lutheran hymnody, and, as an editor, he sought to preserve the fine material already in existence and to call all other good composers to his aid.

TUNE: "Herzliebster Jesu" is from Crüger's "Gesangbuch," published in Berlin in 1640. The tune has appeared in various forms, but the form here is the original.

---

159 HYMN: O Come and Mourn with Me Awhile
TUNE: St. Cross

Author: *Rev. Frederick William Faber*   Composer: *Rev. John B. Dykes*

AUTHOR: For comments on the author, Frederick William Faber, see Hymn 93.

Jesus Christ the Lord

HYMN: This hymn reflects the sentimental realism that the Roman Church magnifies, especially in the matter of our Lord's Passion. It originally appeared in twelve stanzas in a poem entitled "Jesus and Mary."

The critics note that Faber here dwells upon themes about which there is a "noble reticence" in the Gospel records, drawing upon the traditions of the Church rather than adhering to the authentic narratives of the New Testament.

The heart of any true penitent coming into the atmosphere and pictorial details of this Passion hymn will be made conscious of his personal relation to the tragic episode around which the reverent phraseology of the hymn gathers.

COMPOSER: For comments on the composer, John B. Dykes, see Hymn 53.

TUNE: "St. Cross" was composed by Dr. Dykes for this hymn and appeared in "Hymns Ancient and Modern," published in 1861.

---

160   HYMN: Lord Jesus, When We Stand Afar
        TUNE: Penitence

Author: *Bishop William*   Source: *"St. Alban's Tune Book"*
Walsham How

AUTHOR: For comments on the author, William Walsham How, see Hymn 137.

HYMN: This impressive Passion hymn from the heart and the pen of Bishop How was published without a title in his book "Psalms and Hymns," in London in 1854. It has been altered but slightly and forms an admirable model of devotional composition. It is in the form of a prayer addressed to the Lord Jesus. The four stanzas contain three petitions: The first is that, in love for Christ and scorn of self, the view of the cross may enable us to count all else as loss; the second is that the sight of the sufferings of Christ may arouse in us a new hatred of sin; the last is that the Saviour, whose love for the whole world led him to suffer, may give us faith to see the unseen and eternal and be drawn into closer fellowship with the Lord who died but who lives forevermore.

SOURCE: "Penitence" appeared in "The Tune Book as Used at St. Alban's," Holborn, England. No composer is credited for its writing. Very likely, however, it was arranged by Thomas Morley, the organist of St. Alban's, who gave valuable assistance to the editor in harmonizing old English melodies and adapting Gregorian music for congregational use. In the second edition of 1875 it appeared as No. 116 and without name.

TUNE: The general mood of the tune, "Penitence," is contemplative and is well suited for Bishop How's hymn, "Lord Jesus, When We Stand Afar." The hymn should be sung with feeling and not too fast.

161

HYMN: O My Saviour, Lifted
TUNE: North Coates

Author: *Bishop William Walsham How*

Composer: *Timothy Richard Matthews*

AUTHOR: For comments on the author, William Walsham How, see Hymn 137.

HYMN: This hymn by Bishop How, like the one which precedes it, is designed for Passiontide and is adapted for use at Communion seasons, or for other services of devotion and consecration. It embodies the sentiment of Paul, who declared that the love shown toward him by the suffering Saviour had captured his heart and become the dominating passion of his life: "For the love of Christ constraineth us; because we thus judge, that one died for all, therefore all died; and he died for all, that they that live should no longer live unto themselves, but unto him who for their sakes died and rose again."

COMPOSER: For comments on the composer, Timothy Richard Matthews, see Hymn 123.

TUNE: "North Coates," characterized by its exquisite simplicity, was first published by Rev. Timothy R. Matthews in 1862, when it was included in his "Congregational Melodies." Its use in America is quite recent; but whenever it is introduced it is instantly received with approval. In England it is a favorite among children and is included in school collections. It is a wholesome tune, which, notwithstanding its simplicity, has tremendous emotional appeal. For Bishop How's hymn in contemplation of the crucified Saviour its measured lines afford an effective setting.

Jesus Christ the Lord

162

HYMN: Beneath the Cross of Jesus
TUNE: St. Christopher

Author: *Elizabeth C. Clephane*   Composer: *Frederick C. Maker*

AUTHOR: Elizabeth Cecilia Douglas Clephane was descended, as her name may indicate, from the famous Douglas family of Scotland. She was born in Edinburgh in 1830, but spent most of her life in Melrose. Owing to a severe illness in childhood, she always suffered from impaired health; yet her generous and sympathetic disposition led her to devote what strength she possessed, as well as her income, to the services of the needy. Until her death in 1869, she was a most devout member of what was then the Free Church of Scotland.

Five years later an incident occurred which resulted in making her name widely known in Great Britain and America. It was in connection with the campaign conducted by the evangelists Moody and Sankey. Mr. Sankey had cut from a paper a poem written by Miss Clephane, entitled "There Were Ninety and Nine." When asked by Mr. Moody, at the close of a sermon on "The Lost Sheep," to give a message in song, he took this poem from his pocket, placed it on the organ before him, composed the music as he sang, and thus gave to the world a gospel song which shortly attained the widest popularity, and is still the best-known of Sankey's hymns.

HYMN: "Beneath the Cross of Jesus" is part of a poem which appeared first in 1872 in The Family Treasury, a magazine which had a wide circulation in the religious circles of Scotland. The hymn was one of two by the same author. They were printed anonymously, but an editorial note stated that they expressed "the experience, hopes, and longings of a young Christian lately released." These stanzas do indicate the humility, the faith, and the devotion of Miss Clephane whose authorship was subsequently acknowledged, and to whose deep evangelical convictions this hymn attests.

COMPOSER: For comments on the composer, Frederick C. Maker, see Hymn 29.

TUNE: "St. Christopher" was composed for this hymn in "The Bristol Tune Book."

179

His Resurrection

*

163 HYMN: Jesus Christ Is Risen To-Day
TUNE: Easter Hymn

Source: *Latin Hymn*   Source: *"Lyra Davidica"*
(Stanza 4) *Rev. Charles Wesley*

SOURCE: This was originally a Latin hymn of the fourteenth century. For comments on Charles Wesley, the author of stanza 4, see Hymn 26.

HYMN: This resurrection hymn is a priceless possession of the Christian Church. It is indeed *the* Easter hymn. Unfortunately, the authors are absolutely unknown, but it is certain that the hymn is composite and not the creation of any one mind. The stages of its growth can be definitely traced. The first of its four stanzas is based upon the opening couplets of a Latin carol which appears in a manuscript of the fourteenth century. An unknown person translated the carol into English, and it appeared in 1708 in a collection of hymns entitled "Lyra Davidica." The first two couplets, with the second somewhat altered, are as follows:

> "Jesus Christ is risen to-day,
> Our triumphant holiday!
> Who so lately on the cross
> Suffer'd to redeem our loss."

Only these four of the twelve lines of the carol appear in "The Compleat Psalmodist" of John Arnold, published in 1749, but two entirely new stanzas had been added. These stanzas form the second and third of our Easter hymn.

Early in the nineteenth century these three stanzas were published as one of the group of hymns printed at the close of the metrical version of the psalms made by Tate and Brady, and bound in with "The Prayer Book of the Church of England."

The last change consists in the addition of a doxology which had been written by Charles Wesley some years earlier and printed in 1740. It is admirably adapted to the hymn, which, while thus molded by a number of unknown hands, forms a unit and expresses with unique power the glory and the triumph of the resurrection of Christ.

SOURCE: The tune, "Easter Hymn," is found, slightly altered and set to this hymn, in "Lyra Davidica." The composers of the tunes in this work are not indicated. Various names have been proposed

Jesus Christ the Lord

from time to time in connection with this tune, but have not been authentically proved. The collection was an engraved book (*F. H. Sculpsit*), and it is said that only a single copy of the book is known and that its ownership can be traced back only to 1800, when an inscription in the book informs us that it was given by a Mr. Skillern to Dr. Calcott, the famous glee composer. After Calcott's death, at the auction in which his library was sold, the book became the property of William Ayrton, a well-known music critic. At Ayrton's death in 1858 it was sold for eight shillings, sixpence. Two years later it passed into the keeping of the British Museum, the owner receiving a guinea and a half for his treasure.

TUNE: "Easter Hymn" first appeared in "Lyra Davidica," under the title "The Resurrection."

164

HYMN: The Strife Is O'er, the Battle Done
TUNE: Palestrina

Translator: *Rev. Francis Pott*   Composer: *Giovanni P. da Palestrina*

TRANSLATOR: Francis Pott is the translator of this Latin hymn of unknown origin, probably bearing a date much this side of the twelfth century. He was born in Southwark, England, in 1832. After leaving Brasenose College, Oxford, he continued in the active work of parish rector at Northill, Bedfordshire, until an affliction of deafness compelled his retirement. He gave the remainder of his life to the development of hymnology, making large personal contributions to the worship life of his day. He was a member of the first committee that produced "Hymns Ancient and Modern." Later he published "Hymns Fitted to the Order of Common Prayer," an admirable adaptation of hymns specially fitted to the order of worship in the Church of England. He wrote "The Free Rhythm Psalter," seeking to reform the method of chanting. His translations of Latin and Syriac hymns give him a pre-eminent place among the interpreters of the hymnology of the earlier centuries. His most widely known original hymn is "Angel Voices, Ever Singing." Francis Pott died in 1909.

HYMN: This is a hymn in celebration of the victory of immortality over death won by our risen Lord. Born out of the darkness and confusion of the Middle Ages and rising from the heart of an unknown but undismayed singer, it voices for Christian men of all time the hope and joy of the everlasting life through Christ. Horatio Bonar's translation of this hymn in 1857 begins with the line "The battle now is done."

181

Handbook to The Hymnal

COMPOSER: Giovanni Pierluigi Sante da Palestrina (1525–1594) was the son of Pierluigi Sante, a well-to-do peasant, and in the fashion of the time he was called Da Palestrina after his birthplace. He received his training in Rome, where he was influenced by the brilliant master, Orlando di Lasso. He served as chapelmaster in his native town, master of the boys in the Julian Chapel, one of the pontifical singers in the Sistine Chapel, chapelmaster of St. John Lateran, and chapelmaster of the Liberian Chapel of Santa Maria Maggiore. At this time the Church was greatly concerned at the grave abuses which had crept into sacred music. The composers and singers took great liberty in introducing descants and tunes which were unfit for sacred usage, and sometimes lewd and profane words were substituted for the solemn words of the service. Pope Paul IV introduced a reform to abolish these secular elements and to permit only the simple Gregorian chants in unison. The story goes that the Council of Trent delegated Palestrina, already well-known for his compositions, to compose, if possible, some polyphonic music devotional and dignified enough for the church service. Palestrina composed three six-part masses so noble and devotional that there was no thought of abandoning such music. Palestrina, "the savior of church music," was soon appointed composer to the pontifical chapel and later chapelmaster at St. Peter's.

ADAPTER: For comments on the adapter, William Henry Monk, see Hymn 33.

TUNE: "Palestrina" was adapted by William Henry Monk from the "Gloria" of Palestrina's "Magnificat Tertii Toni," published in 1591.

---

165   HYMN: "Christ the Lord Is Risen To-Day"
TUNE: Llanfair

Author: *Rev. Charles Wesley*   Composer: *Robert Williams*

AUTHOR: For comments on the author, Charles Wesley, see Hymn 26.

HYMN: This resurrection hymn by Rev. Charles Wesley is not to be confused with the early hymn "Jesus Christ Is Risen To-Day," based on a Latin composition of the fourteenth century, which inspired Wesley's composition " 'Christ the Lord Is Risen To-Day.' " It appeared first in his "Hymns and Sacred Poems," 1739, with the head-

182

Jesus Christ the Lord

ing "Hymn for Easter." In "Psalms and Hymns," published in 1760, Martin Madan made certain alterations and omitted stanzas 7 to 9, thus forming a hymn of eight stanzas. From this form all later arrangements have been made. It is one of the most popular and widely used of all the many hymns which were composed by Wesley.

COMPOSER: For comments on the composer, Robert Williams, see Hymn 12.

TUNE: For comments on the tune, "Llanfair," see Hymn 12.

---

166   HYMN: The Day of Resurrection
TUNE: Lancashire

Author: *John of Damascus*   Composer: *Henry Smart*

AUTHOR: John of Damascus was born about A.D. 700 and rose to a position of great prominence in the Church. He gave to the Greek Church its standard textbook of dogmatic theology. Aroused by the emperor's order forbidding the ecclesiastical use of images, he issued three letters in behalf of image worship. He later retired to a convent on the west shore of the Dead Sea and devoted the remainder of his days to religious writings. He was a man of wide erudition, was regarded as an able philosopher, and on account of his eloquence he received the title "Chrysorrhous," i. e., "Stream of Gold." He has been canonized by both the Greek and the Latin Churches. Dr. Neale described him as "the last but one of the Fathers of the Greek Church, and the greatest of her poets." He adds, "It is surprising how little is known of his life." That he was born of a good family at Damascus, that he made great progress in philosophy, that he administered his charge under the caliph, that he retired to the monastery of St. Sabas in Palestine, that he was the most learned and eloquent writer with which the iconoclasts had to contend, that at a comparatively late period of life he was ordained priest of the church at Jerusalem, and that he died after 754 and before 787, seems to comprise all that has reached us of his biography.

TRANSLATOR: For comments on the translator, John M. Neale, see Hymn 44.
In support of his High Church views, Dr. Neale in his translations turned not only to the writers of the Church of Rome but also to those of the Orthodox Greek Church. His original studies of these latter authors resulted in the translation of a number of hymns from the Greek, which were published in his volume entitled "Hymns of the Eastern

183

Church." Among those whose compositions were thus presented to the English world, probably none held a place of higher authority than John of Damascus.

HYMN: This resurrection hymn appeared first in "Hymns of the Eastern Church," printed in 1862. It is a free translation of the first of the eight parts of the canon for Easter written by John of Damascus. This has been called "the golden canon" or "the queen of canons." The part from which this hymn has been taken has been pronounced "the grandest piece in Greek sacred poetry." As presented by Dr. Neale, it constitutes a hymn of triumphant joy and exultant faith, setting forth in stirring phrases the deep import of Christ's resurrection.

COMPOSER: For comments on the composer, Henry Smart, see Hymn 61.

TUNE: For comments on the tune, "Lancashire," see Hymn 115.

---

167   HYMN: O Sons and Daughters, Let Us Sing
TUNE: O Filii et Filiae

Author: *Jean Tisserand*   Source: *French Traditional Melody*

AUTHOR: The author of this hymn was a member of the Minorite Brotherhood, a Parisian friar by the name of Jean Tisserand, who died in 1494.

TRANSLATOR: For comments on the translator, John M. Neale, see Hymns 44 and 166.

HYMN: This hymn first appeared in nine stanzas in a pamphlet published sometime between 1518 and 1536. The radiant joy of this hymn, breaking out of the sorrow and darkness of this painful period in the history of the Church and the world, is a thrilling challenge to the present generation.

SOURCE: This tune is from a French traditional melody.

TUNE: The earliest form of this tune, "O Filii et Filiae," is found in "Airs sur les Hymnes Sacrez, Odes et Noels," published in Paris in 1623, where it is used in four parts with the Latin text. The melody, of plain-song origin, is in the eighth mode with a B flat, or

Jesus Christ the Lord

perhaps more strictly speaking in the second mode. The melody appeared in varying forms in the eighteenth century in works including La Feillée's "Méthode du Plain Chant"; a little manual called "A Pious Association," published in London in 1748; and again in "An Essay on the Church Plain Chant," published in 1782 in plain-song notation. It is quite possible for this hymn to move rather briskly when a congregation has become thoroughly familiar with it. To achieve the climax which the fifth stanza deserves, it is well to sing this stanza in unison, with a marked retard on the final alleluias.

---

168 HYMN: Come, Ye Faithful, Raise the Strain
TUNE: St. Kevin

Author: *John of Damascus*   Composer: *Arthur Sullivan*

AUTHOR: For comments on the author, John of Damascus, see Hymn 166.

TRANSLATOR: For comments on the translator, John M. Neale, see Hymn 44 and 166.

HYMN: This Easter hymn is the reproduction of a Greek ode which was found in the canon appointed for St. Thomas' Sunday, written in the middle of the eighth century by John of Damascus. This version was made by Rev. John M. Neale, who followed the original ode much more closely than in the case of most of his translations. He published the hymn first in an article on Greek hymnology in the Christian Remembrancer, of April, 1859. It subsequently was included in many collections of hymns. For it the editors of "Hymns Ancient and Modern," 1861, wrote a closing stanza in the form of a doxology. The original ode by John of Damascus was founded upon "The Story of Moses," Ex., ch. 15. In its first English form the hymn contained four stanzas. In the two-stanza form given in "The Hymnal," the first stanza embodies the comparison of the deliverance wrought by Christ with that of Israel's deliverance under Moses. The next stanza points to the joyous return of spring, as a familiar symbol of the resurrection.

COMPOSER: For comments on the composer, Arthur Sullivan, see Hymn 128.

TUNE: "St. Kevin" appeared in "The Hymnary," which was published in London in 1872. While not among Sullivan's greatest tunes, few others by him are used with more popular approval.

Presbyterians in America have been familiar with it since its inclusion in "The Hymnal" of 1895. The tune is simple and joyous, and effectively expresses the moods and feelings of the Eastertide. It is very useful as a processional.

---

169   HYMN: "Welcome, Happy Morning"
            TUNE: Hermas

Author: *Bishop Venantius*   Composer: *Frances Ridley Havergal*
        Fortunatus

AUTHOR: Venantius Honorius Clementianus Fortunatus, not content with these four imposing names, assumed a fifth, Theodosius, to which in later years was added the title of bishop of Poitiers. This interesting ecclesiastic was far more of a troubadour than a saint. Born near Treviso, Italy, in 530, educated at Ravenna and Milan, he spent most of his life in France, where he died in 609. His career was colorful and romantic. Possessed of a pleasing personality, fond of high living, endowed with poetic gifts, he was popular in all circles. The determining factor in his life was his intimate friendship with Queen Radegundis, who had left her throne to found the Convent of St. Croix at Poitiers. It was due to her influence that he entered the service of the Church and ultimately was appointed bishop. To Radegundis and to Agnes, her former maid, appointed by her as head of the convent, he composed the most extravagant poetic effusions. Much more significant were his hymns to the Virgin. Indeed, he was the "first of the Christian poets to begin that worship of the Virgin Mary which rose to a passion and sank to an idolatry." It is rather surprising that to this author the Church owes some of its best-loved hymns.

TRANSLATOR: For comments on the translator, John Ellerton, see Hymn 20.

HYMN: The Latin poem on which the hymn is based consists of one hundred and ten lines. The thirty-ninth line begins, "*Salve festa dies toto venerabilis aevo*," and is the first line of that portion of the poem of which this hymn, " 'Welcome, Happy Morning,' " by Ellerton, is not so much a translation as a vigorous and popular paraphrase. It is an Easter hymn in which spring is depicted as greeting her risen Lord. "In this sweet poem," says Dr. Schaff, "the whole nature, born anew in the spring, and arrayed in the bridal garment of hope and promise, welcomes the risen Saviour, the Prince of spiritual and eternal life." Only three of the seven stanzas appear in "The Hymnal," but they in-

Jesus Christ the Lord

dicate the exultation and rejoicing of the glad season which the hymn connects with the resurrection of Christ.

COMPOSER: For comments on the composer, Frances Ridley Havergal, see Hymn 56.

TUNE: For comments on the tune, "Hermas," see Hymn 56.

---

170   HYMN: On Wings of Living Light
          TUNE: Mansfield

Author: *Bishop William Walsham How*   Composer: *Joseph Barnby*

AUTHOR: For comments on the author, William Walsham How, see Hymn 137.

HYMN: This hymn by Bishop How appeared first in a collection, "Children's Hymns," published in 1873. Its aim is instruction and exhortation quite as much as worship. The third and fourth stanzas are a fitting application of the Easter story and voice the call to a higher life which is expressed by Paul in his message to the Colossians: "If then ye were raised together with Christ, seek the things that are above, where Christ is, seated on the right hand of God. Set your mind on the things that are above, not on the things that are upon the earth. For ye died, and your life is hid with Christ in God," Col. 3: 1-3.

COMPOSER: For comments on the composer, Joseph Barnby, see Hymn 3.

TUNE: This sturdy tune, "Mansfield," by Barnby, was published in 1890, when it was included in George S. Barrett's "The Congregational Mission Hymnal," for use in the Congregational Union of England and Wales. In that volume it supplied a setting for T. H. Gill's hymn, "Ye of the Father Loved." When "The Home and School Hymnal" was published in London in 1892, it was included in that volume and associated with Bishop How's "On Wings of Living Light." This is a very forceful tune, with a bold and active bass and an arresting melody. The last two musical phrases develop an effective climax of jubilant praise.

Handbook to The Hymnal

His Ascension

*

171   HYMN: Hail the Day That Sees Him Rise
             TUNE: Ascension

Author: *Rev. Charles Wesley*   Composer: *William Henry Monk*

AUTHOR: For comments on the author, Charles Wesley, see Hymn 26.

HYMN: The original hymn by Charles Wesley was published in his "Hymns and Sacred Poems," 1739, under the caption "Hymn for Ascension Day." It contained ten stanzas, the first, second, and fourth of which appear in "The Hymnal." The ascension of Christ as an event distinct from the resurrection should be more fully emphasized by the Christian Church. It signifies not only the withdrawal of our Lord into the sphere of the unseen and eternal, but also his assumption of the place of universal power, Rev. 3:21. Such is the true message of this ascension hymn. The poet sees in this great event the true fulfillment of Psalm 24, and identifies the ascending Christ with "the King of glory," as he calls to mind the words of the ancient hymn of praise:

> "Lift up your heads, O ye gates;
> And be ye lifted up, ye everlasting doors:
> And the King of glory will come in.
> . . . .
>
> Who is this King of glory?
> The Lord of hosts,
> He is the King of glory."

COMPOSER: For comments on the composer, William Henry Monk, see Hymn 33.

TUNE: The tune, "Ascension," was written for the original edition of "Hymns Ancient and Modern," 1861. This setting is much superior to the original Wesleyan setting, which had no alleluias and was of enormous compass, from low B flat to upper G. Here again is a hymn which in a hymn festival or in a service of congregational music would lend itself well to antiphonal singing, the alleluias being relegated to a special group or choir.

Jesus Christ the Lord

172
HYMN: The Lord Ascendeth Up on High
TUNE: Ascendit Deus

Author: *Rev. Arthur Tozer Russell*   Composer: *Johann Gottfried Schicht*

AUTHOR: For comments on the author, Arthur Tozer Russell, see Hymn 156.

HYMN: In this ascension hymn the author embodies the praise of the psalmist, Ps. 68:18, as paraphrased by the Apostle Paul in Eph. 4:8:

> "When he ascended on high, he led captivity captive,
> And gave gifts unto men."

These gifts, according to the apostle, were granted to the Church by the agency of the Holy Spirit, to which truth the author of the hymn refers in the third stanza:

> "Our great High Priest hath gone before,
> Now on His Church His grace to pour."

There is also in the closing line a reference to the description of the great High Priest, given in The Epistle to the Hebrews, as one who "ever liveth to make intercession."

COMPOSER: Johann Gottfried Schicht (1753–1823) was born at Reichenau, Saxony. In 1776, already well trained as an organist and pianist, he studied law at Leipzig. Later, returning to music, he became a pianist at J. Adam Hiller's Liebhaber-Konzerte and at the Gewandhaus concerts, which evolved from them in 1781. He succeeded Hiller as conductor in 1785. In 1810 he followed A. E. Müller as cantor at St. Thomas' Church. He wrote three oratorios, many masses and motets, a *concerto*, cantatas, and a notable choral book with 1,285 melodies, 306 of which were original.

TUNE: "Ascendit Deus" is an original tune which appeared with the hymn "So Hoff Ich Denn mit Festem Mut," in the "Allgemeines Choralbuch," which Schicht edited in 1819. The tune should not be hurried and should be sung at a tempo in keeping with its solidity and dignity.

Handbook to The Hymnal

173 HYMN: See, the Conqueror Mounts in Triumph
TUNE: St. Asaph

Author: *Bishop Christopher*   Composer: *William S.*
Wordsworth   *Bambridge*

AUTHOR: For comments on the author, Christopher Wordsworth, see Hymn 18.

HYMN: Of the hymns which the Church owes to Bishop Christopher Wordsworth, this is regarded as the most noble and majestic. Dr. Julian has declared it to be "the nearest approach in style and treatment to a Greek ode known to us in the English language." The poem as published in Wordsworth's "Holy Year," 1862, was of considerable length. The stanzas chosen for "The Hymnal" are the first three of the five which have been most used. They exhibit the spirit and indicate the character of the poem and form in themselves an anthem of triumphant joy.

COMPOSER: William Samuel Bambridge was born at Waimate, New Zealand, in 1842. At an early age he went to England. For a number of years he sang as a chorister at St. George's, Windsor. After graduating from Oxford, he spent his entire professional career of forty-seven years as music master at Marlborough College, England. After these many years of service and leadership he retired in 1911, but continued his residence at Marlborough until his death in 1923.

TUNE: "St. Asaph," according to James Edmund Jones, of Toronto, Canada, was published in 1872 as a thanksgiving hymn for the recovery of the Prince of Wales (later King Edward VII) from a severe attack of typhoid fever. The illness, which began in November, 1871, continued until February, 1872. Convalescence was long delayed and the United Kingdom was greatly concerned. February 27, 1872, was designated as a day of thanksgiving and a notable service was held at St. Paul's, London, with imposing demonstrations of public joy. The tune is probably best known because of its association with "Through the Night of Doubt and Sorrow." It is a joyous, fluent tune and should be sung with exultation.

Jesus Christ the Lord

His Living Presence

*

174 HYMN: O Thou Great Friend to All the Sons of Men
TUNE: Langran

Author: *Rev. Theodore Parker*   Composer: *James Langran*

AUTHOR: Rev. Theodore Parker, preacher, scholar, reformer, was born in Lexington, Massachusetts, August 24, 1810. He was educated at Harvard, was ordained in 1837, and spent most of his ministry in Boston. Traveling abroad in hope of restoring his health, he died May 10, 1860, at Florence, Italy, where he was buried. With Channing and Emerson he was among the leaders of New England Unitarianism. He believed in God, in human responsibility, and in the immortality of the soul. He was a leading abolitionist, and a great admirer of Garrison, with whom he differed, however, in many views and aims.

HYMN: This hymn should be sung with full faith in Christ as the divine Saviour. In the first stanza his words to the disciples are called to mind: "Ye are my friends, if ye do the things which I command you," John 15: 14. The second and third stanzas refer to his great affirmation, "I am the way, and the truth, and the life: no one cometh unto the Father, but by me," John 14: 6.

COMPOSER: James Langran, Mus.B. (1835–1909), was an English organist. He was born in London and received his instruction from J. B. Calkin and Sir J. F. Bridge. He served successively as organist at St. Michael's, Wood Green; Holy Trinity, Tottenham; and All Hallows (the Parish Church), Tottenham, where he was also instructor at St. Katherine's Training College. He contributed several tunes to "Hymns Ancient and Modern," and acted as musical editor of "The New Mitre Hymnal."

TUNE: "Langran," this beautiful tune of contemplation, inward peace, and quiet strength, was written for "Abide with Me: Fast Falls the Eventide." So associated, it was included in John Foster's "Psalms and Hymns," of 1863, but there bore the name "Evensong." The correct rendering of the tune requires full, broad tones, careful shading, and unhurried tempo. "Langran" is very appropriate for use as an opening sentence or introit. It is so used in "The Hymnal" as Response 8.

175 HYMN: *Strong Son of God, Immortal Love
TUNE: St. Crispin

Author: *Alfred Tennyson*   Composer: *George J. Elvey*

AUTHOR: Alfred, Lord Tennyson, was probably the most famous and truly representative poet of the Victorian era. The son of a clergyman, he was born August 6, 1809, at Somersby, Lincolnshire. In 1828 he entered Trinity College, Cambridge. While still in residence, in 1830, he published "Poems, Chiefly Lyrical." His wide popularity, however, dates from his "Poems" in two volumes, which appeared in 1842. In May, 1850, he published "In Memoriam," and in June of that same year he was married. In November he was appointed to succeed Wordsworth as poet laureate, an appointment which met with unquestioned and universal approval. Among his many familiar poems there might be mentioned "Idylls of the King," "The Princess," "Locksley Hall," and "Maud." In 1884 he accepted a peerage. Tennyson died at Aldworth, October 6, 1892, and was buried in Westminster Abbey.

HYMN: The hymn was taken from the opening stanzas of "In Memoriam," which was written by Tennyson as a tribute to the memory of Arthur H. Hallam, the intimate friend of his early manhood. These opening stanzas are eleven in number, of which the first, fourth, fifth, and seventh have been selected to form this hymn.

COMPOSER: For comments on the composer, George J. Elvey, see Hymn 109.

TUNE: "St. Crispin" was composed in 1862. According to H. Augustine Smith: "It was first published in 'A Selection of Psalm and Hymn Tunes,' edited by E. H. Thorne, 1863. It was composed for the hymn 'Just as I Am, Without One Plea,' and is also used for Bishop How's hymn 'Behold the Master Passeth By.' This tune was used at the funeral of the composer."

---

176 HYMN: O Thou, in All Thy Might So Far
TUNE: Kilmarnock

Author: *Rev. Frederick Lucian Hosmer*   Composer: *Neil Dougall*

AUTHOR: Frederick Lucian Hosmer, D.D., was born in Framingham, Massachusetts, in 1840, was educated at Harvard, and was ordained to a fruitful ministry in 1872. In 1908 he was lec-

Jesus Christ the Lord

turer on hymnody at Harvard. He published "The Way of Life." He died in Berkeley, California, in 1929.

H YMN: The hymn is a singularly simple and direct expression of humble, childlike trust.

C OMPOSER: For comments on the composer, Neil Dougall, see Hymn 28.

T UNE: For comments on the tune, "Kilmarnock," see Hymn 28.

---

177 HYMN: O Son of Man, Our Hero Strong and Tender
TUNE: Charterhouse

Author: *Frank Fletcher*   Composer: *David Evans*

A UTHOR: The author of this hymn, Frank Fletcher, A.M., is an English layman. He was educated at Balliol College, Oxford, where he became distinguished for his brilliant scholarship. He undertook teaching as his life work and has attained extraordinary success in the molding of youth and the management of schools for boys. He has served as assistant master at Rugby, master of Marlborough College, and head master of Charterhouse School, Godalming.

H YMN: This hymn is particularly adapted to appeal to the heroism of youth, and is such a production as might be expected from one who has ever felt a deep sympathy with the aspirations and needs of young Christians.

C OMPOSER: David Evans, Mus.D., has performed for the religious life of Wales in the modern day what Ieuan Gwyllt (John Roberts; see Hymn 183) did in his day. He is a prominent conductor in the great psalmody festivals of Wales, a leading influence in promoting congregational singing, and a notable composer. He was born in 1874 at Resolven, Glamorganshire, and was educated at Arnold College, Swansea; at University College, Cardiff; and at Oxford. In 1903 he became professor of music at University College, and later became senior professor of the University of Wales. His collection of standard hymn tunes, "Moliant Cenedl," reflected a fine musical taste which greatly influenced subsequent collections. His works include the cantata for chorus and orchestra, "The Coming of Arthur"; "Rejoice in the Lord"; "Deffro Mae'n Ddydd," a Welsh choral ballad; "Bro Bugeiliaid," a children's cantata; and many anthems, services, and hymn tunes. He has also made a deep and lasting impression upon the religious life of Wales through his editorship of Y Cerddor, a journal devoted to the cause of music in Wales.

TUNE: This tune, "Charterhouse," is of great breadth and dignity. The melody, which is bold and joyous, is set against a majestic organ accompaniment which requires exact articulation and considerable volume of sound. This type of hymn well represents the modern tune writers of England and Wales, whose influence is increasingly felt and with profit. The tune was written for the words "O Son of Man, Our Hero Strong and Tender," and so used in "The Church Hymnary," published in 1927.

---

178   HYMN: Immortal Love, Forever Full
TUNE: Serenity

Author: *John G. Whittier*   Composer: *William Vincent Wallace*

AUTHOR: John Greenleaf Whittier, the "Quaker poet," was born at Haverhill, Massachusetts, December 17, 1807, and died at Hampton Falls, New Hampshire, September 7, 1892. He began life as a farmer boy and a village shoemaker. With only a meager education he entered upon the profession of journalism about 1828, and subsequently held editorial positions in Boston, Hartford, Philadelphia, and Washington. He was an ardent abolitionist, and served as secretary of the American Antislavery Society, and as editor of its official organ, The Pennsylvania Freeman. In his early years he revealed considerable ability as a writer of verses, and later developed into one of the most truly characteristic of our American poets. His compositions surpassed those of all others in the prominence of their ethical and religious elements. Over fifty hymns found in modern use are attributed to him, practically all of them being extracts from much longer poems.

HYMN: This hymn is a cento arranged from the poem "Our Master," which was printed in the Congregationalist, August 16, 1867. Of the thirty-eight stanzas of the poem, the first, fifth, thirteenth, fourteenth, and sixteenth have been chosen to form the selection found in "The Hymnal." In many books the hymn begins with the fifth stanza:

> "We may not climb the heavenly steeps
>   To bring the Lord Christ down;
> In vain we search the lowest deeps,
>   For Him no depths can drown."

Jesus Christ the Lord

COMPOSER: William Vincent Wallace (1814–1865), noted Irish violinist and composer, was the son of an Irish bandmaster. Even as a boy he played in a theater orchestra in Dublin and later was soloist. The playing of Paganini inspired him to study the violin with devotion, and his concert appearances met with striking success. His life for the most part was spent in travel and adventure. When still a youth he moved to London and at twenty-one years of age he migrated to New South Wales. Later he went to Australia as a pioneer settler. Restlessness led him to continue his wanderings through the East Indies, South America, Mexico, and the United States. He was the composer of several operas. In the year 1850 Wallace lost all his savings through the failure of a New York piano firm, and in the same year he narrowly escaped death in a steamboat explosion. He died in France at the age of fifty-one.

TUNE: "Serenity" is an arrangement from Wallace's "Ye Winds That Waft." In spite of the restless life of the composer, the tune itself well deserves the title "Serenity," and its performance should be smooth and sustained.

---

179   HYMN: We Bear the Strain of Earthly Care
TUNE: Azmon

Author: *Rev. Ozora Stearns Davis*   Composer: *Carl G. Gläser*

AUTHOR: Ozora Stearns Davis, Ph.D., D.D., LL.D., a clergyman of the American Congregational Church, was born at Wheelock, Vermont, July 30, 1866. He was educated at Dartmouth College, graduating in 1889, and at Hartford Theological Seminary. In 1896 he was ordained to the ministry. After a number of pastorates in New England, he served as president of Chicago Theological Seminary from 1909 to 1920. He was moderator of the Congregational Council from 1927 to 1929. Preceding his death on March 15, 1931, Dr. Davis gave to the world a noble example of a Christian's approaching the end of life while in his prime. Under a time schedule set by the usual progress of his disease he continually inspired and challenged the world with his calm spirit and cheering view of the future as death was about to disclose it.

HYMN: The hymn is one of the few which the author has left for the use of the Church. It reflects his Christian faith and breathes the spirit of that faith moving in modern life.

COMPOSER: Carl G. Gläser was born in Weissenfels, Germany, in 1784. His father was his first music teacher. Later he studied at St. Thomas' School, in Leipzig, under Johann Adam Hiller.

August Eberhard Müller taught him piano and Campagnoli taught him violin. In 1801 he took up the study of law, but, music proving to be a greater interest, he gave it up and settled in Barmen, where he taught piano, violin, and voice. He also directed choruses, composed many chorals and songs, and was the manager of his own music store. He died at Barmen in 1829.

ARRANGER: For comments on the arranger, Lowell Mason, see Hymn 18.

TUNE: This tune, "Azmon," is among those introduced into this country from German sources by Lowell Mason. It is found as early as 1839 in Mason's "Modern Psalmody." In Charles S. Robinson's "Songs for the Sanctuary," 1879, it is called "Denfield." Thomas Hastings used a setting of this tune in his "Selah," published in 1856; but he changed the rhythm, beginning with a quarter note on the third beat, making each bar consist of a half note and a quarter note. This tune was known as "Gaston," but with the exception of two tones in the last line it is identical with "Azmon." In "The Methodist Hymnal," this tune has been used since 1867 and in the 1905 edition it is set to the hymn "O for a Thousand Tongues to Sing," one of Charles Wesley's hymns, which has stood first in the books of that denomination for over a hundred years.

---

180   HYMN: O Light, Whose Beams Illumine All
        TUNE: St. Petersburg

Author: *Rev. Edward H. Plumptre*   Composer: *Dimitri Bortniansky*

AUTHOR: Edward Hayes Plumptre (pronounced plum-tree), D.D., a distinguished English clergyman, theologian, and author, was born in London, August 6, 1821. He graduated at Oxford with the highest honors in 1844 and was ordained to the ministry in 1846. He rose in the Church to a position of great eminence. In addition to a number of other positions, he served successively as prebendary of St. Paul's, as professor of exegesis of the New Testament in King's College, as dean of Wells, and as a member of the Old Testament Company for the Revision of the Authorized Version of the Holy Scriptures. His hymns are few in number, but are marked by their stately simplicity, their melody, and their fervor of spirit.

HYMN: This hymn is founded on Jesus' saying, "I am the light of the world," John 8: 12; 9: 5, and on another of his sayings, "I am the way, and the truth, and the life," John 14: 6.

Jesus Christ the Lord

COMPOSER: Dimitri Stepanovitch Bortniansky was born at Gloukoff, in Ukraine, in 1752, and at an early age showed remarkable musical ability. Studying at Moscow, and later at St. Petersburg under Galuppi, he followed his teacher in 1768 to Venice, the Empress Catherine supplying the funds. Later he studied at Bologna, Rome, and Naples. In 1779 he returned to Russia, already well-known for his operatic compositions, and was appointed director of the empress's choir, later called the Imperial Kapelle. Bortniansky had great influence on Russian church music, and to him belongs the credit of having reduced it to a system. He composed for the empress's choir thirty-five sacred *concertos*, ten *concertos* for double choir, and a mass for three voices. Tschaikowsky edited his works, published in ten volumes in St. Petersburg. Bortniansky died in St. Petersburg in 1825.

TUNE: "St. Petersburg" is an adaptation from part of a mass written by Bortniansky in 1822. It is found in a choral book published in Leipzig in 1825, edited by I. H. Tscherlitzky, an organist in St. Petersburg. In this book the tune is used with the hymn "Ich Bete an die Macht der Liebe."

---

181   HYMN: I Know Not How that Bethlehem's Babe
      TUNE: Exeter

Author: *Rev. Harry Webb Farrington*   Composer: *Henry Lowell Mason*

AUTHOR: Major Harry Webb Farrington was born in Nassau, Bahama Islands, July 14, 1880. He graduated from Syracuse University in 1907 and later received the degree of S.T.B. from Boston Theological Seminary and the degree of A.M. from Harvard University. He became interested in work among children and inaugurated the Week Day Church School at Gary, Indiana, in 1914. At the outbreak of the World War he went to France to serve the *Foyers du Soldat* and was given an honorary life commission in the Seventh and Tenth Cuirassiers, 1918-1919. At the close of the war he became a Chautauqua lecturer on religious, educational, and social subjects and became widely known as a speaker for children. It is estimated that he addressed more than two million pupils in the public schools of America. He was a member of the New York East Conference of the Methodist Episcopal Church. When he was in France in 1920 he published a volume of poems. A subsequent volume of his poems was published the next year. He is the author of a number of modern hymns and also wrote books on Franklin, Washington, Lincoln, and Theodore Roosevelt. He died in 1931.

Handbook to The Hymnal

HYMN: The stanzas which compose this hymn were first published as the "Harvard Prize Hymn" for 1910. They have become widely popular for the beauty of their form, the depth of their meaning, and because they comprehend such a vast body of Christian truth in a compass so remarkably small.

COMPOSER: Henry Lowell Mason is the grandson of the famous Lowell Mason. He has been a member of Mason & Hamlin Co., a firm of piano manufacturers, since 1888 and since 1915 its president. He is also the author of small histories of the piano and the American reed organ.

TUNE: "Exeter" was directly inspired by the words with which it is associated in "The Hymnal." In March, 1923, the composer read the hymn in the Boston Saturday Evening Transcript and was impressed by its thought, simplicity, and beauty. "As I re-read it," he writes, "there instinctively came to me a melody—spontaneously and unsought. As the hour was late, and as I did not wish to disturb the members of my family, I did not write it down until the next morning, which was Sunday. The name 'Exeter' was chosen because of my affection for Phillips Exeter Academy, which I attended as a lad."

In rendering the hymn simplicity is most to be desired. As for the tempo, the tune should not drag, nor should it be hurried, but should proceed moderately, evenly, and with no pause between the two phrases of its two periods.

---

182   HYMN: O Son of Man, Who Walked Each Day
        TUNE: Soldau

Author: *Nancy Byrd Turner*   Source: *"Wittenberg Gesangbuch"*

AUTHOR: Nancy Byrd Turner, poet, author, editor, was born in Boydton, Virginia, on July 29, 1880. She was the daughter of an Episcopal minister. She graduated at Hannah More Academy, Maryland, in 1898. In 1916 she joined the staff of The Youth's Companion, in Boston, and served as editor of the children's page from 1918 to 1922. She was a member of the staff of the Independent, in Boston, in 1926, and since 1928 has been a member of the editorial staff of Houghton Mifflin Company. She is the author of a number of books and a contributor to magazines both in America and in England.

HYMN: This hymn expresses a definite Christian experience with sincerity, simplicity, and strength. It was written by request for use in "The Church School Hymnal for Youth," appearing in 1928.

Jesus Christ the Lord

SOURCE: The source is the "Wittenberg Gesangbuch." For comments on German hymnody, see the article, "German Hymn Sources," under "Original Sources," page xxi.

TUNE: For comments on the tune, "Soldau," see Hymn 102.

183
HYMN: Far Off I See the Goal
TUNE: Moab

Author: *Rev. Robert Rowland Roberts*

Composer: *Rev. John Roberts (Ieuan Gwyllt)*

AUTHOR: Robert Rowland Roberts, one of the most distinguished preachers in the Presbyterian Church of Wales, was born at Penmaenmawr in 1865, and was ordained to the ministry in 1891. In addition to the work of his pastorates at Aberdare, Chester, and Cardiff, he served as moderator of the South Wales Association and delivered the Davies Lecture for 1908, dealing with Christian mysticism.

HYMN: At the request of Rev. S. O. Morgan, this hymn was written to be sung to the famous Welsh tune "Moab" and to be included in the revised edition of "The Church Hymnary" of the Presbyterian Churches of Great Britain. It appeared first in a program of praise, used June 29, 1925, at the meeting of the Presbyterian Alliance at Cardiff.

COMPOSER: Rev. John Roberts (Ieuan Gwyllt) was born at Tanrhiwfelen, near Aberystwyth, in 1822, and was ordained to the ministry in the Calvinistic Methodist Church in 1859. He held charges near Merthyr and later at Capel Coch, Llanberis, until he retired in 1869. He died at Vron, near Caernarvon, in 1877. G. Parry Williams writes of him, "As a musician he was unique; incomparable as a musical critic and instructor and an arranger of congregational hymn tunes; and as a conductor of sacred music festivals, he was in a special sense God's gift to Wales." He had a great influence on congregational singing in Wales, since he was the founder of the *Gymanfa Ganu*, or "singing festival," the object of which was to encourage a love for the hymn and the hymn tune. These festivals in turn had a great influence on the educational and religious life of Wales.

TUNE: "Moab" is from the book "Llyfr Tonau Cynulleidfaol." This tune illustrates well the solemn grandeur of the Welsh Congregational tune. It has a strong onward tread, a climax achieved within the range of all voices, and an unmistakable finality in its conclusion. This tune is claimed by many authorities to be the best Welsh tune ever written and one of the greatest hymn tunes in the world.

His Coming in Glory

*

184   HYMN: Lo! He Comes, with Clouds Descending
TUNE: Holywood

Author: *Rev. Charles Wesley*   Source: *J. T. Wade's "Cantus Diversi"*

AUTHOR: For comments on the author, Charles Wesley, see Hymn 26.

HYMN: Few hymns have been more universally used or more altered in form. The original was written by John Cennick (see Hymn 347). The hymn in its original form was first sung in the Moravian Chapel at Dublin, April 20, 1750.

Those hymnologists who have a theory that hymns should not be altered but should be sung as composed would be somewhat surprised by the original verses of Cennick which, for example, began:

> "Lo! He cometh, countless trumpets
> Blow before his bloody sign!
> 'Midst ten thousand saints and angels,
> See the Crucified shine.
> Allelujah!
> Welcome, welcome bleeding Lamb!"

The hymn in its present form contains three of the four stanzas as altered and published by Charles Wesley in his "Hymns of Intercession for All Mankind," 1758. The last two lines, however, are from the original, as Wesley had written:

> "Jah, Jehovah,
> Everlasting God, come down."

A longer form of the hymn, in six stanzas, was prepared by Martin Madan in 1760, combining portions by Wesley with original verses by Cennick. It has been widely popular and has been called "The English 'Dies Irae.'"

SOURCE: For comments on the source, J. T. Wade's "Cantus Diversi," see Hymn 116.

Jesus Christ the Lord

TUNE: The composer of this tune, "Holywood," is unknown. It was printed in "An Essay on the Church Plain Chant," published in 1782, and ten years later in Webbe's "Collection of Motetts." It is found earlier in manuscript form in Wade's manuscript at Stonyhurst College, 1751, and in a similar manuscript, possibly a little earlier, in the Henry Watson Library, Manchester. In the printings mentioned above it is set to the benediction hymn "Tantum Ergo Sacramentum." According to Dr. James Moffatt, the tune seems to have come into usage about the same period as "Adeste Fideles." A slightly different form is found in Gardiner's "Sacred Melodies" of 1815, where it is set to the hymn "Lord, Dismiss Us with Thy Blessing." The tune is characterized by its solidity and by its triumphant note.

---

185   HYMN: The Lord Will Come and Not Be Slow
FIRST TUNE: Old 107th

Author: *John Milton*   Source: *"Scottish Psalter"*

AUTHOR: For comments on the author, John Milton, see Hymn 64.

HYMN: John Milton, who was so famous for the grandeur and extent of his poetic compositions, has had but little influence upon the hymnology of the Church. It is fortunate, however, that this strong hymn has been revived and is being more and more widely used. It does not greatly resemble its original form, but is a cento based on Milton's translation of Ps. 82:4; 85:1–3; 86:5, 6. When but fifteen years of age he had translated Psalms 114 and 136; at the age of forty, when stirred by the stress of the Civil War, he published "Nine of the Psalms Done Into Meter," choosing Psalms 80 to 88. These were exact reproductions of the original, the Hebrew words being printed in the margin, and every English word not in the Hebrew being printed in italics. Five years later he translated Psalms 1 to 8 with much less scrupulous literalism. This cento is said to have been produced by Garrett Horder about 1884. It appeared in his "Worship Song" of 1905 and in "The English Hymnal" of 1906.

SOURCE (First Tune): Until the year 1635 only the proper tunes were given in the various Scottish Psalters, but in that year Andre Hart published an edition with the tunes harmonized in four parts. In the Psalter of 1602 there were three common tunes, tunes which could be sung to any psalm of like meter. In the subsequent editions these common tunes were augmented until in the 1635 edition there were thirty-one such tunes, seven of which were English and twenty-four Scottish. Of the one hundred and eighteen proper tunes, fifty-one are Genevan, thirty-two French, four German, twenty-one English, and ten Scottish. For further comments on the source, see the article, "The Psalters in Early Presbyterian Worship," under "Original Sources," page xv.

TUNE (First): "Old 107th" was an air composed or adapted for this psalm in the "French Psalter," 1543–1544, by L. Bourgeois.

SECOND TUNE: St. Magnus

Composer: *Jeremiah Clark*

COMPOSER (Second Tune): Jeremiah Clark (1670–1707) was one of the outstanding English composers of hymn tunes. Dr. Bridges calls him "the inventor of the modern English hymn tune." Clark was born in London and was a chorister at the Chapel Royal. Subsequently he became organist of Winchester College, of St. Paul's, and joint organist with William Croft, of the Chapel Royal. His physical condition and extreme sensitiveness inclined him to melancholy. Dr. Robert Bridges wrote of Clark's music: "His tunes are beautiful, and have the plaintive grace characteristic of his music and melancholy temperament. They are the first in merit of their kind, as they were first in time; and they are truly national and popular in style." Clark died in London in 1707.

TUNE (Second): In "The Divine Companion," published in 1709, "St. Magnus" appears as an anonymous tune. However, it follows three tunes, the first of which is headed, "The Three Following Tunes by Mr. Jer. Clark," and forms with them one set which is followed, not by further hymns, but by a set of anthems.

---

186   HYMN: Thou Art Coming, O My Saviour
        TUNE: Gwalia

Author: *Frances R. Havergal*   Source: *Welsh Hymn Melody*

AUTHOR: For comments on the author, Frances Ridley Havergal, see Hymn 56.

HYMN: Miss Havergal cherished the expectation of the glorious, personal, visible return of the Lord. This hymn can best be appreciated in connection with such New Testament passages as Heb., ch. 7, which pictures Christ as at once a King and a Priest,

Jesus Christ the Lord

and ch. 9:24–28, where his reappearance is compared to that of the high priest, the golden bells of whose glorious robe could be heard as he was returning from the Holy of Holies. The second stanza brings to mind I Thess. 4:13–18; and the third reëchoes many predictions of universal triumph, such as Psalm 72 and Phil. 2:9–11.

SOURCE: For comments on the source, a Welsh hymn melody, see the article, "Welsh Hymnody," under "Original Sources," page xxii.

TUNE: This setting is a special arrangement of "Gwalia" made by the editors of "The Hymnal." The tune appears in its regular form in Hymn 189. Its association with Miss Havergal's great hymn, "Thou Art Coming, O My Saviour," is fortunate. The arrangement is timely and adequately expresses the majestic lines of the text. "Gwalia" is an old Welsh melody and in 1769 appeared in "The Lock Hospital Collection," which was edited by Martin Madan. In "The Lock Hospital Collection" "Gwalia" bore the name "Love Divine." Under the same name it was included in Rev. H. Parr's "Church of England Psalmody." In that volume the editor distinctly observes that it is a Welsh melody. "Gwalia" is a majestic tune and should be sung with stately rhythm.

---

187 HYMN: The King Shall Come When Morning Dawns
TUNE: St. Stephen

Source: *Greek Hymn*   Composer: *Rev. William Jones*

SOURCE: This was originally a Greek hymn.

TRANSLATOR: John Brownlie, D.D., clergyman, educator, author, and poet, was born at Glasgow in 1859 and was educated at the University of Glasgow and at the Free Church College there. For many years he served as pastor at Portpatrick, Wigtownshire. Deeply interested in popular education, he served as a governor, and for a time as chairman of the board of governors, of the Stranraer High School. He was a careful student of hymnology, particularly of the hymns of the Latin and Greek Churches. In 1899 he published "Hymns and Hymn Writers of the Church Hymnary." Many of his original hymns appeared in "Hymns of Our Pilgrimage Zionward," "Hymns of the Pilgrim Life," and "Pilgrim Songs." His wide scholarship and his genius as a translator were attested by his "Hymns of the Early Church," "Hymns from East and West," and "Hymns of the Greek Church."

Handbook to The Hymnal

HYMN: "The King Shall Come When Morning Dawns" is a free translation of a hymn of the Greek Church. It ranks high among the hymns of the Second Advent. It breathes a spirit of confident expectation and triumphant hope. It should be studied in connection with such Bible passages as Heb. 9:27, 28; I John 3:2; and Rev. 22:7, 17, 20.

COMPOSER: William Jones (1726–1800), an English clergyman who was curate of Nayland, Suffolk, was a writer of church music, including "A Treatise on the Art of Music," published in 1784, and of various theological, philosophical, and scientific works. He was educated at the Charterhouse and University College, Oxford.

TUNE: "St. Stephen" is from "Ten Church Pieces for the Organ," 1789, where the tune appears at the end of the book, set to Psalm 23 and called "St. Stephen's Tune." It is sometimes known as "Nayland" or "Newington."

---

188   HYMN: Come, Lord, and Tarry Not
TUNE: St. Bride

Author: *Rev. Horatius Bonar*   Composer: *Samuel Howard*

AUTHOR: For comments on the author, Horatius Bonar, see Hymn 60.

HYMN: Dr. Bonar was a devoted student of prophecy and believed that the age of glory and of gold would follow the reappearance of Christ. To the promise "Yea: I come quickly," he was ever ready to respond, "Amen: come, Lord Jesus." Such a longing for the returning Christ inspired this Advent hymn. It is based upon such phrases as are found in the closing chapters of Revelation: "Behold, I make all things new"; "I saw a new heaven and a new earth"; "Behold, I come quickly"; "The Spirit and the bride say, Come"; and "The kingdom of the world is become the kingdom of our Lord, and of his Christ."

COMPOSER: Samuel Howard was born in 1710 and died in London in 1782. He was a chorister in the Chapel Royal. Later he was organist at St. Bride's, Fleet Street. Cambridge honored him with the degree of Doctor of Music in 1769. He collaborated with Dr. William Boyce, who was composer to the Chapel Royal and master of the King's Band, in compiling and publishing three large volumes entitled "Cathedral Music." Dr. Howard's musical ability as organist

204

and composer was recognized in this great task which he shared with
Dr. Boyce.

TUNE: "St. Bride" is first found in William Riley's "Parochial
Harmony," where it was set to Psalm 130 and was headed "St.
Bridget's Tune, by Mr. Saml. Howard."

---

189   HYMN: O'er the Distant Mountains Breaking
           TUNE: Gwalia

Author: *Rev. John S. B. Monsell*   Source: *Welsh Hymn Tune*

AUTHOR: For comments on the author, John S. B. Monsell, see
Hymn 7.

HYMN: This hymn, which was published in 1863 under the heading "Second Advent," embodies many of the phrases in the
stirring exhortation of the Apostle Paul and indicates the attitude
of mind which he intimated should characterize those who look for
Christ and love his appearing: "And this, knowing the season, that
already it is time for you to awake out of sleep: for now is salvation nearer
to us than when we first believed. The night is far spent, and the day is
at hand: let us therefore cast off the works of darkness, and let us put
on the armor of light," Rom. 13:11, 12.

SOURCE: For comments on the source, a Welsh hymn tune, see the
article, "Welsh Hymnody," under "Original Sources," page xxii.

TUNE: For comments on the tune, "Gwalia," see Hymn 186.

Praise to Christ the Lord

*

190   HYMN: Crown Him with Many Crowns
           TUNE: Diademata

Author: *Rev. Matthew Bridges*   Composer: *George J. Elvey*

AUTHOR: For comments on the author, Matthew Bridges, see
Hymn 153.

HYMN: This is one of the most spiritual and beautiful of the hymns composed by Rev. Matthew Bridges. The original consisted of six stanzas and appeared in the second edition of Bridges' "Hymns of the Heart," 1851, where it was headed by the text, Rev. 19: 12, in which there occur the words "On his head were many crowns" (King James Version). In its present form of four stanzas, four crowns are mentioned: first that of the "Lamb upon His throne"; second that of the "Lord of love"; third that of the "Lord of peace"; and fourth that of the "Lord of years." The stanzas have been recast and follow the form published in "Church Hymns" and in "The Church of England Hymnbook" of 1880, by Rev. Godfrey Thring. In Bridges' "Passion of Jesus," 1852, this hymn is entitled "Third Sorrowful Mystery, Song of the Seraphs."

COMPOSER: For comments on the composer, George J. Elvey, see Hymn 109.

TUNE: "Diademata" first appeared in "Hymns Ancient and Modern" in the Appendix of 1868. If the primary function of a hymn tune is to reënforce and to convey the feeling of the text, then in "Diademata" and "Crown Him with Many Crowns" we behold a perfect union. The tune fully conveys the triumphant and ecstatic joy of the text, and yet its great dignity and solidity are preserved. It is a tune which organists like to play and which choirs and congregations enjoy singing.

---

191 HYMN: Come, Christians, Join to Sing
TUNE: Madrid

Author: *Christian Henry Bateman* Source: *Unknown*

AUTHOR: Christian Henry Bateman was a clergyman of the Church of England who previously had been a minister of the Moravian Church and then of the Congregational Church. He served as curate in Jersey, in Childshill, Middlesex, and finally at Penymyndd, Hawarden. His supreme work, however, was in the field of hymnody. He edited a hymn book for children under the title "Sacred Melodies for Sabbath Schools and Families," 1843, which reached a circulation of millions and was for many years the book regularly used in the Sunday Schools of Scotland. After taking orders in the Church of England, he published in London "The Children's Hymnal and Christian Year."

HYMN: This hymn, "Come, Christians, Join to Sing," was originally intended for young people, and began, "Come, children, join to sing." In its present form it is well adapted for the use of worshipers of all ages.

Jesus Christ the Lord

SOURCE: The source of this hymn tune is unknown.

HARMONIZER: For comments on the harmonizer, David Evans, see Hymn 177.

TUNE: "Madrid" is of obscure origin. The tune first appeared, according to Dr. Moffatt, under the lengthy heading, "The Spanish Hymn, Arranged and Composed for the Concerts of the Musical Fund Society of Philadelphia, by Benjamin Carr. The Air from an Ancient Spanish Melody. Printed from the Condensed Score of the Society, and Presented to the Composer as a Tribute of Respect and Regard by Some of the Members, his Friends. Philadelphia, 1826." In the preface to this publication, December 29, 1824, is given as the date of performance.

---

192   HYMN: All Hail the Power of Jesus' Name
      FIRST TUNE: Coronation

Authors: *Rev. Edward Perronet*   Composer: *Oliver Holden*
(Stanza 4) *Rev. John Rippon*

AUTHORS: Rev. Edward Perronet was an independent thinker and a bold preacher, whose temper was often harsh and irascible but whose devotion to Christ was unquestioned. His saintly father, who belonged to a family of French refugees, was vicar of Shoreham and a beloved friend and adviser of John and Charles Wesley. He was sometimes called the "archbishop of Methodism." The son was born in 1726 and was educated for the ministry of the Church of England, but under the influence of the Wesleys he became an itinerant Methodist preacher. His bitter antipathy to the Church of England, and his insistence upon separation and upon granting to itinerant preachers licenses to administer the sacraments, led to a separation from the Methodists. He joined the Countess of Huntingdon's Connexion, or sect; but the Countess objected to his violent attacks upon the Church, and he became pastor of a small dissenting congregation at Canterbury, where he died in 1792.

John Rippon, D.D., was born at Tiverton, Devon, April 29, 1751, and was educated for the ministry at the Baptist College, Bristol. In 1773 he became pastor of the Baptist Church in Carter Lane, Tooley Street, London, and over this church he continued to preside until his death, December 17, 1836. He was one of the most influential Dissenting ministers of his time. His collection of hymns, which appeared in 1787, was a famous work. He performed an important service to Baptist hymnody, and is said to have gained for himself an "estate" through the great sale of his works.

HYMN: For many years the origin of the hymn was unknown, but it is now well established as the work of Perronet and constitutes the most notable achievement of the author's life. The original consisted of eight stanzas. The first, seventh, and eighth are printed in "The Hymnal," together with a last stanza which was added by Rev. John Rippon. Each stanza rises to a great climax, and together these stanzas form one of the most stirring and triumphant hymns in the English tongue.

COMPOSER (First Tune): Oliver Holden (1765–1844) was born in Shirley, Massachusetts. He was a carpenter by trade, and, when the British burned Charlestown after the Battle of Bunker Hill, Holden moved there to aid in rebuilding the city and was a resident there for the rest of his life. He was a deeply religious man, a pillar of the church, an organizer and conductor of many singing schools, and a prominent composer of his day. Such was his reputation that when Washington visited Boston in 1789 the city authorized him to write the music and words and train the choir which was to sing the triumphal ode as Washington reached the Old State House. After William Billing's death, he was one of the most popular composers of psalm and hymn tunes in America. Holden edited and published various hymn books, among them "American Harmony," 1793, and "The Worcester Collection," 1797. The fact that Holden wrote hymns as well as tunes is often overlooked. Probably the most widely sung hymn of his compositions is "They Who Seek the Throne of Grace." He lived to be seventy-nine, and his deeply devout nature and creativity to the very last are evidenced by his last words: "I have some beautiful airs running through my head, if I only had strength to note them down."

TUNE (First): "Coronation" was first published in 1793 in "Union Harmony," or "The Universal Collection of Sacred Music," in two volumes. Holden wrote this tune just after the birth of his first-born, a daughter, which probably accounts for the unalloyed joy running through its melodic pattern. The little organ of four and a half octaves on which it was first played is now in the Old State House, Boston.

SECOND TUNE: Miles Lane
Composer: *William Shrubsole*

COMPOSER (Second Tune): William Shrubsole (1760–1806), the son of a farrier, was born in Canterbury, England, and was for seven years a chorister in Canterbury Cathedral. In 1782 he

Jesus Christ the Lord

became organist of Bangor Cathedral, but trouble soon developed because of his sympathy with dissenters, and the following proclamation was issued: "If the William Shrubsole shall be found to frequent any conventicle or religious assembly, where anything is taught which is contrary to the Doctrine or Discipline of the Church of England, the Dean shall be empowered to discharge him from his place of organist." Two months later he was discharged, after which he became organist of Spa Fields Chapel, of Lady Huntingdon's Connexion, which position he retained until his death. While yet a chorister in Canterbury he became a close friend of Perronet. Perronet made him one of the executors of his will, with these words of appreciation: "A fine disinterested affection he has ever shown me from our first acquaintance, even when a proverb of reproach, cast off by all my relatives, disinherited unjustly, and left to sink or swim as afflictions and God's providence should appoint."

TUNE (Second): "Miles Lane," long a favorite in England, is gaining favor in this country. It is more difficult to perform than "Coronation" because of its wide melodic range and interrupted pace. It does, however, achieve true majesty in its stately movement and a thrilling climax in the fourfold repetition of "Crown Him." It was first printed in The Gospel Magazine, of November, 1779, without author's or composer's name. The tune appeared shortly afterwards in Rev. Stephen Addington's "Collection" with Shrubsole's name as composer.

193

HYMN: Rejoice, the Lord Is King
FIRST TUNE: Darwall's 148th

Author: *Rev. Charles Wesley*   Composer: *Rev. John Darwall*

AUTHOR: For comments on the author, Charles Wesley, see Hymn 26.

HYMN: This hymn of Wesley's appeared first in his "Hymns for Our Lord's Resurrection," 1746. Only three of the six original stanzas are used in "The Hymnal," and they form a triumphant pæan of praise to Christ as Lord and King. It is suitable for all services of adoration, as only the last portion of the second stanza sounds the resurrection note and brings to mind the majestic vision of the risen Christ with which the Apocalypse opens, and where is heard the kingly claim, "I am . . . the Living one; and I was dead, and behold, I am alive for evermore, and I have the keys of death and of Hades," Rev. 1:17, 18.

COMPOSER (First Tune): For comments on the composer, John Darwall, see Hymn 50.

TUNE (First): For comments on the tune, "Darwall's 148th," see Hymn 50.

SECOND TUNE: Jubilate

Composer: Horatio Parker

COMPOSER (Second Tune): For comments on the composer, Horatio Parker, see Hymn 19.

TUNE (Second): "Jubilate," with its smooth, yet joyful, melodic progression and its march rhythm, makes a splendid tune for processional use. This tune appeared in the Hymnal of the Episcopal Church in 1894.

---

194 HYMN: Fairest Lord Jesus
TUNE: Schönster Herr Jesu

Source: *German Hymn*   Source: *Silesian Folk Song*

SOURCE: This is a seventeenth century German hymn.

HYMN: "Fairest Lord Jesus" has been known as the "Crusaders' Hymn." It is said to have been sung by the German knights of the twelfth century on their way to Jerusalem. For this beautiful tradition, however, no foundation of fact has been discovered. The words of the hymn cannot be traced earlier than the year 1677, nor the music earlier than 1842. It appeared in "The Münster Hymn Book" of 1677 as the first of "three beautiful selected new hymns." The original form was in five stanzas and began, "Schönster Herr Jesu." It appeared in a greatly altered form in the "Schlesische Volkslieder," published in Leipzig in 1842, with a second stanza which was practically new. The text and melody are said to have been taken down from oral recitation in the district of Glaz. It is this text which forms the basis for the English translation printed by Richard S. Willis in his "Church-Chorals," in 1850. The author of this translation is not known. Another version, entitled "Beautiful Saviour! King of Creation," by Dr. J. A. Seiss, was published in "The Sunday School Book" of the American Lutheran General Council, Philadelphia, 1873.

Jesus Christ the Lord

SOURCE: This tune comes from a Silesian folk-song collection published in Leipzig in 1842.

TUNE: Dr. Hofmann, an editor of the folk-song collection of 1842, writes in the preface: "In the summer of 1836 I visited a friend in Westphalia. Toward evening I heard the haymakers singing: I made inquiries: They sang folk songs which seemed to me worthy of being collected. For this purpose I associated myself with my friend, Richter, and we divided the work between us. He had charge of the musical portion, and I took the rest. How far back this melody goes cannot be determined. It is sung by all classes and all ages, from the shepherd on the hillside to the lisping urchin in the nursery." F. Melius Christiansen, the director of the famous St. Olaf Choir, has arranged an exquisite anthem, "Beautiful Saviour," on the melody of "Schönster Herr Jesu."

---

195   HYMN: The Head That Once Was Crowned with Thorns
TUNE: St. Magnus

Author: *Rev. Thomas Kelly*   Composer: *Jeremiah Clark*

AUTHOR: Rev. Thomas Kelly was a man of deep piety, wide learning, and marked genius. He was born in 1769, the son of an Irish judge, and was educated at Trinity College, Dublin. Destined for the bar he entered the Temple, London, but due to a profound religious experience, his plans were changed and he was ordained in the Established Church. His evangelistic zeal and spiritual fervor displeased the archbishop of Dublin, who forbade him to preach in any church of the diocese. He thereupon withdrew from the Episcopal Church and, as he was a man of wealth, built a number of independent places of worship. He was a magnetic, consecrated, inspiring preacher. He was also a friend of every worthy benevolent and religious cause. He labored in Dublin for about sixty years and died in 1854, at the age of eighty-five. His abiding influence is due to his ability and industry as a musician and poet. His "Hymns on Various Passages of Scripture," 1804, number 765. Among these are some of the finest hymns in the English language.

HYMN: This hymn was published in 1820 with the title "Perfect Through Sufferings," Heb. 2: 10. It is an appeal to believers to be patient in bearing the cross, in view of the sufferings and consequent glory of Christ. The last stanza of the hymn was as follows:

"The cross he bore is life and health,
Though shame and death to him;
His people's hope, his people's wealth,
Their everlasting theme."

COMPOSER: For comments on the composer, Jeremiah Clark, see Hymn 185.

TUNE: For comments on the tune, "St. Magnus," see Hymn 185.

---

196   HYMN: Blessing and Honor and Glory and Power
TUNE: O Quanta Qualia

Author: *Rev. Horatius Bonar*   Source: *La Feillée's "Méthode du Plain Chant"*

AUTHOR: For comments on the author, Horatius Bonar, see Hymn 60.

HYMN: Rev. Horatius Bonar in the third series of his "Hymns of Faith and Hope," published in 1866, included a hymn of eight stanzas, entitled "The Song of the Lamb." In the present form of this hymn, four of these stanzas have been selected and transposed. To appreciate the spirit and message of the hymn it is necessary to read the superb description of the music of heaven contained in Rev., chs. 4; 5, and specifically to note the song in which are united the praises of "every created thing which is in the heaven, and on the earth, and under the earth, and on the sea, and all things that are in them, . . . saying,
    Unto him that sitteth on the throne, and unto the Lamb, be the blessing, and the honor, and the glory, and the dominion, for ever and ever."

SOURCE: For comments on the source, La Feillée's "Méthode du Plain Chant," see Hymn 24.

TUNE: "O Quanta Qualia" in La Feillée's book appears as a plain-song melody in Alcaic meter, set to the hymn of J. de Santeüil, "Regnator Orbis." The tune is probably of older origin than this. It was adapted for use with Neale's translation of "O Quanta Qualia"— "O What Their Joy and Their Glory Must Be"—in "The Hymnal Noted," 1854. While the melody is of seventeenth- or eighteenth-century origin, in its beautiful flow it possesses the characteristics and style of plain chant.

Jesus Christ the Lord

197
HYMN: Majestic Sweetness Sits Enthroned
FIRST TUNE: Nun Danket All' (Gräfenberg)

Author: *Rev. Samuel Stennett*   Composer: *Johann Crüger*

AUTHOR: Rev. Samuel Stennett, son of a Baptist clergyman, was born at Exeter, England, in 1727. In 1748 he became his father's assistant in the pastorate of a church in Little Wild Street, London. Succeeding his father in 1758, he continued as pastor for thirty-seven years, until the time of his death in 1795. He was among the most prominent of the Nonconformist clergymen of the time and won the respect of many political leaders, whom he influenced in support of his principles of religious freedom. He contributed some thirty-eight hymns to the collection of his friend, Dr. John Rippon.

HYMN: "Chief Among Ten Thousand; or the Excellencies of Christ, S. of Sol. 5:10–16" was the title given to this hymn, which was published in Rippon's "Selection" in 1787. There were nine stanzas, the first of which began,

> "To Christ, the Lord, let every tongue
> Its noblest tribute bring."

The fifth stanza in the original is included in many hymnals:

> "He saw me plunged in deep distress,
> He flew to my relief;
> For me he bore the shameful cross
> And carried all my grief."

COMPOSER (First Tune): For comments on the composer, Johann Crüger, see Hymn 158.

TUNE (First): "Nun Danket All' (Gräfenberg)" appeared in the fifth edition of "Praxis Pietatis Melica," published in 1653. The early history of this great work is rather obscure. The first edition was issued between 1640 and 1645, and in one hundred years approximately sixty editions were published. There were forty-five Berlin editions and over twelve Frankfurt editions. The fifth edition was issued in 1653, and Dr. Julian's "A Dictionary of Hymnology" states that this is the earliest perfect Berlin edition that has been found. In these various editions are found some of the finest work of the period, including the first appearances of hymns by P. Gerhardt, J. Franck, and P. J. Spener, and some of the best tunes.

Handbook to The Hymnal

In "Hymns Ancient and Modern" there is an adaptation of this tune by Hately. The form of the tune used in "The Hymnal" is the original.

SECOND TUNE: Ortonville

Composer: *Thomas Hastings*

COMPOSER (Second Tune): Thomas Hastings (1784–1872) from his earliest childhood had a passionate love for music. As a child he was exposed to all the rigors of frontier life. He was born in Litchfield County, Connecticut. According to H. Augustine Smith, in "Lyric Religion," at twelve years of age his family migrated by sleigh and ox sledge to Clinton, New York. In six years he was leading the village choir, and in 1817 he ventured away from the farm and devoted himself to his beloved profession of music. He constantly preached the doctrine that "religion has the same claim substantially in song as in speech," and his lectures, innumerable books, articles, and musical leadership combined to emphasize this viewpoint. He edited a religious journal, The Western Recorder, published in Utica, using its columns to give wider currency to his views. In 1832 Hastings was called to New York by a group of churches which had united in inviting him to make that city his home. From then on, his influence on American church music was great. He is said to have written about six hundred hymns and a thousand hymn tunes, and to have published fifty books of music. Probably his most familiar hymn is "Hail to the Brightness of Zion's Glad Morning." Some of the best-known of his tunes are "Toplady," "Retreat," "Zion," and "Ortonville." His works include "Church Melodies," "Devotional Hymns and Poems," and "The History of Forty Choirs." He collaborated with Lowell Mason in "Spiritual Songs for Social Worship." The University of the City of New York in 1858 gave him the degree of Doctor of Music.

TUNE (Second): "Ortonville" was composed by Thomas Hastings in 1837, and, since its appearance in "The Presbyterian Psalmodist" of 1852, it has been included in all Presbyterian hymnals. Though it is associated with "Majestic Sweetness Sits Enthroned," at first it was set to "O for a Closer Walk with God." The tune is in almost as great favor as Dr. Hastings' "Toplady." Now nearly a hundred years old, "Ortonville" continues as a favorite. It is as simple as a folk song and as popular.

214

Jesus Christ the Lord

198 HYMN: Ye Servants of God, Your Master Proclaim
TUNE: Lyons

Author: *Rev. Charles Wesley*   Composer: *J. Michael Haydn*

AUTHOR: For comments on the author, Charles Wesley, see Hymn 26.

HYMN: This hymn was published in 1744 by Rev. Charles Wesley, and was the first hymn in the section of that hymn book marked "Hymns to be Sung in Tumult." The pamphlet in which it appeared was called "Hymns for Times of Trouble and Persecution."

There had been an outbreak of fierce persecution against the followers of the Wesleys. England was at war with France. The House of Stuart was seeking full restoration. There was fear of an invasion which might bring back the exiled representative of that line and dethrone King George II. The Methodists were actually accused of being Papists in disguise and of working for the cause of the Pretender. Their meetings were dispersed by mobs and their ministers impressed into military service, while the Wesleys were brought before the magistrates for examination.

Amid these disturbances and distresses the hymn "Ye Servants of God, Your Master Proclaim" sounded a note of courage and of unshaken faith. The two stanzas of the original which are omitted are inferior to the four which usually form the hymn. However, they describe quite vividly the threatening "floods" and raging "billows" of the dark "times of trouble." Yet their omission makes the hymn of greater value, as appropriate to all times and occasions when Christian believers may wish to unite in triumphant praise of their Master and Lord.

COMPOSER: J. Michael Haydn (1737-1806) was a brother of the distinguished Franz Joseph Haydn. He was born at Rohrau, in lower Austria, and was first known as a boy soprano, then as a violinist and a pianist, and later as an organist and choirmaster. He himself possessed distinguished gifts which, however, were not equal to those of his brilliant brother, Franz Joseph. He was a warm-hearted, devout man. For a time he lived in Hungary, where his compositions were first published. He became choirmaster first at Grosswardein to the bishop, Count Firmian; then in 1762 at Salzburg to Archbishop Sigismund. He was organist also in the churches of the Holy Trinity and St. Peter in Salzburg. Among other compositions, his writings include one hundred and fourteen graduals, a "Mass in D Minor," a "Lauda Sion," and a "Tenebrae in E Flat."

TUNE: The tune, "Lyons," is an arrangement from Haydn's compositions. It appeared in "The Boston Handel and Haydn Society Collection" as early as 1820, where it was set to "O! Praise Ye the Lord, Prepare a New Song." From that collection it was drawn into denominational hymn books. The arrangement quite likely was made by Dr. Lowell Mason, "who was responsible for the selection of the music and revision of the harmonies."

---

199   HYMN: O for a Thousand Tongues to Sing
TUNE: Richmond

Author: *Rev. Charles Wesley*   Composer: *Thomas Haweis*

AUTHOR: For comments on the author, Charles Wesley, see Hymn 26.

HYMN: These stanzas have been selected and rearranged from the poem written by Charles Wesley to celebrate the first anniversary of his spiritual birth, which he dated May 21, 1738. The original contained eighteen stanzas and was headed "For the Anniversary Day of One's Conversion." Written in 1739, it was published in "Hymns and Sacred Poems" in 1740. The first stanza of the original is the one which appears as the last stanza in "The Hymnal." Most of the several forms in which the abbreviated poem appears begin with the line, "O for a thousand tongues to sing." This line is said to have had its origin in a remark made by Peter Böhler, the Moravian missionary, who, when consulted by Wesley about praising Christ, replied, "Had I a thousand tongues I would praise Him with them all." This hymn has stood first in "The Wesleyan Hymnbook" since 1780. It has held the same place in the official books of the Methodist Episcopal Church from the time of the Church's organization in 1784. It may be interesting to note that in the second line the author wrote, "My dear Redeemer's praise"; and the first line of the third stanza read, "He breaks the power of canceled sin." These original lines are still widely used. The hymn is one of the best existing expressions of the real joy of salvation.

COMPOSER: Thomas Haweis, LL.B., M.D., was born in Truro in 1734, and began the study of medicine with a physician in Truro. Eventually, however, through the influence of the earnest preaching of Rev. Samuel Walker, of St. Mary's at Truro, he resolved to study for holy orders and went to Christ Church, Oxford, and later to Magdalen. In 1757 he was appointed to the curacy of St. Mary Magdalen's Church, Oxford. Later he became rector of All Saints, Ald-

Jesus Christ the Lord

winkle, Northamptonshire, and chaplain to Lady Huntingdon's chapel at Bath. In old age he retired to Bath, where he died in 1820. He published various prose works and a collection of hymns, entitled "Carmina Christo, or Hymns to the Saviour."

ADAPTER: "Richmond" was arranged from the collection "Carmina Christo" by Samuel Webbe (1770–1843), son of the composer of the tune "Melcombe" (see Hymn 31). The younger Webbe studied music under his father and Clementi. He was organist of the Unitarian Church, Paradise Street, Liverpool; the Spanish Ambassador's Chapel, London; St. Nicholas Church, and St. Patrick's Roman Catholic Chapel, Liverpool. He was well-known as a composer of glees, songs, motets, and madrigals.

TUNE: In "Carmina Christo" this tune is used with "O Thou from Whom All Goodness Flows" and in its original form had a repeat of the third line.

---

200   HYMN: O Saviour, Precious Saviour
       TUNE: Angel's Story

Author: *Frances Ridley Havergal*   Composer: *Arthur H. Mann*

AUTHOR: For comments on the author, Frances Ridley Havergal, see Hymn 56.

HYMN: This hymn was written at Leamington, in November, 1870, under the title "Our King; Ps. 45: 11." It was published in a volume of Miss Havergal's poems, "Under the Surface," 1874. She knew what was meant by the Apostle Peter in his words which the first line of this hymn paraphrases: "Whom not having seen ye love; on whom, though now ye see him not, yet believing, ye rejoice greatly with joy unspeakable and full of glory," I Peter 1: 8.

COMPOSER: Arthur H. Mann, Mus.D. (1850–1930), was born in Norwich, England, and was trained as chorister in the cathedral there by Dr. Zechariah Buck. He was organist in various churches, among them St. Peter's, Wolverhampton; Tettenhall Parish Church; Beverley Minster; King's College, Cambridge. Probably his most distinguished service was performed at King's College, famous for its superb choral music. Mann was musical editor of "The Church of England Hymnal." He was also organist at the University of Cambridge and music master of Leys School in Cambridge. Dr. Mann was an acknowledged authority on the music of Handel. In 1894 he and Ebenezer Prout discovered at the Foundling Hospital the original wind parts of Handel's

217

"Messiah," and the oratorio was performed that year at King's College with the reconstructed score. He composed much church music and edited Tallis' famous motet, written for forty voices. He received the degree of Bachelor of Music in 1874 from Oxford, and in 1882 that of Doctor of Music. Dr. Mann was also an honorary A.M. of the University of Cambridge and a Fellow of King's College.

TUNE: "Angel's Story" is named for the hymn by Emily Huntington Miller, "I Love to Hear the Story." The tune was written to be used with this hymn, and first appeared in 1881 in the English "Methodist Sunday School Hymn Book." It has appeared in other collections under the captions "Supplication" and "Watermouth." In recent years the tune has come into wide usage set to Bode's hymn "O Jesus, I Have Promised."

---

201 HYMN: Look, Ye Saints! The Sight Is Glorious
FIRST TUNE: Coronæ

Author: *Rev. Thomas Kelly*   Composer: *William H. Monk*

AUTHOR: For comments on the author, Thomas Kelly, see Hymn 195.

HYMN: This majestic coronation hymn is taken from "Hymns on Various Passages of Scripture," published in 1809 by Rev. Thomas Kelly. Its text is Rev. 11:15: "The kingdom of the world is become the kingdom of our Lord, and of his Christ: and he shall reign for ever and ever." This is among the most popular and widely used of the hymns which have come from the pen of the author. It is regarded as worthy to rank with the best hymns of Watts and Wesley.

COMPOSER (First Tune): For comments on the composer, William H. Monk, see Hymn 33.

TUNE (First): "Coronæ" is a virile and exultant tune. Its range of voice is well adapted for congregational singing. It was written by Dr. Monk in 1871.

SECOND TUNE: Rex Triumphans
Composer: *G. Everett Hill*

COMPOSER (Second Tune): G. Everett Hill was born in Philadelphia in 1864. Although he was by profession a consulting civil and sanitary engineer, and well connected with societies of his

Jesus Christ the Lord

profession in Europe and America, he also has had time to make himself known as an organist. His love for music was innate. It is said of him that he knew the notes of the scale as soon as he knew the letters of the alphabet. When he was five years of age he profited by an older brother's piano lessons, which he made his own by stealing quietly into the room to observe what the instruction was about. After the lesson was over and the teacher gone, he climbed on the piano stool to work at the exercises prescribed for his brother. He studied organ with Mrs. Bunting, organist of Christ Methodist Episcopal Church, and with Dr. David D. Wood, of St. Stephen's Church, Philadelphia. As organist at the Woodland Presbyterian Church, Philadelphia, from 1881 to 1890, he rendered great service. When his profession required him to move to Newport, Rhode Island, he became organist of St. George's Church there, serving until 1898. From 1899 to 1909 he played the organ and drilled four choirs at Grace Chapel, New York City. His home at Orange, New Jersey, is a place of devotion to the divine art.

TUNE (Second): "Rex Triumphans" is a virile setting for "Look, Ye Saints! The Sight Is Glorious." The tune was written while the composer was organist in the Woodland Presbyterian Church, Philadelphia. For years it has been used regularly at the Communion service in that church.

---

202 HYMN: Saviour, Blessèd Saviour
TUNE: David

Author: *Rev. Godfrey Thring*   Composer: *Thomas Morley*

AUTHOR: For comments on the author, Godfrey Thring, see Hymn 38.

HYMN: "Saviour, Blessèd Saviour" was written in 1862 under the heading "The Goal." Its inspiration was the words, "I press on toward the goal unto the prize of the high calling of God in Christ Jesus," Phil. 3:14. In "Hymns Congregational and Others," 1866, it was entitled "Pressing Onwards." The original text contained ten stanzas.

COMPOSER: Thomas Morley was born at Oxford, England, January 1, 1842, where his father conducted a bookbinding establishment. Early evincing an interest in music, he was put in training under L. G. Hayne, and became a proficient organist. In his profession as organist he held many influential positions. While he was organist at St. Alban's, Holborn, London, he contributed substantially to the "St.

Handbook to The Hymnal

Alban's Tune Book" by providing new tunes and by arranging Gregorian music for congregational use. His most creative years seem to have been those spent at Holborn. He is chiefly remembered by the compositions of that period.

TUNE: "David" appeared first in "St. Alban's Tune Book," used at Holborn. The tune is simple in structure, fluent in rhythm, and appealing in melody. It is popular with congregations and is quite readily sung.

---

203   HYMN: O Could I Speak the Matchless Worth
       TUNE: Ariel

Author: *Rev. Samuel Medley*   Composer: *Wolfgang Amadeus Mozart*

AUTHOR: Samuel Medley, a Baptist clergyman, was born in Hertfordshire, England, in 1738, and died in Liverpool, in 1799. In his youth he joined the royal navy. Wounded in a battle in 1759, he was compelled to retire from active service. The reading of a sermon by Dr. Watts about this time led to his conversion. For some years he conducted a successful school. His great desire, however, was to preach, and in 1767 he was called as pastor of a Baptist church at Watford. In 1772 he became pastor of the Byrom Street Church, Liverpool, where he ministered to a large congregation for twenty-seven years. He was the author of a number of popular hymns. Of these it has been said, "Their charm consists less in their poetry than in the warmth and occasional pathos with which they give expression to Christian experience."

HYMN: "O Could I Speak the Matchless Worth" appeared in the third edition of the author's book, "Hymns," under the title "Christ Our King." Of the eight original stanzas the second, sixth, and eighth have been selected for "The Hymnal."

COMPOSER: Wolfgang Amadeus Mozart (1756–1791) was a distinguished Austrian pianist and composer and one of the most instinctive geniuses of all musical history. His genius manifested itself in early childhood to such an extent that his father wrote of him, "Our high and mighty Wolfgang knows everything in this, his eighth year, that one can require of a man of forty." At ten years he was able to read at sight almost anything written for clavier or organ and was composing for orchestra and chorus. His youth was spent in the active musical world and in gaining valuable knowledge from his travels among the great musical centers. To his father, Leopold, himself an excellent and accomplished musician, must be given the credit for the child's early training and development. The father was employed as a musician by

Jesus Christ the Lord

the prince-bishops of Salzburg. Under Sigismund, he was able to travel with his son Wolfgang, but under Hieronymus, who succeeded in 1772, the Mozarts were treated with disdain and finally, in 1781, Leopold was insultingly dismissed.

Wolfgang Mozart possessed the capacity of creating musical masterpieces in his mind and then of setting them down with assurance and certainty. Unfortunately, however, he lacked shrewdness in business affairs and this, combined with a certain volatility in disposition, always left him without a stated professional position, except that of court musician. His marriage in 1782 to Constance Weber, who possessed little practical wisdom and constant ill health, together with financial troubles, embroiled him in sordid cares and difficulties which brought his career to a tragic close at the age of thirty-five. His funeral was a shabby and hasty affair, and he was buried in a pauper's grave.

Mozart is now recognized as one of the great artists of history, both in the dexterity and warmth of his performance and in the neat precision, prophetic texture, and vitality of his composition. His compositions, numbering about six hundred, combine all the best forms and fields of composition in his day with the stamp of his own individuality; and historically he is to be termed the flower of the classical period proper.

ARRANGER: For comments on the arranger, Lowell Mason, see Hymn 18.

TUNE: "Ariel" was arranged from the music of Mozart by Lowell Mason. From two trips to Europe Mr. Mason acquired a mass of Continental music which he adapted for use in his several collections, from which church music has been greatly enriched.

The Holy Spirit

*

204

HYMN: Spirit of God, Descend Upon My Heart
TUNE: Morecambe

Author: *Rev. George Croly*   Composer: *Frederick C. Atkinson*

AUTHOR: George Croly was born in Dublin in 1780 and graduated from Trinity College, Dublin. He is remembered chiefly for his distinguished work in the field of general literature, having thirty-one volumes to his credit. He soon retired from parish work in Ireland and took up his residence in London, where his varied gifts in the field of writing made him notable among the writers of his day. "Salathiel," a work of fiction dealing with the fall of Jerusalem, was said to be the literary sensation of the period, while "Catiline" was considered an outstanding poem of that time. Later he returned to the pulpit of St. Stephen's, in a miserable section of London, a church that had been closed for one hundred years. Here he had a really unique preaching career, in spite of the cobwebs and dust that are described as covering the ceiling and hangings. His uncompromising conservatism and great courage in denouncing liberalism of all kinds brought him great crowds of hearers. It is said that he prepared the collection "Psalms and Hymns for Public Worship," at the request of his people, in 1854. It contained twenty-five psalms, many of which were his own metrical arrangement, together with fifty hymns, ten of which he himself wrote. Unfortunately but few copies are in existence, practically the entire issue being destroyed in a fire. Dr. Croly died suddenly in London in 1860.

HYMN: This hymn is based on the words, "If we live by the Spirit, by the Spirit let us also walk," Gal. 5: 25. It appeared first among the ten original hymns of the author in his "Psalms and Hymns for Public Worship" published in 1854. The hymn moves on levels of deep spirituality, its language betraying an intuitive understanding of the needs of the human heart and its vivid, fervent faith bringing the worshiper to the altar, asking that "one holy passion" fill his being.

COMPOSER: Frederick Cook Atkinson was born at Norwich, England, August 21, 1841. Between the years 1849 and 1860 he served as chorister and assistant organist in the Cathedral of Norwich. He studied music at Cambridge, from which he graduated in 1867, with the Bachelor's degree. Subsequently he became organist and choirmaster of St. Paul's and St. John's Churches at Bradford. From Bradford

222

The Holy Spirit

he was called to Norwich Cathedral, where he was organist from 1881 to 1885. Atkinson died in the year 1897.

TUNE: "Morecambe" was composed for the hymn "Abide with Me: Fast Falls the Eventide." However, it has become widely associated with the present hymn. In "The Plymouth Hymnal" it appears without signature, set to Bonar's hymn "Here, O My Lord, I See Thee Face to Face." The reverent tone of the melody and the chaste harmonies produce a highly fitting mood for this hymn. The somewhat reserved climax of the last line is in perfect keeping with the reverent and humble thought of the text.

---

205   HYMN: Our Blest Redeemer, Ere He Breathed
        TUNE: St. Cuthbert

Author: *Harriet Auber*   Composer: *Rev. John B. Dykes*

AUTHOR: Harriet Auber was of Huguenot ancestry, her great-grandfather being among the refugees who, in 1685, came to England from Normandy after the infamous revocation of the Edict of Nantes by Louis XIV. She was born in London in 1773. Her unusual literary tastes led her to undertake the improvement of the Sternhold and Hopkins versions of The Psalms, which she hoped might be displaced with something more worthy of their lofty themes. In 1829, from her study in a quiet village in Hertfordshire, she wrote "The Spirit of the Psalms." Charles Spurgeon recognized the special quality of her spiritual aspirations and poetic language, and included several of her poems in his collection of tabernacle hymns. Harriet Auber died in 1862.

HYMN: This hymn, first published in 1829 in "The Spirit of the Psalms," has been translated into several languages. It is properly ranked among the chief hymns concerning the Holy Spirit. It is in most modern hymnals and is decidedly popular in American churches.

COMPOSER: For comments on the composer, John B. Dykes, see Hymn 53.

TUNE: "St. Cuthbert" was composed for this hymn in "Hymns Ancient and Modern," 1861.

206   HYMN: Come, Holy Spirit, Heavenly Dove
       TUNE: St. Agnes

Author: *Rev. Isaac Watts*   Composer: *Rev. John B. Dykes*

AUTHOR: For comments on the author, Isaac Watts, see Hymn 22.

HYMN: There are in common use twenty different texts of this apparently immortal hymn of Watts. Written in a time of heated doctrinal debates, this hymn ran the severe gauntlet of the various schools of theologians. John Wesley and his followers objected to the implications of the second stanza, which is here omitted, and Wesley modified the hymn to admit more frankly the presence of the freedom of the will. Whitefield in his collection of 1753 made other changes, as did Toplady in 1776. But the current of Christian devotion, unchanged by the literary alterations of the critics, runs through every stanza of the hymn.

COMPOSER: For comments on the composer, John B. Dykes, see Hymn 53.

TUNE: "St. Agnes, Durham," as it is properly called, was composed for the hymn "Jesus, the Very Thought of Thee," in "A Hymnal for Use in the English Church," 1866, edited by Rev. J. Grey.

207   HYMN: O Spirit of the Living God
       TUNE: Melcombe

Author: *James Montgomery*   Composer: *Samuel Webbe*

AUTHOR: For comments on the author, James Montgomery, see Hymn 11.

HYMN: This hymn, by a man who died in early life on the mission field in the West Indies, was written in 1823 to be used at a meeting of a Yorkshire auxiliary missionary society, held in Salem Chapel, Leeds. Under the title "The Spirit Accompanying the Word of God," it found its place as a missionary hymn in Montgomery's "The Christian Psalmist," published in 1825. Among the four hundred hymns by Montgomery, this holds a high place. "Our apostate race" is pleaded for in the fervent language of one consumed with zeal for all the nations that "hearts of stone begin to beat . . . till every kindred call Him Lord."

COMPOSER: For comments on the composer, Samuel Webbe, see Hymn 31.

TUNE: For comments on the tune, "Melcombe," see Hymn 31.

---

208   HYMN: Holy Spirit, Truth Divine
            TUNE: Mercy

Author: *Rev. Samuel Longfellow*   Composer: *Louis M. Gottschalk*

AUTHOR: For comments on the author, Samuel Longfellow, see Hymn 79.

HYMN: While sharing something of his distinguished brother's gift, Rev. Samuel Longfellow added a deeply devotional element to his poetic writings, as is evidenced in this hymn. It was first issued in the book "Hymns of the Spirit," published in 1864. There is reverence and deep mysticism pervading every stanza, as "Truth," "Love," "Power," and "Right," personified revelations of the Holy Spirit, open toward God the channels for our prayers. The worshiper sincerely using this hymn finds "soul," "heart," "will," and "conscience," enriched by the "dawn" of precious light—a glow warming the heart, a new strength in the will, and a new power in the conscience.

COMPOSER: Louis Moreau Gottschalk (1829–1869) was the son of an English father, a Doctor of Science at Cambridge, Massachusetts, and a French mother, daughter of Count Antoine de Brusle. Young Gottschalk studied the piano at an early age, and when he was twelve went to France to further his musical education. While in that country he made professional tours into France, Switzerland, and Spain. After a period he returned to New Orleans, where he began playing and conducting instrumental concerts. His own compositions include two operas, two symphonies, incidental orchestral compositions, piano pieces, and songs. He was idolized by Spanish America. Although his work is notable for its originality and local color, most of it is forgotten to-day. Gottschalk himself is remembered only as a virtuoso, not as an artist of enduring appeal.

TUNE: "Mercy" is an arrangement of a piano composition by Gottschalk, called "The Last Hope." It has been very popular in its present setting. The emotional qualities of the tune are in an idiom peculiar to popular taste, and the warmth of its harmony lends a simple charm to the hymn which has become endeared to the hearts of thousands of worshipers.

---

209 HYMN: Come, Gracious Spirit, Heavenly Dove
TUNE: Holley

Author: *Rev. Simon Browne*   Composer: *George Hews*

AUTHOR: Simon Browne, a touching figure in early hymnology, writing at intervals when his pathetic delusions forsook him, is the author of this hymn. He was born in Somersetshire in 1680, and, after training under Rev. John Moore, entered the Independent ministry. A peculiar mental malady clouded his life. It is thought that the accidental death of a robber at his hands, together with the death of his wife and son, was responsible for the aberrations that spoiled his peace. He felt that to punish him God had "annihilated in him the thinking substance," that he had lost his moral capacity as well as his intellectual power and had "no more sense than a parrot." In spite of this darkness, there came from his troubled brain about twenty books, including a volume of Apologetics, "Exposition of the First Epistle to the Corinthians," several children's books, a dictionary, and other publications. He was a contemporary of Watts, and in 1741 he published "Hymns and Spiritual Songs, in Three Books, Designed as a Supplement to Dr. Watts," containing 166 hymns.

HYMN: From the author's brilliant mind, disturbed at periods with sad obsessions, comes this singing supplication for "light and comfort from above." The hymn first appeared in Browne's own "Hymns and Spiritual Songs" in 1720. Somewhat altered, it appeared later in Ash and Evans' "Collection" of Baptist hymns, published in 1769. Many another soul burdened with confusion and darkness joins in saying,

> "The light of truth to us display,
> And make us know and choose Thy way."

COMPOSER: George Hews (1806–1873) was a professional musician and a manufacturer of pianos in Boston. From about the year 1830 he was a tenor soloist, a teacher of music, and an organist in that city. He was also a prominent figure in the Handel and Haydn Society there. Beyond this little is known of him.

226

The Holy Spirit

TUNE: "Holley," the composer's best-known tune, appeared in the "Boston Academy Collection," edited by Lowell Mason, and published in 1835. Its soft modulations reflect the mood and thought of the hymn.

---

210   HYMN: O Grant Us Light, That We May Know
TUNE: Quebec

Author: *Rev. Lawrence Tuttiett*   Composer: *Henry Baker*

AUTHOR: Lawrence Tuttiett was born in 1825, at Colyton, in Devonshire. The son of a Royal Navy surgeon, he planned to follow in his father's footsteps. However, after graduating at King's College and also at Christ's Hospital, he turned to the Church, and was ordained in 1848. He gave much of his life to two parishes, one in St. Andrews, another in Perth. He died in St. Andrews after a few years of quiet retirement at Pitlochry. He published several manuals of prayers. A dozen of his hymns are still in common use in England and Scotland. He published, in 1854, "Hymns for Churchmen" and, in 1862, "Hymns for the Children of the Church," as well as several devotional books of merit.

HYMN: This hymn appeared in 1864 in Mr. Tuttiett's volume entitled "Germs of Thought on the Sunday Services." The author is said to have written many of his hymns for the use of parish families in special sorrow or distress. This hymn prays for the light most consoling for those called to pass through seasons of painful misery where human explanations are baffled by pain and darkness— the Light that leads to the "open gate."

COMPOSER: For comments on the composer, Henry Baker, see Hymn 89.

TUNE: For comments on the tune, "Quebec," see Hymn 89.

---

211   HYMN: Thou Power and Peace, in Whom We Find
TUNE: Missionary Chant

Author: *Cecil Frances Alexander*   Composer: *Heinrich Christopher*
Zeuner

AUTHOR: For comments on the author, Cecil Frances Alexander, see Hymn 157.

Handbook to The Hymnal

HYMN: Mrs. Alexander's hymns for children had a profound influence. The original form of the first line of this simple, direct, childlike hymn was "Spirit of God, that moved of old." A literal New Testament phraseology is evident in the author's references to the character, presence, and work of the Holy Spirit.

COMPOSER: Heinrich Christopher Zeuner, who was born in Eisleben in Saxony, on September 20, 1795, came to America in 1824 and settled in Boston, Massachusetts. In Boston his accomplishments as a musician were recognized, and he was encouraged to express himself through an active musical leadership. In that city he learned to know Lowell Mason and other leaders in the profession. Zeuner was elected president of the Handel and Haydn Society for a few months in 1838–1839, an office which Dr. Mason had filled from 1827 to 1832. The creative work of Zeuner seems to have reached its climax in 1832, when his book "American Harp" appeared and passed through several editions. In this collection of nearly four hundred pages, all but five of the tunes were Zeuner's own. The work represented indefatigable study and labor. The book was under the control of the Musical Professional Society of Boston, which commended it to the choirs of America. At the time Zeuner was organist at St. Paul's and organist of the Handel and Haydn Society. Some years later he removed to Philadelphia, where he served as organist of St. Anne's Episcopal Church, and later of the Arch Street Presbyterian Church. Under heavy mental depression, due to harsh criticism of his playing, in November, 1857, he sought a lonely spot in the woods and took his own life. His name is perpetuated by many of his tunes which are still sung.

TUNE: "Missionary Chant" is one of Zeuner's best-known tunes. It appeared as Number 45 in "American Harp," 1832, when it was identified with "Ye Christian Heralds, Go Proclaim." That union is perpetuated in this Hymnal in Hymn 381. The tune is a very adaptable one, which explains its association with many different texts.

212
HYMN: Spirit Divine, Attend Our Prayers
TUNE: Nun Danket All' (Gräfenberg)

Author: *Rev. Andrew Reed*   Composer: *Johann Crüger*

AUTHOR: Andrew Reed, the son of a London watchmaker, was born in 1787, in Butcher Row, London. He worked his way through Hackney College, being employed at the family trade, and later was ordained as a Congregational minister, settling in New Road Chapel, St. George's-in-the-East, his home church. He showed remarkable ability as an organizing leader and soon had to build a more commodious edifice for his growing audiences, calling it Wycliffe Chapel. While devoted to the evangelical gospel in his own church, he also served the larger interests of the community of which he was a part. Through his genius as an organizer and his enthusiasm as a philanthropist, he founded six notable welfare institutions, including asylums and hospitals for orphans, idiots, foundlings, and incurables, at an expense of more than $500,000. His reply to his son, who urged that he write his life story, is quoted by Dr. Moffatt: "I was born yesterday, I shall die to-morrow, and I must not spend to-day in telling what I have done, but in doing what I may for Him who has done all for me." Yale University conferred on him the degree of Doctor of Divinity. His hymns, twenty-one in number, first appeared anonymously in his "Hymn Book" of 1825, and under his own name in his later and larger collection, issued in 1842. He died in 1862.

HYMN: This hymn was sung on a special day of prayer and humiliation appointed by the Congregational Church on Good Friday, 1829, with a view "to promote, by the divine blessing, a revival of religion in the British churches." All the characteristics of a truly wholesome evangelistic hymn are revealed in the stanzas of this hymn.

COMPOSER: For comments on the composer, Johann Crüger, see Hymn 158.

TUNE: For comments on the tune, "Nun Danket All' (Gräfenberg)," see Hymn 197.

---

213   HYMN: Breathe on Me, Breath of God
FIRST TUNE: Rhiw

Author: *Rev. Edwin Hatch*   Source: *"A Students' Hymnal"*

AUTHOR: Edwin Hatch, D.D., who ranks as one of England's most scholarly men, was born in Derby, in 1835. He passed through King Edward's School in Birmingham and, later, Pembroke College at Oxford. From his student days his brilliant gifts as a writer were recognized by the reviews. He was of a Nonconformist family but entered the Church of England and became rector of a parish in London. His learning and scholarship won him conspicuous place in the field of historical research. In 1859 he was called to Trinity College, Quebec, to be professor of classical languages, but returned to Oxford to be vice principal of St. Mary's Hall in 1867. Among learned men the Bampton and Hibbert lectureships are considered high marks of distinguished recognition, and Dr. Hatch's contribution under these appointments was notable. His hymns were few in number, but significant. He died on November 10, 1889.

HYMN: This hymn was published in 1890, after the death of its author, in a volume bearing the title "Towards Fields of Light." It had been used previously in a pamphlet printed by Dr. Hatch in 1878, called "Between Doubt and Prayer." With all his great intellectuality, cultural achievements, and wide academic recognition in England and Europe, he ever remained the docile and humble Christian who here seeks "the perfect life" with God.

SOURCE (First Tune): The source is "A Students' Hymnal," University of Wales, 1923. For comments on Welsh hymnody see the article, "Welsh Hymnody," under "Original Sources," page xxii.

TUNE (First): For comments on the tune, "Rhiw," see Hymn 100.

SECOND TUNE: Trentham

Composer: *Robert Jackson*

COMPOSER (Second Tune): For comments on the composer, Robert Jackson, see Hymn 84.

TUNE (Second): For comments on the tune, "Trentham," see Hymn 84.

---

214 HYMN: Gracious Spirit, Dwell with Me
TUNE: Redhead No. 76 (Ajalon)

Author: *Rev. Thomas Toke Lynch*   Composer: *Richard Redhead*

AUTHOR: For comments on the author, Thomas Toke Lynch, see Hymn 82.

HYMN: This and others of the author's hymns were published in 1855 in "The Rivulet." The hymn reflects the life of illness and parish devotion under very great privation that marked Lynch's church work. Most of his hymns, as is true of this one, were prepared for private use only and when they were introduced into the Congregational Church they caused bitter controversy by reason of their intensely personal and introspective character. Thousands, however, are grateful for

The Holy Spirit

this hymn imploring the presence of the Spirit, with his holiness, grace, and truth, bringing healing, wisdom, and purity into the worshiper's heart.

COMPOSER: Richard Redhead (1820–1901) was a chorister of Magdalen College, Oxford. He was organist of Margaret Chapel (later All Saints' Church), London, from 1839 to 1864; then, until 1894, of St. Mary Magdalene, Paddington. Redhead was in profound sympathy with the Oxford Movement and coöperated with Canon Oakeley in reorganizing the services in Margaret Chapel in the direction of an extreme ritual. They edited the first Gregorian Psalter, with the title "Laudes Diurnae." Some of his other works for the church were: "Church Music," chants, sanctuses, and responses; "Hymns for Holy Seasons"; "The Parish Tune Book"; "The Book of Common Prayer"; "Ancient Hymn Melodies and Other Church Tunes"; "The Cathedral and Church Choir Book." These collections had a leading influence in the music of the Catholic Revival.

TUNE: "Redhead No. 76 (Ajalon)," also known as "Petra" and "Ajalon," appeared without name in Redhead's "Church Hymn Tunes, Ancient and Modern," 1853. It was No. 76 in this collection—hence the name "Redhead No. 76." The tune has long been associated with the hymn "Rock of Ages, Cleft for Me," and is as popular in England as "Toplady" is in this country.

The Holy Scriptures

*

215   HYMN: O Word of God Incarnate
         TUNE: Munich

Author: *Bishop William*   Source: *"Neuvermehrtes Meiningisches*
        Walsham How   *Gesangbuch"*

AUTHOR: For comments on the author, William Walsham How, see Hymn 137.

HYMN: This vigorous lyric was written in grateful praise of the Word of God. It comes from one whose modesty and indifference to worldly honors has made him notable. The fact that he declined a bishopric and great church emoluments without ever discussing it with his wife is an index to the trend of his mind and the spirituality of his life. This is perhaps his best-known hymn, but of the sixty in more or less common use, eight appear in "The Hymnal." This hymn on the Holy Scriptures appeared in the supplement of 1867 to "Psalms and Hymns," by Morrell and How. It encompasses with the faith of a practical, believing Christian all the blessed, rewarding qualities of the "Word of God Incarnate."

SOURCE: "Munich" is an old German choral from the "Neuvermehrtes Meiningisches Gesangbuch" of 1693.

TUNE: "Munich" was first associated with "O Gott, Du Frommer Gott." In Germany it is known as the "Königsberg Choral." Kahn, in his "Die Melodien der Deutschen Evangelischen Kirchenlieder," traces "Munich" back to "Lobsingende Harffe," 1682. In Mendelssohn's "Elijah," it is arranged to "Cast Thy Burden Upon the Lord."

---

216   HYMN: Break Thou the Bread of Life
         TUNE: Bread of Life

Author: *Mary A. Lathbury*   Composer: *William F. Sherwin*

AUTHOR: For comments on the author, Mary A. Lathbury, see Hymn 39.

The Holy Scriptures

HYMN: This hymn is appropriate to accompany either the Communion service or the presentation of the claims of Holy Scriptures upon the thought and life of believers. It comes from the fervent religious experience of a devoted Methodist home. It was written for the late Dr. John H. Vincent, one of the two organizers of the Chautauqua Literary and Scientific Circle, whose vesper services at national headquarters on Chautauqua Lake, New York, were famous for more than a generation. It was for the Chautauqua services that this hymn, together with Miss Lathbury's "Day Is Dying in the West," was written.

COMPOSER: For comments on the composer, William F. Sherwin, see Hymn 39.

TUNE: "Bread of Life" is another of those American tunes widely popular in this country. Its simple and sincere style has endeared it to the hearts of all Christian people. It was written at Chautauqua by Mr. Sherwin. It evinces a reverent and intuitive understanding of the musical demands of the Communion service. It is a striking example of an excellent union of words and music. It is natural that it should be so, as the author and the composer of this hymn were in close association in the work at Chautauqua.

---

217   HYMN: The Heavens Declare Thy Glory, Lord
       TUNE: Uxbridge

Author: *Rev. Isaac Watts*   Composer: *Lowell Mason*

AUTHOR: For comments on the author, Isaac Watts, see Hymn 22.

HYMN: We have in this version of Psalm 19 one of the finest results of the hard-earned literary freedom of our devout religious poets, released from the rigid rules in which tradition had bound the metrical rendering of the psalms. Among 454 psalm versions and hymns by Watts, this lyric translation holds high place as a Christian nature hymn, interpreting the universe as a revelation of the wisdom of God and a promise of the complete sovereignty of his truth and power.

COMPOSER: For comments on the composer, Lowell Mason, see Hymn 18.

Handbook to The Hymnal

TUNE: "Uxbridge" appeared in the "Boston Handel and Haydn Society Collection of Church Music," 1831, set to the words "At Anchor Laid, Remote from Home." This tune has been associated with a great number of hymns. Its solid and majestic style makes it an able musical setting for a large class of hymns. It is found in "The Presbyterian Psalmodist" of 1852, edited by Thomas Hastings, and subsequently in most hymnals. The name "Uxbridge," representing Mason's tune, should not be confused with the earlier psalm tune of this same name, sometimes called "Burford," commonly attributed to Purcell. This may be found in John Chetham's "A Book of Psalmody," published in 1718. There is also another psalm tune by this name in Dibdin's "Standard Psalm Tune Book," of 1857.

---

218 HYMN: Father of Mercies, in Thy Word
TUNE: Beatitudo

Author: *Anne Steele*   Composer: *Rev. John B. Dykes*

AUTHOR: Anne Steele, born in 1716, in Broughton, England, was the daughter of William Steele, a lumberman who occupied without salary the pulpit of the local Baptist church. Through her unusual poetic gifts she became the leading hymn writer of the Baptist Church. She published "Poems on Subjects Chiefly Devotional by Theodosia," in two volumes. In a final edition of her poems were 144 hymns, 34 psalms in verse, and 30 short poems. It was in 1769 that these devotional poems of Miss Steele found their way into the Bristol Baptist "Collection" of Ash and Evans.

A very striking similarity is noted between the author and Miss Havergal. They shared the same fervent spirit of personal evangelism. Miss Steele's hymns dwelt much on aspects of our Lord's sorrow and suffering, while Miss Havergal's portrayed his helpful and saving power here and now, and his victorious Second Coming.

Miss Steele suffered much illness and a great personal sorrow in the tragic death of her *fiancé*. She died in November, 1778.

HYMN: This hymn affords a deep inner view of the Holy Scriptures, reflecting the author's profound experience in the joys and satisfactions found in the Word. It appeared first in "Poems on Subjects Chiefly Devotional," in 1760 and in 1769 it appeared with six stanzas in the Bristol Baptist "Collection" from which the hymn, still widely used, is taken. Christopher's "Hymns and Hymn Writers" repeats the entire twelve stanzas. It is customarily sung in England preceding the reading of the Scripture lesson.

234

The Holy Scriptures

COMPOSER: For comments on the composer, John B. Dykes, see Hymn 53.

TUNE: "Beatitudo" was composed for "How Bright These Glorious Spirits Shine," in "Hymns Ancient and Modern," 1875.

---

219 HYMN: Thy Word Is Like a Garden, Lord
TUNE: Petersham

Author: *Edwin Hodder*   Composer: *Clement William Poole*

AUTHOR: Edwin Hodder was born on December 13, 1837, at Staines, Middlesex County, England, but migrated at nineteen years of age to New Zealand. He was among the pioneer group of idealists that were to make New Zealand in later years a notable sociological laboratory. After returning, he entered the English Civil Service in 1861, from which he retired in 1897 to a quiet but productive literary life in Henfield, Sussex. Many biographies and devotional works came from his pen. His best-known writings are his "Memories of New Zealand Life," 1862, and "The Life of a Century," 1900. His contribution to sacred music is not large, but nevertheless it is significant. In 1863 Hodder issued "The New Sunday School Hymn Book." In this volume were included twenty-seven of his own hymns, among them this one. He died in March, 1904.

HYMN: Out of a rich life of wide travel and observation, Hodder wrote many books. They were devotional biographies as well as travel stories. His hymns collected in 1862 formed a volume which he named "The New Sunday School Hymn Book." This hymn, designed to glorify the variety of form and the versatility of truth in the Holy Scriptures, was written in 1865. Its literary form is unique, in that four striking metaphors are used to describe the noble characteristics of the Word of God: "a garden," "a choir," "an armory," and "a sword." All these figures are recognized as describing the spiritual gifts and moral qualities conferred upon those who have made the Word of God a thing of intellectual and spiritual experience. It is a wholesome antidote to much of the pantheistic and merely aesthetic appreciation of nature.

COMPOSER: For comments on the composer, Clement William Poole, see Hymn 82.

TUNE: For comments on the tune, "Petersham," see Hymn 82.

The Life in Christ

The Call of Christ

*

220   HYMN: Come to the Saviour Now
        TUNE: Invitation

Author: *John M. Wigner*   Composer: *Frederick C. Maker*

AUTHOR: John Murch Wigner was the son of a Baptist clergyman, and was born at Lynn, England, in 1844. He inherited not only his father's poetic talent but also his deep interest in spiritual things. He received his early education in the town of Lynn, in Norfolk. Upon reaching manhood he did not follow his father into the ministry, but, after graduating from London University with the degrees of A.B. and S.B., Wigner found employment in the India Home Civil Service. As a member of his father's church, he became especially interested in the spiritual life of the young people of the parish, and it was for them, as a hymn of invitation, that these words were written.

HYMN: This hymn was first published in the Baptist hymnal of 1880, entitled "Psalms and Hymns." This collection was made by the author's father.
   The first stanza is a direct, personal appeal to sinners to come to our pardoning God, whose glory it is to be plenteous in mercy. The third stanza is the loving call of the great Burden Bearer to all who are sorely tried, grief-stricken, and heavy-laden. One of the deepest tragedies of the Church, reflected in the second stanza, is the multitude of those who have lost their "first love," and have wandered afar and drifted aimlessly.

COMPOSER: For comments on the composer, Frederick C. Maker, see Hymn 29.

TUNE: "Invitation" is a tune about which little seems to have been recorded. It is one of a great host of hymn tunes, products of the late nineteenth century. Whether or not it was originally composed for this hymn is not known, but more fitting music could hardly have been written.

236

The Life in Christ

221 HYMN: Art Thou Weary, Heavy-Laden
FIRST TUNE: Bullinger

Author: *Rev. John M. Neale* Composer: *Rev. Ethelbert W. Bullinger*

AUTHOR: For comments on the author, John Mason Neale, see Hymn 44.

HYMN: This hymn was long believed to be a translation from the Greek of St. Stephen, the Sabaite, but it is mostly an original composition. It was first published in 1862 by Dr. Neale in his "Hymns of the Eastern Church." In 1887 about 2500 persons responded to a questionnaire sent out by the late W. T. Stead, asking for a list of the one hundred best English hymns. This song was tenth in popularity, and without question deserves its high rank. In it poor, weary, sore-distressed, disillusioned humanity hears at last the gracious call of Christ to "come . . . and . . . be at rest." Has this Guide himself gone over the rugged road? What proof is there that he is indeed faithful to his word? Will he receive even me as his follower? To each of these questions a personal testimony is given, but to the final one, "Is He sure to bless?" the triumphant voice of the entire Church—"saints, apostles, prophets, martyrs"—answers, "Yes."

COMPOSER (First Tune): Rev. Ethelbert W. Bullinger (1837–1913) was a clergyman who made music an avocation. He graduated from King's College, London, and was ordained in 1862. As curate he served several parishes. His longest pastorate was at Walthamstow, where he served as vicar of St. Stephen's from 1875 to 1888. He studied music under Dr. William H. Longhurst, Dr. John P. Hullah, and Dr. William H. Monk. His contributions to sacred music have not been extensive and he is remembered chiefly by his tunes. He received the degree of Doctor of Divinity from the archbishop of Canterbury in 1881.

TUNE (First): This tune, "Bullinger," was written in 1874, while Dr. Bullinger was curate at Walthamstow, for "Jesu, Refuge of the Weary." It has been used in Presbyterian Hymnals since 1895. In "The Hymnal" of 1895 the tunes "Stephanos" and "Bullinger" were associated with Dr. Neale's hymn. The relation has been maintained ever since. Even though "Bullinger" is more sentimental than "Stephanos," it is generally preferred among our American congregations.

SECOND TUNE: Stephanos
Composer: *Rev. Henry W. Baker*

COMPOSER (Second Tune): For comments on the composer, Henry W. Baker, see Hymn 99.

TUNE (Second): Of this tune, "Stephanos," Louis F. Benson writes in his "Studies of Familiar Hymns" (Second Series): "'Stephanos' . . . is [the tune] which first attracted attention to the words in 'Hymns Ancient and Modern.' The melody was composed by the Rev. Sir Henry Williams Baker, editor in chief of that book, author also of 'The King of Love My Shepherd Is,' and he asked Dr. Monk, the musical editor, to manage the harmonies for him. It is a good tune when sung deliberately and with feeling."

---

222 HYMN: "Come Unto Me, Ye Weary"
TUNE: Llangloffan

Author: *William Chatterton Dix*   Source: *Welsh Hymn Melody*

AUTHOR: For comments on the author, William Chatterton Dix, see Hymn 135.

HYMN: This hymn was first published in 1867 in an English collection called "The People's Hymnal." Though the first lines of all the stanzas are in the form of a call of Christ to weary, fainting wanderers, with the assurance that Jesus will receive "whosoever cometh," this hymn is not so much an invitation as it is the glad meditation of one who responded long ago to the gracious Voice. The pilgrim calls to mind the years when his heart was sorely oppressed by sin and exults again in the pardon and peace that came, and the present joy that has no end. Having thus tasted of the goodness of the Lord, though conscious of its own unworthiness, the soul casts itself again upon the love of Christ, so boundless and so free.

SOURCE: This tune is from D. Evans' "Hymnau a Thonau." For comments on Welsh hymns, see the article, "Welsh Hymnody," under "Original Sources," page xxii.

TUNE: As the Welsh, with their rich musical nature, learned to adore the Christ, they could scarcely fail to give full scope to their musical talents in sacred song. Taliesin, a Welsh bard of the sixth

The Life in Christ

century, in referring to the hymnology of that period said, "No musician is skillful unless he extols the Lord, and no singer is correct unless he praises the Father." Another said that "in heaven it will be a part of the saints' supremest joy to sing." The first Welsh hymns are probably the work of Davydd Ddu o Hiraddug, canon of St. Asaph. Unlike its effect on the continent of Europe, where it brought about a great outburst of sacred song, the Reformation seems to have had the opposite result in Wales, stilling for a time the desire for sacred song. Late in the sixteenth century singing was revived, but it was not until the rise of Methodism that there came a distinct revival of the love of hymns, and we may regard that as the starting point of modern Welsh hymnology. In singing "Llangloffan," note the annotation at the top of the hymn, "In moderate time." If hurried, it loses the majesty of its rhythm and the appealing force of its minor strain.

---

223   HYMN: Jesus Calls Us: O'er the Tumult
           TUNE: Galilee

Author: *Cecil Frances Alexander*   Composer: *William H. Jude*

AUTHOR: For comments on the author, Cecil Frances Alexander, see Hymn 157.

HYMN: This very popular hymn, published in 1852, was written by Mrs. Alexander, wife of the archbishop of Armagh and primate of all Ireland, and was originally intended for use on St. Andrew's Day. At once the imagination pictures that scene by the Sea of Galilee when Jesus called Simon and Andrew to follow him and "to become fishers of men." In Galilee, Simon and Andrew were summoned for the first time to become followers of Christ; in this hymn, however, the pleading voice of Jesus appeals to those "that are at ease in Zion" and are looking back eagerly on the world's pleasures and its "golden store." In climacteric fashion, we hear the insistent summons to "press on toward the goal unto the prize of the high calling of God in Christ Jesus": "Christian, follow Me"; "Christian, love Me more"; "Christian, love Me more than these." The hymn closes with the eager response of the repentant soul, praying earnestly for strength to "serve and love [Him] best of all."

COMPOSER: William H. Jude, born at Leatherhead, England, in 1851, like many other organists began his musical career by playing in a charitable institution. His first position was at Liverpool in the Blue Coat Hospital. Quite early he became interested in English

Handbook to The Hymnal

musicians, especially Henry Purcell. To revive interest in this great composer, Jude became one of the founders of the Purcell Society and lectured with authority on the works of the man in whose honor the organization was established. His interest in church music was constant and enthusiastic. The Monthly Hymnal, which he edited for some time, was largely the work of his hands. Being a man of community spirit, he assumed the position of organist at Stretford Town Hall, near Manchester, in 1889. As a lecturer on musical subjects, he traveled extensively in Great Britain and some of the colonies, notably Australia. He died in 1892.

TUNE: In America the tune "Galilee" invariably is connected with "Jesus Calls Us: O'er the Tumult." It was composed in 1887. However, like "Evening Praise" or "Chautauqua," its spirit may be readily defeated by too quick a tempo. Conscious of this danger, some editors use other tunes with this hymn. Among them is "St. Andrew," which was composed for the hymn by Edward Henry Thorne in 1875.

---

224 HYMN: Hark, My Soul, It Is the Lord
TUNE: St. Bees

Author: *William Cowper*   Composer: *Rev. John B. Dykes*

AUTHOR: For comments on the author, William Cowper, see Hymn 103.

HYMN: This hymn won recognition after its inclusion in the "Olney Hymns," published conjointly by Cowper and Newton in 1779. As is well known to students of English literature, Cowper's poetry marks an epoch, for, after the high-and-dry rational verses of Pope, Cowper gave expression to real human emotion. Of this the hymn before us is a good example. In it deep personal feeling is revealed in so pure a form that it becomes the expression of the universal lament of Christian men since that day on the shores of Galilee when Christ said to Peter, "Lovest thou me?"

COMPOSER: For comments on the composer, John B. Dykes, see Hymn 53.

TUNE: "St. Bees" was composed by Dr. Dykes for the hymn, " 'Jesus!' Name of Wondrous Love." In 1875 it appeared set to the present hymn in "Hymns Ancient and Modern." The tune had previously found its place in "The Congregational Hymn and Tune Book," 1862.

240

The Life in Christ

HYMN: Behold! a Stranger at the Door
TUNE: Bera

Author: *Rev. Joseph Grigg*   Composer: *John E. Gould*

AUTHOR: Rev. Joseph Grigg, the author of this hymn, was a child of poverty. The date of his birth is uncertain, but the year, 1720, is approximately correct. It is quite clearly established that he was only ten years of age when he wrote the well-known hymn, "Jesus, and Shall It Ever Be."

In his young manhood he learned to be a mechanic, but was not satisfied in his trade. Consequently he gave it up, and in due time entered the ranks of the clergy. In 1743 he became assistant minister of the Presbyterian Church in Silver Street, London. When, four years later, the acting pastor, Rev. Thomas Bures, died, Mr. Grigg resigned and, having married a widow of some means, settled in St. Albans where he engaged in literary work. He wrote a number of hymns, some of which have been quite widely used. He died at Walthamstow, Essex, on October 29, 1768.

HYMN: This hymn was first published in London in 1765 in a collection entitled "Four Hymns on Divine Subjects Wherein the Patience and Love of Our Divine Saviour Is Displayed." With it should be compared the hymn by Bishop How, Hymn 228, for both are based on the same passage of Scripture.

Possibly no other presentation of the seeking Saviour makes a more intimate and direct appeal than that of the vision of John in which he heard Jesus say, "Behold, I stand at the door and knock." At once the imagination grasps the entire picture. Out of the heartbreaks of his own experience the author expostulates with the tardy sinner to receive the matchless Guest and taste the joys no tongue can tell.

COMPOSER: John Edgar Gould (1822–1875) was a man whom the father of Dr. Louis F. Benson honored as "one who has rendered invaluable service to the Church." These sentiments were perpetuated by the son, who many years later testified to the worth of Mr. Gould's hymn tunes by holding up a copy of his "Songs of Gladness," published in 1869, and saying, "This little volume is full of musical treasures." The volume contained more than fifty of Mr. Gould's tunes. Mr. Gould was a versatile composer. He published "Sacred Chorus Book," "The Modern Harp," "The Tyrolean Lyre," "Amphion," and other books. One of his early books is "The Wreath of School Songs," which was published in 1847.

Mr. Gould was the son of Captain Horace Gould, from whom he inherited a brave and generous spirit. In Philadelphia, where he and a friend conducted a music establishment under the name of Gould and Fischer, Mr. Gould was greatly beloved by those whom he called his friends of West Spruce Street. He concludes a letter under date of November 19, 1872, as follows: "I think of our little social gatherings; . . . these are appreciated." The letter closes very affectionately, "Yours, my dear Benson, forever." While on a tour in southern Europe and northern Africa, Mr. Gould died in Algiers in 1875.

TUNE: "Bera," a very useful and beautiful tune, was written in 1849. In "Songs of Gladness" it was associated with "My Soul! What Hast Thou Done for God." Since its inclusion in "The Hymnal" of 1874 no Presbyterian Hymnal has been without it. The tune ranks favorably with Mr. Gould's tunes, "Pilot" and "Gould's Chant." His widow wrote, September 5, 1914, that "Pilot" was the last hymn tune he wrote. He played it on the piano the night before he sailed for Europe and Africa, where he died.

---

226   HYMN: All Ye a Certain Cure Who Seek
TUNE: Ballerma

Translators: *Rev. E. Caswall and Rev. W. J. Blew*   Source: *Old Spanish Melody*

TRANSLATORS: For comments on the cotranslator, Edward Caswall, see Hymn 3.
     Rev. William John Blew was born April 13, 1808. He attended Wadham College, Oxford, where he graduated in 1830 with the degree of A.B. In 1832 he received the degree of A.M. from the same college. He prepared for the ministry, was ordained, and was made curate of Nuthurst and Cocking. Later he was curate of St. Anne's, Westminster, and for a time incumbent of St. John's, near Gravesend. It was undoubtedly due to the influence of the Oxford Movement, which aroused such widespread interest in the Church, that Mr. Blew was led to translate so many of the ancient Latin hymns, many of which were first printed on single sheets for the use of his own congregation. In 1852, with Dr. H. J. Gauntlett he edited "The Church Hymn and Tune Book," a second edition of which was published in 1855. Many of Mr. Blew's translations appeared in this volume.

HYMN: This hymn was taken from "Songs of Syon," edited by G. R. Woodward. The first stanza recalls at once that deep insight into the realities of our human nature that Augustine expressed in the oft-quoted words, "Thou madest me for Thyself, and my heart is restless until it repose in Thee." What a hymn for our confused,

The Life in Christ

searching world to-day! And how suggestive it is of a method of approach for every religious worker, bringing to clear consciousness this inherent quest of the soul and then proclaiming the one tried and certain cure for troubled, sin-sick hearts.

ARRANGER: The father of F. H. Barthélémon was a French Government officer in the Colonial Department, serving in Ireland, and his mother was a member of a wealthy Queen's County family. Barthélémon, who was born at Bordeaux in 1741, served for a time in the Irish Brigade, but because of his evident talent he was induced by the earl of Kellie to study music. He went to England in 1765 and became noted as a concert violinist and conductor. His compositions include the music for "Orpheus" and an oratorio. His acquaintance with Rev. Jacob Duché, refugee rector of Christ Church, Philadelphia, led to his writing the one hymn tune by which he is known. Barthélémon ultimately became a member of the Swedenborgian Church, in which faith he died. His later years were full of misfortune and he died a paralytic.

TUNE: "Ballerma" is thought to be an old Spanish melody, adapted and arranged by F. H. Barthélémon.

227

HYMN: Sinners Jesus Will Receive
TUNE: Berlin

Author: *Rev. Erdmann Neumeister*   Composer: *Claude Goudimel*

AUTHOR: Rev. Erdmann Neumeister was born on May 12, 1671, at Uechteritz, near Weissenfels, where his father was the schoolmaster and organist of the little village. The son was sent to Leipzig University, where he graduated with the degree of A.M. He remained for a time as lecturer in the university, but in 1697 he became assistant pastor at Bibra. A year later full pastoral duties were assigned to him and he was also made superintendent of the Eckartsberg district. His talents won early recognition from the court at Weissenfels and he was appointed tutor in the family of Duke Johann Georg, and soon after became court preacher. In 1706 he was invited by the duke's sister to Sorau where he filled the offices of senior court preacher, counselor, and superintendent for her husband, Count Erdmann II von Promnitz, under whom he enjoyed special favor. From 1715 to his death in 1756 he was pastor of St. James's Church in Hamburg. He was an eloquent preacher and a stanch upholder of traditional Lutheranism against both the Pietists and the Moravians. He wrote 650 hymns, having begun this form of composition in his student days. The claim is also made for him that he originated the sacred cantata and wrote many for his own church.

Handbook to The Hymnal

TRANSLATOR: Emma Frances Bevan, née Shuttleworth, the translator, was the daughter of the warden of New College, Oxford, who afterward was bishop of Chichester. Mrs. Bevan's husband was a banker. Though in early life a member of the Anglican Church, she later joined the Plymouth Brethren.

HYMN: Neumeister wrote these stanzas as the conclusion of a sermon on Luke 15:1. They were first published in "Evangelischer Nachklang" in Hamburg in 1718. Mrs. Bevan published this hymn in 1858 in "Songs of Eternal Life," in which are found many of her translations. The glorious refrain, "Christ receiveth sinful men," is the theme about which this hymn is written. Calvin once asked what part of the Bible it is "with which faith is particularly concerned" and answered that it is "the gratuitous promise in Christ" of "divine benevolence toward us." "God commendeth his own love toward us, in that, while we were yet sinners, Christ died for us." A blessing came to the whole world when John Wesley was able to write, "An assurance was given me that He had taken away my sins, even mine, and saved me from the law of sin and death."

COMPOSER: Claude Goudimel (c.1505–1572) was born at Besançon. He is said to have resided in Rome about 1535, and while there founded a school of music in which Palestrina studied. More recent research, however, disproves his having founded such a school or having had any connection with Palestrina. About 1549 he removed to Paris and formed a musical partnership with Du Chemin. If he had ever lived in Rome his removal would probably have been due to his sympathy with the Reformation, but his conversion to Protestantism has been questioned. He was killed on the night of August 24, 1572, at Lyons as a Huguenot.

TUNE: "Berlin" and all Goudimel's musical writings are peculiarly full and rich, with certain resemblances to Palestrina, and always of extraordinary correctness. The manuscripts of the oldest of his compositions, masses and motets, are in the Vatican and the Oratory of Santa Maria in Vallicella. Goudimel was noted as one of the most eminent composers of music for the Calvinistic psalms and spiritual songs.

The Life in Christ

Answering Christ's Call

*

228   HYMN: O Jesus, Thou Art Standing
TUNE: St. Edith

Author: *Bishop William Walsham How*   Composer: *Justin H. Knecht*

AUTHOR: For comments on the author, William Walsham How, see Hymn 137.

HYMN: Some wonder whether this hymn of Bishop How's may not have been inspired by Holman Hunt's[1] famous painting, Light of the World. This is chronologically possible for the picture was exhibited some thirteen years before the song was written, and, as H. Augustine Smith says in "Lyric Religion," "produced the greatest effect of any religious painting of the century." Even if no direct connection exists, the painting is a most striking comment on the passage of Scripture upon which it and this hymn are based. Hymn 225 is based on the same passage of Scripture. It will be remembered that the imagery of Jesus knocking at the door is in the letter to the lukewarm Laodiceans, Rev. 3:20. The pleading words before us are addressed, then, to thrice-shamed Christian brothers who keep Him standing outside the door.

COMPOSER: Justin H. Knecht (1752–1817) was born in Biberach, Swabia. In 1807, when he was fifty-five years of age, he was called to Stuttgart to conduct the court and theater orchestra. Ten years later he returned to Biberach. He was an organist of considerable ability and, in addition, played the flute, oboe, trumpet, and violin. His compositions and writings include "Le Portrait Musical de la Nature," a symphony having a program comparable to Beethoven's "Pastoral," which it antedates. His "Würtemberg Choralbuch" contains ninety-seven tunes which he contributed. He wrote widely also on composition and theory.

ADAPTER: Rev. Edward Husband (1843–1908), vicar of St. Michael and All Angels in Folkestone, was a musician and composer of note. His lectures on church music brought him into prominence.

[1]While reading the galley proof of this paragraph on shipboard in tropical waters near the Panama Canal, I turned to my deck-chair companion and asked his opinion as to the hyphenating of Holman Hunt's name. He replied that the famous artist had lived two years in the home of his English grandfather while painting this picture and that his father had posed for the figure at the door, the hands and feet being his father's. He said he had in his possession several sketches used in making the picture. The interesting friend was Mr. Arthur H. Clark, the publisher, and it was his opinion that the name should not be hyphenated.—*Editor.*

TUNE: The tune, "St. Edith," appearing in "Handbook to the Church Hymnary," by James Moffatt, as "Knecht" and in some other collections as "St. Hilda," was adapted in 1871 by Husband from a melody by Knecht.

229

HYMN: Thy Life Was Given for Me
TUNE: Old 120th

Author: *Frances Ridley Havergal*   Source: *"Este's Psalter"*

AUTHOR: For comments on the author, Frances Ridley Havergal, see Hymn 56.

HYMN: Though the Scripture text Miss Havergal chose for her hymn was I Sam. 12:24, the actual inspiration, as she herself tells us, came from reading the motto, "I did this for thee; what hast thou done for Me?" which she saw under a picture of the Saviour in the study of a German clergyman. With great plausibility it has been argued that this picture was a copy of the *Ecce Homo* in the gallery at Düsseldorf. An interesting illustration of the deep religious power of this painting is evident in the fact that it was the sight of the original and the reading of the inscription under it that led to the conversion of Count Von Zinzendorf, the great leader of the Moravians. Originally in Miss Havergal's stanzas the first person was used, "I gave my life for thee," as it is found, for example, in the Moody and Sankey "Gospel Hymns." But a surer taste has led to the recasting of the words into the present form.

SOURCE: For comments on the source, "Este's Psalter," 1592, see the article, "The Psalters in Early Presbyterian Worship," under "Original Sources," page xv.

TUNE: From Percy Dearmer's "Songs of Praise Discussed," we learn that "Old 120th" was first found in William Damon's "The Psalmes of David in English Meter," published in 1579, and also in the revised edition of this work, which was published in 1591. It is not, however, found in the majority of the English Psalters before Este's "The Whole Book of Psalmes" published in 1592. Dearmer says that "in 'Ravenscroft's Psalter' it is called an 'Italian Tune,' but from its likeness to the 'Old 77th,' (81st) it might be thought to be an adaptation from the latter. The present form of the melody is that in 'Este's Psalter,'" with a few minor changes. It may be of interest to know that the term "old" is applied to the tunes taken from "Day's Psalter." At first an

The Life in Christ

alternative title was "Proper Tune" or "Church Tune." Later other tunes were written for the songs which were considered equally "churchly" or "proper," so that these titles lost their original appropriateness and were no longer used.

As indicated, the hymn is to be sung rather slowly and with clear, distinct phrasing. There is an opportunity for a strong emotional appeal in the last two lines of each stanza which the descending scale helps to accentuate. Musically, as well as poetically, these lines are solemnly introspective in character.

---

230   HYMN: Just as I Am, Without One Plea
         FIRST TUNE: St. Crispin

Author: *Charlotte Elliott*   Composer: *George J. Elvey*

AUTHOR: Charlotte Elliott (1789–1871) was the daughter of Charles Elliott, of Clapham, England, where her grandfather, Rev. Henry Venn, the famous and greatly beloved evangelical leader, had once been the curate. She must have known him intimately in her childhood for his last years were spent at Clapham. Henry Venn had been a co-laborer with the Wesleys and Whitefield, and also a chaplain of Lady Huntingdon, so Miss Elliott inherited a great evangelical tradition which she and the entire family worthily sustained. Her uncle, Rev. John Venn, who was also a curate of Clapham, presided over the meeting at which the Church Missionary Society was formed in 1799. Among the regular attendants of his church were William Wilberforce and other members of the so-called Clapham Sect, to whose efforts is principally due the abolition of slavery in the British Empire. Miss Elliott entered fully into the innermost beliefs and undertakings of the Evangelical Party and aided them greatly through her many hymns. She was splendidly endowed intellectually, with fine imaginative powers, and was a great lover of poetry and music. Because she was an invalid most of her life she had deep sympathy for those in sickness and sorrow and for them she published "The Invalid's Hymn Book" in 1841, which contained over a hundred of her own songs. The hymn before us was one of these.

HYMN: This is the fifth hymn in W. T. Stead's list of one hundred best English hymns, compiled after receiving over 2500 lists. For a long time the origin of this hymn was said to have been due to a casual word of Dr. César Malan's, of Geneva, Switzerland, when he bade Miss Elliott come to Jesus "just as you are." However, though Dr. Malan influenced her spiritual life greatly, her own nephew by marriage vouches for the following incident as being the true setting: Miss

247

Elliott's brother, Rev. H. V. Elliott, of Brighton, also a writer of valuable hymns, arranged a bazaar to raise money for St. Mary's Hall, an institution founded for the education, at nominal cost, of the daughters of clergymen. Everyone was busy except Charlotte, who was confined to an invalid's couch. Her sense of utter uselessness oppressed her greatly, so much so that she began to wonder whether she was really a Christian. One day when these doubts assailed her she marshaled the certainties of her evangelical beliefs to combat them, and her poetical genius framed them into this great hymn of the free, unmerited salvation through Christ, "the Lamb of God, that taketh away the sin of the world." In after years her brother wrote: "In the course of a long ministry, I hope I have been permitted to see some fruits of my labors; but I feel far more has been done by a single hymn of my sister's." Percy Dearmer, in "Songs of Praise Discussed," has stated that "when she died, more than a thousand letters thanking her for this hymn were found."

COMPOSER (First Tune): For comments on the composer, George J. Elvey, see Hymn 109.

TUNE (First): For comments on the tune, "St. Crispin," see Hymn 175.

SECOND TUNE: Woodworth

Composer: *William B. Bradbury*

COMPOSER (Second Tune): For comments on the composer, William B. Bradbury, see Hymn 106.

TUNE (Second): In ten different books of as many denominations, published during the past twenty-five years and examined by a recent author, Bradbury's tunes appear eighty-eight times. One book contains twenty-one different tunes, and the lowest number represented in any hymnal is three. As "Woodworth" is found in all ten books examined, it would appear to be the most popular of the many tunes written by this composer. "Woodworth," which first appeared in "Psalmistra" in 1849, does not seem to have come into very common use until late in the Sixties. The "Sacred Lute," published in 1864, and "Clariona," published in 1867, both include it. In the Presbyterian Hymnals its first appearance was in "The Hymnal" of 1874. In "Lyric Religion," H. Augustine Smith says that it is one of the tunes that "marks the transition from Lowell Mason's more churchly tunes to the livelier gospel songs that followed." It has retained its popularity, being found in a very large percentage of American hymnals and having the

The Life in Christ

sanction of such editors and critics as Frank Damrosch, Jr., Horatio W. Parker, T. Tertius Noble, and others. Few tunes have so strong a hold on the Church and especially on the older generation.

"Woodworth" should be sung in very moderate time, reflectively and with deep feeling. It is especially important that due regard be given to the phrasing, which will help to prevent a too frequent overemphasis of the strongly rhythmic character of the tune.

---

231 HYMN: Thou Didst Leave Thy Throne and Thy Kingly Crown
TUNE: Margaret

Author: *Emily E. S. Elliott*   Composer: *Rev. Timothy R. Matthews*

AUTHOR: Emily Elizabeth Steele Elliott, born in the year 1836, was the third daughter of Rev. Edward B. Elliott, of Brighton, England. Her father was a man of considerable scholarship and was the author of "Horae Apocalypticae." A number of the daughter's hymns were composed for use in St. Mark's Church, Brighton, and from there went forth to a wider use. For six years she was the editor of The Church Missionary Juvenile Instructor and in its pages many of her hymns appeared, including "Thou Didst Leave Thy Throne and Thy Kingly Crown," which was published in 1870. She had this in common with her well-known aunt, Charlotte Elliott, that she also published a special collection of hymns for the sick. Emily Elliott's work was entitled "Under the Pillow." It was printed in large type, was cheap, and was of convenient size to be slipped under the pillow by those it was designed to cheer and comfort. She died in London in 1897.

HYMN: This hymn was written in 1864 for the choir and school children of St. Mark's Church in Brighton. It appeared in 1880 in Miss Elliott's "Chimes for Daily Service." It is based upon the incident of the birth of Christ in a manger when there was no room for Mary at the inn, Luke 2 : 7. It is appropriate in this section of "The Hymnal," which includes hymns that are answers to Christ's call, for in it the heart of the believer, catching the exulting gladness of the song of the angels, fairly shouts its joyous welcome to the King who comes to bring salvation:

> "O come to my heart, Lord Jesus:
> There is room in my heart for Thee!"

Then, in the same strain of exaltation, the eyes are turned toward the consummation of the Christian hope, when Christ shall come again to reign forever and ever. And again the doors of the heart are opened wide to welcome the King.

COMPOSER: For comments on the composer, Timothy R. Matthews, see Hymn 123.

TUNE: "Margaret" is from "Children's Hymns and Tunes," published in 1876. This tune was composed by Timothy R. Matthews in 1876. Here we have one of the stately dramatic hymns of the Christian faith fittingly set to music that accentuates the tragedy of sacrifice and the glorious triumph of redemption, climaxing in personal acceptance of Jesus as Lord. It permits a variety of renditions. Frequently the hymn is sung by a solo voice, the congregation uniting in the refrain. It also lends itself to dramatization, with special reference to the Christmas season. The reader is referred to H. Augustine Smith's "Lyric Religion," pages 417 to 420, for an illustration of its possibilities. Note especially the strong contrasts: "heaven's arches rang" and "royal degree" set over against "lowly birth" and "great humility." These contrasts, occurring throughout the hymn, can be effectively brought out by appropriate *nuances*, adding greatly to its spiritual appeal.

---

232 HYMN: My God, Accept My Heart This Day
FIRST TUNE: Walsall

Author: *Matthew Bridges*   Composer: Attributed to *Henry Purcell*

AUTHOR: For comments on the author, Matthew Bridges, see Hymn 153.

HYMN: This hymn was written in 1848, the year its author, Matthew Bridges, under the spell of the Oxford Movement, left the Church of England, in which he had been a minister, and followed Cardinal John Henry Newman into the Roman Catholic communion. It first appeared in Bridges' "Hymns of the Heart," but was destined for a much wider sphere of influence and is found in the hymnals of many denominations. There is a striking similarity between the first line of this hymn and the motto found on a seal of John Calvin's, *"Cor meum velut mactatum domino in sacrificium offero"*—"My heart I offer as a sacrifice devoted to God." The emblem on the seal is a heart in a hand, being offered to God. This is an appropriate hymn for the Communion season, especially when new believers are making their first vows and are being received into the Church.

The Life in Christ

COMPOSER (First Tune): One authority writes that "Purcell is as much the boast of England in music as Shakespeare in the drama, Milton in epic poetry, Locke in metaphysics, or Sir Isaac Newton in mathematics-philosophy." He was born in 1658 and died in 1695. It is generally conceded that Purcell is the greatest of native-born English composers. His father and uncle were both musicians of note. He received his musical training from Pelham Humfrey and Dr. John Blow, on whose tombstone was inscribed "Master to the Famous Mr. Henry Purcell." Purcell is said to have composed many of his anthems while a chorister. In 1682 he was promoted to the place of organist at the Chapel Royal. His anthems are still in use. One of the best, "My Heart Is Inditing," was probably composed for the coronation of James II. Charles II sent him to France to study under Lully. In personality he was extremely affable and witty. Many of his writings appear in Dr. Boyce's collection, and also in various collections of Novello's.

TUNE (First): A collection was published by W. Anchors about 1721 under the title "A Choice Collection of Psalm Tunes," and "Walsall" is taken from that collection.

SECOND TUNE: St. Stephen

Composer: *Rev. William Jones*

COMPOSER (Second Tune): For comments on the composer, William Jones, see Hymn 187.

TUNE (Second): For comments on the tune, "St. Stephen," see Hymn 187.

233

HYMN: Jesus, Lover of My Soul
FIRST TUNE: Martyn

Author: *Rev. Charles Wesley*   Composer: *Simeon B. Marsh*

AUTHOR: For comments on the author, Charles Wesley, see Hymn 26.

HYMN: So universal is the appeal of this hymn that its use is world-wide among all denominations. It was written by Charles Wesley shortly after his conversion in 1738 and within a few months of the founding of Methodism. It was first published in 1740 in a collection entitled "Hymns and Sacred Poems," by John and Charles Wesley, and was given the heading "In Temptation." It has also been called "The Sailor's Hymn." The stories are legion that tell of its power to lead men to Christ; and the source of its widespread appeal is not hard to discover, for in it the seeking Christ is portrayed as mighty to save, in tenderest love rescuing storm-tossed and helpless men. Although it is now held by many to be "the hymn of the ages," it is interesting to note that half a century and more passed before it was appreciated. Even John Wesley delayed using it, fearing that the first stanza was too sentimental. The influence of the age of rationalism that abhorred too much enthusiasm and emotion lasted a long time and, as a concession to the taste of the times, in some of the early hymnals the phrase, "Lover of my soul," was changed to "Refuge of my soul."

COMPOSER (First Tune): Simeon B. Marsh (1798–1875) began his musical life at the early age of seven as a member of a children's choir. At twenty he was a teacher of singing. For thirty years he taught classes and conducted singing schools, for the most part in and near Albany, New York, traveling constantly on horseback from town to town and village to village throughout Albany Presbytery. His love for music and for children led him to give them free instruction and he had some considerable influence in introducing music in the public-school curriculum. Marsh's later years were spent at Sherburne as a teacher of music, superintendent of the Sunday School, and choir leader.

TUNE (First): While there have been many attempts to write a tune for the hymn, "Jesus, Lover of My Soul," that would take the place of "Martyn," no other tune has as yet succeeded it in the steadfast affections of the American Church. Hymn and tune seem irrevocably wedded. It is said that in the autumn of 1834 Marsh was *en route* on horseback from Amsterdam, New York, to Johnstown, New York, on his weekly circuit of singing schools when the melody took form. Alighting from his horse, he wrote the notes to the words of John Newton's hymn, "Mary to Her Saviour's Tomb."

SECOND TUNE: Hollingside

Composer: *John B. Dykes*

COMPOSER (Second Tune): For comments on the composer, John B. Dykes, see Hymn 53.

TUNE (Second): This tune, "Hollingside," appeared in 1861 in "Hymns Ancient and Modern" and was written by Dr. Dykes for the hymn, "Jesus, Lover of My Soul." In his parish of St. Oswald's, Durham, Dr. Dykes called his first home "Hollingside Cottage"; hence the name of the hymn.

The Life in Christ

Composer: *Joseph Parry*

COMPOSER (Third Tune): Joseph Parry (1841–1903) started to work in a puddling furnace when he was only ten years old. His musical gifts were apparent at a very early age. With his parents he emigrated to America, but later he returned to Wales, where he became interested in music. His harmonized hymn tune, submitted at the Swansea Eisteddfod, attracted the attention of Brinley Richards, who was successful in raising funds so that Parry might continue his musical education at the Royal Academy of Music. He became professor of music at University College, Aberystwyth, and later lecturer in music at University College of South Wales, Cardiff. Cambridge honored him with the degree of Doctor of Music in 1878. He was to Welsh music what Henry Purcell was to the church music life of England. In 1896 he was awarded £600 by the Eisteddfod for his services to Welsh music. His compositions include the cantatas "The Prodigal Son" and "Nebuchadnezzar"; the oratorio, "Saul of Tarsus"; and scores of hymn tunes. The Welsh collection "Cambrian Minstrelsie" was edited by him. "Merthyr Tydvil" or "Dies Irae," "Dinbych," "St. Joseph," and "Aberystwyth" are among his better-known hymn tunes.

TUNE (Third): "Aberystwyth" takes its name from the town, Aberystwyth, where the composer taught music in University College and where he distinguished himself through his labors for the development of Welsh music.

---

234   HYMN: One Who Is All Unfit to Count
TUNE: Wigtown

Author: *Narayan Vaman Tilak*   Source: *"Scottish Psalter"*

AUTHOR: Narayan Vaman Tilak (1862–1919) was a converted Hindu, a Brahman of high class. Though a Maratha, member of a race commonly considered very practical and unemotional, Tilak had a deeply sensitive soul. Many of his hymns are found in the Marathi hymnal, almost all of those that breathe an intense desire for union and communion with a living God being from his pen. He was an ardent nationalist, saturated with the poetry and traditions of his race, who believed heart and soul in its future contribution to the good of the world. His cousin, Bal Gangadhar Tilak, was, before the coming of Mahatma Gandhi, probably the most effective popular exponent of Indian nationalism.

Handbook to The Hymnal

TRANSLATOR: Rev. Nicol Macnicol, Litt.D. (1870–   ), translator of the hymn, is a distinguished missionary of the United Free Church of Scotland. His many books and articles reveal a profound and sympathetic knowledge of India's religious aspirations. In 1927 he was appointed Secretary of the National Christian Council of India.

HYMN: As Justin Martyr (born about A.D. 100) was until his martyrdom a converted Greek philosopher, and as Augustine's thought is saturated with his pre-Christian Neoplatonism, so Narayan Tilak lived and died a Christianized *bhakti,* one who sought in devoted love to enter into fellowship with God. He himself says that he came to Christ over the bridge of the poetry of Tukaram, a contemporary of John Milton. Here are characteristic translations of two of Tukaram's poems:

> "Ah, Pandurang, if, as men say,
>   A sea of love Thou art,
> Then, wherefore dost Thou so delay?
>   O take me to Thy heart!

> "I cry for Thee as for the hind
>   The faun makes sore lament,
> Nowhere its mother it can find
>   With thirst and hunger spent."

> . . . .

> "How can I know the right—
>   So helpless I—
> Since Thou Thy face has hid from men,
>   O Thou most high?

> "I call and call again
>   At Thy high gate.
> None hears me; empty the house
>   And desolate."

With the cry of the sincere seeker after God in his heart, Narayan Tilak in true Hindu fashion wandered about for ten years in his tireless quest, until his eager soul at last found peace in communion with Christ, the Son of the living God. It is only with this background in mind that one can rightly appreciate his hymn.

SOURCE: For comments on the source, "Scottish Psalter," see the article, "The Psalters in Early Presbyterian Worship," under "Original Sources," page xv.

TUNE: "Wigtown," a new tune for American congregations, is three hundred years old. It appeared in the "Scottish Psalter" of 1635, which Andro Hart published, with suitable tunes harmonized

The Life in Christ

in four parts. "Wigtown" was one of them. Unlike many common-meter tunes, which are characterized by repeated musical phrases, this, without any semblance of repetition, progresses through diverse musical thought to a climactic close. The tune is stately and virile, very formal but by no means without profound feeling. "Wigtown," used twice in this Hymnal, is destined to be widely used and cherished.

---

235   HYMN: Come, Thou Fount of Every Blessing
TUNE: Nettleton

Author: *Rev. Robert Robinson*   Composer: *Rev. Asahel Nettleton*

AUTHOR: Rev. Robert Robinson was born at Swaffham, in Norfolk, England, on September 27, 1735. When his father died, the young lad and his godly mother were left in sore straits. She longed to have her son become a minister of the Anglican Church, but poverty compelled her to apprentice him to a barber and hairdresser in London. He heard a very dramatic sermon of Whitefield's on "the wrath to come," and a sense of fear and dread came over him. On December 10, 1755, as he tells us, he found "peace by believing." From that time he was zealous in the work of the Evangelical Revival. In 1758, while still a member of the Established Church, he began to preach among the Calvinistic Methodists. He served successively in the Methodist, the Independent, and the Baptist denominations. He was a very able and scholarly defender of the Free Churches and wrote with conviction on the theological questions of the day. He died near Birmingham on June 9, 1790.

HYMN: So far as is known, Mr. Robinson wrote only two hymns, both of which are widely current to-day. They are "Mighty God, While Angels Bless Thee" and this hymn. This hymn was written in 1758, only three years after his conversion. It breathes the warm fervor of a new convert in the stirring days of the Wesleyan Revival. It was published the following year in "A Collection of Hymns Used by the Church of Christ in Angel-Alley, Bishopsgate."

COMPOSER: Asahel Nettleton, D.D. (1783–1844), who some believe wrote this tune, was a native of North Killingworth, Connecticut. In 1811, two years after his graduation from Yale, he was licensed to preach and began his preaching ministry, but his ordination did not take place until 1817. He never became a pastor, but devoted himself to evangelistic work, traveling extensively over the New England States, New York, and Virginia. For a brief time he visited in England. He was appointed professor of pastoral theology of the East

255

Windsor Seminary and, although he declined the chair, he lectured there occasionally. Feeling the need of more appropriate hymns for use in his evangelistic meetings, he compiled "Village Hymns," comprising six hundred hymns without tunes. A note, however, stated that a collection of music entitled "Zion's Harp" was the accompanying volume.

TUNE: "Nettleton" did not appear in "Zion's Harp" but rather under the title "Hallelujah" in John Wyeth's "Repository" of 1813. In this copy the melody was carried by the treble, but the bass in the third and fourth lines countered with the words, "Hallelujah, hallelujah, we are on our journey home." The authorship of "Nettleton" is unknown and the consensus of opinion seems to be that Nettleton could not have written it and that his name is his only connection with it. Perhaps some friend or admirer who composed it named it in his honor.

---

236   HYMN: I Heard the Voice of Jesus Say
             TUNE: Vox Dilecti

Author: *Rev. Horatius Bonar*   Composer: *Rev. John B. Dykes*

AUTHOR: For comments on the author, Horatius Bonar, see Hymn 60.

HYMN: This is probably the most widely known and best-loved of the many fine hymns written by Horatius Bonar. It was first published in 1846 in his "Hymns Original and Selected," with the title, "The Voice from Galilee." In 1857 it appeared in the first series of his "Hymns of Faith and Hope" under the same title. The outstanding feature of this hymn is the note of individuality shown in the use of the pronouns "I," "my," "me." While it is perfectly true that "faith . . . worketh by love" the hymn does well to emphasize the Protestant doctrine of an immediate, personal experience of reconciliation to God through union with Christ. Calvin argued against those who conceive faith "to be nothing more than a common assent to the evangelical history," and urged the operation of the Holy Spirit in our hearts "by which Christ, our eternal life and salvation, dwells within us." Behind all of this are the words of Paul, "There is therefore now no condemnation to them that are in Christ Jesus," Rom. 8:1.

COMPOSER: For comments on the composer, John B. Dykes, see Hymn 53.

The Life in Christ

TUNE: "Vox Dilecti" is a tune that presents some musical difficulties and demands careful study, with interpretation, frequent repetition, and illustration of its musical content and possibilities. The first half, in the minor key, and quasi recitative, may well be sung quietly, softly, but, above all, invitingly. The second part, in the strongly contrasting major key, is not only a declaration of ensuing rest and gladness but a grateful acceptance of the invitation. For greatest effectiveness, the second part should be sung softly at first, devoutly and humbly, then built up with a constantly increasing crescendo which climaxes in the last measures. The crescendo should not be marred by a drop in intensity, as so often happens in singing this hymn, but should be sustained throughout the last lines so that this part of the hymn becomes a pæan.

Penitence and Confession

*

237 HYMN: Rock of Ages, Cleft for Me
     FIRST TUNE: Toplady

Author: *Rev. Augustus M. Toplady*   Composer: *Thomas Hastings*

AUTHOR: Rev. Augustus Montague Toplady, the author of "Rock of Ages, Cleft for Me," was born at Farnham, England, in 1740, the year in which Charles Wesley's famous hymn, "Jesus, Lover of My Soul," was first published. We could wish that the Muse of history might expunge from her records the story of the bitter theological controversy between the writers of these two marvelous songs of love and grace. Mr. Toplady's father, a major in the English army, was killed at the siege of Cartagena soon after the birth of his son. For his early education Augustus Toplady attended the Westminster School in London. He received his academic training, however, at Trinity College, Dublin. His conversion occurred soon after graduation—strangely enough, in a barn where a lay preacher of the Wesleyan Methodists was addressing a handful of people. In time Toplady took orders in the Church of England and became vicar of Broadhembury, Devonshire, in 1762. His next and last charge was in London, where he ministered to the French Calvinists. Never robust in health, his frail body was early overtaxed and he died in 1778, shortly after his thirty-eighth birthday. He is said to have been a very forceful preacher, and great congregations were attracted to him. Shortly before his death a friend spoke encouragingly to him, but he replied: "No, no. I shall die. For no mortal could endure such manifestations of God's glory as I have done, and live."

Handbook to The Hymnal

HYMN: In The Gospel Magazine for October, 1775, Mr. Toplady wrote an article containing a message of hope to those who had fallen into sin: "Yet, if you fall, be humbled; but do not despair. Pray afresh to God." A little farther on come the first two lines of this hymn, followed by the last two of stanza 3. So far as is known, this quatrain marks the genesis of the hymn before us. The following March, in the same magazine, Mr. Toplady published a very curious article entitled "A Remarkable Calculation Introduced Here for the Sake of the Spiritual Improvements Subjoined. Questions and Answers Relating to the National Debt." After discussing the enormous debt of England at that time, he concluded that it could never be paid. He then proceeded to calculate the number of sins men commit and showed that, if a man sins once every second, by the time he is fifty years old he would be charged "with 1576 millions, and 800 thousand" transgressions. But even such a debt could be paid, not by us, but by Christ who has "redeemed us from the curse of the law," whose merit will "infinitely overbalance *all* the sins of the *whole* believing world." At the conclusion of the article he gives "A Living and Dying Prayer for the Holiest Believer in the World." This prayer is "Rock of Ages, Cleft for Me." Though strict literary criticism might object to the confusion of images in the hymn, every word and phrase has come to be hallowed in the heart of the Christian Church, for few hymns, if any, express so clearly the great truth that simple trust in the cross of Christ is our only refuge.

COMPOSER (First Tune): For comments on the composer, Thomas Hastings, see Hymn 197.

TUNE (First): The passage of years has dealt hardly with Hastings' tunes, as with many others. From a once considerable representation in American hymnals he is now represented by only three or four tunes, but "Toplady" still has a firm hold on the affections of many worshipers. The year 1830 is the time usually assigned for the composition of this tune. It was published in Hastings' "Spiritual Songs" with this hymn.

SECOND TUNE: Redhead No. 76 (Ajalon)

Composer: *Richard Redhead*

COMPOSER (Second Tune): For comments on the composer, Richard Redhead, see Hymn 214.

TUNE (Second): For comments on the tune, "Redhead No. 76 (Ajalon)," see Hymn 214.

The Life in Christ

HYMN: Jesus, We Are Far Away
TUNE: Agnes

Author: *Rev. Thomas Benson Pollock*   Composer: *Edward Bunnett*

AUTHOR: Rev. Thomas Benson Pollock was born in 1836 and graduated in 1859 from Trinity College, Dublin, from which, four
years later, he also received his Master's degree. His love of poetry
manifested itself even in undergraduate days, when he won the vice
chancellor's prize for English verse. He became a clergyman of the
Church of England in 1861, and held curacies in Staffordshire, in London, and in Birmingham. In the latter city he was curate to his brother,
Rev. J. S. Pollock, vicar of the mission of St. Alban's, Bordesley. This
district was one of extreme poverty, but by most zealous and self-denying
labors the two brothers built up a large congregation and a fine, permanent
work was established. Our author was affectionately known by his people
as "Father Tom." No offers of preferment could induce him to leave his
beloved parish, to which he devoted every energy. Upon his brother's
death, he became vicar, but his strength was exhausted and he survived
him only a few months, dying in 1896.

HYMN: This hymn is a metrical litany from Pollock's collection of
1870. As early as Pliny's famous letter, we find evidence that
antiphonal singing was a regular part of the service of the
Christian Church, and the construction of certain psalms witnesses to the
fact that the Jews sang responsively centuries before our era. The earliest
Christian litanies extant come from the close of the fourth century. They
consist of brief prayers recited by the deacon, to each of which the people
responded, "*Kyrie eleison.*" In the Middle Ages, the litany was more
and more developed and was used in many church processions, especially
in times of national disaster. Though a few examples can be found before
the year 1800, it was only in the middle of the last century that the
metrical litany began to be cultivated by certain members of the Church
of England. At the present time litanies are available for almost all the
feasts and fasts of the church year.

In this hymn there is something profoundly appealing in the repetition
of the direct address to God in the last line of each stanza, "Lord, in
mercy hear us." This repeated prayer also serves a necessary purpose. The
soul, in the deep consciousness of need, is too apt to concentrate attention
on its own distresses, whereas relief comes only when self is forgotten
and faith lays hold on the loving heavenly Father, whose mercy endures.

COMPOSER: Edward Bunnett, Mus.D. (1834–1923), was long an
active figure in the musical life of Norwich, England. He was
chorister in Norfolk Cathedral from 1842 to 1849, and assistant

organist there from 1855 to 1877, when he became organist at St. Peter's, Mancroft, Norwich. For a score of years he conducted the Norwich Musical Union. He was borough organist and organist for the Norwich Musical Festivals. His compositions were mainly for church use.

TUNE: "Agnes" was composed for the hymn, "Jesus, from Thy Throne on High," and was published in "The Hymnal Companion to the Book of Common Prayer," Second Edition, 1877.

---

239   HYMN: Lord Jesus, Think on Me
            TUNE: Southwell

Author: *Bishop Synesius of Cyrene*   Source: *Damon's "Psalter"*

AUTHOR: What a kaleidoscopic period of history is covered by the life of Synesius of Cyrene! Shortly after he was born the great migration of the barbarians began, which broke the frontier of the Roman Empire and, upon the murder of Stilicho, led to the sack of Rome by Alaric in 410. Chrysostom, "The Golden-Mouthed," was hard-pressed in Constantinople shortly after Synesius had appeared as envoy extraordinary to the emperor on behalf of his beloved Cyrene. Jerome and Augustine were at the height of their careers, and before Synesius' death the bigoted Cyril, bishop of Alexandria, shared the guilt of the brutal murder of Hypatia, under whom Synesius studied and whom he greatly admired. Synesius was primarily a man of action, who himself kept watch upon the city walls, who loved the chase and hesitated to be ordained a bishop lest he see his "bows rusting" or his "hounds in idleness." However, he became a very efficient administrator of the affairs of the Church. He died probably about A.D. 430.

TRANSLATOR: The translator of this hymn, Rev. A. W. Chatfield, was an Anglican clergyman who had a distinguished career at Cambridge. Influenced by the Oxford Movement, he became greatly interested in the early Greek Christian poets, many of whose hymns he translated into English.

HYMN: As a student at the feet of the beautiful Hypatia, an interest in philosophy was awakened in Synesius that never died. Plato was the author he loved best and quoted most frequently. But the ecstatic currents of Neoplatonism were sweeping across the philosophic world of his day, and it is in this setting that the hymn before us must be read, if its historic meaning is to be preserved. Between the lines, then, we can sense the Neoplatonic disparagement of the life in the flesh and feel the longing for communion with God whose culmination

The Life in Christ

is the glorious vision of the Eternal. One may use the hymn without hesitation, however, interpreting its phrases in a purely Christian fashion; especially since Mr. Chatfield himself says, "This ode . . . may be considered as a paraphrase or an amplification, rather than an exact translation of the original."

SOURCE: Damon's "Psalter," or "The Psalmes of David in English Meter, with Notes of Four Parts Set Unto Them by Guilielmo Damon," was brought out in London by John Day in 1579.

TUNE: The tunes in Damon's "Psalter" were mainly drawn from earlier Psalters: the "Anglo-Genevan Psalter," 1556; the "English Psalter," by Sternhold and Hopkins, 1562; and the "Scottish Psalter," 1564. Dissatisfied with the simple harmony he had provided for these melodies, Damon recalled as many copies as possible and destroyed them, and a more ambitious effort appeared in 1591. William Damon (c.1540–c.1591) was organist of the Chapel Royal during the reign of Queen Elizabeth. The simple dignity of "Southwell," set to Psalm 45 in the book of 1579, has earned it a place in many succeeding books.

---

240   HYMN: Lord, from the Depths to Thee I Cried
               TUNE: Song 67 (St. Matthias)

Source: *"Scottish Psalter"*   Composer: *Orlando Gibbons*

SOURCE: For comments on the source, "Scottish Psalter," see the article, "The Psalters in Early Presbyterian Worship," under "Original Sources," page xv.

HYMN: This is the metrical translation of Psalm 130 which appeared in the "Scottish Psalter" of 1650. We know that the generation which first sang these words was not dead until the "killing time" came upon Scotland. Many a group of Covenanters at midnight in secluded glens lifted quavering, heartbroken voices to God, using this prayer. And the Lord did hear and answer and gave strength to these warriors of freedom, so that in the end religious liberty was won.

COMPOSER: For comments on the composer, Orlando Gibbons, see Hymn 68.

TUNE: For comments on the tune, "Song 67 (St. Matthias)," see Hymn 68.

241
HYMN: There Is a Fountain Filled with Blood
TUNE: Cowper

Author: *William Cowper*   Composer: *Lowell Mason*

AUTHOR: For comments on the author, William Cowper, see Hymn 103.

HYMN: This hymn was written probably in the year 1771, since it was published during 1772 in R. Conyers' "Collection of Psalms and Hymns." The period from 1765 to 1773 was one of those happier intervals in Cowper's sorely stricken life which was preceded and followed by deepest depression, even mental derangement. On either side of this mountain peak of vision were dark valleys in which the shadows were exceedingly black. When the vision cleared, there came a pæan of praise from Cowper's lips—a veritable, glad hallelujah! In studying this hymn, one should read Mrs. Browning's poem entitled "Cowper's Grave."

COMPOSER: For comments on the composer, Lowell Mason, see Hymn 18.

TUNE: "Cowper" was composed in 1830, and in its present form seems to date from Hastings' "Spiritual Songs," 1832. It has always been associated with this hymn, and earlier names for the tune were "Fountain," "There Is a Fountain," and "Cleansing Fountain." Apparently the composer resented the singing of this tune at more than a moderate pace, for in his later books it is marked "Not too fast."

Dedication and Consecration

*

242
HYMN: Take My Life, and Let It Be
TUNE: Mozart

Author: *Frances Ridley Havergal*   Composer: *Wolfgang Amadeus Mozart*

AUTHOR: For comments on the author, Frances Ridley Havergal, see Hymn 56.

The Life in Christ

HYMN: No comment need be made upon this hymn other than the story given in Mrs. Havergal's own words: "Perhaps you will be interested to know the origin of the consecration hymn 'Take My Life.' I went for a little visit of five days. There were ten persons in the house, some unconverted and long prayed for, some converted, but not rejoicing Christians. He gave me the prayer 'Lord, give me *all* in this house!' And He just *did!* Before I left the house everyone had got a blessing. The last night of my visit . . . I was too happy to sleep, and passed most of the night in praise and renewal of my own consecration; and these little couplets formed themselves, and chimed in my heart one after another till they finished with 'Ever, only, *all* for Thee.'" The hymn was first published in her "Loyal Responses," 1878. In a story of her life, written by her sister, the date given for its composition is December, 1873.

COMPOSER: For comments on the composer, Wolfgang Amadeus Mozart, see Hymn 203.

TUNE: In the long list of compositions by one of the world's greatest composers are many works for church use. The hymn tunes credited to Mozart are arrangements of music not originally in such form. The present tune, "Mozart," is a theme from the "Kyrie" of the so-called "Twelfth Mass" by Mozart, which was not published until 1821 and has been the subject of much argument. It does not yet appear that this music should be definitely attributed to Mozart.

243

HYMN: I Bind My Heart This Tide
TUNE: St. Quintin

Author: *Rev. Lauchlan MacLean Watt*   Composer: *Rev. Henry Parr*

AUTHOR: Lauchlan MacLean Watt, D.D., F.R.S.E., born in the year 1867, comes of sturdy Isle of Skye stock. His courses, both in arts and in divinity, were taken at Edinburgh University, after which, in 1896, he became a minister in the Church of Scotland. Ordained in Turriff, Aberdeen, he was, in 1901, transferred to Alloa and Tullibody; in 1911 to St. Stephen's Church, Edinburgh; and in 1923 to his present ministry in the Glasgow Cathedral. The years 1914–1915 were spent with the Expeditionary Forces, and during 1916–1917 he acted as chaplain to the Forces in France and Flanders. Many will long remember his stirring addresses delivered in this country after the United States entered the war. Two books written at this time deserve mention: "In the

Land of War," which went through three editions, and "The Soldiers' Friend," in eight editions. He has also written upon subjects related to Gaelic history, which is his hobby, but it is in dealing with the inner problems of the soul that his greatest power lies. Many very helpful devotional books have come from his pen, such as "God's Altar Stairs," "Gates of Prayer," "The Saviour of the World," "Prayers for Public Worship," "Life and Religion," et cetera. The present hymn is taken from a book of poems entitled "The Tryst, A Book of the Soul."

HYMN: This hymn, though of very recent date, is surely of Covenanter lineage. We think at once of the ancient Scottish practice, according to which confederates bound themselves together by an oath to uphold one another in a given cause. Of this the "godly band" of the "Lords of the Congregation" in 1557 is a good example. But the best-known "band" is the famous National Covenant of 1638, signed in Greyfriars Churchyard, Edinburgh. Many wrote their signatures in their own blood, while others added to their names the words, "Till death"; and still others raised hands and avowed that they had now "joined themselves to the Lord in an everlasting covenant, that shall not be forgotten." In this hymn, each of the four stanzas binds the heart and soul by a peculiar tie to Christ, to brotherhood with man near or far, to social justice for the poor, and to world-wide peace.

COMPOSER: Rev. Henry Parr was an authority on the psalm and hymn tunes of England, but his own compositions are seldom encountered in modern hymnals. He edited the "Church of England Psalmody," 1847. This is a fine collection, which was the result of much study and research and included a biographical preface. Parr was born in 1815, and after appointments at several churches was vicar of Yoxford, Suffolk, 1872–1894. He died on May 4, 1905.

TUNE: "St. Quintin" was composed in 1834 and was adapted by Edward Shippen Barnes for "Christian Song," 1926, from which it was taken for "The Hymnal."

---

244   HYMN: Blessed Master, I Have Promised
TUNE: Bullinger

Author: *Rev. Charles A. Dickinson*   Composer: *Rev. Ethelbert W. Bullinger*

AUTHOR: Charles Albert Dickinson, D.D., was born at Westminster, Vermont, on July 4, 1849. He graduated from Harvard University in 1876. His ministry in the Congregational Church began when many active pastors were initiating the organization of work with young

The Life in Christ

people. To this the young minister gave careful thought and wrote a number of hymns for young people, some of which appeared in the "Christian Endeavour Hymnal." After he had served several parishes illness compelled him to relinquish the active ministry, and in 1899 he established his residence in Ceres, California.

HYMN: Two hymns of Dr. Dickinson's have achieved wide popularity; they are "O Golden Day, So Long Desired" and this one. The outstanding characteristic of this hymn is the absolute finality of the solemn vow of dedication to Christ. It is "here and now" that the irrevocable decision is made. The only fear is that the flesh may fail, and the one prayer is that strength may always be given "as I need."

> "Save me, Lord, and keep me faithful
> Day by day."

Hearts have been deeply stirred by the use of this hymn at the monthly consecration service of Christian Endeavor societies, for which it was evidently designed.

COMPOSER: For comments on the composer, Ethelbert W. Bullinger, see Hymn 221.

TUNE: For comments on the tune, "Bullinger," see Hymn 221.

---

245 HYMN: Take Thou Our Minds, Dear Lord,
We Humbly Pray
TUNE: Hall

Author: *Rev. William H. Foulkes*   Composer: *Rev. Calvin W. Laufer*

AUTHOR: William Hiram Foulkes, D.D., LL.D., was graduated from the College of Emporia, Kansas, in 1897. Upon completion of his course in the Presbyterian Theological Seminary of Chicago, then McCormick Theological Seminary, he was awarded the Barnardine Orme Smith Fellowship for general excellence and spent the following year in graduate study at New College, Edinburgh. He has held pastorates in the Presbyterian Church, U.S.A., in Portland, Oregon; New York City; and Cleveland, Ohio; and is at present minister of the Old First Church, Newark, New Jersey. In addition to his active parish duties he has been called to responsible positions in the Church at large. Appointed General Secretary of the Board of Ministerial Relief and Sustentation, and later of the New Era Movement, he has also served as a member of the General Council of the Presbyterian Church. Still wider recognition has come in the call to important offices in connection with the International Society of Christian Endeavor, the American Waldensian Society, and the Committee on Coöperation in the Near East. He has been a most successful pastor and an able executive, and his utterances on the public platform and in the press have greatly aided many good causes.

HYMN: From the author we have the following account of the origin of this hymn: "I was standing on the platform of the railroad station at Stony Brook, Long Island, which has been my summer home for many years. One of our young people's conferences was in session. While I was waiting for the train, Dr. Calvin W. Laufer approached me, and, humming a tune, said: 'Dr. Foulkes, we need a devotional hymn for the young people that will challenge their hearts and minds. It has occurred to me that you might be in a mood to write a few verses for such a hymn.' We then hummed the tune together so that I remembered it. As I went in on the train that morning, the words of the first three stanzas came to me almost spontaneously. That evening, as I recall it, I handed them to Dr. Laufer, and he gave them the musical setting of this simple but lovely melody. . . . Several years later, at a young people's conference at Blairstown, the words of the fourth stanza came to my mind as a fitting summary for the other three; so it is found in the later editions of the hymn." The author also has made this comment on the tune: "At that time, the tune was called 'Stony Brook.' Dr. Laufer afterwards changed the name to 'Hall' in honor of our beloved friend, Dr. William Ralph Hall."

COMPOSER: For comments on the composer, Calvin W. Laufer, see Hymn 13.

TUNE: Dr. Laufer wrote this tune at a conference which met at the College of Emporia, Kansas, in 1918, but at the time of composition no hymn was in his mind. A few weeks later, as described above, he hummed the tune to Dr. Foulkes, who quickly wrote the first three stanzas of the hymn. It was published in "Conference Songs," 1918, with a dedication to William Ralph Hall, D.D., for whom the tune is named. It has appeared in several later collections and has become a favorite hymn for consecration services.

The Life in Christ

246

HYMN: Jesus, I Live to Thee
FIRST TUNE: Lake Enon (Mercersburg)

Author: *Rev. Henry Harbaugh*   Composer: *Isaac B. Woodbury*

AUTHOR: The life story of Henry Harbaugh, D.D., is the not uncommon one of poverty, struggle, and achievement. He was born October 24, 1817, near Waynesboro, Franklin County, Pennsylvania, and in his youth worked on the farm, plied the trade of a carpenter, and taught school in order to secure an education. In 1840 he entered Marshall College, then at Mercersburg, Pennsylvania, which later became Franklin and Marshall College at Lancaster. His savings did not suffice for the full course, but in time he became a minister of the German Reformed Church and held pastorates at Lewisburg, Lancaster, and Lebanon, Pennsylvania. In 1864, three years before his death, he was called to the chair of theology in the seminary of his denomination at Mercersburg. While in this position, he advocated what came to be known as "Mercersburg theology," and this type of thought was also championed by him in the Mercersburg Review, which he edited for a time. His published works are numerous, mostly in the realm of theology and church history; and his poetical talent found expression in a book of poems, and in "Hymns and Chants for Sunday Schools," in which his hymns were first published.

HYMN: The central theme of this hymn is the believer's mystical union with Christ, "My life in Thee, Thy life in me," which is but a paraphrase of Paul's thought when he said, "For to me to live is Christ." Luther challenges us with this truth in his "The Freedom of a Christian Man," where he says that only as we are "Christs to our neighbor" are we rightly called Christians. We to-day may hesitate to use Luther's phraseology but the basic truth he expressed must never be forgotten and is splendidly set forth in these stanzas. Though it was not published until about 1861, Dr. Harbaugh wrote the hymn in 1850.

COMPOSER (First Tune): Isaac B. Woodbury, in the comparatively short time he lived, attained considerable eminence as a musician and composer. He was born at Beverly, Massachusetts, October 23, 1819. As a boy he was apprenticed to a blacksmith, but his native gift of music determined for him a different course. At the age of thirteen he moved to Boston and there studied music and learned to play the violin. Possessing a splendid tenor voice, he went to Europe, at the age of nineteen, to prepare for grand opera. Having achieved some success as a ballad singer, he returned to America, to conduct concerts and to teach. He joined the Bay State Glee Club and later organized many singing schools. The States of Vermont and New Hampshire profited by his efficient and enthusiastic leadership. He published "The Dulcimer" in 1850, and other works in 1842 and 1847, and for a number of years he directed the music of the Rutgers Street Church, New York City. Subsequently he went to Europe and, in connection with his search for health, found a great deal of new music, which he incorporated in "The New Lute of Zion," published in 1856, and "The Dayspring," published in 1859. His health being quite precarious, he proceeded in the fall of 1858 to the South. He reached Columbia, South Carolina, and died there October 26, 1858. He had a premonition of the end and shortly before his death said to a friend by his side, "There will be no more music for me until I reach heaven."

TUNE (First): "Lake Enon (Mercersburg)" is one of Woodbury's most beloved tunes. It appeared in "The New Lute of Zion" and later in "The Dayspring." "Lake Enon" is the favorite tune of Mercersburg Academy, where, set to "Jesus, I Live to Thee," it is sung every Sunday just before the sermon. The late head master, Dr. William Mann Irvine, in a letter, under date of August 26, 1920, to Dr. Charles R. Erdman, of Princeton Seminary, described how the students sing it. "The hymn," so the letter states, "must not be sung too fast. Our boys sing the third stanza softly, and pass on into the fourth stanza loudly and triumphantly." The tune is also known as "Mercersburg," a name which was attached to it in a hymnal compiled by Dr. J. H. Odell when he was pastor in Troy, New York.

SECOND TUNE: Trentham

Composer: *Robert Jackson*

COMPOSER (Second Tune): For comments on the composer, Robert Jackson, see Hymn 84.

TUNE (Second): For comments on the tune, "Trentham," see Hymn 84.

---

247   HYMN: Make Me a Captive, Lord
         FIRST TUNE: Llanllyfni

Author: *Rev. George Matheson*   Composer: *John Jones (Talysarn)*

AUTHOR: George Matheson, D.D., LL.D., F.R.S.E., was born in 1842, the son of a successful Glasgow merchant. He attended the University of Glasgow and graduated first in classics, logic, and philosophy. From the age of seventeen he was almost entirely blind, but

The Life in Christ

in spite of this handicap he carried out his plan, already formed, of studying for the ministry. His first parish was at Innellan in Argyllshire, from 1868 to 1886, when he was called to St. Bernard's Parish Church in Edinburgh. Here he ministered for thirteen fruitful years, after which, owing to declining health, he retired and devoted himself to literary work until his sudden death in 1906. The first book published by Dr. Matheson in his blindness was "Aids to the Study of German Theology," and its author was immediately recognized as a philosopher of distinction. His outstanding characteristic as a reconciler is seen clearly in "Can the Old Faith Live with the New?" However, his great power was in another field and his "Representative Men of the Bible" and "Studies in the Portrait of Christ" reveal his deep insight into the depths of the human soul. Yet that which will give him an abiding place in the hearts of Christians through the years to come will not be his books, noteworthy as they are, but his one immortal hymn, "O Love That Wilt Not Let Me Go." No sketch of the life of George Matheson can be complete unless a definite tribute is paid to his sister, his *alter ego*, without whose constant devotion his life work could never have been accomplished.

HYMN: Although he was endowed with marked talent in the realm of speculative theology, it was probably due to his blindness, which thrust him back upon himself, that Dr. Matheson probed more deeply into the springs of Christian personality than into the problems of philosophy. His true insight into the depths of the human soul is finely illustrated in the strong, virile hymn before us. But the highest perfection of personality and the greatest liberty come, and can come, only when every call of the soul glows with a consuming love and loyalty to a Person. Saul strove with all his inner might, but Saul, the persecutor, was the meager result; when, however, he was caught up into a consuming passion for Jesus he became Paul, the great "Apostle to the Gentiles," in whom the very Spirit of Christ was alive again. This hymn was born of the author's own experience, for as Christ's captive he attained true freedom of the soul and a glorious vision of his ever-present Lord.

First published by Dr. Matheson in his "Sacred Songs" in the year 1890, this hymn was entitled "Christian Freedom."

COMPOSER (First Tune): John Jones (1797–1857) was born at Tan-y-castell, Dolwyddelen, Carnarvonshire, and died at Taly-sarn. Largely self-taught, and in earlier years a quarryman, he became a local preacher. Ordained in 1829 by the Welsh Calvinistic (Presbyterian) Church, he came to occupy a foremost place among Welsh pulpit orators. Certain of his hymn melodies have had wide use in Wales and some representation in English collections. The Welsh people are partial to hymn tunes in the minor mode and the custom is to sing them in parts, the alto, tenor, and bass being equally represented. As a result, the melodies of the individual voice parts are often more elaborate than is customary in hymn tunes from other countries.

ARRANGER (First Tune): David Jenkins, for sixteen years identified with the University College of Wales, Aberystwyth, was born at Trecastell, Brecon, in 1849. After a few years of self-training, he studied under Dr. Joseph Parry, one of the most distinguished Welsh musicians of his day, matriculated at Cambridge, where he graduated in 1878. He was active in Welsh singing societies, and won distinction as a competitor and as a judge in their exhibitions of song. He was a versatile composer and has many numbers to his credit. In 1899 he was called as a lecturer on music to the University College of Wales, where his famous teacher, Dr. Parry, had been rendering notable service since 1874. At the time of his death, which was in 1915, he was head of the department of music in the University.

TUNE (First): The tune, "Llanllyfni," was arranged in its present form by David Jenkins. It is a tune of great breadth and unusual possibilities.

SECOND TUNE: Leominster

Composer: *George W. Martin*

COMPOSER (Second Tune): George W. Martin was born in London in 1828, and died there in 1881. He began his musical career as a chorister in St. Paul's Cathedral. Among his later appointments were those of professor of music in the Normal College for Army Schoolmasters, music master in St. John's Training College, Battersea, and organist of Christ Church in the same place. He developed marked ability as a director of large choirs of school children. Unfortunate habits clouded his later years and he died in a hospital and was buried by the parish. "But for one friend," says Dr. Moffatt in "Handbook to the Church Hymnary," "his identity would have been unknown."

HARMONIZER (Second Tune): For comments on the harmonizer, Arthur Sullivan, see Hymn 128.

TUNE (Second): "Leominster," set to this hymn, first appeared in "The Journal of Part Music," Vol. II, 1862, of which Martin was the editor. The present arrangement was made by Sir Arthur Sullivan for his "Church Hymns with Tunes," 1874, where the tune is said to be an old melody, without mention of Martin.

The Life in Christ

248

HYMN: Thine Forever! God of Love
TUNE: Horsham

Author: *Mary F. Maude*   Source: *English Traditional Melody*

AUTHOR: Mrs. Mary F. Maude was the daughter of George Henry Hooper, of Stanmore, Middlesex, England. In 1841 she married Rev. Joseph Maude, vicar of St. Thomas', Newport, Isle of Wight, and later of Chirk, in North Wales, and also an honorary canon of the Cathedral of St. Asaph. Her husband died in 1887. It was through the late Bishop W. W. How, who in early life had also been appointed an honorary canon of St. Asaph, that Mrs. Maude's stanzas first found their way into a church hymnal. In 1864, he and Rev. T. B. Morrell published an enlarged edition of their "Psalms and Hymns," the first edition of which appeared in 1854, and in this work the hymn before us was included.

HYMN: Mrs. Maude was teacher of a class in the Girls' Sunday School of St. Thomas', Isle of Wight. In the year 1847 she was absent for a considerable time and, having the girls much on her heart and mind, wrote weekly letters, at the close of one of which came these almost impromptu stanzas. The next year she published these letters as a little book, entitled "Twelve Letters on Confirmation, by a Sunday School Teacher," and this hymn was placed at the beginning. Four years later it was also printed in "Memorials of Past Years." In the original form there were seven stanzas, those here omitted having special reference to the Day of Judgment, including such petitions as:

> "Thine forever! 'Neath Thy wings
> Hide and save us, King of kings!"

As it was written for the purpose, it is natural that extensive use should be made of this hymn at the time of confirmation in the Episcopal Church, both in England and in America.

SOURCE: This tune is from an English traditional melody.

TUNE: For comments on the tune, "Horsham," see Hymn 95.

249
HYMN: Alas! and Did My Saviour Bleed
TUNE: Martyrdom

Author: *Rev. Isaac Watts*   Composer: *Hugh Wilson*

AUTHOR: For comments on the author, Isaac Watts, see Hymn 22.

HYMN: The title "Godly Sorrow Arising from the Sufferings of Christ" was given to this hymn by Isaac Watts when it was first published in 1707 in his "Hymns and Spiritual Songs." A perfect comment on it is Perugino's painting in the Convent of S. Maria Maddalena dei Pazzi in Florence. Many other masterpieces are so brutally realistic that the attention is absorbed in the bloody cruelty of the deed and in the physical agony of the Crucified. Such pictures principally tell what man's sin has done and does do to the sinless Christ. But the saints have seen much more than that. Saint Catherine of Siena was right when she said, "Nails were not strong enough to hold the God-Man nailed and fastened to the cross, had not love held him there." Yes, he chose the way of the cross for us. Watts and Perugino tell us, not what evil men did to him, but what he did and suffered for love of us. The wide, silent background of the painting induces at once the mood of meditation. The Virgin and Saint Bernard on the one side and Saint John and Saint Benedict on the other give quieting balance and poise to the picture, but each brooding figure is related to and dominated by the cross. Mary Magdalene, a sinner, "such as I," leads us to the redeeming Christ, the object of saving faith, at whose feet one must fall:

"Here, Lord, I give myself away;
'T is all that I can do."

This is the last hymn in this section of "Dedication and Consecration" and in it we reach the climax, for no other hymn expresses so feelingly the reason for consecration to Christ. One can well believe the statement of Dr. Charles S. Robinson that "more conversions in Christian biography are credited to this hymn than to any other."

COMPOSER: For comments on the composer, Hugh Wilson, see Hymn 16.

TUNE: For comments on the tune, "Martyrdom," see Hymn 16.

The Life in Christ

Prayer and Intercession

*

250 HYMN: Lord, What a Change Within Us One Short Hour
TUNE: All Saints

Author: *Archbishop Richard*   Composer: *E. T. Davies*
      Chenevix Trench

AUTHOR: The secret of Archbishop Richard Chenevix Trench's stainless character and lovable disposition may be found in his famous sonnet on "Prayer," which Dr. William Pierson Merrill has arranged as a hymn for this volume. Richard Chenevix Trench came of blended English, Irish, and French-Huguenot stock. He was born in 1807. As preacher, poet, and professor, he gave the world valuable and enduring books, such as his "Notes on the Parables of Our Lord," "Notes on the Miracles of Our Lord," and "Study of Words." As a lad at Harrow he won distinction for his scholarship. His literary labors began while he was a student at Cambridge. In his youth he had a daring and exciting adventure in a plot in behalf of freedom for Spain. The enterprise ended tragically with the capture and death of most of the conspirators, but Trench escaped to the safety of Gibraltar. In 1864 he was consecrated archbishop of Dublin and became foremost in every effort for the community's welfare.

ARRANGER: William Pierson Merrill, D.D., was born in Orange, New Jersey. Graduating from Rutgers College and Union Theological Seminary, he was ordained to the Presbyterian ministry in 1890. Following pastorates in Philadelphia and Chicago, he became, in 1911, pastor of the Brick Presbyterian Church, New York City. He is president of the Church Peace Union, active in the work of The Hymn Society of New York, in constant demand as a college preacher, and the author of several books of which the major theme is world brotherhood through an internationalism transformed by the Christian spirit and ideals. For more than forty years in the active work of the Christian ministry in our great cities, he has come to grips with the actual problems and faces them in a spirit of hope and genuine Christian helpfulness.

HYMN: The poem is a great favorite and has been a blessed reminder to multitudes of the peace and power always available through the practice of prayer. Although it was necessary to alter it for the purpose of song, the message is not changed. The third stanza is an abbreviation of the following lines:

Handbook to The Hymnal

"Why, therefore, should we do ourselves this wrong,
Or others—that we are not always strong—
That we are sometimes overborne with care—
That we should ever weak or heartless be,
Anxious or troubled—when with us is prayer,
And joy and strength and courage are with Thee?"

COMPOSER: E. T. Davies is a well-known Welsh organist, born at Dowlais in 1879. Since 1920 he has been director of music at University College, Bangor, Carnarvonshire. He has conducted choral festivals, composed vocal and instrumental music, and promoted the study and use of Welsh folk songs and literature.

TUNE: "All Saints" was written originally as a quadruple chant for use with long psalms, but subsequently adopted in several Welsh hymnals as an appropriate tune for the hymn, "Aed Sŵn Efengyl Bur Ar Lêd."

---

251   HYMN: Sweet Is Thy Mercy, Lord
TUNE: St. Andrew

Author: *Rev. John S. B. Monsell*   Composer: *Joseph Barnby*

AUTHOR: For comments on the author, John S. B. Monsell, see Hymn 7.

HYMN: John Samuel Bewley Monsell, LL.D., son of the archdeacon of Londonderry, Ireland, is represented in "The Hymnal" by seven hymns, each different from the others and all worthy of a place in the praise book of the Church. They are the best out of seventy-three from his pen, "bright, joyous, and musical." The distinctive feature of this hymn is the play on the words "mercy seat" and "mercy sweet." The Hebrew religion found its center and climax in the Holy of Holies, where was the sacred ark, covered with a slab of solid gold, overshadowed by the cherubim. This was the "mercy seat" and on it was sprinkled once a year the blood of the atonement, a propitiatory sacrifice for the sins of the people. The hymn is adoring praise for the sweet mercy of God which has granted us forgiveness in Christ, the Propitiation for our sins, and not for ours alone but also for those of the whole world.

COMPOSER: For comments on the composer, Joseph Barnby, see Hymn 3.

The Life in Christ

TUNE: "St. Andrew" was composed for these words in 1866 and named for St. Andrew's Church, Wells Street, London, later torn down, where Barnby was organist from 1863 to 1871.

252

HYMN: God of Pity, God of Grace
TUNE: Capetown

Author: *Eliza Fanny Morris*   Composer: *Friedrich Filitz*

AUTHOR: Eliza Fanny Morris, née Goffe, was born in London, in 1821. As her health was delicate, she was brought up in the country. Rural contacts stimulated her fancy and enriched her poetic soul. She edited a "Bible Class Hymn Book." Her published works are "Life Lyrics" and "The Voice and the Reply."

HYMN: This hymn for Lent, in litany form, first appeared in "The Voice and the Reply" in 1858. The volume has a regular progression of Christian experience running through it. It is in two parts, of which the first, "The Voice," consisting of eighteen pieces, sounds the call of God to the spirit of man. The present poem is taken from the second part, "The Reply," consisting of sixty-eight songs, the answer of conscience. The poem is called "The Prayer in the Temple."

COMPOSER: Friedrich Filitz, Ph.D., was born at Arnstadt, Thuringia, in 1804, and died at the age of seventy-two in Munich. He edited two hymnals, and was associated with no less an authority than Ludwig Erk in editing a collection of the best chorals from the sixteenth and seventeenth centuries.

TUNE: "Capetown" was set to "Morgenglanz der Ewigkeit" in "Vierstimmiges Choralbuch Herausgegeben von Dr. F. Filitz," Berlin, 1847. Seven years later the tune was revised and set to the hymn "Lord of Mercy and of Might" in Dr. Peter Maurice's "Choral Harmony."

253

HYMN: I Name Thy Hallowed Name
TUNE: Swabia

Author: *Rev. Louis F. Benson*   Composer: *Johann M. Spiess*

AUTHOR: For comments on the author, Louis F. Benson, see Hymn 29.

Handbook to The Hymnal

HYMN: Dr. Louis F. Benson wrote this hymn at the request of the Musical Editor for use in the "Junior Church School Hymnal" of the Board of Christian Education of the Presbyterian Church in the U. S. A. On the author's final manuscript of the hymn the title given is "When Ye Pray, Say 'Our Father.' " Although written for Juniors, and understandable by them, this hymn has a strength and simplicity that appeals to adult minds. Calvin W. Laufer, in "Hymn Lore," says that it "is based upon The Lord's Prayer, which supplies its framework and determines its content." In defending his interpretation of "Lead us not into temptation" in the couplet in the last stanza, Dr. Benson said, "The only way of escaping temptation is by lifting our desires above the things that tempt us in the lower air to purer air above." The second stanza is a lyric gem.

COMPOSER: For comments on the composer, Johann M. Spiess, See Hymn 20.

TUNE: For comments on the tune, "Swabia," see Hymn 20.

---

254 HYMN: Thou Art the Way: to Thee Alone
TUNE: St. James

Author: *Bishop George W. Doane*   Composer: *Raphael Courteville*

AUTHOR: For comments on the author, George W. Doane, see Hymn 34.

HYMN: In the judgment of many people this is the first of American hymns. It is admirable in its form and highly adaptable to the service of worship. Extensively used in the United States from the first, it has become equally popular in Great Britain. Bickersteth introduced it in 1833. Hall included it in his "Mitre Hymn Book" in 1836 and since then it has been growing in favor. Bishop Doane based his hymn upon our Lord's words in John 14: 6: "I am the way, and the truth, and the life: no one cometh unto the Father, but by me." It is an outstanding example of the strength of monosyllabic words. The hymn contains but twelve words of more than one syllable.

COMPOSER: Raphael Courteville, chorister of the Chapel Royal, had a son of the same name who became one of the children of the Chapel, and then became organist of St. James's, Piccadilly, London, in 1691. His name appears on the church records as organist

276

The Life in Christ

for eighty-one years. His tenure of office was not always peaceful. He was active as a composer of secular as well as of church music.

TUNE: "St. James" is found in "Select Psalms and Hymns for the use of the Parish Church and Tabernacle of St. James's, Westminster," published in 1697. Originally in the key of D, it has gradually been brought down to its present use in the key of A. It is probably one of the first tunes to be named for the patron saint of a church.

255

HYMN: In the Hour of Trial
FIRST TUNE: St. Mary Magdalene

Author: *James Montgomery*   Composer: *Rev. John B. Dykes*

AUTHOR: For comments on the author, James Montgomery, see Hymn 11.

HYMN: James Montgomery, editor and literary critic, a Scotsman so radical in his politics as to be twice cast into prison, is yet remembered for his Christian piety. Of the nine hymns he has contributed to "The Hymnal," this one leads in popularity. The original manuscript of this hymn is dated October 13, 1834. On it are the names of twenty-two persons to whom Montgomery sent copies, together with the dates on which they were sent. Of the four forms of the text extant, that given in Mercer's "Church Psalms and Hymn Book," 1854, is the one most in use. The opening lines have been the subject of controversy, many holding that it is unscriptural to ask Jesus to pray for us. The author himself was evidently not satisfied with the line as it appeared in his original manuscript—"Jesus, pray for me"—for there is a copy of the hymn in his own handwriting, dated April 25, 1835, which reads, "Jesus, stand by me." The line passed through one more change, "Jesus, help Thou me," and in Thring's collection appeared as here, "Jesus, plead for me." The hymn is based upon Jesus' word to Peter in Luke 22:32: "I made supplication for thee, that thy faith fail not."

COMPOSER (First Tune): For comments on the composer, John B. Dykes, see Hymn 53.

TUNE (First): "St. Mary Magdalene" appears in the book of Dykes's hymn tunes to this hymn, with the name "Magdalene," and was so published in Chope's "The Congregational Hymn and Tune Book," 1862.

277

SECOND TUNE: Penitence (Lane)

Composer: *Spencer Lane*

COMPOSER (Second Tune): Spencer Lane was born at Tilton, New Hampshire, on April 7, 1843. He left school at the outbreak of the Civil War to enlist in the army and served more than three years. After the war he entered the Boston Conservatory of Music, afterwards teaching vocal and instrumental music in New York. Later he settled in Woonsocket, Rhode Island, where he opened a music store and took charge of the choir of St. James's Protestant Episcopal Church, which he served for thirteen years. While at Woonsocket he composed hymn tunes and anthems. Mr. Lane had charge of the music of the Congregational Church at Monson, Massachusetts, for about three years. Later he removed to Richmond, Virginia, where he continued for four years. Thereafter he established his residence in Baltimore, Maryland, and became associated with Messrs. Sanders and Stayman, a music firm. During his residence in Baltimore, he had charge of the choir of All Saints' Protestant Episcopal Church for about seven years. He died of apoplexy at Reedville, Virginia, Saturday, August 10, 1903.

TUNE (Second): "Penitence (Lane)" was composed at Woonsocket, Rhode Island, while Spencer Lane was choirmaster there in St. James's Church. One Sunday morning the rector gave him the number of a hymn to be sung at the evening service. Mr. Lane did not like the music and wrote another tune while his wife was preparing dinner. After the evening service, at which it was sung, Bishop Clarke, of Rhode Island, who was present, asked Mr. Lane where he had got the music for the hymn. He replied that it was his own. "That," said the bishop, "will make you famous." It was used at a parish choir festival on "Easter Tuesday, 1879, at 7.30 P.M." At the suggestion of the rector, Rev. Joseph L. Miller, it was sent to Dr. Charles L. Hutchins, who included it in the Episcopal Hymnal of 1879.

---

256 HYMN: Father, in Thy Mysterious Presence Kneeling
TUNE: Henley

Author: *Rev. Samuel Johnson*   Composer: *Lowell Mason*

AUTHOR: For comments on the author, Samuel Johnson, see Hymn 95.

HYMN: "A Book of Hymns for Public and Private Devotion," published in 1846, of which Rev. Samuel Johnson was one of the compilers, first gave this hymn to the public. In some hym-

The Life in Christ

nals it begins with "Saviour" instead of "Father." The author was deeply interested in the Oriental religions, and in some of the hymn's expressions there is a reflection of that feeling after God which Paul mentioned in his speech at Athens, Acts 17: 27. Noteworthy in the hymn is the progress from the sense of the "mysterious presence" of the first stanza, through humility, confession, and trust, to the "dear presence" of the last stanza.

COMPOSER: For comments on the composer, Lowell Mason, see Hymn 18.

TUNE: "Henley" first appeared in Mason's "The Hallelujah," 1854, set to the hymn, "Come Unto Me, When Shadows Darkly Gather." This is one of Mason's most appreciated tunes.

Lowell Mason's son William, long one of the leading piano teachers in this country, went to Leipzig in 1849 to study music. One of his teachers there was Moritz Hauptmann, a famous theorist, and it occurred to Lowell Mason that he would like to have Hauptmann's opinion of some of his pieces. The son hesitated to show the father's comparatively simple hymn tunes to such a celebrity, but, as he tells in his "Memories of a Musical Life," he was surprised and relieved to hear Hauptmann say, "I have examined your father's book with much interest and pleasure, and his treatment of the voices is most musicianly and satisfactory." William Mason said it then dawned upon him that the simplest things are sometimes the grandest and most difficult of attainment.

---

257   HYMN: What a Friend We Have in Jesus
        TUNE: What a Friend

Author: *Joseph Scriven*   Composer: *C. Crozat Converse*

AUTHOR: Joseph Scriven was born in Ireland. As a young man he migrated to Canada. It is told of him that the death of his *fiancée,* who was drowned on the eve of their wedding, led him to seek the comfort of the friendship of Jesus. His religious life found its expression in helpful service of the needy. The following story is given in "More Hymn Stories," by Carl F. Price: "One day in Port Hope, Canada, . . . he was seen on the streets in working clothes, carrying a sawhorse to help some neighbors in need. Two men passed him, one a stranger, the other an acquaintance who spoke to him. The stranger at once inquired if his companion knew that workman, as he was anxious to have some wood cut. The reply came that that was Mr. Scriven, but

279

he would not work for him: 'Because . . . you are able to pay for it. He saws wood only for poor widows and sick people.'" A monument to Scriven's memory, erected by the people of his community, stands near Rice Lake, in Canada.

HYMN: Moffatt's "Handbook to the Church Hymnary" gives this account of the origin of the hymn: "Mr. Scriven wrote the hymn near Port Hope, in Canada, but its authorship remained a secret. 'A neighbor sitting up with him in his [last] illness happened upon a manuscript copy of "What a Friend We Have in Jesus." Reading it with great delight, and questioning Mr. Scriven about it, he said that he had composed it for his mother, to comfort her in a time of special sorrow, not intending that anyone else should see it. Sometime later, when another neighbor asked him if it was true that he composed the hymn, his reply was, "The Lord and I did it between us"' (Ira D. Sankey in 'My Life and Sacred Songs,' p. 279)."

COMPOSER: C. Crozat Converse, LL.D., born at Warren, Massachusetts, in 1832, spent the years 1855 to 1859 as a pupil of eminent music teachers in Leipzig, Germany. On his return to this country, he graduated from the law department of Albany University, and for many years was active as a lawyer in Erie, Pennsylvania. He died at Highwood, New Jersey, in 1918. Though active in law and music, he was also an inventor. He made a strong effort to promote the use of "thou" as a pronoun. Rutherford College gave him the degree of LL.D. in 1895. Theodore Thomas introduced ambitious orchestral compositions by Converse, and conducted his cantata on Psalm 126 in Chicago, but none of his compositions in larger form have survived.

TUNE: "What a Friend" was composed for this hymn and first appeared in "Silver Wings," 1870. In his "Story of the Gospel Hymns" Ira D. Sankey says that after he had completed the manuscript for "Gospel Hymns No. 1," he came across "What a Friend" in a small paper-covered pamphlet of Sunday School hymns published at Richmond, Virginia. As it was by his friend Converse he took out another tune and substituted for it "What a Friend." Thus the last piece to go into the book became one of the most popular—in fact, one of the most popular pieces of the kind ever composed in this country. Its use has been world-wide.

The Life in Christ

Aspiration

*

258 HYMN: "Lift Up Your Hearts!" We Lift Them, Lord, to Thee
TUNE: Woodlands

Author: *Henry Montague Butler* Composer: *W. Greatorex*

AUTHOR: Henry Montague Butler, son of Dr. George Butler, head master of Harrow, was born at Gayton, Northamptonshire, in 1833. He was educated at Harrow and Cambridge, where he won many prizes and became a Fellow. For a time he was a curate at Great St. Mary's, Cambridge, but in 1859 was elected head master of Harrow. He was appointed dean of Gloucester in 1885, and later became master of his *Alma Mater*, Trinity College, Cambridge. He died in 1918. Among his publications were "Ten Great and Good Men," "Some Leisure Hours of a Long Life," and several volumes of sermons.

HYMN: According to Dr. Dearmer, in "Songs of Praise Discussed," this hymn was written by Dr. Butler for "The Harrow School Hymn Book" in 1881. Later the hymn passed to "The Public School Hymn Book" in 1903, and still later to "The English Hymnal" in 1906. Dr. Dearmer considers the hymn a little heavy for schoolboys, but its fine moral passion makes it very desirable for adults.

COMPOSER: For comments on the composer, W. Greatorex, see Hymn 148.

TUNE: For comments on the tune, "Woodlands," see Hymn 148.

---

259 HYMN: O for a Closer Walk with God
TUNE: Dalehurst

Author: *William Cowper* Composer: *Arthur Cottman*

AUTHOR: For comments on the author, William Cowper, see Hymn 103.

HYMN: William Cowper wrote this hymn on December 9, 1769, during the serious illness of his friend, Mrs. Mary Unwin. In a letter written the following day the poet said: "I began to

281

Handbook to The Hymnal

compose the verses yesterday morning before daybreak but fell asleep at the end of the first two lines: when I awaked again, the third and fourth were whispered to my heart in a way which I have often experienced." The hymn first appeared in R. Conyers' "Collection of Psalms and Hymns," 1772. It was included in Toplady's "Psalms and Hymns," 1776, and in "Olney Hymns," 1779. It is a purely English hymn of perfect structure and flowing cadence, based on Gen. 5: 24, "And Enoch walked with God."

COMPOSER: For comments on the composer, Arthur Cottman, see Hymn 143.

TUNE: For comments on the tune, "Dalehurst," see Hymn 143.

---

260   HYMN: O for a Heart to Praise My God
       TUNE: Martyrdom

Author: *Rev. Charles Wesley*   Composer: *Hugh Wilson*

AUTHOR: For comments on the author, Charles Wesley, see Hymn 26.

HYMN: This hymn which has been so widely used in the Church first appeared in Wesley's "Hymns and Sacred Poems," 1742. In 1760 it was included in Madan's "Psalms and Hymns." Five of Wesley's eight stanzas are used in the present volume. Samuel Willoughby Duffield, in his "English Hymns," says: "Fletcher of Madeley says of this hymn, 'Here is undoubtedly an evangelical prayer for the love which restores the soul to a state of sinless rest and Scriptural perfection.' Mr. Christophers tells of an old Congregational minister and his wife who had debated the question of Christian perfection, and who finally made up their minds that, if it consisted in the ability to sing this hymn with the whole heart, they and the Methodists were not far asunder!"

COMPOSER: For comments on the composer, Hugh Wilson, see Hymn 16.

TUNE: For comments on the tune, "Martyrdom," see Hymn 16.

The Life in Christ

261

HYMN: Nearer, My God, to Thee
TUNE: Bethany

Author: *Sarah F. Adams*   Composer: *Lowell Mason*

AUTHOR: Sarah Flower was born at Harlow, Essex, England, in 1805, the younger daughter of Benjamin Flower, an editor. She was married to William B. Adams, an engineer and inventor, in 1834. As a member of a Unitarian congregation in London she contributed thirteen hymns to "Hymns and Anthems," published in 1841 for use in the chapel of Rev. W. J. Fox. The book was edited by her musically gifted sister, Eliza, who furnished sixty-three of the tunes. In the same year Mrs. Adams published "Vivia Perpetua," a dramatic poem in five acts, and in 1845 "The Flock at the Fountain," a catechism for children, with hymns interspersed. She had a striking personality and great intellectual force. Robert Browning was her friend. She contracted consumption while nursing her sister, and died in London in 1848.

HYMN: "Nearer, My God, to Thee" is based on the incident of Jacob's dream at Beth-el, Gen. 28:10-22. In 1887 The Sunday at Home published a list of the one hundred favorite hymns of the day, over 2500 people having sent in their lists. Mrs. Adams' hymn stood in the seventh place. It would still stand near the top of any such compilation. It has been translated into many languages. Often it has been altered, as by the addition of a stanza definitely naming Christ, or by the substitution of a stanza about the Second Coming, or the addition of a doxology to the Trinity. The hymn was a favorite of President McKinley, and of Edward VII, king of England.

COMPOSER: For comments on the composer, Lowell Mason, see Hymn 18.

TUNE: "Bethany" made its first appearance in a collection known as "Sabbath Hymn and Tune Book," 1859. There it is set to this hymn, but the composer is not named, as was frequently the custom in earlier days. Mason's name was attached to the tune in later editions. There has been much comment on the similarity of this tune to the well-known "Oft in the Stilly Night," and in view of Mason's activity in evolving hymn tunes from many sources it may be that his tune was strongly influenced by the older melody.

283

262 HYMN: Lead Us, O Father, in the Paths of Peace
TUNE: Ellingham

Author: *William Henry Burleigh* Composer: *Samuel Sebastian Wesley*

AUTHOR: William Henry Burleigh was born at Woodstock, Connecticut, February 12, 1812, and brought up on a farm at Plainfield. In 1837 he went to Pittsburgh, where he became a printing apprentice and afterwards a publisher. For six years he was editor of The Christian Freeman, of Hartford, Connecticut. Between 1849 and 1855 he was secretary of the New York State Temperance Society. He went to Brooklyn in 1855, as harbor master for the Port of New York, and died there in 1871. His hymns are more generally used in Great Britain than here. He published his "Poems" in 1841, and his widow published an enlarged edition in 1871.

HYMN: This is the only hymn of Burleigh's in this Hymnal. It first appeared in "Lyra Sacra Americana" in 1868, in four stanzas of four lines each.

COMPOSER: For comments on the composer, Samuel Sebastian Wesley, see Hymn 10.

TUNE: "Ellingham" was set to the hymn "Father of Heaven, in Whom Our Hopes Confide," in "A Selection of Psalms and Hymns Arranged for the Public Services of the Church of England, Edited by the Rev. Charles Kemble and S. S. Wesley," 1864.

---

263 HYMN: We Would See Jesus; for the Shadows Lengthen
TUNE: Henley

Author: *Anna B. Warner* Composer: *Lowell Mason*

AUTHOR: In the year 1915 a woman was buried with military honors. This unusual tribute was paid to a nonagenarian, Anna Bartlett Warner, because she and her more famous sister, Susan Warner, had lived on Constitution Island in the Hudson River, near West Point, and for nearly two generations had conducted a Bible class for the cadets of the United States Military Academy. In fact, the sisters came to be regarded as a part of the teaching force of that institution. Anna Warner was born in 1820. She was a novelist of some distinction, writing under

The Life in Christ

the pseudonym of "Amy Lothrop." She edited "Hymns of the Church Militant," and published "Wayfaring Hymns, Original and Translated." Her best-known hymns are "We Would See Jesus; for the Shadows Lengthen," and the song beloved of little children, "Jesus Loves Me! This I Know."

HYMN: The wistfulness of this hymn has endeared it to many. Based upon the incident of the Greeks seeking Jesus, John 12: 20-23, it furnishes fitting expression of the longing of the heart for reality in religious experience. In "The Hymnal" the third and fourth stanzas of the original are omitted. They follow:

> "We would see Jesus: other lights are paling,
>   Which for long years we have rejoiced to see;
> The blessings of our pilgrimage are failing;
>   We would not mourn them, for we go to Thee.
>
> "We would see Jesus: yet the spirit lingers
>   Round the dear objects it has loved so long,
> And earth from earth can scarce unclose its fingers;
>   Our love to Thee makes not this love less strong."

COMPOSER: For comments on the composer, Lowell Mason, see Hymn 18.

TUNE: For comments on the tune, "Henley," see Hymn 256.

---

264   HYMN: Rise, My Soul, and Stretch Thy Wings
        TUNE: Amsterdam

Author: *Rev. Robert Seagrave*   Source: *"The Foundery Collection"*

AUTHOR: Robert Seagrave, son of the vicar of Twyford, Leicestershire, was born in 1693, and followed his father's steps into the ministry of the Church. He graduated from Clare College, Cambridge, in 1714, and took holy orders. Captivated by the Wesleys, he threw himself heartily into their movement to revive the Church. He wrote many letters and pamphlets to awaken the clergy to deeper earnestness in their work. From 1739 to 1750 he was Sunday evening lecturer at Loriners' Hall, London, and also occasionally occupied Whitefield's Tabernacle.

HYMN: "Rise My Soul, and Stretch Thy Wings" first appeared in 1742 in a volume published by Seagrave under the title "Hymns for Christian Worship," partly composed and partly collected from various authors. As the hymn is given here the author's third stanza is omitted and the last has been slightly altered. The omitted stanza is as follows:

> "Fly me riches, fly me cares,
>   Whilst I that coast explore;
> Flattering world, with all thy snares,
>   Solicit me no more.
> Pilgrims fix not here their home;
>   Strangers tarry but a night;
> When the last dear morn is come,
>   They'll rise to joyful light."

SOURCE: The first Methodist hymnal with tunes was "A Collection of Tunes Set to Music, as They Are Commonly Sung at the Foundery," 1742. The "Foundery" was the remodeled foundry which John Wesley had acquired in 1739 and made into the first Wesleyan meetinghouse in London. The book has the reputation of being one of the most poorly printed and ill-adapted books ever prepared for worship purposes. Only one edition was brought out, and it was soon superseded by another and much better collection.

TUNE: Wesley's association with the Moravian Brethren led to his inclusion in "The Foundery Collection," of six chorals from one of their manuals, Freylinghausen's songbook, and "Amsterdam" was one of these. The connection of James Nares with the tune is somewhat hazy, if the account above given be accepted, as the tune is probably older than Nares, who was born in 1715.

Loyalty and Courage

*

265   HYMN: Stand Up, Stand Up for Jesus
          FIRST TUNE: Webb

Author: *Rev. George Duffield*   Composer: *George J. Webb*

AUTHOR: The Duffield family has been noteworthy in Presbyterian church history. Rev. George Duffield (1732–1790) was chaplain in the Revolutionary Army. His grandson and namesake, Rev. George Duffield (1796–1868), held prominent pastorates in Carlisle and Philadelphia, Pennsylvania, in New York City, and in Detroit, Michigan. He was regent of the University of Michigan from 1840 to 1848, and was

The Life in Christ

moderator of the New School General Assembly in 1862. His son, George Duffield, Jr., D.D., author of this hymn, was born in Carlisle, Pennsylvania, in 1818. After his courses at Yale University and Union Theological Seminary, New York, he held pastorates in Brooklyn, New York; Bloomfield, New Jersey; Philadelphia, Pennsylvania; and Adrian, Saginaw City, and Lansing, Michigan. He died in 1888 at the home of his son, Rev. Samuel Willoughby Duffield, pastor of the Westminster Presbyterian Church, Bloomfield, New Jersey. Samuel Willoughby Duffield was the author of "English Hymns: Their Authors and History."

HYMN: A tragic story is connected with Duffield's writing of "Stand Up, Stand Up for Jesus." In the year 1858 a great revival was sweeping across the country. In Philadelphia one of the most active leaders was a young Episcopal clergyman, Rev. Dudley A. Tyng. One Sunday Mr. Tyng had preached to an audience of over five thousand men in Jayne's Hall. On Wednesday he met with a terrible accident which cost him his life within a few hours. Just before his death he sent the following message to the Young Men's Christian Association and the ministers associated with them in the revival: "Tell them to stand up for Jesus." The following Sunday Dr. Duffield read to his congregation the hymn he had written based on the dying message of his friend.

COMPOSER (First Tune): George James Webb was born near Salisbury, England, in 1803. Originally destined for the ministry, he abandoned theology for musical studies, and became organist at Falmouth. Then he decided to come to the United States, and settled in Boston in 1830. Here he soon became allied with Lowell Mason, and his superior musical training stood him in good stead in his various activities as organist, conductor, teacher, and musical editor. He played at the Old South Church, in Boston, was professor of the secular music department of the Boston Academy of Music, conducted orchestral concerts, and was editor with Mason of several collections. On his own account he edited "Scripture Worship," 1834, and the "Massachusetts Collection of Psalmody," 1840. In 1871 he moved to Orange, New Jersey, as did Lowell Mason, and for some years he was active in New York. He died in 1887 in Orange, New Jersey. He belonged to the Swedenborgian Church, and did much for the musical service of the Church of the New Jerusalem. He was a talented and cultured man, with an attractive personality. His daughter, Mary, became the wife of Lowell Mason's son, William.

TUNE (First): "Webb" was composed for a secular song, "'Tis Dawn, the Lark Is Singing," and first published in "The Odeon: A Collection of Secular Melodies," by G. J. Webb and Lowell

Handbook to The Hymnal

Mason, 1837. Its first appearance as a hymn tune seems to have been in "The Wesleyan Psalmist," 1842; then it was used in later Mason and Webb books for the hymn, "The Morning Light Is Breaking."

SECOND TUNE: Miles Animosus

Composer: *Geoffrey Turton Shaw*

COMPOSER (Second Tune): Among the most active leaders in good choir and congregational music in England to-day are the brothers Martin Shaw and Geoffrey Turton Shaw, Mus.D. The latter, born at Clapham and educated at St. Paul's Cathedral Choir School and Derby School, was an organ scholar at Caius College, Cambridge, and was a pupil of Dr. Charles Wood and Sir Charles Stanford. Since 1910 he has been one of His Majesty's inspectors of music in schools. He has composed a great deal of music in many forms.

TUNE (Second): "Miles Animosus" is an example of a modern English tune for unison singing, with a lusty, straightforward air. It may be compared, if one wishes to realize the difference, with the tune "St. Gertrude," by Sir Arthur Sullivan.

---

266 HYMN: A Mighty Fortress Is Our God
TUNE: Ein' Feste Burg

Author: *Rev. Martin Luther*   Composer: *Rev. Martin Luther*

AUTHOR: For comments on the author, Martin Luther, see Hymn 118.

TRANSLATOR: Many translations of the hymn have been made, including a fine one by Carlyle, but the one most popular in this country is that used here, by Frederick H. Hedge, D.D., professor of ecclesiastical history, and later professor of German literature, at Harvard. He was joint editor of "Hymns for the Church of Christ."

HYMN: Luther's famous battle hymn was probably written for the Diet of Spires, 1529, when "the German princes made their formal protest against the revocation of their liberties and thus gained the name of Protestants." Klug's "Gesangbuch," in which the hymn was first published, gave it the title "The Forty-sixth Psalm," of which it is a paraphrase. The hymn spread rapidly over Germany. Gustavus Adolphus had it sung by his whole army before the Battle of Leipzig. It was sung at the Battle of Lützen and on the field of Sedan.

288

The Life in Christ

Frederick the Great called it "God Almighty's Grenadier March." Thomas Carlyle said, "There is something in it like the sound of Alpine avalanches or the first murmur of earthquakes: in the very vastness of which dissonance a higher unison is revealed to us." Another Scotsman, James Moffatt, in his "Handbook to the Church Hymnary," declares that it is "the greatest hymn of the greatest man in the greatest period in German history."

COMPOSER: Luther's interest in music is well-known. As a boy he was a singer. Later he learned to play the flute and the lute. As a monk he studied the music of the great composers of the Roman Catholic Church. The provision of suitable music for worship was one of his first concerns after the great turning point in his life. First came the "Formula Missae," 1523, then the new order for the German mass, 1524, and in the latter year came his first hymnal, "Etlich Cristlich Lider Lobgesang uñ Psalm," which was the first wavelet in the flood of German chorals. Luther had two competent musical assistants, Johann Walther, who was later *Kapellmeister* to the elector of Saxony, and *Kapellmeister* Conrad Rupff. According to Walther, they noted down the choral tunes which Luther invented and played on the flute. In Winterfeld's edition of Luther's "Geistliche Lieder," 1840, may be seen a facsimile of Luther's manuscript of the versification of The Lord's Prayer. At the bottom of the second page he had evidently drawn a staff and noted down a tune for the stanzas, a fact which evidences some proficiency in such matters. Just how many tunes Luther actually composed, and how many he adapted from other sources, will never be known, for in addition to original melodies he and his helpers drew upon plain-song melodies, earlier church melodies, and even secular songs. Many remarks of Luther in regard to church music have been recorded; one of the most typical being: "I am strongly persuaded that after theology there is no art that can be placed on a level with music; for besides theology, music is the only art capable of affording peace and joy of the heart, like that induced by the study of the science of divinity. A proof of this is that the Devil, the originator of sorrowful anxieties and restless troubles, flees before the sound of music almost as much as before the Word of God."

For further comments on the composer, Martin Luther, see Hymn 118.

TUNE: "Ein' Feste Burg" is believed to have first appeared, with this hymn, in a lost songbook of 1529, no copy of which has come to light. It was in Klug's "Geistliche Lieder," Wittenberg, 1535. Not only is it thus one of the oldest chorals, but it is also one of the noblest. Bach founded a cantata upon it; Mendelssohn used it in his "Reformation Symphony"; Wagner in his "Kaisersmarsch"; Nicolai in his overture for a church festival; Raff in an overture. It is even in Meyerbeer's opera, "Les Huguenots," where, as elsewhere, it is the typical Protestant song. That the tune was composed from phrases in the Roman gradual seems to be the consensus of modern opinion, but the credit for the compilation seems to be Luther's.

---

267 HYMN: Faith of Our Fathers! Living Still
TUNE: St. Catherine

Author: *Rev. Frederick W. Faber*   Composer: *Henri F. Hemy*

AUTHOR: For comments on the author, Frederick W. Faber, see Hymn 93.

HYMN: In W. T. Stead's "Hymns That Have Helped" this hymn appears in the double form in which it was first printed, one version for Ireland and one for England. Stead's comment of introduction is interesting: "The following Roman Catholic hymn is a kind of defiant war song, the note of which endears it much to the faithful." By changing a few words it became a Protestant hymn and was included in "Hymns for the Church of Christ." Faber wrote it for his "Jesus and Mary; or, Catholic Hymns for Singing and Reading," 1849.

"The Hymnal" omits one stanza:

> "Our fathers, chained in prisons dark,
> Were still in heart and conscience free;
> And blest would be their children's fate
> If they, like them, should die for Thee."

COMPOSER: Despite his French name, Henri F. Hemy was an Englishman, born at Newcastle-upon-Tyne in 1818. He was organist at St. Andrew's Roman Catholic Church in that city, professor of music at Tynemouth, and teacher of piano and singing at St. Cuthbert's College, Durham. A piano-teaching book which he brought out in 1858 had a remarkable vogue. His "Crown of Jesus Music," 1864, was equally popular. Hemy died in 1888.

TUNE: In English hymnals, where it is not so popular as in this country, "St. Catherine" is known as "Tynemouth." The present arrangement is the work of James G. Walton (1821–1905).

The Life in Christ

268   HYMN: O Jesus, I Have Promised
FIRST TUNE: Day of Rest

Author: *Rev. John E. Bode*   Composer: *James W. Elliott*

AUTHOR: John E. Bode, born in London in 1816, was the son of William Bode, of the General British Post Office. He was educated for the ministry at Eton, Charterhouse, and Christ Church, Oxford. He was first winner of the Hertford Scholarship and tutored at Christ Church for six years. In 1847 he took holy orders and was rector of churches at Westwell, Oxfordshire, and Castle Camps, Cambridgeshire. His published works include "Ballads from Herodotus," "Hymns from the Gospel of the Day for Each Sunday and Festivals of Our Lord," and "Short Occasional Pieces." In 1855 he delivered the Bampton lectures at the University of Oxford.

HYMN: The most interesting feature of this hymn is that it was written for the confirmation service of the author's children, a daughter and two sons. It appeared first in the Appendix to "Psalms and Hymns," published by the Society for Promoting Christian Knowledge.

COMPOSER (First Tune): James W. Elliott as a boy was a chorister in Leamington Parish Church. He became organist at this church, and later held similar positions in other churches, notably at St. Mark's, Hamilton Terrace, London, where he served for thirty-six years. He composed much music, sacred and secular, including popular "Nursery Rhymes."

TUNE (First): "Day of Rest" appeared in "Church Hymns with Tunes," 1874, a book with which Elliott was closely identified. There it was set to "O Day of Rest and Gladness," but in the 1875 edition of "Hymns Ancient and Modern" it was set to "O Jesus, I Have Promised."

SECOND TUNE: Angel's Story
Composer: *Arthur H. Mann*

COMPOSER (Second Tune): For comments on the composer, Arthur H. Mann, see Hymn 200.

TUNE (Second): For comments on the tune, "Angel's Story," see Hymn 200.

Handbook to The Hymnal

269 HYMN: Soldiers of Christ, Arise
TUNE: Soldiers of Christ

Author: *Rev. Charles Wesley*   Composer: *Rev. William P. Merrill*

AUTHOR: For comments on the author, Charles Wesley, see Hymn 26.

HYMN: This fine confirmation hymn was published first in "Hymns and Sacred Poems," in 1749, under the title "The Whole Armour of God." The poem contained sixteen stanzas, twelve of which were later given as three separate hymns in the "Wesley Hymn Book" of 1780. The most popular arrangement is a cento of from four to six stanzas. The entire hymn finds its inception in the thought of the Apostle Paul in Eph. 6: 10-18. It has special appeal to the heroic in Christian living.

COMPOSER: For comments on the composer, William P. Merrill, see Hymn 250.

TUNE: Dr. Merrill has long been known to be keenly interested in the musical service of the Church, and has contributed to it both hymns and tunes. He says that no special circumstances are connected with the composition of "Soldiers of Christ," which first appeared in the Presbyterian Hymnal of 1895.

During the World War a chaplain at Newport wrote to Dr. Merrill that the soldiers and sailors there liked the tune very much, and asked that several thousand copies be printed for their use. Later the chaplain reported that on one day two thousand men, on their way to embark for France, marched down the streets of Newport singing this hymn and tune.

---

270 HYMN: Fight the Good Fight with All Thy Might
FIRST TUNE: Pentecost

Author: *Rev. John S. B. Monsell*   Composer: *Rev. William Boyd*

AUTHOR: For comments on the author, John S. B. Monsell, see Hymn 7.

HYMN: "Fight the Good Fight with All Thy Might" is based on I Tim. 6: 12, and was written for the nineteenth Sunday after Trinity. The hymn appeared in "Hymns of Love and Praise"

The Life in Christ

in 1863, and has become very popular in the English-speaking world. The Episcopal Hymnal of 1889 and the Presbyterian Hymnal of 1895 introduced it in America. Frances A. Jones, of Montreal, states that during the South African War it was heartily sung by congregations of all denominations in England and her colonies. He also says that during the Spanish-American War the hymn came prominently before the American public.

COMPOSER (First Tune): Rev. William Boyd was born at Montego Bay, Jamaica, in 1847. He was educated at Hurstpierpoint, and Worcester College, Oxford, where Baring-Gould was his tutor. As a boy he tried his hand at composition, and at college was an organ student. He was ordained as deacon in 1877 and priest in 1882; from 1893 until his retirement in 1918 he was vicar of All Saints, Norfolk Square, London, where in succession Edward Bairstow and William Wolstenholme were his organists. He died in 1928.

TUNE (First): According to Boyd's story, Baring-Gould asked him to compose a tune to "Come, Holy Ghost, Our Souls Inspire," for a meeting of Yorkshire colliers he had arranged for Whitsuntide. "I walked, talked, slept, and ate with the words, and at last evolved the tune which I naturally named 'Pentecost.' " This was in 1864; the tune remained in manuscript until 1868, when it appeared to "Veni Creator" in "Thirty-Two Hymn Tunes, Composed by Members of the University of Oxford." In 1874 it was revised by the composer's friend, Sir Arthur Sullivan, and set by him to the present hymn in "Church Hymns." Though this was done without even consulting the composer, the tune is now usually associated with these stanzas.

SECOND TUNE: Courage

Composer: *Horatio W. Parker*

COMPOSER (Second Tune): For comments on the composer, Horatio W. Parker, see Hymn 19.

TUNE (Second): The tune, "Courage," a spirited and martial tune by Horatio W. Parker, was composed in 1903. Associated with these words, it appeared in "The Hymnal," which he edited and published that year. It is frequently used as a processional or recessional, and is a commanding number for large choirs and choral groups. Mrs. Parker is under the impression that the present tune was one of the very first her husband wrote.

271 HYMN: The Son of God Goes Forth to War
FIRST TUNE: All Saints New

Author: *Bishop Reginald Heber*   Composer: *Henry S. Cutler*

AUTHOR: For comments on the author, Reginald Heber, see Hymn 41.

HYMN: Bishop Heber began to publish his hymns in 1811. His original design of furnishing songs for the Christian year was carried out after his death, with additions from Jeremy Taylor, Addison, Sir Walter Scott, and others. "The Son of God Goes Forth to War" was written for St. Stephen's Day, to which the second stanza refers. The hymn is full of Scriptural allusions.

COMPOSER (First Tune): Henry S. Cutler (1824–1902) was born in Boston. He studied there and in Europe, specializing in the music of the Established Church. On his return to this country his first appointment was at Grace Church in Boston. In 1852 he became organist and choirmaster at the Church of the Advent, Boston, where his choir of boys and men soon attracted attention, not only for fine singing but also because it was apparently the first surpliced choir in this country. It is said that the then bishop of Massachusetts refused for years to officiate in that church because of its extreme ritualistic features. In 1858 Cutler migrated to Trinity Church in New York, where he introduced a full choral service with vested choir and served as choirmaster for seven years.

TUNE (First): "All Saints New" first appeared, with this hymn, in Rev. J. Ireland Tucker's "Hymnal," 1872.

SECOND TUNE: Crusader
Composer: *Samuel B. Whitney*

COMPOSER (Second Tune): Samuel B. Whitney was born at Woodstock, Vermont, June 4, 1842, and died at Woodstock, Vermont, August 3, 1914. A pupil of J. K. Paine, he became Paine's assistant organist at Appleton Chapel, Cambridge, Massachusetts. In 1871 he became organist and choirmaster at the Church of the Advent, Boston, a position he held for about thirty-seven years. Later, upon resigning, he was appointed director emeritus. Whitney was in the forefront of every movement to improve church music. He aided in the establishment of the Diocesan Choir Guild in 1876, and was its choirmaster for many years. He also organized and conducted many choir festivals. As an organist he was noted for his Bach playing and improvising. He taught organ-playing and lectured at the New England Conservatory of Music.

TUNE (Second): "Crusader" is somewhat more elaborate than the average hymn tune, and may be used effectively as a processional on festal occasions. The short vocal phrases in the third line should not be prolonged, and the sustained E flat in the fourth line may be sung by a few voices, while the other sopranos sing the chief melody in the quarter and eighth notes.

272
HYMN: Who Is on the Lord's Side
TUNE: Armageddon

Author: *Frances Ridley Havergal*   Composer: *John Goss*

AUTHOR: For comments on the author, Frances Ridley Havergal, see Hymn 56.

HYMN: "Thine are we, David, and on thy side, thou son of Jesse," cried Amasai as he and his men forsook the house of Saul to join the cause of David, I Chron. 12: 18. On that stirring incident Miss Havergal based her hymn. It appeared in Home Missions in 1877. She published it the next year in her volume, "Loyal Responses," and later, in 1880, in "Life Chords." Originally there were five stanzas, the third and fifth being omitted in this volume because of the lack of room and because they add nothing to the thought. As the hymn now stands, it is a complete unit in its thought.

COMPOSER: For comments on the composer, John Goss, see Hymn 14.

TUNE: "Armageddon" seems to be an arrangement by Sir John Goss of a tune by Luise Reichardt, which appeared in Part III of Layriz's "Kern des Deutschen Kirchengesangs," 1853. In the present form it is found in the Appendix to W. Mercer's "The Church Psalter and Hymn Book," 1872. Its stirring strains have earned it a place in many hymnals. It was first used in connection with "Onward, Christian Soldiers," and later with the above hymn.

273   HYMN: March On, O Soul, with Strength
TUNE: Arthur's Seat

Author: *George T. Coster*   Composer: *John Goss*

AUTHOR: George Thomas Coster, the author, was born at Chatham, Kent, in 1835. He studied for the Congregational ministry at New College, London, and was ordained in 1859 at Newport, Essex. He held pastorates at Barnstaple, Hull, South Norwood, and Whitby. Among his publications are: "Pastors and People," "Allegories," "The Rhyme of St. Peter's Fall," and "Poems and Hymns." Also, he contributed several poems on Scripture characters to "The Poet's Bible." In 1869 he edited "Temperance Melodies and Religious Hymns."

HYMN: "Who is this that cometh from Edom, with dyed garments from Bozrah? this that is glorious in his apparel, marching in the greatness of his strength?" Isa. 63: 1, is apparently the foundation text of this strong and steadying hymn.

COMPOSER: For comments on the composer, John Goss, see Hymn 14.

TUNE: "Arthur's Seat" appeared as early as 1874 in "Hymns and Songs of Praise," where it is marked "Arranged from Sir John Goss." In the 1895 Presbyterian Hymnal it is given as "Arranged from Sir John Goss, by U. C. Burnap." The name may possibly have some connection with the well-known elevation in Edinburgh, of which Robert Louis Stevenson wrote, "Every now and then as we went, Arthur's Seat showed its head at the end of a street."

---

274   HYMN: Jesus, I My Cross Have Taken
TUNE: Crucifer

Author: *Rev. Henry F. Lyte*   Composer: *Henry Smart*

AUTHOR: For comments on the author, Henry F. Lyte, see Hymn 12.

HYMN: Cross-bearing seemed to be the lot of Henry F. Lyte. His education was obtained only at the cost of severe struggle. After he entered the ministry he was, in his own language, "jostled from one curacy to another," and in his various parishes there was much that was uncongenial to his sensitive spirit. Yet his crosses were nobly borne. This hymn is "the deep and true utterance of the singer's own soul." It was found in a volume of "Sacred Poetry," headed "Lo, we have left all, and have followed thee," Mark 10: 28, and signed "G." In later hymnals it either had the same signature or none at all. The author claimed it by including it in his "Poems Chiefly Religious," 1833.

COMPOSER: For comments on the composer, Henry Smart, see Hymn 61.

TUNE: "Crucifer" had as its original name "Bethany." It first appeared in "Psalms and Hymns for Divine Worship," 1867, where it was used for "Jesus, I My Cross Have Taken."
In W. Spark's "Henry Smart: His Life and Works," the composer's prejudice against what he considered unduly fast congregational singing is emphasized. Smart was an enthusiast in the matter of congregational singing, which under his leadership (from the organ) at St. Pancras Church in London was widely famed. He claimed that the best results were obtained at moderate tempos, and strongly favored unison singing of this melody, with varied organ accompaniment in keeping with the sentiment of different stanzas.

---

275 HYMN: Christian, Dost Thou See Them
TUNE: St. Andrew of Crete

Author: *St. Andrew of Crete*   Composer: *Rev. John B. Dykes*

AUTHOR: St. Andrew of Jerusalem, archbishop of Crete, was born at Damascus about 660. He embraced the monastic life in Jerusalem and was sent to the Sixth General Council at Constantinople, in 680, as the deputy of the patriarch of Jerusalem. He was raised to the archiepiscopate of Crete during the reign of Philippus Bardesanes. For a time he was drawn away by the Monothelite heresy, but afterwards, acknowledging his error, he returned to the orthodox faith. Seventeen of his homilies are extant. He died on the island of Hierissus in 732. His hymns are still sung in the Greek Church.

TRANSLATOR: For comments on the translator, John M. Neale, see Hymn 44.

HYMN: The church owes a debt of gratitude to Rev. John M. Neale for the beauty and skill he has shown in translating Greek hymns. Versification from the prose of ancient liturgies was difficult. The measure of his success is seen in such hymns as "The Day

Is Past and Over," "Art Thou Weary, Heavy-Laden," and "Christian, Dost Thou See Them." They are characterized by great beauty and virility.

COMPOSER: For comments on the composer, John B. Dykes, see Hymn 53.

TUNE: "St. Andrew of Crete" was composed for this hymn, and first published in the Appendix to "Hymns Ancient and Modern," 1868. Comment is often made upon the unusual plan of this tune. The first three stanzas begin with a question, which is set to music in the minor mode, and a melody which seems timid and diffident. The answer to the question, the second half of these stanzas, is set to bold, striding music in the major mode, the mode of confidence and assurance. Dykes perhaps had such a tune in mind when he classified congregational tests into three divisions: "psalms," which were the psalms and canticles of David; "hymns," which were the grand old hymns of the Church; and "spiritual songs," which are "the modern and more emotional hymns, each having its special use. One should supply but not supplant the other." Here, though he was setting one of the ancient hymns of the Church, he applied a modern musical scheme.

276

HYMN: He Who Would Valiant Be
FIRST TUNE: Monks Gate

Author: *John Bunyan*   Source: *English Traditional Melody*

AUTHOR: John Bunyan (1628–1688), the author, was the son of a traveling tinker. However, his father had a fixed residence, making it possible for the lad to attend the village school. Bunyan acknowledged the faults of profanity and lesser sins of dancing and bell-ringing. He served in the Parliamentary army for a short time. Soon after this, he passed through a period of great intellectual struggle. Finally, becoming clear in his faith, he began to preach with powerful effect. After the Restoration he was thrown into Bedford jail, where he spent his time making laces to support his family. During a later imprisonment in Bedford jail he began "The Pilgrim's Progress," which first appeared in 1678. One hundred thousand copies were sold in ten years. "The Holy War" was published in 1682, and the second part of "The Pilgrim's Progress" in 1684. Bunyan had such great influence among the Nonconformists that he was called Bishop Bunyan. His death followed exposure in the rain while on an errand of unselfish service in the interests of an alienated father and son.

The Life in Christ

HYMN: The great allegorist included a number of songs in "The Pilgrim's Progress." Two of them appear in modern hymnals: "He That Is Down Need Fear No Fall" and "Who Would True Valour See," which also is given the title "He Who Would Valiant Be." These two hymns are found in the second part of "The Pilgrim's Progress," in the conversation between Mr. Greatheart and Valiant. "The Church Hymnary" of Scotland retains Bunyan's original stanzas. As the hymn appears here it has been altered in many lines.

SOURCE (First Tune): This tune is from an English traditional melody.

TUNE (First): "Monks Gate" is an adaptation from an English melody, and first appeared, set to this hymn, in "The English Hymnal," 1906. The arrangement is by R. Vaughan Williams.

SECOND TUNE: St. Dunstan's

Composer: *Rev. Charles Winfred Douglas*

COMPOSER (Second Tune): Rev. Charles Winfred Douglas, born in Oswego, New York, February 15, 1867, graduated as Bachelor of Music from Syracuse University in 1891. He entered St. Andrew's Divinity School at Syracuse, and was ordained in 1899. Following 1907, he was canon of St. Paul's Cathedral, Fond du Lac, Wisconsin. He is musical director of the Community of St. Mary, Peekskill, New York, and is one of the editors of the Hymnal of the Protestant Episcopal Church. Canon Douglas has been a church organist for many years and has long been active as editor and compiler of church music for choir as well as for congregation. He has done notable work in the adaptation of Russian and Spanish church music for English-singing choirs.

TUNE (Second): "St. Dunstan's" was written for "The New Hymnal" of the Episcopal Church. It is well suited to the unusual and virile lines of Bunyan's hymn. The tune has no time signature. However, the movement of the music is so direct and fluent that no hesitation is felt in singing the irregular measures. The pattern of the tune calls for forcible and full-toned expression.

---

277   HYMN: Christ of the Upward Way
TUNE: Sursum Corda

Author: *Rev. Walter J. Mathams*   Composer: *George Lomas*

AUTHOR: Walter John Mathams, born in London in 1851, spent his early years at sea. Returning from a voyage, in the course of which he had visited Palestine, he decided to study for the ministry.

Handbook to The Hymnal

In 1874 he entered Regent's Park Baptist College. He served for a time as pastor of Preston, Lancashire. On account of failing health he spent several years in Australia. Returning to England in 1883, Mr. Mathams accepted a pastorate in Falkirk, Scotland. Later, after serving a church in Birmingham, he went to Egypt as chaplain in the army. In 1905 he was admitted to the ministry of the Church of Scotland, serving churches in Stronsay, Orkney, and Mallaig, Inverness. He wrote several popular religious books and one small volume of hymns and poems, entitled "At Jesus' Feet."

HYMN: "Christ of the Upward Way" is a hymn for youth. It deserves to be carefully studied and to be sung thoughtfully and resolutely. Evidently the foundation is the marginal reading of the Revised Version for Phil. 3: 14, "The upward calling of God in Christ Jesus." The last words of the hymn, "Lord, I am here," as indicated in personal correspondence with Dr. Mathams, are based upon a scholastic custom of answering class roll call with the Latin word "*Adsum.*"

COMPOSER: George Lomas (1834–1884), an Englishman, studied music with excellent teachers, Charles Steggall, Sir William Sterndale Bennett, and Sir John Frederick Bridge, but with no intention of making music his profession. He acted as voluntary organist in one church for seven years and in another church for eighteen years. Changing circumstances led Lomas to become a professional musician, and he received the degree of Bachelor of Music at the late age of forty-two. His compositions include a number of hymn tunes and other music for the church service.

TUNE: "Sursum Corda" is set to the hymn "I Lift My Heart to Thee, Saviour Divine," in "The Bristol Tune Book," 1876, to which Lomas contributed a number of tunes. There is no evidence that this was the first appearance of the tune.

---

278   HYMN: Awake, My Soul, Stretch Every Nerve
       TUNE: Christmas

Author: *Rev. Philip Doddridge*   Composer: *George F. Handel*

AUTHOR: For comments on the author, Philip Doddridge, see Hymn 98.

HYMN: Whoever wedded Doddridge's words to Handel's music deserves a debt of lasting gratitude. They belong together and constitute a happy union. The hymn was first published by J. Orton in his edition of Doddridge's hymns in 1755, under the title

300

The Life in Christ

"Pressing On in the Christian Race." One of the earliest collections of hymns in which it was found was a collection by Ash and Evans published in 1769. Since then it has come into general use. It is particularly rich in its Biblical allusions: "Forgetting the things which are behind . . . I press on," Phil. 3:13, 14; "Even so run; that ye may attain," I Cor. 9:24; "So great a cloud of witnesses," Heb. 12:1; "Henceforth there is laid up for me the crown," II Tim. 4:8; and "Shall cast their crowns before the throne," Rev. 4:10.

COMPOSER: For comments on the composer, George F. Handel, see Hymn 120.

TUNE: For comments on the tune, "Christmas," see Hymn 120.

---

279 HYMN: How Gentle God's Commands
TUNE: Dennis

Author: *Rev. Philip Doddridge*   Composer: *Hans G. Nägeli*

AUTHOR: For comments on the author, Philip Doddridge, see Hymn 98.

HYMN: Dr. Doddridge composed many hymns to suit the sermons he preached to his congregation. Some of these hymns have become living sermons that the world will not let die. For the new year nothing is more fitting than "Great God, We Sing That Mighty Hand." Alert Christian spirits will run their race to the tune of "Awake, My Soul, Stretch Every Nerve," while every burdened heart will hold to the comforting peace of "How Gentle God's Commands." In Doddridge's collection of hymns this is Hymn 340, "God's Care a Remedy for Ours." The text upon which it is based is I Peter 5:7: "Casting all your anxiety upon him, because he careth for you."

COMPOSER: Hans Georg Nägeli (1768–1836) was a Swiss, born near Zürich, where he spent most of his life. At an early age he became prominent in musical matters, running a publishing business, composing, organizing the Swiss Association for the Cultivation of Music, and teaching music in public schools. He published the two Beethoven sonatas, Opus 30, Nos. 1 and 2, and incurred Beethoven's righteous anger by inserting two measures of his own in the first sonata. Later in life he wrote and published much on musical subjects. His best-known composition is "Freut Euch des Lebens," 1794.

ARRANGER: For comments on the arranger, Lowell Mason, see Hymn 18.

TUNE: Since Nägeli was a prominent figure in public-school music, Lowell Mason, the father of public-school music in this country, naturally investigated his material with his usual interest. One of the fruits of this study is the arrangement of the present tune, which first appeared in this form in Mason and Webb's "The Psaltery," 1845.

Trust

*

280   HYMN: My Jesus, as Thou Wilt
            TUNE: Jewett

Author: *Rev. Benjamin Schmolck*   Composer: *Carl Maria von Weber*

AUTHOR: For comments on the author, Benjamin Schmolck, see Hymn 21.

TRANSLATOR: For comments on the translator, Jane Laurie Borthwick, see Hymn 30.

HYMN: The Scriptural background of this hymn of trust is Eli's "It is Jehovah: let him do what seemeth him good," I Sam. 3:18; and Jesus' own word: "Not what I will, but what thou wilt," Mark 14:36. Schmolck's life was full of exhausting labors. In later years he was burdened with constant physical sufferings due to cataract and paralysis. "As the olive did not yield its oil before it was bruised, so," said the rabbis, "Israel never produced the fruits of righteousness before the afflictions of God came upon him." The hymn is the product of pain, not simply thought out, but felt. It was published first in "Heilige Flammen," probably in 1704, under the title, "As God Will Is My Aim." Only three of the eleven stanzas of the original hymn are generally used.

COMPOSER: For comments on the composer, Carl Maria von Weber, see Hymn 34.

ARRANGER: For comments on the arranger, Joseph P. Holbrook, see Hymn 62.

The Life in Christ

TUNE: "Jewett" is an arrangement from Weber's "Der Frei-schütz" which was made by Joseph P. Holbrook in 1862. Though other tunes have been used with "My Jesus, as Thou Wilt," "Jewett" has superseded them all, especially in America. It requires confident and prayerful interpretation, for its message is one of trust and comfort.

---

281   HYMN: Be Still, My Soul: the Lord Is on Thy Side
        TUNE: Finlandia

Author: *Katharina von Schlegel*   Composer: *Jean Sibelius*

AUTHOR: Little is known of the author, Katharina von Schlegel. She was head of the Lutheran nunnery at Cöthen, but no such name appears in the records of the institution. From letters written to Heinrich Ernst, Count Stolberg, 1750–1752, it would seem that she was attached to the little court of the duke of Cöthen. This hymn of consolation is the only one of hers to pass into English.

TRANSLATOR: For comments on the translator, Jane Laurie Borthwick, see Hymn 30.

HYMN: In this fine translation Miss Borthwick has given us a hymn of enduring worth. The song carries the thoughts backward to Ps. 46:10, "Be still, and know that I am God"; and forward to I Thess. 4:17, "So shall we ever be with the Lord."

COMPOSER: Jean Sibelius was born December 8, 1865, at Tavaste-hus, Finland. At the age of fourteen he began the study of the violin. In 1885 he was sent to the University of Helsingfors to study law, but he abandoned it before the end of the first semester. Entering the conservatory in 1886, he spent three years in the study of music. From 1889 to 1890 he was a pupil of W. Bargiel and A. Becker in Berlin, later studying with R. Fuchs and K. Goldmark. Returning to Helsingfors in 1893, he became a teacher of composition at the Conservatory of Helsingfors, and also taught at the Orchestral School. It was during this time that his works began to attract attention—so much so that the Finnish Government granted him a pension of six hundred dollars for ten years. In 1900 he accompanied the orchestra on tour and conducted his own works.

The strong individualistic note of Sibelius' music can be traced to the natural power of his themes, combined with marked originality and resourcefulness in their development, and to his native environment. Somberness and tragedy seem to be his prevailing mood, while nature and

Handbook to The Hymnal

the national legends and folklore seem to be his chief sources of inspiration.

TUNE: The tune, "Finlandia," was taken from Sibelius' symphonic poem entitled "Finlandia," and was arranged from that work for "The Hymnal" in 1932. In singing, careful attention should be paid to the shading, especially where unexpected but delightful transitions occur.

---

282   HYMN: I Bow My Forehead to the Dust
TUNE: Pentatone

Author: *John G. Whittier*   Composer: *Henry Walford Davies*

AUTHOR: For comments on the author, John G. Whittier, see Hymn 178.

HYMN: "I am really not a hymn writer," said Whittier, "for the good reason that I know nothing of music. Only a very few of my pieces were written for singing. A good hymn is the best use to which poetry can be devoted, but I do not claim that I have succeeded in composing one." Nevertheless, four of the six Whittier hymns in "The Hymnal" are among the most popular hymns of the day! This hymn is taken from "The Eternal Goodness," a poem of twenty-two stanzas, in which the poet draws away from what he feels to be the harsh conclusions of philosophic thought of his age. In the conscious limitation of human knowledge he turns to the loving-kindness of God, as indicated in the lines:

"To one fixed trust my spirit clings;
I know that God is good!"

On that he rests his soul in hope and peace.

COMPOSER: Henry Walford Davies, LL.D., was born in Oswestry, Shropshire, in 1869. He had a musical heritage from his father, and his musical gifts were indicated in early childhood. He grew up as a chorister in St. George's Chapel, Windsor. From 1890 to 1894 he was a student in the Royal College of Music. From 1903 to 1907 he was the conductor of the London Bach Choir. He received the degree of Bachelor of Music in 1892, and of Doctor of Music in 1894, both from Cambridge. He preserved the best traditions of Welsh church music through his work in the university and schools of Wales. He is a noted composer of hymn tunes and widely recognized as a great leader in community singing. He was knighted in 1922.

The Life in Christ

TUNE: The name of the tune, "Pentatone," refers to the pentatonic scale, which consists of five tones, and is prominent in bagpipe music. Neither the hymn nor the tune is generally known in American churches. The tune was composed for "A Students' Hymnal," which is the hymnal for the University of Wales.

---

283 HYMN: How Firm a Foundation, Ye Saints of the Lord
TUNE: Adeste Fideles

Source: *Rippon's "Selection"*   Source: *J. F. Wade's "Cantus Diversi"*

AUTHOR: The author of this great hymn has hidden himself so carefully that to this day no one surely knows who wrote it. It appeared in Rippon's "Selection," 1787, signed "K." In later editions the name "Kirkham" is appended. In Fletcher's "Collection of Hymns," 1822, it was signed "Kn." In the 1835 edition of the same collection we find "Keen." Spurgeon's hymnal ascribed it to "George Keith." Dr. Julian, in his "A Dictionary of Hymnology," concludes: "The ascription to this hymn must be that of an unknown person of the name of Keen." A man by the name of Robert Keene was precentor in Dr. John Rippon's church.

HYMN: At first the hymn contained seven stanzas. Here it is shortened to four. Samuel Willoughby Duffield's "English Hymns: Their Authors and History" contains the following interesting incident: "Once in the old oratory at evening devotion in Princeton Seminary, the elder Dr. Hodge, then venerable with years and piety, paused as he read this hymn, preparatory to the singing, and in the depth of his emotion was obliged to close his delivery of the final lines with a mere gesture of pathetic and adoring wonder at the matchless grace of God in Christ, and his hand silently beat time to the rhythm instead: 'I'll never, no, never, no, never forsake.'" The hymn was a favorite of Presidents Andrew Jackson and Theodore Roosevelt, and of General Robert E. Lee, and was used at both Roosevelt's and Lee's funerals.

SOURCE: For comments on the source, J. F. Wade's "Cantus Diversi," see Hymn 116.

TUNE: "Adeste Fideles" was first used with the carol, "O Come, All Ye Faithful," a Christmas morning processional. It is sometimes called "Portuguese Hymn," probably because its first use in England was in a Portuguese mission. It is a historic tune in America.

The pioneers lacked songbooks, but this tune was deeply graven on their hearts. They sang it from memory, in their meetinghouses and open-air services, as well as at family worship in the log cabins. Nor was it less popular among more favored people. On Christmas Eve of 1898 it was sung during the Spanish-American War, by American forces near Havana. Thus a song with no name to sponsor it made a great name for itself.

284

HYMN: In Heavenly Love Abiding
FIRST TUNE: Nyland

Author: *Anna Laetitia Waring*   Source: *Finnish Hymn Melody*

AUTHOR: Anna Laetitia Waring (1820–1910) learned Hebrew in order to appreciate the strength and beauty of the Hebrew Psalter, which she read daily. This hymn is steeped in the spirit of the Psalter. Miss Waring was born at Neath, Glamorganshire, Wales, and was brought up in the Society of Friends. She was a woman of childlike faith and joyous disposition. Her interest in the sacramentalism of the Church of England drew her into that fellowship. Early in life she began to write poetry, publishing "Hymns and Meditations by A. L. W." in 1850. She contributed to The Sunday Magazine. Her works are characterized by simplicity and beautiful diction.

HYMN: There is great spiritual comfort in this hymn. Into it is distilled the essence of Psalms 23 and 90. In times of difficulty, in hours of unrest, the hymn has given wings to the heart.

SOURCE (First Tune): This tune is from a Finnish hymn melody.

HARMONIZER (First Tune): For comments on the harmonizer, David Evans, see Hymn 177.

TUNE (First): "Nyland" is an arrangement of a Finnish folk song, which was made by Dr. Evans for "The Church Hymnary," Revised, published in England in 1927. Like many tunes which are based on folk-song themes, it possesses a melody of haunting beauty. It is a people's tune; in a hurried glance at the score one can almost see the rhythmic sway of groups as they sing it. "Nyland" is an effective new setting for Miss Waring's "In Heavenly Love Abiding," and will be welcomed as an alternate tune.

The Life in Christ

Composer: *John Hullah*

COMPOSER (Second Tune): John Pyke Hullah was born in Worcester, England, June 27, 1812, but spent most of his life in London, where he died in 1884. In 1833 he entered the Royal Academy of Music. He was an organist, but made it the real business of his life to popularize vocal music among all people. His training school in Exeter Hall sent out twenty-five thousand trained leaders between 1840 and 1860. He was professor of vocal music in King's, Queen's, and Bedford Colleges. He conducted annual concerts by the metropolitan school children at Crystal Palace. He duplicated in England the work that Dr. Lowell Mason had already done in America. Under his influence there was a vastly increased interest in church music. In 1876 he received the degree of Doctor of Laws from the University of Edinburgh. He edited several books of worship.

TUNE (Second): "Bentley" was especially written for Cowper's "Sometimes a Light Surprises" and was included in "Psalms and Hymns for Divine Worship," published in England in 1867. In America, seven years later, it appeared in the Presbyterian Hymnal of 1874 in association with "Brief Life Is Here Our Portion" and "For Thee, O Dear, Dear Country." It was included in the Hymnal of 1895, and placed opposite "In Heavenly Love Abiding," thus suggesting the relation it sustains in the present Hymnal to those words. The tune was used twice in the Hymnal of 1911. "Bentley," characterized by simplicity of pattern and finely balanced progressions, is unusually mellow and pacifying when written in D flat, as in this Hymnal.

---

285   HYMN: My Faith Looks Up to Thee
        TUNE: Olivet

Author: *Rev. Ray Palmer*   Composer: *Lowell Mason*

AUTHOR: To have written, at the age of twenty-two, a hymn that has outlived a century and spanned the world is achievement enough for any lifetime. That distinction belongs to Ray Palmer, D.D., son of a Rhode Island judge, educated at Phillips Academy, Andover, and graduated from Yale University in 1830. He held Congregational pastorates at Bath, Maine, and Albany, New York. He was Corresponding Secretary of the American Congregational Union from 1865 to 1879, when he retired to Newark, New Jersey. He died there in 1887. He published several books of prose and verse.

HYMN: "My Faith Looks Up to Thee" was written while Palmer was teaching in New York, just after his graduation from college. His own comment was, "I gave form to what I felt by writing, with little effort, the stanzas. I recollect I wrote them with very tender emotion, and ended the last lines with tears." He put the manuscript in his pocketbook, where it remained for some time. One day in Boston he met Lowell Mason, who was busy at that time compiling "Spiritual Songs for Social Worship." Mason asked him if he had a poem for the new book. Palmer gave him his stanzas. In a few days Mason wrote the tune "Olivet," and, again meeting Palmer on the street, said, "Mr. Palmer, you may live many years, and do many good things, but I think you will be best known to posterity as the author of 'My Faith Looks Up to Thee.'"

COMPOSER: For comments on the composer, Lowell Mason, see Hymn 18.

TUNE: "Olivet" was written for "My Faith Looks Up to Thee," and its peculiar fitness has become historic. The hymn and tune present a simple, potent, worshipful sermon on faith in God. The echoes linger long with the worshiper. From the first measure "Olivet" springs to the realms of faith, giving natural voice to the spirit that looks to Him who bore the cross on Calvary.

---

286 HYMN: Jesus, Saviour, Pilot Me
TUNE: Pilot

Author: *Rev. Edward Hopper*   Composer: *John E. Gould*

AUTHOR: Edward Hopper was born in 1818 and graduated from Union Theological Seminary in 1842. His pastorates were at Greenville, New York; Sag Harbor, Long Island; and the Church of Sea and Land, New York City. The latter is attended by many sailors. Lafayette College gave the degree of Doctor of Divinity to Mr. Hopper in 1871. Dr. Moffatt says, "He was found to have died in his study in the act of writing lines on heaven."

HYMN: This poem first appeared in The Sailor's Magazine, 1871, and in the same year it was published in the "Baptist Praise Book." The hymn has become deservedly popular, not only with seagoing folk, but with all voyagers on the sea of life.

COMPOSER: For comments on the composer, John E. Gould, see Hymn 225.

The Life in Christ

TUNE: "Pilot" was written by Mr. Gould for these words. They are artistically fitted in accent, in movement, and in melody. In the slow time you sense the stroke of the oars. In the four recurring slurs of the several voices, in each stanza, you feel the lift of each succeeding wave. Though composed for seamen, and for a special occasion, it is suited for a mother's lullaby, or for any religious service composed of either young or more mature persons. It is one of the first and best of the "gospel hymn" type to find a permanent place in the approved hymnology of the Church. Whatever investment the Church at large has made in mission work for seamen, the Church of Sea and Land has made a signal contribution to all churches through this spiritual hymn of trust.

287

HYMN: I Am Trusting Thee, Lord Jesus
TUNE: Bullinger

Author: *Frances Ridley Havergal*   Composer: *Rev. Ethelbert W. Bullinger*

AUTHOR: For comments on the author, Frances Ridley Havergal, see Hymn 56.

HYMN: This hymn was a favorite of the author and after her death was found in her pocket Bible. Written by Miss Havergal at Ormont Dessous, Switzerland, in September, 1874, it was first published in her volume of poems, "Loyal Responses," 1878, and in "Life Chords," 1880. Long ago Frances Havergal joined "the choir invisible," but her music still brings comfort to the world. The secret of her message was complete surrender and perfect trust in her Lord.

COMPOSER: For comments on the composer, Ethelbert W. Bullinger, see Hymn 221.

TUNE: This contemplative tune is an adequate interpreter of this hymn of Miss Havergal's. When sung in slow time it suggests intimate personal communion, as if the singer and his Saviour were seated side by side, pledged to a trust that is unfaltering. Personal hymns render a special spiritual ministry. In times of cynicism hymns of this type greatly refresh the soul. This hymn serves as a twilight meditation, for an evening service or for the fireside devotions.

For further comments on the tune, "Bullinger," see Hymn 221.

288

HYMN: Cast Thy Burden on the Lord
TUNE: Savannah

Source: *Rowland Hill's "Psalms and Hymns"*

Source: *"The Foundery Collection"*

SOURCE: This hymn is from "Psalms and Hymns," by Rowland Hill. Hymnologists are not pleased with the habit of the famous Rowland Hill, who was one of the many protégés of the generous Lady Huntingdon (1707–1791), of mutilating at his pleasure the hymns of others in the many hymn books he published. This was but a minor weakness in a great evangelist. He was the son of a baronet and was educated at Cambridge, from which he graduated in 1769. Out of his own inherited fortune he built Surrey Chapel on Blackfriars Road, London, where he spent nearly fifty years. He was the greatest outdoor preacher of the period, and his evangelistic tours throughout the Empire were occasions of great crowds and unusual excitement. He was one of the founders of the London Missionary Society. He was a courageous defender of vaccination, having vaccinated thousands himself. His biographies are many and have been popular, as have his volumes of sermons and other writings. His various hymn books were published in 1774, 1783, 1790, 1808, and 1832. They were widely used in popular religious meetings. He died in London in 1833.

HYMN: This hymn, entitled "Encouragement for the Weak," appeared in Rowland Hill's "Psalms and Hymns," 1783. It is Hill's most widely known hymn still in common use. It is a versified interpretation of Ps. 55:22, a hymn of trust the message of which weary souls have sung for 150 years.

SOURCE: For comments on the source, John Wesley's "The Foundery Collection," see Hymn 264.

TUNE: "Savannah" is old enough to be new in many American churches. It is not to be confused with another tune bearing the same name, which is one of Pleyel's chorals. The spiritual challenge of the hymn is such as to compel a careful study of the tune here presented. Like the hymn which it interprets the tune carries a rich heritage of praise from the earlier half of the eighteenth century. Neither the author of the hymn nor the composer of the music is known.

The Life in Christ

289 HYMN: Lead, Kindly Light, Amid th' Encircling Gloom
TUNE: Lux Benigna

Author: *Cardinal John H. Newman*   Composer: *Rev. John B. Dykes*

AUTHOR: John Henry Newman (1801–1890) spent a lonely boyhood in a world of dreams. After graduation from Oxford he obtained a fellowship and became a tutor in Oriel College. He became vicar of St. Mary the Virgin, the University church, and the sermons he preached there made him a power in Oxford and in the world. His striking personality, intellectual gifts, and literary genius gave him a commanding position. Keble's famous sermon on national apostasy, in 1833, drew Newman into the Oxford Movement, of which he soon became the head. His reactionary mind, his antipathy to liberalism, coupled with his failure to revive the Church of England, inclined him more and more toward the Roman Catholic Church. In his own communion the note of authority was lacking. It seemed to be neither apostolic nor Catholic. After some years of mental agony and irresolution, he retracted all that he had ever said against Rome and entered the Roman Church. In his autobiography, "Apologia pro Vita Sua," he gives a striking account of his mental journey and vindicates his sincerity. Leo XIII created him cardinal in 1879 and allowed him to live in England. Universally venerated for his saintly life he passed the last ten years of his career in seclusion.

HYMN: "Lead, Kindly Light, Amid th' Encircling Gloom" was written on a vessel becalmed for one week on the Mediterranean in the month of June, 1833. Newman was on his way from Rome. He had been ill in Sicily. Already uncertainty as to his future was preying on his mind. He was homesick and depressed. It was out of such a mood that this pathetic prayer for guidance was born. The exquisite lyric has been productive of much debate, particularly as to the meaning of the last two lines: By "angel faces" did he mean angels, or the beloved dead, or the lost illusions of youth—those dreams, hopes, fancies, faiths that shine upon us in our early years and then fade into the light of common day? Newman himself answered this in a letter written in 1879 in which he said that he had forgotten just what he did mean by the words. Whatever meaning best suggests the yearning of the soul for guidance in crises of darkness may properly be attached to these words.

COMPOSER: For comments on the composer, John B. Dykes, see Hymn 53.

311

TUNE: "Lux Benigna" was born in the mind of Dr. Dykes as he walked through the Strand in London. It was as if he had seen a rainbow against the cloud of London fog. The poem which Dr. Newman called "The Pillar of the Cloud" was in his mind. It is a cry out of the darkness from a soul in quest of light. The tune is full of entreaty, as is the poem. Cardinal Newman attributed the popularity of the hymn to Dr. Dykes's tune. While it is one of the most difficult tunes for congregational singing, it is universally used. It was a favorite of President McKinley's, and was played by bands and sung by choruses along the route as the body of the martyr President was borne from Buffalo to its last resting place at Canton. A prominent committee of hymnologists selected "Lux Benigna" from other tunes written for this hymn as its best interpreter. It has quickened the pulse beat of many a lonely pilgrim who has kept step with its exalted thought movement.

---

290 HYMN: God of Compassion, in Mercy Befriend Us
TUNE: O Quanta Qualia

Author: *Rev. John J. Moment*   Source: *La Feillée's "Méthode du Plain Chant"*

AUTHOR: For comments on the author, John J. Moment, see Hymn 4.

HYMN: The trust and confidence filling each line of this hymn have their anchorage, as indicated in the last stanza, in the strength of Him who guides the stars in their courses and with whose greatness and might are mingled that compassion and mercy which are ever ready to befriend. The serenity of a Christian's daily life amidst the storms is underwritten by an honest acceptance of the "all-availing" grace of God in Christ.

SOURCE: For comments on the source, "Méthode du Plain Chant," by François de la Feillée, see Hymn 24.

TUNE: "O Quanta Qualia" is an adaptation of a plain-song melody. As such it appeared in La Feillée's "Méthode du Plain Chant," in 1808, set to the hymn, "Regnator Orbis." That it is older than this date indicates is quite generally conceded. In 1854 it was adapted and set to "O What Their Joy and Their Glory Must Be," the original of which was one of a collection made by Abélard for the abbey of the Paraclete, which Héloïse founded near Nogent-sur-Seine.

The Life in Christ

The translation is by Dr. John M. Neale. The tune here is used to words of recent writing. The union formed is pleasing, and has every prospect of long survival. The music calls for fine shading and profound feeling. For further comments on the tune, "O Quanta Qualia," see Hymn 196.

291

HYMN: Whate'er My God Ordains Is Right
TUNE: Was Gott Thut Das Ist Wohlgethan

Author: *Samuel Rodigast*   Composer: *Severus Gastorius*

AUTHOR: Samuel Rodigast was born at Gröben, Germany, in 1649, his father being pastor of the church there. He entered the University of Jena in 1668, from which he received his Master's degree in 1671. He was appointed adjunct of the philosophical faculty in 1676. Thence he went to Berlin in 1680 to become corector of Greyfriars Gymnasium, later to be rector, a post held until his death in 1708.

TRANSLATOR: The hymn is fortunate in its translator, for Catherine Winkworth's translations of German hymns into English are said to be "among the most beautiful ever made. She preserves the beauty and strength of the original."
For further comments on the translator, Catherine Winkworth, see Hymn 6.

HYMN: It is believed that the hymn was written for Samuel Rodigast's sick friend, Severus Gastorius, while Rodigast was at Jena. Gastorius, precentor of the church at Jena, set it to music. It appeared in "Hannoversche Gesangbuch," which was published in 1676. It was said to be the favorite hymn of Frederick William III, of Prussia, and was sung at his funeral by his command. It was founded on Deut. 32:4, and has reminiscences of an older hymn by Altenberg, beginning with the same line.

COMPOSER: Severus Gastorius, of whom little is known, was living in Jena in 1675. At that time he was cantor. He had a devoted friend in Samuel Rodigast, who visited him during a period of severe illness to cheer and comfort him.

TUNE: "Was Gott Thut Das Ist Wohlgethan" was written by Gastorius in 1675 to supply a musical setting for the hymn which Samuel Rodigast had written to comfort him in sickness. It appeared in "Hannoversche Gesangbuch," published in Göttingen in 1676 and later in "Auserlesenes Weinmarisches Gesangbuch," 1681. It has several versions, and some of them do not conserve the original rhythm and melody. The harmonization used in this Hymnal is one of the best and comes from "The Common Service Book" of the United Lutheran Church in America.

Comfort

*

292 HYMN: Call Jehovah Thy Salvation
TUNE: Autumn

Author: *James Montgomery*   Source: *"Psaumes Octante Trois"*

AUTHOR: For comments on the author, James Montgomery, see Hymn 11.

HYMN: This noble hymn, based on Psalm 91, appeared first in James Montgomery's "Songs of Zion," and carried the title "Call the Lord, Thy Sure Salvation." From this same source came a kindred hymn bearing as its title the Scriptural phrase "God Shall Charge His Angel Legions," and also another hymn by the same author, "God's Merciful Guardianship of His People." Remembering the fact that for more than thirty years, through the stormy period of the Napoleonic Wars, Montgomery carried forward the editorship of a paper devoted to human welfare, and was twice sent to prison because of his courageous utterances, it is not strange that in Psalm 91 he found his security, and titled his hymns accordingly.

SOURCE: This tune is from "Psaumes Octante Trois."

TUNE: The melody of the tune, "Autumn," has been traced to the "Genevan Psalter," 1551, in which it was identified with Psalm 42. The tune was introduced to America about the middle of the nineteenth century and was popularized by Dr. Lowell Mason and Dr. Thomas Hastings. Many early church hymnals in this country considered it a Spanish melody. The Presbyterian Hymnal of 1874 so credits it. Twenty years before in "The Hallelujah," 1854, edited by Lowell Mason, it is referred to as a Spanish melody and called "Jaynes." In "The Presbyterian Psalmodist," 1852, edited by Dr. Thomas Hastings, there is an arrangement by V. C. Taylor, which bears the names "Madrid" and "Erith." The version in "The Hallelujah," which probably was improved by Lowell Mason, is very much like the one used in this Hymnal. "Autumn" is a popular and useful tune, and for years has been associated with "Call Jehovah Thy Salvation" and "Guide Me, O Thou Great Jehovah."

The Life in Christ

293   HYMN: Come, Ye Disconsolate, Where'er Ye Languish
        TUNE: Consolation

Authors: *Thomas Moore and*   Composer: *Samuel Webbe*
Thomas Hastings

AUTHORS: For comments on the coauthor, Thomas Hastings, see
Hymn 197.
In this hymn of consoling grace meet the lyric gifts of Thomas
Moore (1779–1852), the Irish poet, and the musical gifts of Thomas
Hastings, an American composer and teacher. Moore's popularity will
live wherever his popular songs "Believe Me, if All Those Endearing
Young Charms," "The Last Rose of Summer," and "Oft in the Stilly
Night" are known. There is some inconsistency between the exalted
spiritual reach of his hymn "Come, Ye Disconsolate, Where'er Ye
Languish" and his reputed lack of personal spirituality. He was born in
Dublin, educated at Trinity College, and went to London in 1799 to
study law, but soon thereafter gave his full time to literature. He was
appointed registrar in the Admiralty Court of Bermuda in 1804. Moore
wrote thirty-two hymns, all contained in one collection entitled "Sacred
Songs." Moore's life reveals so many strange chapters and romantic
incidents that it seems odd that he should ever have been a writer of
hymns. His natural gifts, however, advanced him far in the field of composition, especially in poems of a lyric quality.

HYMN: We owe to Thomas Hastings great praise for composing
the third stanza, regarded by many as the dominant stanza, in
this hymn of consolation. Stanzas 1 and 2 were written by
Moore in 1816, and stanza 3 was added by Hastings in 1832.
"Come, Ye Disconsolate, Where'er Ye Languish" is an example of
an immature poem growing by use into one of the first-rate hymns of
the language. It gains in deep and moving qualities of spiritual comfort
as each stanza in its concluding line rises higher in its affirmation of
God's faithfulness.

COMPOSER: For comments on the composer, Samuel Webbe, see
Hymn 31.

TUNE: "Consolation" is a song out of darkness, bringing assurance
of light to stricken hearts. This tune was probably written in 1763.
It is wedded to Moore's hymn. Few people think of any other
tune as suitable. Twelve of Webbe's tunes are used in American hymnals.
With sweetness and pathos this hymn administers its solace. The hurt of
earth is here overmastered by the healing of heaven. Two other tunes

bear the name "Consolation," the best-known being the Communion hymn set to Mendelssohn's "Consolation," from his "Songs Without Words."

---

294 HYMN: Give to the Winds Thy Fears
TUNE: St. Bride

Author: *Rev. Paul Gerhardt* Composer: *Samuel Howard*

AUTHOR: For comments on the author, Paul Gerhardt, see Hymn 125.

TRANSLATOR: For comments on the translator, John Wesley, see Hymn 63.

HYMN: Each stanza of this hymn begins with a word from Luther's version of Ps. 37:5. Paul Gerhardt wrote especially to the poor, the sick, and the afflicted. Much of his life was lived in anguish of soul, and yet, through it all, he carried his faith and wrote his hymns of confident trust, such as "Give to the Winds Thy Fears."

COMPOSER: For comments on the composer, Samuel Howard, see Hymn 188.

TUNE: For comments on the tune, "St. Bride," see Hymn 188.

---

295 HYMN: There Is No Sorrow, Lord, Too Light
TUNE: Wigtown

Author: *Jane Crewdson* Source: *"Scottish Psalter"*

AUTHOR: Jane Crewdson, the daughter of George Fox, was born at Perraw, Cornwall, England, in October, 1809. At the age of twenty-seven she married Thomas Crewdson, of Manchester. She was never strong physically and finally became a confirmed invalid, suffering greatly. During this period of suffering she wrote several hymns. She died at Summerlands, near Manchester, on September 14, 1863, "leaving behind her the memory of a beautiful Christian life and many admirable verses." It has been said that she truly learned in suffering what she taught in song. "Many felt that her sick room was the highest place to which they could resort for refreshment of spirit and even for mental

The Life in Christ

recreation," according to her husband, who added, "From that apartment came many a letter of earnest sympathy or of charming playfulness."

At the age of forty-two she wrote "Aunt Jane's Verses for Children." One of her volumes of poems, "Lays of the Reformation and Other Lyrics," was published in 1860, and later "A Little While, and Other Poems."

HYMN: Written out of a life of suffering, every word of this invalid's hymn takes on convincing sincerity and spiritual meaning. She is said to have composed this hymn, as she did others, between paroxysms of pain. It appeared in a volume called "A Little While, and Other Poems," published in 1864, and later was printed in "Church Hymns" and "The Church Hymnary." It is a touching approach in absolute confidence to the sympathy of our Lord by one whose hourly and sharpest need tested his sustaining grace. This was the favorite hymn of the late Dr. Jowett, who was at one time pastor of Fifth Avenue Presbyterian Church, New York City.

SOURCE: For comments on the source, "Scottish Psalter," see the article, "The Psalters in Early Presbyterian Worship," under "Original Sources," page xv.

TUNE: For comments on the tune, "Wigtown," see Hymn 234.

---

296   HYMN: Sometimes a Light Surprises
TUNE: Bentley

Author: *William Cowper*   Composer: *John Hullah*

AUTHOR: For comments on the author, William Cowper, see Hymn 103.

HYMN: This hymn of the great poet, William Cowper, carries the additional title "Joy and Peace in Believing." The third stanza is based on the familiar words of Jesus in the Sermon on the Mount, while the fourth reveals the truth set forth in Hab. 3: 17, 18:

> "For though the fig-tree shall not flourish,
> Neither shall fruit be in the vines;
> The labor of the olive shall fail,
> And the fields shall yield no food;
> The flock shall be cut off from the fold,
> And there shall be no herd in the stalls:
> Yet I will rejoice in Jehovah,
> I will joy in the God of my salvation."

317

This was the last hymn sung by the great evangelist of Scotland, Rev. Robert McCheyne, whose zeal for Christ burned with steady flame, even to the hour of his death, when he called for this hymn.

COMPOSER: For comments on the composer, John Pyke Hullah, see Hymn 284.

TUNE: Dr. Hullah has given us a tune well adapted to Cowper's hymn, which is called "a Christian lyric." The well-known melancholy spirit of Cowper is not even suggested in the hymn; nor does a single minor strain sound out in its tonal interpretation. The last word of the hymn, "Rejoice," is the composer's keynote for the tune. The tune was written especially for these words.

For further comments on the tune, "Bentley," see Hymn 284.

Joy

*

297

HYMN: Rejoice, Ye Pure in Heart
TUNE: Marion

Author: *Rev. Edward H. Plumptre*　　　Composer: *Arthur H. Messiter*

AUTHOR: For comments on the author, Edward H. Plumptre, see Hymn 180.

HYMN: This hymn was written in May, 1865, as a processional for a choir festival in Peterborough Cathedral. The hymn carries the moving refrain,

> "Rejoice, rejoice,
> Rejoice, give thanks, and sing!"

This hymn as a poem appeared in Dean Plumptre's "Lazarus, and Other Poems." As a processional hymn, it takes high rank because increasing attention is being given in all Protestant churches to choral uses of both processional and recessional numbers. The tendency, likewise, to omit the so-called formal "anthem" and to enrich the service of worship by the increase of choral amens, introits, and all briefer forms of music is evident. This has a marked effect in turning attention away from man and toward God.

The Life in Christ

COMPOSER: Arthur H. Messiter, one of the best-known and highly esteemed church organists in America, was born at Frome, Somersetshire, England, in 1834. After receiving his early education from private tutors, he devoted his entire time to music. Coming to the United States, he settled in New York City, as organist of Trinity Church. After serving that church for thirty-one years, he retired in 1897. He was an organist and composer of great ability. Several notable books on music were published by him. He edited the Episcopal Hymnal of 1893, a volume which embodied the boy-choir traditions of old Trinity Church. His honorary degree of Doctor of Music was conferred by St. Stephen's College, Annandale, New York. He died in New York City on Sunday evening, July 2, 1916.

TUNE: "Marion" was written in 1883, as is indicated in the hymnal which Dr. Messiter edited. Because of the joyous character of the music the tune won instant recognition. Its association with Dr. Plumptre's "Rejoice, Ye Pure in Heart" is permanent. As a processional hymn it is unsurpassed. It is equally effective for antiphonal singing.

---

298 HYMN: The King of Glory Standeth
TUNE: Gosterwood

Author: *Charitie Lees de Chenez* Source: *English Traditional Melody*

AUTHOR: Charitie Lees de Chenez, the author, was the daughter of Sidney Smith, D.D., the rector of Drumragh, County Tyrone, Ireland. She was born at Bloomfield, in County Dublin, June 21, 1841, was married in 1869 to Arthur E. Bancroft, and later became Mrs. De Chenez. Her hymns have appeared in periodicals and also as leaflets. In 1867 her hymns were published under the title "Within the Veil."

HYMN: This hymn was published, in seven stanzas of eight lines each, in a periodical in 1867, and was entitled "Mighty to Save."

SOURCE: The tune is from an English traditional melody.

TUNE: "Gosterwood" is a bright, virile tune based upon a traditional melody familiar on the Isle of Man. As a folk song it was associated with "The Brisk Young Lively Lad." This arrangement is by R. Vaughan Williams and was made for "The English Hymnal," published in 1906, in which it is used three times. Subsequently it was included in "Songs of Praise." Few recent tune arrangements excel "Gosterwood" for group or congregational singing.

299 HYMN: Since Jesus Is My Friend
FIRST TUNE: Selma

Author: *Rev. Paul Gerhardt*　　Source: *Traditional Melody of the Isle of Arran*

A UTHOR: For comments on the author, Paul Gerhardt, see Hymn 125.

T RANSLATOR: For comments on the translator, Catherine Winkworth, see Hymn 6.

H YMN: In St. Paul's letter to the church in Rome, Rom. 8:31, is found the thought which constitutes the Scriptural basis of this hymn: "If God is for us, who is against us?" This is the beginning of that entire passage, sometimes called "St. Paul's Confession of Faith in the Purposes of God," which concludes with stirring testimony: "For I am persuaded, that neither death, nor life, nor angels, nor principalities, nor things present, nor things to come, nor powers, nor height, nor depth, nor any other creature, shall be able to separate us from the love of God, which is in Christ Jesus our Lord." The translation of this hymn from the original German of Paul Gerhardt is by Catherine Winkworth, an English poet, whose specialty of translations from the German made her a most gifted contributor to the treasury of hymnology. Miss Winkworth, a devoted follower of Christ, consecrated her talents to Christian education and was known always as a radiant disciple and teacher.

S OURCE (First Tune): The tune is from a traditional melody of the Isle of Arran.

A DAPTER (First Tune): Robert Archibald Smith was born at Reading, Berkshire, England, November 16, 1780. Though his musical talents attracted attention quite early, his father, who was a weaver, gave him little encouragement and made him work at the weaver's trade. This work, however, was too confining and endangered the young man's health. More than once his father caught him scribbling musical notes on his loom. Subsequently the father relented and permitted his son to follow his bent. The latter began to teach music in 1803. Being a skillful performer on the violin, the viola, the violoncello, and the organ, he had little difficulty in securing pupils. He also had a fine tenor voice and was consequently appointed precentor and session clerk of the Abbey Church, Paisley, Scotland. Some of his early compositions were musical settings for the verses of his friend Robert Tannahill (1774–1810), a local and popular

The Life in Christ

Scottish poet. Smith was interested in minstrelsy and published six volumes under the title "The Scottish Minstrel." In 1823 he went to St. George's Church, Edinburgh, as leader of psalmody under Dr. Andrew Thomson. He was a successful collector of folk-song melodies and knew how to use them effectively. He understood the Scottish heart and provided Scotland with music characterized by its simplicity of design and solemnity of effect. He died in Edinburgh, January 3, 1829, and was buried in St. Cuthbert's Churchyard.

TUNE (First): "Selma," which is used four times in "The Hymnal" and destined to be greatly appreciated, appeared in 1825 in a hymnal which R. A. Smith edited for use in St. George's Church, Edinburgh. In that book "it is set to Psalm 67, and described as an 'Ancient Scottish Melody. Noted in the Island of Arran, and Harmonized by Mr. Smith.' "

SECOND TUNE: Greenwood

Composer: *Joseph E. Sweetser*

COMPOSER (Second Tune): Joseph E. Sweetser (1825–1873), an English organist, came to America as a young man, when the influence of Lowell Mason and Thomas Hastings was at its height. He was organist of the Church of the Puritans, New York City, then located at Broadway and Fifteenth Street, of which George B. Cheever, D.D., was pastor. Sweetser and George F. Root published, in 1849, a notable book entitled "A Collection of Church Music," which became popularly known as the "Root and Sweetser Collection." Two years later Sweetser and Dr. Cheever published "Christian Melodies." Many of the hymns and tunes of these books were perpetuated by subsequent hymnals, notably by those edited and published by Charles S. Robinson, D.D.

TUNE (Second): "Greenwood" was introduced to American churches through the "Root and Sweetser Collection." In that volume it was associated with "We Lift Our Hearts to Thee." It has been included in all Presbyterian hymnals since 1874. In spite of the fact that it has been called a solemn tune, "Greenwood" has been in constant use since its first appearance.

---

300   HYMN: My Heart Is Resting, O My God
             TUNE: Pentatone

Author: *Anna Laetitia Waring*   Composer: *Henry Walford Davies*

AUTHOR: For comments on the author, Anna Laetitia Waring, see Hymn 284.

HYMN: This hymn reflects in marked degree the qualities of strength and tenderness, vigor and gentleness, courage and submission, seen in the character of Christ. It has been referred to as "The Life of Christ in Song." The noblest tribute to the life of the author of this hymn is that she refrained from all publicity, though constantly creating new evidences of a spiritual "walk with God." Here is a most inspiring presentation of a godly life portrayed in a perfect poem set to moving music.

COMPOSER: For comments on the composer, Henry Walford Davies, see Hymn 282.

TUNE: For comments on the tune, "Pentatone," see Hymn 282.

Peace

*

301 HYMN: Peace, Perfect Peace, in This Dark World of Sin
TUNE: Pax Tecum

Author: *Bishop Edward H. Bickersteth*   Composer: *George T. Caldbeck*

AUTHOR: For comments on the author, Edward H. Bickersteth, see Hymn 62.

HYMN: This hymn was inspired by the Scriptural words, "Thou wilt keep him in perfect peace, whose mind is stayed on thee; because he trusteth in thee," Isa. 26:3. The gamut of life's adversities is run in the seven stanzas of this hymn, with peace abiding at the center and overcoming them all. Sin, duties, sorrows, distance, the unknown, and death itself are met and conquered by that confidence which faith in God bestows. Bishop Bickersteth wrote the words of this hymn at the bedside of Archdeacon Hill, of Liverpool, who was then approaching death with a troubled mind. Eager to comfort his friend, the bishop read the text from Isaiah, and then at once wrote down the words of the hymn as we have them to-day. The son of the author tells us that "the most touching use of this hymn was at the funeral of his brother, at Chiselden, in 1897, when his father was the chief mourner." Thus the hymn written for the comfort of others returned to comfort the author himself.

The Life in Christ

COMPOSER: George Thomas Caldbeck is a one-tune composer. He was born at Waterford, England, in 1852. After studying at the National Model School of Waterford, he entered the Islington Theological College in London to prepare for the ministry and missionary work. While taking his divinity course he served as precentor of the college and before graduating wrote the tune, "Pax Tecum," that perpetuates his memory throughout the world. On account of illness he abandoned the ministry and became a schoolmaster in Ireland. Subsequently he engaged in evangelistic work, itinerated Ireland, and then proceeded to London, where he engaged in open-air preaching. In spite of his scholarly attainments he never seemed to arrive at any degree of substantial success. His most satisfactory achievement was writing "Pax Tecum" for Dr. Bickersteth's "Peace, Perfect Peace, in This Dark World of Sin." Once when haled into court for a technical misdemeanor, the fact that he had written so cherished a tune induced the magistrate to dismiss the case.

ARRANGER: Charles J. Vincent, Mus.D., the arranger of "Pax Tecum," was born in 1852 at Houghton le Spring, Durham, England. As a musician he was to the manner born. His father was an organist and composer of distinction. He received his training at Durham Cathedral and at Leipzig, and he held positions in a number of important parishes. Schirmer and Company, the well-known music corporation, was founded by him, and at first was known as the Vincent Music Publishing Company. Vincent's compositions and books are quite numerous.

TUNE: "Pax Tecum" was composed for "Peace, Perfect Peace, in This Dark World of Sin." A copy was sent to the author, Bishop Edward H. Bickersteth, who included it in the second edition of "The Hymnal Companion to the Book of Common Prayer," 1877, which he edited.

---

302   HYMN: Dear Lord and Father of Mankind
      TUNE: Rest

Author: *John Greenleaf Whittier*   Composer: *Frederick Charles Maker*

AUTHOR: For comments on the author, John Greenleaf Whittier, see Hymn 178.

HYMN: We find here an inspiring poem set to inspiring music. It gathers in its lyric beauty much of the deeper mind and heart of Christ's gospel. It stands with "Immortal Love, Forever Full,"

323

and these two sponsor another, "I Bow My Forehead to the Dust", which closes with that familiar declaration of faith:

> "I know not where His islands lift
> Their fronded palms in air;
> I only know I cannot drift
> Beyond His love and care."

The hymn is a cento from a major poem, "The Brewing of Soma," which describes the foolish ways men employ in seeking God.

COMPOSER: For comments on the composer, Frederick Charles Maker, see Hymn 29.

TUNE: The tune, "Rest," by Frederick Charles Maker, has an unchallenged place as the musical interpreter of the Quaker poet's hymn. Other tunes have been tried, but none compares with this in its adaptation to the message and spirit of the words. It makes resonant the atmosphere of prayer and consecration. In its beginning we sense the confiding intimacy of the worshiper with his heavenly Father. The closing measures lead the soul into reverence, quietude, and peace. The tune bears a helpful message of its own, intensified by its subtle relation to the poet's words.

---

303   HYMN: Immortal Love, Within Whose Righteous Will
        TUNE: Lux Beata

Author: *Rev. Stopford A. Brooke*   Composer: *Albert L. Peace*

AUTHOR: For comments on the author, Stopford A. Brooke, see Hymn 74.

HYMN: This hymn was published in the author's "Christian Hymns," a collection of 269 pieces which he published for the use of his congregation in 1881. "It has a strong likeness to Cardinal Newman's 'Lead, Kindly Light, Amid th' Encircling Gloom,' is in the same meter, and might be called a companion hymn," breathing the same spirit of calm and willing resignation to God's will and trust in his leadership.

COMPOSER: Albert Lister Peace, Mus.D., a distinguished organist, editor, and composer, was born at Huddersfield, England, in 1844. Music was his natural talent. As a boy he was considered a prodigy. He played a church organ at the age of nine, and subsequently held positions at Huddersfield and Glasgow. In the latter place, after having served four other churches in the city, he was appointed to Glasgow Cathedral. In 1897 he was called to St. George's Hall, Liverpool, where he remained until his death in 1912. He was held in such high repute in Scotland that many organs were opened by him. He won distinction by his mastery of the pedals and he was influential in having their range extended. He edited the music of the following hymnals for the Church in Scotland: "The Scottish Hymnal," 1885; "Psalms and Paraphrases with Tunes," 1886; "The Psalter with Chants," 1888; and "The Scottish Anthem Book," 1891. Of his tunes, three are included in "The Hymnal." He died at Blundellsands in 1912.

TUNE: "Lux Beata" is an effective treatment of a difficult meter. The main mood of the tune is that of serenity—perhaps it were better to say serenity and strength. The tune requires careful rendering, and should be sung slowly and with feeling. It was written while Dr. Peace was organist at Liverpool, and within a few years became known on both sides of the Atlantic.

---

304 HYMN: Lead Us, Heavenly Father, Lead Us
     TUNE: Corinth

Author: *James Edmeston* Source: *"An Essay on the Church Plain Chant"*

AUTHOR: For comments on the author, James Edmeston, see Hymn 47.

HYMN: The best-known hymns of James Edmeston are "Lead Us, Heavenly Father, Lead Us" and "Saviour, Breathe an Evening Blessing." Many of his hymns were written for children, and because of their simplicity are admirably adapted to this use. This hymn was specially written for the London Orphan Asylum. It meets all the requirements of a child's hymn, with its objective thought of God as a loving Father tenderly caring for his own. However, its thought roots so deeply in the fundamental things of the Christian faith that it answers equally well the spiritual needs of the old.

SOURCE: "Corinth" comes from that valuable repository of hymn tunes, "An Essay on the Church Plain Chant," published in 1782.

TUNE: In the second part of "An Essay on the Church Plain Chant" the tune, "Corinth," is headed "The Hymn at Benediction." The composer's name is not attached. Some authorities have attributed this tune to Samuel Webbe. Others feel that the melody is of an earlier date and may have been arranged by him.

---

305 HYMN: I Do Not Ask, O Lord, That Life May Be
     TUNE: Submission

Author: *Adelaide Anne Procter*   Composer: *Albert Lister Peace*

AUTHOR: For comments on the author, Adelaide Anne Procter, see Hymn 36.

HYMN: Of this hymn some one has written: "It breathes a spirit of faith in God, and is expressed in unsurpassed beauty." It is a hymn of resignation, and under that title appeared in Miss Procter's "Legends and Lyrics, A Book of Verse," in 1862. The hymn has been criticized for its supineness and placidity, but the criticism is not well founded. On the contrary, the hymn reflects a quiet strength and assurance which indicate that submission and trust in God are always rewarded. On this account its message is comforting and reassuring. The hymn appears in other languages and is destined to live among Christian people everywhere. Miss Procter's most famous poem is "The Lost Chord," set to music by Sir Arthur Sullivan.

COMPOSER: For comments on the composer, Albert Lister Peace, see Hymn 303.

TUNE: "Submission" is a striking illustration of what the composer had in mind when he said, "No definite standard can be applied to all tunes, as each one has its own individual character." Other composers changed the hymn to common meter, presumably in the attempt to make the musical measures smoother. This change destroyed much of the beauty expressed in Miss Procter's own arrangement. Dr. Peace was very successful in writing a tune that is in harmony with the meaning and the spirit of the poem. The difficulty of this task is met by the master's adapting himself and his art to the hymn, rather than by adapting the hymn to more formal musical construction.

The Life in Christ

Love and Communion

*

306 HYMN: O Holy Saviour, Friend Unseen
TUNE: Flemming

Author: *Charlotte Elliott*   Composer: *Friedrich F. Flemming*

AUTHOR: For comments on the author, Charlotte Elliott, see Hymn 230.

HYMN: This hymn on "Clinging to Christ" was written in 1834, shortly after the death of the author's father, and was first published in the 1834 edition of her "Invalid's Hymn Book." The hymn was learned in pain and sorrow, and carries the same power of appeal as does Miss Elliott's better-known hymn, "Just as I Am, Without One Plea." The words of the author tell her full story: "My heavenly Father knows, and he alone, what it is, day after day, and hour after hour, to fight against bodily feelings of almost overpowering weakness and languor and exhaustion, to resolve . . . not to yield to the slothfulness, the depression, the irritability such a body causes me to long to indulge, but to rise every morning determined on taking this for my motto: 'If any man would come after me, let him deny himself, and take up his cross daily, and follow me.'"

COMPOSER: Friedrich Ferdinand Flemming followed music as an avocation. He was born at Neuhausen in Saxony. Quite early he determined on medicine as his life work and studied at Wittenberg from 1796 to 1800, and subsequently at Jena, Vienna, and Trieste. Most of his professional years were spent in Berlin, where he took a keen interest in all musical matters. He composed part songs, especially for male choral groups. He died in Berlin, May 27, 1813.

TUNE: "Flemming" was written about 1810 and formed a part of a musical setting for "Integer Vitae," an ode by Horace. Through its use in singing societies of men, it attracted the attention of hymnal editors who appropriated it. The tune seems to have been introduced to America through the hymnals of Dr. Charles S. Robinson, "Songs of the Sanctuary" and "Laudes Domini."

307 HYMN: O Love That Wilt Not Let Me Go
TUNE: St. Margaret

Author: *Rev. George Matheson* Composer: *Albert L. Peace*

AUTHOR: For comments on the author, George Matheson, see Hymn 247.

HYMN: This most moving and popular hymn came as did Tennyson's poem, "Crossing the Bar," by sudden inspiration, and remains but one of the characteristic marks of the genius of this distinguished Scottish preacher and poet. He said that its writing was "to me a unique experience. . . . This came like a dayspring from on high. I have never been able to gain once more the same fervor in verse. . . . My hymn was composed in the manse of Innellan, on the evening of 6th June, 1882. I was at that time alone. It was the day of my sister's marriage. . . . Something had happened to me, which was known only to myself, and which caused me the most severe mental suffering. The hymn was the fruit of that suffering. . . . The whole work was completed in five minutes, and . . . never received at my hands any retouching or correction." Dr. Matheson did not disclose the nature of the suffering behind the hymn. The statement has been made that it was the failure of the love of the woman to whom he was engaged, who, on learning that he was gradually going blind, said that she would not "go through life with a blind man." This story may be ignored since Dr. Matheson had been blind for twenty-five years. "The hymn . . . is autobiographical" and represents "the consecration of a great soul rising above the despondency caused by" an affliction. The closing words of the hymn have been called "divinely perfect":

> "I lay in dust life's glory dead,
> And from the ground there blossoms red
> Life that shall endless be."

"It was in allusion to these lines that a group of clergymen, who had . . . served as Dr. Matheson's assistants, sent to his funeral a wreath of red roses."

COMPOSER: For comments on the composer, Albert L. Peace, see Hymn 303.

TUNE: "St. Margaret" stands by itself as a fitting expression in music of Dr. Matheson's remarkable stanzas. Other composers have experimented with it; but this tune has universal preference.

The Life in Christ

To make a musical interpretation of a stanza with five lines, complete in itself, without repetition, challenges the initiative and the artistry of a skilled musician. It is probable that Dr. Matheson would say that "St. Margaret" made this hymn famous, just as Cardinal Newman ascribed the popularity of his hymn "Lead, Kindly Light, Amid th' Encircling Gloom" to Dykes's tune "Lux Benigna."

308
HYMN: Love Divine, All Loves Excelling
FIRST TUNE: Beecher

Author: *Rev. Charles Wesley*   Composer: *John Zundel*

AUTHOR: For comments on the author, Charles Wesley, see Hymn 26.

HYMN: This hymn carries from first to last a spontaneous movement of most exalted spiritual power, quite in consonance with Wesley's other and even more famous hymn, "Jesus, Lover of My Soul." It gives the human soul immediate access to the Infinite. The infinite love and grace of God abound everywhere in this hymn. The personal element in Christian experience was set over against the Calvinistic theology then prevailing, and by rebound this preaching and this singing gave the entire Wesleyan era its distinctive power and popularity. The concluding line of this hymn, "Lost in wonder, love, and praise," has been the inspiration of innumerable sermons and hymns.

COMPOSER (First Tune): John Zundel, in his time one of the best-loved organists in America, was born December 10, 1815, at Hochdorf, Germany. Fully equipped as a musician, he came to the United States in October, 1847. He began his career here in the First Unitarian Church, Brooklyn, New York, and in St. George's Church, New York City. On January 1, 1850, he began his famous musical ministry in Plymouth Church, Brooklyn, of which Henry Ward Beecher was pastor, and served the church for nearly thirty years. Before coming to America he was at one time organist at St. Anne's Lutheran Church, St. Petersburg, and bandmaster of the Imperial Horse Guards in St. Petersburg. He and Mr. Beecher were intimate friends and together they rendered a service which influenced the entire country. "We will go to hear Beecher and Zundel," was a current expression of churchgoers. Zundel published, among other works, "The Choral Friend," 1852, and "Christian Heart Songs," 1870. He assisted Mr. Beecher with "The Plymouth Collection," published in 1855. Upon retirement he returned to Germany and died at Cannstadt, July, 1882, in his sixty-seventh year.

Handbook to The Hymnal

TUNE (First): The well-known music of John Zundel has given wings to Wesley's words and carried this song to the ends of the earth. "Beecher" appeared in "Christian Heart Songs." It is written in a popular strain and reflects the influence of Dr. Thomas Hastings and Dr. Lowell Mason. After its appearance, denominational hymnals began to include it, so that now it is one of the best-known tunes in America. It was named "Beecher" in honor of the great pulpiteer.

SECOND TUNE: Love Divine (Le Jeune)

Composer: *George Le Jeune*

COMPOSER (Second Tune): George Le Jeune was born in London in 1871. He came from a musical family, his father being a well-known composer and singing master, as well as organist at Moorfield's Chapel, London. Le Jeune began his musical studies with George Carter, organist of the Cathedral, Montreal, Canada. Subsequently he studied harmony and composition with Joseph Barnby. Upon leaving Montreal, he accepted the position of organist at the Pearl Street Church, Hartford, Connecticut, where he remained until called to St. Luke's, Philadelphia. Removing from Philadelphia in 1876, he spent twenty-eight years in famous St. John's Chapel of Trinity Parish, New York City. In that church he popularized sacred music, and his musical services attracted wide attention. He was a skillful organ recitalist and in frequent demand. He died in 1904.

TUNE (Second): "Love Divine (Le Jeune)" appeared in a collection of twenty-four tunes in 1887. In that publication it was dedicated to one of Le Jeune's best-known pupils, George Edward Stubbs, organist of St. Agnes Chapel, also of Trinity Parish, New York City. The tune is a favorite one for carillon players and may be heard almost any Sunday evening in large cities.

---

309   HYMN: Jesus, the Very Thought of Thee
TUNE: St. Agnes

Source: *Latin Hymn*   Composer: *Rev. John B. Dykes*

SOURCE: This is a Latin hymn of the eleventh century.

TRANSLATOR: For comments on the translator, Edward Caswall, see Hymn 3.

330

The Life in Christ

HYMN: This is one of the large number of medieval hymns still extant which, coming out of the far-away and "dark" centuries, shine with constant glow even now. No literary work of those earlier years is comparable to the lyric poems that yet abide. We have in this present hymn an illustration of devotional poems of the Middle Ages. Even those times could not have been utterly dark. In spite of cruelties and wretchedness, we find in hymns and poems the human spirit "alive and striving." This particular hymn has been attributed to Bernard of Clairvaux. Dr. Schaff calls this "the sweetest and most evangelical (as the 'Dies Irae' is the grandest and the 'Stabat Mater' the most pathetic) . . . hymn of the Middle Ages."

COMPOSER: For comments on the composer, John B. Dykes, see Hymn 53.

TUNE: "St. Agnes" is well adapted to the sentiment and accent of the hymn. The tone is pensive, bordering on pathos. Since the poem represents the knights keeping guard over the Holy Sepulcher at Jerusalem, one can easily imagine them singing quietly, in the night watches. Once learned, this tune almost sings itself. Having learned hymn and tune together, and sensing their exquisite harmony, we wonder why any other composer should attempt to dethrone "St. Agnes" as the accepted interpreter of this most soulful hymn. For further comments on the tune, "St. Agnes," see Hymn 206.

---

310 HYMN: How Sweet the Name of Jesus Sounds
TUNE: St. Peter

Author: *Rev. John Newton* Composer: *Alexander R. Reinagle*

AUTHOR: John Newton was born in London, July 24, 1725. His only schooling was from his ninth to his eleventh year. He was a profligate youth and early in life engaged in the slave trade in Sierra Leone. The writings of Thomas à Kempis and a storm at sea, while he was returning from Africa, were influential in bringing about the conversion of this avowed infidel. He then became a minister in the Established Church of England, and was associated with William Cowper, the poet. Together they published "Olney Hymns." Part of his epitaph, which he himself wrote, is as follows:

"John Newton clerk
once an infidel and libertine
A servant of slaves in Africa
was by the rich mercy of our Lord and Saviour
Jesus Christ
Preserved, restored, pardoned
And appointed to preach the Faith
He had long labored to destroy."

Among the other well-known hymns of Newton are "Glorious Things of Thee Are Spoken," and "Safely Through Another Week." One of Newton's practices might well be emulated by pastors to-day. He gathered all the children of his parish on Thursday afternoons and explained to them the Scriptures.

HYMN: This is one hymn that is probably a paraphrase of the great Latin hymn of Bernard of Clairvaux. Newton's gifts were directness, simplicity, and evangelistic urgency and virility. Perhaps his most famous saying was this: "I remember two things: that I am a great sinner, and that Christ is a great Saviour."

COMPOSER: For comments on the composer, Alexander R. Reinagle, see Hymn 81.

TUNE: For comments on the tune, "St. Peter," see Hymn 81.

---

311   HYMN: I Could Not Do Without Thee
       TUNE: Jesu Dilectissime

Author: *Frances Ridley Havergal*   Composer: *Robert H. McCartney*

AUTHOR: For comments on the author, Frances Ridley Havergal, see Hymn 56.

HYMN: W. Garrett Horder, in "The Hymn Lover," writing of Miss Havergal's hymns, says: "They have done much to foster that warmer and more consecrated type of religion and they help to create a real barrier against all forms of skepticism. One of the best uses of all hymns is to introduce at times into the most stately and formal services these more tender and personal appeals such as this hymn of Frances Havergal brings to us with surpassing grace."

The Life in Christ

COMPOSER: Robert H. McCartney, an English organist, composer, and teacher, was born August 21, 1844. His musical training began early and was of the best. He was a versatile and efficient teacher and became associated with the Music Department, Trinity College, London. He was an organist and choirmaster of ability and served in that capacity in St. James's Church, Wigan, Lancashire. He died December 29, 1905.

TUNE: "Jesu Dilectissime" is one of the best-known tunes by Mr. McCartney. In just what year it was written cannot be definitely stated. Its first appearance in America was in the Episcopal Hymnal edited by Dr. Hutchins and published in 1898. This noble tune, confident, virile, and reassuring, is readily sung.

---

312   HYMN: Ask Ye What Great Thing I Know
        TUNE: Hendon

Author: *Rev. Johann C. Schwedler*   Composer: *Rev. H. A. César Malan*

AUTHOR: Rev. Johann C. Schwedler, the author, was the son of Anton Schwedler, a farmer and rural magistrate of Krobsdorf in Silesia. He entered the University of Leipzig in 1695, and secured his Master's degree from the same university. He became one of the most powerful and popular preachers of his generation, and was especially devoted in the matter of prayers and all forms of liturgy and acts of worship. He frequently called his parishioners to services which began at five o'clock in the morning and continued in relays throughout the day. Schwedler founded an orphanage at Niederwiese. "The grace of God through Christ" was the supreme theme of his sermons and hymns, and "the joyful confidence imparted to the soul that experienced it." His hymn "Wollt Ihr Wissen Was Mein Preis," of which "Ask Ye What Great Thing I Know" is a translation, became the national funeral hymn or anthem in Silesia. Schwedler died during the night of January 12, 1730, and his own hymns were sung at his funeral service.

TRANSLATOR: Schwedler's beautiful hymn was translated by Benjamin H. Kennedy, D.D., LL.D., a distinguished writer and educator. He was born at Summerhill, near Birmingham, England, November 6, 1804. He was educated at King Edward's School, Birmingham, and at Shrewsbury School. In the latter institution Charles Darwin was a fellow pupil. Benjamin Kennedy was a brilliant Latin student and won many honors. He wrote excellent verse and won the Porson Prize at Cambridge. He became a Fellow and classical lecturer at his college. He took holy orders in 1829, and soon after began to teach at Harrow. Seven years later he became head master of Shrewsbury School and raised it to a position of eminence for literary and classical scholarship. He edited "Hymnologia Christiana" and "The Psalter, or Psalms of David in English Verse." Greatly beloved as a teacher, preacher, and lecturer, his latter days were crowned with innumerable honors from universities, churches, and his king. He died in 1889.

HYMN: This is one of two hymns by this mystical German pastor that are in "The Hymnal." Such frank, elemental simplicity as we have in these hymns is characteristic of the group to which Schwedler belonged, which included his neighbors Johann Mentzer, Catherine von Gersdof, and Von Zinzendorf, known as the second founder of the Moravian Brethren, who was the author of over two thousand hymns. A deep personal devotion to Christ, leading at times to extreme fervor and apparently unwise familiarity with sacred emotions, made Schwedler's group of hymn writers outstanding in the period.

COMPOSER: Rev. Henri A. César Malan was born at Geneva, in 1787. After he was educated at Geneva College, he went to Marseilles, with the intention of going into business. However, his intense religious nature led him to return to his native city to prepare for the ministry in the Reformed Church. He was a bold and brilliant preacher, and had a strong following. His public utterances against the formalism of the Church alienated his associates at Geneva College and in the leading churches of the city. Undeterred in his evangelical fervor, he built a chapel in his garden, to which were attracted many visitors from England, France, and Scotland. He was an evangelist of note and was always welcome in the British Isles. As a writer of hymns he was almost as prolific as Watts and Wesley. His influence in England was great, where his tours of healing and evangelism were a comfort to Charlotte Elliott, who, with her friends, gave him loyal support. He was a musician of great ability and is credited with more than a thousand tunes. His outstanding hymnal, "Chants de Sion," 1824, greatly influenced the development of sacred music in France. Malan died at Vandœuvres, near Geneva, in 1864.

TUNE: "Hendon" is one of Malan's most useful tunes. It has been used so widely in America that it seems always to have been associated with the hymnals of all denominations. It is a fresh and joyous tune, of simple pattern and marked sincerity.

The Life in Christ

313   HYMN: My God, I Love Thee; Not Because
        TUNE: Solomon

Author: *Ascribed to Francis Xavier*   Composer: *George Frederick Handel*

AUTHOR: The great missionary saint of the Roman Catholic Church, Francis Xavier, was the son of Don John Giasso and Donna Maria Xavier and was known by his mother's name. He was born at the Castle Xavier, near Pamplona, Spain, on April 7, 1506. He entered the University of Paris at the age of eighteen, and later became a teacher there. There he met Ignatius Loyola, the founder of the Society of Jesus. Xavier became one of the first of Loyola's converts and the most enthusiastic of them all. The Jesuits were founded at Montmartre, near Paris, August 15, 1534. Xavier was with Loyola at Venice, and there became chaplain of the hospital for incurables. He visited Rome and in 1540 left there for his missionary work in India, where his devotion and heroism made his name illustrious for Christ and humanity. He died on December 22, 1552, near Canton, China, after years of service at Travancore, Ceylon, Malacca, and Japan. With the "cross in hand, and a burning zeal in his heart," he carried forward Christ and the Church.

TRANSLATOR: For comments on the translator, Edward Caswall, see Hymn 3.

HYMN: Caswall, the famous translator of Latin hymns, evidently thought that he had come upon a noble lyrical utterance of the great Francis Xavier when he found this hymn. It appeared in a book published in Cologne in 1669 as a version of an old Spanish sonnet. It has been attributed to Xavier because it was thought that a Portuguese version of the sonnet known in India was written by him. Dr. Julian, however, quotes Jesuit scholars in opposition to the Xavier legend. The hymn has surprising popularity even though it deals with the sad and suffering phases of our Saviour's experiences with medieval directness. It undertakes to set pure devotion to the Lord above all possible personal considerations that might taint the faith of a believer.

COMPOSER: For comments on the composer, George Frederick Handel, see Hymn 120.

TUNE: "Solomon" was not written by Handel for this particular hymn. It is adapted from his oratorio, "Solomon," 1748, in which it appears with the lines beginning, "What though I trace each

335

herb and flower." The tune is vigorous and stately, direct and forceful, and convincingly expresses the sentiments and feelings of the hymn with which it is associated.

---

314   HYMN: Jesus, Thy Boundless Love to Me
            TUNE: Stella

Author: *Rev. Paul Gerhardt*   Source: *Old English Melody*

AUTHOR: For comments on the author, Paul Gerhardt, see Hymn 125.

TRANSLATOR: For comments on the translator, John Wesley, see Hymn 63.

HYMN: John Wesley found this hymn by Gerhardt at Herrnhut in 1731, and translated its sixteen stanzas. This translation appeared first in "Hymns and Sacred Poems," 1739, and has grown in usage and popularity with the years until to-day it ranks among the very best of all hymns wherein evangelical truth is underwritten with personal devotion. This hymn is specially fitted for the Communion services, where the sacrament of our Lord makes urgent appeal to the believing heart.

SOURCE: The tune is taken from an old English melody.

TUNE: "Stella" is a very interesting tune, which has been in use in America since the publication of "The Church Hymnal," by Dr. Charles L. Hutchins, in 1872. Two years later it was included in the Presbyterian Hymnal. "The Hymnal," Revised, 1911, uses it as an alternate tune for "Sweet Saviour, Bless Us Ere We Go." When "Easy Music for Church Choirs," a hymnal for Roman Catholic schools, was published in 1851, it was there included as an arrangement, without designating the composer or the source. However, "Stella" is generally conceded to be based on an old English melody. "The English Hymnal," 1906, as well as others which might be indicated, so credits it. The tune is not to be confounded with another bearing the same name and composed by Dr. Horatio W. Parker.

The Life in Christ

315
HYMN: More Love to Thee, O Christ
TUNE: More Love to Thee

Author: *Elizabeth Prentiss*   Composer: *William Howard Doane*

AUTHOR: Elizabeth Prentiss, the writer of this familiar hymn, is thought of by the last generation as the author of a most fanciful but reverently drawn picture of life hereafter, under the title "Stepping Heavenward," published in 1869 and reaching shortly a sale of nearly 100,000 copies. Mrs. Prentiss was a daughter of the devout Dr. Edward Payson, and was born in Portland, Maine, October 26, 1818. Very early she manifested her special facility for writing both prose and poetry. At the age of sixteen she wrote for The Youth's Companion. She was a teacher in Portland, Maine; Ipswich, Massachusetts; and Richmond, Virginia. In 1845 she was married to Rev. George L. Prentiss, who later became professor of homiletics in Union Theological Seminary, New York. Never robust, she died in Dorset, Vermont, on August 13, 1878. She wrote many popular stories, of which "The Flower of the Family" was the first. Her children's books were most successful.

HYMN: This widely used hymn was written in 1869. It was first printed on a fly sheet and later made its appearance in Dr. Hatfield's "Church Hymn Book," 1872. It was written during a time of great personal sorrow in the experience of the author, and reveals her utter dependence on the grace of Christ. It is a tribute to her humble estimate of this, her greatest work, that she kept it many years before anyone knew of its existence. It has been printed in many languages, including Chinese, and the members of the Christian Church of that nation had the words of this poem inscribed on a fan and sent as a token of affection to Dr. Prentiss.

COMPOSER: William Howard Doane was born on February 3, 1832, at Preston, Connecticut. In his early years he was a cotton manufacturer, in business with his father in Norwich, Connecticut, where he also conducted the Harmonic Society. Later he represented his firm in Chicago. Leaving Chicago for Cincinnati, he became head of a large woodworking plant. While engaged in this business, he invented a number of woodworking machines.

In 1862, after recovering from a serious illness, and having been greatly influenced by Fanny Crosby, many of whose hymns he set to music, he began writing hymn tunes. Altogether he compiled over forty songbooks, and wrote some twenty-three hundred songs, ballads, and cantatas. "Silver Spray," 1867, was the most popular Sunday School book of its day. His cantata "Santa Claus" was the forerunner of the many Christmas cantatas now so popular a feature of Christmastide. Dr. Doane won Mr. Sankey to evangelism and it was for Moody and Sankey that his most effective work was done.

The French Government presented Dr. Doane with the badge of the Legion of Honor, in appreciation of his services to religion. He was also given the honorary degree of Doctor of Music by Denison University, Ohio, in which he took a particular interest, endowing its library. He died on December 24, 1915, at South Orange, New Jersey.

TUNE: "More Love to Thee" was composed in 1868. Within a few years, through Dr. Doane's own songbooks and other publications, it became a popular favorite. Gospel song collections, especially those of Moody and Sankey, found it effective in evangelistic meetings. It is not to be confused with an equally successful tune by Theodore E. Perkins, which appears in many hymnals.

---

316   HYMN: Christ, of All My Hopes the Ground
TUNE: Hendon

Author: *Rev. Ralph Wardlaw*   Composer: *Rev. H. A. César Malan*

AUTHOR: Ralph Wardlaw, D.D., was born in Dalkeith, Scotland, in 1779. His father was a merchant and later a magistrate in Glasgow. His fine Scottish mother was from the line of the Erskines. Leaving Glasgow University, he entered the Theological Hall of the Secession Church. He was ordained to the Congregational ministry and held but one parish, Albion Chapel, Glasgow, which he organized on no one's foundation. His great logical and controversial gifts were recognized by his appointment as professor of divinity in the Congregational Theological Hall, Glasgow, where for forty years he was a teacher of marked influence. He left a number of theological works, and in 1803 compiled "A Selection of Hymns for Public Worship." He died in Glasgow in 1853.

HYMN: This is one of eleven of Dr. Wardlaw's own hymns appearing in his "A Selection of Hymns for Public Worship." Coming out of the heart of one of the great controversial leaders of the Nonconformist Church of the period, the hymn breathes the docility and quietude of the humblest Christian.

COMPOSER: For comments on the composer, H. A. César Malan, see Hymn 312.

TUNE: For comments on the tune, "Hendon," see Hymn 312.

The Life in Christ

The Inner Life

*

317   HYMN: As Pants the Hart for Cooling Streams
      TUNE: Spohr

Source: *Tate and Brady's "New Version"*   Composer: *Louis Spohr*

SOURCE: For comments on the source, Tate and Brady's "New Version," see Hymn 19 and the article, "Church Hymns in Great Britain and America," under "Original Sources," page xv.

HYMN: This hymn is dedicated to William III. The artificial style of that period is applied to The Psalms.

COMPOSER: Louis Spohr (1784–1859) was the son of a physician. He played the violin at five years of age and later became concert director of the court of Saxe-Gotha. His wife, also a gifted musician, relinquished the violin because in his opinion it was an instrument unbecoming for a woman. His annual concert tours met with brilliant success, proclaiming him the first virtuoso in Europe. He "tried almost every form of musical composition, and achieved a contemporary success in them all. Few musicians have enjoyed so high a reputation in their own time."

TUNE: "Spohr" is an adaptation of a selection from a solo and chorus in Spohr's oratorio "Calvary." It is a tune of rare grace and charm, admirably fitted to the words "As Pants the Hart for Cooling Streams," with which it has long been associated. It is appearing again with the popularity it so well deserves after a considerable period of disuse.

---

318   HYMN: Let My Life Be Hid in Thee
      TUNE: Weimar

Author: *John Bull*   Composer: *Melchior Vulpius*

AUTHOR: John Bull was the *nom de plume* of J. B. Clipston, a devout and modest curate of the parish of Clipston. He was born in 1777 and died in 1852. He graduated from Oxford in 1801, and in the absence of available records we may conclude that he gave his whole life to the humble ministry of his inconspicuous charge. This is not the Dr. John Bull supposed by some to have written the British national anthem,

339

"God Save the King," which he is said to have played on the organ at Merchant Taylor's Hall, July 16, 1607, as King James was dining there as guest of the company.

HYMN: This hymn on "Consecration to Christ" appeared in the Church of England Magazine in April, 1839. Its mystical thought runs at very deep levels of spiritual understanding and taxes the verbal capacity of our frail and earthly vocabulary. Metaphors alone help us to approximate these profound spiritual experiences.

COMPOSER: For comments on the composer, Melchior Vulpius, see Hymn 92.

ADAPTER: For comments on the adapter, Johann Sebastian Bach, see Hymn 21.

TUNE: "Weimar" appeared in "Ein Schön Geistlich Gesangbuch," 1609, attributed to Vulpius. The name is taken from Weimar in Thuringia, where Vulpius was cantor. In its present form, it is the same as in "Neu Leipziger Gesangbuch," 1682. Its phrasing and rhythm are in the form of a choral. Some variations from the original form are found in works appearing later than 1609, as for instance in "Neue Melodien," 1787. J. S. Bach used it in the "St. John Passion."

As the tune is in choral form, it should be sung slowly and with dignity. Considerable repetition will be necessary before it is fully appreciated and loved, but its power and its sonorous melody will soon endear it to a congregation.

---

319 HYMN: Jesus, These Eyes Have Never Seen
FIRST TUNE: Sawley

Author: *Rev. Ray Palmer*   Composer: *James Walch*

AUTHOR: For comments on the author, Ray Palmer, see Hymn 285.

HYMN: This hymn is among the more widely used hymns of this well-known American hymn writer. It appeared in 1858 in "The Sabbath Hymn Book" and later in "The English Hymnal." While he was pastor of the First Congregational Church of Albany, New York, a version of this hymn was given to Palmer in a mystical manner that scarcely admits of description. In preparing a sermon on Christ, he opened a book that proved to be of special helpfulness, and this trivial

The Life in Christ

incident seized upon his mind as a potent illustration of how Christ's face, as well as his life, is revealed. This hymn is second only to Palmer's hymn, "My Faith Looks Up to Thee," in the esteem of the Church for moral and spiritual beauty.

COMPOSER (First Tune): James Walch, who is especially remembered by his tune "Angelic Voices," also known as "Tidings," was born at Bolton, England, in 1837. In addition to his musical training, he was influenced by the compositions of Dr. John B. Dykes and Sir Joseph Barnby. The influence of the former is especially apparent in Walch's best-known tunes. In addition to being a popular organist, he was a capable orchestral conductor. The tunes that perpetuate his memory are not numerous, but those that remain have enduring value. The voluminous "Church Hymnary of the Congregational Union of England and Wales," which was published in 1887, included three of his compositions. "The Methodist Hymnal" in the United States uses his tunes in connection with six hymns. The hymnals of the Presbyterian Church, as well as of other denominations, also recognize his work. He died in 1901.

TUNE (First): "Sawley" appears in most of the later American hymn books and bears the date of 1860. Among the notable hymnals of England, it appeared in "The Congregational Church Hymnal," 1887. Eight years later it was included in the Presbyterian Hymnal of 1895, and since then in subsequent hymnals of the denomination. "Sawley" was written when Walch was still a young man. It is very much in the style and pattern of Dykes, fluent in movement, and simple in structure.

SECOND TUNE: Osborne

Composer: *Henry Carey*

COMPOSER (Second Tune): Henry Carey, the son of George Saville, Marquis of Halifax, was a versatile musician and dramatist. The date of his birth was about 1692. He studied with Olaus Westeinson Linnert and Thomas Roseingrave. He was quite creative, a gift that exceeded his knowledge of harmony. His music for ballad operas and farces is extensive. Some of his compositions met with success; all of them were interesting. He was a poet of ability and published a volume of verse in 1713. This was enlarged in 1729. Of his compositions, the most popular is his ballad called "Sally in Our Alley," which will transmit his name to posterity. The church music which he wrote was a by-product of his interesting career. He died in Clerkenwell, England, on October 4, 1743. The following day, October 5, 1743, the Daily Post announced his death thus: "Yesterday morning Mr. H. Carey, well known to the musical world for his droll compositions, got out of bed . . .

in perfect health and was soon after found dead. He has left six children behind him." A benefit performance was given for his widow and children on the evening of November 17, 1743, in Covent Garden Theater.

TUNE (Second): "Osborne" was chosen for this Hymnal from "Songs of Praise, Enlarged," published in England in 1931. The tune is an adaptation of one of Carey's melodies. It was used by him in honor of Richard Osborne, a favorite pupil, who died at the age of nineteen, and it bears the name of his departed friend.

---

320 HYMN: Thou Life Within My Life, Than Self More Near
TUNE: Ffigysbren

Author: *Eliza Scudder*   Source: *Welsh Hymn Melody*

AUTHOR: Eliza Scudder, a New England woman, was born in Boston on November 14, 1821. She was a niece of Dr. E. H. Sears, the author of "It Came Upon the Midnight Clear" and other hymns. Dr. Duffield ranks many of her hymns with those of Dora Greenwell and Christina Rossetti, both in the depth of their spiritual feeling and in literary character. Her poems were published in "Hymns and Sonnets, by E. S." in 1880. Miss Scudder died in 1896.

HYMN: This hymn begins with the second stanza of a poem entitled "From Past Regret and Present Feebleness," written in 1871 and published in "Quiet Hours." The deep subjective experience reflected in this hymn is a mark of all Miss Scudder's poems. The lyrical composition in smooth musical measures is of high order and carries an appealing verbal picture of a soul identifying itself with the life of God here and now and sharing His strength in all life's experiences.

SOURCE: For comments on the source, a Welsh hymn melody, see the article, "Welsh Hymnody," under "Original Sources," page xxii.

TUNE: "Ffigysbren," generally known in Wales as "Clod," first appeared in 1840. It is a tune of the simplest construction, both melodically and rhythmically, but, when sung rather slowly, it has a remarkable effect of fugal strength. It appeared in America in "The Harvard University Hymn Book," edited by Archibald T. Davidson in 1926.

The Life in Christ

321 HYMN: O Morning Star, How Fair and Bright
TUNE: Frankfort

Author: *Rev. Philipp Nicolai*   Composer: *Rev. Philipp Nicolai*

AUTHOR: Philipp Nicolai, D.D., was the son of Dieterich Nicolai, a Lutheran pastor at Herdecke in Westphalia. Philipp was born on August 10, 1556. He was educated at the University of Erfurt, and later at Wittenberg. His first preaching was in his father's pulpit. In later pastorates he gave himself in defense of the Lutheran interpretation of the Communion as against the Roman Catholic Mass and likewise the Calvinistic theology. He became pastor of St. Katherine's Church, Hamburg, and exercised wide influence. One of his best-known hymns, "Wake, Awake, for Night Is Flying," was written during a widespread pestilence, 1597–1598, when thousands died, and burials were constant. Nicolai's hymn "O Morning Star, How Fair and Bright," a spiritual wedding song, came to be universally used at marriages. He died in Hamburg, October 26, 1608.

TRANSLATOR: For comments on the translator, Catherine Winkworth, see Hymn 6.

HYMN: It is not difficult to surmise that in this hymn we have some hints of the anxiety in Nicolai's heart arising from his stalwart defense of the altar of his church in Herdecke, 1586, against the return of the Mass, and from his active part in the whole sacramentarian controversy. He prays that the "heavenly Brightness" may shine deeply into his heart and make an altar there. In the last line there may also be some memory of the saddest year in the history of his little town, when in one season some thirteen hundred townspeople died of the plague and were buried, sometimes at the rate of three hundred a month, in the churchyard into which his study window opened. The lyric charm of this hymn is due to the beauty of Miss Winkworth's translation.

COMPOSER: For comments on the composer, Philipp Nicolai, see "Author."

HARMONIZER: For comments on the harmonizer, Johann Sebastian Bach, see Hymn 21.

TUNE: "Frankfort" is taken from another choral. So popular did it become that the melody was chimed out from many a city tower, lines and stanzas of the hymn were printed on common earthenware of the country, and it was in constant use at weddings and festivals. If rendered in unison, with a leading voice, this tune of well-marked time is easy to sing.

---

322   HYMN: 'Mid All the Traffic of the Ways
TUNE: St. Agnes

Author: *John Oxenham*   Composer: *Rev. John B. Dykes*

AUTHOR: A strong spiritual quality distinguishes the work of John Oxenham, the English poet and novelist. His intimate knowledge of church life and a deep religious experience explain the fact that his most popular poems carry the vocabulary of the chancel and altar. He was educated at Old Trafford School, one of the 150 schools of Manchester, and at Victoria University, in which this city of culture takes more pride than in her great textile trade.

As a business man, his life for years was given to travel in Europe and America. Writing, for which he had always shown special proclivity, called him. He began his life of authorship in 1898 when he published "God's Prisoner." This has been followed by a surprisingly large number of novels and books of verse, one of the choicest being "Selected Poems," 1925.

HYMN: This hymn was written during the World War when the sorrow of the human race was most acute. It may easily be accepted as the cry of the heart of the whole human race for a place of rest and "shelter from life's stress."

COMPOSER: For comments on the composer, John B. Dykes, see Hymn 53.

TUNE: For comments on the tune, "St. Agnes," see Hymn 206.

---

323   HYMN: When Shadows Gather on Our Way
FIRST TUNE: Kington

Author: *Rev. Frederick*   Composer: *Rev. F. Llewellyn Edwards*
Lucian Hosmer

AUTHOR: For comments on the author, Frederick Lucian Hosmer, see Hymn 176.

The Life in Christ

HYMN: The inner life of the Christian speaks of its most intimate experiences when recognizing in the first stanza of this hymn the "shadows . . . on our way"; in the second stanza, the "toil and strife" and "roar and din"; in the third stanza, the "burdens sore" and "vexing cares"; and in the fourth, our "faithless" friends. The last lines cry out,

> "O save us from the bitter heart,
> Indwelling Love!"

The hymn is said to have been born out of an early sorrow that ever after shadowed the author's life.

COMPOSER (First Tune): Rev. F. Llewellyn Edwards, born at Kington Magna, Dorset, England, was educated at Lyme Regis, Bath College, and New College, Oxford, where he won the open university prize for Greek verse. He also studied at Ridley Hall, Cambridge, under Bishop Handley Moule. While precentor of St. Paul's Church, Princess Park, he was ordained at Liverpool. Subsequently he held chaplaincies at Seville, Spain, and Nicosia, Cyprus, and then became rector of his native village, Kington Magna, where in 1933 he celebrated the completion of twenty-five years of service. Greatly interested in the worship of the Church, he has consistently sought the improvement of its music. Most of his songs remained unpublished and their use is confined to his parish. Mr. Edwards is an accomplished bell ringer, a member of the "Ancient Society of College Youths," established in 1637, and of the Central Council of Church Bell Ringers. As a bell ringer he took part in muffled peals in Westminster Abbey at the burial of the unknown soldier, and at Queen Alexandra's funeral.

TUNE (First): Some years ago the Dorset Choral Association offered a prize for a new tune to "Our Blest Redeemer, Ere He Breathed," and appointed Dr. Fulford Maitland, formerly musical critic of the Times, as judge. "Kington" won first place. Soon after it appeared in "Songs of Praise," and since then has been included in recent hymn books. Only one other tune of Edwards' is published. "Kington" should be sung in strict time, but not too fast. A retard on the last line will be effective.

SECOND TUNE: St. Cuthbert

Composer: *Rev. John B. Dykes*

COMPOSER (Second Tune): For comments on the composer, John B. Dykes, see Hymn 53.

TUNE (Second): For comments on the tune, "St. Cuthbert," see Hymn 205.

345

324 HYMN: I Sought the Lord, and Afterward I Knew
TUNE: Kerr

Author: *Anonymous*   Composer: *Rev. Calvin W. Laufer*

AUTHOR: The author of this hymn is unknown.

HYMN: This hymn, expressing in striking fashion the self-initiating love of God to which all human efforts to find him are but a response, is attributed by Frank Sealy, editor of "Common Praise," 1913, to Jean Ingelow. This information has not been verified, but the theme of the hymn, the long sentences, the thought of which at times is involved, suggest Jean Ingelow. "The Pilgrim Hymnal" uses it as anonymous, as does "The Harvard University Hymn Book," 1931, the latter suggesting the date of its first publication as 1878.

COMPOSER: For comments on the composer, Calvin W. Laufer, see Hymn 13.

TUNE: On the day that the hymn, "I Sought the Lord, and Afterward I Knew," had been given a place in the new Hymnal, Dr. Laufer was asked to write a tune for it as the old tune was thought inadequate. He complied, and the tune was unanimously adopted by the committee and therefore makes its first appearance in this Hymnal. It bears the name "Kerr," in honor of Dr. Hugh T. Kerr, chairman of the Content Committee of "The Hymnal," 1933.

---

325 HYMN: Be Thou My Vision, O Lord of My Heart
TUNE: Slane

Source: *Ancient Irish Hymn*   Source: *Ancient Irish Traditional Melody*

SOURCE: This hymn is from an ancient Irish hymn.

TRANSLATOR: Mary Elizabeth Byrne is a modern student of Irish poems of religion and coauthor of the "Old and Mid-Irish Dictionary" of the research and honor society of Ireland known as the Royal Irish Academy. She graduated from the National University of Ireland in 1905 and has been engaged as a research worker of the Board

The Life in Christ

of Intermediate Education. She received the chancellor's gold medal in the Royal University in recognition of her authoritative work on the Chaucerian period of English literature. Eleanor Hull, the brilliant author and founder of the Irish Text Society, put this ancient Irish poem into English verse after Miss Byrne had translated it. No one is more competent than Miss Hull to portray the religious longings of the ancient people.

HYMN: Carried by the melody of an ancient ballad of the people, this hymn reflects the deep inner peace and satisfaction of those who have found and followed Christ as a Vision leading on over obstacles and as Wisdom that safely guides to earth's victory and heaven's joys. The quaint metaphors and naïve phrases are characteristic of ancient Irish hymns.

SOURCE: This tune is from an ancient Irish traditional melody.

HARMONIZER: For comments on the harmonizer, David Evans, see Hymn 177.

TUNE: The tune, "Slane," appeared in "The Church Hymnary," Revised. It is truly Irish, and to those with Irish Presbyterian ancestry will become increasingly dear, as it is so eminently characteristic, especially the closing measures. Careful phrasing is essential, although the tempo may well be taken somewhat *rubato*.

There are unique opportunities for delightful *piano* and *forte* contrasts, as for instance in the last line "Waking (*f*) or sleeping (*p*), Thy presence my light." The exultant strain in the third stanza, and the note of aspiration and praise in the fourth, should not be overlooked.

---

326   HYMN: I Am Not Skilled to Understand
TUNE: Ach Gott und Herr

Author: *Dora Greenwell*   Source: *"Neu Leipziger Gesangbuch"*

AUTHOR: For comments on the author, Dora Greenwell, see Hymn 134.

HYMN: No hymns plumb deeper depths of wholesome religious emotion than do those of Dora Greenwell. Her works, "Carmina Crucis," 1869, and "Songs of Salvation," 1873, are ranked by critics among the classics of the devotional life. Her keen intellectual grasp of the great facts and principles of redemption, well illustrated in

347

this hymn, prevented her from being swept into the affirmations of an extreme mysticism. The thought content here is too obvious and simple to need exposition. It is the triumph of an unquestioning faith in the presence of the unexplainable mysteries of salvation and the personal sharing of the legitimate joys of faith long before its subject matter can be rationalized.

SOURCE: This tune was taken from "Neu Leipziger Gesangbuch," 1682.

ARRANGER: For comments on the arranger, Johann Sebastian Bach, see Hymn 21.

TUNE: "Ach Gott und Herr" is traceable to the Pietistic and Moravian activity which took place during the years 1680 to 1757. It is quite probable that it was taken from a folk song and set to appropriate words for use during those great revival gatherings. Here, later, it was undoubtedly found by J. S. Bach, who was deeply stirred by the religious revival of that period.

It should be sung slowly, in choral form, and with marked dignity.

---

327   HYMN: Jesus, I Am Resting, Resting
TUNE: Resting

Author: *Jean Sophia Pigott*   Composer: *James Mountain*

AUTHOR: Jean Sophia Pigott belonged to a well-known Irish family that had been deeply touched by the great Irish revival that swept the island about 1870. So definite were the results that two of the sons went to China as missionaries, one of them to a martyr's grave. Very frail and incapable of strenuous work, Miss Pigott gave herself to writing, painting, and music, for all of which she had talents above the average. For many years she conducted a Bible class for girls. She was led to discard the use of all medicines and rest wholly on her faith for help. She was a devoted follower of the Keswick movement. She died suddenly at thirty-eight years of age. Her several hymns have proved most acceptable. The one here used is considered her best.

HYMN: This meditative hymn, written by Jean Pigott in July, 1875, releases feelings of devotion and spiritual longing that are universal in the human heart. It was written after a convention at Brighton, following which invalidism came upon her. Introspective as the hymn appears to be, it meets well the intimate needs of every con-

The Life in Christ

gregation in corporate worship. Its central thought, from which all its sequences of peace, joy, and happy expectation come, is an intellectual and spiritual rest born of a sense of what God is in the greatness, goodness, and changelessness of his character. There is a childlikeness in its phraseology that especially commends this hymn to every docile Christian in moments of meditation and personal worship.

COMPOSER: Dr. Moffatt in his "Handbook to the Church Hymnary," tells us that James Mountain, D.D., who was born at New Wortley, Leeds, in 1844, was educated for the Congregational ministry at Cheshunt College, and later pursued his studies at Heidelberg and Tübingen. Returning to England, he was ordained and installed at Great Marlow. After a brief period a breakdown in health necessitated his leaving this field and he spent two years recuperating in Switzerland. Moody and Sankey in their English revivals greatly influenced Dr. Mountain and led him to devote his life to evangelism. He spent eight years in mission preaching in England, followed by seven years of evangelistic travels around the world. On his return to England, he spent some twenty years in Emmanuel Church and at St. John's Free Church, Tunbridge Wells. Intensely orthodox, he has been active in a movement for Bible defense and has edited "Newness of Life" and "The Bible Call." Prominent in his musical activity was the editing of "Hymns of Consecration and Faith," from which this tune is taken. The degree of Doctor of Divinity was bestowed on him by Ewing College in Illinois.

TUNE: The gracefulness of movement of the tune, "Resting," if it is not taken too rapidly, makes it one that will charm the average congregation. The tenor score, if well brought out, adds greatly to the beauty of the tune.

---

328   HYMN: My Lord, My Life, My Love
               TUNE: Selma

Source: *"The Yattendon Hymnal"*   Source: *Traditional Melody of the Isle of Arran*

SOURCE: "The Yattendon Hymnal," though composed of but forty hymns, is called by Dr. Dearmer "easily the most distinguished of individual pioneer contributions to modern hymnody." It is the work, both words and music, of England's poet laureate, Robert Bridges. For further comments on Robert Bridges and "The Yattendon Hymnal," see Hymn 158.

349

HYMN: Dr. Bridges, who with all his literary work found time and joy in training the village choir at Yattendon, indicated that he was ignorant of Watts's authorship of "My God, My Life, My Love," 1707, when he made this adaptation. All recognize that the original is greatly enriched in its theme and amplified in its form under the later poet's treatment. It reveals the deep spirituality of Dr. Bridges' thought and bespeaks the sincere personal experience of a Christian man.

SOURCE: This tune is from a traditional melody of the Isle of Arran.

ADAPTER: For comments on the adapter, Robert Archibald Smith, see Hymn 299.

TUNE: For comments on the tune, "Selma," see Hymn 299.

---

329 HYMN: Where Is the Friend for Whom I'm Ever Yearning
TUNE: Herzliebster Jesu

Author: *Archbishop Johann Olaf Wallin*   Composer: *Johann Crüger*

AUTHOR: For comments on the author, Johann Olaf Wallin, see Hymn 17.

HYMN: This hymn by Wallin, the greatest of Swedish hymn writers, appeared in "The Swedish Hymnbook," of which he was editor, in 1819. With it were 150 others of his hymns, besides many of his translations. In this devotional poem we recognize the imagery of a nature lover as well as of a keen spiritual interpreter of the world in which we live. He recognizes the baffling vagueness of nature, yet finally approaches with his sensitive soul the precious secrets that are revealed in "summer winds," singing birds, and "rush" of streams. He comes to the conclusion, as every seeker after God must, that "my prayer can reach Him, but my vision faileth." This and practically all of Wallin's hymns are in common use in Sweden to-day.

COMPOSER: For comments on the composer, Johann Crüger, see Hymn 158.

TUNE: For comments on the tune, "Herzliebster Jesu," see Hymn 158.

The Life in Christ

330 HYMN: And Didst Thou Love the Race That Loved Not Thee
TUNE: Temple Bryan

Author: *Jean Ingelow* Composer: *Robert Alexander Stewart Macalister*

AUTHOR: Jean Ingelow, English poet and novelist, always refused to give details of her personal life. She published her earliest works anonymously. She was born in Boston, Lincolnshire, in 1820, and lived near Ipswich until her permanent removal to London in 1863. This was the year in which her poem "The High Tide" was published and attained instant success. To-day, with the poem "Divided," it shares recognition as the poet's best work. There is in her writings, according to Dr. Moffatt, "a feeling for Nature and a marked power of description, simplicity, pathos, and both depth and truth of religious feeling." Jean Ingelow wrote many novels and fairy stories that charm old and young. She died in Kensington, London, in 1897.

HYMN: This is a cento from a long hymn poem taken from the author's volume of poems published in 1863. There is something exquisite in the simplicity of the language of this hymn, and something intimately understanding in the poet's grasp of the historical and theological features in the narrative of our Lord's human existence and divine character. As a sacred poem this hymn will reward very careful reading.

COMPOSER: For comments on the composer, Robert A. S. Macalister, see Hymn 9.

TUNE: The hymn has found an adequate setting in the tune "Temple Bryan," composed especially for it and for "The Church Hymnary." It exemplifies the improvement evident in recent years in both English and American hymn tunes. This tune should be sung smoothly and with feeling. While it may not be appreciated when first used, yet it is one of those hymns that "grow" with repetition.

---

331 HYMN: What, Ye Ask Me, Is My Prize
TUNE: Wollt Ihr Wissen, Was Mein Preis

Author: *Rev. Johann Christian Schwedler*   Composer: *J. Cammin*

AUTHOR: For comments on the author, Johann Christian Schwedler, see Hymn 312.

351

TRANSLATOR: For comments on the translator, G. R. Woodward, see Hymn 119.

HYMN: This hymn is based on I Cor. 2:2 and Gal. 6:14. It is a translation of Schwedler's hymn, "Wollt Ihr Wissen, Was Mein Preis." It is characterized by the indomitable confidence and joy in the grace of God through Christ that mark all of Schwedler's hymns.

COMPOSER: No information has been discovered concerning the composer of this hymn. Presumably J. Cammin, to whom is ascribed the compilation of the "Melodienbuch von Rautenburg," is responsible for it.

HARMONIZER: The melody was harmonized by G. H. Palmer, one of the many English preacher-musicians of ability. Palmer graduated from Trinity College, Cambridge, in 1868 and immediately entered upon a unique ministry that related him to the work of the parish, pulpit, and choir loft. As an authoritative student in the field of sacred music he has written "The Antiphoner and Grail," "Harmonies of the Office Hymn Book," "The Sarum Psalter," and in addition several fine translations of Latin hymns. This hymn appeared in "Songs of Syon," compiled by Rev. George R. Woodward and published by Schott & Company, London. In the preface, Mr. Woodward states that Mr. Palmer has given "an immense amount of thought, time, labor, and trouble" in reading and revising hymns and tunes as well as in harmonizing many of the tunes included.

TUNE: "Wollt Ihr Wissen, Was Mein Preis" is markedly a tune of praise, well wedded to the words of the hymn, and should be sung exultantly. A strong climax is called for in the last measures, to the words "Jesus, Jesus, Jesus Christ, the Crucified," with appropriate shading on the repeated word "Jesus." This refrain is dignified, yet joyous. The tune is simple in construction and will be sung readily by the average congregation.

332
HYMN: I Need Thee Every Hour
TUNE: Need

Author: *Annie S. Hawks*   Composer: *Rev. Robert Lowry*

AUTHOR: Annie Sherwood Hawks was born in Hoosick, New York, in 1835. During her later residence in Brooklyn she was an active worker in the Baptist church of which Dr. Robert Lowry, who added the refrain to this familiar hymn, was pastor.

The Life in Christ

HYMN: This hymn, so widely sung during the final quarter of the last century, especially in the meetings of Moody and Sankey, was written in 1872 and appeared in Dr. Lowry's "Royal Diadem," 1873, a popular hymn book of the period. It had been sung first in the National Sunday School Association of the Baptist Church, meeting in Cincinnati, for which it may have been prepared. A simple, fervent hymn of personal devotion, confidently claiming the practical values of the Christian faith at every moment of daily life, it continues to hold its place in the informal worship occasions of both home and church.

COMPOSER: Robert Lowry, D.D. (1826–1899), is the author of the words and music of that sentimental hymn "Where Is My Wandering Boy To-Night." To the notable era of informal church music to which the work of Dwight L. Moody and Ira D. Sankey during the final quarter of the last century gave great prominence, Dr. Lowry has made a definite contribution. He was identified with the compilation of eight popular hymn books of the period, which bore such titles as "Bright Jewels" (1869) and "Pure Gold" (1871). His hymns, while appealing strongly to the emotions through their tender sentiment, rested their appeal upon doctrinal tenets deeply embedded in the spiritual experience of the Church. Dr. Lowry underestimated the appeal of his hymns and tunes, and deprecated mention of them, although he could not deny their success. Through his early pulpit service, his six years' professorship at Bucknell University, and his long pastorate in Plainfield, New Jersey, closed by his death in 1899, he considered preaching to be his supreme function, as it certainly was his first love. However, Dr. Lowry wrote many hymn tunes and edited several hymn collections.

TUNE: "Need" first appeared in November, 1872, at a meeting of the National Baptist Sunday School Association.

The Church and the Sacraments

The Church

*

333

HYMN: The Church's One Foundation
TUNE: Aurelia

Author: *Rev. Samuel J. Stone*   Composer: *Samuel S. Wesley*

AUTHOR: Samuel John Stone was born at Whitmore, Staffordshire, England, on April 25, 1839. He received his education at the Charterhouse, London, and Pembroke College, Oxford, receiving from the latter institution the degree of A.B. in 1862 and A.M. in 1872. He served as curate of Windsor, 1862–1870, and curate of St. Paul's, Haggerston, the church over which his father presided, 1870–1874, succeeding his father in the latter year. Mr. Stone published several books, including "The Knight of Intercession, and Other Poems," "Sonnets of the Christian Year," and "Lyra Fidelium." He was a member of the committee on "Hymns Ancient and Modern." He died at the Charterhouse, November 19, 1900.

HYMN: This hymn was written in 1866, when the author was twenty-seven years of age, and was published in his "Lyra Fidelium," a series of twelve hymns on the articles of The Apostles' Creed. It illustrated and enforced the statement, "I believe in . . . the holy Catholic Church." Inspiration for this work seems to have come from Bishop Gray's defense of the Catholic faith in opposition to the teachings of Bishop Colenso. In 1885 the hymn was revised and expanded by the author into ten stanzas for use as a processional in Salisbury Cathedral. Dr. Julian styles it a "magnificent hymn." It has become one of the great processionals of the Church. During the Lambeth Conference in 1888 each of three imposing services, at Canterbury Cathedral, Westminster Abbey, and St. Paul's Cathedral, was opened by the words and music of this hymn, as leaders from every part of the ecclesiastical world moved through the stately aisles. Mr. Stone's contributions to these historic occasions called forth this graceful tribute from the pen of Bishop Nelson from New Zealand:

> "Bard of the Church, in these divided days
> For words of harmony to thee be praise:
> Of love and oneness thou didst strike the chords,
> And set our thoughts and prayers to tuneful words.

· · · · · · · · · · ·

The Church and the Sacraments

From Lambeth towers to far New Zealand's coast,
Bard of the Church, thy blast inspires the host."

COMPOSER: For comments on the composer, Samuel S. Wesley, see Hymn 10.

TUNE: "Aurelia" signifies "golden," and was originally composed for the hymn "Jerusalem the Golden." It appeared first in "A Selection of Psalms and Hymns Arranged for the Public Service of the Church of England, Edited by the Rev. Charles Kemble and S. S. Wesley," 1864. It was probably first set to "The Church's One Foundation" in the Appendix to "Hymns Ancient and Modern," 1868, but now it is quite universally associated with that hymn. When sung to these words it becomes one of our most stately tunes.

---

334 HYMN: O Where Are Kings and Empires Now
TUNE: St. Anne

Author: *Bishop A. Cleveland Coxe*   Composer: *Ascribed to William Croft*

AUTHOR: A. Cleveland Coxe, son of a distinguished Presbyterian minister, was born at Mendham, New Jersey, May 10, 1818. Having graduated from the University of New York in 1838 and from the General Theological Seminary in 1841, he was ordained a deacon in the Protestant Episcopal Church at St. Paul's Chapel, New York City, in 1841 and a rector the following year. He served several important churches, including Grace Church in Baltimore and Calvary Church in New York City. While he was rector of the latter parish, in 1865, he was elected and ordained bishop of the Western Diocese of New York, having previously declined an election as bishop of Texas. He was a scholarly man and wielded a vigorous pen. Several books bear his imprint, including "Christian Ballads," which was published in 1840. Dr. Julian lists seventeen of his hymns. Some of these have been widely used. He was a member of the Hymnal Committee of his denomination from 1869 to 1871, and girded with the authority which this position bestowed he is said to have refused to allow the insertion of his own productions. Bishop Coxe was a militant Christian. The spirit of his life is well expressed in the only other hymn from his pen which "The Hymnal" contains, Hymn 374. He died in 1896.

HYMN: "O Where Are Kings and Empires Now" emphasizes the continuity and the vitality of the Church, bringing to mind the words of Jesus: "The gates of Hades shall not prevail against it." Dr. Duffield refers to an assembly of the General Conference of the

355

Evangelical Alliance, held in New York City in 1873, during which this hymn figured. He quotes an eyewitness: "President Woolsey was giving the opening address. After referring to the prevalent skepticism, he looked up with that peculiar twinkle of the eye which we all recollect— at once expressive of denial and satisfaction—and repeated the first stanza of Bishop Coxe's hymn:

> 'O where are kings and empires now
> Of old that went and came?
> But, Lord, Thy Church is praying yet,
> A thousand years the same.'

For a moment there was silence." This was followed by thunderous applause.

COMPOSER: For comments on the composer, William Croft, see Hymn 2.

TUNE: For comments on the tune, "St. Anne," see Hymn 77.

---

335 HYMN: One Holy Church of God Appears
TUNE: St. James

Author: *Rev. Samuel Longfellow*   Composer: *Raphael Courteville*

AUTHOR: For comments on the author, Samuel Longfellow, see Hymn 79.

HYMN: The author and two other hymns from his pen, Hymns 79 and 208, have already been discussed in these pages. The latter, a beautiful prayer addressed to the Holy Spirit, seems to be the best-known and the most loved of his productions. He also wrote a hymn for the ordination service of Edward Everett Hale.

Samuel Longfellow suffered by comparison with his brother Henry Wadsworth Longfellow. As Dr. Benson, in one of a series of hymn studies, wrote, "The light of his fame has burned, and always must burn, with a paler flame, because nature set it alongside of the far brighter blaze of his brother's renown."

COMPOSER: For comments on the composer, Raphael Courteville, see Hymn 254.

The Church and the Sacraments

TUNE: "St. James" is a durable tune, used twice in this Hymnal. If it is played with brightness, and not dragged, the congregation will sing the last stanza of this hymn with power and assurance. For further comments on the tune, "St. James," see Hymn 254.

336 HYMN: Christ Is Made the Sure Foundation
TUNE: Regent Square

Source: *Old Latin Hymn*   Composer: *Henry Smart*

SOURCE: This hymn came from an anonymous Latin hymn of the seventh century.

TRANSLATOR: For comments on the translator, John M. Neale, see Hymn 44.

HYMN: This hymn has come to us from an unknown Latin writer. It probably had birth in the sixth or the seventh century. The words are what is known as the "Angularis Fundamentum," part of a strong and beautiful Latin poem entitled "Urbs Beata Hierusalem, Dicta Pacis Visio." Several English translations have been made. One of the best of these is that from which the hymn as we have it is taken. The Church is deeply indebted to the translator, Rev. John M. Neale, by reason of this and other hymns which he has brought into our treasury of song from both the Latin and the Greek. The first stanza of the hymn is declarative. The second and third stanzas form a fervent prayer. The hymn closes with an adoring doxology to the triune God.

COMPOSER: For comments on the composer, Henry Smart, see Hymn 61.

TUNE: For comments on the tune, "Regent Square," see Hymn 61.

---

337 HYMN: I Love Thy Kingdom, Lord
TUNE: St. Thomas

Author: *Rev. Timothy Dwight*   Source: *"Williams' Psalmody"*

AUTHOR: Timothy Dwight was born at Northampton, Massachusetts, on May 14, 1752. His mother was a daughter of Jonathan Edwards. He entered Yale College at thirteen years of age and graduated in 1769 at the age of seventeen. He became a tutor at Yale, where he was immensely popular. During his tutorship, at the age of twenty, he published his book "The History, Eloquence and Poetry of the Bible." For a brief period he served as chaplain in the Revolutionary Army and won the admiration of George Washington for patriotism and versatility. In 1783 he was made pastor of the Congregational Church at Greenfield, Connecticut. His *Alma Mater* called him to the presidency in 1795. Dr. Dwight distinguished himself as an educator and author. One of the authorities in this field has said his is "the most important name in early American hymnology." The General Association of Connecticut invited him to revise and complete Watts's "The Psalms of David." This he did, adding thirty-three of his own compositions in a revised edition, including this hymn, which was inspired by, though it could not be said to be a paraphrase of, Psalm 137. The book was published in 1800 and became familiarly known as "Dwight's Watts." Through forty years this man fulfilled his splendid leadership while handicapped by a serious affection of the eyes. During long periods he was unable to read consecutively for fifteen minutes at a time. He died while still president of Yale, on January 11, 1817.

HYMN: This hymn was written while the author was president of Yale College. In it the Church is identified with the Kingdom of God and made an object of love and devotion. We have more stately hymns concerning the Church, but none, perhaps, which carries a more authentic challenge to emotion. Its message is largely subjective, though objectivity is implied. "Tears" and "prayers" and "cares" and "toils" will inevitably open channels of redemptive service.

SOURCE: "Williams' Psalmody" was published by Aaron Williams (1731–1776), a Welshman, a composer of hymns, a music engraver, a music teacher, a publisher of hymns, and clerk of the Scots Church, London Wall.

TUNE: The tune, "St. Thomas," is evidently the second movement of a four-movement tune in Williams' collection of 1762. It is found in "The New Universal Psalmodist," or "Williams' Psalmody," 1770, set to Psalm 48. It appeared in J. F. Wade's "Cantus Diversi," 1751, and in a large number of hymn books appearing since that time. Though one of the oldest tunes in our Hymnal, it has never lost its charm or power. It still is honored as one of the great tunes of the Church because of its unusual singing merit, its strong, emphatic rhythm, its graceful form, and its sturdy forward movement. It should be sung joyously, with sturdy movement and marked rhythm.

The Church and the Sacraments

338 HYMN: City of God, How Broad and Far
TUNE: Mirfield

Author: *Rev. Samuel Johnson*   Composer: *Arthur Cottman*

AUTHOR: For comments on the author, Samuel Johnson, see Hymn 95.

HYMN: The author collaborated with Rev. Samuel Longfellow in the publication of "A Book of Hymns," 1846, and also of "Hymns of the Spirit," 1864. The former was prepared while Longfellow and Johnson were fellow students at Harvard in response to the desire of a young pastor for a more modern hymn book. Though it bore the title, "A Book of Hymns," Theodore Parker, who introduced it to his church, in view of the joint editorship humorously referred to it as "The Book of Sams."

This hymn was found in "Hymns of the Spirit." It is an apostrophe to the Church conceived on the basis of the imagery which was employed in John's vision upon Patmos. The Church is a city with walls and towers and watch fires. There is fine poetic quality in the third stanza.

COMPOSER: For comments on the composer, Arthur Cottman, see Hymn 143.

TUNE: "Mirfield" is in very general use in the hymn books of to-day and may be found in American books of forty years ago. It is a stirring tune, which easily becomes trivial if sung too fast, and without proper accent.

---

339 HYMN: Glorious Things of Thee Are Spoken
TUNE: Austrian Hymn

Author: *Rev. John Newton*   Composer: *Franz Joseph Haydn*

AUTHOR: Perhaps the author never reached a higher level than in this hymn. He did not profess poetic excellence, but at times his rich Christian experience conveyed to his pen both discernment and power. Many of his hymns were autobiographical. They crystallized experiences in the deep places of his soul. We may be certain that he is writing here concerning "streams of living waters" which he has tasted, "cloud and fire" which have revealed the divine Presence to him, "light by night and shade by day" in which he has found comfort. The completeness of his redemption from sin and shame steadied and constrained him to the end. When at eighty years of age he was exhorted to spare himself the fatigue of preaching, he made reply, "What, shall the old African blasphemer stop while he can speak!" (He referred to his having been an African slave trader.)

For further comments on the author, John Newton, see Hymn 310.

HYMN: This hymn appeared first in "Olney Hymns," which was part of the fruitage of a holy friendship between John Newton and William Cowper and a justly famous collection. Newton was curate at Olney, in Buckinghamshire, England, and Cowper became a lay reader in his church. The book included two hundred and eighty of Newton's productions and sixty-eight of Cowper's. It was essentially a revival book. The hymns pulsated with the vitality of faith and consecration. "From them," says Louis F. Benson, in "The English Hymn," "we could reconstruct the actual working of the revival in an English parish under evangelical leadership; and they [the hymns] may be regarded as bringing the hymnody of the evangelical revival to a close. . . . Many of the hymns had been actually a part of the revival services at Olney, being written for special occasions, or to be sung after some special appeal from the pulpit." The book was more than a hymnal for public use; it served widely as an aid for family and private devotions. "At the lowest estimate," says Dr. Benson, "six [of these hymns] must be accorded a classical position: three of Cowper's . . . and three of Newton's." The latter three, he goes on to say, are: "Come, My Soul, Thy Suit Prepare"; "Glorious Things of Thee Are Spoken"; and "How Sweet the Name of Jesus Sounds."

COMPOSER: For comments on the composer, Franz Joseph Haydn, see Hymn 69.

TUNE: The tune, "Austrian Hymn," composed at the request of the prime minister of Austria for a "Hymn to the Emperor," was first used on the birthday of the emperor, February 12, 1797. Some authorities say that it was written after Haydn had heard "God Save the King" in Westminster Abbey, which inspired him to write a national anthem for his own people that would be as appropriate and masterful. The melody seems to be founded on a Croatian folk song. Like the great oratorio "The Creation," the tune was born in faith and prayer.

The hymn was so great a favorite of Haydn's that later he used it as the subject of one of the movements of his famous "String Quartet," No. 77, and it is said to have been the last thing he played before his death.

The hymn is marked, "With exultation," and no better indication of its rendition could be made. It is joyous, inspiring, and devout. It may be used with splendid effect as a stirring processional.

The Church and the Sacraments

340 HYMN: How Glorious Zion's Courts Appear
         TUNE: Irish

Author: *Rev. Isaac Watts*   Source: *"A Collection of Hymns*
                                        and Sacred Poems"

AUTHOR: For comments on the author, Isaac Watts, see Hymn 22.

HYMN: This hymn is an adaptation of a poem written by Isaac Watts and inspired by Isa. 26:1-6. In the original form it was first published in "Watts's Hymns," in 1707, under the title, "The Safety and Protection of the Church." The initial line was printed thus: "How honorable is the place." In 1781, altered to its present form, the hymn appeared in Scotland in a book bearing the imprint "Translations and Paraphrases in Verse of Several Passages of Sacred Scripture, Collected and Prepared by a Committee of the General Assembly of the Church of Scotland." This volume expanded a compilation made in 1745 which had also included "How Glorious Zion's Courts Appear." The book published in 1745, which was authorized only for private use, contained twenty-three of Watts's paraphrases; the 1781 volume, which was used in public services as well, added two of Watts's productions, making twenty-five in all. The hymn has an honorable record. Its career began in the Nonconformist churches of England; it crossed geographical and ecclesiastical boundaries to the Church of Scotland and finally to America.

SOURCE: The source is "A Collection of Hymns and Sacred Poems."

TUNE: For comments on the tune, "Irish," see Hymn 49.

Christian Fellowship

*

341 HYMN: In Christ There Is No East or West
         TUNE: St. Peter

Author: *John Oxenham*   Composer: *Alexander R. Reinagle*

AUTHOR: For comments on the author, John Oxenham, see Hymn 322.

Handbook to The Hymnal

HYMN: These verses come from the pen of a modern English poet who writes with felicity on religious themes. His vision frequently finds the heart of Christian truth and reaches out to the far-flung boundaries of Christian purpose. Here is an example of both. H. Augustine Smith compares Kipling's familiar lines, "East is East and West is West and never the twain shall meet," with this stanza:

> "In Christ there is no East or West,
> In Him no South or North;
> But one great fellowship of love
> Throughout the whole wide earth."

One poem is occupied with rigid racial barriers; the other, while not ignoring these, takes account of the irresistible spirit of brotherhood which is released by the gospel of Christ, a spirit which will eventually break down every barrier. God does not love walls. Christ came to demolish them. "He . . . brake down the middle wall of partition." His work must continue. This poem is part of a pageant entitled "Darkness and Light," which has been used extensively on both sides of the Atlantic.

COMPOSER: For comments on the composer, Alexander R. Reinagle, see Hymn 81.

TUNE: For comments on the tune, "St. Peter," see Hymn 81.

---

342   HYMN: We Come Unto Our Fathers' God
           TUNE: Nun Freut Euch

Author: *Thomas H. Gill*   Composer: *Rev. Martin Luther*

AUTHOR: Thomas H. Gill was born in Birmingham, England, on February 10, 1819. His parents had been English Presbyterians but had espoused the Unitarian faith. He was educated at King Edward's School, in Birmingham, and would have entered Oxford but for the fact that he found himself unable to accept the Articles of the Church of England, subscription to which was then required. He spent his life largely in writing. Among his published works are: "The Fortunes of Faith," 1841; "The Anniversaries" (poems in commemoration of great men and great events), 1858; "The Papal Drama" (an historical essay), 1866; "The Golden Chain of Praise: Hymns," 1869; "Luther's Birthday" (hymns), 1883. He wrote nearly two hundred hymns.

The Church and the Sacraments

One of his earliest intellectual enjoyments was found in the songs of Watts. He loved them and often expressed impatience with those who belittled them. Unitarianism failed to satisfy his hunger for a vital faith and at length he broke with it.

Hymn: This hymn was published by the author in "The Golden Chain of Praise: Hymns." Of its origin he wrote: "The birthday of this hymn, November 22, 1868 (Saint Cecilia's Day), was almost the most delightful day of my life. Its production employed the whole day and was a prolonged rapture." With unassailable credibility, with rare felicity of thought and phrase, and with becoming emotion, this hymn assumes and declares the continuity of divine protection and human praise.

Composer: For comments on the composer, Martin Luther, see Hymn 118.

Tune: "Nun Freut Euch," "Now Rejoice," was written for another Luther hymn and came into use in England with the hymn, "Great God, What Do I See and Hear?" It is generally accepted as Luther's hymn, appearing in "Geistliche Lieder." It is a confident tune, direct in construction, easily singable, and well worth knowing.

---

343 HYMN: Blest Be the Tie That Binds
TUNE: Boylston

Author: *Rev. John Fawcett*   Composer: *Lowell Mason*

Author: For comments on the author, John Fawcett, see Hymn 54.

Hymn: The author, John Fawcett, had for seven years served the church in which he was ordained, in Wainsgate, Yorkshire, England. When in 1772 he was invited to the pastorate of Carter's Lane Church, London, he felt constrained to accept. A farewell sermon had been preached. Wagons loaded for removal to the new parish waited at the door. His people came to say "Good-by." The pathos of their dependence, their expressions of love and tears of bitter grief, were too much for Fawcett and his wife. They could not, they would not, sever so sacred a tie. Furnishings were unloaded and set back in place. Notice of the change of plans was dispatched to London. Later Fawcett wrote this hymn. At a salary of about $125 a year he labored at Wainsgate and nearby Hebden Bridge until his death in 1817, at the age of seventy-eight.

Handbook to The Hymnal

The hymn figured in a life-influencing incident during the early Christian service of Dwight L. Moody. A teacher in his Sunday School who was doomed to death by tuberculosis went with Moody from home to home to plead with the young women of his Sunday School class to give allegiance to Christ. At length the last one yielded and the teacher arranged to leave for his early home the next day. The members of the class assembled for a final gathering and, with emotion which expressed itself in tears and choked voices, they sang:

> "Blest be the tie that binds
> Our hearts in Christian love."

The hymn was published in the author's "Hymns Adapted to the Circumstances of Public Worship and Private Devotion," published in 1782, though it was probably written several years prior to this date, perhaps in 1772. Here there is no definite information.

COMPOSER: For comments on the composer, Lowell Mason, see Hymn 18.

TUNE: "Boylston" is to be found in "The Choir" of 1832 and was named for one of the towns of the composer's native state. It has long been used for this indispensable hymn, "Blest Be the Tie That Binds," and at present is in wider use than "Dennis." It is of interest to note that six of Lowell Mason's tunes appeared in the English "Church Hymnary" of 1927, and none at all in the English "Songs of Praise" of 1931.

---

344   HYMN: Forgive, O Lord, Our Severing Ways
           TUNE: O Mensch Sieh

Author: *John Greenleaf Whittier*   Source: *Bohemian Brethren's "Gesangbuch"*

AUTHOR: For comments on John Greenleaf Whittier, one of the authors of this composite work, see Hymn 178.

HYMN: This hymn is not composed exclusively of Whittier's words, but it carries a large measure of his spirit. The Quaker poet held high ideals of hymn quality and the Church has found in his poems so much beauty, human sympathy, and Christly tenderness, and withal such lyric quality, that it has insisted upon giving them place in its treasury of song. Dr. Julian's "A Dictionary of Hymnology" lists thirty-three of Whittier's hymns. Many of these have been taken from

The Church and the Sacraments

his longer poems in parts and pieced together in order to make the finished product. In the present hymn such phrases as "Our severing ways," "Rival altars," "Wrangling tongues" make vivid our need for unity of spirit and fellowship in service.

SOURCE: The Bohemian Brethren's "Gesangbuch," published in 1566, is frequently referred to in all recent hymnals. The Bohemian Brethren, who were followers of John Huss, have a rich hymnology. The earliest known hymn book extant was compiled for their communion and was probably printed in Prague. A copy of it in the Bohemian Museum of that city bears the date of January 13, 1501. Subsequent hymnals were published in 1505, 1519, 1531, 1541, and 1561. The foundations for congregational song were laid by these people before the Reformation in Germany and Switzerland, where Luther and Calvin were greatly encouraged by these Brethren. From the first, the Bohemian Brethren were deeply concerned about congregational song, and their hymn books were for the worshipers' hands rather than for the choir. They were interested in a purer religious life and published hymns that met popular needs. They encouraged the writing of sacred verse and music that would appeal to the artisan class, young people, and schools of mastersingers which flourished in Germany in the fourteenth, fifteenth, and sixteenth centuries. Secular folk songs were appropriated by the Brethren, and many of these, because of their beauty, have come down the centuries to enrich the worship of to-day. Charles Wesley was inspired by the singing of these truly great people.

TUNE: "O Mensch Sieh" is from the Bohemian Brethren's "Gesangbuch," published in 1566. The version used in "The Hymnal" is an arrangement which appeared in "The English Hymnal" of 1906. While the time of the tune is irregular, the rhythm of it is so obvious that there is no difficulty in singing it. The musical phrases require no time signature. The progressions are natural and unforced. The tune is also known as "Bohemia," indicating by its name how secure is its place in the hearts of the Bohemian Brethren.

---

345   HYMN: Through the Night of Doubt and Sorrow
        TUNE: St. Asaph

Author: *Bernhardt S. Ingemann*   Composer: *William S. Bambridge*

AUTHOR: Bernhardt S. Ingemann wrote this hymn in 1825. He was born in 1789 on the Island of Falster, a Danish possession in the Baltic Sea. He became professor of the Danish language and literature at the Academy of Sorö, at Zeeland, Denmark. He wrote voluminously. In 1851 his works were published in thirty-four volumes. Several historical novels came from his pen, among them "Valdemar the Great and His Men." He was also a poet of some rank. Seven of his hymns were translated into English and published in Gilbert Tait's "Hymns of Denmark." The strength of the lines even after translation bears witness to the author's virile and inclusive faith.

TRANSLATOR: For comments on the translator, Sabine Baring-Gould, see Hymn 35.

HYMN: This seems to be the only piece of the author's work which has attained common use in the English-speaking churches. It is a strong hymn on the subject of Christian brotherhood. The lines fairly throb with vitality, the vitality of conviction and hope and purpose. Christians, whatever their name, whatever their clime, are on a pilgrimage to the Promised Land. There are perils and difficulties; there is struggle and toil. We push on "through the night of doubt and sorrow," but we shall reach our goal. The enthusiasm which the hymn releases is irresistible. It is the enthusiasm of oneness in the whole round of vital Christian experience.

COMPOSER: For comments on the composer, William S. Bambridge, see Hymn 173.

TUNE: For comments on the tune, "St. Asaph," see Hymn 173.

---

346 HYMN: Rise, Crowned with Light, Imperial Salem, Rise
TUNE: Russian Hymn

Author: *Alexander Pope*   Composer: *Alexis T. Lwoff*

AUTHOR: Alexander Pope was born in London, May 21, 1688. He was taught the rudiments of Latin and Greek by Father Taverner, and studied at Winchester and Hyde Park Corner. When he was twelve years of age his parents moved to Binfield, in Windsor Forest, and his studies continued under private auspices. He attained fame as a poet.

Roman Catholic in faith, he had little incentive toward the production of hymns, but he wrote "Messiah," "Universal Prayer," and "Vital Spark," and parts of the first two poems have found their way into our hymn books. This hymn is from "Messiah," which was first published in the Spectator, May 14, 1712, with an introduction by Addison as "A

The Church and the Sacraments

sacred eclogue. . . . Written in imitation of Vergil's 'Pollio.' " It consisted of 107 lines, and from these five different hymns have been taken. Pope died on May 30, 1744.

HYMN: There are two conceptions of the Church. One is vividly pictured in the book of Revelation: "And he . . . showed me the holy city Jerusalem, coming down out of heaven from God, having the glory of God: her light was like unto a stone most precious." The other was beautifully illustrated by Jesus on the night before his death: "Jesus . . . riseth from supper, . . . took a towel, and girded himself. Then he poureth water into the basin, and began to wash the disciples' feet." Each of these conceptions seems to be exclusive. In reality they are interdependent. "Jesus, knowing . . . that he came forth from God, . . . took a towel." Service is rooted in royalty. Royalty releases and increases itself in service. "Whosoever would become great among you shall be your minister." "The crown of life" which imperial Salem wears is fashioned in the compassionate ministries of Christly devotion.

COMPOSER: Alexis T. Lwoff was born in a musical family at Reval in 1799, and seems to have been predestined to an eminent career as a musician. His father was for years the director of the imperial choir at St. Petersburg and held in honor by emperor and people. By entering the army, in which he rose to high rank, Alexis was almost diverted from his life work. Though he rose to be an adjutant to Czar Nicholas I, he succeeded his father as head of the imperial choir in 1836 and continued and increased the traditions of that great organization. When in 1833 a national anthem was written, Lwoff wrote the tune. No musician in Russia understood the canonical services of the Church better than he did. The collection of ritual chants which he published is authoritative to this day. Among his compositions must be included violin *concertos*, operas, and church music. He died in Kovno in 1871.

TUNE: "Russian Hymn" was written for the words "God Save the Czar." The accepted words in the hymn book of to-day are "Rise, Crowned with Light, Imperial Salem, Rise," although this is also a favorite tune for "God the Omnipotent! King, Who Ordainest." This tune is not used so much as it should be. The apparent difficulty for a congregation in the second measure, and in the last measure of the third line, is easily overcome with good leadership by either organ or voice. The hymn itself is too valuable to overlook in these days of increasing Christian fellowship, and this tune, if used a few times in rather close succession, can hardly fail to meet with great favor in any average congregation.

There is a copy of the music of the hymn with Russian words in the Library of Congress, with an autograph presentation, "*De la part du compositeur, A. de Lwoff.*"

347 HYMN: Children of the Heavenly King
TUNE: Pleyel's Hymn

Author: *Rev. John Cennick*   Composer: *Ignaz J. Pleyel*

AUTHOR: John Cennick was born in Reading, England, December 12, 1718. He began life as a surveyor. Of Quaker stock, but brought up in the Church of England, he at length became interested in the Wesleyan movement and became a preacher. After teaching in a school for the children of miners at Kingswood under the direction of John Wesley, he broke with his leader on doctrinal grounds and organized an independent church, which he later led into the Whitefield fellowship. This relation continued until 1745, when he was ordained a deacon in the Moravian Church. His ministry took him to Germany and Ireland.

He wrote many hymns and published several hymn books. Among the latter were: "Sacred Hymns for the Children of God, in the Days of Their Pilgrimage," published in 1741–1742; "Sacred Hymns for the Use of Religious Societies. Generally Composed in Dialogues," published in 1743; "A Collection of Sacred Hymns," published in 1749; "Hymns to the Honor of Jesus Christ Composed for Such Little Children as Desire to Be Saved," published in 1754. Cennick was perhaps the first of Methodism's lay preachers. He died in London on July 4, 1755.

Cennick is the author of the well-known "graces":

Before Meat:

Be present at our table, Lord!
Be here and everywhere adored;
Thy creatures bless and grant that we
May feast in Paradise with Thee.

After Meat:

We bless thee, Lord! for this our food,
But more for Jesus' flesh and blood;
The Manna to our spirits given,
The Living Bread sent down from heaven.

John Wesley had these eight lines of the "Grace Before Meat" and the "Grace After Meat" engraved on the top of his silver teapot, which is still treasured in City Road, London.

HYMN: This hymn first appeared in "Sacred Hymns for the Children of God, in the Days of Their Pilgrimage," and was originally printed with twelve stanzas. "The Hymnal" makes use of the first, second, seventh, and eighth. The hymn has found a place in a large proportion of English and American hymnals in the last

The Church and the Sacraments

one hundred years. It is probably the most popular of Cennick's productions. It reflects the rugged road which his own feet were treading and the gladness which he nevertheless experienced.

COMPOSER: For comments on the composer, Ignaz J. Pleyel, see Hymn 22.

TUNE: "Pleyel's Hymn" is the theme of the slow movement of Haydn's Quartet, Opus 7, No. 4. It has long been associated in books on American hymns with these words: "A cheerful tune to cheerful words." Note the similarity of the first, second, and fourth lines, adding simplicity to the character of the hymn.

Baptism

*

348 HYMN: Saviour, Who Thy Flock Art Feeding
TUNE: Brocklesbury

Author: *Rev. William A. Muhlenberg*   Composer: *Charlotte A. Barnard*

AUTHOR: Rev. William A. Muhlenberg was the grandson of Rev. Frederick Muhlenberg, a Lutheran clergyman and distinguished member of Congress and Speaker of the House of Representatives during both the First and the Second Continental Congress. His great-grandfather, Henry Melchior Muhlenberg, was called "the patriarch of Lutheranism in America." William was born in Philadelphia on September 16, 1796. He graduated from the University of Pennsylvania in 1814 and took holy orders in 1817. He served parishes in Lancaster, Pennsylvania; Flushing, Long Island; and New York City. In 1858 he founded his "hospital-church," St. Luke's, in New York City. He also founded a religious industrial community, known as St. Johnland, on Long Island. He published "Church Poetry," in 1823, "Poems," in 1859, "The People's Psalter," in 1859. He was a member of the subcommittee on "The Prayer Book Collection," published in 1826, included in which was his best-known hymn, "I Would Not Live Alway."

HYMN: This hymn appeared first in "The Prayer Book Collection." We have few hymns which are particularly appropriate for use at the baptism of children. This is one of the best. The picture which it presents, the lamb in the Good Shepherd's arms, is most appropriate and appealing. The hymn has been loved and widely used.

COMPOSER: Charlotte A. Barnard was born on December 23, 1820. In 1851 she married Charles Cary Barnard. About four years later she began to compose ballads and songs under the pseudonym of Claribel. These compositions were for a time extraordinarily popular. She died in Dover, England, on January 30, 1869.

TUNE: "Brocklesbury" probably has some connection with a town of that name near Dover, England. It has long been associated in American books with the hymn, "Jesus, Tender Shepherd, Hear Me," and no tune among the general church hymns is more widely beloved by very little children. It is often used as an evening prayer.

---

349   HYMN: By Cool Siloam's Shady Rill
TUNE: Siloam

Author: *Bishop Reginald Heber*   Composer: *Isaac B. Woodbury*

AUTHOR: For comments on the author, Reginald Heber, see Hymn 41.

HYMN: This is a tender and exquisite hymn for and concerning childhood. It abounds in the striking imagery children love and in the direct address of love and devotion to which children always respond. It is founded upon the following words from Luke 2: 40: "And the child grew, and waxed strong, filled with wisdom: and the grace of God was upon him." The hymn first appeared in The Christian Observer (England) in 1812 and was entitled "Christ a Pattern for Children." Later it was revised by the author and, following his death in 1826, was published in "Hymns Written and Adapted to the Weekly Church Service of the Year." Two stanzas strangely clouded with the gloomy prospects of early death and decay are properly omitted.

COMPOSER: For comments on the composer, Isaac B. Woodbury, see Hymn 246.

TUNE: "Siloam" has a direct and tender beauty that has long made it a favorite for these words. It is to be found in the Presbyterian Hymnal of sixty years ago. Originally it was sung to "Sweet Day, So Cool, So Calm," which George Herbert wrote in a storm at sea.

The Church and the Sacraments

350   HYMN: Father, Hear Us as We Pray
TUNE: Hanna

Author: *Edith F. B. MacAlister*   Composer: *Rev. Calvin W. Laufer*

AUTHOR: Edith Florence Boyle MacAlister is the daughter of Professor Alexander MacAlister, F.R.S., and wife of Sir Donald MacAlister, K.C.B. She is the author of "Uncle Hal." Deeply interested in the religious training of children, she served for a time as superintendent of the Primary Department in the school connected with St. Columba's Presbyterian Church, Cambridge, England.

HYMN: This hymn appeared as a Cradle Roll song in "The Methodist School Hymnal," Wesleyan Methodist Sunday School Department, London. Its first publication in the United States was in "The Church School Hymnal for Youth," published in 1928.

COMPOSER: For comments on the composer, Calvin W. Laufer, see Hymn 13.

TUNE: "Hanna" was composed in 1927 as a musical setting for a hymn written by Dr. Laufer that same year, "Holy Father, God of Might." The tune bears the name "Hanna" in dedication to two very devoted women who were received by Dr. Laufer into the First Presbyterian Church of Union City, Pennsylvania. Dr. Louis F. Benson called attention to the fact that when the alto part is used as the melody it makes a very effective litany. He was also impressed by the fact that each of the four different parts of the tune makes a perfect melody.

---

351   HYMN: Lord Jesus Christ, Our Lord Most Dear
TUNE: Vom Himmel Hoch

Author: *Heinrich von Laufenberg*   Source: *"Geistliche Lieder"*

AUTHOR: The hymn was written by Heinrich von Laufenberg, a priest at Freiburg, Germany. Later he became a monk in the monastery of the Knights of St. John, in Strasbourg. He translated some of the great Latin hymns into German. He also transformed many secular songs of his day into religious songs. Miss Winkworth says of him, "He was a fertile composer and some of his hymns are very graceful and sweet, but many are prolix and fantastic; and though they seem to have been liked in the religious world of his own day they scarcely bear transplanting to ours."

TRANSLATOR: For comments on the translator, Catherine Winkworth, see Hymn 6.

HYMN: This hymn was named a cradle song, or a lullaby. Instead of "This child" the original read, "My child." There were five stanzas in the song, each stanza in the original being followed by the refrain:

"Ah, Jesus, Lord divine,
Guard me this babe of mine."

The hymn as altered will help to make a worshipful setting for the baptism of children.

SOURCE: The source is the book, "Geistliche Lieder." For comments on German hymn melodies see the article, "German Hymn Sources," under "Original Sources," page xxi.

TUNE: For comments on the tune, "Vom Himmel Hoch," see Hymn 118.

The Lord's Supper

*

352 HYMN: Here, O My Lord, I See Thee Face to Face
TUNE: Morecambe

Author: *Rev. Horatius Bonar*   Composer: *Frederick C. Atkinson*

AUTHOR: For comments on the author, Horatius Bonar, see Hymn 60.

HYMN: This is first in a series of eleven hymns which "The Hymnal" presents as suitable for use at the sacrament of the Lord's Supper, by common consent the climax in Christian worship. Additional hymns appropriate to this occasion, such as "When I Survey the Wondrous Cross," "Beneath the Cross of Jesus," "Just as I Am, Without One Plea," will be found in other sections of the book.

The story is told that following the funeral service of Horatius Bonar, as Rev. J. M. Sloan, assistant pastor of the Chalmers Memorial Church, Edinburgh, Scotland, Principal Cairns, and Dr. Cuyler, of Brooklyn,

The Church and the Sacraments

New York, drove in a carriage to Canongate Churchyard, the conversation turned toward Dr. Bonar's hymns. Each spoke of his favorite. The first mentioned was "Here, O My Lord, I See Thee Face to Face."

Bonar's hymns are vital with their author's soul quality. Purity of soul, holiness of life, personal abandon to Christ were part and parcel of the man. The songs were sung to his own soul before they issued from his pen. This hymn was written especially for an elder brother and was first used at the Communion table in the brother's church in October, 1855.

COMPOSER: For comments on the composer, Frederick C. Atkinson, see Hymn 204.

TUNE: For comments on the tune, "Morecambe," see Hymn 204.

---

353 HYMN: Bread of the World in Mercy Broken
TUNE: Eucharistic Hymn

Author: *Bishop Reginald Heber*   Composer: *Rev. John S. B. Hodges*

AUTHOR: For comments on the author, Reginald Heber, see Hymn 41.

HYMN: In vivid phrases the mind is fixed upon the essentials of the sacrament: "Bread of the world," "Wine of the soul," a heart "by sorrow broken," "tears by sinners shed," and in the background, giving significance to it all, a sacrificial cross and a crucified Christ. The hymn first appeared in Bishop Heber's posthumous "Hymns Written and Adapted to the Weekly Church Service of the Year," published in 1827. It has been widely used.

COMPOSER: Rev. John Sebastian Bach Hodges composed the tune for this hymn. According to Rev. A. B. Kinsolving, rector of St. Paul's, Baltimore, John Sebastian Bach Hodges was born in the cloisters of Bristol Cathedral, England, in 1830. His father, Edward Hodges, had received the degree of Doctor of Music from Cambridge University. Sebastian came as a lad with his father to America, studied in Columbia College, New York, and graduated in 1854 from the General Theological Seminary in that city. He served as tutor at Nashotah Theological Seminary, Wisconsin; at the Church of the Holy Communion, in Chicago; and at Grace Church, Newark, New Jersey. In 1870 he was called to the rectorship of St. Paul's, in Baltimore. He abolished the mixed

Handbook to The Hymnal

choir of men and women there and substituted a choir of men and boys. A fine parochial school and a thorough training in music enabled him to make this choir one of the best in America. For thirty-five years he served the parish and the diocese with marked distinction, and wrote more than one hundred pieces of church music, hymn tunes, anthems, and others, in the fine colonial rectory on Saratoga Street. One of his anthems, "Christ Our Passover," is recognized as a composition of rare merit, and his tune to "Bread of the World in Mercy Broken" is sung in many lands. He once published a small book on hymn tunes, now out of print. Dr. Hodges resigned his rectorship in 1905, but lived for nine years longer. He saw the further development under his successor of the fine musical traditions of the parish, a parish which afterwards gave Dr. Miles Farrow to the New York Cathedral of St. John the Divine, and Dr. Channing Lefebvre to old Trinity Church, New York City.

TUNE: "Eucharistic Hymn" came into the Presbyterian Hymnal by way of the Episcopal Church, in whose Hymnal of 1870 it was first used. Its place in the Presbyterian Hymnal is secure since its inclusion in "The Hymnal" of 1895 and subsequent books. Its dominant mood is contemplative and therefore well adapted for the Communion service.

---

354   HYMN: Jesus, Thou Joy of Loving Hearts
       TUNE: Quebec

Source: *Latin Hymn*   Composer: *Henry Baker*

SOURCE: This hymn is a translation of an anonymous Latin hymn, written in the eleventh century.

TRANSLATOR: For comments on the translator and arranger, Ray Palmer, see Hymn 285.

HYMN: The hymn is a translation by Ray Palmer of stanzas 4, 3, 20, 28, and 10 of the Latin poem, "Jesu Dulcis Memoria," a poem of fifty four-line stanzas, the authorship of which is in doubt. Many students have been convinced that it was the work of Bernard of Clairvaux, but a manuscript of the eleventh century attributes it to a Benedictine abbess. Not only is the spirit of the author of the original enshrined in the hymn as we have it here, but also the spirit of Ray Palmer, another of God's noblemen, regarded by many as America's greatest hymn writer. He was a man of sterling character, strong of conviction yet gentle of soul. His love for Christ, his fellowship with Christ,

374

his satisfaction in Christ, and his devotion to Christ are all suggested by the words of this lovely translation. Perhaps the key to the verses is in the lines:

> "From the best bliss that earth imparts
> We turn unfilled to Thee again."

This is one of our most used and best loved Communion hymns, but it is appropriate for devotional meditation at any time.

COMPOSER: For comments on the composer, Henry Baker, see Hymn 89.

TUNE: For comments on the tune, "Quebec," see Hymn 89.

---

355   HYMN: And Now, O Father, Mindful of the Love
       TUNE: Unde et Memores

Author: *Rev. William Bright*   Composer: *William H. Monk*

AUTHOR: Rev. William Bright was born at Doncaster, England, December 14, 1824. He was educated at University College, Oxford, from which he received an A.B. degree in 1846 and an A.M. in 1849. He won the Ellerton theological essay prize in 1848. In 1868 he became Regius professor of ecclesiastical history and canon of Christ Church. He published a number of volumes in his particular field and several devotional books, including "Hymns and Other Poems," in 1866. The latter was revised and enlarged in 1874. He died on March 6, 1901. Dr. Julian, in "A Dictionary of Hymnology," says that "Canon Bright's hymns merit greater attention than they have received at the hands of compilers." He lists seven of his hymns.

HYMN: This hymn was first published in "Hymns Ancient and Modern" in 1875. It is the work of a lover of Christ and one who was able to express his ideas in poetic form. Dignity and reverence are here. Tested knowledge of the Saviour and his sacrificial work is here. Intimate communion with Christ is here. Desire to carry the satisfactions of fellowship out into life and service is here. The hymn is a truly beautiful setting forth of that which the "Beloved Community" should endeavor to experience at the Lord's Supper.

COMPOSER: For comments on the composer, William H. Monk, see Hymn 33.

TUNE: "Unde et Memores" is a highly reverential tune and is characterized by fine musical restraint. The melody at the beginning is low in the scale and suggests a feeling of awe in the presence of great mysteries. It is only toward the end that, with increased volume and higher notes, greater emotion and intense feeling are shown. This quality characterizes many of the tunes of William Monk. A good example is "Eventide," Monk's setting for "Abide with Me: Fast Falls the Eventide."

---

356   HYMN: Be Known to Us in Breaking Bread
FIRST TUNE: St. Flavian

Author: *James Montgomery*   Source: *"Day's Psalter"*

AUTHOR: For comments on the author, James Montgomery, see Hymn 11.

HYMN: Including psalm poems Montgomery wrote a total of four hundred hymns. Most of them were produced during the period of this hymn and later. This hymn first appeared in the "Christian Psalmist" in 1825, entitled "The Family Table," and was republished in "Original Hymns" in 1853 under the same caption. The stanzas refer to a familiar incident at the end of the Emmaus road, Luke 24: 30,31. The author prays for a revelation of Jesus in the breaking of bread, but fears and seeks to avoid the loss of the Revealer:

> "Be known to us in breaking bread,
> But do not then depart."

An unknown author has added to Montgomery's two stanzas three of his own, introducing the hymn with the stanza beginning "Shepherd of souls, refresh and bless." In this form we find it in many hymn books, including the two preceding editions of our own.

SOURCE (First Tune): For comments on the source, "Day's Psalter," see the article, "The Psalters in Early Presbyterian Worship," under "Original Sources," page xv.

TUNE (First): For comments on the tune, "St. Flavian," see Hymn 86.

SECOND TUNE: St. Agnes

Composer: *John B. Dykes*

COMPOSER (Second Tune): For comments on the composer, John B. Dykes, see Hymn 53.

The Church and the Sacraments

T UNE (Second): For comments on the tune, "St. Agnes," see
Hymn 206.

---

357 HYMN: O Bread of Life from Heaven
TUNE: Bread of Life (Warren)

Author: *Anonymous*   Composer: *Samuel P. Warren*

S OURCE: The author of this hymn is unknown. It has erroneously
been ascribed to Thomas Aquinas. It is thought by some that the
Latin poem, "O Esca Viatorum," from which it comes, was written
by a German Jesuit priest of the seventeenth century.

T RANSLATOR: The translator, Rev. Philip Schaff, was born
at Chur, Switzerland, January 1, 1819. He received his education in the German Universities of Tübingen, Halle, and Berlin.
In 1843 the German Reformed Seminary at Mercersburg, Pennsylvania, called him to a professorship in which he served until 1870, when
he accepted an invitation to become professor of sacred literature in
Union Theological Seminary, New York City. He was elected president
of the latter institution in 1887. He died in New York on October 20,
1893.

Dr. Schaff became famous in the fields of church history and dogma.
The American Revision Committee elected him its president. He edited
the original "Schaff-Herzog Encyclopedia." He was a lover of poetry,
especially religious poetry. Among his publications are "Deutsches Ge-
sangbuch," published in 1860, and "Christ in Song," published in 1869.
Collaborating with Roswell D. Hitchcock and Zachary Eddy, he edited
"Hymns and Songs of Praise for Public and Social Worship," in 1874.
He also translated hymns from Latin and German.

H YMN: This hymn moves on a high level of literary excellence
and is charged with deep feeling. In the first stanza Jesus is
addressed as "Bread of life from heaven," "Manna from above."
The second stanza, in consideration of the cup, calls upon him as the
author of a "fount of grace redeeming," a "river ever streaming." The
third stanza breaks through all imagery and takes us in adoring praise to
the feet of the unseen Christ. The form of the hymn is that of a prayer.
It impels us to ask that soul hunger be fed, that thirst be quenched, that
seeking ones be brought to the Object of their quest, and

> "When the veil is rended,
> That we, to heaven ascended,
> May see Thee evermore."

377

Handbook to The Hymnal

Other translations of this Latin poem have been made, the most familiar of which is Ray Palmer's "O Bread to Pilgrims Given."

COMPOSER: Samuel Prowse Warren was the son of an organ builder and at an early age took a great interest in that instrument. While he was still very young he served as organist at the American Church in Montreal. After he had finished college, he studied organ and musical composition under August Haupt and piano under Gustav Schumann in Berlin. Returning to America in 1864, he became organist of All Souls' Church, New York City, in 1865, going to Grace Church in 1867 and to Trinity Church in 1874. In 1876 he returned to Grace Church. In 1895 he became organist of the First Presbyterian Church, East Orange, New Jersey, remaining until his death in 1915.

His musical taste and technical skill were unusual and were graced by his fine character and personality. For many years he was regarded as the dean of American organists. A close student of Bach's works, he exerted a strong influence in the cultivation of taste for that music. His organ transcriptions, church anthems, and settings for Episcopal church services are highly regarded. He had an unusual talent and ability in improvisation. He died in 1915.

TUNE: "Bread of Life (Warren)," by Samuel P. Warren, appeared in the Episcopal Hymnal of 1889, commonly known as the "Tucker Hymnal." It seems to have been written for Dr. Phillip Schaff's translation, "O Bread of Life from Heaven," and is always associated with those words. The music is characterized by great depth of feeling and stateliness of movement. A moderate tempo is suggested.

---

358   HYMN: According to Thy Gracious Word
        TUNE: Dalehurst

Author: *James Montgomery*   Composer: *Arthur Cottman*

AUTHOR: For comments on the author, James Montgomery, see Hymn 11.

HYMN: The hymn was first printed in Montgomery's "Christian Psalmist," published in 1825, under the heading, "This Do in Remembrance of Me," as a poem of six four-line stanzas. In 1853 we find it included in the author's "Original Hymns." The word "testamental" in the third line of the second stanza has been a stumbling-block to certain hymn students and some of the collections have altered the line to read, "Thy cup, Thy precious blood I take." We are to remember the love of Jesus, his sacrificial death, his coming triumph, but

378

The Church and the Sacraments

these are either preparatory or supplemental; our thought is to be chiefly fixed upon him, our crucified, risen, and everliving Lord. Few evangelical hymn books omit this hymn.

COMPOSER: For comments on the composer, Arthur Cottman, see Hymn 143.

TUNE: For comments on the tune, "Dalehurst," see Hymn 143.

---

359 HYMN: For the Bread, Which Thou Hast Broken
TUNE: Agape

Author: *Rev. Louis F. Benson*   Composer: *Rev. C. J. Dickinson*

AUTHOR: For comments on the author, Louis F. Benson, see Hymn 29.

HYMN: The first line of this hymn evokes the Eucharistic atmosphere. It gives thanks for the holy emblems and that for which they stand. The second prays that our lives may be hallowed by the pledge of love, the gift of peace, and the call to heaven. The third takes account of the tie which binds us to those whom we have loved and lost awhile—a tie whose preciousness should be made vivid at the Communion table. The fourth is a prayer for defense, guardianship, and power in our toils for the coming Kingdom. The author is one of the most distinguished among recent hymnologists.

COMPOSER: Rev. Charles John Dickinson is remembered more for his tunes than by any biographical data which is available. He was an Englishman, probably of Irish extraction. Most of his tunes appeared between 1861 and 1873. Five of his best-known tunes were included in the epoch-making Irish Hymnal of 1919. His music is of a high order and indicates technical skill and a broad understanding of what qualities should characterize sacred song. Some of his tunes are well-known in Canada, though not so extensively as in Ireland.

TUNE: "Agape" appeared in the composer's "Hymn Tunes," published in 1861. In that volume it was entitled "Sanctuary." Later it was included in "The Book of Common Praise," the Presbyterian Hymnal in the Dominion of Canada. The dominant mood of the tune is that of contemplation, and therefore it is very useful for the sacrament of the Lord's Supper. The structure of the tune seems to reflect the influence and style of Rev. John B. Dykes, probably the best-known tune composer of the Victorian era.

Handbook to The Hymnal

360 HYMN: 'Twas on That Night When Doomed to Know
TUNE: Rockingham Old

Author: *Rev. John Morison*   Composer: *Edward Miller*

AUTHOR: John Morison, D.D., was born in Aberdeenshire, Scotland, in 1749. His education was received at King's College, at the University of Aberdeen, from which he received an A.M. in 1771. He was called to the parish of Canisbay, Caithness, as minister in 1780. The University of Edinburgh conferred upon him the degree of Doctor of Divinity in 1792. He died at Canisbay on June 12, 1798. In May of 1781 Dr. Morison was added to General Assembly's committee on the revision of the "Translations and Paraphrases." Five of the paraphrases are ascribed to him and two to him and John Logan as joint authors.

HYMN: This hymn is marked by Scottish characteristics. Rugged, Scriptural, calm, it flows much like a stream whose surface fails to evidence its depth. One would not describe the hymn as emotional, but one recognizes the disciplined and controlled feelings which underly its flow. The hymn is a paraphrase of the words of Jesus as he instituted the Lord's Supper on the night on which he was betrayed.

COMPOSER: For comments on the composer, Edward Miller, see Hymn 152.

TUNE: For comments on the tune, "Rockingham Old," see Hymn 152.

361 HYMN: Jesus, to Thy Table Led
TUNE: Melford

Author: *Rev. Robert H. Baynes*   Composer: *M. B. F.*

AUTHOR: Robert Hall Baynes was a devoted son of the English Church, into which he was born in 1831, being the son of the rector at Wellington. He graduated from Oxford in 1856 and was ordained. After serving various parishes in the congested districts of London, among them the perpetual curacy of St. Paul's Whitechapel, he was made Bishop of Madagascar in 1870, but resigned the appointment and became honorary canon of Worcester Cathedral. He was a gifted compiler of sacred poems and wrote many acceptable hymns, of which "Jesus, to Thy Table Led" is the best-known and most widely used. He was editor of several hymn collections, among them "The Canterbury Hymnal," published in 1864; "Home Songs for Quiet Hours,"

The Church and the Sacraments

1878; "Hymns for Home Mission Services," 1879; and "At the Communion Time," a collection of hymns for use at Communion.

HYMN: This hymn appeared originally in "The Canterbury Hymnal," of which Baynes was the editor. It is based upon Eph. 3:19, the words of which constitute the heading under which the hymn originally appeared. The deep sentiment of the passage is the special theme of the second stanza. All the intimate devotional elements that give to our Lord's Supper its profound emotional appeal to the worshiper are itemized and spiritualized in this widely used Communion hymn.

COMPOSER: The composer is unknown.

TUNE: "Melford" is taken from a collection of hymns edited by James Worthington, a public accountant, resident of Philadelphia, whose avocation was hymnology. This collection was published by John R. Rue, Jr., 43 South Fourth Street, in 1886, under the title of "Hymns and Tunes for the Children of the Church." In his preface the editor acknowledges the help of J. H. Hopkins, D.D.; A. G. Mortimer; and W. B. Gilbert, Mus.D., but as no other reference is made to the composers or sources of the hymns used, the signature of "M. B. F." remains unexplained. Dr. Louis F. Benson, in "Christian Song," states in a footnote to the hymn that the manuscript was picked up with others by the same composer in a mass of old papers in a Philadelphia shop. Mr. Warrington, however, in a letter to Dr. Benson dated June 1, 1912, specifically states that the manuscript, along with other tunes by the same composer, was purchased by him from the author, and that "Melford" was the only one so far published.

362

HYMN: A Parting Hymn We Sing
TUNE: Schumann

Author: *Rev. Aaron* Source: *Mason and Webb's "Cantica Laudis"*
 R. Wolfe Composer: *Robert Schumann*

AUTHOR: Rev. Aaron R. Wolfe was born at Mendham, New Jersey, September 6, 1821. He graduated in 1844 from Williams College. College men will recognize the poetic insight of Mr. Wolfe as indicated in a poem written for the fortieth reunion of his class and presented July 1, 1884. The following stanza has the movement of a hymn:

"The world lies backward to our gaze;
The future close at hand;
The hoary heads now catch the rays
That gild the better land."

Graduating from Union Seminary in 1851, he was licensed by the Presbytery of New York on April 9, 1851. From 1852 to 1855 he presided over a school for young women at Tallahassee, Florida. In 1859 he established the Hillside Seminary for Young Ladies at Montclair, New Jersey. This work occupied him until 1872, when he retired. In 1858, under the signature of "A. R. W.," he contributed eight hymns to Hastings' "Church Melodies." Among these was "A Parting Hymn We Sing."

HYMN: This hymn was written for the tenderest of all moments in corporate worship—the moments in which the Lord's Supper concludes. Only the most fitting words can meet the delicate situation in every true worshiper's heart. For this reason this hymn has found its place as an appropriate spiritual response following the Communion service. In a letter Mr. Wolfe says, "I can remember nothing definitely about 'A Parting Hymn We Sing' except that in looking over the lists of topics in hymn books with the idea of endeavoring to supply deficiencies I thought something of this kind might be suitable in rising from the Lord's table." The verses transmute spiritual renewal, which the holy feast has brought, into gratitude and pledged loyalty, into "word and life."

COMPOSER: For comments on the composer, Robert Schumann, see Hymn 78.

TUNE: "Schumann," an arrangement by Mason and Webb, appeared in "Cantica Laudis," which was published in Boston, Massachusetts, in 1850. In that volume it carried the name "White." It was set to "Thou Shalt, O Lord, Descend, and All Thy Kingdoms Bless," and appeared as Hymn 176. The book, "Cantica Laudis," indicates that the tune is an arrangement of something by Schumann, but fails to state what inspired it. As used it is one of the most successful short meter tunes in "The Hymnal," where it appears twice. "Cantica Laudis" was an ambitious effort to take musical subjects and themes from the great masters—Handel, Haydn, Mozart, Beethoven, Schumann, Schubert, Mendelssohn, Gluck, and others—in the hope that choirs and churches "might make sure progress in tasteful cultivation, or in the appreciation, execution, and love of musical truth and beauty."

The Kingdom of God on Earth
Discipleship and Service
*

363 HYMN: "Thy Kingdom Come," on Bended Knee
TUNE: Chesterfield

Author: *Rev. Frederick L. Hosmer*   Composer: *Rev. Thomas Haweis*

AUTHOR: For comments on the author, Frederick L. Hosmer, see Hymn 176.

HYMN: Before this hymn was written there had been a strange lack of hymns concerned with man's duty to his neighbor, and prior to this in the nineteenth century only one based on the petition, "Thy kingdom come." This hymn was written for the commencement exercises at the theological seminary at Meadville, Pennsylvania. Stanzas 3, 4, and 5 show the fitness of the title then given to it, "The Day of God." Thought content and tune join to compel joyous singing. Here is the thrill of assured triumph of the Kingdom. Under the spell of the hymn one feels the world life moving toward righteousness and peace. We should sing as seeing the stars mobilized against all the Siseras in the world, as sensing the dawn of the day promised by God, when righteousness and peace shall abound and abide. Lifted by this song of assurance, devout souls, however cast down, cease to be discouraged.

COMPOSER: For comments on the composer, Thomas Haweis, see Hymn 199.

TUNE: "Chesterfield" is frequently referred to in England as "Richmond." It made its first appearance in 1792 in "Carmina Christo," a book edited by Rev. Thomas Haweis. Dr. Haweis adapted this tune to his words, "O Thou from Whom All Goodness Flows." The last line had florid repeats in the original form.
    This tune is characteristic of the period in which it was written and is one of the best of its type. It is a strong, freely moving melody in this particular version. An alternative version by Martin Shaw appeared in "The Tenor Tune Book," published in 1917.

364   HYMN: O Master, Let Me Walk with Thee
TUNE: Maryton

Author: *Rev. Washington Gladden*   Composer: *Rev. Henry Percy Smith*

AUTHOR: Washington Gladden was a Congregational minister whose most notable pastorate was in Columbus, Ohio, where he built himself into the life of the city as a militant religious leader in social and civic movements. A vigorous writer for periodicals, he did much to mold the thinking of his generation, and his influence was nation-wide. His "Parish Problems" was one of the first books dealing with the programs of the modern Church.

HYMN: Although not written by a hymn writer, this is among the most cherished of all our hymns. For one reason, it fits the modern mood of service. For another, it voices the universal experience of hindering fret and care. And for the strongest reason of all, it has a strain of deep, tender yearning for realized intimacy with the great Companion. These stanzas were not written for use as a hymn but as a poem for quiet meditation, first published in Sunday Afternoon, a magazine of which Dr. Gladden was editor, under the title "Walking with God." A part of the poem, equally strong and tender, revealing the heartaches in a period of controversy, is omitted from the hymn, as not suited for use in church worship.

COMPOSER: Rev. Henry Percy Smith was born in 1825 and died in 1898. Upon his graduation from Balliol College, Oxford, from which he received the degrees of Bachelor of Arts (1848) and Master of Arts (1850), he took holy orders. He was brought under the influence of Charles Kingsley while curate at Eversley, Hants, from 1849 to 1851. He served as perpetual curate of St. Michael's, York Town, Farnborough, Surrey, from 1851 to 1868. He was deeply interested in church music, and while vicar of Great Barnton, Suffolk, composed "Maryton," by which he is remembered. Subsequently, he became chaplain at Cannes and canon of Gibraltar.

TUNE: "Maryton" was composed by Canon Percy Smith for the hymn "Sun of My Soul, Thou Saviour Dear," in "Church Hymns with Tunes" in 1874. The intimate, prayerful melody of the tune makes it particularly fitted to the words as used in this Hymnal. There is a general temptation to drag a melody of this type, and while there should be in no way a feeling of haste this tune is most effective if sung with a smooth-flowing, moderate tempo. Its harmonization makes it effective as a quartet. Dr. Gladden always discouraged new settings to his words and

The Kingdom of God on Earth

clearly indicated a preference for "Maryton," even to the extent of making its use a condition when granting permission for the use of the hymn.

---

365   HYMN: Onward, Christian Soldiers
               TUNE: St. Gertrude

Author: *Rev. Sabine Baring-Gould*   Composer: *Arthur S. Sullivan*

AUTHOR: For comments on the author, Sabine Baring-Gould, see Hymn 35.

HYMN: This hymn was written as a processional for singing children, marching between villages. The author deplored its imperfections and never dreamed of its destined popularity. On one occasion, because objectors to the carrying of a processional cross had prevailed, the last line of the chorus was whimsically changed from "going on before" to "left behind the door"! In the face of rising and widening resentment against whatever might savor of the war spirit, the hymn will live and thrill because it transfigures the war spirit. We have few soldier hymns, and a diminishing demand for them, because of a sense of incongruity between militarism and evangelism which widens with the growing Kingdom. Nevertheless the victories of peace cannot be won save by a heroism and sacrifice surpassing that of soldiers forced to fight and kill. The soul of metaphors and words can be transformed, as under the magic of Paul's inspired pen the ancient fighting man's equipment became transfigured into the whole armor of God. And if marching soldiers, intoxicated by martial music, go forth with passion to their cruel task, how much more should Christian soldiers, their feet "shod . . . with the preparation of the gospel of peace," march to the noblest and most inspiring of all militant rhythms!

COMPOSER: For comments on the composer, Arthur S. Sullivan, see Hymn 128.

TUNE: There is no doubt that Sir Arthur Sullivan's tune, "St. Gertrude," is largely accountable for the popularity of the hymn, "Onward, Christian Soldiers." He composed this hymn to appear in "The Hymnary," published in 1872. While this tune was written for the above book, it first appeared in The Musical Times in December of the preceding year. Since Sullivan composed this tune it has been almost entirely associated with Baring-Gould's words.

366 HYMN: Come, Labor On
TUNE: Ora Labora

Author: *Jane Laurie Borthwick* Composer: *T. Tertius Noble*

AUTHOR: For comments on the author, Jane Laurie Borthwick, see Hymn 30.

HYMN: In the vineyards of the Lord there are always places for those who have the will to work, and in his harvest fields it is still a fact that the laborers are few. The demands of the Kingdom are an increasing rebuke to idleness. Nor is there here any dead line or age limit.

Silvester Horne, the preacher-statesman, was forever bubbling with boyish enthusiasm. Speaking to a friend about a sermon preached before a great audience of "elder blossoms" and "borrowed timers," he challenged his friend to name the text.

" 'Come unto me, . . . and I will give you rest,' " suggested the friend. "No," was the answer.

" 'At evening time there shall be light.' "

"No. No, nothing like these. But this: 'He went . . . in the marketplace . . . and to them he said, Go ye also into the vineyard.' "

This hymn is taken from "Thoughts for Thoughtful Hours," by Miss Borthwick, published in 1857.

COMPOSER: Thomas Tertius Noble was born in Bath, England, May 5, 1867. His greatest reputation has been gained through his being a distinguished organist, although he is also well-known as a composer. From 1884 to 1889 he studied at the Royal College of Music, where he specialized in organ, harmony, counterpoint, and composition. He was organist at All Saints', Colchester, from 1881 to 1889; assistant organist at Trinity College, Cambridge, from 1890 to 1892; organist at Ely Cathedral from 1892 to 1898, and at York Minster from 1898 to 1913. Since then he has been organist and choirmaster at St. Thomas', New York City. He made a recital tour of the Eastern States and Canada in 1913 and also gave recitals at the Panama Exposition in San Francisco in 1915.

In 1898 he founded the York Symphony Orchestra, which he conducted until 1912; with the York Musical Society he revived, after a lapse of seventy-five years, the once famous York Festivals. He acquired the degress of F.R.C.O. and A.R.C.M. Among his many and varied compositions are included a comic opera, a suite for violin and orchestra, a festival cantata, a *concerto* for organ, anthems, services, hymns, and pieces for violin and piano. His "Ora Labora" was written in 1918.

The Kingdom of God on Earth

TUNE: There seems to be no information available regarding the tune, "Ora Labora," except that it first appeared in the new Episcopal Hymnal in 1918. The tune is especially written for unison singing, and is composed in broad, sweeping rhythm. The harmonization of the accompaniment is particularly fine, and from the standpoint of composition the tune is of more than usual merit.

---

367 HYMN: We Thank Thee, Lord, Thy Paths of Service Lead
TUNE: Field

Author: *Rev. Calvin W. Laufer*   Composer: *Rev. Calvin W. Laufer*

AUTHOR: For comments on the author, Calvin W. Laufer, see Hymn 13.

HYMN: In this, one of the newest of our hymns, the recurring thought of every line is finding God and feeling God while serving God. One is reminded of Bishop Simpson's noble phrasing of the task of the Church: "The Church must go into the field with the farmer, into the tent with the soldier, into the forecastle with the sailor, into the pit with the miner, into the counting room with the merchant; it must go into the alleys and purlieus of the city, and grope its way up the rickety stairs and kneel on the bare floor beside the loathesome sufferer. Like the atmosphere, it must press equally on all surfaces of society, like the sea it must crowd into every nook on the shore line of humanity, like the sun it must shine on things foul and low as well as things fair and high. For the Church was redeemed and organized and equipped and commissioned for the moral and spiritual renovation of the whole world."

COMPOSER: For comments on the composer, Calvin W. Laufer, see Hymn 13.

TUNE: "Field" was written by Dr. Laufer at the close of a day when he and his friend, Rev. Herbert H. Field, had broken bread together. The tune was made available for service in September, 1919, in Dr. Field's church, the Flatbush Presbyterian Church, Brooklyn, New York. The tune moves quietly but is strong in beat where the thought requires enhanced expression. As some one has said of it, "It needs no marks of expression; these appear in the rising and falling march of the music." The author and composer being the same person, the tune is naturally an integral part of the words.

387

Handbook to The Hymnal

This hymn is widely used on all occasions and has appeared in "The Century Hymnal" and in "Songs of Life," as well as in fifteen other hymnals.

---

368 HYMN: Lord God of Hosts, Whose Purpose, Never Swerving
TUNE: Welwyn

Author: *Rev. Shepherd Knapp*   Composer: *Alfred Scott-Gatty*

AUTHOR: Rev. Shepherd Knapp was born in 1873, educated at Columbia College and Yale Divinity School, and is at present pastor of the Congregational church of Worcester, Massachusetts. When the hymn was written, he was assistant pastor of the Brick Presbyterian Church, New York City, and wrote the hymn especially for the men's association of that church.

HYMN: This hymn finds inspiration in I Cor. 15:58, "Wherefore, my beloved brethren, be ye stedfast, unmovable, always abounding in the work of the Lord, forasmuch as ye know that your labor is not in vain in the Lord." Jesus' work was not in vain. He finished the work that was given him to do. And God will not swerve from his further purpose. We march and labor in the strength of Him who conquered death and holds in his hand all power in heaven and on earth. The hymn breathes courage, confidence, and gladness.

COMPOSER: For comments on the composer, Alfred Scott-Gatty, see Hymn 110.

TUNE: For comments on the tune, "Welwyn," see Hymn 110.

---

369 HYMN: "Forward!" Be Our Watchword
TUNE: Forward

Author: *Rev. Henry Alford*   Composer: *Henry Smart*

AUTHOR: Rev. Henry Alford, Dean of Canterbury Cathedral, was born in 1810. A most precocious child, he wrote a life of Paul when he was six years old, and at ten he wrote a pamphlet on the subject, "Looking Unto Jesus the Believers' Support Under Trials and Afflictions." He compiled a collection of hymns at eleven, and in his sixteenth

The Kingdom of God on Earth

year he wrote, "I do this day as in the presence of God and my own soul renew my covenant with God, and solemnly determine henceforth to become his, and do his work as far as in me lies." His greatest achievement in the realm of scholarship is his "Greek Testament" with notes. He always desired to go to Palestine, but he was never able to do so; this fact gives special significance to the inscription which he prepared for his tombstone: "The Inn of a Pilgrim Traveling to Jerusalem." He was a member of the New Testament Revision Company.

HYMN: The hymn was written for a festival program of the Canterbury Diocesan Choral Union in 1871 and was based on the words, "Speak unto the children of Israel, that they go forward," Ex. 14:15. Dean Alford was opposed to the processional. However, his accomplished precentor, knowing his gifts, urged upon the dean his duty to write a processional. He was induced to walk the great aisles of the cathedral that he might feel the atmosphere and gather inspiration for a rewriting of the hymn he had submitted. It was immediately used, and has added fame to an already distinguished churchman in a field new to his talents.

COMPOSER: For comments on the composer, Henry Smart, see Hymn 61.

TUNE: "Forward," known in English hymnals as "Smart," has the distinction of having superseded Dean Alford's own tune for his hymn. It was written in 1872 for these words and appeared in "The Hymnary," published that year. Dean Alford's tune, while of considerable merit, was not successful for processional uses. Smart's tune is superior in definiteness of beat and pulse, in melody and harmonization, in movement and spirit. "Forward" is a tune of the people, and as such is appreciated by young and old. It is a valuable tune for festal occasions.

---

370   HYMN: O Lord of Life, Thy Kingdom Is at Hand
       TUNE: Pro Patria

Author: *Rev. Marion Franklin Ham*   Composer: *Horatio W. Parker*

AUTHOR: Rev. Marion Franklin Ham, a preacher with literary gifts and a writer of stories, including many in the Negro dialect, was born on February 18, 1867, at Harveysburg, Ohio. After serving awhile as a newspaper reporter and bank clerk in Chattanooga, Tennessee, he was ordained to the ministry in 1898. From his first pastorate in Chattanooga, from 1898 to 1904, he was called to the First Church of Dallas, Texas, which he served from 1904 to 1909. Since 1909 he has been the incumbent of the Community Church of Reading, Massachusetts.

HYMN: The hymn, "O Lord of Life, Thy Kingdom Is at Hand," was written in the latter part of May, 1912. "One morning," the author states, "I was standing on the front porch of my home and noticed the unusual brightness of the sunlight, playing on the leaves of a maple tree in the yard. The morning was radiant. The whole world seemed full of light, and suggested the theme of the hymn, which is expressed in its first two lines. [On] returning to my study, the stanzas came."

Its first printing was in the Christian Register, of Boston, on January 2, 1913. Later it was included in "The Beacon Hymnal," which was published in 1924.

The hymn is rich in Biblical allusions, references to prophecies, inner Kingdom experiences, the coming glory, the unity of all believers, and the ringing call to present duty. The fine phrasing, the balanced sentences, the spiritual content of all the parts combine to make it a hymn to be studied and sung with joy.

COMPOSER: For comments on the composer, Horatio W. Parker, see Hymn 19.

TUNE: This tune, "Pro Patria," first appeared in the Episcopal Hymnal in 1894. It is a tune best sung in march rhythm, although there is no martial atmosphere. It is one of the solid hymns of the Church.

---

371   HYMN: Lead On, O King Eternal
       TUNE: Llangloffan

Author: *Rev. Ernest W. Shurtleff*   Source: *Welsh Hymn Melody*

AUTHOR: The author, Rev. Ernest W. Shurtleff, a Congregational minister, was born in 1862. He held important American pastorates, but his greatest work was in organizing and developing the American Church at Frankfurt, Germany. He also served the large group of students in Paris, having charge of the Students' Atelier Reunions in Academy Vitti. He and his wife were active in relief work during the World War. He was a musician of ability and has left behind him several volumes of poetry. He died in France, August 24, 1917.

The Kingdom of God on Earth

HYMN: The author's classmates at Andover Theological Seminary, recognizing his poetic gifts, requested that he write a hymn for their graduation in 1887. This hymn was produced and was sung with the emotion which always characterizes graduation exercises. The hymn recalls the days of preparation with their vision and purpose and also reflects the ever-present spirit of eagerness in the graduates for the fields of conquest. The second stanza is especially striking in its vision of victory, and in its understanding of the spiritual forces moving through holiness to the "Amen of peace."

SOURCE: The source is a Welsh hymn melody in D. Evans' "Hymnau a Thonau." For comments on Welsh hymnody see the article, "Welsh Hymnody," under "Original Sources," page xxii.

TUNE: For comments on the tune, "Llangloffan," see Hymn 222.

---

372   HYMN: O Brothers, Lift Your Voices
           TUNE: Lancashire

Author: *Bishop Edward H. Bickersteth*   Composer: *Henry Smart*

AUTHOR: For comments on the author, Edward H. Bickersteth, see Hymn 62.

HYMN: The hymn was written by Bishop Bickersteth, a poet with whom the gift of hymn-writing was hereditary through a noted hymn-writing father. It was written to be used in the Missionary Jubilee of 1848. Printed and circulated in tract form, at first it appeared in his "Psalms and Hymns" in 1858, and in later collections.

A note of confident expectancy characterizes this hymn. Let us lift up our voices and sing songs of triumph *now*, it urges. We war against evils, and strive and fight and build through faith in Him who sees the end from the beginning. The hymn thrills with a conquering faith and carries the overtone of appreciation of the true trophies of battles won for God, goodness, and human happiness.

COMPOSER: For comments on the composer, Henry Smart, see Hymn 61.

TUNE: For comments on the tune, "Lancashire," see Hymn 115.

373 HYMN: Once to Every Man and Nation
TUNE: Ton-Y-Botel

Author: *James Russell Lowell*   Source: *Welsh Hymn Melody*

AUTHOR: The author, James Russell Lowell, was born in Cambridge, Massachusetts, in 1819 and died in 1891 in his beautiful residence, Elmwood, now a much-sought shrine in American life and literature. He graduated from Harvard in 1838 and succeeded Henry W. Longfellow as professor of modern languages and literature in 1855. He was cast for a great character in tumultuous times and gave body, mind, and soul to the great causes, working toward a larger personal liberty and a higher collective destiny for his fellow men. He was editor of The Atlantic Monthly and the North American Review. He was appointed American minister to Spain in 1877, and later was ambassador to the Court of St. James, London. He was one of America's most prolific and purposeful writers. Like Whittier and, in a lesser degree, Longfellow, he wrote with the aims and moral earnestness of an Old Testament prophet against the sins of his generation.

HYMN: The hymn belongs to a historic poem entitled "The Present Crisis," written as a protest against the Mexican War. The poem originally consisted of ninety long lines. It was first used as a hymn in England. Garret Horder, in 1896, made from it a hymn of thirty-two short lines.

This mighty protest against a last-century war is a noble hymn for the times in which we live. It should be often used in the present era of growing antagonism to all wars. It is warm and glowing with Christian ideals and with heroic faith in love's more excellent way of settling international differences.

SOURCE: The source is a Welsh hymn melody. For comments on Welsh hymnody see the article, "Welsh Hymnody," under "Original Sources," page xxii.

TUNE: "Ebenezer (Ton-Y-Botel)," by T. J. Williams, is a tune from "Llawlyfr Moliant," published in 1890. The alternate name, "Ton-Y-Botel," is used almost exclusively. It is claimed by a widely credited legend that this tune was so named because it was found in a bottle washed ashore on the Welsh coast during a storm. This legend, however, is entirely without foundation. The tune is very simple in its structure and is formed throughout by imitations of the first bar. The melodic sequence is characteristic of many Welsh tunes.

The Kingdom of God on Earth

374   HYMN: We Are Living, We Are Dwelling
        TUNE: Blaenhafren

Author: *Bishop Arthur Cleveland Coxe*   Source: *Traditional Welsh Melody*

AUTHOR: For comments on the author, Arthur Cleveland Coxe, see Hymn 334.

HYMN: This hymn was written when the author was only twenty-two years old. It was composed in the stress of the same stirring times in which Lowell wrote "The Present Crisis." It is nobly adapted to a situation wherein a keen Christian conscience senses the breaking of a new day for Kingdom ideals. Here is reflected the thrill that comes with the motive of striving to serve, not merely one's own generation, but also the generations to come. We become builders of the Kingdom that is to be.

The hymn is suitable for singing in an emotional atmosphere created by a message of challenge to renewed and uttermost consecration to the Christian task.

SOURCE: For comments on the source, a Welsh hymn melody, see the article, "Welsh Hymnody," under "Original Sources," page xxii.

TUNE: The tune, "Blaenhafren," is apparently named for a farm or homestead. However, no information can be found regarding it.

---

375   HYMN: When Wilt Thou Save the People
        TUNE: Commonwealth

Author: *Ebenezer Elliott*   Composer: *Josiah Booth*

AUTHOR: The author, Ebenezer Elliott, was born in Yorkshire, England, in 1781 and lived in Sheffield, the center of that industrial life whose abuses shocked his soul. He was an ironmonger. He wrote his poems for a newspaper in Sheffield, and rejoiced in being known as the bard of the poor. He was called "The Corn Law Rhymer." His passion for social justice was an embodiment of the spirit expressed in Micah 6: 8. His poems had much to do with moving the British Government to repeal the bread tax in 1846.

393

HYMN: This hymn was published posthumously in a volume of Elliott's poems, issued in 1850. It was never intended to be used as a hymn. It found its way into "The Congregational Church Hymnal" in 1887 and into other hymnals later. Written to incite reforms of unhappy conditions in a particular era, the hymn is suitable to any age calling for movements for the betterment of the people. Every stanza comes to a climax in the cry, "God save the people." Here is the spirit of Emerson's poem "God Said, 'I Am Tired of Kings,'" turned into a rhythmic prayer. This business man author made himself a voice for the inarticulate cry of the downtrodden. His hymns should arouse all Christians to a realization that in God's sight persons are of more value than property.

COMPOSER: Josiah Booth was born in 1852 and died in 1929. He was educated at Oxford and the Royal Academy of Music. He was organist from 1868 to 1876 at Banbury, and from 1877 to 1918 at Park Chapel (Congregational), Crouch End, London. He was the composer of over a hundred hymn tunes, many of which are still in use. He also helped to edit "The Congregational Church Hymnal," which appeared in 1888, and was musical adviser to the committee responsible for "The Congregational Hymnary," published in 1916. For forty years he led the musical portion of the services at Park Chapel, not only with great technical skill but with rare appreciation of the spiritual uses of music.

TUNE: "Commonwealth" is said to have been written in ten minutes, but is considered Josiah Booth's most famous tune. At breakfast one morning he opened a letter in which was contained the hymn, "When Wilt Thou Save the People," for which the writer wanted a tune. Mr. Booth read the verses, turned to the piano, and immediately played the now familiar "Commonwealth," writing it down directly afterwards. On being interviewed shortly before his death, he passed over the manuscript to his interviewer, pointing out that not one note had been altered since its hurried writing many years before.

Missions

*

376   HYMN: Go, Labor On: Spend, and Be Spent
TUNE: Pentecost

Author: *Rev. Horatius Bonar*   Composer: *Rev. William Boyd*

AUTHOR: For comments on the author, Horatius Bonar, see Hymn 60.

The Kingdom of God on Earth

HYMN: This hymn was written in 1843, under the title "The Useful Life." Its immediate purpose was to encourage a group of workers in a mission, where the besetting temptation, in view of the dismal surroundings and in the presence of results that gave little or no indication of progress, was to say, "What is the use?" How difficult it is to keep on working without visible results, when other laborers in more favorable conditions report large returns! We need very frequently to remind ourselves that it is God who gives the increase, and that in processes invisible to us God is working toward the harvest. Dr. Jowett, being asked to define vision, said, "It is seeing the harvest when the snow is on the ground." This is a good hymn to sing when the ground is frozen.

COMPOSER: For comments on the composer, William Boyd, see Hymn 270.

TUNE: For comments on the tune, "Pentecost," see Hymn 270.

---

377   HYMN: Jesus Shall Reign Where'er the Sun
TUNE: Duke Street

Author: *Rev. Isaac Watts*   Composer: *John Hatton*

AUTHOR: For comments on the author, Isaac Watts, see Hymn 22.

HYMN: This hymn was written before missionary interest had been awakened. It was the first lyric call to the Great Commission. It was used in 1862 under most dramatic circumstances, as described by G. I. Stevenson in his "Hymn Book Notes." Five thousand natives of Tonga, Fiji, and Samoa, who had forsaken paganism to become Christians, gathered under the banyan trees for divine worship. The solemn service began with the singing of this hymn. On this occasion King George, the sable chief of the South Sea Islands, was present and later drew up a constitution transforming a pagan régime into a Christian government.

Watts's title for the hymn was "Christ's Kingdom Among the Gentiles." He was interested in every possible advance toward brotherhood. He pleaded for a new type of hymn suitable to this advance. He said, "We preach the gospel and pray in Christ's name, and then check the aroused devotions of the Christians by giving them a song of the old dispensation."

COMPOSER: John Hatton, composer of "Duke Street," was born probably in Warrington, England. He died in 1793 in St. Helen's, the place of his residence, in the township of Windle. He lived on the street whose name he gave to the one tune by which his name is known. His funeral service was held in the Presbyterian Chapel of St. Helen's.

TUNE: "Duke Street," while of English origin, has such wide use in America that it seems to be an American product. It was included in one of the earliest publications of the Boston Handel and Haydn Society. In that organization's hymn book, under the date of 1820, it was associated with "Lord, When Thou Didst Ascend on High." It seems to have been included in all the hymnals of the Presbyterian Church. Its first appearance was in the year 1793, when it was included in Henry Boyd's book, "A Select Collection of Psalm and Hymn Tunes." Its association with Watts's "Jesus Shall Reign Where'er the Sun" goes back many years.

378

HYMN: Christ for the World We Sing
TUNE: Trinity (Italian Hymn)

Author: *Rev. Samuel Wolcott*   Composer: *Felice de Giardini*

AUTHOR: The author, Rev. Samuel Wolcott, a Congregational minister, was born in South Windsor, Connecticut, on July 2, 1813. He graduated from Yale in 1833. After two years as a missionary in Syria failing health compelled him to return to America, where he served as pastor of a number of important churches. It is interesting that he never attempted to write a hymn until he was fifty-six years old, and then wrote over two hundred before he died at Longmeadow, Massachusetts, on February 24, 1886.

HYMN: The author wrote that this hymn was suggested by a motto over the pulpit in a church in Ohio where a Y. M. C. A. convention was in session. The motto was "Christ for the World, and the World for Christ." Walking through the streets on his way home from the meeting, the hymn took shape in his mind. It has been adopted by Yankton College as the opening hymn for each term. It might well be adopted by every Christian as the opening sentiment for each new day.

COMPOSER: For comments on the composer, Felice de Giardini, see Hymn 52.

TUNE: For comments on the tune, "Trinity (Italian Hymn)," see Hymn 52.

The Kingdom of God on Earth

379 HYMN: Heralds of Christ, Who Bear the King's Commands
TUNE: National Hymn

Author: *Laura S. Copenhaver*   Composer: *George William Warren*

AUTHOR: Mrs. Laura Scherer Copenhaver, born in 1868 at Marion, Virginia, lived all her life in the town of her birth. To Marion College, which was founded by her father, she has given more than thirty years as a teacher of English literature. Because of her interest in the educational and missionary interests of the Church, she has constantly served as a lecturer and conference leader. In this capacity she has lectured at Lake Geneva, Wooster, Blue Ridge, Lakeside, and St. Petersburg. She has been instrumental in developing handicraft and pageantry among the young women of the Southern mountains. Through magazine articles, verses, and hymns she has extended her influence throughout the country.

HYMN: "Heralds of Christ, Who Bear the King's Commands" was first used in a conference at Northfield, Massachusetts, and was later published by the Women's Missionary Society of the United Lutheran Church. The missionary program of the women of the Methodist Episcopal Church North for one entire year was built around this hymn. It was so used by the Southern Presbyterian Church in its program for 1934. Of the hymn Mrs. Copenhaver states the following:
"In writing 'Heralds of Christ' I was moved with a sense of unity with all the builders of the King's highway in other lands and ages. Missionaries and ministers were frequent guests at the college and the missionaries were especially interesting to me. Romance hung about them."

COMPOSER: For comments on the composer, George William Warren, see Hymn 153.

TUNE: George William Warren's tune, "National Hymn," appeared in the "Hymnal for the Episcopal Church," in 1894. Printed copies of the tune, with words by Rev. Daniel C. Roberts, sent to the late Dr. Benson by Dr. Warren, bear this notation at the top: "As sung at the Columbian celebration service at St. Thomas's Church, New York, Sunday morning, October 9, 1892." This was probably the first time the hymn was used in a service. It is one of the finest processional hymns in the whole realm of hymn tunes. Its unique feature is the trumpet introduction and interludes throughout the number. Dr. Warren has caught here a rare combination of that quickening appeal which comes from a martial air, with an undercurrent of sanctity and reverence. No one can possibly sing this hymn without a quickening of the pulse because of its martial rhythm, yet not in one measure does that profoundly religious inspiration which produced the hymn forsake it.

---

380   HYMN: From the Eastern Mountains
TUNE: Valour

Author: *Rev. Godfrey Thring*   Composer: *Arthur H. Mann*

AUTHOR: For comments on the author, Godfrey Thring, see Hymn 38.

HYMN: Because of references in the first stanza to the Wise Men, this noble hymn is too often classified as only a Christmas hymn. Rather it should be sung often through the entire year. There is a wideness in its reach that touches a great variety of human experiences. In it we sing of the Light that must shine in every heart before God can have his way with human life. Its inclusiveness makes its message appropriate for Christians, for wanderers, for children, for the aged, for all who seek to walk in the Light.

COMPOSER: For comments on the composer, Arthur H. Mann, see Hymn 200.

TUNE: "Valour" is a virile, forward-moving tune. In the main body of the tune there is not a single repetition of phrase. Only in the refrain is there a recurrence of the two phrases with which the tune opens. The music is Anglican and reflects the proportions and atmosphere of cathedral environs. "Valour" was introduced to American churches by Episcopal hymnals. This is its first inclusion in "The Hymnal" of the Presbyterian Church.

---

381   HYMN: Ye Christian Heralds, Go Proclaim
TUNE: Missionary Chant

Author: *Rev. Bourne H. Draper*   Composer: *Heinrich Christopher Zeuner*

AUTHOR: The author, Rev. Bourne H. Draper, was born in Cumnor, near Oxford, England, in 1775. Early poverty delayed his preparation for an entrance into the ministry. He was of a Church of England family, but becoming a printer's apprentice in Oxford, at the

The Kingdom of God on Earth

Clarendon Press, he became affiliated there with the Baptist Church, which he joined. By the help of Dr. John Ryland, head of the Baptist Academy at Bristol, he was able to pursue his studies. In 1804 he was ordained as pastor of the Baptist church of Chipping-Norton. He was a man of great piety and poetic gift. Numerous fugitive poems appeared in magazines under his initials. His books for children together with his devotional works and volumes of sermons number thirty-six in all.

HYMN: The hymn was originally a hymn of seven stanzas, written as a farewell to missionaries. It was compiled from a poem beginning "Sovereign of worlds, display Thy power." The origin and authorship were for a long time uncertain. It was found in Elias Smith and Abner Jones's "Hymns for the Use of Christians," published in Portland, Maine, in 1805, under the title, "On the Departure of the Missionaries. By a Bristol Student." This "Bristol Student" has been identified as Rev. B. H. Draper. The characterization of missionaries as Christian heralds is true to the vocabulary of the gospel commission. Since we are His witnesses how can we think of our rank among men as other than Christian heralds? The hymn is used rarely except in America.

COMPOSER: For comments on the composer, Heinrich Christopher Zeuner, see Hymn 211.

TUNE: For comments on the tune, "Missionary Chant," see Hymn 211.

---

382 HYMN: O Zion, Haste, Thy Mission High Fulfilling
TUNE: Angelic Songs

Author: *Mary Ann Thomson*   Composer: *James Walch*

AUTHOR: The author of this hymn is Mary Ann Thomson. Mrs. Ethel B. Owen, of Philadelphia, the daughter of Mrs. Thomson, writes of her mother: "My mother, whose maiden name was Faulkner, was an Englishwoman, born in London in 1834 and deeply interested in her church from girlhood. She was brought up in an old-fashioned London rectory." She came to the United States as the wife of John Thomson, first librarian of the Free Library of Philadelphia. Out of a deep spiritual culture, she contributed many hymns to the various journals of the Protestant Episcopal Church. She died in 1923.

HYMN: The author thus describes the writing of this hymn: "I wrote the greater part of the hymn, 'O Zion, Haste, Thy Mission High Fulfilling,' in the year 1868. I had written many hymns before. One night while I was sitting with one of my children who was ill of

Handbook to The Hymnal

typhoid fever, I felt impelled to write a missionary hymn to the tune of the hymn, 'Hark! Hark, My Soul! Angelic Songs Are Swelling.' I could not then get a refrain I liked. I left the hymn unfinished for about three years. I finished it by writing the refrain which now forms part of it. I do not think it is ever sung to the tune for which I wrote it. I feel much indebted to the composer of the tune, 'Tidings,' [Angelic Songs] for writing so inspiring a tune to my words."

COMPOSER: For comments on the composer, James Walch, see Hymn 319.

TUNE: In 1875, James Walch, an English organist and composer, conceived the idea of writing a tune for "Hark! Hark, My Soul! Angelic Songs Are Swelling." This he did in spite of the fact that the words were already associated with two well-known tunes. He had little hope that a third tune, however good, would gain even the slightest recognition. This however, proved to be the case. Mr. Walch at first failed entirely in his purpose, just as Mrs. Thomson had previously failed at first with her words, "O Zion, Haste, Thy Mission High Fulfilling," which are the words used here. In the providence of God, however, Walch's tune, "Angelic Songs," also known as "Tidings," and Mrs. Thomson's words found each other. The union was favored from the beginning, and continues to this day.

---

383 HYMN: Send Thou, O Lord, to Every Place
FIRST TUNE: Isleworth

Author: *Mary C. Gates*   Composer: *Samuel Howard*

AUTHOR: Mary C. Gates, a descendant of the only daughter of Roger Williams, was born in Rochester, New York, February 14, 1842. Through her father, who was William S. Bishop, she sprang from a family distinguished for culture and public service. The spirit of her ancestors was in her and an eminent career was inevitable. After receiving a liberal education she became identified with Leroy Female Seminary as an instructor, and remained there several years. In the year 1873 she married Dr. Merrill E. Gates, afterwards president of Rutgers College, at New Brunswick, New Jersey, and still later of Amherst College, at Amherst, Massachusetts. For many years she served on the Women's Board of Foreign Missions of the Reformed Church in America, and in that capacity her services were gratefully recognized throughout the denomination. She was a versatile writer and a frequent contributor to The Christian Intelligencer, The Independent, The Youth's Companion, and The Atlantic Monthly. She died on December 17, 1905.

400

The Kingdom of God on Earth

Of her, Denis Wortman, D. D., wrote the following lines: "The characteristic of her poems is their evangelical nature. She lives in the great world of nature, but her particular home is with the Nazarene. She has a personal affection for Jesus, like Mary and Martha, and like them she makes him the guest of her home and of her heart."

HYMN: "Send Thou, O Lord, to Every Place" was written for a missionary convention of the Christian Endeavor Society in 1890, where it was first introduced and used. It has become the author's best-known hymn. The hymn is one of clear vision of the spiritual needs of the world. The Great Commission of the Lord to go forth is expressed as an intense prayer that God may send "swift messengers," "men whose eyes have seen the King," to heal "the bruised and broken hearts" of the world. The lines and couplets of the hymn are very direct and challenge self-sacrificing service and devotion. The hymn is widely used in missionary meetings and conventions and has been influential in securing recruits for the foreign field.

COMPOSER (First Tune): For comments on the composer, Samuel Howard, see Hymn 188.

TUNE (First): The tune, "Isleworth," by Samuel Howard, is from "Melodies of the Psalms of David According to the Version by Christopher Smart," where it is set to the words of Psalm 6. It is written in the minor mode, with rather complicated harmonization. It is most effective if sung in unison. Although "Elmhurst" is the more commonly known tune to the hymn, "Send Thou, O Lord, to Every Place," "Isleworth" is included in the new Hymnal because of its unusually fine harmonies.

SECOND TUNE: Elmhurst

Composer: *Edwin Drewett*

COMPOSER (Second Tune): Edwin Drewett was born in 1850 in London and died in 1924. He studied at the Royal Academy and for many years was organist of Harecourt Congregational Chapel, London. Later, from 1893 to 1905, he played in the German Lutheran Church at Dalton. From 1905 until the war broke out in 1914 he played at the German Embassy Church, Brompton; and from 1917 until his death he played at King Charles the Martyr, Tunbridge Wells.

TUNE (Second): There is very little known regarding the tune, "Elmhurst," except that it was originally written by Edwin Drewett for the hymn "O God of Mercy, God of Might" and appeared first in "The Congregational Church Hymnal," published in 1887. It is used in "The Hymnal" of 1933 as an alternate tune to "Isleworth."

Handbook to The Hymnal

384 HYMN: Fling Out the Banner! Let It Float
TUNE: Waltham

Author: *Bishop George W. Doane*   Composer: *J. Baptiste Calkin*

AUTHOR: For comments on the author, George W. Doane, see Hymn 34.

HYMN: St. Mary's School, at Burlington, New Jersey, desired a hymn appropriate to the raising of a school flag. Bishop Doane, head of the school at the time, was greatly interested in religious poetry and hymns and it was largely through his influence that Keble's "Christian Year" was introduced into America. Bishop Doane supplied the flag-raising hymn in 1848 and gave to the world one of the most popular of its missionary hymns. He was often known as the missionary bishop of America. One of his great sermons was preached in 1837 on the theme, "The Missionary Charter of the Church." It is interesting to note that his son, William Croswell Doane, at one time bishop of Albany, is the author of one of our well-known hymns, "Ancient of Days, Who Sittest Throned in Glory."

The setting for the present hymn is taken from Ps. 60: 4:

"Thou hast given a banner to them that fear thee,
That it may be displayed because of the truth."

COMPOSER: John Baptiste Calkin was born in London on March 16, 1827, and died in the same city on May 15, 1905. He was a pianist, organist, and composer, having been taught by his father, James Calkin. He was organist and precentor of St. Columba's College, Navan, Ireland. Later he became organist of Woburn Chapel, London; of Camden Road Chapel; and of St. Thomas', Camden Town. He was also a professor at the Guildhall School of Music and the Croydon Conservatoire. Among the many works which he published are included hymn tunes, services, anthems, songs, and organ music.

TUNE: "Waltham" appeared first in "The Hymnary," published in England in 1872. In a comparatively short time it appeared in other books published in Scotland and America. It is usually associated with the hymn "Fling Out the Banner! Let It Float." Its martial swing and the ease with which it can be sung place it in the category of popularity with "St. Gertrude" and "Webb." This tune is well fitted for processional use.

402

The Kingdom of God on Earth

385

HYMN: From Greenland's Icy Mountains
TUNE: Missionary Hymn

Author: *Bishop Reginald Heber*   Composer: *Lowell Mason*

AUTHOR: For comments on the author, Reginald Heber, see Hymn 41.

HYMN: Reginald Heber, aged thirty-six, minister at Hodnet, England, was visiting his father-in-law, Dean Shipley, at Wrexham over Whitsunday, in 1819. It was customary in those days to accompany a special offering with a special hymn. By order of the king an offering was to be taken on this Sunday for the Society for the Propagation of the Gospel in Foreign Parts. On Saturday afternoon a few friends were gathered in the library. The dean asked his talented son-in-law to compose something appropriate for the offering on the morrow. Heber gladly consented and withdrew to the other end of the room. After fifteen minutes or so Dr. Shipley asked if he had written anything, and he replied by reading aloud what we now know as the first three stanzas of the hymn. Although his listeners were satisfied he declared that the thought was not complete and retired to write the fourth stanza. The dean was so pleased with it that he refused to allow other stanzas. The hymn was printed that same evening with only one correction in the manuscript, the substitution of "heathen" for "savage" in that much-discussed second stanza, which is omitted in this edition. It is interesting to note that when the manuscript was later sold it brought forty-two pounds, considerably more than the offering on that Whitsunday.

COMPOSER: For comments on the composer, Lowell Mason, see Hymn 18.

TUNE: "Missionary Hymn" appeared in "The Boston Handel and Haydn Society Collection," published in 1829. It was composed by Lowell Mason, who also edited the book in which it appeared. After its appearance in that book it spread through all denominations in a wide variety of hymn books, including Sunday School collections. The fluency of the melody, with its carol-like simplicity, has contributed much to its popularity. Since the range of the melody is within the scope of the average singer there is always full-voiced congregational support.

403

386 HYMN: O Son of God, Our Captain of Salvation
TUNE: Donne Secours

Author: *Rev. John Ellerton* Source: *"Genevan Psalter"*

AUTHOR: For comments on the author, John Ellerton, see Hymn 20.

HYMN: In 1871 a hymn book was published bearing the simple title, "Church Hymns," edited by Bishop How, John Ellerton, and others. This hymn, which had been written on April 5 of that same year, appeared in this book. It can be used with good effect in those services where the anniversary of a pastorate is observed. It very aptly illustrates the description of Ellerton's writings as given in Dr. Julian's "A Dictionary of Hymnology": "The words which he uses are generally short and simple; the thought is clear and well stated; the rhythm is good and stately. Ordinary facts in sacred history and in daily life are lifted above the commonplace rimes with which they are usually associated, thereby rendering the hymns bearable to the cultured, and instructive to the devout." "It is no exaggeration to say that his [Ellerton's] hand may be traced and his voice heard in every hymn book of importance during the last thirty years before his death," says H. Augustine Smith.

SOURCE: For comments on the source, "Genevan Psalter," see the article, "The Psalters in Early Presbyterian Worship," under "Original Sources," page xv.

TUNE: "Donne Secours" was composed or adapted by L. Bourgeois, John Calvin's choirmaster, in the "French Psalter" of 1551. It is a nobly impressive melody and one of the finest examples of Genevan tunes.

---

387 HYMN: O Christ, Forget Not Them Who Stand
TUNE: Missionary Chant

Author: *Margaret E. Sangster* Composer: *Heinrich Christopher Zeuner*

AUTHOR: The name of Margaret E. Sangster, née Munson, has been associated with religious prose and poetry for three generations. The granddaughter who bears the name, an author also, writes thus of her grandmother:

"My grandmother was born in New Rochelle, New York, of Scotch-

The Kingdom of God on Earth

Irish parentage on Washington's Birthday, 1838. She married my grand-father in the years just before the Civil War.

"Her church affiliations were always close but the denomination was not always the same. Grandmother usually joined the church that she most liked in the town in which she, at the moment, resided, but she was an active member and worker in any church that held her letter. At the time of her death she was a member of the Congregational Church; before that she had been a member of the Dutch Reformed Church. She died in 1912.

"Grandmother was a prolific writer, although during the last ten years of her life she was almost totally blind. She was contributing editor to half a score of magazines. Her verse was something of a side line with her. She wrote verse easily and whenever the spirit moved her. Oddly enough, it is her verse that will probably live longest."

Under the title "From My Youth Up" she wrote, in her old age, her autobiography, a charming volume found in many libraries.

HYMN: In these four couplets the missionary as he stands in the vanguard of the battle of the Kingdom is most vividly portrayed. He who knows the literature of the missionary enterprise will catch a vision of these heroes courageously moving on "in flood, in flame, in dark, in dread." The hymn is beautiful in its simplicity and directness. The unusual word "vanguard" might stand as its title. It is a prayer uttered in the language most appropriate to petition and thanksgiving.

COMPOSER: For comments on the composer, Heinrich Christo-pher Zeuner, see Hymn 211.

TUNE: For comments on the tune, "Missionary Chant," see Hymn 211.

---

388   HYMN: From All That Dwell Below the Skies
       TUNE: Lasst Uns Erfreuen

Author: *Rev. Isaac Watts*   Source: *"Geistliche Kirchengesäng"*

AUTHOR: For comments on the author, Isaac Watts, see Hymn 22.

HYMN: This hymn as we now have it first appeared in 1781 in the "York Pocket Hymn Book," edited and published by Robert Spence, a Methodist class leader and bookseller living at York, England. The shortest psalm, Psalm 117, is the subject of this beautiful hymn. The first two stanzas, which are stanzas 1 and 3 in "The Hymnal," are unaltered from Watts's "The Psalms of David," published in 1719. Later some one added two other stanzas. Thus in one composition both psalm and hymn are united. This hymn exemplifies Watts's mission. Wearied with the poor singing in the Southampton Nonconformist church, he determined, in spite of ridicule, to attempt better paraphrases and even hymns of his own. He had courage coupled with great ability. He was a grandson of a naval commander who, rather than surrender, blew up his ship and perished with it. Isaac honored his family traditions. Afflicted with ill health through most of his seventy-four years, he accomplished a variety and quality of work that puts all the world in his debt. Dr. Johnson said of him, "He has provided instruction for all ages, from those who are lisping their first lessons to the enlightened readers of Malebranche and Locke; he has left neither corporeal nor spiritual nature unexamined; he has taught us the art of reasoning and the science of the stars." There are twenty hymns and two responses by Isaac Watts in this Hymnal.

SOURCE: For comments on the source, "Geistliche Kirchengesäng," see Hymn 13.

TUNE: For comments on the tune, "Lasst Uns Erfreuen," see Hymn 13.

---

389   HYMN: The Morning Light Is Breaking
        TUNE: Webb

Author: *Rev. Samuel F. Smith*   Composer: *George J. Webb*

AUTHOR: Samuel F. Smith, whose name is always thought of in connection with "My Country, 'T is of Thee," was born within sound of the Old North Church chimes in Boston on October 21, 1808, just two years after the "haystack prayer meeting" at Williams College. After graduating from Harvard in the same class with Oliver Wendell Holmes he began his theological seminary course at Andover, where he was a student in 1832. He was ordained as pastor of the Baptist church at Waterville, Maine, in 1834; he served also as professor of modern languages in the college there, which later became known as Colby College. He had a rare gift for acquiring languages, of which he knew not less than fifteen. At the age of eighty-six he was looking for a suitable textbook in order to take up the study of Russian. In 1842 he became pastor of the First Baptist Church of Newton Center, Massachusetts, where he remained pastor for twelve years and where he lived the rest of his long life. For fifteen years he was secretary of the Missionary

The Kingdom of God on Earth

Union. It is interesting to note that the author of our best-loved and most-sung national hymn had such a vision of the Kingdom of God that he wrote one of the most popular missionary hymns. Both hymns were written in the same year.

HYMN: In 1832 exciting news was coming from Adoniram Judson in Burma. After years of suffering and discouragement he was writing home that the light was breaking and many were accepting Christ. Young Samuel Smith, just twenty-four years old at the time, caught the enthusiasm from these letters and felt that the triumph of the cross was near. Although Dr. Smith never went to the foreign field he sent to Burma a son, who said of this hymn: "It has been a great favorite at missionary gatherings and I myself have heard it sung in five or six different languages in Europe and Asia. It is a favorite with the Burmans, ... from whose lips I have heard it repeatedly."

COMPOSER: For comments on the composer, George J. Webb, see Hymn 265.

TUNE: For comments on the tune, "Webb," see Hymn 265.

---

390   HYMN: From Ocean Unto Ocean
        TUNE: Lancashire

Author: *Rev. Robert Murray*   Composer: *Henry Smart*

AUTHOR: Robert Murray was born in the rugged highland district a few miles north of Truro, Nova Scotia, December 25, 1832. As a little boy he was richly endowed with a poet's imagination. It is said that he read theology and wrote poetry before he was ten years old. After graduating from the Free Church college at Halifax, of which he was later a governor for many years, he was licensed to preach. However, all recognized that his great pulpit was the religious press. For fifty years he was editor of the Presbyterian Witness, one of the most influential journals of the maritime provinces. His poetry, often appearing anonymously in his paper, found its way into the church hymnals; this hymn and "Lord, Thou Lov'st the Cheerful Giver" were included in "The Church Hymnary" published in 1898. Dr. Murray died December 10, 1910.

HYMN: It probably will be found that the hymns which truly live are those that grow out of the deepest convictions of their authors' lives. This fine home mission hymn is a perfect example of this fact. For many years Dr. Murray was an outstanding advocate in Canada of a united Christian Church that should carry the "good news" to every part of the Dominion. Of the Hymnal published by the Presbyterian Church of Canada in 1897, Dr. Louis Benson wrote, "It had the felicity of bringing forth a hymn writer of Canadian Presbyterianism, Dr. Robert Murray, of Halifax, whose home mission hymn, 'From Ocean Unto Ocean,' has already proved its usefulness." We, south of the border, may well sing this Kingdom hymn with our sister Church of the north.

COMPOSER: For comments on the composer, Henry Smart, see Hymn 61.

TUNE: For comments on the tune, "Lancashire," see Hymn 115.

---

391 HYMN: Hail to the Brightness of Zion's Glad Morning
TUNE: Wesley

Author: *Thomas Hastings*   Composer: *Lowell Mason*

AUTHOR: For comments on the author, Thomas Hastings, see Hymn 197.

HYMN: In the year 1832 there was in the Church a rising enthusiasm for missions. Nowhere was it expressing itself more impressively than in the hymns which were being written. "Hail to the Brightness of Zion's Glad Morning" and "The Morning Light Is Breaking" were written in the same year, and have much the same hope and enthusiasm. Although Thomas Hastings is said to have written more than six hundred hymns and composed more than a thousand tunes, it is possible that he will be remembered longest as the author of these lines, which Dr. Ninde has called "a missionary lyric, by common consent, the best of all his hymns." "If we take the aggregate of American hymnals published during the last fifty years," says a writer in Dr. Julian's dictionary, "or for any portion of that time, more hymns by him [Hastings] are found in common use than by any other native writer." In this hymn are associated the names of two men who did as much as, if not more than, any others in America to develop sacred music—Lowell Mason and Thomas Hastings. Hastings, with Thomas Bradbury, may be said to have founded Sunday School hymnology, publishing together sixty different books, whose sales totaled more than ten million copies. Two years before he wrote this hymn Hastings composed the music to which "Rock of Ages, Cleft for Me" is most generally sung. This universally loved tune, a great missionary hymn, and the generally known arrangement of Thomas Moore's lines, "Come, Ye Disconsolate, Where'er Ye Languish," are

The Kingdom of God on Earth

enough to make the name of Thomas Hastings live as long as our faith sings its way into the hearts of men.

As a boy Hastings had moved from Connecticut with his parents to the rough frontier life of Oneida County, New York. He early developed a taste for music, and in 1866 he began teaching it, conducting choirs and singing classes in Troy and Utica. Finally, in the very year this hymn was written, he was called to New York City to direct several choirs. The last forty years of his life were spent there in increasing usefulness.

COMPOSER: For comments on the composer, Lowell Mason, see Hymn 18.

TUNE: The tune "Wesley" is a simple, straightforward melody, with an unusually bright rhythm. Mason's fame as a hymn-tune composer has reached its heights with more familiar and renowned melodies, such as "Sabbath," "Missionary Hymn," and "Boylston," but the merit of "Wesley" as a hymn tune is unquestionable.

---

392   HYMN: Thou, Whose Almighty Word
TUNE: Fiat Lux

Author: *Rev. John Marriott*   Composer: *Rev. John B. Dykes*

AUTHOR: Rev. John Marriott was born in 1780 at Cottesbach, near Lutterworth, England, famous in history as the place of John Wycliffe's death. After studying at Rugby he entered Christ Church College at Oxford, from which he graduated in 1802. The following year he was ordained a minister of the Church of England. For many years he was associated as tutor and chaplain with the family of the duke of Buccleuch, who presented him with the living at Church Lawford, Warwickshire. Due to ill health, however, he moved to the more genial climate of Devonshire, where he was finally settled as curate at Broadclyst. He died there in 1825. He was a friend of Sir Walter Scott, who dedicated to him the second canto of "Marmion."

HYMN: The sons of John Marriott, who published a volume of their father's sermons in 1838, indicate that this hymn was written about 1813. It was printed anonymously after his death in The Friendly Visitor in July, 1825, under the title, "Missionary Hymn." A few of his hymns appeared in his lifetime, without his permission. This is the only hymn that has been widely used, but to have written such glorious lines as these is sufficient to keep a man's memory alive in the Church. The first stanza is addressed to God the Creator, the second to

Christ the Redeemer, and the third to the Spirit of truth and love, closing with the ascription to the Trinity. This hymn by John Marriott unites the praise of the Trinity with the universal spread of the gospel.

COMPOSER: For comments on the composer, John B. Dykes, see Hymn 53.

TUNE: The tune, "Fiat Lux," first appeared in "Hymns Ancient and Modern," Enlarged Edition, in 1875. It was composed for the hymn with which it is united here. It is most effective if sung in a full, fervent tone. It is more than slightly suggestive of the tune used for "God Save the King" and "My Country, 'T is of Thee," and has many of the fine qualities of that melody.

Stewardship

*

393 HYMN: Son of God, Eternal Saviour
TUNE: In Babilone

Author: *Somerset Corry Lowry*   Source: *Dutch Traditional Melody*

AUTHOR: Somerset Corry Lowry was born in Dublin, Ireland, in 1855. He received his education at Repton and Trinity Hall, Cambridge, being ordained to the ministry of the Church of England in 1879. He was the vicar of North Holmwood; St. Augustine's, Bournemouth; Wonston; and St. Bartholomew's, Southsea. He published several devotional books and a collection of "Hymns and Spiritual Songs." He died in 1932.

HYMN: This is one of seven hymns of the author which are mentioned by Julian as being in contemporary hymnals. In 1898 Lowry wrote for Queen Victoria's annual service in memory of the prince consort the hymn, "O Saviour, Once Again the Ebbing Year." The hymn, "Son of God, Eternal Saviour," was written in 1893 and appeared in the magazine Goodwill in February, 1894. It was included in the 1904 edition of "Hymns Ancient and Modern." There is here a stateliness in diction that is attractive, and a beautiful simplicity and directness set the hymn apart as an outstanding hymn of stewardship.

SOURCE: The source is a Dutch traditional melody.

TUNE: For comments on the tune, "In Babilone," see Hymn 93.

The Kingdom of God on Earth

394
HYMN: We Give Thee But Thine Own
TUNE: Schumann

Author: *Bishop W. Walsham How* Source: *Mason and Webb's "Cantica Laudis"*

AUTHOR: For comments on the author, W. Walsham How, see Hymn 137.

HYMN: In Prov. 19: 17 is found the line, "He that hath pity upon the poor lendeth unto Jehovah," which underlies the thought of this hymn:

> "Whate'er for thine we do, O Lord,
> We do it unto Thee."

But certainly the author had in mind also Jesus' words about the cup of cold water in his name. This hymn may be appropriately used by the minister as a prayer in connection with the taking of the offering, or may be sung by the congregation or choir in dedication of the offering. It is among the most familiar and best-loved of How's many hymns. In the closing year of Bishop How's life he was chosen to write a national hymn for the British Empire's observance of Queen Victoria's Jubilee in 1897.

SOURCE: For comments on the source, Mason and Webb's "Cantica Laudis," see Hymn 362.

TUNE: For comments on the tune, "Schumann," see Hymn 362.

395
HYMN: O My Father, I Would Know Thee
TUNE: St. Helen's

Author: *Harriet Osgood Munger* Composer: *Robert Prescott Stewart*

AUTHOR: Harriet King Osgood Munger was born in Salem, Massachusetts, on March 14, 1857. She was educated in the private schools in Salem and entered Wellesley College in the first year of its founding. Owing to ill health she was unable to continue her course, and turned to the study of art. Several years of training abroad followed her courses at the Boston Museum of Fine Arts School. In the early eighties she became a teacher in the Burnham School for Girls, at Northampton, Massachusetts. In 1889 she was married to Theodore T. Munger,

Handbook to The Hymnal

D.D., the famous pastor of the United Church of New Haven, Connecticut. From that time she was indefatigable in the work of the parish as well as of her home. She organized the Pleasant Sunday Afternoon Class, held at an hour of the day when mothers were free. She took the lead in starting the New Haven Nurses' Association. After the death of her husband in 1910 she returned to her old home at Salem, where she continued to live a highly useful life until her death in 1925.

HYMN: Doubtless this hymn, which appeared first in the calendar of the Mungers' church on October 7, 1894, was written during the author's life in the manse at New Haven. She was frequently a contributor to The Congregationalist. The second stanza of the hymn,

> "I would turn my highest powers
> Into service sweet;
> For all my ministry to others
> Make me meet,"

is beautifully illustrated by her own later years. Late in life she took lessons in *Braille* and attained such a high degree of skill that she won high praise from the national *Braille* headquarters. For five years she spent two to three hours a day in this work, sending several completed books to Washington.

COMPOSER: Robert Prescott Stewart, Mus.D., was born in Dublin, Ireland, on December 16, 1825. He was educated as a chorister of Christ Church Cathedral, and became organist there in 1844. In the same year he was appointed organist of Trinity College, Dublin. From this time on his promotions were many and rapid. He became conductor of the Dublin University Choral Society in 1846, professor of music in Dublin University in 1861, and conductor of the Dublin Philharmonic. He was honored with a musical doctorate in 1844, at which time the Choral Society presented him with his graduate robes and a jeweled baton. He was a prolific writer and composer, and in recognition of his work was knighted in 1872. "The Irish Church Hymnal," published in 1876, which he edited, is a fitting memorial of his devotion to the cause of worship. Crowned with honors, he died in Dublin on March 24, 1894.

TUNE: "St. Helen's" was composed for "Art Thou Weary, Art Thou Languid," and in connection with that hymn appeared in "The Irish Church Hymnal." This fact explains the confident and comforting mood of the music. For a tune of small compass it is a work of art. The hymn calls for fine shading and should be sung prayerfully and in moderate time. It is of interest to note that the tune is also associated with "I Am Trusting Thee, Lord Jesus."

The Kingdom of God on Earth

396   HYMN: Saviour! Thy Dying Love
                TUNE: Something for Jesus

Author: *Rev. Sylvanus D. Phelps*   Composer: *Rev. Robert Lowry*

AUTHOR: Rev. Sylvanus Dryden Phelps was born at Suffield, Connecticut, May 15, 1816, and graduated from Brown University in 1844. Ten years later he became pastor of the First Baptist Church at Hartford, where he remained for twenty-eight years. He became editor of the Christian Secretary, published in Hartford, and was the author of several volumes of poems, including hymns. This one hymn alone is in popular use.

HYMN: These words of sincere devotion might not have been preserved had they not had the good fortune to be wedded to the tune to which they are always sung. Robert Lowry, gathering hymns for a Sunday School songbook under the title, "Pure Gold," met Mr. Phelps one day and asked for a contribution. These lines, which had been printed in the Watchman and Reflector ten years before, were given to Lowry, and upon appearing they became immediately popular. On Dr. Phelps's seventieth birthday Dr. Lowry, the composer of the tune, sent a note of congratulation to him which read as follows: "It is worth seventy years even if nothing comes of it but one such song, which the world will keep on singing after its author shall have passed away." This hymn is now found in practically all hymnals and collections of gospel songs.

COMPOSER: For comments on the composer, Robert Lowry, see Hymn 332.

TUNE: "Something for Jesus" was composed in 1872. At that time Rev. Robert Lowry was pastor of a Baptist church in Lewisburg, Pennsylvania, and professor of literature in Bucknell University. It has always been associated with "Saviour! Thy Dying Love," by Rev. Sylvanus D. Phelps, written in 1862. It appeared in "Gospel Hymns, No. 1," published in 1875. Of the tune Dr. Phelps was accustomed to speak gratefully as follows: "Dr. Lowry has given wings to my hymn."

397 HYMN: I Thánk Thee, Lord, for Strength of Arm
TUNE: O Jesu

Author: *Rev. Robert Davis*   Source: *"Hirschberg Gesangbuch"*

AUTHOR: The author, Rev. Robert Davis, is a child of the manse. He was born at Beverly, Massachusetts, July 29, 1881, the son of Rev. William H. and Emma Meacham Davis. He received his Bachelor's degree from Dartmouth in 1903, spent the next year in graduate study at Harvard, and returned to his *Alma Mater* to teach in the English Department for one year. The next three years he spent at Union Theological Seminary, taking at the same time his Master's degree from Columbia. From 1910 to 1917 he was pastor of the Englewood Presbyterian Church, in Englewood, New Jersey. When the war broke out he went overseas with the Red Cross, and since 1920 has been living in Margaux, France.

HYMN: Just as the first half of the nineteenth century brought forth most of the great missionary hymns, so the first half of this century is seeing the birth of many hymns touched with the social spirit of the gospel. It is interesting to note that these beautiful verses were written when the author was an assistant pastor of the Brick Presbyterian Church, New York City. They are typical of the best idealism of the young men and women of the day—appreciative of the blessings they enjoy but deeply intent to share them with others.

SOURCE: The source is a melody in "Hirschberg Gesangbuch." For comments on German hymnody see the article, "German Hymn Sources," under "Original Sources," page xxi.

TUNE: For comments on the tune, "O Jesu," see Hymn 79.

---

398 HYMN: O Lord of Heaven and Earth and Sea
TUNE: Almsgiving

Author: *Bishop Christopher Wordsworth*   Composer: *Rev. John B. Dykes*

AUTHOR: For comments on the author, Christopher Wordsworth, see Hymn 18.

HYMN: Bishop Wordsworth wrote this hymn while he was at Westminster. That part of his work which commands the highest interest of the hymnologists is "The Holy Year," a collec-

The Kingdom of God on Earth

tion of hymns for every season of the church year. Though he was a great scholar, Bishop Wordsworth's hymns are noted for their simplicity. Canon Ellerton declared that this hymn is "not in the least poetical, full of halting verses and prosaic lines, and yet of such true praise, so genuine, so comprehensive, so heartfelt, that we forget its homeliness."

COMPOSER: For comments on the composer, John B. Dykes, see Hymn 53.

TUNE: "Almsgiving," by John B. Dykes, A.M., Mus.D., is a widely used tune. While it was composed for "O Lord of Heaven and Earth and Sea," it has been associated with various texts. The pattern of the tune is simple and the melody suggests a meditative mood.

---

399   HYMN: Lord, Speak to Me, That I May Speak
TUNE: Canonbury

Author: *Frances R. Havergal*   Composer: *Robert Schumann*

AUTHOR: For comments on the author, Frances R. Havergal, see Hymn 56.

HYMN: No hymn of consecration is more widely sung than this. It accurately bespeaks the character of the author. All her life was consecrated to God. Speaking of the day in 1853 when she was confirmed in the Worcester Cathedral, she wrote, "I committed my soul to the Saviour, and earth and heaven seemed bright from that moment." She named this hymn "A Worker's Prayer," and connected it with Rom. 14:7: "For none of us liveth to himself." Some one has noted that the hymn is a study in verbs—speak, lead, feel, strengthen, teach, fill, tell, show. Although the first person is used often, none of the blessings sought are selfish. This hymn is sung at commencement each year by the graduating class of the Chicago Presbyterian Seminary. From the seven volumes of Miss Havergal's poetry there are many hymns that will live in all the hymnals. Eleven of them are presented in this volume.

Miss Fanny Crosby, who has always had a large place in every book of gospel hymns, treasured the lines written to her by Miss Havergal:

> "Dear blind sister over the sea
> An English heart goes out to thee;
> We are linked by a cable of faith and song
> Flashing bright sympathy swiftly along."

COMPOSER: For comments on the composer, Robert Schumann, see Hymn 78.

TUNE: "Canonbury" is an arrangement from Robert Schumann's "Nachtstück," Opus 23, No. 4. Schumann has been called a singing nightingale. The melodic quality of his hymns is evidently responsible for the characterization. This tune is a happy combination of beauty and solidity. At the time the "Nachtstück" appeared Schumann was at his best. Writing of his experiences on March 15, 1839, he said: "I used to rack my brains for a long time, but now I scarcely ever scratch a note. It all comes from within, and I often feel as if I could go playing straight on without ever coming to an end."

Brotherhood

*

400 HYMN: The Light of God Is Falling
TUNE: Greenland

Author: *Rev. Louis F. Benson*   Composer: *J. Michael Haydn*

AUTHOR: For comments on the author, Louis F. Benson, see Hymn 29.

HYMN: This is one of Dr. Benson's noblest hymns. It reflects not only deep love for Christ but sincere love for his fellow men. The rhythm is stately and melodious, carrying both dignity and cheerfulness. The major theme is that Christ is in the common things of life and every humble duty is transformed by the light of his divine presence. Psalms 1 and 15, the Sermon on the Mount, and many passages from the prophets and from the New Testament describe the man pictured in the second stanza. Six characteristics are given of the man who "dwells in God's own country." All are positive and constructive, being fruits of the tree of righteousness. The author emphasizes generosity, honesty, helpfulness, loyalty to right and truth, as supreme qualities of the citizen of the Kingdom. One who is fruitful in these good things is a colaborer with God and "tills the Holy Land." Such a follower of the Master has a deep concern for the crowds "in toil and pain and sin." As they find each other in the Elder Brother, they will share in the coming of the Kingdom.

The Kingdom of God on Earth

In the last stanza the host of the redeemed in glory unite their prayers with the living, pointing to the cross and to Him who ever leads his people on, in whom alone we find true brotherhood.

COMPOSER: For comments on the composer, J. Michael Haydn, see Hymn 198.

TUNE: "Greenland" is an arrangement from J. Michael Haydn, a younger brother of the great Franz Joseph. It first appeared in B. Jacob's "National Psalmody," which was published in England in 1819. Jacob was organist of the famous Surrey Chapel, London, whose pastor, Rowland Hill, popularized hymn-singing. In this he was supported by his organist, who collected popular melodies and arranged them for use in public worship. This is a stirring tune and has a climactic close.

401

HYMN: Rise Up, O Men of God
TUNE: Festal Song

Author: *Rev. William Pierson Merrill* Composer: *William H. Walter*

AUTHOR: For comments on the author, William Pierson Merrill, see Hymn 250.

HYMN: This hymn is a simple, direct, rugged challenge to men. It bids them stand firm in the faith and be strong as loyal soldiers of the King. The spirit of the hymn opposes mere pious sentiment, mere outward profession, mere lip service, mere social "good times" in the name of religion as offering any kind of substitute for reality.

> "Have done with lesser things;
> Give heart and soul and mind and strength
> To serve the King of kings."

Not in their own strength, however, but under the uplifted cross of Christ, following in his steps, must Christian men do their part to "bring in the day of brotherhood and end the night of wrong."

COMPOSER: William Henry Walter, an American composer, was born in Newark, New Jersey, in 1825 and died in 1893. In that city he served as organist in one of the Episcopal churches. From there he was called to an Episcopal church in New York City. His professional skill attracted the attention of Columbia University, where he became the organist of the college in 1856. Later he was honored with the doctorate in music by the institution he served so acceptably.

TUNE: "Festal Song" is a spirited tune. It opens with a unison phrase that moves forward in stately and virile part singing. It supplies the challenging hymn, "Rise Up, O Men of God," with a forceful and active musical setting. The tune was first published a year after the composer's death. It appeared in the revised and enlarged edition of the Episcopal Hymnal, published in 1894, and in subsequent hymnals of that denomination, including the new Hymnal.

---

402 HYMN: Let There Be Light, Lord God of Hosts
TUNE: Pentecost

Author: *William M. Vories*   Composer: *Rev. William Boyd*

AUTHOR: The author, William M. Vories, is a lyric voice of our own day. While he is but little known he speaks as a man of deep and genuine religious feelings and high aspirations. He pours out his heart in passionate supplication for the true peace born of mutual Christian love in the heart of man.

HYMN: This hymn appropriately enough is copyrighted in the name of the American Peace Society. It voices the prayer of a suffering world drenched with the blood of men and chilled with the fear of war. Our youth, challenging the futility of war, is singing hymns like this in testimony of dedication to the discipline of peace. It seeks light first for each heart: "Make us Thy ministers of life." Then it recognizes the call to brotherhood, to "rejoice with them that rejoice" and "weep with them that weep." The hymn is a prayer for the perfect love that "casteth out fear." The Church needs to pray with great humility and earnestness the words with which the hymn closes, "God, give Thy wayward children peace!"

COMPOSER: For comments on the composer, William Boyd, see Hymn 270.

TUNE: "Pentecost" is a tune of simple structure, yet a thrilling bugle call to action. It was composed in 1864 by Rev. William Boyd for the hymn, "Veni Creator." Its first appearance was in "Thirty-Two Hymn Tunes, Composed by Members of the University of Oxford," published in 1868. In 1874 it was set to Dr. John S. B. Monsell's well-known hymn, "Fight the Good Fight with All Thy Might." The tune lends itself to a spirited and dignified rendition.

The Kingdom of God on Earth

403   HYMN: O Brother Man, Fold to Thy Heart Thy Brother
         TUNE: Welwyn

Author: *John Greenleaf Whittier*   Composer: *Alfred Scott-Gatty*

AUTHOR: For comments on the author, John Greenleaf Whittier, see Hymn 178.

HYMN: The hymn is an impassioned plea for brotherliness and human kindness. It embodies the spirit of the words, "Let us not love in word, neither with the tongue; but in deed and truth," I John 3: 18. See also John 13: 35; 15: 12; James 1: 27. These passages are reflected in the various stanzas. Stanza 2 tenderly refers to John as "he whom Jesus loved" while stanza 3 has a beautiful reference to Jesus "who went about doing good," Acts 10: 38. Stanza 4 is prophetic, not only of the liberation of the slave but of the bursting of the fetters of fear, ignorance, superstition, hatred, and war. Over all these things Christian love will finally triumph. This is one of six of Whittier's hymns in "The Hymnal."

COMPOSER: For comments on the composer, Alfred Scott-Gatty, see Hymn 110.

TUNE: For comments on the tune, "Welwyn," see Hymn 110.

---

404   HYMN: Come, Kingdom of Our God
         TUNE: Garden City

Author: *Rev. John Johns*   Composer: *Horatio W. Parker*

AUTHOR: Rev. John Johns was born at Plymouth, England, on March 17, 1801. He entered the Presbyterian Church and served for many years in Liverpool as "minister to the poor," where he gave himself in loyal devotion to the service of the humble and needy. He fell a victim to the fever that was raging in the district where he labored, and died on June 23, 1847. He was a man of fine poetic gifts. He published three volumes of poems but his memory is best cherished because of the offering of his heart and life in the service of the Master among the poor.

HYMN: The hymn is a prayer for the coming of the Kingdom of God on earth. Each stanza prays in marked sequence for the virtues and graces, for all life and for all tribes and nations, that are to mark the achievement of God's Kingdom on earth. The hymn is a simple and sincere expression of prayerful desire for the fulfillment of

The Lord's Prayer: "Thy kingdom come. Thy will be done." It is the more impressive since the life of the author was spent in humble effort to help to answer this prayer in his own field of labor.

COMPOSER: For comments on the composer, Horatio W. Parker, see Hymn 19.

TUNE: "Garden City" was written by a man who was greatly interested in the development of worshipful congregational singing. To that end he opposed the sentimental type of tune which has been encouraged by many publishers. Dr. Parker's tunes are all of a stately, virile order, leading some to feel that they are for the choir rather than the pew. Experience proves the contrary. "Garden City" is one of his most popular tunes. It was composed in 1890 and, set to the words, "Come, Kingdom of Our God," appeared in the Episcopal Hymnal of 1895. Dr. Parker ranks as one of America's greatest teachers and composers.

---

405 HYMN: Lift Up Our Hearts, O King of Kings
TUNE: Truro

Author: *Rev. John Howard Masterman*   Source: *T. Williams*
"Psalmodia Evangelica"

AUTHOR: John Howard Masterman, D.D., Bishop of Plymouth, England, since 1923, was born in 1867. After graduating from St. John's College, Cambridge, Bishop Masterman served the Church and the academic world with great distinction. He has had a useful career as clergyman, educator, lecturer, and author.

HYMN: This hymn is a prayer for the uplifted heart, for the "brighter hopes and kindlier things," for the open vision of a better world to come, for "holier dreams of brotherhood." Stanza 2 is a confession of human failure, and stanza 3 is a humble prayer for God's gift of a purer and a nobler life. It is a hymn expressing tenderly the deep longing of a sympathetic heart for the rule of the good and holy will of God over the troublesome affairs of men. Such a hymn fits the needs of our modern age.

SOURCE: The source is T. Williams' "Psalmodia Evangelica."

TUNE: For comments on the tune, "Truro," see Hymn 114.

The Kingdom of God on Earth

406   HYMN: Eternal Ruler of the Ceaseless Round
          TUNE: Unde et Memores

Author: *Rev. John W. Chadwick*   Composer: *William H. Monk*

AUTHOR: Rev. John White Chadwick, author and poet, was born at Marblehead, Massachusetts, in October, 1840. His forbears were fisher folk, while his own father belonged to the high seas. Naturally Chadwick felt near to these humble folk of the sea. His vigorous character, breezy manner, and frank and open countenance made him a part of the seafaring group. He began life as an apprentice to a shoemaker. Yearning for something different, he entered the State Normal School at Bridgewater, later Phillips Exeter Academy, and finally Harvard Divinity School, from which he graduated in 1864. He was called to a pulpit in Brooklyn, New York, which he occupied all his life. He died in 1904.

A certain mysticism is seen in his poetry, of which he published four volumes. He was a great lover of literature and wrote on various subjects. He was a man of strong conviction and of ardent desire for unity in all that breaks down wrong and builds up right. This hymn is a splendid reflection of his character.

HYMN: This hymn was written on June 19, 1864, for the senior class at Harvard Divinity School, Cambridge, Massachusetts, of which Chadwick was a member. It was written at the darkest hour in our nation's life, and called for peace and good will while the civil strife and sectional hate were splitting wide the North and South. Adoration of God the Father precedes a strong emphasis of human brotherhood. A mystic longing for oneness in him and with one another pulses through every line of the hymn. This is one of the worthiest of hymns dealing with the grace of brotherhood.

COMPOSER: For comments on the composer, William H. Monk, see Hymn 33.

TUNE: For comments on the tune, "Unde et Memores," see Hymn 355.

---

407   HYMN: Master, No Offering
          TUNE: Love's Offering

Author: *Rev. Edwin P. Parker*   Composer: *Rev. Edwin P. Parker*

AUTHOR: Rev. Edwin P. Parker was born in Castine, Maine, January 13, 1836. He graduated from Bowdoin College and from Bangor Theological Seminary, becoming pastor of a Congregational church in Hartford, Connecticut. He cherished a keen interest in Christian hymnology and edited various collections of hymns. This is his only hymn in our collection. He died in 1925.

HYMN: This hymn was born out of the daily pastoral experience of the author. It was written to be read at the close of a Sunday sermon when, as is often the case, the lofty aspirations of the hour seem to call for a release through poetry rather than through prose. The hymn was first published in 1889 in "The Christian Hymnal." The author provided the tune as well as the text. A fine, tender sentiment of spiritual fellowship saturates the hymn. It breathes a deep devotion to God, out of which comes sincere love for man. The last line of each stanza registers the hymn's final sequence of resignation and devotion.

COMPOSER: For comments on the composer, Edwin P. Parker, see "Author."

TUNE: "Love's Offering" was composed by Rev. Edwin P. Parker for his own words in 1888. At the time he was pastor of the Second Congregational Church of Hartford, Connecticut. At his own request he also had charge of the music of his church. He composed for his choir many tunes and arrangements of classic themes.

The City

*

408   HYMN: The Fathers Built This City
            TUNE: Patmos

Author: *Rev. William George Tarrant*   Composer: *Henry J. Storer*

AUTHOR: Rev. William George Tarrant is another of the surprisingly large number of pastor musicians whose musical ability and interest went hand in hand with their parish programs. He was born in England in 1853 and became pastor of the Wandsworth Unitarian Christian Church. His literary ability was indicated by his editorship of The Inquirer from 1888 to 1897. He was highly esteemed as a hymnologist of sound judgment and was one of the editors of "The Essex Hall Hymnal," published in 1890 and revised in 1902.

HYMN: This most unusual hymn has the city as its theme of prayer and praise. It is a striking challenge to city builders and dwellers. It turns from the usual wail of pessimism and distrust of those who see the city as the plague spot of civilization and sounds the

The Kingdom of God on Earth

note of gratitude, hope, and obligation in the presence of the modern city. The city as a by-product of our gregarious humanity represents both the best and the worst in our civilization. With all its amazing power for good and evil the city must be taken for God! Boston, New York, Philadelphia, Chicago, and San Francisco are supreme opportunities for everything noble and good in collective humanity, if the children of the fathers who laid the foundations of these cities will make vital and effective the principles of Christian faith and its saving program amidst the "hive of toiling men." The hymn is admirably adapted for use in religious or patriotic meetings.

COMPOSER: Henry J. Storer, born in 1860, is an American organist and composer. During his professional career he resided at Albany, New York, and in Cambridge and Belmont, Massachusetts. As a teacher of harmony, counterpoint, and composition he had a large clientele in Boston and vicinity. For years he was associated with The Musician, published by Oliver Ditson Company, Boston, as reader and critic. Though he has written numerous organ numbers, songs, and anthems, he is best remembered by his tunes, of which he has more than twenty in various hymnals.

TUNE: "Patmos" was composed in 1891 and first printed in "The Church Hymnal" in 1894. In that book also appeared three other tunes by Mr. Storer, none of which, however, is so well-known as this. Both the Methodist Hymnal, published in 1905, and the Presbyterian Hymnal, published in 1911, include it.

---

409   HYMN: O Holy City Seen of John
TUNE: Morwellham

Author: *Rev. W. Russell Bowie*   Composer: *Charles Steggall*

AUTHOR: Rev. Walter Russell Bowie is the rector of Grace Episcopal Church, New York City. He was born in Richmond, Virginia, in 1882, graduating from Harvard University and the Episcopal theological seminary at Alexandria. His ministry is marked by the sympathy and breadth of his churchmanship and his courage in confronting social and industrial situations with the uncomprising standards of the Christian religion. His authorship has been widely recognized, particularly through his "The Children's Year," "The Master of the Hill," "The Inescapable Christ," "When Jesus Was Born," as well as other books. His poems are few but effective.

423

Handbook to The Hymnal

HYMN: The hymn is a visualization of the Holy City, the builder and maker of which is God, in contrast to the previous hymn, which deals with the city built by the fathers. The Holy City seen by the seer on Patmos, Rev., ch. 22, is here visualized in its beauty and holiness over against the shame of man-made cities, with their lust, suffering, and despair. That we may have grace to build the City of God here on earth is the prayer of the third stanza. The last stanza gives us assurance that this City not only is in the mind of God but will come to glorious realization on earth. The undaunted faith of the hymn is an assurance of the final realization of this hope.

COMPOSER: Charles Steggall, Mus.D., is said to have trained more organists than any other teacher in England. He was born in London, June 3, 1826. His musical education was received at the Royal Academy of Music, where he studied under the distinguished Sterndale Bennett. As an organist he served Christ Church, Maida Hill; Christ Church, Lancaster Gate; and Lincoln's Inn Chapel. For half a century he was the chief professor of the organ at the Royal Academy of Music, a position which he held from 1851 to 1903, when he resigned. The return to Bach, a movement that continues to this day, had his cordial support. His lifelong interest in church music expressed itself in anthems and hymn tunes, and in editorial work. He succeeded William H. Monk as musical editor of "Hymns Ancient and Modern," proofs of which he was reading at the time of his death. He died in London, June 7, 1905.

TUNE: "Morwellham" is an exultant tune and a most fitting setting for Dr. Bowie's fine text, "O Holy City Seen of John." It appeared in the third edition of "The Hymnal Companion" published in 1890. In that volume it was associated with Anna L. Waring's hymn, "Father, I Know That All My Life." The tune is new to America. In "The Hymnary" of the United Church of Canada, "Morwellham" is used three times.

---

410   HYMN: Where Cross the Crowded Ways of Life
         TUNE: Germany

Author: *Rev. Frank Mason North*   Source: *William Gardiner's "Sacred Melodies"*

AUTHOR: Frank Mason North, D.D., LL.D., was born in New York City, November 3, 1850. He graduated from Wesleyan University in 1872, and was ordained to the ministry of the Methodist Church. He served as editor of The Christian City and was deeply interested in the work of city missions. This is a city mission hymn in the

The Kingdom of God on Earth

best sense. It reflects the author's warm interest in the work of missions, for Dr. North served not only as secretary of city missionary work of the Methodist Episcopal Church in New York, but from this service he entered the secretaryship of foreign missions of his Church.

HYMN: This hymn was written upon the urgent request of Professor Caleb T. Winchester, of Wesleyan University, who was then engaged in the preparation of the Methodist Hymnal. Meeting Dr. North in 1902, the professor urged him to write a missionary hymn for the new book. Dr. North had recently preached on the text, "Go ye therefore unto . . . the highways," Matt. 22:9. In his sermon he had presented the appealing challenge of the crowds of people thronging open squares and streets in New York and in European cities. With yearning heart he had watched the people come and go. Thus the first line was suggested, "Where cross the crowded ways of life." Christ returning from the Mount of Transfiguration and healing the young man suggested the lines:

> "O Master, from the mountain side,
> Make haste to heal these hearts of pain."

The hymn was first published in 1903 and quickly found its way into many standard hymnals.

SOURCE: The source is William Gardiner's "Sacred Melodies." William Gardiner was born at Leicester, England, March 15, 1770. Though he became an assistant to his father, who was a stocking manufacturer, he was always a musician at heart. In his youth he composed songs and duets, which were published under the *nom de plume* of W. G. Leicester. Later he developed a great interest in the compositions of the best foreign composers, especially those of Germany. Under the title "Sacred Melodies," of which he published six volumes, he introduced to England many sacred lyrics which have since been arranged into useful hymns. Among his books are the following: "The Music of Nature," published in 1832; "Music and Friends," published in 1838; and "Sights in Italy," published in 1847. He died at Leicester on November 11, 1853, at the fine old age of eighty-four.

TUNE: "Germany," known in England as "Walton," is from Gardiner's "Sacred Melodies." The volume attributes it to Beethoven. The original, however, has not yet been identified. Even Gardiner admitted that he could not point out where he found it.

The Nation

*

411

HYMN: O Beautiful for Spacious Skies
TUNE: Materna

Author: *Katharine Lee Bates*   Composer: *Samuel A. Ward*

AUTHOR: Katharine Lee Bates, a professor of English literature at Wellesley College, who died in 1929, is the author of this beautiful hymn. Karl Price, in "One Hundred and One Hymn Stories," tells us she wrote it in 1893 while on a western trip in which she visited the World's Columbian Exposition in Chicago. "The patriotic impressions made upon her mind by the wonderful White City she bore westward with her as she journeyed to Colorado; and when at last she stood on the summit of Pike's Peak and beheld the far-spreading panorama below and the spacious skies above, her soul was stirred by the thought of the greatness and the God-given destiny of America. These lines were set ringing in her heart, and into a noble poem she has woven the beauties of that mountain-top vision."

HYMN: This is not only one of the most popular but also one of the most beautiful of our patriotic hymns. It is patriotism at its best. In beautiful language the greatness, riches, and beauty of our country are thankfully recounted. The first half of every stanza lends itself to such recounting, while the second half offers prayer for its purity, and God's continued grace. The last stanza gives an exalted picture of the realization of the dream of the patriots and of that nobler, freer, and more brotherly America for which every true patriot longs and prays. With the repetition of the prayer of the first stanza the hymn comes to a tender and impressive close.

COMPOSER: Samuel A. Ward, who is remembered by his tune, "Materna," was born in Newark, New Jersey, December 28, 1847. In that city he built up a lucrative business, selling pianos, organs, and musical supplies. His store continued for more than twenty-five years and was the center for music lovers, exerting great influence in fostering the musical life of Newark. Mr. Ward was director of the Orpheus Club for fourteen years. He died in Newark, September 28, 1903.

TUNE: "Materna," now associated with different texts, was originally written for "O Mother Dear, Jerusalem." As such it appeared in the Episcopal Hymnal which was published in 1892. Three years later the same setting was preserved in "The Hymnal," pub-

The Kingdom of God on Earth

lished by the Presbyterian Church in 1895, and in "The Hymnal," Revised, published in 1911. During the World War the tune became associated with Miss Bates's hymn and, in spite of the fact that other tunes have been composed for it, seems to retain popular approval. On a post card mailed under date of January 17, 1895, and addressed to Louis F. Benson, D.D., Mr. Ward states that the tune was composed in 1882.

4I2
    HYMN: My Country, 'Tis of Thee
    TUNE: America

Author: *Rev. Samuel F. Smith*   Source: *"Thesaurus Musicus"*

AUTHOR: For comments on the author, Samuel F. Smith, see Hymn 389.

HYMN: One writer says of Samuel F. Smith that "he is at once the most patriotic and the most cosmopolitan of hymn writers." It may also be said of this hymn that it is at once the most devotedly patriotic and the most universally beloved of our patriotic songs. It has carried the nation through the Civil War, the Spanish-American conflict, and the terrible years of the World War. In our public schools it has been one of the powerful factors in unifying the minds and hearts of the children of our varying racial and linguistic groups and binding them together in a common love for our country and its ideals. Simple, dignified, direct, it is obvious why it has become the song of the people.

SOURCE: The source of the tune, "America," is the "Thesaurus Musicus."

TUNE: The tune, "America," the British "National Anthem," is of obscure origin. The melody, or similar melodies, have been known in England for several centuries. "Much time and pains," writes Dr. Benson, "have been spent in investigating the matter, but these questions still remain unanswered." It has been claimed for Henry Carey, but the claim cannot be established. He is supposed to have sung it as early as 1740, but neither the "Thesaurus Musicus" of 1740 nor The Gentlemen's Magazine of 1745 gives him credit. With some measure of support it has been maintained that "it was written for the Catholic Chapel of James II." While there is doubt about the origin of the tune, it is gratifying to know that Great Britain and America are one in spirit when they sing it.

HYMN: God Bless Our Native Land
TUNE: Dort

Authors: (Stanzas 1 and 2) *Siegfried A. Mahlmann*   Composer:
          (Stanza 3) *William E. Hickson*   *Lowell Mason*

AUTHORS: Siegfried A. Mahlmann seems to have been the original author of the sentiments of this hymn as it appeared in England and America. He wrote it in German as a patriotic hymn for Saxony sometime before his death in 1826.

William Edward Hickson, one of the authors of this hymn, was born in London and became a bootmaker in Smithfield, England. Retiring from business, he gave himself to a life of writing and philanthropy and did much to promote popular interest in singing. He was a friend of popular education and worked to improve conditions of labor in industry. He issued several song manuals and other books dealing with the history of music. He died at Sevenoaks, Kent, in 1870.

HYMN: As to the origin of this popular hymn there has been no little controversy. It has been ascribed to Rev. C. T. Brooks, who is said to have translated it from the German about 1832, while he was a student of theology at Cambridge, Massachusetts. It has also been ascribed to Rev. J. S. Dwight, of Harvard University. However, the authorship of Siegfried A. Mahlmann seems finally to have been established, at least for the first two stanzas, while for the last stanza credit goes to William Edward Hickson, of England. Various versions of this hymn exist both in England and in America.

The hymn is an earnest prayer for God's care and blessing for our nation, which in stanza 3 is expanded to include all nations, that they may live together in true brotherhood and good will.

COMPOSER: For comments on the composer, Lowell Mason, see Hymn 18.

TUNE: "Dort," by Lowell Mason, while not a great tune, has so long been associated with the worship of the American people that it is destined to survive. Now more than a hundred years old, its simplicity and directness will perpetuate it. "Dort" was published in Dr. Mason's "Spiritual Songs" in 1832. Since its appearance in the Presbyterian Hymnal of 1874 it has been included in all subsequent hymnals of the denomination. In "The Hymnal" of 1895 it was used twice. It was included again in "The Hymnal," Revised, of 1911.

The Kingdom of God on Earth

414 HYMN: God of Our Fathers, Whose Almighty Hand
       TUNE: National Hymn

Author: *Rev. Daniel C. Roberts*   Composer: *George William Warren*

AUTHOR: Daniel C. Roberts, D.D., was born at Bridgehampton, Long Island, New York, on November 5, 1841. He graduated from Kenyon College in 1857, served as a private in the Civil War, and was ordained a clergyman of the Protestant Episcopal Church in 1866. He wrote this hymn in 1876 for the centennial Fourth of July celebration at Brandon, Vermont.

HYMN: This hymn was first included in the Protestant Episcopal Hymnal in 1892. It is a stately hymn, full of beauty and majesty, both in words and in music. It acknowledges God as the Creator of the universe and as the One who has led us as a nation, and prays that his protection and blessing may still abide with us and that our lives may be filled with "love and grace divine." It is a noble hymn, worthy of a great patriotic occasion, and rich and joyous if properly played, especially the trumpet accompaniment.

COMPOSER: For comments on the composer, George William Warren, see Hymn 153.

TUNE: For comments on the tune, "National Hymn," see Hymn 379.

---

415 HYMN: O Lord Our God, Thy Mighty Hand
       TUNE: America Befriend

Author: *Rev. Henry van Dyke*   Composer: *Rev. William Pierson Merrill*

AUTHOR: For comments on the author, Henry van Dyke, see Hymn 5.

HYMN: This is a noble hymn, full of poetic feeling, dignity, and strength. Stanza 1 acknowledges God as the giver of freedom and prays for further guidance. Stanza 2 prays for the country, for its various states, for its cities, and for the diverse races that here have found a home. Equality and justice form the burden of prayer of the third stanza, while the last stanza prays for all mankind, until Jesus shall reign in holiness "o'er hill and vale, from sea to sea." It is a patriotic hymn of a high order.

COMPOSER: For comments on the composer, William Pierson Merrill, see Hymn 250.

TUNE: "America Befriend" was composed by William P. Merrill, D.D., in 1912, at the request of Nolan R. Best, then editor of The Continent, who felt that Dr. Henry van Dyke's patriotic hymn, "O Lord Our God, Thy Mighty Hand," needed a tune of its own. Hymn and tune were printed in The Continent that same year. They were also included in "Songs of the Christian Life," compiled by Charles H. Richards, and published in New York City in 1912.

---

416 HYMN: Not Alone for Mighty Empire
TUNE: Hyfrydol

Author: *Rev. William Pierson Merrill* Composer: *Rowland Hugh Prichard*

AUTHOR: For comments on the author, William Pierson Merrill, see Hymn 250.

HYMN: This is a truly noble hymn born out of the spirit of the America of the early twentieth century, but in its essence applicable to every great nation. Not material things form the true cause of thanksgiving, but spiritual treasures and realities.

The Christian patriot is indeed proud of the mighty empire, the bounteous harvests, the victorious army and navy, the great past of our history. All these he appreciates with exalted gratitude, but far above and beyond these are the spiritual things, the real treasures which have made the nation great: the things unseen, the conquests of the spirit, the priceless gift of freedom, the home, the church, the school, the open door of opportunity to brave and free men. For the great army of faithful souls who have "passed and left no name," for the idealists who have inspired the nation and the patriots who have sacrificed for it, for the courageous voices, whether in pulpit or in press, that have been "loyal to the living Word"— for all these "heroes of the spirit" we should ever give devout thanks to God. The hymn closes with an uplifting prayer. There is danger of strife between race and creed, class and faction. Subsequent years have shown the reality of this danger felt by the author. We need "faith in simple manhood," and should pray earnestly with the Christian patriot, "God of justice, save Thy people."

The Kingdom of God on Earth

COMPOSER: For comments on the composer, Rowland Hugh Prichard, see Hymn 113.

TUNE: "Hyfrydol," which appears in simpler harmonization as Hymn 113, in this instance was arranged by one of the editors of "The English Hymnal," published in 1906. Very rich harmony and more vivid movement characterize this version. It is a vigorous Welsh tune and has the beauty and strength of the Welsh hills in it. Together with full organ it should be sung with dignity and nobility. The last two braces of music should have the benefit of a crescendo. It is a weighty, rugged tune, but smooth in movement.

---

417   HYMN: Judge Eternal, Throned in Splendor
        TUNE: Rhuddlan

Author: *Rev. Henry Scott Holland*   Source: *Welsh Traditional Melody*

AUTHOR: Henry Scott Holland, D.D., Litt.D., theologian and preacher, was born at Ledbury, Herefordshire, England, on January 27, 1847. He studied at Eton and at Balliol College, Oxford, and was appointed canon at St. Paul's, in 1884, on Gladstone's recommendation. His interest in social and economic problems was profound. He had a large share in the founding of the Christian Social Union and was editor of The Commonwealth from 1895 to 1912. In 1911 he was appointed *regius* professor of divinity at Oxford, where he was influential in raising the required intellectual and spiritual standards for the divinity degrees. In spite of many physical infirmities he was an untiring worker. The World War broke his spirit and undermined his health and on March 17, 1918, he died at Oxford. He was a great lover of music and while canon of St. Paul's greatly enriched its musical life. He wrote many books, among them a life of Jenny Lind.

HYMN: This is the only hymn, so far as is now known, that this gifted man wrote. It voices the two major themes of his life's thought and work—evangelism and social service. The hymn is a prayer for the nation, primarily for the British Empire, but so universal in its spirit that our nation also finds it suitable to its spiritual needs, especially in these days of crisis. The first stanza is general, calling upon the holy and eternal Judge to purge the realm of evil things, even if it be with the "living fire of judgment"—not with judgment alone, however, but also with solace and healing. The second stanza is particular and takes

431

Handbook to The Hymnal

up the burden of the oppressed and underprivileged, the teeming crowds of the great city as well as the lonely strugglers on the prairies and in the forests. The third stanza closes with the prayer that God's holy will may be done, that our darkness may be dispelled by the light from his Word, and that the entire national life may be cleansed and purified through the glory of the Lord.

SOURCE: The source is a Welsh traditional melody. See the article, "Welsh Hymnody," under "Original Sources," page xxii.

TUNE: "Rhuddlan" is an arrangement of a Welsh traditional melody known as "Dowch i'r Frwydr," "Come to Battle." This arrangement is from the well-known English hymnal, "Songs of Praise." It also appeared in "The English Hymnal," published in 1906. The tune is strong of beat and may be used effectively as a processional. It appeared in 1800 in Edward Jones's "Musical Relicks of the Welsh Bards."

---

418   HYMN: Braving the Wilds All Unexplored
             TUNE: Marcus Whitman

Author: *Rev. Robert Freeman*   Composer: *Rev. William Pierson Merrill*

AUTHOR: Robert Freeman, D.D., was born in Edinburgh, Scotland, on August 4, 1878. He received his early education in Edinburgh and came to the United States in 1896. He is a graduate of Allegheny College, Meadville, Pennsylvania, and of Princeton Seminary. The College of Wooster has conferred on him the degree of Doctor of Letters. He first served in Baptist churches in McKeesport, Pennsylvania, and Binghamton, New York. Later he became pastor of the Lafayette Avenue Presbyterian Church, Buffalo, New York, and since 1911 he has been pastor of Pasadena Presbyterian Church, Pasadena, California. He is president of the board of trustees of Occidental College, Los Angeles, director of San Francisco Theological Seminary, and was moderator of the Synod of California. He is the author of several books and many poems. Among his books are: "The Hour of Prayer," "The Land I Live In, and Other Verse," "New Every Morning," "What About the Twelve?"

HYMN: This is a worthy memorial to Marcus Whitman and those whom he represents, a sturdy hymn with martial air and heroic appeal. The voice of the pioneer speaking from these lines challenges. The words, written by the pastor of a great church on the Pacific Coast, and the tune, by the pastor of an equally great church on the

432

The Kingdom of God on Earth

Atlantic Coast, together strongly challenge the Church of America of to-day to be worthy of its great heritage.

COMPOSER: For comments on the composer, William Pierson Merrill, see Hymn 250.

TUNE: The tune, "Marcus Whitman," was written on request in 1927 by Dr. Merrill. "On a Friday," he states, "my wife telephoned from the house to my study at the church, telling me that Dr. John A. Marquis, secretary of the Board of National Missions, wanted me to write a tune for a new hymn written by Dr. Robert Freeman, of Pasadena, California, in celebration of the 125th anniversary of the founding of the Board. He said the tune was needed by the following Monday, three days off. I called Dr. Marquis and told him one could not thus write tunes on demand. He said he would send me the hymn anyhow. I received the hymn Saturday morning. Busy all that morning, I did not look at it until I was walking home at noon. At once it captivated me by its fine swing, rhythm, and highly religious tone. By the time I had reached my door, a walk of less than ten minutes from the church, the tune had formed itself in my mind, at least the main part of the melody. I recall that the last two lines came first. I worked at it that afternoon, mailed it to Dr. Marquis that night, and it was used at the celebration Monday morning."

419

HYMN: O God of Earth and Altar
TUNE: Llangloffan

Author: *Gilbert K. Chesterton*   Source: *Welsh Hymn Melody*

AUTHOR: Gilbert Keith Chesterton, one of England's foremost literary men, was born on May 29, 1874, in Kensington, and makes his home in Beaconsfield, near London. He is known throughout the English-speaking world as an author, journalist, pamphleteer, propagandist, and poet. He is a fearless critic of much that is modern in art and literature and is an ardent champion of the "merry old England" of a former day. In 1922 he entered the Roman Catholic Church. He has traveled and lectured in the United States. As the author of a large number of volumes he is always strongly individualistic and unconventional, interesting and provocative.

HYMN: Mr. Chesterton wrote this hymn in 1906 for "The English Hymnal." In its spirit of earnestness, solemn warning, and call to repentance, it reminds one strongly of Kipling's "Recessional" of 1897. Although "O God of Earth and Altar" was written with

433

Handbook to The Hymnal

British conditions in mind, it deals with human needs that are elemental and world-wide. Its appropriateness to modern American conditions is striking. The form and vocabulary of the hymn is as direct as the prayers of The Psalms. Its major promise is that God is the God not only of the altar and the temple, but of the earth also, and is concerned with the public and private sins of men and nations and with the problems of human welfare.

> "Our earthly rulers falter,
> Our people drift and die;
> The walls of gold entomb us,
> The swords of scorn divide."

These phrases in their vivid language are truly descriptive of the sins and shortcomings of modern states.

SOURCE: The source is a Welsh hymn melody from D. Evans' "Hymnau a Thonau." For comments on Welsh hymnody see the article, "Welsh Hymnody," under "Original Sources," page xxii.

TUNE: "Llangloffan" is a Welsh melody of wide use. It is a tune of great breadth and vigorous pulse, sincere and convincing in mood. The melody is clearly defined and readily sung. In 1865 it appeared in D. Evans' "Hymnau a Thonau." The tune is used three times in this Hymnal.

---

420 HYMN: God the Omnipotent! King, Who Ordainest
TUNE: Russian Hymn

Authors: *Henry F. Chorley*   Composer: *Alexis Lwoff*
Rev. John Ellerton

AUTHORS: For comments on the author, John Ellerton, see Hymn 20.
Henry F. Chorley was born on December 15, 1808, in Lancashire, England. Part of his education was received in Liverpool, where he made the acquaintance of Mrs. Hemans and other literary persons whose friendship he enjoyed. As a literary critic, he was of sound judgment, discriminating taste, manly independence, and utmost sincerity. Among his best friends was Charles Dickens, whom he greatly admired. He is described by a biographer as "upright, sincere, generous, and affectionate; irritable and opinionated, but essentially placable; an acute and courageous critic, a genuine if incomplete artist, a warm-hearted, honorable gentleman."

434

The Kingdom of God on Earth

HYMN: This is a free rendering of the famous Russian national hymn, of which various versions are extant in English. In August, 1870, during the Franco-Prussian War, Rev. John Ellerton wrote a paraphrase of it. It was first published in "Church Hymns" in 1871.

The hymn expresses deep reverence and adoration, even abject submission, reflecting the deeply religious spirit, coupled with the holy awe before majesty and power, so characteristic of the Russian people before the great revolution. It also voices the sorrow of a people longing for freedom and happiness, while expressing their consciousness of their own failings. The final stanza consists of a triumphant pæan of joyful exultation, prophetic of the day when all the people shall dwell together in peace and safety,

> "Singing in chorus from ocean to ocean
> Peace to the nations, and praise to the Lord."

The cry of the people for peace rises through words and music, making this one of the most touching of peace hymns.

COMPOSER: For comments on the composer, Alexis Lwoff, see Hymn 346.

TUNE: For comments on the tune, "Russian Hymn," see Hymn 346.

World Friendship and Peace

*

421   HYMN: O God of Love, O King of Peace
FIRST TUNE: Cannons

Author: *Rev. Henry W. Baker*   Composer: *George Frederick Handel*

AUTHOR: For comments on the author, Henry W. Baker, see Hymn 99.

HYMN: The hymn is a devout and earnest prayer for peace and world friendship, accompanied by humble confession of sin. Hope and trust can be lodged in none other than God, on whose faithful word we can ever rest. The prayer of the last stanza is that our hearts may be united in holy love and heavenly peace, as are the holy ones in heaven.

Handbook to The Hymnal

C OMPOSER (First Tune): For comments on the composer, George Frederick Handel, see Hymn 120.

T UNE (First): "Cannons" was originally used with Charles Wesley's hymn, "Sinners, Obey the Gospel Word." It is one of three hymns written by Handel for words by Wesley. "Cannons" is a challenging and commanding tune, and should be sung with marked rhythm. The pause at the end of the third line should be sustained. The last line should be positive and deliberate.

SECOND TUNE: Quebec

Composer: *Henry Baker*

C OMPOSER (Second Tune): For comments on the composer, Henry Baker, see Hymn 89.

T UNE (Second): For comments on the tune, "Quebec," see Hymn 89.

---

422 HYMN: Light of the World, We Hail Thee
TUNE: Meirionydd

Author: *Rev. John S. B. Monsell*   Source: *Welsh Hymn Melody*

A UTHOR: For comments on the author, John S. B. Monsell, see Hymn 7.

H YMN: Those who knew Dr. Monsell intimately see in the appeal of this hymn to light and beauty a reflection of his indomitably happy, buoyant spirit as a Christian. He was in rebellion against hymns clouded in gloom or music lacking warmth and fervency. His beautiful household was touched with a certain gayety which he felt went with "the beauty of holiness." Of the more than three hundred hymns written by Dr. Monsell, this has the widest use in America. The hope for the Kingdom of God on earth, for true world friendship and peace, is not in man but in God, and comes from Him who is the true Light of the world. It is a hymn worthy to be sung by the Church of Christ in all lands and at all times, but never more so than now, though it was written during the time of the Civil War.

S OURCE: The source is a Welsh hymn melody. See the article, "Welsh Hymnody," under "Original Sources," page xxii.

The Kingdom of God on Earth

TUNE: For comments on the tune, "Meirionydd," see Hymn 156.

423　HYMN: These Things Shall Be: a Loftier Race
FIRST TUNE: Depauw

Author: *John Addington Symonds*　Composer: *Robert G. McCutchan*

AUTHOR: John Addington Symonds was born in Bristol, England, in 1840. He left behind him at Harrow and Oxford brilliant records as a student. He spent his entire life handicapped by bodily weakness that circumscribed his professional ambitions. Fighting tubercular tendencies, he early fled to the foothills of the Alps and there spent the rest of his life in most remarkable literary productivity and sacrificial service in the interest of the Swiss people. He wrote in six volumes an authoritative story of the "Renaissance in Italy." He was an authority on Dante as well as on the Greek poets, Shakespeare, and the English drama. He translated the autobiography of Cellini, sonnets by Michelangelo, and the works of other noted Italians. A chill caught in Rome, where he had gone to forget a sorrow, brought to its close his very remarkable career. Symonds died in 1893.

HYMN: The hymn is four stanzas taken from the fifteen that constitute a poem by Symonds, entitled "A Vista." The poem belongs to a volume of poems published in 1880, bearing the title, "New and Old: A Volume of Verse." For a generation these stanzas have been used for festival hymn services and general public meetings, being especially popular during the tense days of the World War. The hymn was regarded with such significance that the League of Nations Union made wide distribution of it in popular song sheets used in the war camps. Mrs. Vaughan, the poet's daughter, indicates that the hymn was doubtless "thrown off hurriedly during some moment of deep longing . . . for the betterment of the people." Note the word "inarmed," which some have suggested as a misprint. It means "arm in arm" and gives special meaning to the entire stanza. The hymn is in full accord with the prophetic visions of the sure coming of the Kingdom of God among men.

COMPOSER (First Tune): Robert G. McCutchan was born at Mt. Ayr, Iowa, on September 13, 1877. He studied at Park College and at Simpson College. From the latter he graduated with the degree of Bachelor of Music. Subsequently he continued his musical education in Berlin and Paris. Upon his return to America he became associated with Baker University and continued there from 1904 to 1910. In that institution, in addition to organizing the conservatory of music, he

437

Handbook to The Hymnal

taught singing. At present he is the dean of the school of music associated with De Pauw University, in Greencastle, Indiana.

TUNE (First): "Depauw," by Dean McCutchan, of De Pauw University, is a tune of recent origin, having appeared in 1930. It is perhaps the best tune associated with John Addington Symonds' hymn, "These Things Shall Be: a Loftier Race." The music is hopeful, vigorous, and commanding. It truly expresses and intensifies the words of this hymn.

SECOND TUNE: Truro

Source: *T. Williams'*
"Psalmodia Evangelica"

SOURCE (Second Tune): The source is T. Williams' "Psalmodia Evangelica."

TUNE (Second): For comments on the tune, "Truro," see Hymn 114.

---

424 HYMN: Turn Back, O Man, Forswear Thy Foolish Ways
TUNE: Old 124th

Author: *Clifford Bax*   Source: *Melody in "Genevan Psalter"*

AUTHOR: Clifford Bax was born in London in 1886, and lived during his youth in Germany, Belgium, and Italy. In these countries he studied art, to which his earlier passion drew him; later he turned to dramatic literature, a realm in which he achieved distinction. He wrote many plays in which music had a large part, and also poems, sketches, and a volume of recollections, "Inland Far," published in 1925. Bax died in 1932.

HYMN: The hymn was written in 1919, while the author's soul was filled with the futile tragedies of the World War. He makes a strong plea for repentance from the sinful and foolish ways which lead to destruction. Like the blows of a hammer the words fall, "Turn back, O man, forswear thy foolish ways." In spite of the flame of reason which crowns the brow of man, in spite of the lessons of history, he still goes on in his foolish ways, still fails to hear the gentle voice of God which speaks in his bosom.

"Earth might be fair and all men glad and wise.

. . . .

Would man but wake from out his haunted sleep."

438

The Kingdom of God on Earth

This call to repentance rises with holy indignation from the soul of the poet, who sees what ruin man's folly and wrath have wrought, and sees as well what good will and brotherly kindness might do.

SOURCE: For comments on the source, a melody in the "Genevan Psalter," see the article, "The Psalters in Early Presbyterian Worship," under "Original Sources," page xv.

TUNE: "Old 124th" has been subjected to many different arrangements since its appearance in the "Genevan Psalter." It is one of the best tunes that appeared in that book. In England and Scotland it has been popular with all Nonconformist bodies. In the "Genevan Psalter" it was set to Psalm 124. When the duke of Savoy attacked Geneva and was repulsed the grateful people sang it. Through "Day's Psalter," published in 1563, in which it was included, it has found its way to the Church at large. It is an exceptional setting for this hymn by Clifford Bax.

425

HYMN: Thy Kingdom Come, O Lord
TUNE: St. Cecilia

Author: *Rev. Frederick L. Hosmer*   Composer: *Rev. Leighton G. Hayne*

AUTHOR: For comments on the author, Frederick L. Hosmer, see Hymn 176.

HYMN: "Thy Kingdom Come, O Lord," by Frederick L. Hosmer, D.D., was written in 1904 under the title "The Prophecy Sublime." After its inclusion in "The Hymn and Tune Book" it began to be widely used. The hymn is as direct as the prayer, "Thy kingdom come," of which the verses are but an expansion. The hymn is so broad and universal in its spirit that all can join in it, for it goes beyond the bounds of creed and race and seeks to embrace the whole family of mankind. It lends itself easily to union gatherings in the interest of Christian unity and world friendship. It embodies the highest ideals of the Kingdom of God on earth, but these will be realized, not through man's good will and effort alone, but through the grace of God in Christ Jesus.

COMPOSER: Rev. Leighton G. Hayne, Mus.D., was a trained musician. He was born at St. David's Hill, Exeter, England, in 1836 and died at Bradford in 1883. He was a son of the manse and was educated at Eton and at Queen's College, Oxford. He was ordained to the ministry in 1861. At the university he conducted the chorus and was public examiner in the school of music. From 1868 to 1871 he was organist at Eton. In 1871 he became rector of Mistley and vicar of Bradfield, Essex. He wrote many hymns and was one of the editors of "The Merton Tune Book."

TUNE: "St. Cecilia" is from "The Merton Tune Book," which was compiled for the church of St. John Baptist, Oxford. In that collection it was composed for Dr. Bonar's hymn, "Thy Way, Not Mine, O Lord." It is an appealing and prayerful tune.

---

426   HYMN: Father of All, from Land and Sea
TUNE: Almsgiving

Author: *Bishop Christopher Wordsworth*   Composer:
Rev. John B. Dykes

AUTHOR: For comments on the author, Christopher Wordsworth, see Hymn 18.

HYMN: This hymn is four stanzas selected from a long poem by Bishop Wordsworth, the nephew of the great poet. The poem was written and read at the church congress held at Nottingham in 1871. When one recalls that Bishop Wordsworth, with great labor and rare taste, selected for "The Holy Year" hymns for every worship opportunity offered by the church calendar, one realizes the spiritual capacity and devotion of the man in matters of public and private worship. This hymn is an earnest prayer for Christian unity, written in the spirit of John, ch. 17. It is direct, sincere, fervent, a Scriptural prayer hymn in which all believers may gladly join.

COMPOSER: For comments on the composer, John B. Dykes, see Hymn 53.

TUNE: For comments on the tune, "Almsgiving," see Hymn 398.

The Life Everlasting

*

427   HYMN: Ten Thousand Times Ten Thousand
       TUNE: Alford

Author: *Rev. Henry Alford*   Composer: *Rev. John B. Dykes*

AUTHOR: For comments on the author, Henry Alford, see Hymn 369.

HYMN: It was inevitable that, sooner or later, the Christian spirit should break forth into song in hymns about heaven, with the beautiful imagery of the book of Revelation as their inspiration. But it was strangely slow in doing so. There were hymns in praise of the Triune God, of Jesus, of the Virgin; hymns in honor of saints and martyrs; morning and evening hymns in large numbers. At last, somewhere in the sixth or seventh century, we come upon the "rugged but fine old hymn," "Urbs Beata Hierusalem" ("Blessed City, Jerusalem"), in which a very limited use was made of Rev., ch. 21, in connection with Eph. 2: 20; I Peter 2: 5.

But it was not until several centuries later that this alluring theme began to come fully into its own in Christian hymnody, and then against a dark background. Out of the cloisters of those days came songs set in a minor key. They dwelt upon the evils of a wicked and a darkened world and the tremendous solemnities of the Last Judgment, turning then, for consolation, to the glories and the joys of the heavenly land. Bernard of Cluny's "De Contemptu Mundi" ("On Contempt of the World"), from which our "Jerusalem the Golden" is taken, is the classic example.

Hymns of this character make a strong appeal to the heart, for they are born of what the Germans call "*Heimweh*," "longing for home." They are good for the soul in some of its states. Too much indulged, their effect is morbid and enervating, producing discontent with life, fostering gloom and despair of the present, and weakening the fighting spirit so essential in Christian living.

This hymn, written as a processional for saints' days, originally consisted of but three stanzas, the fourth being added in 1870. The hymn in its complete form was sung at the author's funeral in 1871. With glowing faith and joy the first three stanzas celebrate the complete and everlasting consummation of Christ's redeeming work. The fourth stanza drops back into the longing of earth's exiles for home and the speedy coming of the Kingdom.

441

COMPOSER: For comments on the composer, John B. Dykes, see Hymn 53.

TUNE: "Alford" was composed for this hymn in the revision of "Hymns Ancient and Modern," published in 1875. In a letter to Mrs. Dykes on the occasion of the composer's death, Sir Henry Baker said, "We are going to sing only his tunes to every hymn all next Sunday, and the 'Dies Irae' after evensong for him, followed by 'Ten Thousand Times Ten Thousand.'"

This hymn should be sung with marked rhythm. As a processional, for which it is admirably suited, the time should be a little faster, with two pulses to each measure.

---

428   HYMN: Upward Where the Stars Are Burning
        TUNE: Bonar

Author: *Rev. Horatius Bonar*   Composer: *John Baptiste Calkin*

AUTHOR: For comments on the author, Horatius Bonar, see Hymn 60.

HYMN: "*Sursum corda!*" ("Lift up your hearts!") So rang the call to worship in the ancient liturgies. "*Habemus ad Dominum.*" ("We lift them up unto the Lord.") So we do when we sing this hymn with spirit and understanding. Unlike so many hymns about heaven, it is pure praise—no discontent with life, no selfish satisfaction in the thought of escape from the want and woe of earth or of the delights of the redeemed—all pure praise of Him who is the Author of the life everlasting.

This hymn is part of a poem of five stanzas entitled "Upward." It is found in numerous hymnals.

COMPOSER: For comments on the composer, John Baptiste Calkin, see Hymn 384.

TUNE: "Bonar" has been included in the hymnals of the Presbyterian Church since 1895. The tune was composed in 1867, a year after Dr. Bonar's hymn, with which it is associated, was written. It is of interest to observe that both tune and hymn were introduced to America through Sunday School hymnals. In its present setting it appeared in two such collections in 1876, "The New Hymnary" and "The Book of Praise," both published by Bigelow and Main, New York City. Dr. Charles H. Richards, in 1880, included it in "Songs of Christian

The Life Everlasting

Praise," also published in New York. After that date nearly every new hymnal gave it recognition.

Like the words, the tune is hopeful and joyous in character. When introduced to America, it was arranged as a carol for unison singing. In singing it, special attention should be given to the last two braces of music, which are climactic and call for broad tonality and decisive articulation.

---

429 HYMN: For All the Saints Who from Their Labors Rest
FIRST TUNE: Sarum

Author: *Bishop William Walsham How*   Composer: *Joseph Barnby*

AUTHOR: For comments on the author, William Walsham How, see Hymn 137.

HYMN: The original hymn consists of eleven stanzas. It is a great favorite, not only with congregations but with hymnologists, being found in every important collection. Few of these, however, print all the stanzas. It was written for use on saints' days and is one of the many hymns for which we are indebted to the "bishops and other clergy" of the Church of England. It has the long time sense. As we read it, and much more when we sing it, we seem to be living in history. The past merges with the present and the future. We are, for the moment, living members of a vast fellowship that extends beyond the borders of earth and time into the eternal heavens, a fellowship that knows both the agony of mortal strife and the joy of victory. Singing, our voices become part of the Church's "unending song."

COMPOSER (First Tune): For comments on the composer, Joseph Barnby, see Hymn 3.

TUNE (First): This tune, "Sarum," was composed for "The Sarum Hymnal" for these words of Bishop How in the year 1869. This hymnal was a collection of hymns and tunes for use in the diocese of Salisbury—hence the name. In choosing the time for this tune, the whole notes in the alleluias must be taken into consideration. If it is too slow, the congregation will not be able to sing each alleluia easily in one breath.

SECOND TUNE: Sine Nomine

Composer: *R. Vaughan Williams*

COMPOSER (Second Tune): Ralph Vaughan Williams, Mus.D., is one of the most distinguished living British composers. He was educated at Trinity College, Cambridge; the Royal College of Music, London; and in Paris and Berlin. Most of his works were composed after his thirtieth birthday. He entered the World War as a private and later held a commission in the artillery. He has done excellent work in collecting and editing folk songs and carols, chiefly from East Anglia and Herefordshire. His compositions reveal a strong melodic gift, a severe and noble style, and great originality. They have a strong flavor of the English folk music which he has studied so thoroughly and enthusiastically. He was musical editor of "The English Hymnal," published in 1906, and a coeditor with Martin Shaw and Percy Dearmer of "Songs of Praise," published in 1925.

TUNE (Second): "Sine Nomine" was composed for these words for "The English Hymnal." This tune may not be easy for congregational singing at first, due to the irregular values of the notes. But if choir and congregation sing in unison as directed, the result will be heartening.

---

430 HYMN: O What Their Joy and Their Glory Must Be
TUNE: O Quanta Qualia

Author: *Pierre Abélard*   Source: *La Feillée's*
                                        "Méthode du Plain Chant"

AUTHOR: Pierre Abélard was born in 1079, in Le Pallet, France, of a noble Breton family.

He was intended by his parents for the military profession. By nature a thinker, he chose philosophy and theology, becoming one of the most famous disputants and teachers of his time. His brilliant lectures attracted crowds of students from all over Europe. He was a courageous challenger of old ideas. His success as a teacher is indicated by the fact that nineteen cardinals and two popes came from the ranks of his pupils. But his life was strangely and repeatedly broken through his romance with Héloïse, his young pupil. The pair fled from Paris to Brittany, and there were privately married. Bending before the storm of condemnation, Abélard became a monk and Héloïse took the veil, eventually becoming abbess of a nunnery.

Among the figures of the Middle Ages there is none more arresting than that of Pierre Abélard—philosopher, theologian, monk. Brilliant, proud,

The Life Everlasting

passionate, harried by powerful enemies, he had a spectacular and tragic career. Sins that overwhelmed him were many and grave. So were the sorrows that humbled, softened, and purged him.

Driven from pillar to post, Abélard died in a monastery on his way to Rome to plead his cause before the pope in the year 1142.

T RANSLATOR: For comments on the translator, John Mason Neale, see Hymn 44.

H YMN: This celebrated hymn was one of more than one hundred which Abélard wrote for use at evening prayer in the abbey of the Paraclete, of which Héloïse was abbess. His hymns were long lost, but in 1838 six were found in the Vatican, and later ninety-seven came to light in the Royal Library at Brussels.

S OURCE: For comments on the source, La Feillée's "Méthode du Plain Chant," see Hymn 24.

T UNE: For comments on the tune, "O Quanta Qualia," see Hymns 196 and 290.

---

431 HYMN: Hark! Hark, My Soul! Angelic Songs Are Swelling
TUNE: Pilgrims (Smart)

Author: *Rev. Frederick W. Faber*   Composer: *Henry Smart*

A UTHOR: For comments on the author, Frederick W. Faber, see Hymn 93.

H YMN: This hymn was published in Faber's "Oratory Hymns" in 1854, in seven stanzas of four lines each, with a refrain. Several lines have been improved by alterations now generally accepted. Canon Ellerton indicated that he did not know the meaning of "pilgrims of the night," but this does not invalidate the poetry. The hymn makes a strong appeal to the spirit of the average worshiper and its popularity is very genuine and widespread.

C OMPOSER: For comments on the composer, Henry Smart, see Hymn 61.

T UNE: "Pilgrims (Smart)," written by Henry Smart, first appeared in "Hymns Ancient and Modern" with Faber's words.

When choir leadership is not strong it will be conducive to more whole-hearted singing on the part of the congregation if this tune is played in the key of E flat, rather than E major.

445

Handbook to The Hymnal

432 HYMN: We Know Not a Voice of That River
TUNE: Achnasheen

Author: *Christina G. Rossetti*   Composer: *Charles H. Lloyd*

AUTHOR: For comments on the author, Christina G. Rossetti, see Hymn 133.

HYMN: This highly mystical hymn is taken from the author's large volume of meditations on the book of Revelation, entitled "The Face of the Deep." It is obviously suggested by Rev. 22:1. The mystical river may be "too full for sound and foam," but through the words of the hymn we seem to hear its rhythmical murmur,

"Where forever and ever and ever
It flows to no sea."

COMPOSER: The composer, Charles Harford Lloyd, A.M., Mus.D., was educated at Rossall School and at Magdalen Hall, Oxford. He was organist of Gloucester Cathedral and then of Christ Church, Oxford. After 1892 he was precentor of Eton College. In 1914 he became organist of the Chapel Royal. He edited "Church Hymns" in 1903.

TUNE: "Achnasheen" is a tune of interesting pattern. The unusual meter of the words is skillfully expressed in the music, which is fluent in movement, exquisite in sentiment, and of intimate mood. The confidence and wistfulness of Miss Rossetti's hymn are nobly revealed and amplified. The union of words and tune seems to have been introduced to America by Louis F. Benson, D.D., in his hymnal, "Christian Song," which was published in 1926.

---

433 HYMN: O Love That Lights the Eastern Sky
TUNE: Vittel Woods

Author: *Rev. Louis F. Benson*   Composer: *Bradley Keeler*

AUTHOR: For comments on the author, Louis F. Benson, see Hymn 29.

HYMN: In thought and word this hymn is reminiscent of "Crossing the Bar." It has for its background the author's summer home at Northeast Harbor, Maine. It was written in Philadelphia on February 11, 1923, and was first published in Dr. Benson's private collection of hymns in 1925.

446

The Life Everlasting

Dr. Calvin W. Laufer, in "Hymn Lore," says: "Although of recent origin, the hymn has already received widespread acceptance. At a musical festival at Canterbury Cathedral it was sung by a chorus of nine hundred voices. . . . It has been translated into French for use in the Catholic cathedral at Lausanne. It is appreciated also in Paris, Baden-Baden, and elsewhere in Europe. In America it appears in several hymnals, among which are 'Christian Song' and 'The Church School Hymnal for Youth.' . . .

"In it the author reflects upon the changing aspects of life, which supply . . . abundant reason for joy."

COMPOSER: Walter Bradley Keeler, pianist and composer, was an intimate friend of Dr. Louis F. Benson, whom he esteemed highly as a hymn writer and hymnologist. He lived in Switzerland and divided his time between Lausanne and Paris, paying short visits to America. Greatly appreciating Dr. Benson's hymns he set many of them to music of his own composition. He was interested in talented young composers and made provision in his will for a trust fund at one of our American universities to aid them while in training. He died in Europe on November 11, 1933.

TUNE: "Vittel Woods" came as an inspiration to Mr. Keeler while he was hiking in Vittel Woods, Switzerland. Dr. Benson's beautiful hymn, "O Love That Lights the Eastern Sky," was in his mind when he wrote the tune. He sent a copy to Dr. Benson, who used it in his "Hymns," published in 1925, and in "Christian Song," published in 1926. Two years later it was included in "The Church School Hymnal for Youth." It was Dr. Benson's wish that his words and this tune should always be associated.

---

434   HYMN: The Sands of Time Are Sinking
TUNE: Rutherford

Author: *Anne Ross Cousin*   Composer: *Chrétien Urhan*

AUTHOR: Anne Ross Cundell was the daughter of a Scottish physician, David Ross Cundell, who served in the British Army during the Napoleonic wars and was an assistant surgeon at the Battle of Waterloo. Anne, born in 1824, was a highly gifted person, becoming especially proficient in music and languages. The theological controversies stirred up by the Tractarian Movement sent her from the Episcopal Church to the Presbyterian. She married a minister of the Free Church, Rev. William Cousin. Her hymns are characterized by a hopeful, loving, grateful spirit.

Handbook to The Hymnal

HYMN: This hymn is a mosaic composed of passages from "Letters and Dying Sayings," by Samuel Rutherford. Mrs. Cousin's daughter tells how her "mother fitted the pattern of her verses line by line as she sat at her sewing"—a peculiar way of producing a hymn. But it must be admitted that the result is surprisingly beautiful and satisfying. The hymn consists of nineteen stanzas only three of which are used in "The Hymnal."

Rutherford was a quaint Covenanter minister, born about 1600. He was a powerful defender of Calvinistic doctrine and fought the Nonconformity Acts of Parliament. While stricken with a mortal disease he was summoned by Parliament to answer to a charge of treason in 1661. He replied, "I am summoned before a higher Judge and judicatory: that summons I behove to answer; and, ere a few days arrive, I shall be where few kings and great folks come."

COMPOSER: Chrétien Urhan was born near Paris in 1790, and spent most of his life in that city. He was organist of the Church of St. Vincent de Paul. He was self-taught in music until the age of fifteen, when he played for the Empress Josephine. The empress was so impressed by the youth's talent that she made it possible for him to study with the best masters. For years he played the *viol d'amore*, an instrument even then out of use. Urhan was a man of great religious scruples. He dressed like a clergyman and lived the life of an ascetic. For thirty years he played as solo violinist in the Opéra Française yet he is said never to have looked in the direction of the stage, so deep were his religious scruples. He was a genuine artist, a man of wide culture, and a composer of originality. "Chants Chrétiens" is a collection of popular tunes from which this one has been taken.

ARRANGER: Edward F. Rimbault, a noted English organist, scholar, and collector of music has arranged this tune. The present version is much altered from the original.

TUNE: When playing "Rutherford," the organist must take care not to rush singers at the ends of the phrases or in the middle of lines 1, 2, and 3, each of which ends in a short note.

---

435 HYMN: Jerusalem the Golden
FIRST TUNE: Ewing

Author: *Bernard of Cluny*   Composer: *Alexander Ewing*

AUTHOR: Of a man with so celebrated a name as Bernard of Cluny, surprisingly little is known. He was born probably in Morlaix, Brittany, very early in the twelfth century. Both parents are said

448

The Life Everlasting

to have been English. He became a monk in the great abbey of Cluny, famous for the beauty of its buildings and the splendor of its services. There, for all we know, he continued to live until his death at an unknown date. His sole claim to fame is the long poem, "De Contemptu Mundi" ("On Contempt of the World"), from which our hymn is taken. Other hymns from the same poem, not in our Hymnal, are "Brief Life Is Here Our Portion" and "For Thee, O Dear, Dear Country."

TRANSLATOR: For comments on the translator, John M. Neale, see Hymn 44.

HYMN: This is a golden hymn about the Golden City. Though he spent his life shut in a monastery, Bernard knew what was going on in the world about him. His poem is a savage satire upon the vices and follies of the Church and of the human society of his time. It is too frank and realistic to be translatable. Against a dark background we have this lovely picture of the celestial city and its "sweet and blessed" countryside, "that eager hearts expect."

Dr. Neale's version was first published in a thin little volume, entitled "The Rhythm of Bernard de Morlaix, Monk of Cluny, on the Celestial Country," published in 1858. Owing to the extreme difficulties presented by the Latin meter, we have a paraphrase rather than a translation. The beautiful imagery of The Revelation of John comes into its own in our hymns about the life everlasting.

COMPOSER (First Tune): Alexander Ewing was a native of Aberdeen, Scotland. He studied law at Marischal College, but later went to Heidelberg, Germany, to study music. He was closely identified with the Haydn Society of Aberdeen and the Harmonic Choir. He specialized in madrigals and anthems. He joined the army, and served in the Crimean War and also in China, becoming a lieutenant colonel. On the Sunday after his death in Taunton in 1895, and also at his funeral, this tune was sung.

TUNE (First): After a rehearsal of one of the choral societies with which Col. Ewing was affiliated, he presented "Ewing" in manuscript, with copies of the voice parts, to the conductor, and requested that it be sung. Thus his only tune was started on a long career. It was first printed on single sheets in 1853 in triple time. In the first edition of "Hymns Ancient and Modern" the meter was changed to common time and this alteration was universally adopted. The composer never approved of this change, of which he used to say, "It now seems to me a good deal like a polka."

This hymn will be better suited for congregational singing if the organist will play it a half, or even a whole, tone lower. In its present key

449

few besides the sopranos of the choir will be able to sing the third line with its F sharp on the words "joys" and "awaits."

SECOND TUNE: Urbs Beata

Composer: George F. Le Jeune

COMPOSER (Second Tune): For comments on the composer, George F. Le Jeune, see Hymn 308.

TUNE (Second): "Urbs Beata" ("The City Beautiful") was composed in 1887 after Le Jeune had come to St. John's Chapel. By repeating the first four lines of the hymn, the composer has made possible a refrain for his tune.

This is a choir tune *par excellence* and a fine processional. It should be sung with two pulses to the measure. The high notes in the refrain are for the choir only. Should the congregation be expected to join in on this hymn, it would be well for the organist to omit these notes when he is playing the tune before the singing.

---

436   HYMN: O Mother Dear, Jerusalem
TUNE: Materna

Author: *"F.B.P."*   Composer: *Samuel A. Ward*

AUTHOR: Who wrote this quaint and lovely old hymn is not known. Dr. Neale accepts the "information" furnished him by Mr. David Sedgwick, distinguished hymnologist, that the letters "F. B. P." stand for Francis Baker, Pater (Priest), who was for some time imprisoned in the Tower of London. But William T. Brooke, in Dr. Julian's "A Dictionary of Hymnology," says that this is "a pure guess and cannot be received. The writer, probably a Roman Catholic of the sixteenth century and possibly a priest, remains unknown."

HYMN: Owing to the varying forms in which this hymn, or some portions of it, are found in old and modern texts, its history is confused. Its original source is a passage from "The Meditations of St. Augustine." In this passage he describes in great detail the joys and glories of the New Jerusalem, using the imagery of the Apocalypse.

With this as his inspiration, F. B. P. wrote a hymn of twenty-six four-line stanzas beginning, "Jerusalem, My Happy Home." It is found in manuscript form in the British Museum. The manuscript is undated, but is of the latter part of the sixteenth or the beginning of the seventeenth century. The three stanzas of eight lines each printed in "The Hymnal"

450

The Life Everlasting

are taken word for word from F. B. P.'s hymn, except the first line of the first stanza, which reads, as in many texts, "O Mother Dear, Jerusalem."

COMPOSER: For comments on the composer, Samuel A. Ward, see Hymn 411.

TUNE: For comments on the tune, "Materna," see Hymn 411.

---

437   HYMN: I Heard a Sound of Voices
TUNE: Patmos

Author: *Rev. Godfrey Thring*   Composer: *Henry J. Storer*

AUTHOR: For comments on the author, Godfrey Thring, see Hymn 38.

HYMN: Dr. Julian says that this hymn was written in 1886 and published by Novello and Company, with music by H. S. Irons, in the same year. It took its place at choral festivals and appeared in "Church Hymns" in 1903. The hymn theme is evidently taken from Rev. 7:9, 10, which is an outline drawing of the most picturesque and noble aspects of heaven as revealed to John.

COMPOSER: For comments on the composer, Henry J. Storer, see Hymn 408.

TUNE: For comments on the tune, "Patmos," see Hymn 408.

---

438   HYMN: Sunset and Evening Star
TUNE: Crossing the Bar

Author: *Alfred Tennyson*   Composer: *Joseph Barnby*

AUTHOR: For comments on the author, Alfred Tennyson, see Hymn 175.

HYMN: "'Crossing the Bar,'" said Lord Tennyson's son and biographer, "was written in my father's eighty-first year, on a day in October when we came from Aldworth to Farringford. Before reaching Farringford he had the moaning of the bar in his mind, and after dinner he showed me this poem written out. I said, 'That is the crown of

451

your life's work.' He answered, 'It came to me in a moment.' He explained the 'Pilot' as 'that Divine and Unseen who is always guiding us.' A few days before my father's death he said to me, 'Mind you put "Crossing the Bar" at the end of all editions of my poems.' "

It is sometimes carelessly read and quoted as though it contemplated death as arrival in port. But the idea is exactly the opposite, startling in its boldness and grandeur. It pictures the soul, in death, as putting out to sea, on a never-ending voyage of discovery and activity with the Chief Pilot at the helm, hitherto unseen, but now seen "face to face."

COMPOSER: For comments on the composer, Joseph Barnby, see Hymn 3.

TUNE: A committee of the Free Church of Scotland engaged Sir Joseph Barnby to set Tennyson's words to music for "The Home and School Hymnal" in 1892. The tune, "Crossing the Bar," first appeared in this country in the Presbyterian Hymnal of 1895.

The changing moods of the words are well expressed in the music— so much so that the composition resembles an unaccompanied quartet anthem. Freedom in regard to both time and shading should characterize its singing.

---

439   HYMN: Sooner or Later: Yet at Last
TUNE: Ultima

Author: *Christina G. Rossetti*   Composer: *Rev. James Moffatt*

AUTHOR: For comments on the author, Christina G. Rossetti, see Hymn 133.

HYMN: Much thought of death tends to darken and paralyze life. Other generations have erred in this point. They have deliberately dwelt in "the valley of the shadow." Not so the present generation. It obscures the thought of death. The result is life lived at short range and thus deprived of some of its most exalted and powerful motives.

Much of the cheapness and sordidness of the life of our day is due to an unwillingness to face frankly and courageously this stern fact in our present existence.

COMPOSER: James Moffatt, D.D., Litt.D., was educated at the Academy, University, and Free Church College, Glasgow. He was ordained in 1896. After holding several pastorates he became Jowett lecturer in London, in 1907. He was Yates professor of Greek and the New Testament in Mansfield College, Oxford, from 1911 to 1915; professor of church history in the United Free Church College, Glasgow, from 1915 to 1927. He is now Washburn professor of church history in Union Theological Seminary, New York City. He was a member of the Revision Committee of "The Church Hymnary."

TUNE: "Ultima" was composed for these words of Christina Rossetti by Dr. Moffatt. The tune is simple and straightforward, with a range of only five tones.

---

440   HYMN: Now the Laborer's Task Is O'er
               TUNE: Requiescat

Author: *Rev. John Ellerton*   Composer: *Rev. John B. Dykes*

AUTHOR: For comments on the author, John Ellerton, see Hymn 20.

HYMN: This hymn was written for and first published in "Church Hymns," published in 1871 by the Society for the Promotion of Christian Knowledge. The author said: "The whole hymn . . . owes many thoughts and some expressions to a beautiful poem of the Rev. Gerard Moultrie's, beginning, 'Brother, now thy toils are o'er.' This poem is found in 'The People's Hymnal.'"

Certain lines, in the first stanza, and, indeed, the entire hymn, are in striking contrast with Tennyson's "Sunset and Evening Star," where death is regarded as a putting out to sea. (See the comments on Hymn 438.)

COMPOSER: For comments on the composer, John B. Dykes, see Hymn 53.

TUNE: "Requiescat" was written by Dykes for the hymn, "Now the Laborer's Task Is O'er," by Ellerton. It appeared first in the 1875 edition of "Hymns Ancient and Modern."

The organist must be flexible as to time and movement in playing the third line of the music, which is the phrase ending on the word "last." This is wise in view of the quickly changing harmonies and the need for breathing.

Children's Hymns

*

441 HYMN: With Happy Voices Singing
TUNE: Tours

Author: *Rev. William George Tarrant*   Composer: *Berthold Tours*

AUTHOR: For comments on the author, William George Tarrant, see Hymn 408.

HYMN: This hymn was written in 1888. It is adapted for children of all ages. Breathing the spirit of youth it is sensitive to the beauties of nature. Set to a lovely, singable tune, it specially provides a worship response for little children. Never sacrificing its stateliness and dignity to weak sentimentality, as do many children's hymns, it brings the little worshipers with kindled imagination and a simple concept of God to a most joyous expression of praise.

COMPOSER: For comments on the composer, Berthold Tours, see Hymn 111.

TUNE: For comments on the tune, "Tours," see Hymn 111.

---

442 HYMN: I Think When I Read That Sweet Story of Old
FIRST TUNE: East Horndon

Author: *Jemima Luke*   Source: *English Traditional Melody*

AUTHOR: Jemima Thompson Luke, born in 1813, was the daughter of Thomas Thompson, one of the founders of the British and Foreign Sailors' Society. Her father on one occasion offered twenty pounds as a prize for fifty simple gospel hymns. This was won by James Edmeston, who during his life wrote over two thousand hymns. In her youth Jemima Thompson intended to become a missionary to India, but ill health prevented. She never lost her interest in foreign missions and for a time edited a missionary paper for children. In 1843 she married Rev. Samuel Luke, a Congregational minister. She died in 1906.

HYMN: This hymn was printed in The Sunday School Teacher's Magazine in 1841. Mrs. Luke wrote it to the music of the Greek air, "Salamis," which was singing in her heart. Concerning the

454

origin of the hymn she herself indicated that she was traveling on missionary work a distance of five miles in a stagecoach. "It was a beautiful spring morning, it was an hour's ride, and there was no other inside passenger. On the back of an old envelope I wrote in pencil the first two of the verses now so well known, in order to teach the tune to the village school, supported by my stepmother, . . . which it was my privilege to visit. The third verse [the fourth stanza here] was added afterwards to make it a missionary hymn."

Two other stanzas not often in current use were added, the second reading as follows:

"But thousands and thousands who wander and fall
Never heard of that heavenly home;
I should like them to know there is room for them all
And that Jesus has bid them to come."

SOURCE (First Tune): The source is an English traditional melody.

TUNE (First): "East Horndon" is similar to a folk tune, "The Fisherman," given in the Journal of the Folk Song Society, Vol. I. The melody should be sung in a smooth, flowing style. The director should beat two slow pulses to the measure, not six rapid ones.

SECOND TUNE: Sweet Story

Source: *A Greek Folk Song*

SOURCE (Second Tune): The source is a Greek folk song.

ARRANGER (Second Tune): For comments on the arranger, William B. Bradbury, see Hymn 106.

TUNE (Second): The tune, "Sweet Story," is closely knit with the words of Mrs. Luke. On hearing the tune, she took a fancy to it and "searched Watts and Jane Taylor and several Sunday School hymn books for words to suit the measure, but in vain." It was for this reason that she wrote the words, which were published in 1841. The hymn should be sung in simple, unhurried style.

443

HYMN: I Love to Tell the Story
TUNE: I Love to Tell the Story

Author: *Katherine Hankey*   Composer: *William G. Fischer*

AUTHOR: Katherine Hankey, the author of "I Love to Tell the Story," was a woman of culture and consecration. She was a member of a small group, known as the Clapham Sect, dedicated to evangelistic enterprises. At an early age she became interested in Sunday School work in London and Croydon. Her influence with shopgirls in London was great and many of them who attended her Bible classes became workers in the Church. Some of her best hymns were inspired by her experiences as a Sunday School teacher and by her desire to help those whom she had recruited. Miss Hankey belonged to a family of means, her father being a banker in Clapham, where she was born in 1834. In the midst of her increasing work she found it necessary to go to Africa to nurse an invalid brother. While there she became interested in missions and upon her return to England was moved to devote the proceeds of her writings to Christian stations in foreign lands. She published several books and a volume of hymns. Her best-known hymns are "Tell Me the Old, Old Story," "I Saw Him Leave His Father's Throne," and "I Love to Tell the Story." When she died in London in 1911 she was mourned throughout the entire world. "I Love to Tell the Story," which has been translated into many languages, perpetuates her memory.

HYMN: "I Love to Tell the Story" was written in 1866. It was popularized by the Moody and Sankey evangelistic campaigns in England and America. Mr. P. P. Bliss included it in "Gospel Songs," which was published in Cincinnati, Ohio, in 1874. A year later a joint collection of gospel songs was made by Mr. Bliss and Ira D. Sankey, which was introduced at the great Moody meetings in Brooklyn Rink and in the old Pennsylvania Railroad depot in Philadelphia. Vast throngs became acquainted with Miss Hankey's hymn, which in the meanwhile had had a refrain added and had be comewedded to a tune by William G. Fischer, of Philadelphia. It soon proved to be one of those gospel songs that penetrated music halls and churches, and was whistled by converts on the street.

COMPOSER: William G. Fischer, of German extraction, was born in Baltimore, Maryland, on October 14, 1835. Early in his youth he came under the influence of the singing schools which were conducted under the leadership of Dr. Lowell Mason, Dr. Thomas Hastings, and their followers. He learned to read music in a church singing class, and later studied harmony, the piano, and the organ. For a while he was associated with J. B. Lippincott, in Philadelphia, and learned

456

Children's Hymns

the bookbinding trade. By dint of personal effort and perseverance he became a successful teacher of choirs and conductor of singing societies. In 1865 he was elected teacher of music in Girard College, where he served for ten years. He and John E. Gould opened a piano store and music house which did a lucrative business in Philadelphia. After Mr. Fischer retired in 1898, the firm was continued by a son.

In the main Mr. Fischer's name is perpetuated by his gospel songs, of which he wrote about two hundred. He was a man of inspiring presence and in demand as a conductor of choral groups at conventions and revival meetings. In 1876 he led a chorus of one thousand voices in connection with the Moody and Sankey meetings in Philadelphia. He died in Philadelphia on August 13, 1912.

TUNE: "I Love to Tell the Story" was written in 1869. Soon after its composition, Chaplain McCabe, later Bishop McCabe, visited the composer's place of business and was introduced to the tune. He gave it his approval. Within a year it found its way into gospel song collections and became a popular favorite at revival meetings. Of the many hymns of this type, it is one of the few that is included in the more stately hymnals of the Church.

---

444 HYMN: It Fell Upon a Summer Day
TUNE: Childhood

Author: *Rev. Stopford Augustus Brooke*   Source: *"A Students' Hymnal"*

AUTHOR: For comments on the author, Stopford Augustus Brooke, see Hymn 74.

HYMN: This hymn appeared first in Dr. Brooke's "Christian Hymns," published in 1881. It consisted of ten stanzas of four lines each and was entitled "Christ Blessing Little Children." The words of Scripture are woven closely into the text of the hymn, which gives it considerable educative value. When asked by a mother when she should begin the education of her child, then four years old, a clergyman replied, "Madam, you have lost three years already."

SOURCE: The source is the book, "A Students' Hymnal," University of Wales, 1923. For comments on Welsh hymnody see the article, "Welsh Hymnody," under "Original Sources," page xxii.

TUNE: "Chiidhood" was written for use with this hymn in "A Students' Hymnal." It was composed with a number of other tunes in the book "by a small community of minds, in some cases

457

by as many as five." The editor, who, however, was finally responsible in each case, was Sir Walford Davies, Mus.D., LL.D., one-time professor of music at the University College of Wales; organist of St. George's, Windsor; and master of music to the king. He was knighted in 1922.

The problem of phrasing in this tune is a real one. If a very moderate time is not selected the singers will soon become breathless, inasmuch as a sustained note does not occur at any double bar until the last one. As for the word phrases, which do not always come at the double bars, some may desire to make slight breaks in the music to emphasize the meaning of the words. In any case it is necessary to establish and maintain a certain steadiness of time throughout.

445
HYMN: Father, Lead Me Day by Day
TUNE: Lyne

Author: *Rev. John Page Hopps*   Source: *"Magdalen Chapel Hymns"*

AUTHOR: John Page Hopps (1834–1912) was born in London and educated at the Baptist College of Leicester. After a brief ministry in Leicestershire, he became connected with the Church of the Saviour in Birmingham. He served in several parishes, including Glasgow. He is the author of many books, generally controversial in character. He long continued his editorship of The Truthseeker, which he founded in 1863. His hymn books, eight in number, were designed for school, missionary, and congregational uses. Many charming hymns for children are found in his collections.

HYMN: The author calls this "a child's prayer for divine guidance." Its vocabulary and sentiment are childlike and its praying stanzas express the heart's desire of childhood, with its untroubled trust in God. It has had wide use through the National Sunday School Union of Great Britain. It should find its way into the hearts of our tiniest worshipers. Two stanzas of the original hymn are omitted.

SOURCE: The source is "Magdalen Chapel Hymns."

TUNE: "Lyne" originally was set to the hymn "Let Us with a Gladsome Mind." Whether or not it originated in the hymn-singing movement of Magdalen Hospital and similar institutions, which gained great impetus in 1758 and resulted in the composition of many new tunes, cannot be definitely ascertained. The tune is sometimes labeled simply "Magdalen Hymns, 1860."

Children's Hymns

446 HYMN: When Mothers of Salem
TUNE: Athlone

Author: *William Medlen Hutchings* Composer: *Robert Newton Quaile*

AUTHOR: The author, William Medlen Hutchings, was born in 1827 and died in 1876. He was a printer and publisher in London and a member of the Congregational Church.

HYMN: "When Mothers of Salem" was written for the anniversary service of St. Paul's Chapel Sunday School, Wigan, in 1850, and was printed in a revised form in the Juvenile Missionary Magazine in 1850. It has been used extensively in the churches of England, Scotland, and Canada. It was one of the first gospel songs for children.

COMPOSER: Robert Newton Quaile came into prominence in the year 1911, when the well-known book "The Methodist Sunday School Hymnal" was published in London. In that hymnal, which has proved to be a valuable depository of hymns and tunes for young people, three tunes by Mr. Quaile were included. They are of undoubted merit and have won the favorable attention of hymnal editors. Mr. Quaile, now engaged in business at Mallow, County Cork, Ireland, is a son of the manse, and was born in 1867. His father, Rev. William Quaile, an Irish Methodist minister and an able preacher, gave his son a liberal education and had him trained at Wesley College, Dublin. Robert Newton Quaile follows music as an avocation. Though his tunes are not numerous, those that have won public favor bear the marks of skilled workmanship.

TUNE: "Athlone" is an excellent setting for "When Mothers of Salem." Associated with these words it first appeared in "The Methodist Sunday School Hymnal," published in England in 1911. It is a tune of exquisite feeling and simple structure and effectively expresses the text of the hymn, which for some reason or other had been associated with a famous German festal song, "Crambambuli." This tune has proved a deliverance.

447 HYMN: I Love to Hear the Story
TUNE: Gosterwood

Author: *Emily Huntington Miller*   Source: *English Traditional Melody*

AUTHOR: The author, Emily Miller, née Huntington, was the daughter of a Methodist minister. She was born in Brooklyn, Connecticut, on October 22, 1833. She graduated from Oberlin College in 1857 and became the wife of Professor John E. Miller in 1860. She was a writer of both prose and verse and specialized in literature for children. She was the editor of The Little Corporal, a children's magazine which later became St. Nicholas. Among her score of books were the popular stories of "Captain Frith," "Little Neighbors," and a volume of poems, "From Avalon and Other Poems." She became dean of women at Northwestern University in 1891 and was given the honorary degree of L.H.D. by the institution in 1909. Among her most popular hymns are "Enter Thy Temple, Glorious King," written for the dedication of a church in Akron, Ohio, in 1861, and the above hymn, widely used in England and America.

HYMN: This hymn appeared in 1867 in the magazine, The Little Corporal, of which Mrs. Miller was editor. It is said to have been composed under a sudden inspiration within the brief space of fifteen minutes. It is supposed to have been suggested by Katherine Hankey's familiar hymn, which was written a few months before this, and was immediately accepted as a gospel hymn. The hymn is in perfect harmony with the natural joyousness and outspoken frankness of childish love. However, it expresses the passion of every true disciple of Christ.

SOURCE: The source is an English traditional melody.

TUNE: "Gosterwood" appeared first in "The English Hymnal," published in 1906, and is an arrangement by R. Vaughan Williams. The folk tune from Surrey was known as "The Valiant Lady" and also as "The Brisk Young Lively Lad." This setting probably came from a favorite ballad air of the seventeenth century, entitled "When the Stormy Winds Do Blow." Many variants have been found, all of which end with eight bars of the tune and the words, "When the stormy winds do blow." Two of these are the "Shepherd's Song" from Gloucestershire and John Davy's famous "Bay of Biscay."

Because of the joyful character of the tune it would be easy to sing it too fast. A steadily moving time, which allows the singers to get in all the notes clearly and comfortably, should be chosen.

Children's Hymns

448 HYMN: The Shepherds Had an Angel
TUNE: May Song

Author: *Christina G. Rossetti*   Source: *Traditional English Carol*

AUTHOR: For comments on the author, Christina G. Rossetti, see Hymn 133.

HYMN: These beautiful verses are new as a hymn. They appear in Christina Rossetti's "Sing Song," a nursery-rime book. It is inscribed "For My Godchildren" and entitled "A Christmas Carol." The poem consists of nine stanzas of six lines each. The first line of stanza 4 in the poem reads, "Nearer and nearer day by day," and is changed to read in the hymn, "Lord, bring me nearer day by day." Other Christmas carols in "Sing Song" are: "Before the Paling of the Stars," "In the Bleak Midwinter," "What Can I Give Him, Poor as I Am," and "Love Came Down at Christmastime."

SOURCE: The source is a traditional English carol.

TUNE: "May Song" was a Somerset folk tune, entitled "Heave Away, My Johnny," which has been arranged by Cecil Sharp. The original has been abbreviated and reharmonized to furnish the arrangement used here for Christina Rossetti's text. It should be sung with marked rhythm, particular care being taken to avoid a slowing of the time in the third line on the words, "Home from far."

---

449 HYMN: Jesus, Tender Shepherd, Hear Me
FIRST TUNE: Dijon

Author: *Mary Lundie Duncan*   Source: *Old German Melody*

AUTHOR: The author, Mary Lundie Duncan, was the daughter of a Scottish minister, Rev. Robert Lundie, of Kelso, and was born at Kelso in 1814. She married Rev. William Wallace Duncan, the son of Henry Duncan, D.D., reputed to be the organizer, in 1836, of the first savings bank. Her sister became the wife of Horatius Bonar, that prince of Scottish hymn writers, and a student under Thomas Chalmers in the University of Edinburgh. Mrs. Duncan died suddenly in 1840, leaving two small children.

Mary Duncan was a most remarkable character. Her contemporaries compared her brilliant mind, overflowing personality, and devout spirit to those of Madame Guyon, the "evangelist of quietism." Her hymns, written for her little ones, appeared after her death in "Memoir," prepared by her mother. They were twenty-three in number and were issued in 1842 under the title, "Rhymes for My Children." "Jesus, Tender Shepherd, Hear Me" is her best-known hymn.

HYMN: Sung by generations of little children at their bedsides, this hymn holds a unique place among evening hymns for children. In every word it breathes the childlike spirit. In its trustfulness and intimate feeling for God as the tender Shepherd caring for his lambs throughout the night, the hymn reveals the author's intuitive understanding of the child's feeling of dependence on God and mystical understanding of him.

SOURCE (First Tune): The source is an old German melody. See the article, "German Hymn Sources," under "Original Sources," page xxi.

TUNE (First): This tune, "Dijon," is from "Liederbuch für Kleinkinderschulen . . . Herausgegeben von Theodor Fliedner, 1842." The melody, which was set to the words, "*Müde bin ich, geh' zur Ruh*," has here been slightly altered from the original.

SECOND TUNE: Brocklesbury

Composer: *Charlotte A. Barnard*

COMPOSER (Second Tune): For comments on the composer, Charlotte A. Barnard, see Hymn 348.

TUNE (Second): For comments on the tune, "Brocklesbury," see Hymn 348. It is easy for children to sing "Brocklesbury," in a jerky, detached style, with an accent on every syllable. Probably they will make the melody more flowing if the accompanist plays over the tune, thinking of two pulses only in each measure and keeping the melody smooth and sustained.

---

450   HYMN: Around the Throne of God in Heaven
       TUNE: Children's Praises

Author: *Anne H. Shepherd*   Composer: *Henry E. Matthews*

AUTHOR: Anne Houlditch Shepherd was the daughter of Rev. Edward H. Houlditch. She wrote over sixty hymns, which were published under the title, "Hymns Adapted to the Comprehension of Young Minds," published in 1836. She wrote two novels which attracted considerable attention in her day: "Ellen Seymour" and "Reality."

Children's Hymns

HYMN: This hymn was first published in the author's "Hymns Adapted to the Comprehension of Young Minds," 1836, together with sixty-three other hymns of her own writing. It has been sung around the world in many languages. Robert Moffat, the famous missionary, translated it into the Bechuana language in 1838.

COMPOSER: Of Henry E. Matthews, born about 1820, known as the composer of the beautiful tune, "Children's Praises," little is known. His nationality is a matter of controversy but many editors feel that he was an American and known to Dr. Lowell Mason and Dr. Thomas Hastings. At all events, it was Dr. Hastings who had much to do with popularizing this one tune that perpetuates Matthews' name. In England Mrs. Shepherd's words, "Around the Throne of God in Heaven," are consistently associated with an anonymous tune called "Glory," which appeared in the "Tune Book to the Hymns and Chants for Sunday Schools." Though Matthews' tune has frequently been called "Glory," it must not be mistaken for the English tune.

TUNE: "Children's Praises" has had long usage in American churches and Sunday Schools. The tune was arranged in 1853. Three years later, in 1856, Dr. Thomas Hastings included it in "The Presbyterian Psalmodist." It met with instant popular approval, and in order to make it more widely known to Presbyterian Sunday Schools it was printed in The Presbyterian Sabbath School Visitor under date of September 1, 1857. Within the next decade it was included in more than a dozen hymnals for the Sunday Schools of the land. In some of these it appeared anonymously; but in the majority of them the editors ascribed it to Henry E. Matthews. It was first set up in carol form.

---

451   HYMN: So Here Hath Been Dawning
TUNE: Hardwick

Author: *Thomas Carlyle*   Source: *English Traditional Melody*

AUTHOR: The author of this hymn, Thomas Carlyle, was one of the unique characters of Scottish life. Carlyle, the son of a stonemason, was born in poverty in Ecclefechan in 1795. His godly parents expected their son to enter the Presbyterian ministry. After studying at Annan Academy and the University of Edinburgh, where he showed amazing avidity for reading, he gave up his purpose of entering the ministry. He taught school but not successfully. He entered upon law, hoping to reach the Scottish bar. This choice also proved unsatisfactory. He was ordained to be a writer. Amid hardship and penury he determined to follow literature. This he did in the face of poor remuneration and lack of appreciation. He stands out as one of the greatest literary figures of a very notable period. He finally came into his own and left to the world a noble bequest in "The French Revolution," which he called "truth clad in hell fire"; "Sartor Resartus"; and scores of essays, poems, criticisms, and literary productions. A place of honor was offered for his body in Westminster Abbey, but in harmony with his well-known desire for simplicity he was laid to rest in the village in which he was born.

HYMN: This tender hymn comes as a surprise to most readers of this grim, vehement Scottish writer. It reflects his love of beauty in nature, which his abrupt and rugged manners never obscured. It was published in his "Miscellaneous Essays" and was marked as a children's hymn when introduced into "Songs of Praise," published in 1925. Carlyle was profoundly religious and hated the materialism that he felt was sapping the reality of faith all around him. He challenged everyone everywhere, even in this little hymn, with the great responsibility of living and the necessity of sanctifying every day with a holy purpose.

SOURCE: The source is an English traditional melody.

TUNE: The tune, "Hardwick," is from Cecil Sharp's "English Folk Carols." It was noted by him from Mr. Henry Thomas at Chipping Sodbury. The portion of the tune here used is only the chorus of the original and there are alterations in the notes as well as in the harmony.

---

452   HYMN: Saviour, Teach Me, Day by Day
             TUNE: Posen

Author: *Jane E. Leeson*   Composer: *Georg C. Strattner*

AUTHOR: Jane E. Leeson (1807–1882) was a celebrated member of the Catholic Apostolic Church. Later she entered the Roman Catholic Church. She believed that her hymns were produced under divine inspiration, direct and creative. She published several books of hymns for children: "Infant Hymnings," "Hymns and Scenes of Childhood," and "The Child's Book of Ballads." Of her personal history nothing is known.

Children's Hymns

HYMN: This hymn was first published under the title "Obedience" in the author's "Hymns and Scenes of Childhood," published in 1842. It consisted of four stanzas of eight lines each.

Perhaps Miss Leeson's most popular hymn, much used in Great Britain, is "Loving Shepherd of Thy Sheep," the first stanza of which reads:

> "Loving Shepherd of Thy sheep,
> Keep Thy lamb, in safety keep;
> Nothing can Thy power withstand,
> None can pluck me from Thy hand."

COMPOSER: Georg C. Strattner (1650–1705), a German musician of ability and an admirer of Joachim Neander, of Bremen and Düsseldorf, came to popular attention as the editor of the fifth edition of Neander's "Bundeslieder," which was published at Frankfurt and Leipzig in 1691. By that time Neander, the first important hymn writer of the German Reformed Church, had been dead eleven years, and a cult of admirers had risen up to perpetuate his memory and his works. His hymns were collected and set to music, and the whole five editions which followed are in the Royal Library at Berlin. From these books other hymnals of worth were made. Strattner was a guiding spirit in this work and contributed tunes of his own composition.

TUNE: "Posen" appeared in the fifth edition of Neander's "Bundeslieder," published in 1691, and from there it has won acceptance throughout the world. It is a short tune of vigorous beat and in popular mood. Over against a striking melody is an interesting and forceful bass. Many texts have been associated with the tune, and "Saviour, Teach Me, Day by Day" is one of the most successful. "Posen" has always been popular with young people. It is equally successful, however, with adults, who have appropriated it. An early arrangement, which was made by J. A. Freylinghausen in 1705, was used in the Hymnal of 1911.

453

HYMN: Gentle Mary Laid Her Child
TUNE: Tempus Adest Floridum

Author: *Joseph Simpson Cook*   Source: *Medieval Spring Carol*

AUTHOR: The daughter of the author, in writing to the editor, indicates that Rev. Joseph Simpson Cook, S.T.D., was a pastor in the Methodist Church and later in the United Church of Canada. He was born in Durham County, England, in 1860, and died on May 28, 1933, in Toronto, Canada. He graduated from Wesleyan College of McGill University in Montreal. He wrote constantly, and left unfinished an important work on Biblical interpretation. His lyrical writing seems to have been limited to fugitive poems of a deeply religious character, of which this hymn is one.

Hymn: This beautifully conceived children's hymn carries the narrative of the birth of Jesus in the simplest possible language and in almost perfect lyric measures.

Source: The source is a spring carol of the fourteenth century.

Arranger: Ernest MacMillan was born in 1893 in Toronto, Canada, the son of a Presbyterian minister. His lifelong study has been hymns. At the age of thirteen Ernest was sent to England for study with Alfred Hollins. He passed the fellowship examinations for the Royal College of Organists at seventeen. After attending the University of Toronto he returned to England for further study. While he was on a walking tour of Germany the World War broke out. He was arrested with his companion and placed in Ruhleben Camp for the duration of the war. During this time he composed music for Swinburne's "Ode to England," for which he was granted the degree of Doctor of Music by Oxford University while he was still in Germany. At present he is principal and musical director of the Toronto Conservatory of Music.

Tune: This melody, "Tempus Adest Floridum," usually sung to Dr. John Mason Neale's rendering of the legend of "Good King Wenceslas," was originally a spring carol. It appears in "The Oxford Carol Book" with the free translation of the original, "Spring Has Now Unwrapped the Flowers." It appeared in "Piae Cantiones," a book printed by Theodoricus Petri in 1582, the object of which was to preserve in Sweden in the Reformed days the medieval songs and carols.

It will best be sung simply and softly as a lullaby, forgetting the hilarious mood often introduced with the more familiar Christmas words.

---

454 HYMN: Once in Royal David's City
TUNE: Irby

Author: *Cecil F. Alexander*   Composer: *Henry J. Gauntlett*

Author: For comments on the author, Cecil F. Alexander, see Hymn 157.

Hymn: This hymn was published in Mrs. Alexander's "Hymns for Little Children," in 1848. It was based upon the words in The Apostles' Creed, "Who was conceived by the Holy Ghost,

Children's Hymns

born of the Virgin Mary." Her hymn "There Is a Green Hill Far Away" was based on the words, "Suffered under Pontius Pilate, was crucified, dead, and buried" and her hymn "Every Morning the Red Sun" was composed around the phrase, "And the life everlasting." Mrs. Alexander excelled in the writing of hymns for little children. Concerning Mrs. Alexander's children's hymns, William G. Brookes says: "A need was felt for something more simple, and in 1848 Mrs. Alexander published her 'Hymns for Little Children.' They were charmingly simple and tender, clear in dogma, and of poetical beauty, combining the plainness of Watts with the feeling for and with childhood of the Taylor sisters."

COMPOSER: Henry J. Gauntlett (1805–1876) was organist of his father's church at nine years of age. He prepared for the law and followed that profession until he was thirty-nine years old, when he gave it up to devote himself to music. The archbishop of Canterbury conferred on him the degree of Doctor of Music. Of him Mendelssohn said, "His literary attainments, his knowledge of the history of music, his acquaintance with acoustical laws, his marvelous memory, his philosophical turn of mind, as well as his practical experience, rendered him one of the most remarkable professors of the age." He edited many hymn books and wrote thousands of tunes.

TUNE: "Irby" was originally written for this hymn and first appeared in "Christmas Carols," in 1849. In Dr. Gauntlett's "Hymns for Little Children. . . . Set to Music with Piano Accompaniment," published in 1858, it was set for one voice with piano accompaniment. This hymn should not be sung too fast because of the many fast-moving notes in the melody as well as in the other parts.

455
HYMN: Angel Voices, Ever Singing
TUNE: Angel Voices

Author: *Rev. Francis Pott*   Composer: *Arthur S. Sullivan*

AUTHOR: For comments on the author, Francis Pott, see Hymn 164.

HYMN: This very widely used hymn appeared in Pott's "Hymns Fitted to the Order of Common Prayer," published in 1866. It was written for "the dedication of an organ and the meeting of choirs." The theme is drawn from the adoration of the angels about the throne of God. The call is to the complete dedication of all human powers and arts to the service and worship of God. Such dedication, the author felt, must precede all worthy worship.

467

COMPOSER: For comments on the composer, Arthur S. Sullivan, see Hymn 128.

TUNE: The tune, "Angel Voices," was written in 1872. Dr. Pott objected to it on the grounds that it was written "with the first stanza alone in mind, and the rest of the hymn in contrast therewith." It has received criticism from various sources, but in the American Church the tune has wide popularity.

The director should beat two slow pulses to each measure for this melody. It should be sung in stately, even time.

---

456   HYMN: Golden Harps Are Sounding
        TUNE: Hermas

Author: *Frances R. Havergal*   Composer: *Frances R. Haverga*

AUTHOR: For comments on the author, Frances R. Havergal, see Hymn 56.

HYMN: This is an Ascension Day hymn based on Eph. 4:8:
"When he ascended on high, he led captivity captive,
And gave gifts unto men."

It was written in 1871. In the "Memorials of Frances Ridley Havergal," by her sister, we read in one of her letters her own account of how she looked upon her talent for hymn-writing. She says: "I shall look up and thank Him, and say, 'Now, dear Master, give me another to rime with it, and then another'; and then perhaps he will send it all in one flow of musical thoughts, but more likely one at a time, that I may be kept asking him for every line. There, that is the process, and you see there is no 'I can do it' all. That isn't his way with me. I often smile to myself when people talk about 'gifted pen' or 'clever verses,' because they don't know that it is neither, but something really much nicer than being 'talented' or 'clever.'" Nearly every poem would verify the above. Some instances are given. "When visiting at Perry Barr she walked to the boys' schoolroom, and being very tired she leaned against the playground wall while Mr. Snepp went in. Returning in ten minutes, he found her scribbling on an old envelope, and at his request she handed him the hymn just penciled, 'Golden Harps Are Sounding.'"

COMPOSER: For comments on the composer, Frances R. Havergal, see Hymn 56.

Children's Hymns

TUNE: For comments on the tune, "Hermas," see Hymn 56.
The earlier setting under Hymn 56 is a different harmonization, in which the key is one half tone lower. It would be better suited, therefore, for use as a congregational hymn. When "Hermas" is used for a choir processional, the higher key is preferable.

457

HYMN: Brightly Gleams Our Banner
TUNE: St. Theresa

Author: *Rev. Thomas J. Potter*   Composer: *Arthur S. Sullivan*

AUTHOR: The author, Rev. Thomas J. Potter, was born in 1827 and died in Dublin in 1873. He became a priest of the Roman Catholic Church in 1857. Later he achieved a brilliant career as a teacher in the chair of pulpit eloquence and English literature in the Foreign Missionary College of All Hallows, in Dublin. He was the author of many volumes dealing with the art of preaching, such as "The Spoken Word, or, The Art of Extemporary Preaching"; "Sacred Eloquence, or, The Theory and Practice of Preaching"; and "The Pastor and His People."

HYMN: This hymn, the author's most popular one, was taken and altered for Protestant uses from "The Holy Family Hymns," published in 1860. It was recast in "Psalms and Hymns" in 1867 and 1869. This is a greatly abbreviated form of the original. The first stanza carries majestically the spirit of a brilliant processional, of which the Protestant Church knows little. But in the remaining stanzas the atmosphere changes and in the humility of true devotion the life of service is portrayed with prophetic foretokens of heaven and victorious rest.

COMPOSER: For comments on the composer, Arthur S. Sullivan, see Hymn 128.

TUNE: Like the tune "Angel Voices," Hymn 455, this tune has afforded the critics the opportunity to chide Sullivan for writing deliberately to touch the heart of the multitude. "A relaxing of reverent restraint" is said to be his weakness. Sir Henry Hadow, describing such a melody in "Music as an Element in Worship," remarks that there is "too much ease in Zion." Nevertheless the spiritual influences of "St. Theresa" are widely recognized throughout the Church.
It is a slow processional with two pulses to each measure. However, only the first beat of the measure should be stressed; otherwise words like "banner" will be distorted by having accents fall on both syllables alike.

Handbook to The Hymnal

458 HYMN: Saviour, Like a Shepherd Lead Us
TUNE: Sicilian Mariners

Author: *Anonymous*   Source: *Sicilian Melody*

AUTHOR: This hymn appeared anonymously in "Hymns for the Young," published in 1832 by Miss D. A. Thrupp. Miss Thrupp, whose children's hymns have been extensively used, was born in London on June 20, 1779, and died there on December 14, 1847. Her unyielding purpose to avoid undue personal publicity has robbed her of the praise she deserves. Her earlier hymns, strikingly adapted to the worship experience of children, appeared in Wilson's Friendly Visitor and Children's Friend, under the name "Iota." She compiled "Hymns for the Young" for the Religious Tract Society in 1830. This hymn has been ascribed, and with some degree of credibility, to Henry Francis Lyte (1793–1847). (See the comments on Hymn 12.)

HYMN: The original version of this hymn has the word "tenderest" instead of "tender" in stanza 1, line 2. What John Wesley says of children's hymns in a preface dated 1790 is applicable to-day: "There are two ways of writing or speaking to children: the one is to let ourselves down to them; the other, to lift them up to us. Dr. Watts has written in the former way, and has succeeded admirably well, speaking to children as children, and leaving them as he found them. The following hymns are written on the other plan; they contain strong and manly sense, yet expressed in such plain and easy language as even children may understand. But when they do understand them, they will be children no longer, only in years and stature."

SOURCE: The source is a Sicilian melody.

TUNE: For comments on the tune, "Sicilian Mariners," see Hymn 54.

Special Seasons and Services

Thanksgiving and Harvest

*

459   HYMN: Now Thank We All Our God
             TUNE: Nun Danket

Author: *Rev. Martin Rinkart*   Composer: *Johann Crüger*

AUTHOR: Rev. Martin Rinkart (1586–1649), dramatist, composer, poet, and pastor, was a man of sterling character. Seeking to secure an education, he supported himself by his music while studying theology. Completing his studies at Leipzig he eventually returned to Eilenburg, the town of his birth and boyhood, to be the parish minister. There he lived and labored for thirty-two years. A terrible pestilence raged in 1637, followed by a severe famine. Eight thousand people died in the town in one year and of these Pastor Rinkart buried over four thousand.

When, in the course of the Thirty Years' War, the Swedish army captured the town and demanded a huge ransom, Rinkart went to the enemies' camp to intercede. On being rebuffed, he came back to his church, called the people to prayer, and then again visited the camp, where he secured a compromise.

Rinkart wrote six dramas of Luther and the Reformation, the material of which was later adapted by Lessing.

TRANSLATOR: For comments on the translator, Catherine Winkworth, see Hymn 6.

HYMN: Tradition relates this hymn, written at about the conclusion of the Thirty Years' War, to the making of final peace. Moffatt says that the tradition is groundless. Ecclus. 50: 22-24 furnishes the basis for the hymn. It was sung at the dedication of Cologne Cathedral in 1887, at the Diamond Jubilee of Queen Victoria in 1897, and at the laying of the corner stone of the Reichstag Building in Berlin by William I in 1884.

This hymn has been called the German "Te Deum." It is sung in the German churches on New Year's Eve. The first two stanzas were composed as a grace before meat to be used in the author's own family.

COMPOSER: For comments on the composer, Johann Crüger, see Hymn 158.

TUNE: "Nun Danket" is a tune known the world over. The recent Japanese Hymnal has given it prominent place, as have hymn books of other lands. The melody of this tune is from Johann Crüger's "Praxis Pietatis Melica," of which more than fifty editions were published between 1650 and 1750. The third edition of this work appeared in 1648, and in it this melody appeared. It has had many versions, and one of the best is by Mendelssohn in his "Lobgesang."

---

460 HYMN: Come, Ye Thankful People, Come
TUNE: St. George's, Windsor

Author: *Rev. Henry Alford* Composer: *George J. Elvey*

AUTHOR: For comments on the author, Henry Alford, see Hymn 369.

HYMN: This is the most widely accepted of Dean Alford's hymns. It appeared in 1844 in his "Psalms and Hymns." It is marked by the pronounced musical rhythm that characterizes Alford's work and is above the usual level of his hymns in its poetic qualities. The content of the hymn sweeps broadly through the whole régime of God's grace manifest in his present worldly blessings and in his eternal salvation.

COMPOSER: For comments on the composer, George J. Elvey, see Hymn 109.

TUNE: For comments on the tune, "St. George's, Windsor," see Hymn 109.

---

461 HYMN: We Praise Thee, O God, Our Redeemer, Creator
TUNE: Kremser

Author: *Julia Bulkley Cady Cory* Source: *Old Netherlands Melody*

AUTHOR: Julia Bulkley Cady Cory is the daughter of J. Cleveland Cady, one of the noted architects of New York City. Mr. Cady was the superintendent of the Sunday School of the Church of the Covenant, affiliated with the Brick Presbyterian Church, New York City, where his daughter was an active member.

HYMN: This hymn was first used at a Thanksgiving service in the Brick Presbyterian Church of New York City in 1902, when Dr. William R. Richards was pastor. The organist, J. Archer Gibson,

Special Seasons and Services

had found the music, set to militaristic and unchristian words. He
lamented the fact and called it to the attention of Miss Julia Bulkley Cady.
At his request she composed these joyous words for the Dutch tune. A
Christmas stanza was later added.

There is solid grandeur here, coupled with a quick meter. Worthy
words and noble music make this hymn sing itself into the memory. It is
in the "grand style," with a touch of Puritan austerity that is associated
with autumn weather and the New England Thanksgiving Day.

SOURCE: The source is an old Netherlands melody.

COMPILER: Adrianus Valerius, compiler of "The Collection" of
Netherlands songs, in which the hymn appears, was born at
Middelburg, The Netherlands. Most of his life was spent at
Veere, where from 1606 until his death, on January 27, 1625, he held legal
offices. His collection of songs was published at Haarlem in 1621 and 1626.
Special value is given to this collection because Valerius noted the tunes
as they were sung and added short sketches as to how they were inspired.

TUNE: This old Netherlands melody, known as "Kremser," goes
back to 1625. The tune is an interesting study in musical diction,
simple in style and characterized by phrases and progressions that
undulate like the waves of the sea. It has been a popular hymn since the
seventeenth century. Whether sung with the measured, stately tones of a
choral, or the gayer mode of a festival traditional, the rendering of it is an
inspiring event.

---

462   HYMN: O God, Beneath Thy Guiding Hand
       TUNE: Duke Street

Author: *Rev. Leonard Bacon*   Composer: *John Hatton*

AUTHOR: Dr. Leonard Bacon was born of missionary parents in
1802. His birthplace was the trading post of Detroit, then one of
the points on the frontier in constant peril. After nine years of
pioneer life the lad was sent to live with his uncle, a physician at Hartford,
Connecticut. He graduated at Yale and Andover Seminary, and in 1825
was ordained and installed as pastor of the Centre Church, New Haven,
Connecticut. He was appointed to the chair of theology in Yale Divinity
School in 1866, which he held until 1871. He was one of the founders of the
New York Independent, the most influential American weekly religious
journal of the last half of the nineteenth century. Leonard Bacon was a
leader in the early discussions in opposition to slavery, and in his leader-

ship in courses of moral reform he was true to his rugged Puritan convictions. As a writer of hymns and a most intelligent compiler, he has rendered great service to the Church. While a student in the seminary he compiled "Hymns and Sacred Songs for the Monthly Concert." He died on December 23, 1881.

HYMN: On April 25, 1833, the bicentennial of Connecticut and of the Centre Church was celebrated. Dr. Bacon not only delivered the main historical address but took the theme of his sermon as the basis for this hymn. How well the spirit of the Pilgrim Fathers is voiced in this hymn! We have but to read from Edward Winslow's own words: "Our corn [wheat] did prove well; and God be praised, we had a good increase of Indian corn [maize]. Our harvest being gotten in, our Governor sent four men on fowling, that so we might, after a special manner, rejoice together after we had gathered the fruit of our labors. Many of the Indians came amongst us, and among the rest Massasoit, with some ninety men whom for three days we entertained or feasted."

COMPOSER: For comments on the composer, John Hatton, see Hymn 377.

TUNE: For comments on the tune, "Duke Street," see Hymn 377.

---

463 HYMN: Praise, O Praise Our God and King
TUNE: Monkland

Author: *John Milton*   Arranger: *John B. Wilkes*

AUTHOR: For comments on the author, John Milton, see Hymn 64.

EDITOR: For comments on the editor, Henry Williams Baker, see Hymn 99.

HYMN: This hymn from England's chief compiler, Henry Williams Baker, is based on Psalm 136, as versified by John Milton. According to his biographies, Milton put the psalm into musical form when he was fifteen years of age, while attending St. Paul's School, London. It appeared in 1645 in his "Poems in English and Latin." There are various versions, all based on Milton's hymn. The hymn is but one of four of Baker's that, according to Dr. Julian, "are the highest strains of jubilation." Most of Baker's hymns are exceedingly plaintive,

Special Seasons and Services

sometimes even sad. The hymn is given here as it appeared in "Hymns Ancient and Modern," published in 1861, of which Sir Henry Baker was the editor.

ARRANGER: For comments on the arranger, John B. Wilkes, see Hymn 64.

TUNE: For comments on the tune, "Monkland," see Hymn 64.

---

464   HYMN: We Plow the Fields, and Scatter
       TUNE: Wir Pflügen

Author: *Matthias Claudius*   Composer: *Johann A. P. Schulz*

AUTHOR: The author, Matthias Claudius (1740–1815), a friend of Goethe, was educated at Jena, where the current rationalistic influences turned him from theology to law. He became a journalist and editor. In 1776 he was appointed commissioner of agriculture and manufactures for Hesse Darmstadt. In 1777 a severe illness brought him a deep religious experience and conversion. He turned to newspaper-editing with a new interest and introduced much poetry in a religious strain, exercising a great influence on the religious life of the country. He had a desperate struggle with poverty, but in 1788 was appointed by the Danish crown to a position as bank auditor.

TRANSLATOR: The translator of this favorite Thanksgiving hymn, sung everywhere by children, is Jane Montgomery Campbell, a daughter of an Episcopal clergyman in Paddington, a part of London. She was unusually gifted in poetical and musical matters. She shared with her father in the work of the parish and trained choirs of children in the singing of hymns and in other ways lent aid to the work of enriching the worship life of the community. She collaborated with Charles S. Bere in the preparation of hymn and choral collections, "The Garland of Songs," published in 1862 and "Children's Chorale Book," 1869. Along with these volumes she produced one of her own containing translations, and her own hymns used in her London parish work with children. This highly consecrated and endowed woman died in 1878.

HYMN: This hymn is an adaptation of "The Peasants' Song" in "Paul Erdmann's Feast," a sketch by Claudius, who, as a trained journalist, presents a charming picture of the simplicity and piety of a north German harvest festival. "They sang the Peasants' Song as here follows," he writes. "I don't know what sort of effect the song has when it is read, but I know well what that was when the peasants sang it.

475

The music, they said, was Italian. I have set it down as well as I could catch it. Let any one improve it, or make another one."

The original hymn is in seventeen four-line stanzas, with a refrain to each. In 1800 a Hanover schoolbook carried stanzas 3-10 of Claudius' song to the now-famous music by Schulz. Ever since this happy rearrangement the hymn has had an extraordinary popularity in German. It came to England in Miss Campbell's translation in 1861.

COMPOSER: Johann A. P. Schulz was a contemporary of Matthias Claudius, whose hymn, "We Plow the Fields, and Scatter," he helped to make famous. He was born at Lüneburg, Germany, in 1747. Contrary to the wishes of his father, who intended him to enter the ministry, he ran away from home to prepare for a musical career. He successfully begged Kirnberger, of Berlin, to accept him as a pupil. Under the latter's instruction Schulz laid the foundation for a successful musical career. After traveling in France, Italy, and Germany, he became musical conductor for Prince Henry, of Prussia, at Rheinsberg from 1780 to 1787. Seven years of conducting, from 1787 to 1794, were given to the Danish Court at Copenhagen. He wrote songs, operas, oratorios, and instrumental music. He died at Schwedt, on June 10, 1800.

TUNE: "Wir Pflügen" is a festive tune and justly famous. It appeared in "Lieder für Volkschulen," issued in Hanover, Germany, in 1800. It was introduced to England in The Bible Class Magazine for November, 1854. Since Jane Campbell's excellent translation of the text was made in 1861, it has been widely used in England and America.

465
HYMN: God of Mercy, God of Grace
TUNE: Ratisbon

Author: *Rev. Henry F. Lyte*   Source: *Old German Melody*

AUTHOR: For comments on the author, Henry F. Lyte, see Hymn 12.

HYMN: This joyous paraphrase of Psalm 67 was written by a gifted author who even as a student three times won the prize for an English poem. Ministering all his life to the needs of a small country parish, Lyte was specially qualified to voice the gratitude of rural people for the generous returns of nature. While there is a universal inclusiveness in the call to worship in this hymn, it has specially in mind the call to gratitude for the fruits of the earth. The hymn was first printed in 1834, appearing in Lyte's "The Spirit of the Psalms." Five of the author's hymns are in "The Hymnal."

Special Seasons and Services

SOURCE: The source is an old German melody, arranged in J. G. Werner's "Choralbuch." For comments on German hymnody see the article, "German Hymn Sources," under "Original Sources," page xxi.

ARRANGER: The arranger, J. G. Werner, was born in 1589 in Holland. In the year 1614 he became master in the Löbenicht School at Königsberg. There he edited the "Königsberg Gesangbuch," to which he contributed a number of hymns. Werner's psalm versions are designated "Psalters German."

TUNE: "Ratisbon" is a German melody, taken from the "Choralbuch" of J. G. Werner, published in 1815.

The New Year

*

466 HYMN: Ring Out, Wild Bells, to the Wild Sky
     TUNE: Jordan

Author: *Alfred Tennyson*   Composer: *Joseph Barnby*

AUTHOR: For comments on the author, Alfred Tennyson, see Hymn 175.

HYMN: In the death of Arthur Hallam, Tennyson had lost his best friend. In "In Memoriam" he traces his grief through successive Christmas celebrations and, after over a hundred poetic sections, bursts into this song of confident affirmation at the opening of a new year. Through the mazes of his grief and doubt he wanders, plagued by the implications of the new struggle between science and religion, until, at last, with a "hope that never lost her youth," he comes to faith in God.

> "That God, which ever lives and loves,
>   One God, one law, one element,
>   And one far-off divine event,
> To which the whole creation moves."

In this hymn, which is from section 106, the poet turns from the past and his own private grief and looks to the future, with its hopes for mankind. The mood is heightened and the bells, wild and jubilant, ring out as though "the closing cycle" were already beginning. The powers that work for good are those that unite men, while the feeling that grief isolates and is harmful moves the poet to rise above it.

477

"My father expressed his conviction," wrote Tennyson's son, "that the forms of the Christian religion would alter, but that the spirit of Christ would still grow from more to more in the roll of the ages,

> " 'Till each man find his own in all men's good,
>   And all men work in noble brotherhood!' "

COMPOSER: For comments on the composer, Joseph Barnby, see Hymn 3.

TUNE: "Jordan," known in English hymnals as "Cantate Domino," appeared in "The Hymnary" of 1872. It was composed for Dr. Monsell's "Sing to the Lord a Joyful Song," but has been found a successful setting for other texts, such as "The Lord Is Come, on Syrian Soil" and "Ring Out, Wild Bells, to the Wild Sky." The tune represents Barnby at his best. Credit must be given to the Protestant Episcopal Church for introducing it to America.

467

HYMN: From Glory Unto Glory
TUNE: Hoyte (St. Columba)

Author: *Frances Ridley Havergal*   Composer: *W. Stevenson Hoyte*

AUTHOR: For comments on the author, Frances Ridley Havergal, see Hymn 56.

HYMN: This hymn of personal consecration at the opening of the New Year is one of about fifty of Miss Havergal's hymns in common use in both England and America. It was written on December 24, 1873, while she was living at Winterdyne. It was used first as a New Year's leaflet and then published in a volume of poems, entitled "Under the Surface." It contained twenty stanzas of four lines each. Miss Havergal indicated to Dr. Julian that the hymn was reminiscent of "that flash of electric light, when I first saw clearly the blessedness of true consecration, December 2, 1873. I could not have written the hymn before. It is a wonderful word from 'glory unto glory.' May we more and more claim and realize all that is folded up in it." The author wrote "For More Exceeding" as a sequel to this hymn in 1876.

COMPOSER: William Stevenson Hoyte, who is the author of a volume entitled "A Book of Litanies, Metrical and Prose, with an Evening Service and Accompanying Music," was born in England in the year 1844. He was organist of All Saints, Margaret Street, London, from 1868 to 1907. His tunes are not numerous, but are of a high order.

TUNE: "Hoyte," also known as "St. Columba," was composed during the composer's incumbency as organist at All Saints, London. The usual date assigned to it is 1889. It is a stirring tune of optimism and good cheer. As a processional it is effective. It is a fortunate setting for Miss Havergal's hymn, "From Glory Unto Glory," and gives it noble expression.

---

468 HYMN: Standing at the Portal
TUNE: The New Year

Author: *Frances Ridley Havergal* Composer: *Arthur H. Mann*

AUTHOR: For comments on the author, Frances Ridley Havergal, see Hymn 56.

HYMN: Rev. James Davidson, vicar of St. Paul's, Bristol, England, writing of Miss Havergal's hymns, says: "She lives and speaks in every line of her poetry. Her poems are permeated with the fragrance of her passionate love of Jesus. . . . The burden of her writings is a free and full salvation, through the Redeemer's merits, . . . and her life was devoted to the proclamation of this truth by personal labors, literary efforts, and earnest interest in foreign missions." This hymn was written January 4, 1873, six years before her death, and published in "Under the Surface" (1874) and in "Life Chords" (1880). It is a New Year's hymn, with all the characteristics of resignation and hope that mark Miss Havergal's poetry.

COMPOSER: For comments on the composer, Arthur H. Mann, see Hymn 200.

TUNE: "The New Year" is a stately processional tune, written in popular style, well-balanced phrases, and moving cadences. In structure the music is Anglican, of stirring harmony and thrilling progression. The parts between a fluent melody and undulating bass are equally well done, and result in a tune of unusual merit.

---

469 HYMN: Break, New-Born Year, on Glad Eyes Break
TUNE: Nox Praecessit

Author: *Thomas H. Gill* Composer: *John Baptiste Calkin*

AUTHOR: For comments on the author, Thomas H. Gill, see Hymn 342.

Handbook to The Hymnal

HYMN: According to Dr. William Ellis Thompson, a walking stick handed down from one of Gill's Puritan ancestors and dating from 1692 was the inspiration of this New Year's hymn, which was written one Sunday afternoon. Thomas Gill was born a Unitarian and was, consequently, debarred from the English universities. Educated in Nonconformist schools, he rigorously opposed ritualism, though he later joined the Established Church. Of martyr ancestry, he lived to be eighty-seven. At seventy-five, when his eyesight was threatened, he said, "I am grateful for the gift of a remarkable memory."

"Poetic fervor, devout emotion, lyric meaning" characterize Gill's work. His high standard for hymns is expressed in sentiments like these: "Hymns are not meant to be theological statements . . . nor even enunciation of precepts. They are utterances of the soul in its manifold moods of hope, fear, joy, sorrow, wonder, love, and aspiration." They should be characterized by "liveliness and intensity of feeling; directness, clearness, and vividness of utterance; strength, sweetness, and simplicity of diction; and melody of rhythm. . . . Excessive subtlety, excessive ornament should be avoided."

COMPOSER: For comments on the composer, John Baptiste Calkin, see Hymn 384.

TUNE: "Nox Praecessit" is a vigorous tune. For this reason it has always been associated with bright and joyful texts. It was composed for "Bride of the Lamb! Awake, Awake" in 1873, and in that year appeared in "The Christian Hymnal," published in England. It has also been associated with Barton's "Walk in the Light: So Shalt Thou Know." It is a fine setting for this New Year's hymn by Thomas H. Gill.

---

470 HYMN: Great God, We Sing That Mighty Hand
TUNE: Wareham

Author: *Rev. Philip Doddridge*   Composer: *William Knapp*

AUTHOR: For comments on the author, Rev. Philip Doddridge, see Hymn 98.

HYMN: This hymn is from Doddridge's (posthumous) "Hymns Founded on Various Texts in the Holy Scriptures" (1755), where it is headed "Help Obtained from God. Acts XXVI. 22. For the New Year." It is a hymn of great dignity and, while gratefully reminiscent of the past year and its mercies, is thoughtful at the threshold of the new year. It is written in the spirit of the prayer of fiery John Hunter, who

480

wrote "Hymns of Faith and Life," one of which (Hymn 507) is included in "The Hymnal":

"Almighty Father, as we keep holy time under the deepening shadows of the closing year, we thank Thee for all that it hath brought to us of mercy and truth. Let not the experiences of our past days be lost upon us. Fix in our minds every lesson of faith and duty which Thou hast been teaching us. Grant unto us, before the record of this year hath been finished and sealed, a very honest and deep desire to live according to Thy will, as it hath been made known to us in Jesus Christ our Lord. Amen."

COMPOSER: William Knapp, as his name indicates, was probably of German extraction. He was born at Wareham, England, in 1698. He was concerned about congregational singing and exerted great influence in improving it by his tunes and anthems. He was sometimes referred to as "a country psalm singer." An accomplished musician, he served as organist at Wareham and at Poole. At the latter place he was parish clerk of St. James's for thirty-nine years and was referred to in The London Magazine for 1742. While he published several important works, his memory is perpetuated by his tune "Wareham," which, according to Dr. James Moffatt, "is one of the best congregational tunes ever written."

TUNE: The period of old syllabic tunes continued for more than 250 years, during which small musical progress was made. Within the first half of the eighteenth century came the beginning of English hymnology, and with it new departures in hymn-tune music. From this time on the old tunes were called "psalm tunes"; the new ones were designated as "hymn tunes," in which hymn and hymn tunes appear together. This demand grew out of the Lutheran Reformation in Germany and Methodism. The change in form appears in such tunes as "Wareham," by William Knapp, 1738. The ruggedness of the old tunes was much softened. The new tunes were more flowing, often in triple time, and introduce "passing" or "nonchordal," which were unknown to the syllabic tunes. These newer hymns are marked by more elaborate harmonies. "Wareham" first appeared in Knapp's book "A Sett of New Psalms and Anthems" (1738). It was composed for the sacrament of the Lord's Supper, and was set to Ps. 36: 5-10.

471

HYMN: All Beautiful the March of Days
TUNE: Forest Green

Author: *Frances Whitmarsh Wile*

Source: *English Traditional Melody*

AUTHOR: Frances Whitmarsh Wile was born in Bristol Valley, New York, in 1875. Her literary friendships included the poets and hymn writers, Dr. W. C. Gannett and Dr. F. L. Hosmer. In their search for a hymn properly reflecting the spiritual values of the winter season, Mrs. Wile was appealed to, with the result that this poem, entitled "All Beautiful the March of Days," was produced.

HYMN: Brought up in this charming rural area, where the mails came but once a week and where, in the great winter snowfall that characterizes the region, nature for long winter months lays "a silent loveliness on hill and wood and field," the author in her beautiful hymn achieved the atmosphere of Whittier's "Snow-Bound," with an added element of reverence and gratitude to God that becomes worship.

SOURCE: "Forest Green" is from "The English Hymnal," which was published in 1906. It is an arrangement by R. Vaughan Williams from a folk song called "The Plowboy's Dream."

TUNE: This is a bright and joyful tune, and has been joined with a variety of texts, as, "O Little Town of Bethlehem," "The Summer Days Are Come Again," and "All Beautiful the March of Days." Summer, winter, and Christmas are associated with its inspiring music.

Laying of a Corner Stone

*

472

HYMN: Christ Is Our Corner Stone
TUNE: Unity

Source: *Old Latin Hymn*

Composer: *R. Huntington Woodman*

TRANSLATOR: John Chandler was born in Surrey, England, June 16, 1806. He graduated from Oxford in 1827 and was ordained in 1831. He became vicar of Witley, the town where he was born, in 1837. He takes rank with the foremost of our modern translators of hymns. He sought to set over against the ancient prayers in the liturgy hymns born out of the same period of religious life. Thus he was led to

Special Seasons and Services

make a real contribution to hymnology from these ancient sources. Perhaps forty of his Latin translations are in common use. The fields through which his scholarship carried him are evidenced by the following titles of his books: "The Hymns of the Primitive Church," 1837, followed by a second volume in 1841 and later by "Life of William Wykeham," and "Horae Sacrae," the last being prayers and meditations of English divines. He died at Putney in 1872.

HYMN: This is a free but admirable translation of a seventh or eighth century Latin hymn probably taken from the Paris Breviary of 1643. The original text is in two parts, both used as hymns, the latter part especially popular in American churches. The first part is "Urbs Beata Hierusalem"; the second part, the present hymn "Angularis Fundamentum." The entire hymn by long tradition belongs to the service of dedication, the second part being especially appropriate for the services in connection with the laying of the corner stone of a church.

COMPOSER: Raymond Huntington Woodman, the composer of the tune, "Unity," was born in Brooklyn, New York, January 18, 1861. He was the son of an organist and at an early age became assistant to his father, who held a position at Flushing, Long Island. Besides becoming a student at the College of New York City, he received his early musical training from his father. Later he studied four years under Dudley Buck and then spent a period of time in Paris as a pupil of César Franck. In public life Dr. Woodman has been a member of the faculty at the Metropolitan College of New York City and served as musical editor of the New York Evangelist, professor of music at Packer Collegiate Institute, and head of the theory department of the American Institute of Applied Music. He is a Fellow and Warden of the American Guild of Organists. He has been a prolific composer, and his compositions include numerous songs, choral works, cantatas, and works for piano and organ.

TUNE: "Unity" was especially written for the Presbyterian Hymnal of 1895 and for the words, "Christ Is Our Corner Stone." Since then it has been included in all subsequent hymnals of the denomination. The dominant mood of the tune is festive, thus making it an appropriate setting for use at the laying of a corner stone for a church.

473 HYMN: O Thou, Whose Hand Has Brought Us
TUNE: Day of Rest

Author: *Rev. Frederic William Goadby*   Composer: *James W. Elliott*

AUTHOR: Rev. Frederic William Goadby was the son of a Baptist minister of Leicester, England, where he was born August 10, 1845. He received his theological training at Regents' Park College, and received a Master's degree from London University in 1868, becoming a pastor the same year at the Baptist Church in Bluntisham, Hunts, where he remained until 1876. An untimely death in 1880 at thirty-five years of age cut short what evidently was to have been a brilliant pastoral career. Before his early death Goadby's literary gifts were beginning to be recognized through his contributions to the periodicals of his day and by his hymns.

HYMN: This hymn is most specific in all its references to the "opening of a place of worship," for which purpose it was written. It appeared first in "The Baptist Hymnal" in 1879. It appropriately gives praise for every generous heart and every willing hand that the finished building represents. It closes asking that "the busy toiler," burdened with his daily routine, may "rise to the things above."

COMPOSER: For comments on the composer, James W. Elliott, see Hymn 268.

TUNE: For comments on the tune, "Day of Rest," see Hymn 268.

Dedication of a Church

*

474 HYMN: Founded on Thee, Our Only Lord
TUNE: Mendon

Author: *Rev. Samuel F. Smith*   Source: *German Melody*

AUTHOR: For comments on the author, Samuel F. Smith, see Hymn 389.

HYMN: This hymn of dedication for a sanctuary, with some six hundred others, came from the fertile pen of Rev. Samuel F. Smith, who is best known by the hymn "My Country, 'T is of

Thee." In a letter dated December 14, 1894, the author said, "This hymn ["Founded on Thee, Our Only Lord"] was written a few weeks since to be used at a young men's social union in Boston." The Boston Evening Transcript of February 14, 1925, states, however, that the hymn was written by Dr. Smith for use in the dedication of the house of worship of the Rosendale Baptist Church, June 17, 1889. Dr. Smith, according to this account, was one of thirteen persons who assembled in the home of Amasa Wood and organized that same church, March 13, 1875. The hymn is doubtless suggested by the word of Christ that he would build his Church upon a rock. In the first and last stanzas the figure of a rock is employed to represent the impregnable character of the Church's foundations. The majesty and power of divinity are set forth in the light of God's redeeming love.

As a hymn of worship and devotion it possesses dignity and worth. "Founded on Thee, Our Only Lord" is eminently suitable for use in the dedicatory service of a Christian house of worship, as an expression of those changeless verities for which the unshaken Church fittingly stands.

ARRANGER: Samuel Dyer, the son of a Baptist preacher, was born November 4, 1785, at Wellshire, England. He studied music under the guidance of Thomas Walker, of London, a distinguished chorister, and in 1811 came to New York to follow a musical career. After spending a year in New York City, he removed to Philadelphia, where he became a well-known choir leader and teacher, as well as a conductor of oratorio music. Several times he visited his native land for study and research. While residing in Baltimore, Maryland, he published his "New Selection of Sacred Music," which was a valuable work used from the New England States to the Gulf. He died in Hoboken, New Jersey, July 20, 1835.

TUNE: "Mendon" is based upon a German melody. It seems to have first appeared in the "Supplement of Samuel Dyer's Third Edition of Sacred Music" (1824). Later, with some revision, it was included in the fourth edition. Subsequently it was revised by Dr. Lowell Mason, who is supposed to have given the tune its name.

---

475   HYMN: All Things Are Thine; No Gift Have We
TUNE: Herr Jesu Christ

Author: *John Greenleaf Whittier*   Source: *"Pensum Sacrum"*

AUTHOR: For comments on the author, John Greenleaf Whittier, see Hymn 178.

HYMN: To the pen of the immortal Quaker poet Whittier the Church is indebted for this warmly devotional hymn, for use in connection with the dedication of a house of worship. It was written for the opening of Plymouth Church, St. Paul, Minnesota, in 1873, and appeared in print in 1875 in the collection entitled "Hazel Blossoms." It was also embodied in Horder's "Congregational Hymns" in 1884 and was published in Whittier's "Complete Poetical Works," 1876. It is a well-phrased ascription of gratitude to the divine Architect, properly worded in the mood of human weakness and humility, with a dignified invocation of the manifest presence of divine and "tender Fatherhood." By a gentle hand the Quaker poet leads his fellow worshipers out of the emptiness of bare walls into an inner shrine resplendent with the living Presence. The hymn is couched in simple, pleasing phrases; is winged by a gliding, gentle rhythm; and is mystically and emotionally satisfying.

ARRANGER: For comments on the arranger, Johann Sebastian Bach, see Hymn 21.

TUNE: "Herr Jesu Christ" appears in "Pensum Sacrum" published in Görlitz in 1648. The collection contained 267 Latin odes and 80 melodies. The melody under discussion here was set to six odes. In 1651 it became associated with the hymn, the first words of which give it its name. This was the "Gothaer Cantional." The version used in this book is by Bach as it appeared in his "Vierstimmige Choralgesänge" (1765–1769).

---

476 HYMN: Thou, Whose Unmeasured Temple Stands
TUNE: St. Anne

Author: *William Cullen Bryant*   Composer: *Ascribed to William Croft*

AUTHOR: The author, William Cullen Bryant, who was born November 3, 1794, in Cunnington, Massachusetts, is best known as an eminent American poet of the early part of the nineteenth century. He died on Long Island, July 12, 1878, in his eighty-fourth year. During his lifetime, he wrote more than twenty hymns.

HYMN: The hymn, "Thou, Whose Unmeasured Temple Stands," was written in 1835 for the dedication of a chapel in Prince Street, New York City, and is the most widely known of Bryant's hymns. It was introduced into Great Britain in 1837 and was included in Beard's "Collection." In its present form, somewhat changed from the original, it appeared in "The American Presbyterian Psalter and Hymns," Richmond, Virginia, in 1867 and also was included in Horder's "Congregational Hymns," London, 1884. Bryant aptly begins his dedicatory verse by a direct and impressive invocation of the great "Thou." The element of objectivity in worship, as well as its subjective aspects, is here presented. When the sense of the divine Presence fades from the temple, its glory, and inevitably its power, disappear. The hymn runs the gamut of human moods and needs to which the sanctuary of God is designed to minister. The divine blessing is implored for those who err, for those who sorrow, and for those who tremble and are fearful. Firmness is besought to complete the quality of faith, and warmth is coveted to kindle love into a sacred flame. Within the consecrated shrine tranquillity and peace abide. "The storm of earthborn passion dies."

COMPOSER: For comments on the probable composer, William Croft, see Hymn 2.

TUNE: For comments on the tune, "St. Anne," see Hymn 77.

---

477 HYMN: O Thou Whose Glory Shone Like Fire
TUNE: Solothurn

Author: *George A. Warburton*   Source: *Swiss Traditional Melody*

AUTHOR: George A. Warburton, whose hymn, "O Thou Whose Glory Shone Like Fire," has been given a place in "The Hymnal," was English-born, coming to America with his father, a blacksmith, and settling in Auburn, New York. With a deeply religious family background, George soon became interested in Christian work and finally dedicated himself to the work of the Young Men's Christian Association, serving as secretary in Watertown and Syracuse, New York, but coming to his most extended service of twenty-five years in the Railroad Men's Building in New York City. After a brief interval in a business enterprise with his son, he became secretary of the Toronto Association, leading in campaigns for several buildings and directing welfare activities in the great Canadian camps in the World War.

HYMN: The hymn, with its melody to be sung in unison, fitting men's voices, and in sustained tempo, is replete with suggestions of those social ministries to which the Y. M. C. A. has so largely devoted itself. They are all rooted, in the author's mind, in the presence of the great "Thou."

In the ministry of the Master, George Warburton found the theme for the dedication of an edifice devoted to the welfare of young men. Human compassion, motivated by the indwelling Spirit of Christ, breathes through the four stanzas of this hymn. His homelessness is made the motive for providing them a home. His sorrow in the night, with its consequent longing for the love of a human friend, is made the touchstone of friendship between man and man. By his "life and words" which were "one," with their qualities of strength and manliness and holiness, men may be shown how they, too, may and ought to live.

SOURCE: The source is a Swiss traditional melody.

TUNE: "Solothurn" is a Swiss traditional melody, which since its appearance in "The English Hymnal" (1906) has won favor with hymnal editors in England and America. It was first introduced to the Presbyterian denomination through "The Church School Hymnal for Youth" (1928). It is used three times in "The Hymnal." The tune is of simple pattern and skillfully conserves the traditional character of the original melody. The singing of it, which should be buoyant and joyous, should be well supported by broad tonal registrations of the organ.

Dedication of an Organ

*

478 HYMN: All Nature's Works His Praise Declare
TUNE: Bethlehem

Author: *Rev. Henry Ware, Jr.*   Composer: *Rev. Gottfried W. Fink*

AUTHOR: Rev. Henry Ware, Jr., was a well-known New England minister and later a professor of theology. He was born in 1794 and graduated from Harvard in 1812. Ralph Waldo Emerson was his assistant pastor in 1829. Four years after his death in 1843, four volumes of his works were published, which included a large number of hymns. "All Nature's Works His Praise Declare," under the caption "Opening of an Organ," appeared in Horder's "Congregational Hymns," London (1884). Several others of Mr. Ware's hymns deal with special occasions in the life of the church, such as the dedication of a sanctuary, the laying of a foundation stone, the opening of a place of worship; a notable hymn, "Great God, the Followers of Thy Son," was written for the ordination of Jared Sparks, the historian, when he became pastor of the Unitarian Church in Baltimore, Maryland, in 1819. "All Nature's Works His Praise Declare" is, fittingly, to be sung "with a spirit of joy." The universe itself is vocal with praise—"a voice in every star" and a song in every fleeting breeze. The range of praise extends from "sweet music" to "the thunder and the shower" and the voice of "the stormy sea." The denizens of the sea and the birds of the sky add their voices to the "loud chorus." It is only, however, when human voices and human skill add their notes that the symphony of praise is complete.

COMPOSER: Rev. Gottfried Wilhelm Fink is known as a composer and author of textbooks on the theory of music. His theoretical works are published in German and consist of contributions to Schilling's "Lexicon der Tonkunst"; a collection of one thousand songs and choruses to be used in the home; and also textbooks in the study of harmony and *solfeggio*. He was born March 7, 1783, at Sulza, in Thuringia, and was educated as a chorister at Naumburg. In 1842 he became professor of music in the University of Leipzig. As a prolific writer on musical subjects he contributed to many papers and journals of the day. His leading musical works were the "Musikalischer Hausschatz der Deutschen," a collection of hymns and songs (1843), and "Die Deutsche Liedertafel" (1846). He died at Halle, August 27, 1846.

TUNE: "Bethlehem," composed in 1842, was published in Fink's collection of the following year. The tune is in popular style and pattern and always successful for large choruses or congregations. Joy is its prevailing mood.

Dedication of Memorial Gifts

*

479 HYMN: Let Children Hear the Mighty Deeds
TUNE: Dundee

Author: *Rev. Isaac Watts*   Source: *"Scottish Psalter"*

AUTHOR: For comments on the author, Isaac Watts, see Hymn 22.

HYMN: This hymn first appeared in Watts's "Psalms" (1719). It is a liberal paraphrase of Psalm 78. Set to the stately tune of "Dundee," the hymn is most fitting for the dedication of memorial gifts. God's ancient glories in the mighty deeds which he performed of old are to be told by each generation to its successor, enriched by the record of his repeated and enlarged wonders and powers. Their memorial is not to be primarily a record of their deeds but of his almighty power. It is only when the jewels of our loving gifts are strung upon the thread of his purposes that they become invested with continuing and lasting significance. If, upon first thought, Isaac Watts's paraphrase might seem to divert the worshiper from a suitable contemplation of the gift, it is only in order that the glory of the divine Giver of all might be fully set forth and, therefore, all giving in his name be invested with a nobler joy.

SOURCE: For comments on the source, "Scottish Psalter," see the article, "The Psalters in Early Presbyterian Worship," under "Original Sources," page xv.

TUNE: For comments on the tune, "Dundee," see Hymn 98.

Installation of a Pastor

*

480   HYMN: O Thou Who Makest Souls to Shine
      TUNE: Solothurn

Author: *Rev. John Armstrong*   Source: *Swiss Traditional Melody*

AUTHOR: The author, John Armstrong, D.D., was born at Wearmouth, England, August 22, 1813. He was the eldest son of his father, who was a physician. He graduated from Lincoln College, Oxford, in 1836, and became rector of St. Paul's, Exeter, in 1841. In 1853 he was consecrated as bishop of Grahamstown, South Africa. He died on May 16, 1856. His memoirs by T. T. Carter were published in 1857. "The Pastor in His Closet," a volume published in 1847, includes the hymn "O Thou Who Makest Souls to Shine."

HYMN: The light of the ministry, according to this hymn, is from souls that shine with light from brighter worlds. Their radiance of spirit must come from heavenly sources. Whether they teach or learn, they must depend upon the divine benediction. For the young minister the hymn covets a heart that is both pure and wise, and the graces of "faith, hope, and love, all warmed by prayer." As ministers themselves are trained for the life above and beyond, they will be best fitted to prepare their people for such a life. It is, however, in their pastoral offices that their ministry rises to its climax, and for their faith-

Special Seasons and Services

fulness God's blessing is besought. Like all hymns written nearly one hundred years ago, Armstrong's verse in this installation hymn lacks something of vividness in its sense of social responsibility. Yet its roots go down into the unchanging realities of the gospel ministry, and the truth it symbolizes is fresh from age to age.

SOURCE: The source is a Swiss traditional melody.

TUNE: For comments on the tune, "Solothurn," see Hymn 477.

---

481 HYMN: God of the Prophets! Bless the Prophets' Sons
TUNE: Toulon

Author: *Rev. Denis Wortman*   Source: *"Genevan Psalter"*

AUTHOR: Denis Wortman, D.D., L.H.D., was born in Hopewell, New York, April 30, 1835, and died in 1922. He was a graduate of Amherst College in 1857 and of New Brunswick Theological Seminary in 1860, in which year he was ordained a minister of the gospel in the Reformed Church in America. He held pastorates in Brooklyn, Philadelphia, and Schenectady, New York, and spent twenty years in the pastorate. For seventeen years he was the Secretary of Ministerial Relief of his denomination and in 1901 was president of its General Synod. In 1888 "Reliques of the Christ" was published from his pen, and in 1903 "The Divine Processional."

HYMN: At the centennial of New Brunswick Theological Seminary in October, 1884, Dr. Wortman sent this message on behalf of the class of 1860, of which he was a member: "May I take the liberty of sending you the enclosed verses; a very humble attempt to express the prayer that our Class of 1860, and indeed all loyal sons of New Brunswick Seminary, lift to God at this unusual anniversary, for His blessing upon her and all who go forth from her instructions." The original "Prayer for Young Ministers" contained seven stanzas, four of which appear in "The Hymnal." With a telling Old Testament reference to Elijah and Elisha, the hymn moves forward into the midst of the days in which men now live. There is no suggestion of a waning glory for the Church or its ministry here, but the call for a "nobler, stronger" service.

The last three stanzas of Dr. Wortman's hymn pray for a prophetic, priestly, and apostolic ministry.

491

SOURCE: For comments on the source, "Genevan Psalter," see the article, "The Psalters in Early Presbyterian Worship," under "Original Sources," page xv.

TUNE: "Toulon," which has been traced to the "Genevan Psalter" of 1551, is one of the most famous tunes in "The Hymnal." It has been ascribed to C. Goudimel, who may have had nothing more to do with it than harmonizing the melody. Because of its association with Psalm 124, it is known in English hymnals as "Old 124th." In England, where it is especially popular among Nonconformist bodies, it was introduced through Day's "Whole Booke of Psalmes" in 1563.

---

482 HYMN: Lord of the Church, We Humbly Pray
TUNE: Magdalen College

Author: *Edward Osler*   Composer: *William Hayes*

AUTHOR: For comments on the author, Edward Osler, see Hymn 10; on Charles Wesley, see Hymn 26.

HYMN: "Lord of the Church, We Humbly Pray" comes from the fertile mind and soul of Edward Osler but is based on a hymn of Charles Wesley's. This hymn is to be used in a convocation of the church where the gospel ministry is being set forth in a service of ordination or installation. It glows with fervor and evangelical faith. The congregation is yearning for the blessing of God to rest upon one about to accept the solemn vows of ordination and installation, not omitting a direct allusion to "the Saviour's blood." It supplicates divine help for the ministry that it may "preach the truth of God." It also prays that ministers may live to God alone, and finally receive the word, "Well done," continuing their ministry of "praise and bliss and love" throughout all eternity.

COMPOSER: William Hayes, Mus.D. (1706–1777), the composer of the tune "Magdalen College," was trained as a chorister in the Gloucester Cathedral, and served as organist in St. Mary's Parish at Shrewsbury, England. Later he became organist at Worcester Cathedral and Magdalen College, Oxford, where he remained for forty-three years. In 1741 he was appointed professor of music at the University of Oxford.

His musical compositions consisted of twelve ariettas and two cantatas, which were published in 1735, and a number of anthems and metrical psalms for use in Magdalen College chapel.

Special Seasons and Services

TUNE: "Magdalen College" was composed for use in the chapel of the college at Oxford. It was originally set to Merrick's version of Psalm 122, and published in 1774. It is a virile tune, marked in progression, and finely ranged for either male voices or congregational singing. It is popular at Magdalen College, where it is considered Hayes's best-known tune.

Installation of a Minister of Music

*

483   HYMN: Come, O Thou God of Grace
TUNE: Trinity (Italian Hymn)

Author: *William E. Evans*   Composer: *Felice de Giardini*

AUTHOR: Rev. William Edwin Evans, an American Methodist minister who later entered the Protestant Episcopal Church, was born in Baltimore, Maryland, July 11, 1851. He was an active pastor in several churches of the Methodist Church, South, and was chaplain of Randolph-Macon College, where he was educated. His poems are fugitive contributions to periodicals.

HYMN: Dr. Evans' hymn partakes of the robust characteristics of that familiar hymn of anonymous source, "Come, Thou Almighty King." The first stanza of this hymn utters the notes of adoration and invocation in which the "God of grace" is besought to "descend" and to cause this temple reared to him to be filled with his majesty. In the second stanza the divine presence and blessing are invoked to enrich and ennoble the songs and anthems which God's waiting people raise. In the third stanza the hymn leads the worshipers to hear God's own voice, who alone can "give success," who only can "the truth impart." In the concluding stanza the divine Trinity is adored as the worthy object of all praise, unto whom "glad songs" are to be sung and to whom "glad hearts" are to be brought, in token of that time when the praises of earth shall be crowned with celestial fullness. Dr. Evans' fine hymn of invocation and praise discloses traces of Welsh fervor, and is Scriptural in its flavor. It will not be confined to dedicatory services.

COMPOSER: For comments on the composer, Felice de Giardini, see Hymn 52.

TUNE: For comments on the tune, "Trinity (Italian Hymn)," see Hymn 52.

493

Marriage

*

484

HYMN: O Perfect Love, All Human
      Thought Transcending

TUNE: Perfect Love

Author: *Dorothy Blomfield Gurney*   Composer: *Joseph Barnby*

AUTHOR: Dorothy Frances Gurney, née Blomfield, was born in London in 1858. Her father was Rev. Frederick George Blomfield, rector of St. Andrew's, Undershaft, London, and his father, in turn, was Bishop Blomfield, of Chester and London. Miss Blomfield married Gerald Gurney, whose father, Rev. Archer Gurney, was a hymn writer of merit. With her husband, Mrs. Gurney was received into the Roman Catholic Church in 1919, at Farnborough Abbey. She has published two volumes of poems and "A Little Book of Quiet."

HYMN: The hymn "O Perfect Love, All Human Thought Transcending" was written by Mrs. Gurney in a quarter of an hour one Sunday evening in 1883 at Windermere. It was written to be used at the marriage of her sister. Since 1889 it has been associated with Sir Joseph Barnby's tune "Perfect Love." The invocation of "perfect Love" and, in turn, "perfect Life" to keep tryst with those who are about to set forth upon their romantic wedded way is apt and singularly felicitous. Not only are the divine graces invoked but their human counterparts in "tender charity" and "steadfast faith," in "patient hope" and "quiet, brave endurance," are simply but solemnly summoned. The minor note of "earthly sorrow" is not disregarded but is finally lost in the symphony of peace and glory begun here and consummated in "eternal love and life." Such a hymn sincerely sung, in the mood born of a spiritual understanding of the realities of wedded life, would transform many a marriage, setting it free from leaden ties and giving it heavenly wings.

COMPOSER: For comments on the composer, Joseph Barnby, see Hymn 3.

TUNE: "Perfect Love" is an arrangement from an anthem which Sir Joseph Barnby composed in 1889 for the marriage of the duke and duchess of Fife. Mrs. Gurney's words have been associated with this tune since its appearance, making this hymn one of the best wedding hymns extant. All modern hymnals include it.

494

Special Seasons and Services

485
HYMN: O Love Divine and Golden
TUNE: Blairgowrie

Author: *Rev. John S. B. Monsell*   Composer: *Rev. John B. Dykes*

AUTHOR: For comments on the author, John S. B. Monsell, see Hymn 7.

HYMN: Among the few effective marriage hymns this has found a permanent place. In the common vernacular the hymn reflects the universal blessing of married love for throne or cottage and prays in tender, direct language for the "hands united" and the "hearts made one." Its practical phraseology in no wise mars the reverential dignity of the hymn. It first appeared in "Hymns and Miscellaneous Poems," one of eleven volumes of poems from Monsell's pen, published in Dublin in 1837. From this hymn was taken "Love Divine and Tender," another of the three hundred hymns of this prolific writer.

COMPOSER: For comments on the composer, John B. Dykes, see Hymn 53.

TUNE: "Blairgowrie," while not showing Dykes at his best, represents him in a fluent, popular style that has won for the tune wide acceptance. It is a tune of well-balanced phrases, happy turns, and pleasing cadences. For congregational singing it is unexcelled. It has been associated with various texts. In the Hymnal of 1911 it was used twice: with John Monsell's words, "O Love Divine and Golden," and with Oswald Allen's "To-Day Thy Mercy Calls Me." It was composed in 1872.

Schools and Colleges

*

486
HYMN: Behold a Sower! from Afar
TUNE: Forest Green

Author: *Rev. Washington Gladden*   Source: *English Traditional Melody*

AUTHOR: For comments on the author, Rev. Washington Gladden, see Hymn 364.

HYMN: This hymn first appeared in "The Pilgrim Hymnal" in 1904. It is founded on a faith that all real knowledge comes from God. As the prophets of old made known God's truth and prepared the way for a better world, so the growth of knowledge gives us confidence in a brighter and better future.

SOURCE: For comments on the source of this tune, see Hymn 471.

TUNE: For comments on the tune, "Forest Green," see Hymn 471.

---

487 HYMN: Come, My Soul, Thou Must Be Waking
TUNE: Columbia College

Author: *F. R. L. von Canitz*   Composer: *George William Warren*

AUTHOR: The author, Friedrich Rudolph Ludwig von Canitz, was born November 27, 1654, and was educated at the Universities of Leyden and Leipzig. Elector Friedrich Wilhelm made him a member of his personal staff in 1677 and Emperor Leopold I made him a baron in 1698.

TRANSLATOR: The hymn was translated into English by Rev. Henry J. Buckoll, A.M. (born September 9, 1803, and died at Rugby, June 6, 1871), who was probably the editor of the first edition of the Rugby School "Collection" of hymns. He translated a number of German and Latin hymns. His hymns and translations are mostly found in hymnals of the public schools.

HYMN: This is a hymn to the glories of a new day and bears a striking similarity to Psalm 19. While especially suitable for use in schools or colleges, it is fitted for opening the day by any group of Christians. Dr. Arnold, in his book, "Christian Life" (1841), says that this hymn was born out of a life "distinguished alike by genius and worldly distinctions, and by Christian holiness." He further tells how, when the last morning dawn broke in upon the sick chamber of its author as he neared the end, the latter asked to be supported to the window that he might look once again upon the rising sun. As he looked he cried, "If the appearance of this earthly and created thing is so beautiful . . . , how much more shall I be enraptured at the sight of the unspeakable glory of the Creator himself!"

COMPOSER: For comments on the composer, George William Warren, see Hymn 153.

TUNE: This tune, "Columbia College," was composed when George William Warren was organist at Columbia University. It is in his hymnal, which was used at St. Thomas' Church and also at St. Bartholomew's Church in New York City. The tune requires that it shall be sung very broadly. It was written for male voices, and this original purpose of the tune should be borne in mind in unison singing. The tune appeared in "The Tucker Hymnal" in 1894, in "The Grace Church Hymnal" in 1909, and in "The Columbia University Hymnal" in 1922.

488

HYMN: Be Strong
TUNE: Song 24

Author: *Rev. Maltbie D. Babcock*   Composer: *Orlando Gibbons*

AUTHOR: For comments on the author, Maltbie D. Babcock, see Hymn 70.

HYMN: The fugitive writings of Dr. Babcock were after his death gathered in a volume, under the title "Thoughts for Everyday Living," published in 1901. This hymn is a poem which was included in this popular volume. It is an expression of Dr. Babcock's own philosophy of life, and might well be called the battle cry of a happy warrior whose life was dominated by his faith in God. To a young pastor asking advice as to the wisdom of his leaving a quiet parish in a small town to accept a call to the pulpit of a large city church, Dr. Babcock emphasized his lifelong love of the strenuous struggle by saying, "If you wish a nest stay where you are, but if you wish an arena accept the call." The young man was John Timothy Stone, and the call was to Dr. Babcock's own pulpit in Baltimore.

COMPOSER: For comments on the composer, Orlando Gibbons, see Hymn 68.

TUNE: "Song 24" is a tune in a serious mood. Its melody has been called "grave" and its harmony "broad and virile." It was written for "The Hymnes and Songs of the Church," by George Wither, which was published in 1623. In that collection it was set to a paraphrase of Lam., ch. 1. The editors of "The Hymnal" saw in this ancient song the quality and character of music that would more adequately express Dr. Babcock's hymn, "Be Strong." By adding the first two measures the tune was made available. It should be sung in unison and with dignity.

489 HYMN: Father of Men, in Whom Are One
TUNE: St. Lo

Author: *Henry Cary Shuttleworth* Source: *Old Breton Melody*

AUTHOR: The author, Henry Cary Shuttleworth, was the son of Rev. Edward Shuttleworth, and was born in the vicarage of Egloshayle, Cornwall. He was educated at St. Mary Hall and Christ Church, Oxford. He was appointed rector of St. Nicholas, Cole Abbey, London, in 1883. He was also professor of pastoral and liturgical theology and lecturer in ecclesiastical history and English literature. He was much interested in hymnology and wrote several books on it. He compiled a small appendix to "Church Hymns," for use in St. Nicholas Church, in which several of his own hymns appeared.

HYMN: It is easy to understand how out of a heart so deeply burdened for the poor and downtrodden of London as was that of the author this deeply sympathetic Christian hymn should come. Shuttleworth was a follower of F. D. Maurice and Charles Kingsley in the Christian Socialist Movement in the Guild of St. Matthew and served as one of the assistants in St. Paul's Cathedral. This hymn was written for use by the Friendly Societies. It finds an almost universal echo in the higher life of the college campus to-day. It appeared with music by the author in The Church Monthly in 1898 and was in the St. Nicholas, Cole Abbey, Hymnal.

SOURCE: The source of this tune is an old Breton melody.

TUNE: This tune, "St. Lo," an old Breton melody, was introduced to this Hymnal from "School Worship," published in London in 1926. The simple, diatonic tune has the peculiarity of having the irregular structure of three-bar phrases. It has a range of but a sixth and should be sung in a quiet manner. It will be effective as a unison hymn.

---

490 HYMN: O Thou Whose Feet Have Climbed Life's Hill
TUNE: St. Magnus

Author: *Rev. Louis F. Benson* Composer: *Jeremiah Clark*

AUTHOR: For comments on the author, Rev. Louis F. Benson, see Hymn 29.

Special Seasons and Services

HYMN: This hymn was written by Dr. Benson in February, 1891, at the request of the committee compiling the Hymnal of 1895. It was desired for use in the colleges. It originally appeared with the tune "Log College," written for it at Dr. Benson's request by George William Warren. The hymn comprehends in sympathetic fashion the aspirations of the student and seeks to identify with all his longing the satisfactions that come only through the life and lesson of the "Master of our schools." The imagery throughout is true to academic life and experience.

COMPOSER: For comments on the composer, Jeremiah Clark, see Hymn 185.

TUNE: For comments on the tune, "St. Magnus," see Hymn 185

Memorial Days
*

491   HYMN: Now Praise We Great and Famous Men
          TUNE: Ach Gott und Herr

Author: *Rev. William G. Tarrant*   Source: *"Neu Leipziger Gesangbuch"*

AUTHOR: For comments on the author, William G. Tarrant, see Hymn 408.

HYMN: This hymn fills a need in the worship services of the many memorial occasions with which American life is filled. It is a hymn of gratitude to God for his gift of "the wise and brave and strong, who graced their generation." It magnifies our debt to "peaceful men of skill," who, "rich in art, made richer still the brotherhood of duty." To praise our worthy fellow men who have builded for us the structure of our civilization is but another way of acknowledging our debt to God for what we have inherited from the ages.

SOURCE: The source of this tune is a melody in "Neu Leipziger Gesangbuch," 1682.

ARRANGER: For comments on the arranger, Johann Sebastian Bach, see Hymn 21.

499

TUNE: For comments on the tune, "Ach Gott und Herr," see Hymn 326.

Travelers

*

492   HYMN: Eternal Father, Strong to Save
             TUNE: Melita

Author: *William Whiting*   Composer: *Rev. John B. Dykes*

AUTHOR: William Whiting was born on November 1, 1825, at Kensington, London, and died in 1878. He was master of Winchester College Choristers' School.

HYMN: This hymn is used at the United States Naval Academy at Annapolis and on English ships, and a beautiful translation appears in the hymn book of the French navy. It was written in 1860, and, with some alterations, was used in the standard English church collection, "Hymns Ancient and Modern." It is a translation from a Latin hymn, being a triune litany addressed to Father, Son, and Holy Spirit.

COMPOSER: For comments on the composer, John B. Dykes, see Hymn 53.

TUNE: The tune, "Melita," was composed for Whiting's hymn, to be included in "Hymns Ancient and Modern" (1861). It gives a feeling of great profundity by its use of the low registers of the voice, and the clear, straightforward harmonic structure. The sense of the depth of the sea is present in the musical effect.

Orisons

*

HYMN: In the Early Morning
TUNE: Celestial Voices

Author: *Ida F. Leyda*   Composer: *R. F. Lloyd*

AUTHOR: Ida F. (Mrs. H. M.) Leyda is superintendent of the Primary Department of the Presbyterian Sunday School in Wapello, Iowa. While living in Chicago she had charge of the Children's Division of the State Sunday School Council of Religious Education and published three songbooks: "Carols," "Melodies," and "Junior Hymns and Carols." She wrote this hymn for use in connection with the graded lessons on God's gifts of day and night, hoping, as she says, "to interpret religiously to little children these gifts," and to stir in them an appreciation of God's provision for play and recreation in the daytime and rest at night.

HYMN: The hymn is suitable for either morning or evening use, day and night being spoken of as God's gifts.
A child can understand this simple hymn, for it deals with that which comes within his day-by-day experience. Children should learn to love the night, with its gift of rest and the opportunity of watching for the stars, "the Scriptures of the skies," of which Longfellow sings in "Evangeline":

> Silently one by one, in the infinite meadows of heaven,
> Blossomed the lovely stars, the forget-me-nots of the angels.

The alternation of day and night played an important part in primitive religions. The Greek poets described in lovely phrases the coming of Aurora, the dawn. Christianity has a place in its hymns for the response awakened by nature in the human heart. The Master doubtless loved to greet the sunrise on the hills of Galilee.

This is an orison of thanksgiving rather than a petition. It is well that our prayers should reflect this spirit of gratitude for "days of gladness" and "rest of night."

COMPOSER: Richard Francis Lloyd is the composer of "Celestial Voices." When "The Congregational Hymnary" (London, 1916), a volume of more than a thousand hymns appeared, it included three tunes by this composer; namely, "Winton," "Clairvaux," and "Rock of Ages." Mr. Lloyd, son of the late Richard John Lloyd, Litt.D., was born at Liverpool, England, May 27, 1871. Obtaining scholarships in organ-playing and harmony, he entered the Liverpool College of Music, where he studied composition under the late Dr. W. H. Hunt. He graduated with the degree of Bachelor of Music. Upon graduation he was appointed, in 1903, organist and choirmaster of Sefton Park Presbyterian Church, Liverpool, during the ministry of Dr. John Watson (Ian Maclaren). He completed in 1934 thirty-one years of service in this church.

TUNE: "Celestial Voices" was composed for "The Methodist School Hymnal." It was introduced to the Presbyterian Hymnal of 1933 through "The Hymnary" (1930) of Canada. Its association with Ida F. Leyda's text is fortunate, for it well expresses and amplifies its sentiments and moods. The tune was originally set to a hymn of communion and prayer, written by Marie Corelli, the first lines of which are:

> In our hearts celestial voices
> Softly say.

494

HYMN: Jesus, Kneel Beside Me
TUNE: Eudoxia

Author: *Rev. Allen Eastman Cross*   Composer: *Rev. Sabine
Baring-Gould*

AUTHOR: Rev. Allen Eastman Cross, now retired, lives in Manchester, New Hampshire, where he was born in 1864. In a personal letter dated January 1, 1934, he says: "I have a place of retreat, just outside the home city of Manchester. It looks like a cabin on a high hill, but to me 'Pinecrest' is . . . an observation post, a place of meditation, and a mystic shrine. When I gave up the ministry of the pulpit, to give myself to the ministry of writing, I came back here, and for seven years I have tried to re-create old writings, that still had sparks of life, and to compose living poems and essays."

Mr. Cross was educated at Phillips Andover Academy and Amherst College. "I chose the calling of the ministry in the last year of college life, with the simplest and most audacious motive, to help God to help people," he writes. After graduating from Andover Theological Seminary, he began his ministry in the Congregational Church at Cliftondale, Massachusetts, afterwards going to the Park Congregational Church in Springfield. Later he was associate pastor for ten years with the famous Dr. George A. Gordon in the Old South Church in Boston. His last pastorate began in 1914, in the First Congregational Church of Milford,

Orisons

Massachusetts. After eleven years there he retired in 1925. He is the author of a volume of poems, "Pass On the Torch."

HYMN: In 1907, in a time of extreme personal worry and strain, Dr. Cross wrote this "lyric prayer," which he calls "The Great Companion." In the personal letter cited above he writes: "I felt the ineffectualness of my prayer life and the ineffectiveness of workaday service. The Son of Man seemed to possess all I lacked. I was drawn to him by sheer difference as well as by far-off kinship. I turned to him as to a superlative companion and spoke out of my need." Later, when the Old South Sewing Club of the historic Old South Church in Boston asked for a hymn to be sung at the annual meeting, April 9, 1907, he gave them these verses, to be used with the tune "Merrial," by Barnby. It has been repeatedly copied in calendars and anthologies as well as in articles and books. He says that the account in Luke 11:1 influenced his thought: "And it came to pass, as he was praying in a certain place, that when he ceased, one of his disciples said unto him, Lord, teach us to pray."

The first three stanzas successively voice the aspiration that Jesus will kneel, work, and watch beside the petitioner in the three periods of the day—dawn, noon, and night.

COMPOSER: For comments on the composer, Sabine Baring-Gould, see Hymn 35.

TUNE: The tune, "Eudoxia," is supposed to be a German melody, but has never been identified. It is a simple, pleading melody. One might assume that it had been written for children on account of its marked simplicity. It has a range of but five tones. Though marked 4/4, it has a grouping of only two pulses in the bar and will best be sung in this manner.

---

495 HYMN: May the Grace of Christ Our Saviour
TUNE: Evening Prayer

Author: *Rev. John Newton*   Composer: *John Stainer*

AUTHOR: For comments on the author, John Newton, see Hymn 310.

HYMN: Any devotional expression coming from one who so long had known the bitterness of sin in his own life and its evil power among the seafaring men with whom he had fellowship will be marked by deepest emotion. "Amazing Grace," "In Evildoing I Took

503

Delight," and others of Newton's hymns are the irresistible outgoing of a heart whose freedom had been hard bought.

"The triple benediction contains in solution the Christian doctrine of God which was crystallized later in the Trinitarian doctrine of the creeds," according to W. F. Howard in "The Abingdon Bible Commentary." It has become so commonplace that unfortunately but few worshipers are conscious of its real meaning. Paul mentions first the grace of Christ, for it is through him that we realize God as Father. Grace is kindness freely bestowed. In speaking of the love of God we mean that ultimate reality is not blind force or fate, but that the power back of existence is not only life but moral and personal life. Through the Spirit's influence we are brought into union and fellowship with Christ and the Father, and with men.

COMPOSER: For comments on the composer, John Stainer, see Hymn 130.

TUNE: Stainer was very fond of children, and wrote many tunes for them, of which this simple, exquisite tune, "Evening Prayer," is one. It was originally set to the words "Jesus, Tender Shepherd, Hear Me," and appeared in the first edition of "The Church Hymnal." Stainer was a keen student of psalmody and he modeled his tunes after the older psalm tunes.

---

496   HYMN: The Lone, Wild Fowl in Lofty Flight
TUNE: Comavon

Author: *H. R. MacFayden*   Composer: *Philip James*

AUTHOR: The author, Rev. H. R. MacFayden, is a minister of the Presbyterian Church in the United States at Pinetops, North Carolina. He was born in Bladen County, North Carolina, on February 1, 1877. His father was a Presbyterian pastor. This is the only hymn which he has written.

HYMN: The author evidently had in mind the lines from William Cullen Bryant's "To a Water Fowl":

> He who, from zone to zone,
>   Guides through the boundless sky thy certain flight,
> In the long way that I must tread alone,
>   Will lead my steps aright.

The hymn was written while he was a field worker for Nashville Presbytery. He noticed the announcement of a nation-wide hymn-writing contest in The Homiletic Review. In a personal letter, dated February 16, 1934, he writes: "The hymn was written on a quiet Sunday afternoon in the fall or early winter of 1925 and sent to the Review. It was forgotten until I was surprised with an announcement that I had been awarded the third prize in the contest."

The Brief Statement of the Reformed Faith, printed in the front of "The Hymnal" (pages xlii, xliii), contains this statement: "We believe that God is revealed in nature, in history, and in the heart of man." This is a hymn which brings us face to face with the God of nature.

COMPOSER: Philip James, the composer, was born in New York City in 1890. He has distinguished himself in many musical lines. His compositions are of a highly refined and sensitive type, rich in color and emotional effect. He has held, in recent years, several important positions as organist of prominent churches in New York and its suburbs, but of late has been principally occupied in orchestral conducting and radio work, and is now instructor in the department of music at Columbia University. His orchestral compositions show great talent. During the World War he was in active service, reaching the rank of lieutenant. After the armistice he became associated with "Pershing's own band" at Chaumont, eventually becoming its bandmaster.

TUNE: The tune, "Comavon," is a sturdy, choral-like melody, though harmonized in modern style. It has a sense of two pulses to the bar, though the signature is 4/4. It should be thus sung. It has something of the feeling of an old traditional Jewish melody. The small limit of the melody gives a feeling of solemnity.

---

497   HYMN: My Master Was So Very Poor
             TUNE: My Master

Author: *Harry Lee*   Composer: *Karl P. Harrington*

AUTHOR: In efforts to locate and identify Harry Lee, the author of this widely used hymn, recourse was had to the Copyright Division of the Congressional Library, to the Personnel Department of the War Department, and to various bureaus and libraries. All was unavailing. If the writer of this hymn is still living, he must find great joy in the spiritual service his hymn is rendering.

HYMN: The antithetical arrangement of this hymn most impressively sets before us the paradoxical situations in our Lord's life. It is in keeping with Paul's striking statement, "For ye know the grace of our Lord Jesus Christ, that, though he was rich, yet for your sakes he became poor, that ye through his poverty might become rich," II Cor. 8:9. The poverty of the surroundings at Jesus' birth is contrasted with the grandeur of the kings who came to worship him. He shared his bread with the poor, and the divine resources that were his were placed at their disposal.

COMPOSER: Karl Pomeroy Harrington was born June 13, 1861. He studied music in America and abroad. He has been instructor in Latin in several universities, and organist at Stamford and Hartford, Connecticut, and elsewhere. He has been president of the Festival Chorus and also its director at Bangor, Maine. He has composed songs and other music. He is the author of a number of books on classical and musical topics. He is a member of and a leading spirit in The Hymn Society of New York.

TUNE: The tune, "My Master," was written at the request of the editor of the "Junior Church School Hymnal" (1927). The union with Harry Lee's beautiful hymn proved so satisfactory that it was used in "The Church School Hymnal for Youth" (1928). The tune should be sung in smooth rhythm. There should be no pause at the end of the first line, thus preserving the rhythm. The tune sings best in 6/4 time, with the accent recurring in every other bar.

---

498   HYMN: I Am Not Worthy, Holy Lord
TUNE: Leicester

Author: *Rev. Henry Williams Baker*   Composer: *William Hurst*

AUTHOR: For comments on the author, Henry Williams Baker, see Hymn 99.

HYMN: There is a place in corporate worship for such a personal hymn as this, which in words of sincerity and heart-searching opens the door of the human heart to the divine Visitor.

The sense of unworthiness, or true humility, is one of the essential characteristics of the Christian way of life. The modern mood, with its emphasis upon self-expression and its deprecation of anything like an inferiority complex, challenges this attitude. But throughout the ages saints of greatest moral power have always been remembered for their own consciousness and confession of imperfections.

This hymn, based on Matt. 8:8, was written in 1875 for the Revised Edition of "Hymns Ancient and Modern."

Orisons

COMPOSER: William Hurst, the composer of this hymn, is a non-professional musician of Leicester, England. He was born in 1849. Though engaged in business, he is a patron of music and has given himself unselfishly to the promotion of sacred music through the churches of his own region.

TUNE: The tune, "Leicester," was written by Hurst for the Revised Edition of "Hymns Ancient and Modern." It is of moderate range, dignified and reverent, and should be sung rather quietly to express its suppliant character.

---

499 HYMN: Through Love to Light! O Wonderful the Way
TUNE: Finlandia

Author: *Richard Watson Gilder*   Composer: *Jean Sibelius*

AUTHOR: Richard Watson Gilder was a popular speaker in the universities and on commemorative occasions. Harvard, Yale, and Princeton gave him honorary degrees. He was born in Bordentown, New Jersey, on February 8, 1844, the son of Rev. William Henry Gilder, a Methodist minister, who conducted a seminary for girls. He served for a time in the Civil War as an army chaplain and as a private in the First Philadelphia Artillery, after which he entered railroad service as a paymaster. In 1865 he embarked upon a literary and editorial career, and five years later became managing editor of Scribner's Monthly. He was the president of the New York Free Kindergarten Association, president of the Fellowship Club, an organization of artists and writers, and an ardent worker in city reform. Later he succeeded Dr. J. G. Holland as editor of Century. He published several volumes of poems. "I am a poet," he said. "I would rather be that than all the rest put together."

HYMN: This hymn tells of the quest for certainty and the assurance that there is an answer to the search. In a sense it may be said to illustrate the Master's words, "He that doeth the truth cometh to the light, " John 3: 21. Through love we can trust God and find that, although the way leads through darkness, it does not end there but opens into light. Life to Gilder was not a blind alley but a thoroughfare.

COMPOSER: For comments on the composer, Jean Sibelius, see Hymn 281.

TUNE: For comments on the tune, "Finlandia," see Hymn 281.

500 HYMN: Beloved, Let Us Love: Love Is of God
TUNE: Grandpont

Author: *Rev. Horatius Bonar*   Composer: *John Stainer*

AUTHOR: For comments on the author, Horatius Bonar, see Hymn 60.

HYMN: Each stanza of the hymn opens with the injunction, "Beloved, let us love." "Love is of God," "love is rest," "love is light" are some of the declarations of this simple hymn, one of the few in this book retaining five stanzas. Such lines as,

> "For they who love,
> They only, are His sons, born from above"

takes us into the heart of John's Gospel.

This hymn comes from the volume "Communion Hymns," published in 1881. The sacrament of the Lord's Supper was lovingly cherished by this great Scottish minister as a supreme act of worship.

COMPOSER: For comments on the composer, John Stainer, see Hymn 130.

TUNE: This tune, "Grandpont," is within the range of a fifth. It is simple, direct, and unornamented. It will best be sung with the broad feeling of two beats to the bar, which will cause the music to flow with a smooth, even quality. It should not be sung *forte*, but with great reverence.

This tune was composed for this hymn and was included in the first edition of "The Church Hymnary."

---

501 HYMN: Not So in Haste, My Heart
TUNE: Dolomite Chant

Author: *Bradford Torrey*   Source: *Austrian Melody*

AUTHOR: Bradford Torrey was born at Weymouth, Massachusetts, in 1843 and was a well-known American ornithologist and nature writer. After teaching two years, he entered business in Boston, and from 1886 to 1901 was on the staff of The Youth's Companion. After

Orisons

his retirement he lived in Santa Barbara, California, where he died in
1912. Two years before his death he wrote for The Atlantic Monthly a
delightful article describing his tramps in the Yosemite Valley. His first
book on "Birds in the Bush," in 1885, was followed by several others,
among them being "Nature's Invitation," published in 1904. His "Field
Days in California" was published the year following his death. He edited
the "Journal" of Henry D. Thoreau.

Hymn: This is an exquisite call to patience. It evidences the quiet
attitude of the student of nature, born of his experiences with
the furtive life of the out of doors. To study birds the author had
to learn to be quiet.

Long ago the psalmist wrote, "Be still, and know that I am God," but
we are not always heedful of this advice.

Many lines in this hymn, such as,

> "The feet that wait for God
> Are soonest at the goal,"

are worthy of memorization and quoting. Some worshipers of speed and
haste may not relish the emphasis upon patience in this hymn, but it has
a message that this generation should heed. Emerson used to ask, "Why
so in haste, little man?" The lover of nature who thinks God's thoughts
after him gets a new perspective on life. He realizes that the universe discloses a divine purpose through the ages.

Source: The source of the tune, "Dolomite Chant," is an Austrian
melody.

Harmonizer: Joseph Thomas Cooper, the friend of and collaborator with Bishop Edward H. Bickersteth, was one of the
most active organists of his day. He held various positions as
organist in London and vicinity. He wrote numerous articles on hymnody
and church music. Many of his papers appeared in Evening Hours, a
periodical edited by Bishop Bickersteth. The "Chant Book Supplement"
had his editorial oversight, as also "The Hymnal Companion," a revised
and enlarged edition of which was published in 1877. Joseph T. Cooper
was born in London, May 25, 1819; there he followed his profession, and
there, on November 17, 1879, he died.

Tune: The melody of "Dolomite Chant" has the peculiar rhythmic
freedom of folk-song material. Its low register enables it to be sung
with reverence and the spirit of supplication. It should not be hurried, especially in the 3/2 bars, and also at the end. It requires a marked
legato throughout. The tune first appeared in Bishop Bickersteth's
"Hymnal Companion to the Book of Common Prayer" in 1877.

502

HYMN: Round Me Falls the Night
TUNE: Seelenbräutigam

Author: *Rev. William Romanis*   Composer: *Adam Drese*

AUTHOR: Rev. William Romanis was born in 1824. He graduated from Emmanuel College, Cambridge, with highest honors in 1846 and in 1849 he won his Master's degree. He became a master in the classical department of Cheltenham College and later a curate at Atminster and St. Mary's, Reading. In 1863 he became vicar at Wigston Magna, Leicester, and in 1888 at Twyford, Hants. After a few fruitful years of retirement he died in 1899. His volume of sermons, under the title "Sermons Preached at St. Mary's, Reading," passed through two editions.

HYMN: This hymn appeared in the Wigston Magna School Hymnal in 1878. It is a hymn of trust for the evening time, coming from the pen of a competent writer who seems to have but few hymns to his credit. Dr. Julian indicates but three as being in common use. Each stanza of the hymn contains a prayer for reassurance in the darkness of the night. The first stanza craves comfort from the vision of God's face; the second, from the speaking of his voice; and the third, from the protecting embrace of his fatherly arms.

The psychologist tells us that it is of great value before going to sleep to give one's subconscious self helpful and exalted suggestions. This would be an excellent hymn to repeat before dropping off to slumber. It breathes the spirit of trust and confidence, as the last lines indicate:

"Sure from every ill
Thou wilt guard me still."

COMPOSER: Adam Drese, to whom the tune "Seelenbräutigam" is attributed, was born in Thuringia in 1620 and died in Arnstadt on February 15, 1701. He became *Kapellmeister* at Weimar and later held various positions at Jena. He was greatly impressed by the writings of Spener and Luther. He wrote a number of hymns and chorals, fourteen of which are in Georg Neumark's "Fortgepflanzter Musikalisch-poetischer Lustwald," published in Jena in 1657.

TUNE: The tune, "Seelenbräutigam," has a peculiar accent on the second beat of the bar, due to the first beat's being divided. It has an air of antiquity about it. It should not be hurried, but sung with the breadth of choral style. Its spirit and effect are quiet and chant-like.

Orisons

503

HYMN: O Lord, Turn Not Away Thy Face
TUNE: Cheshire Tune

Author: *Rev. John Marckant*   Composer: *Ascribed to John Farmer*

AUTHOR: John Marckant was a country clergyman in England nearly four centuries ago. He contributed to "The Complete Psalter" of Sternhold and Hopkins, published by John Day (1562). The record shows that he was incumbent of Clacton Magna in 1559, the year following Queen Elizabeth's accession. From 1563 to 1568 he served at Shopland, Essex.

Julian's Dictionary states: "He is known only as the author of one or two small pieces: a political poem on Lord Wentworth, 1558–9; a New Year's gift intituled, 'With Speed Return to God'; and 'Verses to Divers Good Purposes,' circa 1580–1." The old metrical version of The Psalms shows that he was the author of the paraphrases of Psalms 118, 131, 132, 135, in the "Old Version" of 1562. His full name is printed in the edition of 1565.

HYMN: These two brief stanzas contain in somewhat archaic language much of the gospel message: The mercy gate is open wide "to those that do lament their sin." One thinks in this connection of the picture of the wicket gate in Bunyan's "The Pilgrim's Progress."

This hymn originally bore the interesting designation, "The Lamentation of a Sinner." It has the distinction of being one of the oldest English hymns in "The Hymnal." It appears in the "songs" that were appended to Sternhold and Hopkins' "Old Version," John Day's edition, and has been sung since 1560. Its existence and use show that hymns had already found their way into the worship of the churches at that early date.

COMPOSER: "Cheshire Tune" is attributed to John Farmer. Thomas Este, who was among the first publishers of music, was a famous printer, born about 1540. His first work as a music printer was "Sonnettes and Songs Made Into Music of Fyve Parts. By William Burd." In 1588 he published a collection of Italian madrigals, known as Este's "Musica Transalpina," in which the tunes were harmonized. Este's "The Whole Booke of Psalmes," published in 1592, gave two tunes, "Winchester" and "Chesshire," by John Farmer. The latter was set to Psalm 146. "Cheshire Tune" has been made from this melody. But little is known of Farmer. He was one of at least twelve composers employed by Este to harmonize the tunes for his "Whole Booke of Psalmes," and at one time was organist of Christ Church Cathedral, Dublin. He was recognized as a skilled harmonizer.

TUNE: This melody should be sung with a sense of two beats in the bar. Farmer employed the "tiercé de Picardie," ending the harmony in major. The tune is plain, and does not admit of any attempt at varied interpretation.

---

504   HYMN: None Other Lamb, None Other Name
TUNE: All Hallows

Author: *Christina G. Rossetti*   Composer: *Frederick Luke Wiseman*

AUTHOR: For comments on the author, Christina G. Rossetti, see Hymn 133.

HYMN: This hymn appeared in 1892. It is a portion of a meditation on the apocalyptic vision of the Lamb recorded in Rev. 5:6. Christina Rossetti was disappointed in love because her *fiancé* entered the Roman Catholic Church. Suffering under many burdens, this cloistered spirit poured out her heart in confession of deep need and entire dependence upon Him besides whom there is "none other Hope in heaven or earth or sea." Augustine declared, "My heart is restless until it repose in Thee." The hymn echoes this thought: "Nor heaven have I, nor place to lay my head, nor home, but Thee." This hymn is introspective, but its spiritual intentions and literary excellence make it most valuable in public worship.

COMPOSER: Frederick Luke Wiseman is Secretary of the Home Mission Department of the Wesleyan Methodist Church. He was born in 1858 and educated at Didsbury College, England. He was assistant tutor in Hebrew at this college, superintendent of the Birmingham Central Mission, and, from 1887–1913, minister of the Central Hall, Birmingham. He was president of the Wesleyan Conference in 1912–1913 and president of the National Council of Evangelical Free Churches in 1914. His musical compositions include "Songs of the Twelve Hours."

TUNE: "All Hallows" is an effective musical setting for Christina G. Rossetti's hymn, "None Other Lamb, None Other Name." It is a hopeful tune and requires careful shading. The temptation to accelerate the tempo must be guarded against. The concluding line of four syllables calls for heightened feeling and emotion.

Orisons

505   HYMN: Now Woods and Fields Are Sleeping
         TUNE: Nun Ruhen Alle Wälder (Innsbruck)

Author: *Rev Paul Gerhardt*   Composer: *Heinrich Isaak*

AUTHOR: For comments on the author, Paul Gerhardt, see Hymn 125.

TRANSLATOR: For comments on the translator, George R. Woodward, see Hymn 119.

HYMN: Out of a gloomy career shadowed by the horrors of the Thirty Years' War and disturbed by the absence of any settled position of service until near the middle of his life, Paul Gerhardt wrote this hymn of evening quiet and introspection. In it he rises above the sorrows that harassed him in the long illness and death of his wife and the early death of his four little children. The second stanza includes commendation to God for nightly care of "friends and kindred nearest." We may well learn serenity through trust from Gerhardt, under whose portrait at Lubben are inscribed in Latin the words: "A Theologian Sifted in Satan's Sieve."

COMPOSER: Heinrich Isaak was an eminent contrapuntist, probably of German origin, who was born about 1455 and died in Florence in 1517. He was organist and *Kapellmeister* to Lorenzo the Magnificent. Later he was *Kapellmeister* at the court of Maximilian I at Vienna. One of the peculiarities of his work is the frequent appearance of the melody in the soprano, a comparatively unusual procedure for the time.

HARMONIZER: For comments on the harmonizer, Johann Sebastian Bach, see Hymn 21.

TUNE: This tune, "Nun Ruhen Alle Wälder," also called "Innsbruck," is the harmonization used by Bach in his "St. Matthew Passion." The melody has a stately, dignified feeling throughout, and should be sung with the eighth note to a beat—in other words, eight beats to a bar.

506   HYMN: Lord Jesus Christ, with Us Abide
         TUNE: Ach Bleib Bei Uns

Author: *Rev. Nicolaus Selnecker*   Source: *Early German Melody*

AUTHOR: Nicolaus Selnecker was born at Hersbruck, Germany, December 5, 1532. At the age of twelve he became organist in the Kaiserburg Chapel in Nürnberg. At the University of Wittenberg, where he received a Master's degree in 1554, he was the favorite pupil of Melanchthon. In 1557 he was appointed second court preacher at Dresden. In 1565 he became professor of theology at Jena, and later at Leipzig. He became the center of many theological controversies, writing, in German and Latin, 175 theological and controversial works. He helped to build the great Motett Choir of St. Thomas' Church in Leipzig, which later was conducted by Johann Sebastian Bach. Rev. James Mearns, in Julian's "A Dictionary of Hymnology," says of him: "Amid the manifold changes and chances of his life he found inspiration and consolation in the study of and recourse to the Psalter, and in his love of music. . . . His German hymns partake for the most part of the objective churchly character of the hymns of the Reformation period, and indeed contain many reminiscences of them. . . . A genuine piety, a deep and fervent love to the Saviour, and a zeal for the best interests of his Church on earth, are expressed in clear, flowing and musical style."

HYMN: This hymn was written in 1611. Many translations of this hymn have appeared, differing slightly, all carrying the author's earnest spirit of pleading for the comfort of God's presence in the darkness of approaching night. The hymn echoes the invitation of the two bewildered disciples at the end of the walk to Emmaus, while its second stanza reveals the deep yearning of the old debater's heart for a peace that he never found among his brethren, from whom he so sharply differed.

SOURCE: The source of this tune is an early German melody.

ARRANGER: For comments on the arranger, Johann Sebastian Bach, see Hymn 21.

TUNE: This tune is an old German melody, found in the "Geistliche Lieder," Leipzig, 1539. It was elaborated by Bach, and is found in his "Choralgesänge." It also appears in Calvisius' "Hymni Sacri Latini et Germanici," 1594, in the alto, as a descant to another melody set to the hymn, "Danket dem Herrn Heut' und All' Seit."

507
HYMN: Dear Master, in Whose Life I See
TUNE: Solothurn

Author: *Rev. John Hunter*   Source: *Swiss Traditional Melody*

AUTHOR: John Hunter was born in Aberdeen in 1848, and was a baptized child of the Church of Scotland. Owing to poverty, he left school to become a draper's apprentice at the age of thirteen. In 1859 a religious revival touched his soul with a profound influence and turned him toward the ministry. He was not able to meet the scholastic requirements of the presbytery, so he entered the Nottingham Congregational Institute and Spring Hill College at Birmingham, where he spent but five years, all told, in preparation before being ordained and beginning his work. Later his intense evangelical convictions encountered intellectual difficulties from within and he shifted from the old positions in which he had been brought up. Nothing, however, quenched his evangelical fervor and he accepted with great sacrifice heavy responsibility in critical situations in Glasgow and finally in the old Weigh House Church in London. Beneath the burdens of this field and the sorrows of the World War he died in 1917, at sixty-nine years of age.

HYMN: This hymn appeared originally in the monthly paper of the author's own Trinity Church, Glasgow. Later it was published in "Hymns of Faith and Life" (1896). The hymn is worthy of intensive devotional study. It reveals the religious aspiration of the spiritually-minded leader.

SOURCE: The source of the tune is a Swiss traditional melody.

TUNE: For comments on the tune, "Solothurn," see Hymn 477.

508
HYMN: My Spirit Longs for Thee
TUNE: Fingal

Author: *John Byrom*   Source: *Irish Traditional Melody*

AUTHOR: John Byrom, A.M., F.R.S., was born in Manchester, England, on February 29, 1692. He belonged to a merchant's family of good standing and was sent to Merchant Taylors' School and Cambridge University. He became a Fellow at Trinity College in 1714, and in 1716 traveled in Europe, settling for the study of medicine at Montpellier. His career as a physician, however, did not develop. He had an inventive genius and created as early as 1723 a system of shorthand-writing. His shorthand system was not printed until after his death, and it never gained wide use. He came under the influence of William Law, the God-fearing Jacobite who refused to swear allegiance to George I. In 1729 he read Law's famous book, "Serious Call to a Devout and Holy Life," which was the means of converting Samuel Johnson and stirring profoundly both Wesleys. In 1793, Byrom published two volumes of poems, a few of which came into use as hymns.

HYMN: This hymn, the theme of which is "No Rest but in God," is taken from Byrom's "Miscellaneous Poems," printed in 1793. The particular poem to which the hymn belongs is in two parts, entitled, respectively, "The Desponding Soul's Wish" and "The Answer." To the first part, "My spirit longs for Thee," the second part answers, "Cheer up, desponding soul." Byrom was a layman of profound mystical experience and ranks among the good hymn writers of his day.

SOURCE: The source of this tune is an Irish traditional melody.

ARRANGER: Leopold L. Dix, born in 1861, is a graduate of Trinity College, Dublin, a lawyer by profession and a musician by avocation. He has composed numerous hymn tunes specially for the Hymnal of the Irish Episcopal Church. He has been active as a composer and arranger in many fields in musical activity.

TUNE: "Fingal" is arranged from an Irish traditional air and is very modal in character, being in the Æolian, or natural minor, mode of D, with the natural seventh. This tonality gives the tune a strong feeling of antiquity, and thus it requires a plain, churchly manner of performance, with no attempt at color or modern effects.

---

509 HYMN: Before the Day Draws Near Its Ending
TUNE: Sunset

Author: *Rev. John Ellerton*   Composer: *George Gilbert Stocks*

AUTHOR: For comments on the author, John Ellerton, see Hymn 20.

HYMN: Among the fifty hymns from Ellerton's pen this hymn takes high rank, both for its emotional content and for its literary style. We have here an "afternoon" hymn—"before the day draws

Orisons

near its ending." It was written for a Festival of Choirs at Nantwich, a market town in Cheshire, in April, 1880. After being published in the "Nantwich Festival Book" it passed into the "Westminster Abbey Hymn Book" in 1883. The threefold thought of God in the second stanza is as "Light," "Truth," and "boundless Mercy." In the third stanza the hope is expressed that finally we may

> "Sing that song before Thee
> Which none but Thy redeemed can learn."

This line is based on Rev. 14:3: "And no man could learn the song save the hundred and forty and four thousand, even they that had been purchased out of the earth."

COMPOSER: George Gilbert Stocks, Mus.D., born in 1877, was formerly organist at Almondbury and teacher at St. Edward's School, Oxford. Since 1912 he has been head music master at Repton School. He has composed a number of hymn tunes, and in 1924 published "Hymns for Use in Chapel."

TUNE: This tune, "Sunset," is really in 7/2 time, though there is no signature at the beginning. Each bar is a combination of a four and a three measure, which is an unusual rhythm for a hymn. But this melody is entirely singable. Care must be taken, therefore, to place the accent on the second syllable of "before" and on the first syllable of "ending," on the first syllable of "evening" and on "sky."

---

510   HYMN: As Now the Sun's Declining Rays
       TUNE: St. Columba (Irish)

Author: *Rev. Charles Coffin*   Source: *Old Irish Hymn Melody*

AUTHOR: Charles Coffin was born at Buzancy (Ardennes) in 1676. He is one of the few French hymn writers whose poems have become a part of the worship material of America. In striking contrast to the influence of Germany in this field has been the meagerness of the French influence. Coffin was principal of the college at Beauvais in 1712, succeeding the historian Rollin. He became rector of the University of Paris in 1718. In 1727 he published some of his Latin poems, for which he was already noted. In 1736 the bulk of his hymns appeared in the "Paris Breviary," an authoritative directory of worship in the Roman Catholic Church. In the same year he published "Hymni Sacri Auctore Carolo Coffin." In 1755 a complete edition of his works was issued in two volumes. In the edition of 1736 his hymns numbered about one hundred.

Handbook to The Hymnal

TRANSLATOR: For comments on the translator, John Chandler, see Hymn 472.

HYMN: This hymn is a translation by John Chandler of a Latin hymn by Charles Coffin. It was used by Chandler in his "Hymns of the Primitive Church" (1837).

SOURCE: The source is an old Irish hymn melody from Dr. Petrie's Collection.

TUNE: For comments on the tune, "St. Columba (Irish)," see Hymn 145.

---

511 HYMN: Ere I Sleep, for Every Favor
       FIRST TUNE: Thanet

Author: *Rev. John Cennick*   Composer: *Rev. Joseph Jowett*

AUTHOR: For comments on the author, John Cennick, see Hymn 347.

HYMN: This is one of the popular hymns of this very prolific hymn writer, who passed through an unusual variety of religious experience.
This two-hundred-year-old evening hymn is for use before going to sleep. It expresses gratitude for every favor experienced during the day. It ends with the typical reminder of death, "Till Thou hence remove me," which the hymn writers of two centuries ago felt necessary to incorporate in the ending of many of their hymns.

COMPOSER (First Tune): Rev. Joseph Jowett (1784–1856) was the musical rector of the parish of Silk Willoughby, Lincolnshire. Among his works were "Lyra Sacra"; "Select Extracts from the Cathedral Music of the Church of England for One, Two, Three, and Four Voices" (London, 1825); and "A Manual of Parochial Psalmody" (London, 1832).

TUNE (First): "Thanet" is from Jowett's "Parochial Psalmody." The tune is exceedingly simple, being within the range of a fifth, and has a reiterated modulation, stressing the third and fourth lines of the poem.

Orisons

SECOND TUNE: Cwmdu

Composer: *David Emlyn Evans*

COMPOSER (Second Tune): The composer of the second tune, David Emlyn Evans (1843–1913), was an amateur composer of distinction, winning seventy Eisteddfod prizes and publishing several cantatas, madrigals, anthems, and the like. For thirty years he was editor of a musical monthly, Y Cerddor, and musical editor of the Welsh Congregational "Caniedydd" (1895) and of the Wesleyan Welsh hymnal, "Llyfr Tonau." He was an important music critic, and also the compiler of a text book on harmony.

TUNE (Second): "Cwmdu" is a tune of unusual pattern and meter but of exquisite sentiment. The concluding musical phrase should develop a slight crescendo and then close with diminishing volume. As a setting for the words, "Ere I Sleep, for Every Favor," "Cwmdu" appears in "The Church Hymnary," Revised, published in 1927.

---

512 HYMN: O Saviour, I Have Naught to Plead
TUNE: Gwyneth

Author: *Jane Crewdson*   Composer: *John Price (Beulah)*

AUTHOR: For comments on the author, Jane Crewdson, see Hymn 295.

HYMN: This hymn, written for the sick room shortly before Mrs. Crewdson's death, appeared in "A Little While and Other Poems." Out of her long invalidism she was able to measure the "exceeding need" of the Saviour as well as his "exceeding love." The second stanza contrasts the short, rapidly passing span of human need with the eternal love that "lasts forevermore." One of her friends said, "More than half a century of patient suffering went to the making of her [Mrs. Crewdson's] hymns."

COMPOSER: The composer, John Price, a noted Welsh musician, was born in Llangammareh in 1857. He was chorister at Beulah, Breconshire, when but ten years of age. He was graduated from the Tonic Sol-fa College in 1879 and for fifty years has led a creative and highly coöperative musical life in Wales. His anthems and hymn tunes are widely sung.

TUNE: The tune, "Gwyneth," was composed by Price for Charlotte Elliott's hymn "Just as I Am, Without One Plea."

513

HYMN: My Jesus, Pierced for Love of Me
TUNE: Nu Wol Gott Das Unser Gesang

Source: *"Paderborn Gesangbuch"*   Source: *German Melody*

SOURCE: The source is "Paderborn Gesangbuch," 1726.

TRANSLATOR: For comments on the translator, George R. Woodward, see Hymn 119.

HYMN: This translation by Rev. George R. Woodward, from the German of more than two centuries ago, is a prayer of thankfulness for the love of Jesus. The second stanza is a request for his presence, coupled with a confession of unworthiness. The third stanza is based upon Psalm 42:

> "As the hart panteth after the water brooks,
> So panteth my soul after thee, O God."

SOURCE: The source is a sixteenth-century German melody.

HARMONIZER: For comments on the harmonizer, George R. Woodward, see Hymn 119.

TUNE: "Nu Wol Gott Das Unser Gesang" is a sixteenth-century melody harmonized by Rev. George R. Woodward, of England. It appeared in his interesting hymnal, "Songs of Syon," which was published in London in 1923. An explanatory word appended to the tune in that volume traces it to "Leisentrit," 1584. The music is contemplative in character and very effective for unison singing.

Responses

Opening Responses: Introits

*

I-2   RESPONSE: Come, Dearest Lord, Descend and Dwell
          TUNE: Ein Kind Geboren

Author: *Rev. Isaac Watts*   Source: *Old German Carol*

AUTHOR: For comments on the author, Isaac Watts, see Hymn 22.

RESPONSE: The first sixteen Responses are designed for use at the opening of a church service when something briefer than a regular hymn is found desirable. They begin appropriately with two stanzas by Watts, taken from one of his most familiar and widely used hymns. The hymn was evidently suggested by, and is in a sense a paraphrase of, Eph. 3: 17-21.

SOURCE (First Tune): This tune is from an old German carol. See the article, "German Hymn Sources," under "Original Sources," page xxi.

TUNE (First): "Ein Kind Geboren" is not the original tune, but is derived from a German carol tune found in Klug's "Geistliche Lieder zu Wittemberg" (1543). A later form appeared in Lossius' "Psalmodia, Hoc Est Cantica Sacra Veteris Ecclesiae Selecta" (1553), and may be found in "The Oxford Book of Carols" (1928). This later tune was originally a descant to the older one, but gradually displaced the parent melody. The first line of the present version is that of the newer tune, the rest being nearer to the original.

When the natural phrasing of the tune and the natural phrasing of the text do not coincide, it is better to phrase according to the words rather than according to the music. The hymn would indicate a more or less gradual ascent from a quiet invocation to a climax of inexpressible joy.

SECOND TUNE: Federal Street
Composer: *Henry K. Oliver*

COMPOSER (Second Tune): For comments on the composer, Henry K. Oliver, see Hymn 90.

Handbook to The Hymnal

TUNE (Second): For comments on the tune, "Federal Street," see Hymn 90.

---

3 RESPONSE: O Come, Let Us Worship and Bow Down

Source: *Psalm xcv. 6*   Composer: *Edward Shippen Barnes*

SOURCE: The source is Ps. 95:6. During the crusades the ringing phrases of this psalm were familiar throughout Europe and the Holy Land as the battle cry of the Knights Templars. Verse 6 has probably been more used than any other words as the call to worship in the Christian Church through all the centuries. It was inscribed by Christian Friedrich Schwartz, the brilliant young German pastor whom the Danish Missionary Society sent to India in 1750, over the portal of his Mission Church of Bethlehem at Tranquebar.

COMPOSER: For comments on the composer, Edward Shippen Barnes, see Hymn 70.

TUNE: This music was composed by Mr. Barnes for the "Junior Church School Hymnal" (1926). If sung slowly and quietly it will tend to counteract the restless, wandering thoughts of the congregation, and focus the attention upon the one central thought, namely, that of the presence of God.

---

4 RESPONSE: O Come, Let Us Worship and Bow Before the Lord

Composer: *Petr Iljitch Tschaikowsky*

SOURCE: The words of this response are taken from the Service of the Russian Church, calling on the congregation to worship and on the risen Lord to hear and save.

COMPOSER: Petr Iljitch Tschaikowsky was born in Votkinsk, Russia, in 1840 and died in St. Petersburg in 1893. He was one of the greatest of all modern Russian composers. He composed in all forms. His six symphonies are all of importance, the "Pathétique" being his greatest success. Also, he composed beautiful chamber music and many strong overtures. The overture of "Romeo and Juliet" is the best of these.

TUNE: These are the first few measures from an anthem written for the "Liturgy of St. John Chrysostom" of the Russian Church. This music should be sung with a strong tone and with a stately,

522

Responses

majestic rhythm, symbolizing thus the almighty power of God. The complete anthem, edited by N. Lindsay Norden, of Philadelphia, is published with an English text by J. Fischer & Bro., New York City.

---

5   RESPONSE: The Lord Is in His Holy Temple

Composer: *Rev. Calvin W. Laufer*

SOURCE: The source is Hab. 2:20. Habakkuk's sublime appeal to the inhabitants of the earth to bow in silent awe before the majesty and power of the God of Israel is here set to music in fine harmony with the devotional character of the words.

COMPOSER: For comments on the composer, Calvin W. Laufer, see Hymn 13.

TUNE: This music should be sung slowly and without undue accent on the first beats of the measure. A good *legato* throughout should be observed, with care to avoid the appearance of forced expression.

---

6   RESPONSE: The Lord Is in His Holy Temple

Composer: *E. Edwards*

SOURCE: The same text as in Response 5 is here set to a peculiarly effective chant.

COMPOSER: The composer, E. Edwards, is an Anglican organist, of whom no biographical information is available.

TUNE: The music is that of a typical Anglican chant. It should be sung, with the tempo befitting worship and adoration and not too fast, in such a way that serenity and calm will inspire the congregation to an expectant mood.

7   RESPONSE: Father of Lights, in Whom There Is No Shadow
     TUNE: Welwyn

Authors: *Elizabeth Wilson*   Composer: *Alfred Scott-Gatty*
         Helen Thoburn

AUTHORS: One of the authors of this response, Miss Elizabeth Wilson, entered the work of the Young Women's Christian Association in 1889 and continued with this organization until 1928, serving for some years in India. On her retirement she returned to her home town at Appleton, Wisconsin, where she was ordained as a minister of the Methodist Episcopal Church. The other, Miss Helen Thoburn, was also a Y.W.C.A. secretary, a member of the Madison Avenue Presbyterian Church of New York. Her service with the Association was divided between China and this country, in the work of interpreting America to China and China to the world. She died in 1931.

RESPONSE: The hymn from which this stanza is taken has long been widely used in Young Women's Christian Association circles. This is the first occasion on which it has been introduced into a church hymnal. The hymn was written as a recessional for a pageant, "The Ministering of the Gift," which Miss Thoburn was preparing for the Fourth National Convention of the Association held in Richmond, Virginia, April, 1913. Late one afternoon Miss Thoburn came into Miss Wilson's office with some words which she had written to J. Albert Jeffery's tune, "Ancient of Days." (See Hymn 58.) Miss Wilson suggested the connection between the Giver and his greatest Gift in terms of light, the Father of lights and the Light of the world. With this thought as a basis, before the afternoon was over the hymn was written.

COMPOSER: For comments on the composer, Alfred Scott-Gatty, see Hymn 110.

TUNE: This response is a good opening form of praise for evening, although there is no reason why it cannot be used at any service. Considering either the darkness of the night or the darkness of men's minds, it is fitting to sing about the "Father of lights" with a buoyant spirit. The tempo suggestion, "Moderately slow," does not prevent the time from proceeding with a joyous spring that indicates an assurance that the Father will supply enlightenment.

For further comments on the tune, "Welwyn," see Hymn 110.

Responses

8
RESPONSE: Father, the Watches of the Night Are O'er
TUNE: Langran

Source: *"Disciples' Hymn Book"*   Composer: *James Langran*

SOURCE: This is a morning prayer from "The Disciples' Hymn Book," expressing gratitude to God for his care over us through the night and asking for his continued protection through "the watches of the day."

COMPOSER: For comments on the composer, James Langran, see Hymn 174.

TUNE: "Langran," although written for an evening hymn, is obviously appropriate for the morning service. The first stanza moves calmly but firmly to a song of gratitude for God's protection. The second stanza, recognizing the trials of the future, ends with a prayer for poise and peace. This attitude suggests a quiet cadence. For further comments on the tune, "Langran," see Hymn 174.

9
RESPONSE: Lord, for the Mercies of the Night
TUNE: Farrant

Author: *Rev. John Mason*   Composer: *Richard Farrant*

AUTHOR: The author, John Mason, was born in England, the son of a dissenting minister, about 1645. He graduated from Clare Hall, Cambridge, in 1664. The last twenty years of his life, until his death in 1694, were spent in Water-Stratford, where he was rector of the parish church. He was widely known, both as an eloquent preacher and as a writer of hymns and other devotional literature. His friend Richard Baxter called him "the glory of the English Church." About a month before his death he saw in a dream a vision of Christ and on the following Sunday preached a sermon which he entitled "The Midnight Cry," in which he proclaimed the near approach of the Second Advent. The rumor spread that the event was to occur in Water-Stratford. Multitudes flocked into the town and for several weeks great excitement prevailed, with all the phenomena of intense religious enthusiasm. The excitement had scarcely begun to subside when Mason died.

He was one of the earliest hymn writers of the English Church, and for two hundred years a considerable number of his hymns were widely used. His main contribution to hymnology, however, lies in his unmistakable influence on Watts and Wesley and other later writers.

RESPONSE: This, like the preceding, is a morning hymn, thanking God for the mercies of the night past and praying that the new day and all our days, here and hereafter, may be dedicated to his praise.

COMPOSER: Richard Farrant (c.1530–1580) served in the Chapel Royal during the reigns of Edward VI, Mary, and Elizabeth, except for five years when he was master of choristers at St. George's Chapel, Windsor. He is chiefly remembered for his beautiful service in G minor and for two anthems, "Call to Remembrance" and "Hide Not Thy Face." His works show him a worthy contemporary of Christopher Tye (d.1572) and Thomas Tallis (d.1585).

TUNE: "Farrant" is adapted from the anthem "Lord, for Thy Tender Mercies' Sake," usually attributed to Richard Farrant. This hymn of dedication and praise demands virile interpretation and should move with a broad, majestic stride.

---

10   RESPONSE: Approach, My Soul, the Mercy Seat
            TUNE: Dalehurst

Author: *Rev. John Newton*   Composer: *Arthur Cottman*

AUTHOR: For comments on the author, John Newton, see Hymn 310.

RESPONSE: In "Approach, My Soul, the Mercy Seat," we have one of Newton's most familiar and popular hymns. It is found in the "Olney Hymns," a collection of hymns by Newton and his friend Cowper. The original hymn contained five stanzas.

COMPOSER: For comments on the composer, Arthur Cottman, see Hymn 143.

TUNE: Joined with the present text, this introit is effective if sung quietly by the entire congregation. Introspection should be stimulated by a smooth, quiet performance. A silent reading of the text, before or after singing, is recommended.

For further comments on the tune, "Dalehurst," see Hymn 143.

Responses

II

RESPONSE: Lord, We Come Before Thee Now
TUNE: Horsham

Author: *Rev. William Hammond*   Source: *English Traditional Melody*

AUTHOR: The author, William Hammond, was born in Battle, Sussex, England, in 1719, and educated at St. John's College, Cambridge. In 1743 he joined the Calvinistic Methodists and two years later the Moravian Brethren. He died in London in 1783. Besides writing original hymns, many of which were once widely used, he was among the first to publish translations of the old Latin hymns.

RESPONSE: This hymn was originally written for the purpose here suggested, to be used at the opening of a church service. In it the people voice their plea that God will hear their prayers, inspire their songs, and speak to them through his Word.

SOURCE: The source is an English traditional melody.

TUNE: Too often hymns of this type are sung with a false emotion, indicating thoughtlessness or hypocrisy. The nature of the text suggests a steady forward pressure in the tune.
For further comments on the tune, "Horsham," see Hymn 95.

12

RESPONSE: Jesus, Where'er Thy People Meet
TUNE: Simeon

Author: *William Cowper*   Composer: *S. Stanley*

AUTHOR: For comments on the author, William Cowper, see Hymn 103.

RESPONSE: This hymn was written for the opening of the Great House at Olney as a place for prayer meetings at the time when Cowper was living at Olney with his friend John Newton. At that time the practice of holding a public service of worship anywhere except in a properly consecrated church was less familiar than it is now. Cowper opens this hymn with a defense of the propriety of the practice and gives assurance that God's presence is not limited to particular places.

COMPOSER: Samuel Stanley (1767–1822) was for a long time a leading musician in Birmingham, England. His opinions on the correct performance of Handel's music were quoted authoritatively for many years after his death. Under his leadership the musical services of Ebenezer Chapel, in Steelhouse Lane, became widely known. During his lifetime he published two sets of hymn tunes. After his death a third volume was published. "Simeon" was one of the first set, published about 1796.

TUNE: "Simeon" was published at Birmingham, England, 1802, and was associated with one of Watts's hymns. It is equally appropriate for morning or evening. Confidence in the promises of God should be reflected in the music by a strong, unwavering tone.

---

13   RESPONSE: Jesus, Stand Among Us
           TUNE: Bemerton (Caswall)

Author: *Rev. William Pennefather*   Composer: *Rev. Friedrich Filitz*

AUTHOR: William Pennefather was born in Dublin and educated at Trinity College in his native city. In 1841 he was ordained, and later held various incumbencies both in Ireland and in England. He was the author of many hymns, most of them written specifically for use at conferences held under his direction in Barnet and Mildmay.

RESPONSE: This hymn is a simply expressed prayer for the presence of Christ and his Spirit, appropriate for the opening of any service.

COMPOSER: For comments on the composer, Friedrich Filitz, see Hymn 252.

TUNE: The first two measures of "Bemerton" accord with the sentiment of the hymn, indicating a quiet quest for the Holy Spirit within each heart, and should be sung with that thought in mind. A brighter quality in the last stanza should correspond to the sentiment of hope there expressed.

---

14   RESPONSE: Let All Mortal Flesh Keep Silence
           TUNE: Picardy

Source: *"Liturgy of St. James"*   Source: *French Traditional Carol*

TRANSLATOR: For comments on the translator, Gerard Moultrie, see Hymn 112.

Responses

RESPONSE: These six lines, with their Biblical air of simplicity and sublimity, are taken from the so-called "Liturgy of St. James," an ancient liturgy of the Syriac Church. The response bears evidence of having been composed in its various parts somewhere from the fourth century to the eighth.

TUNE: "Picardy" is a French carol, probably of the seventeenth century. Contrary to most French carols, there is no childlike gayety to be found in this tune, whether it be sung fast or slowly. It is harmonized in somewhat modal style and has the feeling of a plain song.

It must be sung very slowly. Its character appears rather somber but also dignified and stately. If sung fast the somberness changes to a certain harshness. All tunes change their character somewhat with a considerable change of speed, but here the conversion is remarkable and denotes an unusual tune.

---

15   RESPONSE: Shepherd of Mortals, Here Behold
          TUNE: Diman

Composer: *Joseph E. Sweetser*

RESPONSE: This exquisite stanza addressed to the "Shepherd of mortals" is of great beauty and simplicity. Its introduction here as an introit is unusual. Humility, aspiration, and expectation could not be more felicitously expressed. Most effective is the last line, "O Man of Nazareth, be our guest!"

COMPOSER: For comments on the composer, Joseph E. Sweetser, see Hymn 299.

TUNE: "Diman" is suitable for a children's service because of the simplicity of the words and music. It should be kept in mind that when an unaccented syllable such as "tals" in the word "mortals" leaps to a comparatively high pitch, one should carefully avoid giving undue accent to that syllable. Maintain an accent in singing that would be proper in speech.

---

16   RESPONSE: May You Who Enter Here
          TUNE: St. Issey

Author: *Anonymous*   Source: *English Traditional Melody*

RESPONSE: This is a blessing, to be sung suitably by the choir, imploring God's presence in the hearts of the worshipers. This hymn by an unknown writer appeals to the worshipers to come to

God by the way of the Crucified, with purged hearts and eyes open to the vision of complete redemption in him.

TUNE: England is said to be richer in traditional folk songs than is any other country. Of this English folk music, born of the hearts of the people, "St. Issey," with its simplicity and charm, is a peculiarly appealing example. The original melody appeared in the "Fitzwilliam Virginal Book," published about 1600. It became very popular in the sixteenth and seventeenth centuries and was frequently mentioned in plays and other writings. This arrangement was made for "The English Hymnal" of 1906.

Because of the key, the tempo, and the melodic cadences, this tune is apt to be interpreted in a mournful manner. The hymn contains elements of mystery and seriousness, but resurrection rather than death is the ultimate message of the text. With this in mind the last phrase must necessarily move to a strong climax.

Prayer Responses

*

17   RESPONSE: Come, My Soul, Thy Suit Prepare
      TUNE: Savannah

Author: *Rev. John Newton*   Source: *Rev. John Wesley's "The Foundery Collection"*

AUTHOR: For comments on the author, John Newton, see Hymn 310.

RESPONSE: This is the first of a series of five responses suggested for use before or after a spoken prayer. In the mood of the One Hundred and Third Psalm, the worshiper calls his own soul to praise and to a renewed confidence in Christ's willingness and power to answer prayer. "Congregational song," writes Dr. Louis F. Benson in "Christian Song," "becomes spiritual only as each individual Christian brings his personal offering to the sanctuary, and contributes it to the common song of brotherhood." This hymn is a definite call for the prayerful and joyous contemplation of God in worship.

SOURCE: For comments on the source, John Wesley's "The Foundery Collection," see Hymn 264.

Responses

TUNE: For comments on the tune, "Savannah," see Hymn 288. The response may be effectively used as a preliminary to a period of silent prayer, in either a formal or an informal service of worship.

---

18   RESPONSE: May the Words of My Mouth

Source: *Hebrew Traditional Melody*

RESPONSE: This response is based on Ps. 19: 14, a peculiarly fine example of ancient Hebrew music, with a devotional quality reminiscent of the days when great choirs sang at the Temple festivities. It is incorporated in a service ritual for the synagogue edited by Rev. Max Graumann (d. 1933), for many years cantor of the West End Synagogue, New York. It will be found especially effective when rendered by a soloist, preferably contralto.

SOURCE: The source is an old Hebrew melody.

TUNE: This Hebrew traditional melody in the minor mode may be sung by a soloist, a choir, or a congregation, before the usual pastoral prayer of the ordinary church service. The smooth musical phrases should be sung with unhurried but hopeful feeling. Though the music is in a quiet mood, it is also intense and aspirational.

---

19   RESPONSE: Hear Thou in Love, O Lord, Our Cry

Composer: *Felix Mendelssohn*

RESPONSE: These familiar and deservedly popular measures are taken from Mendelssohn's oratorio, "Elijah." At the close of Part I, after the destruction of the prophets of Baal, the people, at Elijah's direction, look for rain and voice their plea in the music of this refrain.

COMPOSER: For comments on the composer, Felix Mendelssohn, see Hymn 11.

TUNE: This short musical phrase from the works of Felix Mendelssohn was used as the ending of the tune "Intercession New," by William Hutchins Callcott, 1867. It fits the words in a most appealing way, and could be used most appropriately at the conclusion of a service of prayer. As the harmony is essential to the beauty of the music, a choir ought to be used along with the congregation, if the people desire to sing the response.

---

20   RESPONSE: May the Words of My Mouth

Source: *Traditional Serbian Melody*

RESPONSE: This response, like Response 18, is based on Ps. 19:14.

SOURCE: The source is a traditional Serbian melody.

TUNE: This traditional Serbian melody is reminiscent of the musical mode of the Greek Orthodox Church. With its simple yet fundamental harmonization it can best be used where there is a choir well trained in the art of clear enunciation and the effective presentation of spiritual feelings.

---

21   RESPONSE: O Thou Who Hearest Every Heartfelt Prayer
        TUNE: Morecambe

Composer: *Frederick C. Atkinson*

RESPONSE: This is a simple and gracefully expressed petition for God's blessing on a Sunday service, appropriate for use as a response in connection with the opening prayer.

COMPOSER: For comments on the composer, Frederick C. Atkinson, see Hymn 204.

TUNE: This response would appear to be most suitable to the quiet of the evening service of worship, before the pastoral prayer of the minister. The tune, being usually well known, will be sung heartily in most churches.

For further comments on the tune, "Morecambe," see Hymn 204.

Responses

Responses to Scriptures

*

22   RESPONSE: O Lord, Open Thou Our Eyes

Composer: *John Camidge*

SOURCE: This response is based on Ps. 119:18.

RESPONSE: This is a response suitable for use by the choir or by the congregation in connection with the reading of the Ten Commandments or Christ's summary of the law or any other Scripture portion.

COMPOSER: John Camidge (1735–1803) was for forty-three years (1756–1799) organist at York Minster, England, and was widely known both for his playing and for his compositions. He was succeeded by his son Matthew, who served until 1842, and he in turn by his son John, who more than rounded out the century, serving until 1859. All three were notable as composers of church music.

TUNE: This tune is a very simple musical statement, the strength of which is in its simplicity. This response is more suitable for congregational use than one of an elaborate type, and should be sung with an increasingly forceful crescendo.

23-24   RESPONSE: Thy Word Have I Hid in My Heart
FIRST TUNE: Selma

Source: *Psalm cxix*   Source: *Melody from the Isle of Arran*

SOURCE: The response is based on Ps. 119:11, 12.

RESPONSE: These verses lend themselves readily to use in connection with the reading of the law or any portion of the Scriptures.

HARMONIZER (First Tune): For comments on the harmonizer, R. A. Smith, see Hymn 299.

533

TUNE (First): The traditional Scottish melody which in Hymn 299 is adapted to a conventional short-meter hymn is here adapted to two verses in the irregular rhythm of the Authorized Version of The Psalms.

For further comments on the tune, "Selma," see Hymn 299.

SECOND TUNE: Cheshire Tune

Source: *"Este's Psalter"*

SOURCE (Second Tune): For comments on the source, "Este's Psalter," see Hymn 503.

TUNE (Second): For comments on the tune, "Cheshire Tune," see Hymn 503.

---

25   RESPONSE: Teach Me, O Lord, the Way of Thy Statutes

Composer: *William Henry Hewlett*

SOURCE: This response is based on Ps. 119:33.

RESPONSE: Many of the psalms are spontaneous bursts of song, exultant in spirit, lyric in quality. But the long poem from which this response is taken is very different. It is a quiet meditation on the Word of God. The author conceives the Word, not as something written in a book, though it comes often through "statutes," "judgments," "commandments," "testimonies," in the Scriptures; the Word itself is to him a creating, communicating energy or spirit from God, which speaks in the human soul to guide, to warn, to heal, to quicken, or to bless. The verse here given is a prayer admirably suited to follow the reading of the Bible, for it expresses both the desire to learn and the purpose to do the will of God, to be taught "the way of thy statutes" and to "keep it unto the end."

COMPOSER: William Henry Hewlett was born in Bath, Somerset, England, in 1873. He studied piano, organ, and theory in Toronto, Berlin, and London. Principal of the Hamilton Conservatory of Music, since 1922 he has been conductor of the Elgar Choir, Hamilton, and is an ex-president of the Canadian College of Organists. He served on the Hymn Book Committee of the former Methodist Church of Canada, and later on the Hymnal Committee of the United Church of Canada. He is a composer of church and piano music.

Responses

TUNE: This music was written to these words and included in "The Hymnary" (Canada, 1930). The response is very appropriate to follow the reading of the Ten Commandments, and may be sung either by choir or by congregation.

Offertory Responses

*

26   RESPONSE: All Things Come of Thee, O Lord

Composer: *Ludwig van Beethoven*

SOURCE: The source is I Chron. 29:14.

RESPONSE: The historic setting of this verse is significant. King David was assembling the material with which Solomon might build a Temple for God. Gathering the people together, he told them that he himself had given gold and silver—"because I have set my affection to the house of my God." Then he asked, "Who then is willing to consecrate his service this day unto the Lord?" The people and their leaders responded with great generosity and "rejoiced, for that they offered willingly" their gold and silver and precious stones for the house of the Lord. Then the king offered a prayer, vs. 10–19, in which he blessed Jehovah as the Source of all good, "Both riches and honour come of thee, and thou reignest over all; and in thine hand is power and might." Then, in a characteristic burst of humility, David uttered these words: "But who am I, and what is my people, that we should be able to offer so willingly after this sort? for all things come of thee, and of thine own have we given thee." A reading of this whole chapter will make vivid the beautiful spirit of true consecration which this response expresses.

COMPOSER: For comments on the composer, Ludwig van Beethoven, see Hymn 5.

TUNE: This is one of the most widely used offertory responses, and is usually sung by a congregation during the presentation and consecration of the offering.

27 RESPONSE: All Things Are Thine: No Gift Have We
TUNE: Herr Jesu Christ

Author: *John Greenleaf Whittier*   Source: *"Pensum Sacrum"*

AUTHOR: For comments on the author, John Greenleaf Whittier, see Hymn 178.

RESPONSE: The Quaker poet, who disclaimed being a hymn writer because, as he said, he was not at all musical, has nevertheless given us some of our most beautiful hymns. The one from which these lines are taken is from a less familiar poem written for the opening of a new church in Minnesota in 1872. It was first published in Horder's "Congregational Hymns" in 1884, but has not had wide circulation. In the first stanza, here used as a response, Whittier has taken the idea of consecrating to God what comes from God, voiced by King David (see Response 26), and with characteristic simplicity has expressed it in verse which is both reverent and singable.

SOURCE: For comments on the source, "Pensum Sacrum," see Hymn 475.

ARRANGER: For comments on the arranger, Johann Sebastian Bach, see Hymn 21.

TUNE: For comments on the tune, "Herr Jesu Christ," see Hymn 475.

---

28 RESPONSE: The Sacrifices of God Are a Broken Spirit

Source: *Psalm li*   Source: *Tonus Regius*
From the Lutheran Service

SOURCE: The source is Ps. 51:17.

RESPONSE: These words recall us from thoughtless giving. They come from one of the profoundest prayers in the Bible, which expresses "the voice of the penitent soul in all ages." The psalmist, overwhelmed by a sense of guilt, knows that no gesture of benevolence on his part can earn any merit for him in the sight of a righteous God. Shame and humiliation submerge his soul and no formal

Responses

procedure will bring him any relief. Nothing less than forgiveness, utterly undeserved, granted out of God's compassion for the sinner, will avail. This, surely, is the secret of the gospel's power!

> "Not the labors of my hands
> Can fulfill Thy law's demands."

SOURCE: The source is the "Tonus Regius" from the Lutheran Service.

TUNE: The nature of this offertory response would indicate its best usefulness to be in connection with a Communion service, where a quiet and subdued presentation of gifts is to be desired.

29-30 RESPONSE: Bless Thou the Gifts Our Hands Have Brought
FIRST TUNE: Deus Tuorum Militum

Author: *Rev. Samuel Longfellow*   Source: *Grenoble Church Melody*

AUTHOR: For comments on the author, Samuel Longfellow, see Hymn 79.

RESPONSE: It is not what we do, but what God does, that counts. It was not what Paul and Barnabas had done among the Gentiles, but "what miracles and wonders God had wrought among the Gentiles by them," Acts 15:12. We give our gifts, we make our plans, we do what we believe to be God's will; but unless he himself works with and through us all our struggles for accomplishment are futile.

SOURCE (First Tune): The source is a Grenoble church melody.

TUNE (First): This dignified old Grenoble church melody, "Deus Tuorum Militum," will greatly enhance the spiritual force of the presentation of offerings when sung by a congregation as its ushers return in a body with the gifts in their hands.

SECOND TUNE: Llangollen (Lledrod)
Source: *Welsh Hymn Melody*

SOURCE (Second Tune): This melody is taken from "Llyfr Tonau Cynulleidfaol" (1859).

TUNE: As in much of the Welsh music, a great deal of the charm of the tune, "Llangollen (Lledrod)," is dependent on the harmony. Hence this response would be an excellent variation where the usage of a church depends upon the choir to furnish the musical portion of the service.

31-32 RESPONSE: We Give Thee But Thine Own
FIRST TUNE: Windermere

Author: *Bishop W. Walsham How*   Composer: *Arthur Somervell*

AUTHOR: For comments on the author, W. Walsham How, see Hymn 137.

RESPONSE: Here, in four short lines, is the whole principle of stewardship. This response voices the humble recognition of God's bounty to us and our direct responsibility to him for the use we make of his gifts. Written in 1858, the hymn of which this is the first stanza was first published six years later. The joy of Christian giving is the joy of sharing with our fellow men and so of giving to Him who gives to us all that we have.

COMPOSER (First Tune): Sir Arthur Somervell, A.M., F.R.C.M., Mus.D., was born in the Lake District of England, at Windermere, June 5, 1863. He was educated at King's College, Cambridge, and studied music with Sir C. V. Stanford. His musical education was continued in Germany, and at the Royal College of Music in London, where he later taught harmony and counterpoint. Since 1901 he has been inspector of music for England, Wales, and Scotland, for the Board of Education.

TUNE (First): "Windermere," named after the composer's birthplace, was specially written for "The English Hymnal" of 1906, to the words of the hymn used in this response.

SECOND TUNE: Selma
Source: *Melody from the Isle of Arran*

SOURCE (Second Tune): The source is a melody from the Isle of Arran.

ARRANGER (Second Tune): For comments on the arranger, R. A. Smith, see Hymn 299.

538

Responses

TUNE (Second): For comments on the tune, "Selma," see Hymn 299.

---

33   RESPONSE: To Do Good, and to Distribute, Forget Not

Composer: *Jonathan Battishill*

SOURCE: This response is based on Heb. 13:16.

RESPONSE: Offerings like those we make in our gifts of worship are superficial unless our "sacrifice" is something more than "the fruit of our lips" or the depositing of money in a plate. The author therefore here adds the deeper note: "But to do good and to communicate [literally, "share," or, as it is rendered here, "distribute"] forget not: for with such sacrifices God is well pleased." This response might well be used before the offering is taken.

COMPOSER: Jonathan Battishill was born in London, May, 1738, and died at Islington, December 10, 1801. He entered upon his musical career at a very early age as a chorister in St. Paul's Cathedral. He later became deputy organist in the Chapel Royal. He was organist successively in two of London's parish churches, and was also conductor and harpsichordist at Covent Garden.

TUNE: This response, in chant form, might be used effectively by a choir, after the minister has offered his dedicatory prayer, prior to the taking of the offering.

---

34   RESPONSE: O Dearest Lord

Source: *Bohemian Brethren Traditional*

RESPONSE: Properly the offertory is not the "taking of a collection," nor yet the presenting of money for use in the church, but the consecration to God of ourselves as well as our possessions, what we keep for our own use as well as what we give for the church's use. The offering has been called "the great central act of worship." It should be a glad and solemn moment in the service, instead of the routine matter it so easily becomes, and in it not only our gifts, which for all their usefulness are mere symbols, but also

"Our songs of praise,
The prayers we raise,"

539

and all that we do and think in this hour should be offered up to God for his acceptance and blessing. This holy act of comprehensive worship is suggested in the brief sentence of this response.

SOURCE: This is a Bohemian traditional melody of undoubted worth. Its composer is not known.

TUNE: Plainly intended for congregational use, this fine response fits into various forms of taking the offering. The harmony should be sung if at all possible.

General Responses
*

35   RESPONSE: To Him Who Sits Upon the Throne
        TUNE: St. Magnus

Author: *Rev. Isaac Watts*   Composer: *Jeremiah Clark*

AUTHOR: For comments on the author, Isaac Watts, see Hymn 22.

RESPONSE: This verse is apparently taken from a little-known hymn by Dr. Watts. It is an "ascription of praise," such as those given in "The Book of Common Worship," Revised, pages 203, 204, and is, indeed, a paraphrase of the last of these, which is taken from Rev. 5:13: "Blessing, and honour, and glory, and power, be unto him that sitteth upon the throne, and unto the Lamb for ever and ever." This is a response which might be used at the close of one of the prayers or at the conclusion of the service of worship.

COMPOSER: For comments on the composer, Jeremiah Clark, see Hymn 185.

TUNE: For comments on the tune, "St. Magnus," see Hymn 185.

Responses

36 RESPONSE: O Bread of Life from Heaven
TUNE: Bread of Life (Warren)

Author: *Anonymous*   Composer: *Samuel P. Warren*

TRANSLATOR: For comments on the translator, Philip Schaff, see Hymn 357.

RESPONSE: For comments on the response, "O Bread of Life from Heaven," see Hymn 357.

COMPOSER: For comments on the composer, Samuel P. Warren, see Hymn 357.

TUNE: For comments on the tune, "Bread of Life (Warren)," see Hymn 357.

---

37 RESPONSE: Father, Fill Us with Thy Love
TUNE: Horsham

Source: *English Traditional Melody*

RESPONSE: This response suggests the mystic relation between Christians and their Lord concerning which Jesus had so much to say at the Last Supper, John, chs. 14 to 17. At the close of his prayer on that occasion Christ prayed "that the love wherewith thou hast loved me may be in them, and I in them." Against such a background, as well as that of Paul's great prayer in Eph. 3:17-19, the true significance of this response is to be seen. It is a prayer for a union with God in which the bond is "the love of God, which is in Christ Jesus our Lord," Rom. 8:39.

SOURCE: The source of this tune is an English traditional melody.

TUNE: For comments of the tune, "Horsham," see Hymn 95.

38 RESPONSE: A Holy Stillness, Breathing Calm
TUNE: Landskron

Source: *"Bohemian Hymnal"*

RESPONSE: "Be still, and know that I am God," Ps. 46:10, is a command we too seldom obey. One business man, in a group of younger men who were being asked for suggestions as to how to make Sunday worship more helpful, said, "I sometimes wish the minister would stop talking during the prayers and let me think my own thoughts." In some of our churches deliberately planned silences occur at various points in the service, and many people feel that "it creates an atmosphere in which it is easy and natural to hear the voice of God." "My soul," says the psalmist, "wait thou only upon God; for my expectation is from him."

SOURCE: This tune is found in the "Bohemian Hymnal" of 1531.

TUNE: "Landskron" would be an excellent conclusion to a period of silent prayer, the end of which would be indicated by the playing of the first chord on the organ.

---

39 RESPONSE: Day by Day
TUNE: Stonethwaite

Author: *Richard of Chichester*   Composer: *Arthur Somervell*

AUTHOR: Richard of Chichester was one of the beacon lights of early Christian culture that shone in the dismal darkness of the Middle Ages. He was born in Droitwich in 1197, and died at Dover in 1253. His zeal as a student carried him through Oxford, Paris, and Bologna, the outstanding centers of learning of the period. His learning was recognized by his being made chancellor of Oxford University, while his religious devotion was rewarded through his appointment as chancellor of Canterbury. His election as bishop of Chichester is said to have offended Henry III on account of his stern moral standards and rigid ideas as to church discipline. The Church canonized Richard in 1262.

RESPONSE: This quaint and beautiful hymn is admirably adapted for a response following prayer or to stand alone in any order of worship. Triple phrases in the last line bring this hymn prayer into the realm of practical Christian experience in that it asks that we may all love and follow our Lord more "clearly," "dearly," and "nearly."

Responses

COMPOSER: For comments on the composer, Arthur Somervell, see Response 31.

TUNE: "Stonethwaite" is of recent origin. It was especially written for the words of Richard of Chichester, and included in the enlarged edition of "Songs of Praise" (London, 1931). As the words of the text are of irregular meter, considerable skill was necessary to express them. The difficulty was overcome by providing a tune that is semirecitative, unforced and natural musical conversation.

40

RESPONSE: Praise to the Holiest in the Height

TUNE: Hebdomadal

Author: *Cardinal John H. Newman*   Composer: *Bishop Thomas Banks Strong*

AUTHOR: For comments on the author, John Henry Newman, see Hymn 289.

RESPONSE: The great English ecclesiastic, who was also a poet and something of a musician, had for some time been under a vivid apprehension of approaching death. As a matter of fact, he lived for thirty-five years beyond this period of apprehension. As he meditated calmly on the experience which he believed awaited him, a sudden inspiration came to him to write a poem setting forth in dramatic form the vision of a Christian's death on which his imagination had been dwelling. This was "The Dream of Gerontius," written in 1865 and published in The Month for May and June of that year. It was later set to music by Sir Edward Elgar, but when it first appeared it was widely read as a poem. One writer "knew a poor stocking weaver who on his deathbed made his wife read it to him repeatedly." General "Chinese" Gordon prized it highly, and had a well-marked copy with him when he met his death at Khartoum. Newman was deeply touched by this and transferred Gordon's pencil marks to his own copy.

COMPOSER: Thomas Banks Strong was born in London, 1861. He attended Westminster School and Christ Church, Oxford. After his ordination in 1885, he became successively Bampton lecturer in 1895; dean of Christ Church, 1901–1920; vice chancellor of Oxford University, 1913–1917; bishop of Ripon, 1920–1925; and bishop of Oxford in 1925. Bishop Strong served as one of the editors of "The Oxford Hymn Book."

TUNE: "Hebdomadal" appeared in "The Oxford Hymn Book" (1908) as the musical setting for "Praise to the Holiest in the Height."

Closing Responses

*

41   RESPONSE: Now May He Who from the Dead
TUNE: Solitude

Author: *Rev. John Newton*   Composer: *Lewis T. Downes*

AUTHOR: For comments on the author, John Newton, see Hymn 310.

RESPONSE: This prayer hymn, based on the benediction with which our Communion service closes, is taken from Heb. 13:20. Nothing is known of the circumstances of its composition, but it may have special reference to the awful experience which preceded Newton's conversion in 1748, when at the age of twenty-three, a godless, reckless sailor, he spent a frightful night steering a water-logged vessel in the face of apparently inevitable death. He brought the ship through without loss of life, but he never forgot the experience, and he knew afterwards, if not at the time, that he was "dead" in his sins, both during that dreadful night and later when for six years he was master of a slave ship. If ever a man had a right to believe that he had been "quickened" with Christ, it was John Newton, and his hymn about Him

"who from the dead
Brought the Shepherd of the sheep"

expresses the sense of security which the saved Christian feels, and is a fitting prayer to sing at the close of a service. It was first published in "Olney Hymns" in 1779.

COMPOSER: Lewis T. Downes, born in 1827, was an organist in Providence, Rhode Island.

TUNE: The tune, "Solitude," was written for these words. Where it is not feasible to have a recessional, this well-harmonized tune, sung by a choir, would make a beautiful close to a service of worship, after the benediction was pronounced, especially if it is customary for the people to be either seated or kneeling.

Responses

42 RESPONSE: Honor and Glory, Power and Salvation
TUNE: Coelites Plaudant

Source: *Rouen Church Melody*

RESPONSE: The noble words of this ascription of praise, sung to the ancient melody given, rise in majesty and spiritual aspiration toward the culmination of all worship as realized in the "triune, eternal."

SOURCE: The source is a Rouen church melody.

TUNE: The tune, "Coelites Plaudant," is an old Rouen church melody. Where it is the practice of a congregation to remain standing after the benediction, this stirring melody would be well adapted to close the morning service. This tune is one of the innumerable folk songs that grew out of the musical church life of France, especially in the area under the influence of the Rouen Cathedral.

---

43 RESPONSE: Lord, Let Us Now Depart in Peace
TUNE: Trust

Composer: *Rev. George W. Torrance*

RESPONSE: This brief prayer includes allusions to several beautiful and familiar Bible passages. First, the "Nunc Dimittis" in Luke 2:29–32, which has been sung for so many centuries in many lovely musical settings: "Lord, now lettest thou thy servant depart in peace." The second line suggests the words of Jesus, "Where two or three are gathered together in my name, there am I in the midst of them," Matt. 18:20. "The brightness of Thy face" in the third line might refer either to the Mosaic benediction, with its "The Lord make his face to shine upon thee, and be gracious unto thee," Num. 6:25, or Paul's wonderful expression in II Cor. 4:6, where he speaks of "the light of the knowledge of the glory of God in the face of Jesus Christ." The final petition echoes the parting promise of Jesus, "Lo, I am with you alway, even unto the end of the world," Matt. 28:20.

COMPOSER: George William Torrance was born in 1836 at Rathmines, near Dublin, Ireland. He died at Kilkenny, Ireland, August 20, 1907. He began his career as a chorister in Christ Church Cathedral, Dublin. Later he became an organist and, after studying for a time in Leipzig, was ordained and emigrated to Australia, in 1869, where he remained until 1897, returning to Ireland to fill various church positions until his death.

T UNE: The tune of this response is called "Trust." This quiet closing response is well suited to the evening service, the harmony being most effective.

---

44   RESPONSE: Now May the Light That Shone in
Jesus Christ Our Lord
TUNE: Benediction

Author: *Anonymous*   Composer: *Henry Barraclough*

R ESPONSE: Here is a benediction which brings the idea of Jesus as the Light of the world into the closing thought of a service. It suggests an inner radiance rather than a light shining upon the path. Perhaps the author had in mind the passage, referred to in the comment on Response 43, in which Paul says, "God, who commanded the light to shine out of darkness, hath shined in our hearts, to give the light of the knowledge of the glory of God in the face of Jesus Christ," II Cor. 4: 6. There is an allusion also to the prologue of John in which the Word, who was in the beginning with God and was God, is identified with "the true Light, which lighteth every man," John 1: 9.

C OMPOSER: Henry Barraclough, the eldest son of Joseph Heaton Barraclough and Sara Jane (Metcalfe) Barraclough, was born December 14, 1891, at Wrose Hill, Windhill, near Shipley, Yorkshire, England. He began his musical studies at the age of five years, and by the age of fifteen played the organ for churches and schools. In January, 1914, he was engaged as pianist by J. Wilbur Chapman, D.D., and Charles M. Alexander, evangelists, continuing with them in their campaigns in England, Scotland, and the United States, until he enlisted in the United States Army, November, 1917. Mr. Barraclough has held several official positions in the Presbyterian Church, and now serves as manager of the Administration Department of the Office of the General Assembly. He served as organist and choirmaster at Hermon Presbyterian Church, Frankford, Philadelphia, 1919–1921. At present he is choirmaster in the Tioga Presbyterian Church, Philadelphia, a position which he has held since November, 1931.

T UNE: "Benediction" was composed to anonymous words found in a small devotional pamphlet in January, 1932. The opening musical phrase is used as the basis for the following three lines, rising in the scale to emphasize the progression of ideas, then being lowered for the final line to obtain a quietly sustained conclusion. Choirs with basses of good sonority may obtain a fine effect by allowing them to proceed down the entire musical scale beginning with the third line of the response.

---

45   RESPONSE: Father, Give Thy Benediction
           TUNE: Alla Trinita Beata

Author: *Rev. Samuel Longfellow*   Source: *"Laudi Spirituali"*

AUTHOR: For comments on the author, Samuel Longfellow, see Hymn 79.

RESPONSE: This is the first stanza of another of Samuel Longfellow's hymns, and it has all the depth and beauty which are characteristic of his work. Printed at first anonymously in 1864, in a collection called "Hymns of the Spirit," it has never been widely used. The whole stanza apparently had its origin in the words of Paul written from his Roman dungeon: "The Lord is at hand. Be careful for nothing; but in every thing by prayer and supplication with thanksgiving let your requests be made known unto God. And the peace of God, which passeth all understanding, shall keep your hearts and minds through Christ Jesus," Phil. 4: 5-7.

SOURCE: The source is "Laudi Spirituali."

TUNE: "Alla Trinita Beata" is an adaptation by Charles Burney (1726–1814) of a melody found in a manuscript collection, "Laudi Spirituali," at Florence, Italy. These hymns had their origin during the thirteenth century and were based on plain song, influenced by the popular music of the period.

Chanting and Plain Song

Chanting

A chant is not a hymn melody to which a text is fitted, but a series of tones to which the words of a psalm or canticle are recited. Chanting is, therefore, rhythmical reading and the words are of prime importance. They should be sung at a uniform rate of speed throughout, with every syllable clearly enunciated; weak syllables should not be slighted, nor strong syllables unduly prolonged.

Plain Song

Three ancient hymns have been included in their plain song settings. Plain song is rhythmical speech. The verses are not divided into measures by bar lines; these are used only to indicate the ends of phrases.

No time signature is indicated; the notes themselves represent the relative time values of the syllables. When a syllable extends over more than one note, the stems of the notes are joined.

548

Ancient Hymns and Canticles

*

46   CHANT: O Come, Let Us Sing Unto the Lord

Source: *Psalm xcv*   Composer: *William Boyce*

SOURCE: This chant, known as the "Venite," is based on Psalm 95.

CHANT: This was the battle hymn of the Knights Templars and
was sung on many a field of conflict in the Holy Land.
    The psalm originally ended, "The sheep of His hand." This is
much the better ending, with the strong note of loving confidence.
    "The Book of Common Prayer," 1552, which was widely used by
the Reformed Church of Scotland before the introduction of John
Knox's "Book of Common Order," provided for the singing of this psalm
after the versicles and responses which followed The Lord's Prayer and
the "Assurance of Pardon" in the Sunday Morning Order of Worship.

COMPOSER: The composer, William Boyce, Mus.D. (1710–1779),
has been called the last of the Old English School of church composers. Son of a cabinetmaker, he became chorister at St. Paul's
Cathedral, London, and subsequently organist in several London churches.
As his great gifts gave him prominence, he became conductor of the
famous "Three Choirs" festival, one of the organists of the Chapel Royal,
composer to the Chapel Royal, and master of the king's band. Throughout his life he was afflicted with a growing deafness, which finally caused
him to relinquish some of his appointments, but he continued his work
with the utmost fortitude. In his latter days he turned to the compiling of
his famous "Cathedral Music," which has been a treasure-trove to musicians ever since his day. He is described by Dr. Moffatt as an "amiable
man, of blameless life."

TUNE: From an artistic standpoint, the musical content of the
Anglican chant is slight and the form of the chant stereotyped.
This makes detailed description of each chant difficult and perhaps
unnecessary. Chants differ principally in the impressions they create, as of
ruggedness and strength, joy, sorrow, reflection, meditation. Thus a chant
to accompany a particular canticle should be chosen with proper care, as
it should reflect the general sentiment of the words. The fact that the
musical content is necessarily slight does not prevent chanting from producing a profound and moving effect when sympathetically performed.
This chant is of a strong type suitable to the "Venite."

Handbook to The Hymnal

47-48 CHANTS: Additional Chants to the "Venite"

Composer, Chant 47: *Richard Goodson*
Composer, Chant 48: *Richard Farrant*

COMPOSER (47): Richard Goodson (1655–1718) was appointed organist of New College, Oxford, in 1682, and in that year succeeded Edward Lowe as organist of Christ Church Cathedral and professor of music in the University. On his death, his son, of the same name, succeeded him in both posts. It is difficult to determine which of these men was the composer of this chant.

COMPOSER (48): For comments on the composer, Richard Farrant, see Response 9.

---

49 CHANT: We Praise Thee, O God

Composers: *Thomas Attwood*
Matthew Camidge
Rev. William H. Havergal

SOURCE: The "Te Deum Laudamus" was called "The Songe of Austyn and Ambrose," because of the legend that it had its inspiration at the baptism of Augustine by Ambrose, the two saints improvising and singing alternately.

Niceta, bishop of Remesiana, 392–414, has been cited as the probable author (i.e., of Parts I and II). Niceta was a contemporary and friend of Prudentius, author of "Ye Clouds and Darkness, Hosts of Night," who was one of the greatest of all early Latin Christian poets.

But the "Te Deum" is more probably of gradual growth, or, at least, of composite authorship.

CHANT: This is the most famous hymn, not of Biblical origin, of the Western Church. The Eastern Church does not know it in a Greek form. Although the first ten verses exist in Greek, these appear to be a translation from the Latin.

It is composed of three parts:

I. In praise of the Trinity. Verses 1-13.
II. In praise of the Redeemer. Verses 14-21.
III. Suffrages (short petitions) principally from The Psalms, originally said after the hymn but later written as part of it. Verses 22-29.

From the standpoint of sentiment, the first section, that of praise, seems to close with verse 15, that of history and doctrinal belief with verse 23,

550

Ancient Hymns and Canticles

that of supplication with verse 29. This, at least, was the traditional manner of assigning different chants to this long hymn for many years. The chant is slightly altered in this book in accordance with recent research.

The strength and beauty of the "Te Deum" are enhanced if it is sung in its original form, i.e., Parts I and II. It is a glorious old hymn of the Church, majestically gathering up much of the Christian heritage from The Apostles' Creed and from the Preface, the "Sanctus," and the "Gloria in Excelsis" of the Communion Office. It is not strange that Martin Luther placed it third, putting only The Apostles' Creed and the Nicene Creed before it as the great confession of faith.

Shakespeare, it has been pointed out, recognized it as the fitting hymn for great occasions, such as coronations and the celebration of victory. For instance, he made King Henry V, in the hour of triumph, exclaim:

> "Do we all holy rites:
> Let there be sung '*Non nobis*' and '*Te Deum.*'"

COMPOSERS: Thomas Attwood (1765–1838) was one of the outstanding organists and composers of his time. His extended works show force and originality and their music has frequently a highly descriptive quality, as in his famous anthem, "They That Go Down to the Sea in Ships." His father was a musician and a coal merchant. As a chorister of the Chapel Royal, Attwood came under the notice of the Prince of Wales, afterwards George IV, who sent him abroad for tuition under great masters. In Vienna he was a favorite pupil of Mozart. In 1796 he became organist of St. Paul's Cathedral and one of the first professors of the Royal Academy of Music. He was one of the first in England to recognize the genius of Mendelssohn.

Matthew Camidge (1758–1844) was one of a family of Yorkshire musicians. He succeeded his father, John, as organist at York Minster.

For comments on the third composer, William H. Havergal, see Hymn 97.

---

50   CHANT: O Be Joyful in the Lord

Source: *Psalm c*   Composer: *Rev. Henry Aldrich*

SOURCE: This chant, known as the "Jubilate Deo," is based on Psalm 100.

CHANT: "The Book of Common Prayer," 1552, which is of peculiar interest to Presbyterians, provides the One Hundredth Psalm ("Jubilate Deo") as an alternative to the "Benedictus," when the latter occurs in some other part of the Order of Morning Prayer.

It is essentially a song of thanksgiving. Hence it is more appropriate for festival than for penitential seasons. Originally it came before the lesson and not, as now, after it.

The metrical version, "All People That on Earth Do Dwell," with its tune from the "Old Version," gives us the famous "Old Hundredth," with its wealth of associations.

COMPOSER: This chant, perhaps the most popular setting of the "Jubilate Deo," was composed by Rev. Henry Aldrich (1647–1710), a man of great and varied gifts. He was an authority on theology, logic, architecture (some ancient Oxford buildings being from his plans), heraldry, and music. In the music library of Christ Church, Oxford, exists a comprehensive study, in manuscript, dealing with the art of music from the points of view of history, physics, and harmony. Aldrich became eventually vice chancellor of the University.

51-52   CHANTS: Additional Chants to the "Jubilate Deo"

Composer, Chant 51: *William Byrd*   Source, Chant 52: *Oxford Chant*

COMPOSER (51): William Byrd was born in Lincoln, in 1538. He became "one of the most illustrious figures of an age when the musical glory of England was at its height." In 1563 he was organist of Lincoln Cathedral, in 1569 a member of the Chapel Royal. A steadfast Roman Catholic, he was, in those troublous times, permitted to retain his office in the Chapel Royal, and became one of the most distinguished writers of church music that England has ever known. His death took place in 1623 in London.

SOURCE (52): The Oxford Chant is an anonymous composition, concerning which no information is available.

53-54   CHANT: Blessèd Be the Lord God

Source: *Luke i. 68-79*   Composer, Chant 53: *Joseph Barnby*

Composer, Chant 54: *Ludwig van Beethoven*

SOURCE: This chant is based on Luke 1: 68-79. The text of this and the other Scriptural canticles entered the Prayer Book from the Great Bible of 1539, rather than from the later and, to us, more generally familiar King James Version of 1611.

Ancient Hymns and Canticles

CHANT: The "Benedictus" is particularly appropriate as the canticle following the New Testament lesson. As one writer points out, it is the last prophecy of the old dispensation and the first of the new, and provides a key to the evangelical interpretation of all prophecy. It is an acknowledgment of the communion of saints under both dispensations. In one edition of the first Prayer Book a rubric describes the "Benedictus" as a "thanksgiving for the performance of God's promises."

COMPOSER and TUNE (53): This brilliant and effective chant, equally useful and even more appropriate as a setting to the "Venite" or the "Magnificat," is the composition of Joseph Barnby. (See Hymn 3.)

COMPOSER and TUNE (54): This tune is an adaptation from Beethoven. For comments on the composer, see Hymn 5.

---

55   CHANT: O All Ye Works of the Lord

Composer: *T. Tertius Noble*

SOURCE: This canticle was originally a part of the Septuagint, the Greek version of the Old Testament, where it was inserted between vs. 23 and 24 in Dan., ch. 3, as the song of the three men in the fiery furnace.

CHANT: The "Benedicite" was early used as a canticle in morning worship. The first Prayer Book ordered its use in Lent instead of the "Te Deum." In the Scottish Prayer Book of 1637 the "Benedicite" was replaced by the Twenty-third Psalm.

COMPOSER: For comments on the composer, T. Tertius Noble, see Hymn 366.

TUNE: The "Benedicite," on account of its length, has been a difficult canticle to which to supply music. This setting of Dr. Noble's may be sung in a reasonably short time, with no distortion of accent.

---

56   CHANT: My Soul Doth Magnify the Lord

Source: *Luke i. 46-55*   Composer: *Joseph Barnby*

SOURCE: This chant, known as the "Magnificat," is based on Luke 1 : 46-55.

CHANT: In the West the "Magnificat" is said or sung at evensong. Since the time of Saint Benet it has been sung at vespers. But there is nothing in the canticle itself which confines it to this service. In fact, the Eastern churches sing the "Magnificat" with the morning canticles.

The "Magnificat" has been used in the English Church for at least eight hundred years.

COMPOSER: For comments on the composer, Joseph Barnby, see Hymn 3.

TUNE: This is a melodious and sensitively musical chant for the "Magnificat." It is also an excellent setting for the "Benedictus."

57-58   CHANTS: Additional Chants to the "Magnificat"

Composer, Chant 57: *Thomas Purcell*
Composer, Chant 58: *Richard Woodward*

COMPOSER (57): Thomas Purcell, who died in 1682, was a member of a famous family of English musicians which at a slightly later date produced the renowned Henry Purcell. He was attached in various musical capacities to the Chapel Royal, and it is on record that he had difficulty at times in collecting his salary. He is known for a few chants, some of which have survived to the present day.

COMPOSER (58): Richard Woodward (1744–1777) held positions of importance in Dublin, where his father was a vicar choral of Christ Church and St. Patrick's Cathedrals. Richard eventually became vicar choral of St. Patrick's and organist at Christ Church. He left a volume of "Cathedral Music," but only his chants are now in general use.

---

59   CHANT: Lord, Now Lettest Thou Thy Servant

Source: *Luke ii. 29*   Composer: *John Blow*

SOURCE: This chant, known as the "Nunc Dimittis," is based on Luke 2: 29-32.

Ancient Hymns and Canticles

CHANT: The "Song of Symeon," has been used as an evening canticle from the earliest age. The "Apostolic Constitutions" mention it. Since the first Prayer Book, 1549, it has been sung after the second lesson at evensong.

COMPOSER: John Blow (1648–1708), the composer of this simple and dignified chant, was a voluminous composer of church music and reached, during his lifetime, the details of which are rather sparse, the high position of organist of Westminster Abbey and also that of one of the three organists of the Chapel Royal. In 1679 he either resigned or was dismissed from his position at Westminster to make room for Purcell, upon whose death in 1695 he was reappointed. He served there the rest of his life. His birthplace was probably North Collingham, Nottinghamshire, near Newark.

60-61   CHANTS: Additional Chants to the "Nunc Dimittis"

Source, Chant 60: *Tonus Peregrinus*
Composer, Chant 61: *Rev. William Felton*

SOURCE (60): The "Tonus Peregrinus" is an irregular mode, additional to the eight in common use in plain chant. Its beautiful melody has made it very popular in the Anglican service. Its origin and history are obscure. It seems to have been composed for some special occasion. It is used in the Catholic Liturgy to the psalm "In Exitu Israel," the missionary psalm, which may account for its title, "The Pilgrim's Tone."

COMPOSER (61): Rev. William Felton (c. 1715–1769) held various positions of a musical nature at Hereford Cathedral and was also chaplain to the princess dowager of Wales. He was distinguished in his day as a composer for and performer on the organ and harpsichord. He also published methods of instruction for the above instruments. His *concertos* were imitative of Handel, who, it is said, refused to allow his name among Felton's patrons.

62-63   CHANT: Lift Up Your Hearts

Composer, Chant 62: *John Merbecke*
Composer, Chant 63: *John Camidge*

SOURCE: Brightman gives Lam. 3:41 as the source of the "Sursum Corda."

CHANT: The "Sursum Corda" is common to all liturgies. It is one of the liturgical formulas of which we have the earliest evidence. Cyprian quotes it and its answer. We find it in the "Apostolic Constitutions." The invitation to give thanks is the proper introduction for the great eucharistic prayer. The Jewish grace before meals contains exactly our form: "Let us give thanks unto the Lord our God."

COMPOSER (62): John Merbecke, Mus.D. (1523–c.1585), was organist at St. George's Chapel, Windsor, and his life was not without the dangers, imprisonments, and excitements of the time, in his case on account of "heretical" writings, such as his concordance of the Scriptures. In later life he became more of a theologian than a musician, considering church music a "vanity." With the establishment of the second Prayer Book in 1552, which did not command singing as the first had done and also altered the ritual, a portion of Merbecke's work was necessarily thrown out of use.

TUNE (62): The earliest settings, after the Reformation, of portions of the Anglican Service began about 1544, perhaps with that of Stone. The earliest complete setting was that of John Merbecke, in 1550. This was a unison setting, principally derived from the simpler Gregorian chants. The essential value of Merbecke's treatment lies in his study of the rhythmic treatment of the English language as opposed to Latin. His object was to supply a "playne tune" for the daily Offices of the Church. Subsequent harmonizations or accompaniments of his setting have been frequent, Stainer's being in wide use. Later accompaniments have attempted to preserve more accurately the modal atmosphere considered appropriate. The title of Merbecke's work was "The Booke of Common Praier Noted."

COMPOSER (63): For comments on the composer, John Camidge, see Response 22.

64-66   CHANT: Lord, Have Mercy Upon Us

Source, Chant 64: *Lutheran Service of* 1528
Composer, Chant 65: *John Merbecke*
Source, Chant 66: *"Serbian Liturgy"*

CHANT: This chant is known as the "Kyrie." The three petitions, "Lord, have mercy upon us," "Christ, have mercy upon us," and "Lord, have mercy upon us," are known as "the lesser litany." The early litanies always began with the words, *Kyrie eleison* ("Lord,

Ancient Hymns and Canticles

have mercy upon us"); hence the "Kyrie" came finally to be called the litany itself.

"*Kyrie eleison*" is the only Greek formula remaining in the Latin worship forms. But it does not seem to be a survival from the days when all was Greek, because we have no certain reference to it until the middle of the fourth century.

SOURCE (64): This is the "Shorter Kyrie" in the Episcopal Service. It comes from a Lutheran Service of 1528. Luther founded his music upon (1) plain song, and (2) choral and choral-like folk song. He had no objection to the Catholic plain chant when he considered it suitable for his purposes, and this example is obviously from that source. It is widely agreed that Luther composed no music whatever, but he was an editor and adapter of taste and discernment, and also employed the best musical talent, notably that of Johann Walther (1496–c.1570).

COMPOSER (65): For comments on the composer, John Merbecke, see Chant 62.

SOURCE (66): This chant is taken from a Serbian liturgy. The mystical liturgy of the Eastern Church has followed an independent development from its earliest days. It is a tradition of dignity and usually of simplicity, and is not unaffected by its modal origin. This is true even in some of the comparatively recent anthems of Tschaikowsky, Rachmaninoff, and others.

67-68 CHANT: Responses After the Commandments

Source, Chant 67: *Ancient*
Composer, Chant 68: *George J. Elvey*

CHANT: The second "Book of Common Prayer," 1552, was used in Scotland, having been revised under strongly Calvinistic influences. John Knox once said that he "could think well of it." In this Prayer Book the Decalogue was added to the Communion Office and the Kyries adapted as responses. These are directly traceable to the Calvinistic "Liturgia Sacra" of Valler and Pullain.

SOURCE and TUNE (67): This is the "Kyrie," as opposed to the "Shorter Kyrie," in Episcopal usage. The setting is ancient, apparently from a Gregorian chant, concerning which details are lacking.

COMPOSER and TUNE (68): This is a melodious and popular setting by George J. Elvey. For comments on the composer, see Hymn 109.

69 CHANT: Glory to God in the Highest

Source: *Luther's Service of* 1524

CHANT: "The Angelic Song," heralding the Nativity of Christ, is based on Luke 2: 14. It is a "Gloria in Excelsis" of irregular form, from Luther's Service of 1524. It is of plain-chant origin. See Chant 64.

---

70 CHANT: Glory Be to God on High

Source: *Old Scottish Chant*

CHANT: The "Gloria in Excelsis" is an early hymn of the Greek Church which appeared not later than the fourth century and possibly as early as the second. It is found in its present form among the psalms and canticles at the end of the "Codex Alexandrinus."

His liturgical genius prompted Crammer to move it from the beginning to the end of the liturgy in the Prayer Book of 1549.

TUNE: This chant, known as "Old Chant" or "Old Scottish Chant," is the best-known setting of the "Gloria in Excelsis." In spite of its universal use, it is extraordinarily difficult to find any authentic information as to its origin or antiquity. It is very like one used at York Minster, and probably other English cathedrals, which is known merely as "Scottish Chant." Its simple outline suggests a possible origin in plain chant.

---

71 CHANT: Holy, Holy, Holy

Composer: *Thomas Attwood*

CHANT: This is an enlarged form of the "Sanctus." The words "full of the Majesty of Thy glory" occur in the "Te Deum"; the last sentence is from Matt. 21: 9.

This form of the "Sanctus" is used in the Communion Service of our Presbyterian "Book of Common Worship."

COMPOSER: For comments on the composer, Thomas Attwood, see Chant 49.

Ancient Hymns and Canticles

72-74   CHANT: Holy, Holy, Holy

Composer, Chant 72: *Peter C. Lutkin*
Composer, Chant 73: *John Merbecke*
Composer, Chant 74: *A. S. Cooper*

CHANT: The "Tersanctus," or "Trisagion," is the early Christian appropriation of an older Jewish Doxology of the synagogue based on Isa. 6: 3. This is the form as found in the Communion Office of the "Book of Common Prayer."

COMPOSER and TUNE (72): The musical life of the composer, Peter Christian Lutkin (1858–1931), with the exception of thorough study in Berlin, Vienna, and Paris under the best masters, was spent in Chicago, where he was brought up. After holding important positions in that city as organist, conductor, and teacher, he became dean of the School of Music in Northwestern University in 1895. His life was thereafter identified with a remarkable development of that school, and much emphasis was placed upon church music, valuable bulletins being frequently issued from the University upon that subject. Lutkin was also a composer of note, and the "Sanctus" here presented is a good example of the charming type of composition he could produce with simple means.

COMPOSER (73): For comments on the composer, John Merbecke, see Chant 62.

COMPOSER and TUNE (74): This is a simple choral setting much used in the Episcopal ritual. Information as to the composer, A. S. Cooper, is not available.

75-77   CHANT: O Lamb of God

Composer, Chant 75: *John Merbecke*
Source, Chant 76: *Lutheran Service of* 1528
Composer, Chant 77: *Giovanni Pierluigi
da Palestrina*

SOURCE: This chant, known as the "Agnus Dei," is based on John 1: 29.

Handbook to The Hymnal

CHANT: The use at the Communion of John the Baptist's greeting of our Lord is natural and appropriate. In the old Roman breviary it was sung at the time of the breaking of the bread. In the Antiochene Liturgy it is said by the pastor. It occurs also in the "Gregorian Sacramentary." In the "Scottish Euchologion," "Book of Common Order," the "Agnus Dei" precedes the Communion collect and the "Sursum Corda."

COMPOSER (75): For comments on the composer, John Merbecke, see Chant 62.

SOURCE (76): This is an altered form of the "Agnus Dei," from a Lutheran Service of 1528. See Chant 64.

COMPOSER (77): For comments on the composer, Giovanni Pierluigi da Palestrina, see Hymn 164.

78-80 CHANT: Glory Be to Thee, O Lord

Composer, Chant 78: *John Merbecke*
Composer, Chant 79: *Anonymous*
Composer, Chant 80: *Thomas Tallis*

CHANT: The "Book of Common Prayer," 1549, as does also the present Scottish Liturgy, ordered "Gloria Tibi" to be said or sung before the reading of the Gospel and "Gratia Tibi" after it. Settings of the "Gloria Tibi" are sung before the reading of the Gospel in the Communion Service of the Episcopal Church.

COMPOSER (78): For comments on the composer, John Merbecke, see Chant 62.

COMPOSER (79): Chant 79 is an anonymous composition.

COMPOSER (80): Thomas Tallis' setting is second in importance only to that of Merbecke. Its date is 1552. Tallis may be considered the chief of the founders of the harmonized Anglican chant.
For further comments on the composer, Thomas Tallis, see Hymn 42.

Ancient Hymns and Canticles

81   CHANT: Thanks Be to Thee, O Christ

Composer: *Thomas Tallis*

CHANT: "Gratia Tibi" is an altered version of the response option-
ally sung after the Gospel reading. See Chants 78–80.

COMPOSER: For comments on the composer, Thomas Tallis, see
Hymn 42.

———————

82   CHANT: O Gladsome Light
TUNE: Nunc Dimittis

Source: *Old Greek Hymn*   Composer: *Louis Bourgeois*

TRANSLATOR: This is Robert Bridges' translation of the famous
Greek hymn, "O Gladsome Light," also given beautiful expression
by Longfellow and many others. For further comments concerning
Robert Bridges, see Hymn 158.

CHANT: This "Candlelight Hymn" is, probably, with the exception of the canticles, the "Tersanctus," and such passages, the
oldest Christian hymn. It is still sung in the Greek Church as an
evening hymn.

Dr. Dearmer says: "It is quoted by Basil, who died in 379, as of unknown authorship and date; and we know that in the second century
hymns were sung at cockcrow and lamplighting. Its very simple words
have proved a difficulty to many translators. The most familiar [transla-
tion] has been Keble's." (See Chant 83.)

COMPOSER: For comments on Louis Bourgeois, the composer of
this dignified hymn, see Hymn 1.

———————

83   CHANT: Hail, Gladdening Light
TUNE: Sebaste

Source: *Old Greek Hymn*   Composer: *John Stainer*

TRANSLATOR: For comments on the translator, John Keble, see
Hymn 31.

CHANT: This Greek vesper hymn comes from entirely unknown sources, out of the victorious life of the third-century Church. It comes bearing the traditional name of "Candlelight Hymn," being sung in the churches at lamplighting. Basil, who is known as one of the four "Greek doctors" of the Greek Church, and at his death in 379 was bishop of Cæsarea, quotes the hymn, indicating that it was even then of unknown origin. It has survived without the prestige of notable authorship, entirely upon the purity and loftiness of its concept of worship of the blessed Trinity in the shadows of the closing day. (See Chant 82.)

COMPOSER: For comments on the composer, John Stainer, see Hymn 130.

TUNE: Stainer's setting of the hymn, "Sebaste," is a smoothly flowing and attractive combination of hymn and chant. The music used here was composed for this text and included in "Hymns Ancient and Modern," 1875.

---

84   CHANT: O Splendor of God's Glory Bright
            TUNE: Proper Sarum (Mode I)

Author: *Ambrose of Milan*   Source: *"The Yattendon Hymnal"*

AUTHOR: Ambrose, one of the great bishops of the Western Church like John Calvin, studied law before entering the service of the' Church. He was early appointed governor of the district in northern Italy of which the principal city is Milan. He was such an ardent defender of the faith against the Arians that, upon the death of the bishop of Milan in 374, he was by acclamation elected bishop. As bishop, he manifested rare balance of character, combining justice with mercy, "firmness with gentleness."

Ambrose greatly improved the music of the Church. While scholarship cannot concede that he had any part in the composition of the "Te Deum," nevertheless it is not strange that tradition should associate so great a name with so great a hymn.

For further comments on the author, Ambrose of Milan, see Hymn 32.

TRANSLATOR: For comments on the translator, Louis F. Benson, see Hymn 29.

CHANT: This is a splendid translation of the famous hymn of Ambrose, Archbishop of Milan (340–397), whose musical efforts were among the most important in the formation of the early plain chant.

Ancient Hymns and Canticles

SOURCE: The "Sarum Hymnal," from which the tune is originally taken, was the most valuable storehouse of the ancient English liturgy, following the method of plain chant but containing its own peculiar forms. It has preserved a record of the national taste at a time of which there is little other record. "The Yattendon Hymnal," from which this tune was taken, is a rare and recondite collection of antiquities.

---

85   CHANT: Of the Father's Love Begotten
      TUNE: Divinum Mysterium

Author: *Aurelius Clemens Prudentius*   Source: *Medieval Plain Song*

AUTHOR: Aurelius Clemens Prudentius was "one of the best and most prolific of early Latin Christian poets." He was a native of Spain. Like Ambrose and John Calvin, he too studied law. He held important administrative positions. In his fifty-seventh year he entered a monastery and devoted himself to the work on which his fame and the gratitude of the Church rest. His works formed the basis for much of the music in the ancient breviaries and hymnaries. This great hymn is in the York and Hereford Breviaries, as well as in others in Europe.

TRANSLATORS: For comment on the translators, John Mason Neale and Henry W. Baker, see Hymns 44 and 99, respectively.

ARRANGER: For comments on the arranger, Charles Winfred Douglas, see Hymn 276.

TUNE: This ancient hymn tune, "Divinum Mysterium," with its magnificent plain-chant melody, is usually found among Christmas hymns. It has been arranged in rhythmical form in several hymn books in 6/4 or 3/4 time, an arrangement more practical for congregational use.

---

86   CHANT: Father, We Praise Thee
      TUNE: Proper Sarum (Mode VI)

Author: *Gregory the Great*   Source: *"The Yattendon Hymnal"*

AUTHOR: For comments on the author, Gregory I, see Hymn 24.

Handbook to The Hymnal

TRANSLATOR: For comments on the translator, Percy Dearmer, see Hymn 24.

HYMN: This hymn is the translation by Dr. Dearmer, one of the outstanding students of hymnology of our day, of a Latin hymn ascribed to Gregory I (540–604). Its ancient quaintness and simplicity of expression have been preserved in the translation. It is a morning hymn, imploring preservation and direction, not merely through the day but through life, even unto heaven, "where Thy saints united joy without ending."

It was Gregory the Great who is said to have nailed to the altar at Rome a copy of the "Antiphonarium," his official liturgic pattern and guide in the musical services of the churches, and to have sent hymns and chants through the wilds of the North and West by his missionaries. It was Gregory's influence that for all time shaped the worship forms of the Church.

SOURCE: This plain song is from "The Yattendon Hymnal." It is very old, probably of the eleventh century, and appears in Leofric's "Collectarius," but does not occur in books of continental Europe. Its great beauty has been recognized for centuries, and its association with the eleven-syllable line, the Sapphic proper, is most fanciful and effective.

87-92   CHANTS: Amens

Source, Chant 87: *Greek Liturgy*
Source, Chant 88: *Traditional*
Source, Chant 89: *Danish*
Source, Chant 90: *Traditional*
Composer, Chant 91: *John Stainer*
Composer, Chant 92: *Philip James*

CHANT: "Amen" is an old Hebrew formula, which the Christian Church took over from the worship of the synagogue. Justin Martyr, in his "First Apology," says that when the president has ended the prayers and thanksgivings all the people present cry out saying, "Amen." The word "Amen" in the Hebrew language means, "So be it."

From time immemorial it has been the custom of both Jews and Christians, at the close of prayer offered by the minister, to say "Amen," or, "So be it." This is the people's indorsement or appropriation of what has been said in their stead. "It is like signing one's name to a document,"

564

Ancient Hymns and Canticles

says Dr. James Moffatt, "not a thing to be done casually. Yet in many congregations the 'Amen' is left, at the end of the prayers and the benediction, to the minister, or, if it is used, it is uttered with an offhand air, so that it sounds like an anticlimax, whereas it should gather up the full heart of the people."

The disuse of the Amen by the people, and of The Lord's Prayer, the "Gloria Patri," and the minister's kneeling at prayer, were all part of the general decadence in worship which followed upon the rejection of the Scottish Liturgy of 1637. Two centuries were to pass before our Church was to begin the movement for the recovery of our heritage of reformed yet universal Christian worship as exemplified in the Orders of Worship of Schwarz, Bucer, Calvin, Pullain, À Lasco, and "The Book of Common Prayer," 1552.

SOURCES (87–90): The "Twofold Amen," Chant 87, is taken from the Greek liturgy.

The "Threefold Amen," Chant 88, is a traditional response, anonymous.

The "Threefold Amen," Chant 89, is derived from anonymous Danish sources.

The "Dresden Amen," Chant 90, was immortalized by Wagner in his opera "Parsifal." It was in traditional use long before his day, however, at the Dresden court, and was freely used by Mendelssohn in his "Reformation" symphony. Its origin is obscure.

The "Sevenfold Amen," Chant 91, has long been the most popular elaborate setting of the "Amen." It is generally used as the final Amen of a service. This "Amen" was used at the funeral service of Stainer.

The "Wykagyl Amen," Chant 92, is a twofold Amen, modern in feeling.

COMPOSER (91): For comments on the composer, John Stainer, see Hymn 130.

COMPOSER (92): For comments on the composer, Philip James, see Hymn 496.

---

93   CHANT: Glory Be to the Father

Source: *Second Century*   Source: *Old Scottish Chant*

CHANT: This was called the "Lesser Doxology," the "Gloria in Excelsis" being the "Larger Doxology." The first portion of the "Gloria Patri" goes back to the beginning of Christendom; the second was probably added in the sixth century. Its Trinitarian language is derived from Christ's Great Commission in Matt. 28: 19. Though it has been used in various parts of the service, its chief place for many centuries has been after the psalm.

SOURCE: A portion of the "Old Scottish Chant" discussed in Chant 70 is used for this "Gloria Patri."

94-95

CHANT: Praise God from Whom All Blessings Flow
TUNE: Old Hundredth

Author: *Bishop Thomas Ken*   Source: *"Genevan Psalter"*

AUTHOR: For comments on the author, Thomas Ken, see Hymn 42.

HYMN: This Doxology, which closes both the "Morning Hymn" and the "Evening Hymn" of Bishop Ken, has become so universally adopted as to be known as a Protestant "Te Deum." In America it has voiced for the people as has no other Doxology their feelings of gratitude and sense of God's presence and power in moments of crisis and achievement. It was a typical use of this noble hymn when, in 1858, after the unexpected news of the successful laying of the Atlantic cable had been received, a thousand men at a college dinner in Andover, Massachusetts, rose and sang it. Bishop Ken sang his morning and evening hymns with this Doxology to the accompaniment of viol or spinet, but to tunes not handed down. To be accepted as a worthy and popular verbal channel of praise for the Church for two hundred years betokens immortality for any hymn.

ARRANGER (94): For comments on the arranger, Louis Bourgeois, see Hymn 1.

TUNE (94): The original musical rhythm of the "Doxology" is here given.
    For further comments on the tune, "Old Hundredth," see Hymn 1.

TUNE (95): This is the same melody as Chant 94, in the rhythm familiarly associated with "Old Hundredth" at the present time.